TORY INSURGENTS

Tory Insurgents

THE LOYALIST PERCEPTION
AND OTHER ESSAYS

Revised and Expanded Edition

Robert M. Calhoon, Timothy M. Barnes, and Robert S. Davis

IN COLLABORATION WITH
Donald C. Lord, Janice Potter-MacKinnon,
and Robert M. Weir

THE UNIVERSITY OF SOUTH CAROLINA PRESS

© 1989, 2010 University of South Carolina

The Loyalist Perception and Other Essays was published
by the University of South Carolina Press, 1989
This revised and expanded edition is published by
the University of South Carolina Press
Columbia, South Carolina 29208

www.sc.edu/uscpress

Manufactured in the United States of America

19 18 17 16 15 14 13 12 11 10
10 9 8 7 6 5 4 3 2 1

Library of Congress Cataloging-in-Publication Data
Calhoon, Robert M. (Robert McCluer)
  Tory insurgents : the loyalist perception and other essays / Robert M.
Calhoon, Timothy M. Barnes, and Robert S. Davis ; in collaboration with
Donald C. Lord, Janice Potter-MacKinnon, and Robert M. Weir. — Rev.
and expanded ed.
      p. cm.
  Rev. ed. of: The loyalist perception and other essays. Columbia, S.C. :
University of South Carolina Press, c1989.
  Includes bibliographical references and index.
  ISBN 978-1-57003-890-7 (cloth : alk. paper) — ISBN 978-1-57003-920-1
(pbk : alk. paper)
  1. American loyalists. 2. United States—Politics and government—
1775–1783. I. Barnes, Timothy M. II. Davis, Robert Scott, 1954– III. Lord,
Donald C. IV. Potter-MacKinnon, Janice, 1947– V. Weir, Robert M.
VI. Calhoon, Robert M. (Robert McCluer) Loyalist perception and
other essays. VII. Title.
  E277.C23 2010
  973.3—dc22
                        2010003403

for
Jack P. Greene
and in memory of Jack Barnes,
Don Higginbotham, and Heard Robertson

Contents

Preface

In 1989 *The Loyalist Perception and Other Essays* reprinted eleven previously published articles and essays. I had coauthored four of its chapters, one each with Timothy M. Barnes, Donald C. Lord, Janice Potter (now Potter-MacKinnon), and Robert M. Weir. These collaborative chapters reappear in this expanded volume, which has become still more collaborative. Barnes and I here collaborate on another chapter, one of the longest in the book and published here for the first time. Over the past quarter century, Robert S. Davis has emerged as the preeminent historian of loyalism in frontier Georgia and South Carolina, and he contributes two chapters extensively revised especially for this volume. With the assistance of Barnes and Davis, my 1991 essay on Carolina loyalism as viewed by the Irish-born patriots Aedanus and Thomas Burke is reprinted here with a new concluding section, as is a chapter and the epilogue from my long out-of-print *The Loyalists in Revolutionary America, 1760–1781* (1973).

The new material and new authorship of this edition strengthens our conviction that *ideas* leading toward *action* and finally maturing into settled patterns of *practice* remain the configuration of loyalist scholarship. Thus part 1, "Ideas," introduces an array of pre-Revolutionary loyalists and one loyalist-leaning neutralist. Chapters 2 through 6 portray William Smith, the visionary yet closeted theorist of a different kind of empire than the one he sensed was threatened with revolutionary disruption in 1776; Thomas Hutchinson, who waged a tenacious and intelligent struggle to exile the Massachusetts Assembly and Council from Boston until legislative leaders and the British government could appreciate the value of disciplined colonies governed by disciplined imperial institutions; Egerton Leigh, the sexual adventurer and vice admiralty judge in South Carolina who provoked his kinsman Henry Laurens to take the moral and ethical measure of imperial officialdom; Joseph Galloway, the architect of a reform empire superficially like William Smith's but rooted in quite different insecurities from those troubling the New York councillor; and, finally, Robert Beverley, the Virginia planter who styled himself in 1775 "as sorrowful spectator of these tumultuous times." Here we add, as an appendix, the long letter containing that self-portrait.

Introducing these biographical chapters is the title essay of the original collection, "The Loyalist Perception," positing patterns of *principle, accommodation,* and *doctrine* as a framework of pre-Revolutionary loyalism. The opening chapter contains new material on the place of the loyalists in the political structure of the Mother Country. These new passages argue that *principled loyalism* was nourished by association with the talented if myopic upper levels of the British imperial bureaucracy, that *accommodating loyalism* imbibed the flexible and professed openness of the Rockingham Whigs, and that *doctrinaire toryism* was an extension of the stability of Anglican parish life in England. Part 1 now concludes with a chapter from *The Loyalists in Revolutionary America* on moderate patriots, neutralists, and moderate loyalists in the years from 1774 and 1777, exploring the uses of reason in political upheaval—the beginning, as readers will see in chapter 9, of growing moderation on both sides of the revolutionary divide.

While part 1 emerged from the scholarship of the 1960s and early 1970s, part 2, "Action," echoes the concern of historians from the mid- to late-1970s and into the 1980s with human activity. Thus social historians of the Revolution considered the Revolution a learning process in which ideas came to permeate the behavior of groups of people within American society. The printers and writers of anonymous essays in the garrison town press discussed in chapters 8 and 9 were one such group. Another much larger group included thousands of loyalists in arms discussed in chapters 10, 11, 12, and 13.

Three of the six chapters in part 2 are new to the collection. Timothy M. Barnes and I originally wrote "Loyalist Discourse and the Moderation of the American Revolution" for the first, and as yet unpublished, volume in a new history of discourse in America. Davis's chapter on Kettle Creek, "Loyalism and Patriotism at Askance," and his biographical study of the patriot John Dooly are in fact companion pieces in which, as Professor Davis demonstrates, loyalists and patriots mirrored in each other's emotions, aggressions, and identities. Originally published in the online *Journal of Backcountry Studies* and in the *Georgia Historical Quarterly,* respectively, they have been revised especially for this book.

Finally, in part 3, "Practice," we present loyalist scholarship from the mid-1980s to the early 2000s on the culmination of Revolutionary history as thoughtful *action,* or *practice.* My collaboration with Barnes began in 1975 when our paths crossed at the American Antiquarian Society where we discovered evidence identifying John Witherspoon as the instigator of mock ritual humiliations of the loyalist printers Benjamin Towne and James Rivington. Our 1985 article on Witherspoon did not include the extensive political, social, cultural, and ethical context that we had reconstructed. Much of that context ended up on the cutting room floor only to be swept up and reintroduced as the interpretive framework of my 1987 essay "The Reintegration of the Loyalists and the Disaffected." Barnes's collaboration in framing this essay is here belatedly acknowledged. Part 3, and in a sense the second edition as a whole, concludes with "A Special Kind of Civil War," the longer portion of the epilogue and conclusion from *The Loyalists in Revolutionary America.*

Between 1997 and 2002, Kenneth G. Anthony helped conceptualize both this book and a companion volume on political moderation; during the final two years of the preparation of both books, Marguerite Ross Howell served as project manager and capably oversaw myriad editorial details. Ed Roush and Karen S.

Walker offered insights and encouragement. The authors also acknowledge with appreciation the assistance of Catherine S. "Cat" McDowell of the Digital Projects Office, Walter Clinton Jackson Library, University of North Carolina at Greensboro, Sallie Harlan, Lynne Landwehr, Jess Shelander, Deanna Slappey, Richard Smallwood, Karen Walker, and the support of the University of North Carolina at Greensboro Research Council and the George Washington Distinguished Professorship in History in 2005–8 from the North Carolina Society of the Cincinnati.

ROBERT M. CALHOON

Introduction

The American Revolution was a prolonged and complex event that encompassed several kinds of conflict within the British Empire and American society. Some of these conflicts were central to the attainment of American independence; others were tangential to that process; and still others were part of a pervasive atmosphere of conflict and change throughout the Atlantic world of the eighteenth century. The American colonists who opposed the Revolution, the loyalists, were caught up in all of these changes; characterizing the loyalists' experiences illustrates the complexity of the Revolution and the vitality of loyalist scholarship.

The central conflicts of the Revolutionary era arose from Great Britain's decisions in the 1750s and 1760s to centralize control of the Empire and to secure subordination of the colonies to British authority. Britain's tightening of customs enforcement, imposition of the Stamp Act, and use of Townshend duties revenue as a slush fund to pay the salaries of Crown officials normally paid by the colonial assemblies were the heart of the conflict within the Empire. Those controversies swirled around prominent colonists and future loyalists who held positions as royal governors, lieutenant governors, royal councillors, judges, and attorneys general. They found themselves in the painful position of defending parliamentary statutes that they regarded as harsh and harmful to the well-being of the Empire; they became caught in the middle of clumsy efforts to prosecute patriot activists in the courts or to use British troops to enforce civil order. In these ways, colonists who held Crown offices unwittingly became the point men for a new, tougher royal administration. Underlying those policies were beliefs, ideas, and practices to which Crown supporters in America had to accommodate themselves. These included the doctrine of parliamentary supremacy, familial rhetoric about the British Empire as a Mother Country with her colonial children, and a rising level of prosperity fed by British credit and colonial debt. Loyalists did not usually regard Parliament as supreme, but they viewed the British legislature as the embodiment of the political will of the British nation and a dynamic constitutional force within the Empire. They too could take offense at the notion of the colonists as permanent children of the British parent, but they were also aware that acts of adolescent willfulness only postponed British recognition of colonial maturity. Aware of the fragility of commercial prosperity within the Empire, they fretted about the dangers and hazards of foregoing British military protection and commercial support. The loyalists therefore sought to forestall an ideological collision between the regime-oriented values of Parliament and the Crown and the growing libertarianism of colonial politics. When the collision finally occurred in 1774 with the enactment of the Coercive Acts punishing Boston and Massachusetts for the destruction of taxed tea the preceding December, the loyalists produced several imaginative plans for reforming the British Empire; they pointed with alarm to the growing polarization in colonial-imperial relations; and in a few instances they affirmed conservative principles of hierarchy and submission of social inferiors to their superiors in human affairs.

The Revolution did not occur in a vacuum nor was its impact restricted to the British institutions in America that it overthrew or to the new republican ones it created. The Revolution spilled into areas of American life only tangentially connected to the question of empire versus independence. The Revolution occurred within a triracial society of European immigrants and their descendants, Native American Indians, and African American slaves and free blacks. When Lord Dunmore, royal governor of Virginia, called on slaves of rebellious planters to win their liberty by taking up arms in behalf of the king in November 1775, eight hundred slaves responded and made their way to the British base at Norfolk. Slave owners throughout Virginia and Maryland justifiably feared that thousands of others were poised to follow had a favorable opportunity arisen. In South Carolina a free black ship pilot named Thomas Jeremiah was overheard in 1775 telling another black man that "there is a great war coming [that will] help the poor Negroes." South Carolina patriot leaders brutally executed Jeremiah as an example to other blacks who might share his vision of racial justice and his estimate of the division between British officials and Carolina whites. Ever since the 1740s, the British had cultivated North American Indian tribes as allies against the French. Britain also discovered that through diplomacy, colonial governments could obtain Indian lands needed for the expansion of the white population. The Revolution presented tribes with close ties to the British government—notably the Mohawks in New York and the Creeks, Cherokees, and Seminoles along the southern frontier—with the ambiguous and dangerous choice of being British allies and virtual British subjects in the American Revolutionary war or remaining neutral. Those tribes that chose to fight for the Crown then faced the still more dangerous choice of subordinating themselves to British military commanders or operating as independent fighting forces protecting Indian interests. For agents of the British Superintendents of Indian Affairs and other frontier loyalists, the Indians' presence became a military asset, while their ambiguous relationship to the Crown became a source of white loyalist insecurity.

Racial minorities were not the only relatively powerless, victimized people who looked to the British Crown for protection during the War for Independence. A variety of ethnic minorities and other marginal groups in American society resisted being coerced into supporting the patriot cause. These included highland Scots settlers in North Carolina; Quakers and German pietist groups in Pennsylvania, North Carolina, and Connecticut; and poor white yeoman farmers—often caught up in Methodist revivals—in places like the Delmarva Peninsula of Maryland, Delaware, and Virginia. The lines separating outright loyalists from politically indifferent and apolitical people were thin and indistinct. Often the militarization of American life after 1775 exacerbated local feuds. Such antagonisms erupted in northern New Jersey in 1776 and in Georgia and the Carolinas in 1779–81 as the British military occupied those regions. Racial, ethnic, and social instability—the byproducts of the expansionism and exploitive energies of colonial society and the pluralism of its humbler immigrants—seriously jeopardized the Revolutionary cause and created whole new categories of lower-class and marginal loyalists.

In addition to reconstructing what the loyalists did to oppose the Revolution and which groups deliberately joined—or were drawn into—the anti-Revolutionary movement, certain conditions of life in America retarded opposition to British rule, just as others accelerated it. For example, colonial society during the second and third quarters of the eighteenth century became increasingly Anglicized as British styles, products, and national hubris infiltrated American life. People who benefited from this development tended to celebrate British dominance and often became loyalists during the Revolution. These people often felt that disorderly colonial growth needed the stabilizing hand of British regulation. Anglican clergymen who resented the discourtesy and seeming crudeness of Protestant dissenter sects, critics of land speculation who detested the political power of the landed aristocracy, and ethnic minorities fearful of being swallowed up by the English-stock majority all looked to British authority as necessary for the discipline of colonial society. As family life became less restrictive after mid-century—amid prosperity and social expansion—young men struck off on their own at earlier ages rather than waiting to inherit the estates of their fathers. This development prompted some to decry the decline in the authority of fathers over their children just as it inspired others to regard the autonomy of young men as a healthy kind of individualism. Growing generational tension occurred at the very time British officials on both sides of the Atlantic employed familial rhetoric to characterize the colonies themselves as children of the parent, or Mother Country, and as opposition politicians in the colonies used it to denounce the oppression of the colonies by British authorities as unbefitting a loving, protective parent.

The most pervasive reality in late colonial life was the colonists' sense of their own provincialism: their dependence on, and remoteness from, the metropolitan center of British life. Provincialism made some colonists hypersensitive to indications that decay and corruption in British life were eating away at the vitals of imperial institutions and values. It underscored their feeling of helpless dependence on the economic power of the British nation and their feeling of excessive dependence on British credit. British opposition figures such as the notorious John Wilkes—libertarian, rake, and political rabble-rouser—acquired sensational followings in the colonies. The centralizing policies of the British ministry and bureaucracy, especially of the Treasury, suggested that the British constitution and the "rights of Englishmen" were in danger of being replaced or subverted. People who looked to Parliament and the Crown to expand the power of the Empire, and thereby control disturbances within colonial culture, were predisposed to support Britain when the Revolution erupted.

The same provincialism that impelled some colonists to desire a new order, centered on American rather than British values, drove others to yearn for an imperial solution to the problems of life on the periphery of the Empire. They looked to Parliament and the Crown to expand the power, wealth, and even boundaries of the Empire and to bring back the halcyon days of the Seven Years' War when British dynamism and determination linked people throughout the king's dominions in a common cause. "Seagirt Britannia! mistress of the isles!" rhapsodized one Maryland loyalist in the early 1770s:

> Where Faith, and Liberty, united reign;
> Around whose fertile shores glad Nature smiles,
> And Ceres crowns with gifts the industrious swain! . . .
>
> And, when again our colours are unfurl'd,
> May Britons nobly join one common cause!
> With rapid conquests strike the wondering world,
> In firm support of Liberty and Laws.[1]

That vision of a world made whole and coherent and vibrant by British institutions and imperial expansion was also an antidote to disequilibrium in the colonies and an inspiration to thousands of loyalists who rallied to the royal standard during the War for Independence.

Historical understanding of the conflicts inherent in the American Revolution owes much to research and writing on the loyalists during the past quarter century. The essays reprinted in this book played a modest part in the loyalist leavening of the texture of Revolutionary scholarship. Published over more than four decades, they sought to map the terrain between the private, inner, subjective awareness of the loyalists and the public, external, objective dilemmas imposed on them by the Revolution. The title essay, "The Loyalist Perception,"[2] explores that terrain and locates three ideal types of pre-Revolutionary opposition to colonial resistance: principled, accommodating, and doctrinaire. "The Loyalist Perception" seeks to capture the ideas that were the essence of these three positions, to establish the interrelations between them, and to date their demise after 1776.

The next five chapters explore various oppositions to, and criticisms of, the pre-Revolutionary movement. Chapter 2, "'The Constitution Ought to Bend': William Smith, Jr.'s, Alternative to the American Revolution,"[3] interprets a treatise on the nature of the British Empire written by a knowledgeable New York politician and historian, William Smith, Jr., during the midst of the pre-Revolutionary controversy. Smith's criticisms of the imperial constitution were more radical than those of most colonial whigs, and his sense of political equanimity and survival hinged on the capacity of statesmen on both sides of the Atlantic to reconstruct imperial administration in light of growing American power and maturity.

A still closer view of the legal and political—as well as psychological—bonds holding the Empire together is provided in the discussion by Robert M. Calhoon and Donald C. Lord of the controversy over the removal of the Massachusetts General Court from Boston, 1769–72.[4] That article examines the minute and subtle contemporary analysis of the royal instructions governing the conduct of royal governors in America. One of those instructions directed first Governor Francis Bernard and then his successor, Thomas Hutchinson, to assemble the Massachusetts Assembly in Cambridge rather than Boston as a gesture of disapproval of the assembly's actions. Who was bound by those instructions—the governor or the whole provincial government—and the room an instructed governor had for maneuver in such a situation became central issues in the dispute. The chilling effect of government by instruction on the colonial exercise of political liberty and responsibility became the highly charged atmosphere in which the removal controversy occurred. Before a face-saving compromise could be effected, questions about the nature of representative government and the duty of public officials to respect the "public good" tested the integrity of both colonial democracy and imperial rectitude.

The moral issues defined clinically in the removal controversy in Massachusetts spilled into a messier political conflict in South Carolina when Egerton Leigh, notorious plural officeholder, became embroiled in disputes over customs enforcement and legislative control of the purse. A friend, kinsman, and close associate of Henry Laurens, Leigh demonstrated a kind of moral obtuseness in his conduct as judge, husband, and imperial operator that epitomized for the native South Carolina elite the corrupt nature of British rule. In "'The Scandalous History of Sir Egerton Leigh,'"[5] Robert M. Weir and Robert Calhoon examine this uproarious case study of the redefinition of public ethics in the pre-Revolutionary debate.

Smith, Hutchinson, and Leigh each achieved a measure of prestige in colonial politics by mastering the rules of the political game; each was victimized by a failure to sense how rapidly those rules were changing during the late 1760s and early 1770s. Joseph Galloway, ally of Benjamin Franklin and Speaker of the Pennsylvania Assembly, misjudged this situation still more grievously. "'I Have Deduced Your Rights': Joseph Galloway's Concept of His Role, 1774–1775"[6] examines his famous, though not fully understood, Plan of Union for the British Empire against the background of his ambition and immense appetite for behind-the-scenes maneuvering.

The misperception of political reality and the abruptly clogged channels of political communication in the late pre-Revolutionary debate apparent in chapters 1 through 4 prepare the way to an understand the writings of a wholly apolitical critic of colonial resistance, Robert Beverley of Virginia. "'Unhinging Former Intimacies': Robert Beverley's Perception of the Pre-Revolutionary Controversy, 1761–1775" explores the coming Revolution from the vantage point of a man innocent of any thirst for power or appreciation for political ideas. Beverley's flatfooted

efforts to defend his political neutrality and to condemn political activism provide a kind of mirror image of Revolutionary mobilization in Virginia. Immobilized by the actions of others, Beverley saw at close range the character and
intensity of patriot resistance. Beverley was, in fact, one of many moderate patriots, neutralists, and loyalists who between 1774 and 1777 sought a middle way out
of the Revolutionary crisis. Their "uses of reason in political upheaval" was the
subject of chapter 15 in *The Loyalists in Revolutionary America, 1769–1781* (1973),
a chapter that anticipated chapter 9 in this book, Barnes and Calhoon's essay
"Loyalist Discourse and the Moderation of the American Revolution," and also
Calhoon's *Political Moderation in America's First Two Centuries* (2009).[7]

Beverley was one of many moderate patriots, neutralists, and moderate loyalists who sought a way around the impasse between the authority of the Mother
Country and the traditional liberties of American colonists. A perspective on that
effort, chapter 7 brings to conclusion the exploration of loyalist ideas. Previously
published in *The Loyalists in Revolutionary America, 1760–1781* (1973), this chapter seeks to convey the apprehension, even terror, of watching the Empire self-
destruct from inflexibility and rigidity on both sides of the imperial controversy.[8]

Ideas have unpredictable consequences, and no one foresaw in 1775–76 the
extraordinary military and psychological struggles that the War for Independence
would unleash. As, during the war, loyalists continued to think about their plight
and their need for continued British rule, the concrete tasks of supporting military campaigns and undermining the cohesion and morale of the patriot regime
made loyalism into a program of *action*. Newspapers were a critical battleground.
Chapter 8, "The Character and Coherence of the Loyalist Press," surveys loyalist
polemical journalism from the pre-Revolutionary period through the War for
Independence.[9] Using Daniel Leonard's allegation that the Continental Congress
was a repository of "disaffection, petulance, ingratitude, and disloyalty" as a point
of departure, Janice Potter-MacKinnon and Robert Calhoon show how these four
concepts constituted the intellectual and ethical universe within which loyalist
polemicists lived. Chapter 9, an essay published here for the first time, contrasts
the harsh polemicism of the garrison town loyalist press in the 1770s with a growing moderation between 1780 and 1782. Unbeknowst to each other, both patriots
and loyalists in the later stages of the War for Independence came to value moderation as a force for civility, humanity, and wisdom.

The price Americans paid, loyalists and patriots alike, for their political con-
victions came into sharp focus as the military struggle spilled from formal battle-
grounds and into civilian neighborhoods. Chapter 10, on the "nature" of the
war,[10] and chapter 11, on the southern, western, and northern peripheries of the
military conflict,[11] discern the same apprehension and anguish in small skirmishes
and in sweeping geopolitical strategic thinking by the British and their loyalist
surrogates. Thomas Jefferson was not simply flattering George Washington when
he declared that Washington's surrender of military and political authority to

Congress in 1783 "probably prevented this Revolution from being closed, as most others have been, by a subversion of that liberty it was intended to establish."[12] No one during the Revolutionary War knew for certain whether the blessings of constitutional government could be snatched from the jaws of post-Revolutionary disorder. In his study of violence and military conflict in the Georgia backcountry, Robert S. Davis suggests, first in chapter 12 on the skirmish at Kettle Creek, that whigs and tories alike expected the white-Indian conflict as well as the pro-British–pro-American conflict to continue for decades into the future irrespective of which side prevailed in the struggle for independence. That prospect meant that the frontier would have to be governed, if at all, by local truces. And in chapter 13, his companion study of the frontier patriot John Dooly, Davis shows how conflicting cross-currents of ambition, land hunger, vengeance, wildly shifting fortunes of war, and benumbing misfortunes for families such as the Doolys made Revolutionary warfare in Georgia into a tragedy of Shakespearean proportions. The British were not out to win hearts and minds but to draw upon already existing support for the king's cause that they mistakenly believed still existed in America. They believed that they were rescuing their loyal subjects from anarchy and that the colonists would show their gratitude by rushing to the British army where they could be sneered at, abused, underpaid, and distrusted. Kettle Creek and John Dooly illustrated that the British leaders were wrong; a majority of Americans in 1779 were willing to risk everything for the new nation, while the remaining loyalists were American ethnic groups, some of them even criminal elements, wanting a return of British colonial protection more than an opportunity to die for king and country.[13]

As patriots tried to deal with their own internal opponents and as loyalists reacted to their victimization, the ideas and actions of both sides evolved into *practices* shaped by the needs and interests of both groups. Barnes and Calhoon began a long association after discovering evidence that John Witherspoon, Presbyterian divine from Scotland, president of the College of New Jersey, and delegate to the Continental Congress, sought to spin the news story of Revolutionary allegiances to the patriots' advantage. Chapter 14, "Moral Allegiance: John Witherspoon and Loyalist Recantation," places the Witherspoon story in the context of moral republicanism, the creation of a blessed community revolutionary saints.[14] The complex cultural circumstances underlying this episode did not make their way into that article, but they do provide the internal structure for chapter 15, "The Reintegration of the Loyalists and the Disaffected"—a paper originally presented at a conference at Johns Hopkins University in 1985 on the short-term consequences of the American Revolution.[15]

Chapter 16, which concludes this edition, is adapted from *The Loyalists in Revolutionary America, 1760–1781,* and it considers the loyalist experience as a social process involving civil war, national liberation, and ultimate sources of authority.[16]

Notes

1. William Eddis, *Letters from America,* ed. Aubrey C. Land (Cambridge, Mass.: Belknap Press of Harvard University Press, 1969), 71–72.

2. Robert M. Calhoon, "The Loyalist Perception," *Acadiensis* 3 (Spring 1973): 3–14.

3. Robert M. Calhoon, "William Smith Jr.'s Alternative to the American Revolution," *William and Mary Quarterly,* 3rd ser., 22 (January 1965): 105–18.

4. Donald C. Lord and Robert M. Calhoon, "The Removal of the Massachusetts General Court from Boston, 1769–1772," *Journal of American History* 55 (March 1969): 735–55.

5. Robert M. Calhoon and Robert M. Weir, "The Scandalous History of Sir Egerton Leigh," *William and Mary Quarterly,* 3rd ser., 26 (January 1969): 47–74.

6. Robert M. Calhoon, "'I Have Deduced Your Rights': Joseph Galloway's Concept of His Role," *Pennsylvania History* 35 (October 1968): 356–78.

7. Robert M. Calhoon, "'Unhinging Former Intimacies': Robert Beverley's Perception of the Pre-Revolutionary Controversy, 1761–1775," *South Atlantic Quarterly* 68 (Spring 1969): 246–61.

8. Robert M. Calhoon, *The Loyalists in Revolutionary America, 1760–1781* (New York: Harcourt Brace Jovanovich, 1973), 175–87.

9. Janice Potter and Robert M. Calhoon, "The Character and Coherence of the Loyalist Press," in *The Press and the American Revolution,* ed. Bernard Bailyn and John B. Hench (Worcester, Mass.: American Antiquarian Society, 1980), 229–72.

10. Robert M. Calhoon, "Civil, Revolutionary, or Partisan: The Loyalists and the Nature of the War for Independence," in *Military History of the Revolution,* ed. Stanley J. Underdal (Washington, D.C.: Office of Air Force History, 1976), 94–108.

11. Robert M. Calhoon, "The Floridas, the Western Frontier, and Vermont: Thoughts on the Hinterland Loyalists," in *Eighteenth-Century Florida: Life on the Frontier,* ed. Samuel Proctor (Gainesville: University Presses of Florida, 1976), 1–15.

12. Thomas Fleming, *The Perils of Peace: America's Struggle for Survival after Yorktown* (New York: Smithsonian Books / Collins, 2007), 322.

13. An earlier version of this work appeared as "Lessons from Kettle Creek: Patriotism and Loyalism at Askance on the Southern Frontier," *Journal of Backcountry Studies* 1 (May 2006); available online at http://library.uncg.edu/ejournals/backcountry/Vol1No1/Kettle_Creek_Loyalists.pdf (accessed June 4, 2009).

14. Timothy M. Barnes and Robert M. Calhoon, "Moral Allegiance: John Witherspoon and Loyalist Recantation," *American Presbyterians: The Journal of Presbyterian History* 63 (Fall 1985): 273–84.

15. Robert M. Calhoon, "Aedanus Burke and Thomas Burke: Revolutionary Conservatism in the Carolinas," in *The Meaning of South Carolina History: Essays in Honor of George C. Rogers, Jr.,* ed. Clyde N. Wilson and David Chesnutt (Columbia: University of South Carolina Press, 1991), 50–66.

16. Calhoon, *Loyalists in Revolutionary America,* 502–6.

1
Ideas

One

The Loyalist Perception

ROBERT M. CALHOON

The nature of loyalism in the American Revolution is an intractable historical problem, in part, because the loyalists appeared in several distinct social and political settings: pre-Revolutionary colonial society, rebellious American states, the various parts of the British Empire to which they fled, and the post-Revolutionary republic where still more reemerged as respectable citizens. In each of these contexts the loyalists revealed different facets of the values, attitudes, and characteristics which accounted for their adherence to the Crown. While it is dangerous to read back into the loyalists' Revolutionary experience things they said in retrospect, it is also misleading to assume that the loyalists revealed everything they had to say about themselves under the intense pressures of specific crises in the pre-Revolutionary controversy or later during the Revolution itself.

While a perceptive kind of comparative history will be needed to bring together the pieces of the loyalist puzzle, it is also important to explore as analytically as possible the loyalists' perception of reality, the structure of their values, and the pattern of their rational and emotional responses within each of the historical contexts from which they operated. Historians dealing with the loyalists have, for the most part, asked questions about the location and condition of identifiable groups of loyalists, the thrust of loyalist rebuttals to specific tenets of whig belief, and the political and social conditions which made some colonists unusually dependent on British authority for their security and identity. Another kind of question should probe the loyalists' view of themselves and focus on their own statements of self-consciousness and self-awareness. Pre-Revolutionary critics and victims of a colonial resistance felt conscious of certain political and social *roles* which they tried to play as the imperial controversy progressed; they wrestled with the *dilemma* of adapting, improving, relaxing, or intensifying their performance of those roles as the pre-Revolutionary movement made those roles increasingly awkward; as each individual realized that he was not going to regain his former authority, influence, or equanimity, he communed within himself and gave some expression to the *anguish* he felt. The loyalists' understanding and presentation of their roles, dilemmas, and anguish in letters, pamphlets, oratory, state papers, and in the way they dealt with public issues and devised strategies for defending themselves revealed a coherent view of external events and their own character in time of crisis.

A useful tool in the examination of this kind of loyalist testimony is the concept of *perception,* the process of giving structure to thought and sensations. Perception seeks explanations and patterns in the random data the senses detect in a social situation: it uses language "to determine or at least to influence what one notices around him": it is a process which creates categories and "category-systems" in the mind. Perception deals with a man's self-image, emotional and intellectual dexterity and stamina, the imperatives govern his conduct in times of crisis and the predispositions which operate in periods of routine. By treating pre-Revolutionary opponents of colonial resistance as verbalizing, category-building, reflective, self-conscious figures, one can gain access to the interior of their political thought.[1] As the pre-Revolutionary critics and opponents of colonial resistance responded to the crises of that period, they constructed three reasonably distinct models of political reality. One was the enunciation of principle, the repeated statement of legal, historical, and constitutional rules which bound the Empire together and necessarily circumscribed colonial liberty. A second was the search for accommodation, the belief that grounds for compromise existed and could be discovered and exploited through the use of good sense and prudence. A third was the appeal to doctrine, the sometimes shrill, uncompromising insistence that all colonial resistance and remonstrance was morally wrong and aesthetically abhorrent.

Thomas Hutchinson was, of course, the preeminent loyalist enunciator of principle, combining a sure grasp of fundamentals with a sensitivity for intricacies. "I have but one set of principles upon government in general and the constitution of this province in particular. There must be one supreme legislature in every state." He admitted, however, that "it is a very difficult matter to determine any certain proportion of freedom necessary to the happiness of a subordinate state."[2] He devoted a lifetime to the search for that "certain proportion of freedom" and we know a great deal about the depth and nature of that commitment from Edmund S. Morgan's analysis of Hutchinson in the Stamp Act crisis, Malcolm Freiberg's dissection of his ambition and his self-doubts, Clifford K. Shipton's defense of his rectitude, and Bernard Bailyn's discovery of his constitutional acumen.[3] What this fragmented, somewhat static, portrait lacks is an appreciation of Hutchinson's emotionality—the passions which integrated his roles and aspirations and aggravated his suffering. One way to fill this void is to focus, not only on his manifest principles, ambitions, and skills, but also on the strange paradoxes and polarities of his political character.[4]

The strongest of those polarities was his belief that he was primarily a defender of colonial liberty and that prudent submission to British authority was a subtle strategy for preserving that liberty. As Edmund Morgan showed in 1948, Hutchinson privately came close to denying the legitimacy of the entire Grenville program and stated categorically that it did infringe on inherent colonial rights;

yet in 1770 he privately proposed a horrifying set of coercive measures for Britain to impose on Massachusetts. Hutchinson was never conscious of any contradiction. The coercion he sadly recommended was intended to have a stunning, sobering effect on the shortsighted and excited men and inaugurate a stabilizing period and thereby strengthen Massachusetts' capacity to resist British encroachments.[5] Hutchinson's tremendous personal reserve created the very suspicions which kept his political life in upheaval; against his aloofness, however, tugged his ambition to provide decisive public leadership. He candidly spoke of this tension in his character during his dispute with the General Court over the Boston Resolves in 1773:

> If I am wrong in my principles of government or in the inferences I have
> drawn from them, I wish to be convinced of my error. I have laid before
> you the principles of your constitution. If you do not agree with me I wish
> to know your objections. They may be convincing to me or I may be able
> to satisfy you of the insufficiency of them. In either case, I hope, we shall be
> able to put an end to those irregularities which shall ever be the portion of
> a government where the supreme authority is controverted.[6]

In 1773, that was exactly the kind of dialogue Hutchinson sought to have with his contemporaries—a healing exchange in which he prescribed the premises of the discussion. He could emerge just that far, but no further, from his private contemplation of the issues of liberty and authority.

Hutchinson struggled intelligently with these conflicting impulses toward withdrawal and involvement. He resisted the temptation to dismiss whig argument with superficial rebuttals; he regarded the complexity of the pre-Revolutionary debate with great seriousness; this polarity pitted his dismay against his intellect and curiosity. It enabled him to be at once withdrawn and self-conscious and also capable of seeing himself in a larger context. When he became fully engaged in the task of understanding a tenet of whig belief, Hutchinson brought to his work the full force of his highly controlled emotionality. During the protracted dispute from 1769 to 1772, over the removal of the General Court from Boston, he tried to breathe life and vitality into the notion that the royal instructions to colonial governors were a positive benefit to the political life of the province. As he elaborated his explanation, the Crown's prerogative became an intimate, all-embracing, pervasive, organic influence which transmuted mobility and finesse to otherwise static executive authority. In turn the governor's receptiveness, discretion, and intelligence in responding to imperial directives determined their effectiveness. Hutchinson constructed an idealized minuet between Crown and governor which was almost poetic and sensuous in its structure and intricacy.[7] Hutchinson, significantly, conceived of British power as a throbbing, expansive force which could permeate and activate his own behavior as governor. Colonial leaders conceived of British power in exactly the same fashion; as Bernard Bailyn observes, they were transfixed by the "essential . . . aggressiveness" of political power and by its "endlessly propulsive tendency to expand itself beyond legitimate boundaries.[8] Confident that he could serve as a channel and instrument of British authority without damaging the liberty of his province, Hutchinson only succeeded in confirming his enemies' deepest fears about the capacity of the Crown to insinuate itself into the political life of the province.

Hutchinson's insistence on principle and his calculated style of debate and exposition distinguished him from William Smith, Jr., and other moderate critics of colonial resistance who shunned dispute over principle and sought practical, improvised accommodation with Britain. In 1767, Smith devised a constitution for the British Empire which he believed should be a malleable instrument which could accommodate the growing political maturity of the colonies.[9]

His ability as a constitutional theorist and diagnostician complemented a different set of Smith's predispositions during the pre-Revolutionary period: his fondness for the intricate strategies which his fellow councillors employed in competing for the ear and trust of successive royal governors, especially William Tryon who arrived in 1771. After one protracted struggle Smith believed he had won Tryon's confidence and made him suspicious of the rival Delancey faction. "I shall feed that spirit," he exulted in a moment of revelation, "to disentangle him from a fear of Council and Assembly." During the Tea crisis in December 1773, he tried to use the same methods to guide Tryon's hand during a hazardous period. He besieged Tryon with suggestions on how to avoid violence if the tea was landed or how to prevent its unloading if violence was unavoidable. The destruction of the tea in Boston took the decision out of Tryon's hands and launched a new period of greater crisis for royal officials. "It must mortify Tryon who had spoken so vauntingly and assured the government of the landing" of the tea, Smith noted with customary care. But he was much more aware that his own attempts to guide Tryon's hand had been of little practical value to the governor. "Tryon will think I animated him to render him unpopular," he lamented; "how dangerous it is to give private advice."[10]

Smith appeared in 1774–1775 simply to be a conservative gravitating to the right of his former allies in the Livingston faction; in reality he was wholly engrossed in working out the implications of his chosen roles as constitutional analyst and behind-the-scenes manipulator of government and party policy. He wrote and circulated numerous essays on the constitutional and tactical problems facing colonial leaders and propounded an almost clinical set of negotiating tactics, which included "feeling the pulse of the ministry," proceeding "without a word about rights," and exercising exquisite tact and timing. When all this came to naught he responded by writing his longest and most moving exposition of the issues of the Revolution, one which juxtaposed a scathing indictment of British policy and defense of colonial liberty with an absolute refusal to sanction armed rebellion. The conflict between the two commitments reduced him to an abject state of intellectual immobility long before his apparently opportunistic conversion to the British cause. "I persuade myself," he told an inquisitive committee of safety on July 4, 1776, "that Great Britain will discern the propriety of negotiating for a pacification." He could not relinquish the hope that the elusive search for accommodation would transfix the lives of other men as completely as it had his own.[11]

The enunciation of principle often reflected a concern with law and the details of imperial administration while the search for accommodation expressed an awareness of the subtleties of colonial politics. In contrast, the appeal to doctrine came from men on the periphery of political life and imperial government. Eschewing legal and practical objections to colonial resistance, they focused directly on the immortality and ugliness of discontent. The high Anglican polemicists were, of course, the quintessential doctrinaire loyalists and Bailyn has most effectively shown that their writings struck with jugular accuracy at the most significant tenets of whig theory. In Samuel Seabury's vivid denunciation of violence and intimidation, Jonathan Boucher's taut authoritarian logic, and Thomas Bradbury Chandler's breathtaking endorsement of subordination, Bailyn found "wrathful epitaphs" to an "ancient, honorable, moribund philosophy" of order and obedience.[12]

Seabury's fame as a polemicist rests on his colorful and pugnacious denunciation of whig tactics for enforcing the Continental Association boycott on trade with Britain in late 1774 and early 1775. But his vivid language has distracted attention away from the systematic argument which formed the core of the *Letters of a Westchester Farmer*—the nature of perception itself. Seabury was fascinated with the way in which the mind handles sense impressions and organizes them into concepts. He beseeched his readers to practice enough sophistication to subject each new impression of rebellion to careful and critical scrutiny. Unless men assessed the future implications of their actions and appreciated the power and destructiveness of mass contagion, they could not prudently restrain their enthusiasms nor calm the passions of their fellow men. The root of the problem was the finite capacity of the mind and the limitless appeal of false political ideas. "At present politics seems to engross almost every body," he complained in 1769, "and leaves no room for more serious and important reflection." The result by 1774 was a "sullen, sulky obstinacy" which "takes possession of us. . . . Preposterous pride! . . . It degrades instead of exalting our characters" and was the product of "all the *insidious arts* that evilminded and *designing* men can possibly make use of." Only by assuming a posture of aloof, watchful skepticism could a man avoid contamination from glib, appealing, but unsupportable patriot contentions. In the midst of a long series of obtuse propositions—one, for example, resurrected virtual representation in terms which no politically knowledgeable loyalist would have defended—Seabury abruptly related the discussion to his central concern. "That you will perceive the force of this reasoning," he told his polemical rival, Alexander Hamilton, "I cannot pretend to say. A person . . . with jaundice sees no color but yellow. Party heat, the fever of liberty, may vitiate the mind as much as jaundice does the eyes."[13]

Hutchinson, Smith, and Seabury only suggest the distinctiveness of the ideas, beliefs, sensibilities, and patterns of response exhibited by men who enunciated principle, searched for accommodation, or appealed to doctrine during the pre-Revolutionary controversy. Although principle, accommodation, and doctrine were not mutually exclusive categories into which men can be placed, the leading prominent opponents of colonial resistance and the most widely circulated anti-whig ideas of the pre-Revolutionary period almost all adhere to one of these three modes of thought and feeling. Principle, accommodation, and doctrine were orientations and assumptions which gave direction and focus to men's thinking and conduct. In some cases individuals shared more than one of these orientations. John Wentworth of New Hampshire was preeminently a man of accommodation with his warm association with the Rockingham Whigs, thorough contempt for the policies and style of officials like Lord Hillsborough, and primary concern for the interests of his province. He gracefully adapted to a substantial reduction in his family's power in New Hampshire during his governorship. He had a rare degree of serenity which enabled him—without a trace of ambivalence—to contemplate the use of military force to uphold British authority and accept without apparent bitterness his own exile from America. No other loyalist embodied so fully as Wentworth a congenial attachment to both principle and accommodation.[14]

In most cases, a man who partook of more than one of these orientations was dominated by one particular view of political reality and borrowed incidentally from the others. Joseph Galloway desperately wanted to engineer single-handedly an imperial compromise in 1774. The structure of his ideas about the preservation of liberty and the scope of his ambition to heal the Empire in one brilliant stroke dictated that he pronounce rigid principles about the nature of the Empire and that he insist on the complete acquiescence of other colonial leaders to his leadership. When men did not listen to his explanations of principle and liberty and ignored his pretensions to leadership, they created an unexpectedly severe dilemma: they shattered his image of himself as a master of political theory and public persuasion. Galloway then replaced this shattered self-image with one still more magnificent and yet also consistent with his initial posture as an advocate of accommodation and enunciator of principle: "I have deduced your rights and explained your duties. I have laid before you the constitutional extent of parliamentary jurisdiction. I have pointed to the mode which you ought to pursue for a restoration of those rights." His concept of role and the dilemma in which it placed him compelled Galloway to locate all of the wisdom necessary to a solution of the imperial impasse in his own mind. At each stage his perception undermined his advocacy of accommodation and intensified his insistence on principle.[15]

Orientations toward principle, accommodation, or doctrine not only overlapped, they also cut across without completely severing other intellectual alignments during the pre-Revolutionary controversy. Alan Heimert has associated rationalist theology with loyalism or with lukewarm, insensitive support of the whig movement.[16] In direct conflict with the Calvinist whigs, the rationalist clergy neither believed that British policy sprang from utter human depravity nor believed that confession and repentance was an integral preliminary stage in the defense of American liberty. To the rationalist clergy sin afflicted the thoughtless and unreflective. In political terms the sins which needed confessing and forgiving in 1774–1775 were "turbulent desires, secret views of fostering party spirit, lust for unjust dominion, and impatience with lawful government."[17] In elaboration of Heimert's thesis it must also be pointed out that rationalists were subdivided into accommodating and doctrinaire loyalist positions. The accommodating rationalists included Anglicans like William Smith and Jacob Duche and Congregationalists like Gad Hitchcock and Daniel Shute. They endorsed just enough remonstrance to bring colonial discontent to British attention but not so much as to exacerbate the conflict. The doctrinaire rationalist clergy led by Boucher, Chandler, Myles Cooper, and Seabury eschewed this search for a moderate position: political opposition was not an instrument which men might employ responsibly; its "bitterness and wrath and anger and clamour and evil speaking . . . bitter ungodly spirit toward those who differ . . . in things civil or religious" were intrinsically evil, explained the Rev. Samuel Andrews of Connecticut in 1775. The "confidence" and sense of "girding" for righteous conflict which he saw all around him—which the accommodating rationalists wanted to dignify, channel and moderate—blinded men in Andrews's view, to the truth that political change was the prerogative of God and not of men."[18]

Just as Andrews felt compelled to look squarely at the moral earnestness of his whig contemporaries, most pre-Revolutionary loyalists felt driven to discover and articulate a single quintessential insight into the causes of the Revolution and of their own plight. The reconstruction of their perception leads directly to each man's discovery of some central truth about himself and the Revolution. For Egerton Leigh, it came when he discovered that he could relate every step in South Carolina's political and constitutional development to some stage in his own humiliation and downfall. Once he sensed that unity and coherence in South Carolina history, he could at the same time write a trenchant account of the province's political development and also establish his own identity by accentuating the very presumptions about himself that most outraged Charleston's planter-merchant elite and made him a pariah.[19] Jonathan Sewall's withering contempt for the whig protest in Massachusetts reflected a conflict he had felt throughout his adult life: tension between his intellectual distinction and courage on the one hand and his insecurity about his social and political preeminence on the other. He developed an ironic, slightly cynical, and sometimes bemused dismay over any exuberant human enterprise. These defenses protected him from the kind of volcanic eruptions of rage that racked his friend and ally Peter Oliver. Sewall's insight enabled him to recognize the source of disorder in Massachusetts, which "is, I say, so truly astonishing, so entirely out of the course of nature, so repugnant to the known principles which most forceably actuate the human mind that we must search deeper for the grand and hidden spring. . . . This is an enthusiasm in politics like that which religious notions inspire, that drives men on with an unnatural impetuosity [and] baffles and confounds all calculation grounded upon rational principles."[20]

The loyalist perception of the coming of the American Revolution consisted of brilliantly incisive but partially formed and almost stillborn political fears, apprehensions, uncertainties, impulses toward obstruction, and sensations of ambivalence, immobility, and helplessness. This fragmentation and lack of coalescence in pre-Revolutionary loyalist ideology testified to the fragility of elaborate political ideas in eighteenth-century America and the rapid mortality rate of particular formulations of thought as public men continually struggled to revamp slightly out-of-date intellectual postures. In a political culture that took ideas very seriously, this instability cast marginal political figures such as the critics and victims of pre-Revolutionary protest into an excruciating position. This unstable, fluid political culture not only dominated the eighteenth century—as Jack P. Greene's two articles on colonial pessimism and anxiety dramatically emphasized—but elements of this malady continued well into the nineteenth century and provided much of the distraught energy expended by James M. Banner's Federalists and Fred Somkin's Fourth of July orators.[21]

With the commencement of hostilities in 1775 and the declaration of American independence in 1776, the discrete categories—conservatism and defense of the established order—tended to dissolve. War and the creation of new state governments widened the scope of the conflict and caught thousands of previously obscure men in the machinery of internal security. The people that William H. Nelson calls the "Tory Rank and File" were clusters of "cultural minorities" scattered along the geographical and social periphery of American life: religious pacifists, pro-British Indian traders, backcountry southern farmers, unassimilated ethnic minorities, as well as isolated individuals everywhere impelled by custom, instinct, greed, accident, resentment, or bad luck to oppose independence.[22] They expressed their opposition to the Revolution in more elemental ways than did their counterparts in the pre-Revolutionary controversy. As the War for Independence created loyalist communities in occupied New York, Charleston, and Philadelphia and as communities of exiles formed in England and Canada, a new sense of loyalist identity emerged: the loyalists' ironic discovery that they were victims of both American aggression and British incompetence. An understandable, if somewhat irrational, paranoia became a positive force in shaping post-Revolutionary loyalist behavior. It engendered a tough, realistic, and implacable determination to surmount the difficulties of rebuilding their lives and constructing a new political social order in British North America. The pre-Revolutionary loyalist perception was only one ingredient in this long and fascinating process. But if this interpretation of the stages of loyalist thought is a valid preliminary diagnosis of the historical problem, then the riches of the Loyalist Papers Project may well fuel a far-reaching inquiry into the comparative intellectual history of colonial America, Revolutionary America and England, and post-Revolutionary Canada.[23]

Author's Note (1988)

By the time I wrote this essay, the correct name of the organization mentioned in the last sentence was the Program for Loyalist Studies and Publications, Robert A. East and James E. Mooney, executive and associate directors. While the complete photocopying of loyalist manuscripts, envisioned by the project, was not feasible because of funding limitations, the project did compile and publish *A Bibliography of Loyalist Source Material in the United States, Canada, and Great Britain*, ed., Gregory Palmer (Westport, Conn.: Meckler Publishing, 1982).

Author's Note (2008)

The principle/accommodation/doctrine conceptualization has held up fairly well over the years. Admittedly no one has strongly invoked it or critically questioned its validity. Nevertheless this formulation now needs fine-tuning.

Principled loyalism received substantial reinforcement in 1973, the same year this essay was first published, when my teacher, Jack P. Greene, published the then newly discovered manuscript treatise by William Knox, "Considerations on the great Question, what is to be done with America?" Knox was Whitehall's chief authority on colonial administration and also a Georgia loyalist with property and connections in the buffer colony between South Carolina and East Florida. Written in 1778 or early 1779, Knox's treatise sought a deeper explanation as to why the war had not been the cakewalk he and other imperial officials had assumed it would be and, specifically, why more colonists had not rallied to the royal standard.

"The causes . . . are inherent in the Constitution," Knox speculated, and by "Constitution" he meant literally the materials from which the colonial system had been put together—or *constituted*. "Opulence" and geographic "greatness" had instilled into colonial thinking the idea that the colonies were "distinct" rather than subordinate communities. Love of monarchy had atrophied in North America and habits of reliance on their "connection" with the British state never put down deep roots. The earliest settlers knew "poverty" and lived in a "mean condition," which, from the outset, instilled abhorrence of British taxes and distaste for the accoutrements of royal government. The abundance of lawyers in the colonial elite was an "important and fatal cause of the predominancy of Democratic power." Concessions early charters made to religious dissenters undermined religious as well as social "hierarchy." Finally the ignorance of Crown officials about these very manifestations of imperial weakness spawned "mistakes" in imperial governance that could be corrected only by laying down "a new foundation upon Principles of Wisdom, Justice, and solid Policy" giving "happiness" to the colonists sufficient to "render equally their Inclination and their interest to continue [as] Members of the British Empire."

What stands out in *that* enunciation of loyalist principle is the admission that loyalism was a persuasion dependent on enlightened statecraft. Had I been more alert to Knox's newly surfaced insights as I completed "The Loyalist Perception," this essay would have focused more on statecraft than on provincial political identity. (See Jack P. Greene, ed., "William Knox's Explanation for the American Revolution," *William and Mary Quarterly*, 3rd ser., 30 [April 1973]: 293–306, and "The Deeper Roots of Colonial Discontent: William Knox's Structural Explanation for the American Revolution," in *Understanding the American Revolution: Issues and Actors* [Charlottesville: University Press of Virginia, 1995], 10–17.)

Likewise, doctrine, the final element in the loyalist perception, has been powerfully reinforced by subsequent scholarship: J. C. D. Clark, *English Society, 1688–1832: Ideology, Social Structure, and Political Practice* (Cambridge: Cambridge University Press, 1985), and Clark's companion volume, *English Society, 1660–1832: Religion, Ideology, and Politics* (Cambridge: Cambridge University Press, 2000), argue that high toryism was normative throughout rural England and that this healthy development accounted for the stability of British politics during what Robert R. Palmer has called "the age of the democratic revolution." While the majority of Americans in the 1770s and 1780s had moved beyond the pale of Clark's sense of political reality in England, had I looked more closely at English toryism in the scholarship of the 1980s, I would have better appreciated the bedrock of political support in England on which the North ministry, and its loyalist allies, depended.

Finally, whither accommodation? When the accommodating loyalists beheld the Rockingham Whigs, they perceived the kind of British political leadership that could save the colonies from revolution and keep Americans content under mild imperial rule. Rockingham Whiggery was a mirror in which the accommodating loyalists saw their fondest dreams. In Eliga H. Gould, *The Persistence of Empire: British Political Culture in the Age of the American Revolution* (Charlottesville: University Press of Virginia, 2000), the Rockingham party was not mentioned. But a closer reading revealed that the Rockingham Whigs were not in his book because they were not products of the political culture of their times. Rich, idealistic, and intellectually ambitious, they had no need of imperial grandeur and hierarchy to complete their identity and no cause to be mindful of the fragility of the Hanoverian regime Robert Walpole and George I had socially constructed in the 1720s and 1730s as a special trusteeship for factional politicians later in the century. The historic moderation of the Rockingham Whigs and their colonial clients obscured the political culture of their times.[24]

Repealing the Stamp Act and instituting negotiations for peace in 1782 represented the outer limits of their capabilities. In 1766 they took the pressure off the accommodating loyalists; in 1782 they set in motion the negotiations that nudged the Continental Congress toward loyalist conciliation and which Parliament sweetened with a grant for loyalist compensation.

Notes

1. This paragraph is based on a variety of writings in social psychology and phenomenology. Jerome S. Bruner, "Social Psychology and Perception," in E. E. Maccoby et al., eds., *Readings in Social Psychology* (New York, 1958), pp. 85–94 and Roger Brown, *Social Psychology* (New York, 1965), chapter 12 both discuss the major recent writings in the field and quotations are from the Bruner article. See also Frank P. Chambers, *Perception, Understanding, and Society* (London, 1961), p. 51; Maurice Merleau-Ponty, *The Primary of Perception* (Evanston, Ill., 1964), p. 25; Zevedi Barbu, *Problems in Historical Psychology* (New York, 1960), pp. 20–22; the extensive discussion of work on motivation in Robert F. Berkhofer, *A Behavior Approach to Historical Analysis* (New York, 1969), pp. 55–67. This scholarship meshes closely with several recent historiographical articles: Samuel H. Beer, "Casual Explanation and Imaginative Re-enactment," and Bruce Kuklick, "The Mind of the Historian," both in *History and Theory*, 3 (1963): 6–29 and 8 (1969): 313–31, and John Dunn, "The Identity of the History of Ideas," *Philosophy*, 43 (April, 1968): 85–104.

2. Hutchinson to Rev. Eli Forbes, October 16, 1773, and to John Hely Hutchinson, February 14, 1772, Hutchinson Letterbooks, vol. 27, pp. 556–57, 296–300, Massachusetts Archives, State House, Boston (available in typescript at the Massachusetts Historical Society, Boston).

3. Morgan, "Thomas Hutchinson and the Stamp Act," *New England Quarterly*, 21 (1942): 459–92; Freiberg, "How to Become a Colonial Governor," *Review of Politics*, 21 (October, 1951): 646–56; Shipton, *Sibley's Harvard Graduates* (Cambridge and Boston, 1933–1975), vol. 7, pp. 383–13; B. Bailyn, *Ideological Origins of the American Revolution* (Cambridge, Mass., 1967), pp. 121–23.

4. John A. Garraty, ed., *Interpreting American History: Conversations with Historians* (New York, 1970), vol. 1, p. 74.

5. Morgan, "Thomas Hutchinson and the Stamp Act," pp. 487–92; Donald C. Lord and Robert M. Calhoon, "The Removal of the Massachusetts General Court from Boston, 1769–1772," *Journal of American History*, 55 (1969): 728, n. 9, see below, chapter 3.

6. Hutchinson, *Speeches of . . . Governor Hutchinson to the General Assembly . . .* (Boston, 1773), pp. 13–14; see also his "Dialogue between a European and an American [Englishman]," Hutchinson Papers, vol. 28, p. 102, Mass. Arch.

7. Lord and Calhoon, "The Removal of the General Court," pp. 747–48, 753–54.

8. Bailyn, *Ideological Origins*, p. 56.

9. Robert M. Calhoon, ed., "William Smith's Alternative to the American Revolution," *William and Mary Quarterly*, 3rd ser., 22 (1965): 105–18, see below, chapter 2.

10. W. H. W. Sabine, ed., *Historical Memoirs from . . . 1763 to . . . 1776 of William Smith* (New York, 1956), pp. 118, 156–64.

11. Sabine, *Historical Memoirs*, pp. 224–28c, 271–77, 279.

12. Bailyn, *Ideological Origins*, p. 312; a highly original but gingerly examination of high Tory ideology is Michael D. Clark, "Jonathan Boucher: The Mirror of Reaction," *Huntington Library Quarterly*, 33 (1969): 19–32.

13. Seabury to Rev. Daniel Burton, December 17, 1769 and March 29, 1770, Society for the Propagation of the Gospel Papers, Fulham Palace, London; ms. sermon, Lambeth Palace, London; Clarence Vance, ed., *Letters of a Westchester Farmer* (White Plains, N.Y., 1930), pp. 152, 72–75, 104, 111–12, 116.

14. Wentworth to Dr. Belham, August 9, 1768, Wentworth Letterbooks, New Hampshire Department of Records and Archives, Concord, N.H., quoted extensively in L. S. Mayo, *John Wentworth . . .* (Cambridge, 1921), pp. 122–24.

15. Robert M. Calhoon, "'I have deduced your rights': Joseph Galloway's Concept of his Role, 1774–1775," *Pennsylvania History,* 25 (1968): 356–78, see below, chapter 5.

16. Alan Heimert, *Religion and the American Mind: From the Greater Awakening to the Revolution* (Cambridge, Mass., 1966).

17. William Smith, *The Works of William Smith, D.D.* (Philadelphia, 1803), vol. 2, p. 123.

18. Samuel Andrews, *A Discourse Showing the Necessity of Joining Internal Repentance with the External Profession of It . . .* (New Haven, Conn., 1775), pp. 15–18.

19. Robert M. Calhoon and Robert M. Weir, "'The Scandalous History of Sir Egerton Leigh,'" *William and Mary Quarterly,* 3rd ser., 26 (1969): 47–74, see chapter 4 below.

20. Sewall to General Frederick Haldimand, May 30, 1775, quoted in Jack P. Greene, ed., *Colonies to Nation, 1763–1776* (New York, 1967), pp. 266–68.

21. Jack P. Greene, "Search for Identity: An Interpretation of the Meaning of Selected Patterns of Social Response in Eighteenth-Century America," *Journal of Social History,* 3 (1970): 189–220, and Greene, "Political Mimesis: A Consideration of the Historical and Cultural Roots of Legislative Behavior in the British Colonies in the Eighteenth Century," *American Historical Review,* 75 (1969): 337–67; James M. Banner, *To the Hartford Convention: The Federalists and the Origins of Party Politics in Massachusetts, 1789–1815* (New York, 1970), and Fred Somkin, *Unquiet Eagle: Memory and Desire in the Idea of American Freedom, 1815–1860* (Ithaca, N.Y., 1967).

22. See W. H. Nelson, *The American Tory* (Oxford, 1961), chap. 5.

23. On these patterns, see Wallace Brown, *The Good Americans: The Loyalists in the American Revolution* (New York, 1969), chap. 6; Mary Beth Norton, *The British-Americans: The Loyalist Exiles in England, 1774–1789* (Boston, 1972).

24. See Robert McCluer Calhoon, *Political Moderation in America's First Two Centuries* (Cambridge, 2009), pp. 74–81.

"The Constitution Ought to Bend"

William Smith, Jr.'s, Alternative to the American Revolution

ROBERT M. CALHOON

During the mid–eighteenth century various men proposed improvements in the administration of the colonies. Martin Bladen, Sir William Keith, Benjamin Franklin, James Abercromby, Henry McCulloh, Thomas Pownall, and Francis Bernard were only the more prominent advocates of reform.[1] Most of these writers sought either to streamline colonial administration or to provide mechanisms by which the colonies might better contribute to the defense of the Empire. Franklin, Pownall, and Bernard seemed to sense that more extensive reforms might be needed to bridge the growing gap between colonial practice and imperial theory; but even their proposals did not pay sufficient attention to changes in colonial politics and the new aspirations of American leaders. Just how drastic a change was necessary in imperial institutions and in the assumptions of British officials about colonial politics was suggested by William Smith, Jr., a New York lawyer, historian, and councillor,[2] in his "Thoughts upon the Dispute between Great Britain and her Colonies," printed here below.

Composed between 1765 and 1767 during the Stamp Act crisis and its aftermath, Smith's "Thoughts" drew upon two decades of study and activity in New York politics.[3] He had long been aware of the implications of the rise of the lower houses of provincial assemblies, which, he reasoned, was at the heart of most problems between the colonies and the Mother Country. New York assemblymen, he noted in 1756, were "tenacious in the Opinion that the Inhabitants of this Colony are entitled to all the Privileges of *Englishmen*" and "have a Right to participate in the legislative Power." Royal governors operated on the contrary assumption that the assembly existed only by the sufferance of the Crown. "It is easy to conceive," he predicted, "that Contentions most naturally attend such a Contradiction of Sentiments." These two opposing conceptions of the status of the lower houses persisted, Smith explained, because no one saw the problem as a whole. Colonial officials would not take the claims of the assembly seriously, and colonial representatives were preoccupied with mundane problems like "the Regulation of Highways, the Destruction of Wolves, . . . and the Advancement of the other little Interests of the particular Counties which they . . . represent."[4]

The furor in New York over the Grenville program confirmed Smith's fears. First the Sugar Act, then a long dispute between Lieutenant Governor Cadwallader Colden and the New York legal profession over an appeal to the Privy Council, and finally the Stamp Act dangerously antagonized the province. The ostensible cause of the crisis, as Smith and others noted, was the fear that British taxation would enable Parliament to "take away all we have."[5] But Smith believed that the root of the problem lay much deeper, and his peculiar contribution was to demonstrate how the structure of the Empire contributed to conflicting assumptions of British and colonial leaders about colonial rights and obligations.

Smith therefore based his "Thoughts" on the premise that the colonies' contribution in the Seven Years' War and their growing maturity entitled them to a generous redefinition of their place in the Empire. To have supposed that such a readjustment could be accomplished by commercial restrictions or Parliamentary taxation was, in Smith's judgment, "palpable Blundering." As colonial opposition to the Grenville program mounted, Smith noted how both sides appealed to their respective interpretations of the British constitution. The colonists invoked the rights of Englishmen, and the British replied that the virtual representation of the colonies in Parliament amply protected those rights. Such appeals to constitutional precedent, he contended, were futile: "the Truth is, that the Empire, long after the Constitution was formed, acquired a *new, adventitious State.* . . . The Question therefore is not, what the Constitution was, or is, but what, present Circumstances considered, it ought to be." In the place of fruitless contention about constitutional rights, both sides should seek common ground in the mutual advantages provided by the wealth of the Empire. In order for the colonies to survive and flourish and Britain to maintain its power, "the Constitution (be it what it will) ought to bend, and *sooner or later* will bend." Because Smith remained detached from any particular interpretation of the constitution, he conceived of it as a malleable, flexible set of doctrines which men should adapt to meet changing circumstances.[6]

The recognition by all parties that the constitution of the Empire should remain flexible was, in Smith's view, only a first step. He also wanted boldly to reconstruct imperial institutions. Reiterating the view that the provincial preoccupations of assemblymen precluded the broad vision needed to govern America, he suggested the creation of a continental parliament to supplement the assemblies, drawing members from all of the mainland colonies including Quebec, Nova Scotia, and the Floridas. He also envisioned an American council appointed by the Crown and a Lord Lieutenant modeled on that post in Ireland.

Smith's "Thoughts" assumed that only tangible, workable changes in the structure of the Empire could create a more stable political atmosphere. The constitutional debate revealed to him an unnatural state of anxiety, growing out of the colonists' fears about their political rights and British concern for the security of its economic stake in the colonies. The chief virtue of his approach, he believed, lay in his recognition of that insecurity and his desire to alleviate it effectively.

Smith's "Thoughts" therefore aimed all of its proposals toward the object of rebuilding confidence. His immediate purpose was to abolish the necessity for Parliamentary taxation of the colonies by transferring that authority to the new American parliament. He proposed that the Crown should present the American legislature with an annual requisition. The new legislature would then apportion the sum among the various colonies, leaving the raising of the revenue to the provincial assemblies. Significantly, the American parliament would deal in these fiscal matters, not with the Parliament at Westminster, but directly with the Crown. Having secured an exemption from Parliamentary taxation in return for this annual contribution, the colonies would then acknowledge Parliamentary authority over them in all other fields.

The problems of taxation and imperial defense were secondary to Smith's main purpose. He was chiefly interested in analyzing the sources of distrust within the Empire. He attributed the lack of confidence between British and colonial leaders in large part to the proliferation of colonial assemblies. They could neither function effectively nor command British respect because they attracted inferior men, were subject to provincial pressures, and could not cope with problems affecting the colonies as a whole. If, however, colonial institutions were inadequate, taxation by Parliament was no solution. The advocates of virtual representation, Smith observed, were motivated by ignorance and an "overweaning Attachment to their own Interest." To prevent imperial disintegration, politicians on both sides had to visualize the Empire as a whole, anticipate its future development, and then create institutions capable of meeting present and future needs. The expansion of the colonies across the continent had only begun, he noted, while British power had probably reached its zenith. This sense of the future motivated his belief in constitutional reform. British self-interest required a durable link with the colonies, and America could exploit the resources of the continent more effectively if it could exchange raw materials for British goods. Therefore, he concluded, while both sides needed 'the Empire, the British probably had a greater interest in preserving it than did the colonies. The authors of "The American Whig, No. V,"—probably Smith and William Livingston—carried this analysis a step further by defining the seaboard colonies and inland territories as an "indispensable substratum of empire" which required for its "foundation . . . a *regular American Constitution*."[7] This declaration of nascent manifest destiny in Smith's "Thoughts" and "The American Whig" added a new dimension to the discussion of colonial rights by turning the prospect of American expansion into a compelling argument for constitutional reform.

The subsequent career of Smith's "Thoughts" was less interesting than the content of the document itself. Appointed to the Council in New York in 1767, Smith found himself increasingly concerned with provincial affairs, particularly with a protracted struggle within the Council over the distribution of certain disputed lands situated between New York and New Hampshire. He did attempt to have provisions of his plan incorporated in a petition to the House of Lords in

December 1768, but the assembly deleted it.[8] His interest in it revived, however, when General Frederick Haldimand expressed interest in the proposal in 1775 as the imperial crisis moved to its climax. Smith sent the General a copy of his "Thoughts" and Haldimand forwarded it without comment to Lord Dartmouth, Secretary of State for the Colonies.[9] In August 1775 the plan received further attention when a published letter—written in 1769 by Thomas Hutchinson to Hillsborough, Dartmouth's predecessor as Colonial Secretary—spoke of "an Expectation of an American Parliament" by someone in New York. Hutchinson ridiculed the idea because it compromised the supremacy of Parliament. Smith presumed that Hutchinson had not seen his manuscript, but he did recall mentioning its contents to Hutchinson's friend, Andrew Oliver.[10] A few days after he saw the newspaper account of Hutchinson's letter about his plan, Smith heard a rumor that Lord Mansfield had prepared proposals for reconciling the colonies. Smith immediately assumed that his plan was "the Ground work" of Mansfield's recommendations, and he further assumed that Hutchinson's garbled version of the "Thoughts" or Haldimand's complete text had received serious consideration in London.[11]

Though Smith's "Thoughts" in fact received little if any attention from British officials, he remained convinced that inadequate mechanisms of Empire were at the bottom of the imperial crisis. His "Thoughts as a rule for my own Conduct, at this melancholy Hour of approaching Distress," written a few weeks before independence, was a painstaking résumé of the failure of the institutions of the Empire to accommodate both British and colonial aspirations. As in his earlier "Thoughts," he here located the crux of the problem in a structural flaw of the Empire. "As no Provision was made for constituting an Impartial Judge between [the colonies and the Mother Country]," he lamented, "their Controversies are therefore to be decided by Negotiation and Treaty, or on an Appeal to the Lord of Hosts by Battle."[12]

Few contemporaries read Smith's "Thoughts," and even Haldimand and Dartmouth did not appear to appreciate its importance.[13] But it is an instructive source on the coming of the Revolution. It shows that Smith—an informed, reflective eighteenth-century American—was capable of looking at the constitution, not as a doctrine to obey nor a reality to accept, but as a tool to adapt, improve, and "bend." Because Smith believed that individuals had the ability to perceive and the duty to correct flaws in the constitution, his memorandum minimizes the importance of impersonal, historical forces and enhances the role of individual initiative in colonial politics. Smith might well have agreed with Charles H. McIlwain's well-known view that the American Revolution resulted from "a collision of two mutually incompatible interpretations of the British constitution"[14] or at least the constitution of the British Empire. But unlike the legalistic writers upon whom McIlwain depended, Smith's analysis attributed the constitutional impasse more to the intellectual rigidity among leaders on both sides than to a contradiction of principles.[15]

Two copies of the "Thoughts," one in Smith's handwriting, are preserved among the Dartmouth Papers in the William Salt Library, Stafford, England.[16]

Thoughts upon the Dispute between Great Britain and her Colonies.

They who speak of the Union between these Countries, barely as of Importance, and even of *vast* Importance, do not express themselves properly. He who knows, that *one third* Part of the Commerce of Britain, depends upon her Colonies; and that if this is lost, she is ruined, will talk of the Union, as essential to the very Existence of the Empire.

What then are we to think of the present Quarrel? It is a Dissease that affects Life. And as it spreads fast, the Remedy must be speedily administered. A solid Dominion must be founded in Love and Interest. The affection of three Millions of Subjects, situated as we are, if once lost, will scarce ever be regained.

The last War was a glorious one. To *Individuals* it has been profitable; and if our Successes are wisely improved, it will be so to the *Nation,* the vast Increase of the Public Debt notwithstanding.

By the Conquest of Canada, Great Britain was supposed to acquire the Dominion of all North America; and thenceforth to be in a Condition, to seize the West India Islands at Pleasure, humble France and Spain and secure the Tranquility of Europe.[17] But is the Rescue of the Continent from France, the ensuring of it to Great Britain? Surely something more was to be done after the War ceased. The Colonies when delivered from the Enemy, were to be secured to their Protectors.

It was palpable Blundering, to imagine that this could be effected by unusual, exceptionable Taxations, and an embarrassed, partial Commerce. The Minister fell into this Error, in a Fright at the Amount of the national Debt, and for want of Knowledge concerning the Nature and State of our Trade.

He presumed that the Colonies were now out of their Infancy, able to stand upon their Legs, and to give Aid to the Mother Country.

The vast Wealth acquired from us in the Circuits of Commerce were not considered. What respected our Defense from the Enemy abroad, and the Savages at Home, and the internal support of Government, ing[r]ossed all his Attention.

It is agreed that if the Colonies enjoy a free Trade, it will bear Impositions, that may vastly relieve the Charges of the Empire.

A direct Tax was devised in 1764, but not without some Diffidence. A Year's Notice was given, before the burden was actually imposed.

This is the Origin of the controversy. Much has been written upon the Subject. Both Countries fly to the Constitution, for Arguments in Support of Tenets, *diametrically* opposite to each other. On the Part of America, there is a Claim to all the Rights of Englishmen; whence it is inferred, that no Tax can be laid upon them without the Consent of their Assemblies: Great Britain on the other Hand, attempts to justify her Measures, by admitting the Principle, but denying the Consequence; for She contends, that the Americans are *virtually* represented, by the Commons of Great Britain.

It is not proposed to enter into this Controversy here. Let it suffice to observe, that the Litigants on both Sides, seem to be insensible, that the constitutional Principles they appeal to, were established before the Colonies were discovered, and that some of them argue, as if we were in the same Predicament, with a *County* of the Old Realm of England; whereas the Truth is, that the Empire, long after the Constitution was formed, acquired a *new, adventitious State.* And the Question therefore is not, what the Constitution was, or is, but what, present Circumstances considered, it ought to be.

Britain having made a vast Accession to her Dominion, by Discovery, by Conquest and by Cession, the Disputants, instead of spending their Time, in collecting Arguments, all chargeable with a Non Sequitur, should have pointed to Measures conducive to the common Weal of both Countries; because to that [end][18] the Constitution (be it what it will) ought to bend, and *sooner* or *later* will bend; unless it is the Design of Heaven to infatuate and destroy us as a Nation.

The Colonies became separate, and with respect to each other independent Societies, by *Accident;* neither the Crown nor the Nation, had any Design in Splitting the Dominions into so many different, petty Governments. Thro' *Necessity* each acquired *Legislative* Powers, in a Mode somewhat similar to the grand Pattern in the Parent Country. There seems to be no Reason to doubt, but that if the whole Continent of North America, had been antiently asked for by one Company; suppose for Instance the Virginia Company in 1606, the Grant would have passed; and *one* Assembly been constituted, to make Laws for this immense Region.

The Case is however otherwise, the Continent consists of Sixteen or Seventeen Colonies and Provinces, under the immediate Government, of almost as many little Parliaments made up of a Governor and a Council differently appointed, and an Assembly of Delegates, chosen by the People.

None can deny, that the Colonies ought to bear some Part of the Public Burdens. If the Royal Requisitions for Aids are to be made to each, the Objections are obvious and unanswerable,

1st The Empire will become too complex, popular and unwieldy;

2ly Persons utterly incompetent for its Affairs, will participate in its Councils; and,

3ly The Empire will be perpetually distracted, and in Danger of a Dissolution, from a want of *Uniformity in Design.*

The Advocates for the British Supremacy, had these Consequences in full View. The Prospect filled them with Terror. We ought to ascribe the fictitious, virtual Representation they talk of, to their Consternation, and *not to*

Malice. But their Scheme is manifestly defective; because it does not provide for the Safety of the Colonies; It discovers an overweaning Attachment to their own Interest; and being partial, tends to work the Disunion we all dread, as ruinous to the whole Empire.

America supplicates for Relief; and if she desires no more, than the Parliament's ceasing to act, upon the Principle of unbounded Sovereignty, and that the Crown may again recur, to the old Course of Requisitions to each Colony, the guilt of partiality will be our's.

Let any Man well consider the three Objections, to such a Form of Government above mentioned, and he must be convinced, that it cannot give Stability to so vast an Empire.[19]

If our Experience has not yet furnished Arguments from *Facts,* against such a Distribution of Power, tis because we were formerly too feeble and exposed, to give the Assistance that will *soon* be justly due, and certainly expected.

The present Contentions are the *first,* in the Train of tragical Consequences, inevitably flowing, from *too manifold a Partition,* of the *Legislative* Authority of the Empire.

It is of Necessity then, that a Constitution be devised, friendly to every Branch of the great Whole, and linking Great Britain and her Colonies together, by the most indesoluble Ties.

As the Contest arose, from a Foresight of the Inconveniences, attending a Resort to so many *separate* Assemblies, the most obvious Remedy seems to be, a Consolidation of all these little, continental Parliaments into *one.*

It is not proposed to annihilate the Assemblies, but that there be a Lord Lieutenant as in Ireland, and a Council of at least Twenty four Members, appointed by the Crown, with a House of Commons, consisting of Deputies chosen by their respective *Assemblies,* to meet at the central Province of New York, as the Parliament of North America.

A Parliament is no Novelty; and therefore we shall not be perplexed in settling its Powers, and the Privileges of the several Branches. Let it be in general understood, that to this Body the Royal Requisitions for Aids are to be made, and that they are to have Authority, to grant for all, and to settle the Quotas of each; leaving the Ways and Means to their separate Consideration, unless in Cases of Default.

The Number of the Council may depend upon the Royal Pleasure; but to preserve their Independency, they ought to be Men of Fortune, and hold their Places for Life; with some honorable Distinctions to their Families, as a Lure to prevent the Office from falling into Contempt.

The Number of the Delegates, will naturally be proportioned to the comparative Weight and Abilities, of the Colonies they represent. The two Floridas, Rode Island, Nova Scotia and Georgia ought each to have five. New Hampshire, Marriland, North Carolina and Quebec seven. South Carolina and New Jersey eleven. New York, Pennsilvania and Connecticut twelve and Massachusets Bay and Virginia fifteen.[20]

The whole House will thus consist of one hundred and forty one Members. A small Number, considering the Importance of their Trust. Besides Accident, Business and Disease will Occasion the Absence of many. They may be afterwards increased, when the Colonies are become more populous and desire it. The Crown to retain its antient Negative, and the British Parliament its Legislative Supremacy, in *all Cases* relative to *Life Liberty and Property,* except in the Matter of Taxations for *general Aids,* or the immediate, internal Support of the American Government.[21]

This Project is manifestly free from all the Objections, that lay either against that, which subjects American Property to the British Disposition; or the other, which asks that each Colony, should participate *so largely* in the Councils of the Empire, as to have the Power of refusing Aids; tho' thought necessary for the common Safety, by the *united Voice* of Great Britain and all the Rest of her extensive Dominions.

It may be said of every one of the Colonies, that our Assemblies are unequal to the Task, of entering into the Views of so wise, and so great a Nation as Great Britain is, and from which we are so far removed. Indeed it is not to be expected from an Infant Country, many of those Assemblymen represent little obscure Counties, and are themselves at Streights for a bare Livelyhood. Besides, the scant Districts of the respective Provinces, bring the several Branches of the Legislature into too great a Familiarity, for the Purposes of good Government; and open the Door to frequent Bickerings and Discords, in which the common Interest will be too often sacrificed, to private Piques or partial Aims, and the Royal Voice drowned in the Dinn of Faction, or the Clamours against an obnoxious Governor.

But in a Parliament, chosen *not by the Counties,* but by the *Representatives* of the Colonies, we shall collect the Wisdom of the whole Continent, and find the Members acting upon Principles, doubly refined from popular Lees, and with a Liberality unbiassed by the partial Prejudices, prevalent in the little Districts by which they were sent.

Unspeakable Advantages will also flow, from the Introduction of a *dignified* Government, into a Country long neglected, and where, on Account of its being little known to Great Britain, and the diversity of their Colony Constitutions, many Disorders have crept in, in some Instances dangerous and detrimental to the Colonies, and their British Creditors, and derogative of the just Rights, and many Prerogatives of the Crown, most friendly to Peace and good Order.

But the Capital Advantages of this Scheme, will be the Recovery of the Colonies, to a firm Confidence in the *Justice* and *Affection* of the Parent State. And by opening to her the Conduits of sure, full and constant Information, enabling her so to regulate and improve this vast, dependant, growing

Territory, as to unite every Branch of the Empire, by the Cords of Love and Interest, and give Peace, Health and Vigor to the whole.

There are several Reasons, why this Measure should be *speedily* attended to.

I   The Colonies are universally agitated, by Suspicion, Fear and Disgust; and doubling by their own Growth in less than thirty Years, will in *Fifty*, equall the Inhabitants of Great Britain and Ireland. Unforeseen Events in Europe, may accelerate this momentous Increase[.]

II   By the dissentions in the Mother Country, her rapid Advance in Luxury, the American Attention to Manufactures, the Alarming Extent of the National Debt, the democratical Assendancy of the Commons, and many other Causes, Great Britain seems to have passed the Zenith of Her Glory, without some great Change in the system of her Affairs.

III   If these [sic] is a Recourse to the Establishment of a Dominion, founded *only in Fear,* it can last no longer, than till the controuling Power, is distressed by a general War; and the Revisal of the Contest for Liberty at such a Crisis; must be tragical indeed. Members to a Parliament in Europe, the Americans never will send; and every other Scheme, but one as agreeable to them as that now recommended, would soon prove to be but a temporary Palliative and meer Quack Medicine.

IV   The Colonies will never be less assuming than at present. If the Disgusts now raised, should continue, we may become a Nest for the disaffected and designing, even in Great Britain and Ireland; Now we demand only an Exemption from *Parliamentary Taxations* as a Right, recognizing at the same Time, the Supremacy of Great Britain, in *every other Instance* and particularly her Sovereignty in Commerce.[22] It is therefore her Interest to lay a solid Foundation for her Dominion by a voluntary and durable Compact. What we ask as a Favor at present, may be after a few Years offered and refused.[23]

I am sensible that a Jealousy of the Power, which a Union of our Councils would create, may prevent Great Britain from concurring in the Erection of a *third Parliament,* for the Government of the Empire. But this very Jealousy, is Part of the National Disease, and will if it continues, be the Ruin of us all.

If she Means to oppress her Colonies, their common Danger, will in Spite of all Opposition unite them together. The late offensive Laws are a Proof of it, and all History verifies the Position. But if she abandons her partiality, and generously consults the common Weal, What Ground can there be for Jealousy. When once secured in our Property, our Affection will revive; and ten Thousand Cords may be contrived, to tie us together by the Knot of Interest. Prosperity may indeed make us wanton; but Provinces rarely rebell, till the Yoke of Oppression galls, and a deaf Ear to their Complaints, has begot a sullen Abhorrence of their Masters.

It has been apprehended by some, that some extensive Colonies, like an overgrown Child, will exhaust the Parent. The Cases of the antient

Phoenicians, and modern Spaniards, have been mentioned on this Occasion. But all that read History, are not able to apply it, and make the proper Distinctions.

If Great Britain is to be ruined as these Speculatists suppose by the Flight of her Inhabitants to America, 'tis high Time to set the new House in Order, for their comfortable Accommodation, and welcome Reception. The Colonies are growing up, with many distinguishing Peculiarities; and tho' they may be now easily drawn into an harmonious Uniformity, yet by a little longer Negligence, their Prejudices will grow obstinate and humoursome.

If any unforeseen Catastrophe in Europe, should render their favorite Islands, no longer tenable in that Quarter, they may retreat to America; and the Present, is the most Advantageous Season, for laying a solid Foundation, for the speedy Re-establishment of a Dominion, which no Power upon Earth will be able to annoy.

But tho' the Wars in Asia, drove the feeble and defenceless Phoenecians to Carthage, and the Mines of Mexico and Peru depopulated Spain, Yet Great Britain by a wise Conduct, may improve her Colonies, even for the Increase of her own Population, as well as the Aggrandizement of her Power.

Every Body knows, that the Number of her Inhabitants is vastly inhanced since the Discovery of the New World; and can any Man be ignorant, that this is owing to the Augmentation thereby given to her Commerce?

The same Causes will produce the same Effects. The Spanish Emigrations drained the old State, chiefly, because they sent her *Money* instead of *Merchandise*. Spain was converted into a Castle of Indolence; She acquired *Silver* and *Gold* from her colonies, but not *real Wealth*.

If Great Britain is attentive to her own, and the Trade of her Colonies, she may dismiss all Fears of our Increase. Nay it will be then her Interest, to incourage our Increase.

One cannot take the State, Nature, Climates and prodigious Extent of the American Continent into Contemplation, without high Prospects in favor of the Power, to which it belongs. It is sufficient to be the *Granary* of all the Rest of the British Dominions. Fed by our Plough, Britain might attend more to the Cultivation of Sheep. By that Staple, and the Collection of raw Materials *from* us and *by* us, she may convert her own Island, as it were, into one great Town of Manufacturers, undersell every other Nation in Europe, and maintain and exalt her Supremacy, until Heaven blots out all the Empires of the World.

Author's Note (1988)

Smith's plan received more attention than I realized when I wrote this article. For citations to discussions of his ideas, see Robert M. Calhoon, *The Loyalists in Revolutionary America, 1760–1781* (New York, 1973), p. 520. The historian William Gordon had access to a draft of the plan sometime before 1776 and transcribed it; Gordon's transcription mysteriously found its way into the papers of John Adams, prompting Adams's modern editors to attribute it to Gordon, see Robert J. Taylor, ed., *Papers of John Adams* (Cambridge, Mass., 1977), vol. 2, pp. 419–28. At the request of the editor of the *William and Mary Quarterly*, I shortened the title of this article by deleting the quoted words; here the original title is restored.

Notes

1. On proposals to rationalize the institutions of the Empire see in general Charles M. Andrews, *The Colonial Period of American History*, vol. 4 (New Haven, Conn., 1938): 412–13; on Bladen, see Jack P. Greene, "Martin Bladen's Blueprint for a Colonial Union," *William and Mary Quarterly*, 3rd ser., 17 (1960): 516–30; on Keith, see Roy N. Lokken, "Sir William Keith's Theory of the British Empire," *The Historian*, 25 (1963): 403–18; on Franklin, see Gerald Stourzh, *Benjamin Franklin and American Foreign Policy* (Chicago, 1954), pp. 48–82; on Abercromby, see Andrews, *Colonial Period of American History*, vol. 4, pp. 409–11; on McCulloh, see [Henry McCulloh], *Proposals for Uniting the English Colonies on the Continent of America; . . .* (London, 1757) and Jack P. Greene, "'A Dress of Horror': Henry McCulloh's Objections to the Stamp Act," *Huntington Library Quarterly*, 26 (1962–63): 253–62; on Pownall, see John A. Schutz, *Thomas Pownall . . .* (Glendale, 1951), pp. 181–214, and Caroline Robbins, *The Eighteenth-Century Commonwealthmen* (Cambridge, Mass., 1959), pp. 311–19; on Bernard, see Edmund S. and Helen Morgan, *The Stamp Act Crisis: Prologue to Revolution* (Chapel Hill, N.C., 1953), pp. 7–20. See also Richard Koebner, *Empire* (Cambridge, Eng., 1961), pp. 86–90, 105–13, 130–41, 147–48 and in general chaps. 3 and 4. Stourzh's study of Franklin and Koebner's posthumously published study have done more than any other works to identify the structure and purposes of empires as categories of eighteenth-century thought.

2. In 1963 I consulted Dorothy Rita Dillon, *The New York Triumvirate . . .* (New York, 1949); William H. W. Sabine's introduction to the *Historical Memoirs from 16 March 1763 to 9 July 1776 of William Smith* (New York, 1956), pp. vii–xii, I–II; Milton M. Klein's introduction to *The Independent Reflector . . .* (Cambridge, Mass., 1963), pp. 14–17; and L. F. S. Upton's introduction to *The Diary and Selected Papers of Chief Justice William Smith, 1784–1793* (The Champlain Society, *Publications*, XLI [Toronto, 1963]), vol. 1, pp. xxvi–xxxiii.

3. The composition of the proposed continental government is summarized in "Memoir of the Honourable William Smith, Written by His Son ["William Smith of Canada"], in William Smith, *The History of the Late Province of New-York, from Its Discovery, to the Appointment of Governor Colden, in 1762*, vol. 1 (New York, 1829), pp. xi–xxiii. The manuscript bears the notation, "written in 1767," but was probably composed in 1765. Many of its ideas appeared in Smith's letter to the Rev. George Whitefield, Dec. 6, 1765, Dartmouth Papers, I ii, 820, William Salt Library, Stafford, England. An unnamed English visitor to New York reported in early November 1765 that he found Smith hard at work on a critique of colonial administration and policy in the light of the Stamp Act crisis. See Rockingham Papers, Wentworth-Woodhouse Muniments, R 24/34, Sheffield City Library, Sheffield, Eng. The fullest discussion of Smith's proposals is in Professor Upton's introduction to Smith's Diary, vol. 1, pp. xxvi–xxxiii.

4. "The Political State" [in ca. 1756], in William Smith, *The History of the Province of New York from the First Discovery to the Year 1732*, Appendix, chap. 5 (London, 1757), pp. 241–43.

5. Smith to Whitefield, Dec. 6, 1765, Dartmouth Papers, I ii, 820. See also Milton M. Klein, "Prelude to Revolution in New York: Jury Trials and Judicial Tenure, *William and Mary Quarterly,* 3rd ser., 17 (1960): 439–62.

6. A remarkably similar analysis of the economic potential and political needs of the Empire, gleaned from *The Wealth of Nations,* appears in E. A. Benians, "Adam Smith's Project of an Empire," *Cambridge Historical Journal,* I (1923–25): 249–83.

7. "The American Whig, No. V," *New-York Gazette, or Weekly Post-Boy,* Apr. II, 1768. The "American Whig," a series of polemics against Thomas Bradbury Chandler's demands for an American bishop, was edited and largely written by Smith's close friend and political ally, William Livingston. "No. V" contained this striking digression on the structure of the Empire and has been attributed to Livingston in Carl Bridenbaugh, *Mitre and Sceptre . . .* (New York, 1962), pp. 306–7; however, Smith and Livingston probably collaborated on this number since its arguments and style dovetail so closely with those of Smith's "Thoughts." Chandler himself suspected Smith of sharing authorship of previous issues of the "American Whig." See Chandler to Samuel Johnson, Apr. 7, 1768, in Herbert and Carol Schneider, eds., *Samuel Johnson, President of King's College: His Career and Writings* (New York, 1929), vol. 1, pp. 436–38, and, particularly, Koebner's perceptive discussion of this issue of the "American Whig in *Empire,* pp. 171–72.

8. Dec. 13, 1768, in Smith, *Historical Memoirs, 1763–1776,* pp. 49–50.

9. Smith to Haldimand, July 4, 1775, Dartmouth Papers, II, 1353.

10. Smith, *Historical Memoirs, 1763–1776,* pp. 235–36; *Pennsylvania Journal* (Philadelphia), Aug. 9, 1775.

11. Smith's information about Mansfield was incorrect. Mansfield made no recorded recommendations about reconciling the colonies in 1775, but he had advocated important conciliatory features of the Quebec Act of 1774, and Smith probably confused the two activities. See Reginald Coupland, *The Quebec Act: A Study in Statesmanship* (Oxford, 1925), pp. 10, 32, 49–50, 100.

12. Smith, *Historical Memoirs, 1763–1776,* pp. 271–77. On Smith's elaborate analysis of the Revolutionary crisis from 1774 to 1776, see William H. W. Sabine, "William Smith and His Imperial 'Compact,'" *Manuscripts,* 8 (1956): 315–18; William H. Nelson, *The American Tory* (Oxford, 1961), pp. 123–25; Upton, ed., *Diary,* pp. xxxi–xxxiii; and Smith, *Historical Memoirs, 1763–1776,* pp. 188–90, 209, 224–25, 228–28c, 235–37, 239–41, 242–51, 257–59, 261–63, 265–66, 271– 77, 279–83.

13. It is not clear how a London merchant, Brook Watson, came to possess an unsigned, abbreviated version of Smith's "Thoughts" which he sent to Dartmouth in January 1775. Historical Manuscripts Commission, *Fourteenth Report,* Appendix, Part 10 (London, 1895), p. 262.

14. Charles H. McIlwain, *The American Revolution: A Constitutional Interpretation* (New York, 1923), p. 5.

15. On Smith's later constitutional ideas, see Oscar Zeichner, "William Smith's 'Observations on America,'" *New York History,* 23 (1942): 328–40; Hilda Neatby, "Chief Justice William Smith: An Eighteenth-Century Whig Imperialist," *Canadian Historical Review,* 28 (1947): 44–67; and Upton, ed., *Diary,* pp. xxxiii–xl.

16. Dartmouth Papers, II, 1353, 1354.

17. I have been informed that the Value of the West India Product imported into France in 1754, was near ten Millions Sterling. How immense the Profits on the European Sales! She holds these Sources of Wealth at the Mercy of Great Britain. By Expeditions

from the Continent of America, any of these Islands may be easily overwhelmed and reduced. [Smith's Note.]

18. One or more words were apparently omitted inadvertently; the bracketed word has been supplied by conjecture.

19. Its affairs are now directed by more than Twenty Parliaments. What a Multitude of Souls to one Body! [Smith's Note.]

20. From separate Requisitions to the Island Colonies, we have no Inconveniences to apprehend. It is easy to command their Wealth by a commercial Police. They are besides absolutely dependant upon Great Britain and the Continent of America. They owe their Safety to the Protection of the one, and the Supplies of the other, and must of Necessity belong to the Power that rules both. They can never revolt while the present Union subsists. [Smith's Note.]

21. No other than such a *limited Sovereignty* is exercised over Ireland, tho' a conquered Country. [Smith's Note.]

22. This will be consistent with our Exemption from Her Taxations, if the Duties go into the Province Treasuries, or are passed to our Credit, on the Royal Requisitions. [Smith's Note.]

23. These considerations were staples in the discussion of the nature of the Empire. Smith probably drew these ideas from Franklin's essay, "Observations concerning the Increase of Mankind, Peopling of Countries, &c." See Leonard W. Labaree and Whitfield J. Bell, Jr., eds., *The Papers of Benjamin Franklin,* 4 (New Haven, Conn., 1961): 227–34. Both men agreed that colonial population would double within every generation and that this increase compelled Britain to reform the political system of the Empire. Both feared that concentrations of urban population would encourage the decline of public virtue as was already evident in Britain. See especially [Smith], "A brief Consideration of New-York . . . ," Jan. 18, 1753, in Klein, ed., *The Independent Reflector,* pp. 103–8. Another loyalist who proposed imperial union as a means of averting the American Revolution, Joseph Galloway, also defended this policy on the grounds that colonial population would increase by tenfold within the coming century. Galloway to Richard Jackson, Aug. 10, 1775, Dartmouth Papers, II, 1031.

The Removal of the Massachusetts
General Court from Boston, 1769–1772

Robert M. Calhoon

and Donald C. Lord

On June 14, 1769, Governor Francis Bernard ordered the Massachusetts General Court to leave its traditional seat in Boston and to reassemble in Cambridge for the remainder of its session. When Lieutenant Governor Thomas Hutchinson, on March 8, 1770, summoned the Court to meet in Cambridge, he provoked a constitutional crisis in Massachusetts and instigated a controversy which lasted for more than two years.[1] Hutchinson claimed that his royal instructions required him to remove the Court from Boston's turbulent influences. The Court, in turn, challenged the power of the Crown to interfere in the provincial matter of calling, proroguing, and dissolving the assembly. It further questioned whether Hutchinson was actually bound by an explicit instruction and suspected him of harassing the Court out of whimsy. In the process of demanding the Court's return to Boston, the house of representatives and council enunciated Lockean doctrine and alleged that the continued removal from Boston jeopardized the liberty of the province and violated the compact between Massachusetts and the Crown.

The struggle forced Hutchinson to justify the Crown's authority to dictate the location of the Court and to explain the obligations which a Massachusetts royal governor owed to the Crown and to the province. He knew that the removal of the Court was a risky step—one which would provide his enemies with a dramatic grievance. At the same time, he was so disturbed by the erosion of royal authority in the province that he was determined to preserve one of the Crown's prerogatives from further deterioration. Thus, until he could coax from the Court a tacit acknowledgment of the validity of the Crown's prerogative to instruct the governor on the use of his powers, Hutchinson was determined to resist all efforts to compel him to return the Court to Boston. When he finally did return the Court to its traditional seat in June 1772, it was by no means clear whether the Court had won a victory or the governor had secured a qualified, moral triumph by upholding the prerogative for two years. The question of victory became a moot point, however, when fresh controversies in 1773 and 1774 overshadowed the more restrained argument created by the removal of the Court. The inconclusive end of the dispute, the short distance from Boston to Cambridge, and the sometimes tedious semantic haggling over terms like "inconvenience" tended to obscure the significance of the struggle. The controversy provoked both Hutchinson and the Court to conduct a particularly acute inquiry into the sources and disposition of power in Massachusetts politics.

The contest originated with a royal instruction to Bernard, drafted in July 1768, which stated that because a "licentious and unrestrained Mob" dominated Boston, the governor could assemble the Court in Salem or Cambridge for its next session. Such "lenient and persuasive Methods," it continued, might discredit Massachusetts' radical leaders in the eyes of the province's inhabitants. Bernard doubted whether the removal would have any practical effect and considered this rebuke to Boston a necessary gesture. After weighing the problem, he assembled the Court in Boston in June 1769; and he did not remove it to Cambridge until it persisted in denouncing the presence of British troops in Boston. In Cambridge, the house completed its resolutions condemning Bernard's administration and included a brief complaint about the removal from Boston.[2]

When Bernard left for England later in the summer of 1769, Hutchinson was uncertain whether he should continue to assemble the Court in Cambridge. Bernard's proclamation on July 15, 1769, proroguing the Court until early 1770, mentioned neither Boston nor Cambridge as the place of its next meeting. An instruction to Hutchinson, dated December 9, 1769, directed him to call the Court to Cambridge unless he thought there were contrary reasons "of such a nature to outweigh these considerations." Distressed by the uncertainty, he wrote to Thomas Gage that, if left to his own discretion, he would not remove the Court from Boston.[3] In London, Bernard had discussed Massachusetts affairs with Lord Hillsborough and had participated in drafting the December 9 instruction. He sent Hutchinson a candid explanation of its meaning:

> You will . . . receive Directions for calling the Assembly at Cambridge, but not so peremptory as to oblige you to do it if you should think it best to have it at Boston. . . . I recommended a peremptory Order that you might be more able to apologise for it. But it was answered that this amounted to a peremptory Order, if your Opinion did not direct you to counteract it, in which Case you was left at Liberty to do what you thought for the best. But if you thought it best to obey it, you might quote it as a positive Order.[4]

Although subsequent instructions specifically forbade Hutchinson from returning the Court to Boston,[5] he probably assumed that he still possessed discretionary authority to do so as soon as the Court ceased to challenge the prerogative of the Crown to instruct a governor on the location of an assembly. An instruction dated July 3, 1771, reiterated that discretion; and Hutchinson's hands were probably not completely tied at any time during the controversy.[6] In 1775, he explained cryptically and probably accurately that "I never said I had a positive instruction" to keep the Court in Cambridge "but that I had such instruction as made it necessary."[7] Fortunately for Hutchinson, his discretion was effectively hidden by a circular letter of 1768 to all royal governors which prohibited them from showing any part of an instruction to an assembly or council. Bernard, in December 1769, pointedly reminded Hutchinson of that restriction and added that it would prevent the Court from learning of "the discretionary Power given to you."[8]

However Hutchinson may have interpreted his instructions concerning the location of the Court, he realized that the removal from Boston was only a temporary and partial expedient. Pessimism about the feasibility of restoring tranquility to Massachusetts politics by any conventional methods pervaded his thinking during the controversy. In March 1770 he offered to resign in order to make way for a new governor with greater stature and more sweeping powers. He recommended to the Crown that Parliament should discipline Massachusetts by outlawing combinations which resisted enforcement of British law, by imposing oaths to support British authority on all colonial legislators and councillors, and then by appointing only British noblemen as royal governors for periods of not more than three years. "Nothing but a sharp external force," he concluded, "will bring Boston to a state of due subordination."[9]

Protests against the removal of the Court confirmed his analysis of unrest in the province. The controversy, he later wrote in his *History of the Colony and Province of Massachusetts-Bay,* tended "to alienate the people from their connexion with the parent state, and to reconcile them to an independency both of crown and parliament." His letters at the time used much the same language; and he described the controversy as a "determined design to wrest from the Crown every power which the people do not think convenient," "confirming . . . our principles of independence." In one sense, Hutchinson's apparent foresight is misleading, for by *independence* he meant only the autonomy which the Court was seeking in 1770. However, he did understand clearly how explosive the presumptions of the Court could become if the Crown challenged them directly. "I think it must puzzle the wisest heads in the Kingdom to restore America to a State of Government and Order," he wrote at the close of a letter on the removal of the Court. "In general I can say that the wound may be skinned over but can never be healed until it be laid open to the bone. Parliament must give up its claim of Supreme Authority . . . or the Colonies must cease from asserting a Supreme Legislative power within themselves." Ever sceptical of his ability to make any lasting contribution, Hutchinson saw the removal of the Court as one way of "skinning over" the wound of disobedience in Massachusetts.[10]

Hutchinson's concern was justified. When the house assembled in the "new chapel" and the council met in the library of Harvard College in Cambridge on March 15, 1770, the messages of both chambers revealed a well-stocked arsenal of constitutional and practical objections to the Court's removal from Boston. Though mild in comparison with its later views, the house's initial arguments indicated the road which lay ahead. Arguing that the removal was an infraction of the representatives' essential rights as "Men and Citizens" as well as those "derived to us by the British Constitution and the Charter of this Colony," the house presented a plea for the return of the Court to Boston. The message further complained that the removal was inconvenient both for the members of the Court and for Harvard College.[11] These problems could be remedied, the house argued, if the lieutenant governor would use the power which he "alone" possessed to restore the Court to its "ancient Place, the State House at Boston." Hutchinson protested that he alone did not have the power to return the Court to Boston because he was bound by the King's instructions. The house retorted that while the power to call the Court had once belonged to the Crown, it had been given as a "Grant in Favor" to the governor. The house regarded the governor's sole exercise of this power, free from any Crown supervision, as a protection of the province's liberty. Hutchinson's removal of the Court, therefore, at the behest of a "Ministerial Mandate," eroded one of the province's basic rights. Lest Hutchinson believe that the house stood alone in its conflict with him, the council announced that while it was concerned with the "preservation of the Royal Prerogative," it was also anxious about the good of the people. The Court itself, the council declared, could advise the governor on the proper place to hold the assembly. The house then asked to see Hutchinson's alleged instructions. He replied that he was forbidden to reveal their contents.[12]

By refusing to show his instructions to the house, Hutchinson forced his opponents to adopt a new line of attack. A committee informed the governor that even if he had instructions, these ought not "to be deemed of sufficient Force to invalidate the Law." The House of Commons in 1749 and 1751 had given weight to this argument by refusing to endow royal instructions with the force of law. Even more important, the committee argued, was an act of 1698 which established the form of the writ used for summoning the General Court; the writ specifically designated Boston as the seat of the Court. Hutchinson quickly observed that the words "The Town of Boston" in the writ, like the words "William the Third," were understood to be mere matter of form. Just as quickly, the house resolved that all the words in the writ, like "William the Third," which by their nature were changeable, were form; those words that were not changeable by their nature, like "a certain Place," were "fix'd and perpetual."[13]

Each side had stated its basic position, but the house faced a circumstance that could weaken its position—the necessity of doing legislative work. If the house refused to consider constituents' petitions which had accumulated, it might lose public support and strengthen Hutchinson's hand. *"Only from absolute Necessity"* the house turned to its business, and it denied that any precedent had been established which acquiesced in the removal from Boston.[14] Practical necessity forced the house to alter its tactics but not to abandon its principles. On April 7, 1770, Hutchinson had asked for laws to strengthen the executive courts because of disturbances in Gloucester. The house replied that the continued presence of British troops in Boston—dispatched there because of rioting against customs officials in June 1768—and the removal of the Court from its "ancient and legal Seat" were bold attempts to intimidate the province and infringe upon its liberty. The house was, therefore, "employed in Matters which concern the very Being of the Constitution" and had no time for questions of executive jurisdiction. In this intransigent mood the assembly was dissolved the following day for annual spring elections. The newly elected house gave little promise of accommodation; Boston, in particular, showed its defiance by returning Thomas Cushing, Samuel Adams, and John Hancock—all outspoken opponents of Hutchinson's removal of the Court.[15]

The "Boston Instructions," adopted unanimously shortly after the election as a guide for the town's representatives, further demonstrated Boston's determination to resist Hutchinson's actions. The instructions warned of alarming signs of a "deep-laid and desperate plan of imperial despotism" which would destroy the "BRITISH CONSTITUTION" and protested against the removal of the Court in violation of "ancient usage and established law." A section of the instructions, drafted by Josiah Quincy, presented a legal argument against Hutchinson's use of the oral instructions; Quincy cut through the ambiguity surrounding the term "prerogative" and directly debated against that concept. Ever since Englishmen had repudiated the "mystical jargon" about divine-right rule, Quincy asserted, the prerogative had ceased to be a subject "too delicate" for public discussion. Only laws passed by Parliament or by a colonial assembly could compel a subject's obedience, he argued. The King's prerogative was therefore only binding when it did not exceed or conflict with the law, and indeed it was hedged about with statutes specifically limiting its use. By tradition, moreover, the prerogative could never be used in any way harmful to the interests of the subject. William Blackstone's definition of prerogative, Quincy declared, encompassed these restrictions; the prerogative was "'the discretionary power of acting for the public good, where the positive laws are silent, [and] if . . . abused to the publick detriment, . . . is . . . unconstitutional.'" Drawing upon these doctrines, Quincy drove his argument to its conclusion: if the removal of the Court did not violate "the principles of crown law" or provincial laws which designated Boston as "the seat of government," not even a "Crown lawyer" could prove that the removal served in any way the interests of the people.

The Boston Instructions were a formidable attempt to construct a legal formula for attacking the royal instructions. First English usage, then Parliamentary and provincial laws, and finally the public good stood as limits to the prerogative. If an encroachment slipped by one line of defense, it was sure to collide with the next barrier against arbitrary rule. Implicit in the formula was another tenacious safeguard—the assumption that the Crown bore the burden of evidence to show that an action did not violate the public good, or law, or tradition.[16]

"The doctrine advanced in this piece of rant," Hutchinson wrote of the Boston Instructions, "may as well be advanced against the King's assent to our laws or his appointing a Governor as against the removal of the Court from Boston by His

Majesty's order." Determined not to be baited into rash action, he concluded that only the "artful management" of the house by the Boston members could account for its message of April 23. Thus he sought to convince other members of the Court of the integrity of his position. Even before the Boston Instructions, for example, he tried to convince the council that he had not summoned the Court to Cambridge on his own volition nor did he "have reason to think that the [Crown's] motives for ordering it to be done now cease." While he denied personal responsibility for the Court's removal, he insisted in the same breath that he alone could decide when the Crown's attitude on the question might change. It was a delicate position that could be sustained, he wrote Bernard, only so long as the Court did "not know that I had any discretion left in the matter." He pleaded, therefore, that his letters to the ministry be kept secret.[17]

When the new Court assembled on May 31, 1770, the conflict was renewed. Speaking for the house, Hancock presented the lieutenant governor with a message that challenged the precedents Hutchinson had sought to establish for the removal of the Court to Cambridge. In addition to a meeting in 1747 when the Court had met at Cambridge following the burning of the Boston Town House, Hutchinson had discovered and publicized two other precedents for his action— one in 1721 and another in 1729. In both cases the Court had met at Salem. But the house countered that the Court had met in Salem in 1721 because a smallpox epidemic plagued Boston. The removal, therefore, was for the public good! The 1729 removal was dismissed as an illegal step to which the house had never acquiesced. In neither case would the house grant precedents. Hutchinson's summons was still considered an illegal attempt to make instructions supersede the law.[18]

Hutchinson was not so easily cornered. He uncovered another precedent: the Court had met in Salisbury in 1737. Unfortunately for his case, the council later proved that the Court had met willingly at Salisbury to settle a boundary dispute with New Hampshire. Hutchinson still insisted that his actions were legal. Neither he nor the Crown, he told the Court, intended to make instructions supersede the law. He conceded that the prerogative was not to be used for injury, and he could see none in the removal of the Court. It was preposterous to believe, he stated, that the King had no power to control the government through instructions.[19] Significantly, before Hutchinson could defend the prerogative, he had admitted that it was to be used for the public good and that instructions did not supersede the law—two constitutional concepts dear to the leaders of the Court. Since Hutchinson still refused to show his instructions to the Court, the house resolved by a vote of ninety-six to six that the removal from Boston was an injury to the province and necessitated the Court's continued refusal to do business. The house further resolved that all future election writs contain the words "TOWN-HOUSE AT BOSTON."[20]

Admitting his chagrin at the size of the vote, Hutchinson tried to explain that he had acted as an obedient servant of the Crown. He reminded his opponents that, as speaker of the house in 1747, he had cast the deciding vote on a bill to rebuild the Town House in Boston after fire had destroyed the old structure. Then he had acted for his constituents, now he acted for his king. The house pounced on this boast and cited it as evidence that the lieutenant governor himself had once considered Boston the most convenient location of the Court. The house's new statement of reasons for refusing to do business further argued that, regardless of circumstances in 1747, the present attack on the liberty of the province made the Court's return to Boston imperative. The representatives had no guarantee that Hutchinson would not move them from one remote part of the province to another "till he shall have worried them into a Compliance with some arbitrary Mandate." Moreover, the province's records, located in Boston, were necessary tools for the Court's work.[21]

Frequent complaints about the inconvenience of meeting outside Boston encouraged Hutchinson to believe that the house was "giving up the claim of Right and urging only the Inconvenience" of the removal, "that they are silenced as to the illegality" of the meeting in Cambridge.[22] The house's messages in June, however, drew no such distinction. Instead, the representatives mounted a more systematic attack on the foundations of the royal prerogative. Hutchinson's actions, they declared, were admittedly the exercise of a discretionary power; "Such is the Imperfection of human Nature, as to render discretionary Power, however necessary, always . . . dangerous." They insisted that the "commons," or popularly elected branch of the legislature, ought to be as free as any other part of the government, for the "democratical Branch is at least as important to the People and the Constitution as the monarchical and the aristocratical." Hutchinson labeled this presumption an attempt to undermine the prerogative by making the house the sole judge of its exercise. At this point, the council came to the defense of the house; the Court, it insisted, valued the prerogative fully as much as did the governor because the prerogative existed for the public good. If the removal of the Court damaged the interest of the province, then it became the responsibility of the Court to so inform the governor; and it was his duty to act upon this information. The decision to return the Court to Boston, the council agreed, remained with the governor; but his only proper source of guidance was the advice of the Court. Coming to the crux of the argument, the council observed that the charter gave the governor "full power" to summon, prorogue, or dissolve the Court, and the Crown had no business interfering in the decision.[23]

The council, Hutchinson replied, obviously did not understand the concept of the public good; that principle, he observed dryly, "is the great Purpose for which Government is instituted" and not merely the license for actions of the legislature.[24] Certain that a correct reading of the charter would leave no doubt about the propriety of the Crown's actions, he solicited a favorable legal opinion from Attorney General Jonathan Sewall. The term "full power" in the charter, Sewall explained, was intended "merely to exclude all claims from any Authority within the Colony"; and it in no way precluded the Crown's instructing the governor to exercise the prerogative in a particular manner. A year later, an anonymous writer,

"Aequitas," probably Sewall himself, presented the most cogent constitutional defense of Hutchinson's conduct. He sought to determine "the end and design" of the governor's office under the charter and maintained that the charter, as a grant from the King, necessarily protected the royal prerogative. Although the governor exercised some of his powers at his own discretion and others according to expressed instructions, "all acts of prerogative should be in the Governor's name ... for the sake of consistency." None of the governor's executive actions, "Aequitas" insisted, were immune from royal supervision for the simple reason that the Crown retained the power to dismiss a governor. Moreover, since the King had the power to dismiss a governor who failed to uphold royal policy, the province would be reduced to chaos if the King were not permitted to tell a governor what was expected of him. Royal instructions did require "unlimited obedience," "Aequitas" continued, and there was nothing sinister in that requirement; such power was "no farther extensive than is necessary to relieve the King" from continual involvement in Massachusetts affairs.[25]

This interpretation of the charter by Hutchinson and Sewall convinced the house to reconsider conspiratorial implications of its removal from Boston. Samuel Adams drafted the house's message, which was presented to the governor on August 1, 1770, and reiterated the chamber's resolution not to do business for fear that the King's ministers might misuse instructions to alienate the sovereign from his people and thus violate the terms of the compact between Massachusetts and the Crown. The house did not believe, Adams wrote, that the King had ordered the removal because no correspondence had been forwarded to prove this contention. He also denounced the constitutional opinions of Hutchinson's legal advisor. According to the charter, Adams argued, not even the king-in-council could settle disputes between the branches of the provincial legislature because there was no provision in the charter for such an appeal. The opinion of the attorney general, therefore, was not binding in Massachusetts. At this point in the argument, Adams introduced the strongest use of natural law yet attempted by the Court: because there was no provision in the charter to settle this dispute, the parties involved must turn to the only standard common to all, the public good. According to Locke, he continued, the people had the right to oppose all abusive exercises of legal and constitutional prerogatives of the Crown. Because there was no place on earth to appeal such abuses, the people could only "appeal to Heaven." Adams did not think such an appeal was necessary at that time, nor did he deny that royal instructions ought to be obeyed. They would cease to be binding, however, when they injured the people. These qualifying considerations did not weaken his argument, for once Hutchinson accepted the Court's standard of the public good, there was no need to push the argument further. The governor could judge what was good for the public, since the people could always inform him of any injury to them; and Hutchinson had merely to act upon this information. Adams added that the province had gone to great expense to raise a new town house in Boston. What assurance did men have that the "next Freak of a capricious Minister will not remove the Court to some other place"? On an even more alarming note, Adams boldly claimed that the house of representatives possessed the same rights in Massachusetts as the House of Commons in Great Britain; but now he feared that these rights, and the Massachusetts charter itself, were threatened by the "the subtle Machinations, and daring Encroachments of wicked Ministers." These sinister figures, Adams concluded, had given the Court ample reason to resist its removal. Consider, he said, the pattern of recent intimidation against Massachusetts—extended vice admiralty jurisdiction, swarms of customs officials, the Boston Massacre. Only a vigilant legislature stood between the people and further acts of tyranny.[26]

Hutchinson accepted this challenge to constitutional debate. The Court had vigorously restated the fundamental tenets of New England political theory: the ultimate responsibility of a magistrate to serve the interests of the people, and the duty of their representatives to thwart the efforts of a magistrate who became the tool of the Crown or other special interest.[27] In the light of those principles, the Court's refusal to do business was a legitimate way of compelling Hutchinson to reconsider the interests of the province and dissuading him from continuing his assaults against the public good. Hutchinson did not contradict this interpretation of the compact; rather he sought to show that this dictum was not applicable to his removal of the Court from Boston. He first reviewed the precedents for the removal of the Court, the form of the writ for summoning the assembly, and the legal opinion that he had solicited. He dismissed the Court's use of Locke's compact theory, "detached as it is from the rest of the Treatise," because he knew of "no Attempts to enslave or destroy you." Rather than be drawn into a debate on the meaning of Locke's doctrines, Hutchinson presented his own understanding of the compact between the people and the Crown.[28]

The central cause of the impasse, Hutchinson declared, was that the Court considered the "charter as a Compact between the Crown and the People of the Province" and wanted "one Party to the Compact to be held and not the other." He assured the Court that by calling it into session he had fulfilled his obligations under the charter and that it was the Court which, by refusing to reciprocate and proceed with its business, had failed to meet its obligations to the province. Moreover, he argued, the Court had chosen to define the charter in a manner which placed no burdens on itself and limited only the authority of the Crown and the governor. This devious conduct, he explained, not only was damaging to the immediate needs of the province but also was openly hostile to the operation of the Crown's prerogative. The Court now appeared to Hutchinson to be claiming a novel, unlimited power to decide whether any exercise of the prerogative served the interests of the province. Behind this ambition he perceived an ominous presumption: the notion that the Crown could not compel a governor to obey its instructions. Thus, he argued, the governor was repeatedly forced to use the one power at his disposal—the very one the Court wanted to limit—that of continuing to call the Court to meet in Cambridge so long as it refused to do business and denied the force of the prerogative. Until then, he warned, "it is not in my Power to remove you to Boston ... without a further Signification of his Majesty's Pleasure." If he were convinced, however, "that removing the court from Boston was an Encroachment upon your [the Court's] natural or constitutional Rights, I would not urge my Commission or Instructions to justify ... doing it; *but I must make my own Reason and Judgment My Rule and not yours.*"[29]

In Hutchinson's view, the compact between the Crown and the people could function only if the Court relinquished its role as an enemy of the prerogative. Once the Court acquired the power to exercise final review over any use of the prerogative—once it was freed from the responsibility of persuading the governor and securing his voluntary acquiescence—then the balance of power within the province would shift dangerously toward legislative domination over the Crown. Recognizing that the removal issue had revealed fresh disagreements in Massachusetts about the proper location of power within the province, Hutchinson declared that if the Court's opinion were to prevail against the position of the Crown, then "to what Purpose was this or any other Reserve in the Charter made to the Crown?" With the words ringing in the legislators' ears, Hutchinson again prorogued the Court.[30]

Proroguing the Court settled nothing. When it was summoned again to Cambridge on September 26, 1770, Hancock presented Hutchinson with the house's request to return the Court to "its ancient and legal Seat." Hutchinson ignored this request and informed the house that it had pressing business, since many provincial statutes, particularly revenue laws, had expired. His request elicited no positive response, but what Hutchinson failed to accomplish by rhetoric, he advertently achieved by obeying another one of his instructions. On orders from General Gage, Castle William, overlooking Boston Harbor, was occupied by British troops. In order to protest this provocative action, the house voted fifty-nine to twenty-nine to return to business. The representatives resolved that the garrisoning of Castle William, based on instructions from London, was another unconstitutional use of prerogative power. Only for this reason, the house agreed to transact routine business and to protest, at the same time, against Gage's order. When this work was completed, Hutchinson prorogued the Court. He remarked on this temporary victory; the house had failed to impeach his conduct or force him to give up any part of the Crown's prerogative.[31]

The Court met at Cambridge twice in 1771, from April 3 to 25 and from May 29 to July 5. By this time Hutchinson's appointment as royal governor was official, and during both sessions the removal controversy merged with the beginning of a fresh conflict over his new, independent salary from the Crown. In 1769, the house had provoked Bernard to remove the Court to Cambridge when it refused to provide any funds for the operation of the administration, and in Cambridge the house voted unanimously to deny Bernard his salary. During the impasse over the removal of Court in 1770, the house refused to pay Hutchinson's salary and expenses as lieutenant governor. In 1771, Hutchinson withheld his assent from bills compensating him £831 for his services as lieutenant governor and from a new grant of £1,300 to him as governor. When the house demanded an explanation on April 25, 1771, Hutchinson revealed that he was receiving an independent salary from the Crown.[32] In the face of this unprecedented challenge, Samuel Adams and James Otis fell to bickering over tactics. Adams wanted the house to refuse to do business outside of Boston; Otis, on May 29, 1771, impatiently replied that the governor had the power to assemble the Court "where he pleased," and he prevailed on the house to reject Adams's motion and send a conciliatory message to Hutchinson stressing the inconvenience of sitting in Cambridge.[33] This deviation scarcely represented what one observer called "Otis's Conversion to Toryism."[34] Nor did it indicate a fundamental division among the leaders of the house over the principles at stake in the removal controversy, for by June 18, Otis, Adams, Hancock, and Speaker Cushing reached agreement on a new message to Hutchinson. The message combined, in a unified argument, the house's objections against two uses of prerogative power—the removal from Boston and the governor's new, independent salary. The governor's power to assemble, prorogue, and dissolve the Court was so great—and in the past two years had been so much abused—that "the Safety of the People requires . . . a Check" on the executive. According to the charter, the house declared, the "free Gift" by the Court guaranteed that the people could influence a governor. Now the removal from Boston and the independent salary threatened "a free Assembly" subjugated to "arbitrary Edicts and Mandates."[35] On July 5, 1771, Hutchinson prorogued the Court and kept it prorogued until April 8, 1772, thereby eliminating repetition of protests in the journal of the house against his conduct. He also warned Hillsborough that the continued removal from Boston was beginning to hurt the Crown's interests because the Boston representatives were working to prevent any compromise of the dispute which would rob them of an effective grievance.[36]

Throughout the prorogation of the Court, Samuel Adams kept the issue alive in the pages of the Boston *Gazette*. Writing as "Candidus," he reminded his readers that "the Tyrants of Rome were Natives of Rome," just as Hutchinson was a native of Massachusetts. Royal instructions, he declared, could make the charter a scrap of paper. Indeed, by relinquishing his power to the secretary of state, Hutchinson had become a "*pimp* rather than a governor." Adams warned against attempts to lull the province into "that *quietude* . . . by which *slavery* is always preceded . . . ," for the people must not sleep while their "system of free government is changing." Under the pen name of "Valerius Popicola" ("Valerius, friend of the people"), Adams sharpened and restated his Lockean views. He argued that if the people of a state had not consented to the authority over them, no such authority existed. If Massachusetts were part of the body politic of Great Britain, it should be consulted in its lawmaking; if Massachusetts were a separate body politic, it should make its own laws. Adams was quickly challenged on this point. "Those who see [the royal instructions] as an infringement of our Liberties," a Hutchinson supporter retorted, "seem to look upon this province as an absolutely free and independent state. . . . But this objection will vanish when it is considered that we are not more than a subordinate province." By seeking to deny the governor any "freedom or independence" in adhering to royal instruction, the writer continued, the Court was grasping for "absolute and uncontrollable" power.[37]

The struggle returned to the legislature when the house met in Cambridge on April 8, 1772. Worried by the length and direction of the controversy, Hutchinson was conciliatory and cautious. As he explained to Hillsborough, he was determined to return the Court to Boston for reasons of convenience if the Court would refrain from questioning the Crown's prerogative to determine its meeting place. He convinced Hancock to present a petition for removal to Boston along these lines, but the motion was soundly defeated.[38] The key to the situation, Hutchinson then concluded, lay in what the house could be induced to leave unsaid in their petitions. He was, however, determined not to omit from his own pronouncements a vindication of the royal prerogative, for "if I had said nothing to them of their denying the King's authority to instruct the Governor, I think they . . . would have triumphed in having carried their Point." Whatever his views on the prerogative, Hutchinson sincerely desired an end to the impasse. In early June 1772, in an interview with Hancock and Speaker Cushing, Hutchinson advised them that he would act upon any petition from the house which did not deny the King's authority to instruct the governor. He promised to overlook any other "frivolous objections" which the house might "insist upon . . . to save appearances," such as the inconvenience of meeting in Cambridge, the obligation of the governor to be guided solely by the public good, "and the like." According to Hutchinson's version of the interview, Hancock and Cushing agreed to these terms but warned that Samuel Adams might try to upset the arrangement by insisting on a denunciation of the prerogative. Hutchinson endorsed this strategy and cautioned them against Adams's "art and insidiousness."[39]

To no one's surprise, Adams did induce the house to insert into its address the accusation that the removal of the Court to Cambridge had been unnecessary. Hutchinson asked only for a clarification of the veiled accusation. The house replied that its message was sufficiently clear and required no explanation. Hutchinson could not retreat from this semantic dispute; "what appears to you to be sufficiently plain," he countered, "appears to me to be doubtful and equivocal." He could not determine with certainty whether the message denied the prerogative of the Crown to instruct the governor. But Hutchinson believed that Adams had outwitted him. Many representatives, he feared, were unaware that their message might be construed as questioning the prerogative, and they would accuse him of breaking his promise to return the Court to Boston if the house would ask him to do so solely for reasons of convenience. Pressed by his own supporters to act expediently, Hutchinson kept the house sitting for ten days and then summoned the council. He asked its members whether they considered the return of the Court to Boston to be consistent with the governor's obligations to the King. As Hutchinson anticipated, the council agreed that the step was legal, and the

Court was recalled to Boston. Thus two years of conflict ended on an undecisive note. The Court was jubilant, but Hutchinson wrote to John Pownall that he had "Manifested to the people of the province" his "strict regard to the king's instructions," which he felt would strengthen him in his future contests with the Court.[40]

The controversy over the removal of the Court from Boston was at once an illuminating and perplexing episode in pre-Revolutionary Massachusetts politics. It was, clearly enough, one of the last of a long series of colonial protests against the use of royal instructions as a legal basis for harassment of a refractory assembly. The resourcefulness of Hutchinson and Bernard in interpreting the instructions in the most opportunistic manner and in defending their legality with painstaking precision underscores Leonard W. Labaree's contention that by the 1770s the instructions, even in the hands of an able governor, were archaic, inflexible methods of imperial administration.[41] Moreover, the controversy was almost certainly the major cause of the grievance in the Declaration of Independence accusing the King of calling "together legislative bodies at places unusual, uncomfortable, and distant from the repository of their public records for the sole purpose of fatiguing them into compliance with his measures."[42]

The struggle further modifies the deceptive appearance that the years 1770–1772 were a period of quiet in Massachusetts when resistance against British authority nearly collapsed.[43] Though it lacked the violence and explosive polemics of protests in the 1760s, the controversy over the removal of the Court revealed continuing and unresolved tension between British and colonial concepts of liberty and order. However, while the characterization of the early 1770s as a *quiet period* fails to account for that tension and consequently overlooks its potential for further political turmoil, it does rest upon some undeniable evidence. Boston's activist politicians did become increasingly divided over tactics in 1771 and 1772.[44] These disagreements influenced the later stages of the removal controversy in May 1771 when the Court proceeded to do business despite Samuel Adams's objections and, a year later, when Hancock and Cushing negotiated secretly with Hutchinson. While his use of these differences was a tribute to Hutchinson's tenacity and skill, he knew that he could extract only limited advantage from his opponents' differences over tactics; and when the house only partially muted its attacks on the prerogative in June 1772, he seized the opportunity to be done with the dispute. On balance, then, the controversy might well appear to have reached its climax in August 1770 and, thereafter, to have become a stalemate for nearly two years while both Hutchinson and the Court searched for the terms of a face-saving but inconclusive retreat from positions each had unwisely chosen to defend. It might also appear that the Court protested its removal from Boston because it had no serious grievances left to agitate after nonimportation collapsed in October 1770.

Beneath this appearance of indecisiveness and triviality, however, the removal controversy was a protracted, serious inquiry into the nature of the prerogative. The development of the debate forced both of the participants to define more precisely their responsibilities and the principles which each believed should govern the use of power in provincial affairs. The most striking quality of the controversy—the extraordinary amount of time and effort expended on a relatively minor issue—is itself an important clue to the essential meaning of the dispute. The Court, torn between a traditional and novel mode of resistance,[45] preferred to construct an unsystematic set of tangible precedents. Its tenacious clinging in its messages to phrases like "according to usage" and "ancient and legal seat" emphasized the preservative, traditional sources of the Court's favorite ideas. Hutchinson's tenacity in rebutting these specific arguments, and the alarming implications of his version of prerogative power, compelled the Court to formulate a more comprehensive justification for resistance. The Court first argued that the removal was an attempt to give the instructions the force of law in Massachusetts, and then it discovered the more sinister intention of the Crown to emasculate the assembly's will to resist other encroachments.

Hutchinson contributed substantially to this heightened awareness of the implications of the prerogative. His defense of it was a frightening recital, all the more because his dry, legalistic style was at once precise and suggestive. Unintentionally but vividly he depicted an intimate and constant communication between the ministry and the governor and a pervasive influence that was as far-reaching as a governor's receptiveness and malleability would allow it to become. This notion of the prerogative corresponded exactly with the conception of power which Bernard Bailyn has found in pre-Revolutionary ideology where "most commonly the discussion . . . centered on its essential aggressiveness: its endlessly propulsive tendency to expand itself beyond legitimate boundaries."[46] The Crown's attempt to punish Boston by removing the Court and, to a greater extent, Hutchinson's compelling demonstration of the political processes at work forced the Court to move beyond the defensive appeal to precedent and to articulate more fully than at any previous time the vague but sweeping doctrine that the prerogative could be used only to serve the public good, that the public good was equivalent to the happiness and security of the people, and that only the people's representatives could determine when their happiness and security were served or endangered. That idea was dynamic and contagious. New exercises of the prerogative starting in 1771—independent salaries, the garrisoning of Castle William, and Hutchinson's refusal to assent to a law which would have taxed Crown officials[47]—provoked the Court to borrow extensively from the 1770 debates in order to construct, from traditional practice and the theory of compact, a new set of limitations on the use of the prerogative.

In early 1773, Hutchinson and the Court again debated a basic constitutional question—the extent of Parliamentary power—in their celebrated clash over the Boston Resolves. The removal controversy may have influenced that debate by conditioning both sides to eschew peripheral differences and to proceed at once to the heart of their disagreement about the meaning of the British constitution. Certainly the removal controversy reinforced the predisposition among public men in pre-Revolutionary Massachusetts—and during a period of constitutional strife—to conceive of institutions as players in a moral drama. Hutchinson regarded the removal as virtuous, disinterested discipline by the Crown of a willful colonial assembly; the Court questioned the virtue of any exercise of imperial authority which was based on such lofty presumptions. Some of the participants seemed to sense that the exposure of political evil and the execution of prudent countermeasures was an uncertain undertaking. For as the dispute ended, an anxious undercurrent appeared in some of their assessments of the outcome. Hutchinson must have felt a sharp twinge of doubt when he predicted that the Court, in forthcoming battles over independent Crown salaries, would remember and respect the tenacity he had shown during the removal controversy. Likewise, Councillor James Bowdoin may have betrayed a certain nervous exhilaration as well as jubilance when he declared in October 1772 that "the removal of ye General Assembly to Boston, as well as from it, has proved alike ineffectual to bring them to an acquiescence with ministerial measures. The air of Cambridge & of Boston is equally unsuitable" to affect the vision of Massachusetts representatives.[48]

Notes

1. Previous treatments of the removal of the Court include Robert E. Brown, *Middle-Class Democracy and the Revolution in Massachusetts, 1691–1780* (Ithaca, N.Y., 1955), pp. 269–92; John Cary, *Joseph Warren: Physician, Politician, Patriot* (Urbana, Ill., 1961), pp. 101–2; Clifford K. Shipton, *Sibley's Harvard Graduates: Biographical Sketches of Those Who Attended Harvard College . . .* (14 vols., Boston, 1933–1975), vol. 8, pp. 188–91; John F. Burns, *Controversies between Royal Governors and their Assemblies in the Northern American Colonies* (Boston, 1923), pp. 195–210; John C. Miller, *Sam Adams: Pioneer in Propaganda* (Boston, 1936), pp. 242–53; Thomas Hutchinson, *The History of the Colony and Province of Massachusetts-Bay,* Lawrence Shaw Mayo, ed. (3 vols., Cambridge, 1936), vol. 3, pp. 202, 242, 256; Douglass Adair and John A. Schutz, eds., *Peter Oliver's Origin & Progress of the American Rebellion: A Tory View* (San Marino, 1961), pp. 99–100; Lawrence Henry Gipson, *The British Empire before the American Revolution* (14 vols., New York, 1958–1968), vol. 12, pp. 43–44. For a convenient collection of some of the major documents in the controversy, see Hutchinson, *History of the Colony and Province of Massachusetts-Bay,* vol. 3, pp. 370–404.

2. Lord Hillsborough to Francis Bernard, July 30, 1768, March 24, 1769, Instructions to Provincial Governors of Massachusetts, transcripts, vol. 8, pp. 2422–27, 2439–40 (Massachusetts Historical Society, Boston); *Journal of the Honorable House of Representatives of His Majesty's Province of the Massachusetts-Bay, in New England, Begun and Held at Boston, in the County of Suffolk, on Wednesday the Thirty-First of May, Annoque Domini, 1769* (Boston, 1769–1770), pp. 20, 56–60, 80–87; Bernard to Hillsborough, Aug. 6, 1768; Bernard to Richard Jackson, April 8, 1769; Bernard to John Pownall, April 23, 1769; Bernard to Hillsborough, May 15, 1769, Francis Bernard Papers, vol. 7, pp. 19–23, 163–66, 274–76, 282–85 (Harvard College Library, Cambridge). Quoted by permission, Harvard College Library.

3. Hillsborough to Thomas Hutchinson, Dec. 9, 1769, Instructions to Provincial Governors, vol. 8, p. 2449; Hutchinson to Thomas Gage, Feb. 25, 1770, Hutchinson

Letterbooks (Massachusetts Historical Society, transcripts), Massachusetts Archives, vol. 26, pp. 445, 448 in Boston, where two regiments of British troops were stationed at the end of 1769.

4. Bernard to Hutchinson, Dec. 5, 1769, Bernard Papers, vol. 8, pp. 28–30.

5. Hillsborough to Hutchinson, July 6, 31, Aug. 4, 1770, Instructions to Provincial Governors, vol. 8, pp. 2462–64, 2467, 2469.

6. Hutchinson later alluded to a "conditional" instruction superseding the July and August 1770 dictates (Hutchinson, *History of the Colony and Province of Massachusetts-Bay*, vol. 3, p. 243), probably the instruction of July 3, 1771 (Instructions to Provincial Governors, vol. 8, pp. 2543–44). In June 1771, he had considered returning the Court to Boston, but the house's message of June 19, 1771, which attacked the prerogative, forced him to change his mind. Hutchinson to Israel Williams, Dec. 2, 1771, Israel Williams Papers (Massachusetts Historical Society, Boston). It is unclear from the letter to Williams whether the message of June 19 provoked the Crown to rescind Hutchinson's discretionary authority or whether the July 3, 1771, instruction subsequently convinced him that the house's message eliminated, for the time being, conditions under which he could use his discretion. No further instructions which indicated the extent of his discretion have been found except one drafted ten days before he finally summoned the Court to Boston. It was received too late to have affected that decision. It referred to unspecified "Conditions upon which you *alone* are authorized to assemble" the Court at Boston (Instructions to Provincial Governors, vol. 8, pp. 2565–66) and probably noted the terms of the July 3, 1771, instruction. See also Hutchinson's "Account and Defense of his conduct and actions in Massachusetts, 1764–1774," pp. 4–7 (Massachusetts Historical Society, Boston).

7. Peter Orlando Hutchinson, comp., *The Diary and Letters of His Excellency Thomas Hutchinson* (2 vols., London, 1883–1886), vol. 1, pp. 525–26.

8. Instructions to Provincial Governors, vol. 8, p. 2428; Bernard to Hutchinson, Dec. 5, 1769, Bernard Papers, vol. 8, pp. 28–30.

9. Malcolm Freiberg, "How to Become a Colonial Governor: Thomas Hutchinson of Massachusetts," *Review of Politics*, 21 (Oct. 1959): 655–56; Hutchinson to Pownall, March 21, 1770; Hutchinson to Pownall, June 8, 1770, Massachusetts Archives, vol. 26, pp. 464, 502–503, and Boston *Gazette*, June 19, 1775; Hutchinson to Bernard, March 25, 1770, Hutchinson Letterbooks, vol. 26, pp. 471–72, and Boston *Gazette*, June 5, 1775.

10. Hutchinson, *History of the Colony and Province of Massachusetts-Bay*, vol. 3, p. 243; Hutchinson to Pownall, July 27, 1770, Massachusetts Archives, vol. 26, p. 524; Hutchinson to Thomas Whately, Oct. 3, 1770, Massachusetts Archives, vol. 27, pp. 11–12, 21.

11. The Harvard Corporation soon complained that the use of the College for so controversial a purpose encroached upon the independence of the institution; only after Hutchinson's adroit intervention with the Board of Overseers, of which he was a member, did that body decline by a vote of eight to seven to make a similar protest. Harvard Corporation to Hutchinson, May 3, 1770; Hutchinson to Harvard Corporation, May 14, 1770, Miscellaneous Manuscripts, vol. 13 (Massachusetts Historical Society, Boston); Hutchinson to Hillsborough, May 3, 1770, Massachusetts Archives, vol. 26, pp. 476–77; Samuel Eliot Morison, *Three Centuries of Harvard, 1636–1936* (Cambridge, Mass., 1946), pp. 136–37. For Hutchinson's comments on the meeting of the overseers on May 1, 1770, see transcript, UA II, 27.70, Harvard University Archives; Hutchinson to Bernard, May

3, 1770, Massachusetts Archives, vol. 25, pp. 416–17; Shipton, *Sibley's Harvard Graduates,* vol. 10, pp. 149–50.

12. *Journal of the . . . House of Representatives of . . . Massachusetts-Bay . . . 1769,* pp. 90–97.

13. *Journal of the . . . House of Representatives of . . . Massachusetts-Bay . . . 1769,* pp. 90–97; Massachusetts *Gazette,* March 29, 1770. The issue was debated further in "Verus," Massachusetts *Gazette and Boston Weekly News-Letter,* May 16, 1771, and [Benjamin Prescott] *A Free and Calm Consideration of the Unhappy Misunderstandings and Debates . . . Between . . . Parliament and . . . Colonies* (Salem, Mass., 1774), pp. 50–51.

14. *Journal of the . . . House of Representatives of . . . Massachusetts-Bay . . . 1769,* pp. 99–102.

15. *Journal of the . . . House of Representatives of . . . Massachusetts-Bay . . . 1769,* pp. 139, 178–81.

16. *Boston Town Records, 1770 through 1777* (Boston, 1887), 27–32. John Cary, *Joseph Warren,* p. 101, identified Quincy as the author of the legal arguments in the resolves. William Blackstone, *Commentaries on the Laws of England* (4 vols., Philadelphia, 1771–1772), vol. 1, p. 252. Quincy did not identify Blackstone as the author of this quotation, but merely referred to "our lawbooks"; the quotation is correct. Blackstone credited the definition to Locke—"*For Prerogative is nothing but the Power of doing publick good without a Rule.*" See Peter Laslett, ed., *John Locke: Two Treatises on Government* (Cambridge, Eng., 1960), p. 396.

17. Hutchinson to [?], May 22, 1770; Hutchinson to Bernard, March 25, 1770, Massachusetts Archives, vol. 26, pp. 489–90, 471–72.

18. *Journal of the Honorable House of Representatives of His Majesty's Province of Massachusetts-Bay in New-England, Begun and Held at Harvard-College in Cambridge in the County of Middlesex, on Wednesday the Thirtieth Day of May, Annoque Domini, 1770* (Boston, 1770–1771), pp. 6–7.

19. *Journal of the . . . House of Representatives of . . . Massachusetts-Bay . . . 1770,* pp. 12–13.

20. *Journal of the . . . House of Representatives of . . . Massachusetts-Bay . . . 1770,* pp. 6–7, 10–11, 15–22.

21. *Journal of the . . . House of Representatives of . . . Massachusetts-Bay . . . 1770,* pp. 23–32. In 1729–1730, the house met variously at Cambridge, Salem, Roxbury, and George Tavern on Boston Neck, and in 1737 at Salisbury from August 10 to October 20; it is interesting to note that in 1637, at the height of the Antinomian controversy, John Winthrop managed to have the General Court removed from Boston, which was the center of Anne Hutchinson's supporters, to Newton (later Cambridge), where he regained the office of governor by defeating Mrs. Hutchinson's ally, Sir Henry Vane.

22. Hutchinson to Pownall, May 30, 1771, June 8, 1770; Hutchinson to Hillsborough, June 8, 1770; Hutchinson to Thomas Hood, June 8, 1770, Massachusetts Archives, vol. 27, p. 174, vol. 26, pp. 502–504. At this point Hutchinson, deeply involved in efforts to secure a delay of the Boston Massacre trials, commented that "a jovial celebration of the Festival at Boston in opposition to me for carrying the General Court to Cambridge" had "diverted" public attention away from radical demands for an immediate trial of Captain Preston and his soldiers. The unusually sarcastic tone of that remark suggests, however, that at this time Hutchinson did not really minimize the seriousness of the removal

controversy. L. Kinvin Wroth and Hiller B. Zobel, eds., *Legal Papers of John Adams* (3 vols., Cambridge, Mass., 1965), vol. 3, p. 12.

23. *Journal of the . . . House of Representatives of . . . Massachusetts-Bay . . . 1770*, pp. 25–31, 32–37, 39–43.

24. *Journal of the . . . House of Representatives of . . . Massachusetts-Bay . . . 1770*, pp. 49–51.

25. *Journal of the . . . House of Representatives of . . . Massachusetts-Bay . . . 1770*, pp. 58–59. The relevant passage in the charter stated: "the Governour . . . shall have full power and Authority from time to time as he shall Judge necessary to adjourne Prorogue and dissolve all Great and General Courts or Assemblyes met and convened as aforesaid." Francis N. Thorp, ed., *The Federal and State Constitutions, Colonial Charters and other Organic Laws . . . 1492–1908* (7 vols., Washington, 1909), vol. 3, p. 1879. "Aequitas," Massachusetts *Gazette and Boston Weekly News-Letter*, July 18, 1771. See also "Constitutionalists" and "Publius," Massachusetts *Gazette and Boston Weekly News-Letter*, Feb. 21, May 23, 1771; Catherine B. Mayo, ed., *Additions to . . . Hutchinson's History of Massachusetts-Bay* (Worcester, 1949), p. 39.

26. *Journal of the . . . House of Representatives of . . . Massachusetts-Bay . . . 1770*, pp. 63–71; Harry Alonzo Cushing, ed., *The Writings of Samuel Adams* (4 vols., New York, 1904–1908), vol. 2, pp. 19–35.

27. For a searching analysis of New England Lockean sermons on restraining the magistrate, see Richard Buel, Jr., "Democracy and the American Revolution: A Frame of Reference," *William and Mary Quarterly*, 21 (April 1964): 169–70.

28. *Journal of the . . . House of Representatives of . . . Massachusetts-Bay . . . 1770*, pp. 58–61, 73–78.

29. *Journal of the . . . House of Representatives of . . . Massachusetts-Bay . . . 1770*, pp. 58–61, 73–78. (italics added).

30. *Journal of the . . . House of Representatives of . . . Massachusetts-Bay . . . 1770*, pp. 58–61, 73–78.

31. Brown, *Middle-Class Democracy*, pp. 275–76; *Journal of the . . . House of Representatives of . . . Massachusetts-Bay . . . 1770*, pp. 80–82, 85–87, 89–91, 97–99, 170–82. Henry Young Brown to Hutchinson, Nov. 28, 1770, Massachusetts Archives, vol. 25, pp. 453–54.

32. Gipson, *The British Empire before the American Revolution*, vol. 12, p. 44.

33. *Journal of the . . . House of Representatives of . . . Massachusetts-Bay . . . 1769*, pp. 20, 42; *Journal of the Honorable House of Representatives of His Majesty's Province of Massachusetts-Bay in New England, Begun and Held at Harvard-College in Cambridge in the County of Middlesex, on Wednesday the Twenty-Ninth Day of May, Annoque Domini 1771* (Boston, 1771–1772), p. 242; Shipton, *Sibley's Harvard Graduates*, vol. 11, p. 282.

34. A remark by John Chandler, quoted in John Adams's diary, entry for June 2, 1771, L. H. Butterfield and others, eds., *Diary and Autobiography of John Adams* (4 vols., Cambridge, Mass., 1961), vol. 2, p. 20.

35. *Journal of the . . . House of Representatives of . . . Massachusetts-Bay . . . 1771*, pp. 62–64.

36. *Journal of the . . . House of Representatives of . . . Massachusetts-Bay . . . 1771*, pp. 177; Hutchinson to [?], June 5, 1771; Hutchinson to Hillsborough, June 22, 1771; Hutchinson to Pownall, June 22, 1771; Hutchinson to Jackson or Whately [?], July 19, 1771, Massachusetts Archives, vol. 27, pp. 180–81, 188–89, 197–98.

37. "Candidus," Boston *Gazette,* Sept. 9, 23, 30, Oct. 14, 1771; "Valerius Popicola," Boston *Gazette,* Oct. 28, 1771; Miller, *Sam Adams,* p. 253; Cushing, *Writings of Samuel Adams,* vol. 2, pp. 204–12, 222–29, 237–45, 256–64; "Chronus," [Henry Caner] Massachusetts *Gazette and Boston Weekly News-Letter,* Jan. 2, 1772.

38. *Journal of the . . . House of Representatives of . . . Massachusetts-Bay . . . 1771,* pp. 119–20; Samuel Adams to James Warren, April 13, 1772, Massachusetts Historical Society, *Collections,* 72 (Boston, 1917): 10–11. For Hutchinson's strategy prior to the session, see his letters to Pownall, Oct. 14, 1771, and to Hillsborough, March 12, 1772, Massachusetts Archives, vol. 27, pp. 240, 301–302.

39. Hutchinson to Hillsborough, April 10, 1772, Massachusetts Archives, vol. 27, pp. 315–16; Hutchinson to Pownall, June 15, 1772, Massachusetts Historical Society, *Proceedings,* 19 (Boston, 1881–1882): 138.

40. Hutchinson to Pownall, June 15, 1772, Massachusetts Historical Society, *Proceedings,* vol. 19, p. 138; Hutchinson to Hillsborough, June 15, 1772; Hutchinson to James Gambier, June 30, 1772, Massachusetts Archives, vol. 27, pp. 344, 354–55; Hillsborough to Hutchinson, Aug. 7, 1772, Instructions to Provincial Governors, vol. 8, pp. 2568–69.

41. Leonard Woods Labaree, *Royal Government in America: A Study of the British Colonial System Before 1783* (New Haven, Conn., 1930), pp. 446–48.

42. On two other occasions during the reign of George III, an assembly was removed from its traditional seat—in South Carolina in 1772, when the Commons House was moved from Charleston to Beaufort during the Wilkes fund controversy, and again in Massachusetts in May 1774, when General Gage, Hutchinson's successor, removed the Court in Salem. See Jack P. Greene, "Bridge to Revolution: The Wilkes Fund Controversy in South Carolina, 1769–1775," *Journal of Southern History,* 29 (Feb. 1963): 37; Gipson, *The British Empire before the American Revolution,* vol. 12, p. 150. Of these disputes, the 1770 removal of the Court was by far the most widely known. It was discussed in Boston in 1775, when some of Hutchinson's stolen correspondence relating to the affair was published. See Boston *Gazette,* June 5, 1775. When Hutchinson read the Declaration of Independence, he assumed that it referred to his removal of the Court; and his wry *Structures upon the Declaration of the Congress at Philadelphia* (London, 1776), pp. 14–15, asked how the Court could have been "fatigued" while idly refusing to do business.

43. See John C. Miller, *The Origins of the American Revolution* (Boston, 1943), pp. 315–25.

44. Cary, *Joseph Warren,* pp. 98–113.

45. The same ambivalence is discussed in Richard D. Brown, "Massachusetts Towns Reply to the Boston Committee of Correspondence, 1773," *William and Mary Quarterly,* 25 (Jan. 1968): 36–38.

46. Bernard Bailyn, *The Ideological Origins of the American Revolution* (Cambridge, Mass., 1967), p. 56.

47. See Gipson, *The British Empire before the American Revolution,* vol. 12, pp. 43–47.

48. James Bowdoin to Pownall, Oct. 24, 1772, Massachusetts Historical Society, *Collections,* sixth series, 9 (Boston, 1897): 297. See the discussions of the Crown's prerogative as a source of anxiety, instability, and conflict from the 1730s to the 1750s and the moral implications of those struggles in Bernard Bailyn, *The Origins of American Politics* (New York, 1968), pp. 69–73, 136–52.

Four

"The Scandalous History of Sir Egerton Leigh"

Robert M. Calhoon
and Robert M. Weir

"I am a down-right *Placeman,*" Egerton Leigh declared in 1773. Shortly thereafter, with equal candor, Thomas Lynch, a delegate from South Carolina to the First Continental Congress, and a man of sound judgment, described him as the greatest "Rascall among all the Kings Friends."[1] That South Carolinians of Lynch's stature had come to regard the terms placeman and rascal as virtually synonymous was largely because Leigh appeared to share both roles, and his notorious quarrel over vice-admiralty matters with the merchant Henry Laurens, though not always fully understood, has long been familiar to students of early American history.[2] What has hitherto been generally overlooked, however, is that Leigh was one of the most able Crown servants in the colony prior to the Revolution and that his early achievements appeared to establish firmly his position in local society. Indeed, the contrast between this early promise and later disgrace has the fascination of classical tragedy as well as considerable historical significance.

Certainly, Leigh was not the only Crown officeholder to find the difficulties of the pre-Revolutionary period insurmountable, but his unique vantage point and qualifications made him an unusually perceptive interpreter of the forces which helped to destroy him. His career, his awareness of the political hostility which he aroused, and his introspective contemplation of his own dilemma, illustrate the complexity of loyalist motivation and, in addition, illuminate several facets of the pre-Revolutionary period in South Carolina.

In 1753, at the age of twenty, Leigh arrived in South Carolina with his father, the newly appointed chief justice. Doubtless under the latter's benign aegis, Leigh quickly launched a brilliant career. He began to practice law immediately and, aided by a short term as clerk of the Court of Common Pleas—a position which gave him valuable contacts among the legal profession—he rapidly built up a very successful private practice.[3] With equal speed, he accumulated public honors and offices. In January 1755 he was elected to the Commons House of Assembly by St. Peter's parish; reelected in 1757, he retained this position until January 1760 when he took a seat on the Council.[4] In the meantime, on November 3, 1755, he was appointed surveyor general of the province. Six years later he became judge of the Charleston Vice-Admiralty Court, and in 1765 he became the attorney general.[5]

Wealth and social position accompanied his professional rise. From 1756 to 1765 his private law practice yielded between £1,000 and £1,200 sterling per year, and his official positions probably more than doubled this amount. As a result his income was among the largest in the colony.[6] Although somewhat more aggressive in acquiring offices than land, between 1757 and 1763 he accumulated grants totaling 1,800 acres, bought a 500-acre plantation on the Santee River, and purchased more than 2 acres in Ansonboro, a rapidly developing community north of Charleston.[7] Moreover, in 1756 he married Martha Bremar, the daughter of Martha and Francis Bremar. The elder Martha was Henry Laurens's sister; Francis had been a merchant associate of Laurens and a member of the Commons House.[8] If the marriage to Laurens's niece did not bring immediate wealth to Leigh—which it probably did not—it did help to cement a friendship between the two men and thereby ensure that for more than a decade Leigh would handle much of Laurens's legal business.[9] Leigh, a cultured man whose versatile talents included considerable ability as a musician as well as a poet and prose writer, rented a house in Charleston and furnished it with an extensive library, which soon totaled more than 800 volumes, a large organ, and a magnificent collection of paintings, including works by Veronese and Correggio.[10] The parishioners of St. Philip's elected him a vestryman, and he became a commissioner of the provincial free school in Charleston. In 1765 the local Masons elected him deputy grand master and heir apparent to the provincial grand master, Benjamin Smith, the respected speaker of the Commons House of Assembly.[11]

It was an amazing performance. In a dozen years Leigh, at the age of thirty-two, had vaulted into the very top ranks of local society. Only a fortuitous combination of circumstances could account for such phenomenal success. A relative lack of competition helped, for there was a dearth of educated men to fill public offices in the colony. Family connections certainly contributed: Egerton's father, Peter, had been high bailiff of Westminster before becoming chief justice of South Carolina. Despite later stories of misconduct as high bailiff—none of which was proved—the elder Leigh seems to have retained sufficient influence at Whitehall to further his son's advancement, and his name was usually mentioned in solicitations in behalf of the young Leigh.[12]

Hard work also furthered Egerton Leigh's career. He allocated his time carefully and therefore paid more attention to his private law practice and the lucrative duties of the surveyor generalship than he did to responsibilities which he discharged gratis, such as service in the Commons. During his term in the House he seldom appeared when attendance was voluntary, though he performed required duties conscientiously enough to become a relatively prominent figure.[13] Somewhat surprisingly, although his power to appoint deputy surveyors—and he had squadrons of them—gave him control of considerable patronage, Leigh does not appear at this time to have been interested in using this power to advance his career.[14] Perhaps he did not need to and instead aimed at goals where popular support was of little value. Certainly he succeeded in impressing men who had the political and economic power to help him. High regard for his ability and character seems to have been the most important cause of his rapid professional advancement. Governor William Henry Lyttelton's enthusiastic recommendation of him as a rising young lawyer of "unblemished reputation," not influential family connections, secured Leigh's appointment to the Council.[15] Even after the break between the two friends, Laurens continued to respect Leigh's natural ability, although he vigorously condemned his judgment and his morals. For example, during the admiralty affair Laurens, a sternly moral but shrewd judge of men, noted that "if he had resolution enough to with stand the temptations of high Life [he] would be an admirable Man." What Laurens probably realized was that Leigh had mortgaged his future income for present consumption. Nevertheless, Laurens had earlier trusted his friend implicitly. When Leigh went to England in 1764, Laurens wrote merchant correspondents there, recommending him as a worthy man "for whome I bear the highest regard" and authorizing them to lend him whatever sums he might need, up to the limits of Laurens's own credit.[16]

The Stamp Act crisis, however, triggered severe financial and political problems for Leigh. Its most immediate impact was to cut off practically all of his income for nearly six months. The inability to obtain stamps brought business in the Court of Commons Pleas to a standstill, closed the Vice-Admiralty Court, and prevented the granting of lands. But a sense of duty, or perhaps the hope of future reward, influenced Leigh more than concern over his immediate loss of income. Alone among the lawyers of Charleston in the spring of 1766 he argued against reopening the Court of Common Pleas without stamped paper. When Chief Justice Charles Shinner reported to the ministry on the conduct of local officials during the crisis, he censured virtually everyone except Leigh.[17] But opposition to opening the Court endeared him to few. When the nature of Shinner's report became public knowledge, gossip quite naturally (and probably correctly) marked Leigh as the instigator of Shinner's accusations and dealt his popularity another serious blow. Leigh's private law practice never recovered.[18] Consequently, he became dependent upon his Crown offices for financial rewards and a sense of importance. The need to retain these pursuits therefore obsessed him, but his tenaciousness increasingly appeared to put private interest before the public welfare, thus further estranging him from the local community. In short, he was caught in a vicious circle.

The next step in Leigh's downfall was also a by-product of the Stamp Act crisis. In the spring of 1766 the Commons, hoping that the Rockingham ministry might be willing to make further concessions to the colonies, undertook a comprehensive review of various problems confronting South Carolina. Leigh's recent role had made him and his offices conspicuous. Among other sources of concern, the House therefore noted that Leigh and some of his fellow royal officers held positions which were partly designed to check each other. A man who sought to occupy simultaneously all of Leigh's offices risked entangling the colony, as well as himself, in many unnecessary difficulties—Laurens warned his friend against the pitfall. The Commons House, always wary of power which did not appear properly limited, took more direct action by ordering Charles Garth, its agent in London, to ask the ministry to remove Leigh from some of his offices.[19] Leigh ignored the friendly advice, attributed the actions of the Commons purely to resentment at his conduct during the Stamp Act crisis, and mobilized his friends in London in his behalf. They apparently succeeded. Lord Shelburne, who actually sympathized with the attitude of the House, informed Garth that Leigh could not be deprived of any of his offices because no charges of misconduct had been brought against him. It was, however, a Pyrrhic victory for Leigh.[20]

In the spring of 1767 a new customs collector, Daniel Moore, a former member of Parliament for the borough of Great Marlow, arrived in Charleston and opened Pandora's box. It is possible that Moore was primarily dedicated to serving his country by tightening up the customs service in South Carolina, but it is probable that he was more interested in enriching himself by the same means.[21] At any rate, he adopted questionable practices which may have actually violated the law. Enraged local merchants responded with an avalanche of suits, complaints, and information against him in the Courts of Common Pleas, General Sessions, and Vice-Admiralty. Within six months Moore fled to England, but not before his activities brought into the Vice-Admiralty Court what the *South Carolina Gazette* correctly termed "as difficult causes as perhaps ever came before that court in America."[22] In all likelihood no one could have coped with them successfully. Certainly Leigh failed, although within the limits set by the desire to protect his position he tried to render just and equitable verdicts.

Four cases marked Leigh's progress into an ever-deepening morass. On June 19, 1767, he released the *Active*, a coasting vessel seized for failing to clear properly. The crux of Leigh's decision was his statement that because the navigation acts were not intended to "lay any unnecessary Restraint" on legitimate commerce, they should not be rigidly applied to intracolonial trade.[23] The decision was certainly reasonable and Leigh believed it to be praiseworthy, but officialdom thought otherwise. Concerned about the precedent which the decision might set, the Lords of the Treasury referred the matter to the British attorney and solicitor generals who considered the verdict much too lenient.[24] Leigh had overreached himself, and even before he learned of the full reaction to his decision, he realized that unless he gave more support to customs officials he would jeopardize his judgeship.[25] In the next case he therefore relied upon a technicality to acquit Moore of a charge filed by local merchants that he had demanded illegal fees. Leigh, however, believed that Moore's underhanded conduct merited a sharp reprimand.[26] The remaining cases involved the *Broughton Island Packet* and the *Wambaw*, two coasting schooners belonging to Henry Laurens, which had been seized under almost identical circumstances because they had not cleared as Moore demanded. But the ballast in the *Wambaw* was saleable; that aboard the

Broughton Island Packet was not. The difference enabled Leigh to engineer a compromise by condemning the former vessel and releasing the latter. Moreover, Leigh neglected to declare "a probable cause of seizure," i.e., that reasonable grounds had existed for believing that the discharged schooner had been operating in violation of the law.[27] The omission opened the way for Laurens to recover his losses on the one vessel by suing for damages in the case of the other—something that Laurens's lawyers immediately recognized. Given the context of the whole affair and the fact that Leigh was an experienced judge, it is difficult to believe that his apparent oversight was unintentional.[28]

Leigh's attempt to make his compromise as equitable as possible proved to be a fatal mistake. Laurens sued George Roupell, the customs searcher who had made the actual seizure. Although Roupell had been a member of the Commons House and for nearly twenty years a respected customs official,[29] he was now unable to find a private lawyer to defend him and Leigh, as attorney general, consequently acted for his fellow Crown officer. However, as Roupell later complained to the customs commissioners, "he had left such an opening when Judge, that the attorney general could not close it again," and the jury awarded Laurens a judgment which Roupell was unable to pay. Nor did the temporary collector who succeeded Moore, Roger Peter Handaside Hatley, feel free to pay the sum from customs funds without the authorization of his superiors. Roupell thus faced going to jail,[30] but on June 17, 1768, Hatley deliberately delayed receiving a bond for goods already aboard the *Ann*, a large vessel belonging partly to Laurens, so that Roupell could seize it. Acting through intermediaries, Roupell then offered to release the ship if Laurens would surrender his demand for damages. Laurens refused, and Leigh faced a serious dilemma.[31] On the one hand, because local customs officials had been filing a stream of complaints against him,[32] he could not hope to retain his office unless he protected Roupell. On the other hand, because the officers had so obviously resorted to subterfuge, it was extremely difficult to justify declaring a probable cause of seizure. The problem appeared almost insoluble, but Leigh devised a rather ingenious way out. He forced Roupell to take the seldom used oath of calumny, a declaration that his actions were not motivated by malice. The bond had not been posted; the vessel was technically in violation of the law; Roupell swore that he had acted in good faith; *ipso facto* there was a probable cause of seizure; and on July 11, 1768, Leigh so certified when he discharged the vessel, noting that he had a "Strong Suspicion that there was more of design and Surprise on the part of some officers than of any intention to commit fraud on the part of the Claimant. . . ."[33]

Throughout the whole series of cases Leigh had really acted as an arbitrator and, considering the pressures upon him, a reasonably fair one. At the time many South Carolinians may have understood this, and the *South Carolina Gazette*, a newspaper not noted for its partiality to officers of the Admiralty Court, reported that the "equitable decree" regarding the *Ann* "seems to have given general satisfaction."[34] But in attempting to protect himself while extricating everyone else from their own difficulties, Leigh had succeeded chiefly in making himself vulnerable for, as Roupell put it in a complaint to the customs commissioners, "no Judge of Admiralty can make a Court of Equity of it upon all occasions, which for this year past has been the case."[35]

Laurens understood the situation as well as Roupell and was equally dissatisfied. He attacked Leigh in a pamphlet titled *Extracts from the Proceedings of the Court of Vice-Admiralty.* Leigh defended himself with *The Man Unmasked,* a personal attack on Laurens who in turn countered with a new edition of the *Extracts* which contained an appendix in reply to Leigh. These pamphlets cannot be dismissed as mere scurrilous polemics. In a sense both Leigh and Laurens were fighting for professional and political survival. Each took the matter with utmost seriousness, and the pamphlets therefore reveal much about the men involved.

Leigh clearly expected that Laurens would understand the pressures that he was under and make allowances for them: that, given the circumstances, he had done the best he could for him and that the part of a relative and a friend was to help one through a difficult situation by remaining quiet. Knowing full well that he was vulnerable—throughout the entire proceedings he had tried to stifle complaints against his decisions—and knowing that Laurens knew this, Leigh was not only panic-stricken at being pilloried in the press, he was also horrified at Laurens's apparent ingratitude and Iago-like betrayal. He had, Leigh declared, violated their long friendship and family ties and cruelly endangered the livelihood of Leigh's wife, seven children, and mother-in-law. "Every man who reads his book, must perceive the motive," Leigh explained. "Under the specious shew of an *exalted kind of virtue,* which regards no law, no friendship, no alliances, no ties of blood," Laurens had attempted "to gain a *popular name*" and to sacrifice "the fame of a man in the meridian of his days."[36]

It was true that Laurens for various reasons had found himself out of step with a good part of the community during the early 1760s and that he realized that his conduct during the admiralty affair redeemed him in the eyes of many persons.[37] Nevertheless, in attributing Laurens's behavior to a lust for popularity, Leigh considerably oversimplified the matter. Laurens had been unfairly treated by the customs officers; the whole affair had been very expensive and time-consuming; it had forced him to postpone an intended trip to England; and he was a busy man whose attitude toward the use of time was the essence of the Puritan ethic. Equally important, while the *Ann* was loading, he left Charleston for his Georgia plantations after writing to his correspondents in England, "As I have been very attentive to the general Interest I beg you will not be under any apprehensions of mismanagement on Account of my absence. . . ." While he was gone, goods were put aboard the ship that led to its seizure. Moreover, Laurens had earlier lost his temper at Moore, who was an elderly man, and twisted his nose on a crowded street—a widely publicized episode that mortified Laurens after he had cooled down.[38] In short, he had good reason to be irate over the whole business and to feel that both his reputation as a merchant and his self-respect as a man of honor were at stake. Most important, all of these personal considerations contributed to his willingness to perform what he considered to be his duty. There can be no doubt that throughout his entire career Laurens possessed an amazingly deep commitment to the public welfare and a heroic sense of duty, though like other human beings he could interpret the one and exercise the other from his own limited vantage point. He and his contemporary South Carolinians were profoundly sceptical of the ability of fallible mortals to use power wisely. Because neither kings nor commoners were divine their power should be hedged about by proper limits. As a single judge in a court without a jury, Leigh's powers were potentially dangerous. That he had placed his own self-interest above his duty in failing to curb the customs officers proved that he could not be trusted with these powers. Thus self-interest and personal considerations combined to reinforce Laurens's belief that the admiralty jurisdiction as it was constituted in America invited arbitrary exercises of power. Friend or no friend, Leigh and his court had to be attacked for the sake of the commonweal.[39]

It would be a mistake to dismiss Laurens's point of view as a mere rationalization. It would be equally erroneous to see Leigh's reaction as entirely a matter of wounded feelings or of tactical maneuver designed to discredit Laurens. Fundamentally, what was at issue were two basically different conceptions of what constituted morality in a public officeholder. To Leigh morality was something personal, intimate, almost clannish. The preservation of family ties and the protection of friends took precedence over abstract considerations of right and wrong, while ingratitude was the most heinous of sins. For Laurens the priority was reversed: virtue, duty, and the common good transcended all other considerations, even the obligations of friendship and family.

Irrespective of which might be considered a higher form of ethics, Leigh's system was poorly adapted to the glare of publicity, and the episode of the Vice-Admiralty quarrel proved a disaster to him. Laurens made a point of demonstrating the inherent conflicts between Leigh's multiple roles which involved him at various times in the same cases as a private lawyer, as attorney general, and as judge. Roupell made the same point in complaints to the customs commissioners and succeeded where the whole Commons House had earlier failed. The ministry directed Leigh to resign either as Vice-Admiralty judge or attorney general. Leigh resigned the less lucrative judgeship and did his best to make the resignation appear voluntary, but without much success.[40] Two years later Leigh also gave up his private practice in the Court of Chancery on which he sat as a member of the Council. The reason for his action is not entirely clear, but it is worth noting that one of the parties in his last case was another Crown officer, George Saxby, the receiver general of quitrents. Perhaps Leigh was forced to resign; perhaps, remembering the admiralty affair, he thought it prudent. Whatever the reason, he did not give up much—his chancery business was already very small.[41]

More important than the loss of judgeship was the increasing isolation from the community that his declining private practice reflected. Part of his alienation was the result of his stand during the Stamp Act crisis, part came from his questionable conduct and the adverse publicity of the admiralty cases, and part was largely a matter of personality. Insecure and therefore hypersensitive, flamboyant, witty, erudite, and arrogant, he possessed an unfortunate knack for unnecessarily irritating people. For example, while he was presiding over the cases of the merchants against Moore, a rumor reached him that the merchants had acted as a group in order to intimidate him by their combined wealth and influence. Infuriated, Leigh unleashed a barrage of sarcastic accusations before checking the accuracy of his information, which was false. Understandably, the merchants were offended.[42]

Whatever its causes, the growing hostility toward Leigh increasingly meant that his sins were magnified and his good deeds overlooked. Although by the late 1760s the road was not entirely downhill, Leigh was now so estranged from the local leaders that his minor triumphs—unlike his earlier successes—often appeared to be victories of an outsider, achieved at the expense of the community. While still judge, he had responded to complaints against supposedly exorbitant charges in the Vice-Admiralty Court by reducing fees, but he received little credit for his action. Conversely, although the Commons House seemed to begrudge him every penny, he forced it to more than double the salary first offered to him in lieu of fees under a new court system planned for the backcountry. The reason for his success as a negotiator was his credible threat to secure disallowance of the act establishing the courts unless he was more adequately compensated. The price of his victory was a conviction among many South Carolinians that he did indeed put his private interest before the public welfare.[43] A success of a different kind, for which he paid a different price, was his purchase in 1767 of a fine plantation, 553 acres seven miles up the Cooper River from Charleston. Significantly, he seems to have named it "The Retreat." However, it proved to be more of a headache than a consolation. Its purchase price put a severe strain on his dwindling income and he sold it within four years.[44] Even his election as grand master of the local Masons in January 1768 was less of an achievement than it might have appeared to be, for as deputy provincial grand master since 1765 Leigh was already in line to succeed Benjamin Smith when he retired in 1767 because of ill-health.[45]

Despite these apparent successes, Leigh was only too well aware that his fortunes had suffered an amazing reversal since 1765. Quite understandably he blamed Laurens for many of his troubles, but Leigh was too intelligent not to realize that the source of his difficulties went much deeper: that the tensions of the last few years had made it impossible for Crown officers to function effectively unless they had the power to command respect. Impotent threats only brought contempt, as Leigh had painfully discovered when he futilely tried to block publication of Laurens's *Extracts* by threatening to cite him for contempt of court and sue for libel.[46] Public support made Laurens impregnable; the lack of it rendered Leigh vulnerable.

Leigh sought refuge behind the mysteries of the law. He maintained that Laurens had revealed his ignorance of the law when he had accused the Vice-Admiralty judge of inconsistent rulings in the cases of the *Wambaw* and the *Broughton Island Packet*. The difference between the cases, Leigh replied, was perfectly apparent to his trained legal eye. If Laurens could not see that difference, it only proved that he was "in a strange element, clearly out of his depth, perplexed by an enquiry foreign to the whole study and labour of his life." Leigh's definition of his craft involved more than mere technical knowledge and practice. Law was a calling requiring an elaborate initiation. Outsiders could never be expected to comprehend its wisdom. Laurens's attacks on Leigh only reassured him how "every departure, from the regular system to which we are bred . . . from that track which nature or our parents chose for us . . . will only involve us in a . . . perplexity of inextricable mazes."[47] Leigh's plea for the higher wisdom of lawyers revealed major weaknesses which he most wanted to disguise. In his eyes, indecision became judicial deliberation. The contempt with which men viewed his conduct became the ignorance of laymen about legal processes. The widespread sympathy among South Carolina leaders for Laurens's plight became blindness to Leigh's right as a royal official to deference and respect.

Laurens's criticisms, Leigh argued further, were not merely personal differences; they undermined the whole structure of law and the administration of justice. Sheltering himself within legal tradition, he tried to explain how judicial processes worked. The king was the source of justice, distributing it through the realm through the work of judges, all fallible men. The system of appeal—as well as precedent and procedure—served to correct judges' human errors. Inevitably, he explained, defeated parties accused the judge of bias. When they did so, they set themselves above the law and subverted the constitution. Attacks on judges endangered the community because slandered jurists had no means of retaliation. Laurens, Leigh concluded, misunderstood both the relation between the courts and society and the actual merits of his own case. Actually, he had been treated very well, Leigh observed. He therefore had no real grounds for complaint, and his accusations were "wild, inconsistent, irregular, and strange."[48]

In the final analysis, however, Leigh's defense rested on a plea that his professional dignity entitled him to a special construction of his actions. "When seizures are made," he explained, "the [Vice-Admiralty] judge is presumed to be totally indifferent to the parties in the dispute; charity supposes likewise that he is influenced only by his sense of duty."[49] If he had made errors, they were errors of judgment, not of evil intent. Brought before the bar of public opinion, he could, in effect, only avow that his intentions had been good and plead for mercy. For a proud and sensitive man such impotence must have been a humiliating, frustrating experience.

What was so galling was that he could not bring most South Carolinians to recognize his own wise and constructive propensities. The trouble seemed to be that most persons did not understand the principles of human behavior. Men were difficult to analyze because they were a "mixture of so much *goodness* and so much *baseness* ... a compound of opposite *qualities, humours,* and *inclinations.*" When faced with this problem, the average man, Leigh believed, simply counted a person's good and bad qualities, deducting one total from the other "as we do in vulgar arithmetic." Leigh proceeded differently: "I ... sift out ... the first ruling principle of the man, and then ... carry in my eye his leading passion, which I separate from the other parts of his character, and then observe how far his other qualities, good and bad, are brought to support *that.*"[50]

Recognition from the Crown, he hoped, would help him command respect because it would compel men to take seriously his "leading passion" of service to the King and thereby dissuade them from simply compiling his alleged misdeeds. Perhaps the triumph of a peerage could redeem everything. In the spring of 1771 he therefore set sail for England where he pestered the King's advisor, the Earl of Rochford, to recommend him. Receiving little encouragement, he finally resorted to a presumptuous maneuver. He told Rochford that if the King did not grant him a royal honor before his ship sailed for South Carolina in ten or twelve days, he would then return to Charleston "under a patient Expectation that Royal Favour will be extended to me in due time." The twelve days passed without a summons from the palace, but Rochford did not disabuse Leigh of the presumption that he could force the King's hand in this manner. Six weeks later, on September 14, 1772, George III granted his hard pressed servant a baronetcy, though not a peerage.[51]

While in England Leigh also seems to have received other favors. At least he made pregnant a girl in his household, an orphan who was his own ward, his wife's sister, and Henry Laurens's niece. Who seduced whom is a question that will probably always remain unanswerable.[52] Nevertheless, two points can and should be made. First, a kind of poetic injustice was involved: Leigh believed that Laurens had attempted to destroy his reputation and had thereby violated family ties, while Leigh's incestuous conduct violated family ties and struck at the reputation of Laurens's family. Second, Leigh's attempts to hide the affair were astonishingly clumsy. He and the girl returned separately to South Carolina. When her time to deliver was near, he put her aboard a vessel bound for England whose captain was an acquaintance of Laurens. Although Leigh enjoined the girl under threat of dire penalties not to contact her uncle, it seems almost incredible that a man of his intelligence did not realize that Laurens would learn of the affair. Indeed, Laurens himself realized as much when he wrote, "Nothing is too Wicked for him to *attempt,* even when Detection and Judgement are at his Threshold— He is the most Wicked Man and the greatest Fool that ever I heard or Read of, in a Man of tolerable Education and Sense."[53]

Not only Laurens but all of Charleston soon discovered what had happened. Before the vessel was out to sea the girl went into labor. When the captain attempted to put her ashore, Leigh prevented it. She gave birth with no midwife in attendance, and the baby died within the week. Laurens termed it murder and suspected that Leigh had hoped that without proper care the mother would die as well.[54]

Whether or not Laurens's suspicions were justified, Leigh's conduct was indefensible, and he became a social pariah, reduced to associating chiefly with Fenwick Bull, another recently fallen Crown officer who had been horsewhipped and ostracized for attempting to bribe a jockey into fixing a horse race.[55] No baronetcy could help Leigh now—it could only further disgust South Carolinians with the administration that appeared to honor him. (Laurens correctly suspected that Leigh had probably purchased his title, but by this point in the pre-Revolutionary controversy, most colonial observers simply regarded the title as a genuine expression of the Crown's esteem for Leigh.) Thus John Adams recorded in the diary which he kept during the First Continental Congress: "He [Thomas Lynch] entertained us with the scandalous History of Sir Egerton Leigh—the Story of his Wife's Sister, . . . and all that. There is not says Lynch a greater Rascall among all the Kings Friends. He has great Merit, in this Reign."[56]

Whatever merit he possessed, Leigh had become ineffectual, and—certainly in South Carolina—a positive liability as a servant of the Crown. Although the powers and prestige of the Council had been waning for more than a decade, it had been a consistent source of support for royal officers who tried to uphold imperial measures. When Leigh became the senior member and president, the Council and its measures were identified with a man who was already considered to be beyond the pale. Moreover, because he led the upper house into imprudent, if not irresponsible, actions, there appeared to be some foundation for the charge that Council "Business is generally done by a small Junto, under the Direction of a man desperate in Fortune, abandoned in Principle, and ruined in Reputation."[57] Leigh's presidency therefore materially accelerated the complete eclipse of the South Carolina Royal Council.

The final round of the battle between the Commons House and the Council stemmed from the Wilkes fund controversy which arose in 1769 when the Commons dispatched a donation from provincial funds to the Society of Supporters for the Bill of Rights in England, a group supporting John Wilkes. Again, Leigh found himself drawn into controversies begun by other men. In 1773 he tried to take the initiative after the Crown and successive governors had failed to induce the Commons to relinquish its claim to sole control of provincial expenditures. For nearly four years the Crown had forbidden governors to assent to a tax bill unless it included a clause prohibiting the treasurer from transmitting public funds out of the province.[58] On his return from England Leigh took matters into his own hands. Acting on information supplied by Henry Perroneau, one of the public treasurers, he prodded the Council to prepare a report which blamed the depleted state of the provincial treasury on the Commons for its refusal to enact an acceptable money bill. Somewhat later, two members of the Council—John and William Henry Drayton—prepared a report criticizing the recent conduct of the upper house and, in effect, praising the Commons for its stand. The Draytons' manifesto appeared in the *South Carolina Gazette*. Infuriated at this opposition, Leigh as president of the Council ordered the arrest of the paper's printer, Thomas Powell, for violating the privileges of the upper house.[59] The Commons exploded in protest, and two local justices of the peace—both members of the Commons— immediately ordered Powell's release on the grounds that because the councillors held their positions at the pleasure of the Crown, the Council was in reality an appendage of the executive and therefore not an independent house of the legislature possessing the power of commitment for contempt. Powell and one of his supporters then sued Leigh but lost when the chief justice, a member of the Council, ruled that that body was an upper house of the provincial legislature and within its rights in enforcing its privileges.[60] But the Commons House transmitted a vigorous denunciation of the Council's actions to the ministry and most South Carolinians continued to believe that the justices of the peace had the better of the argument. As a result of its apparently unwarranted and arbitrary behavior, the Council sank even lower in public estimation.[61]

In the meantime, the Powell affair had made Leigh's own position completely intolerable. During a meeting of the upper house the volatile William Henry Drayton reportedly called Leigh a damn fool to his face—a remark which the journal does not record. It does show, however, that the members felt it necessary at this time to adopt a series of "Remembrances for Order and Decency to be kept in the Upper House of Assembly," one of which stipulated that "all personal sharp and taxing Speeches [ought to] be forborn." Worse yet, Edward Rutledge, who made his name as a patriotic lawyer by representing Powell during the proceedings, denounced Leigh unmercifully in open court. On top of all these difficulties, in the spring of 1773 the ministry ordered a temporary embargo on the granting of lands in all royal colonies, and Leigh's income as surveyor general vanished.[62] What was to be gained by remaining in South Carolina was obviously no longer worth the price. Therefore, Leigh arranged for an allowance of £500 sterling per year from James Simpson who would act as attorney general in Leigh's absence. Then, having apparently delayed his departure in an unsuccessful attempt to avoid encountering Laurens in London, Leigh sailed for England on June 19, 1774.[63]

While waiting to depart he wrote an account of political events in South Carolina and sent the manuscript to London where in January 1774 it was anonymously published as a pamphlet titled *Considerations on Certain Political Transactions of the Province of South Carolina*. Leigh's defense of the Council and attack upon the conduct of the lower house enraged Henry Laurens, who correctly guessed the author's identity. Laurens and Ralph Izard, also then in London, therefore enlisted Izard's friend, Arthur Lee, to compose an *Answer to the Considerations on Certain Political Transactions of the Province of South Carolina.*[64]

Even Dr. Alexander Garden, who was relatively unsympathetic to the Commons in the Wilkes fund controversy, thought that Lee's *Answer* was an effective rebuttal, though he considered Egerton Leigh the better literary stylist.[65] Nevertheless, even though his position was too extreme for a future loyalist like Garden,

Leigh's analysis of the situation in South Carolina was shrewd and perceptive. There was good reason for the quality of his observations.

While he was a member of the Commons House it had been engaged in one of its periodic controversies with the upper house, and Leigh had served on a committee appointed to report whether or not the Council ought to be considered an upper house.[66] His service on this committee, his general experience in the Commons, and his membership in the Council gave him unusual insight into the workings of the political system in the colony. As a result, his analysis of the Wilkes fund controversy contained a highly sophisticated study of the nature of political change in South Carolina, and in particular it went to the heart of the matter in its discussion of the Commons's ascendancy from the 1720s to 1770s. Stripped of Leigh's attempts at self-justification, his pamphlet presented an analytical explanation of how the Commons House expanded its power. He took pains to delineate specific elements in the collective behavior of the assemblymen: the steady accumulation of power throughout the history of the legislature, the careful nurturing of precedents by the Commons, the tenacity with which assemblymen performed their functions and clung to their powers, the gratification they derived from the common endeavor, the absolute impasse between the Commons and the Crown which the additional instruction on provincial finance imposed on their struggle, the dependence of the Council's status as an upper house upon form rather than function, the hopeless tactical position of the Council once Powell had been released, and the supreme importance which the Council placed on its dignity after the bases for that dignity had disappeared.

As an opponent of the Commons, Leigh, significantly, acknowledged primacy of constitutional principle as a motivation of the House's actions in the Wilkes fund controversy. He based his case on the undesirability and impropriety of the Commons's extension of its fiscal powers "beyond the original . . . intention of those from whom they derive their whole authority."

Every political power, he reminded the assemblymen, had in its nature some limit beyond which it ought not to be extended. The constant temptations of men "to be misled by passion, fancy, or caprice" made these limits necessary and justified the Crown and Council in opposing the Wilkes fund grant or any repetition of it.[67] Neither conspiracy nor self-interest had any central place in Leigh's indictment. Rather the Commons's action had proceeded from folly, ignorance, and childish fascination with "a *factious* Club of Men . . . at the London Tavern"— as he styled the pro-Wilkes society. Leigh readily conceded the accuracy of the Commons's body of precedents, dating back to 1737, for their power to appropriate public funds. "In order to combat these Facts," he argued, "let us . . . reflect what slow advances *Infant Societies* of Men make towards Regularity or Perfection." The feeble efforts of early provincial government to cope with its problems scarcely justified subsequent attempts by the Commons to spend public funds on any purpose whatever. These admitted "Precedents, therefore, of new Communities are of very little weight." Most early examples of spending by the Commons dealt with mundane matters like the salaries of the clergy or the encouragement of silk production.[68] By admitting the legalistic nature of the Commons's appeal to its early development, Leigh recognized the central fact about the province's political history, and he thereby deprived himself of grounds for strong rebuttal. He denounced the exercise of the Commons's power; he could not, however, deny the existence of that power.

Leigh not only comprehended the constitutional ingredients of the Commons's ascendancy; he also understood its dynamic character. The success of its efforts and the sheer pleasure of maneuver and struggle reinforced the ambitions of its members and produced "baneful effects." Noting the constant agitation of provincial politics since the Stamp Act crisis, he explained that "human nature . . . cannot bear a constant Tide of flattering Successes without becoming Insolently Saucy, and Arrogantly Vain." This emotional dimension of politics explained why the Wilkes fund controversy had proceeded from one impasse to another in "*Geometric Progression*." As it developed, both the Commons and Council, he recalled, held tightly to their commitments. The Council insisted that as an upper house it could refuse assent to money bills, while the assemblymen remained "tenacious in their Rights as they conceived them." The additional instruction, prohibiting the governor from assenting to any money bill which did not forbid the treasurer to send money out of the province, prevented any compromise and reinforced the Council's intransigent position. The additional instruction confirmed a situation to which men on both sides were already committed. Thus the issue became "Whether the King is to recall . . . his Instruction; or the People submit to a check for an unconstitutional Application of the Public Treasure." "Justice as well as Prudence," he declared, "require us to yield the point." A gesture of obeisance by South Carolina, Leigh realized in 1773, was needed to restore the vigor of British authority in the province.[69]

Leigh derived his accurate assessment of the changes in South Carolina politics which, in part, had destroyed him politically and would contribute substantially to the coming of the Revolution there from the same self-centered and rigid quality of mind which blinded him to his opponents' values. He realized that the protests against the Council's arrest of Powell were also a personal attack against his exercise of the Council's power. Vainly seeking the support of Lieutenant Governor William Bull, he called the suit by Powell and one of his supporters against him "the unprecedented Insult which is intended to be cast on the Second or Middle branch of the Legislature [the Council] . . . for an Act done by me as President."[70] Leigh insisted that his chief motive in arresting Powell was to uphold the dignity of the Council and thereby preserve the constitution of the province. That dignity, apart from an admittedly shadowy similarity with the British House of Lords, consisted of the sacrifices made by its members. The lack of emoluments, public scorn of its proceedings, danger of arbitrary dismissal, and, now, the Wilkes fund controversy completed the sacrificial process in which Leigh took such pride. The Council, he pleaded, could not hope to maintain itself as a viable institution much longer if men in the province could publicly violate its prerogatives, if no court would enforce its decisions, and if men looked on it as an agent of oppression. "What security can such a Branch of the Legislature have," he demanded, "when . . . General Opinion proclaims, that a Place in Council is a kind of alienation from the concerns and interest of the People?"[71] He was incredulous that South Carolinians should consider him as alienated from their society, but at the same time he retained an especially acute awareness that in performing what he considered an honorable function in the politics of the province he had helped place himself, the Council, and the interests of the Crown directly in the way of the consuming flame of political opposition.

In part, Leigh had written his pamphlet in the hope of vindicating the Council and himself against the accusations of the Commons House. He also doubtless hoped that his performance would attract the favorable attention of the ministry, but his success was meager. Everyone was preoccupied by the chain of events that followed the Boston Tea Party and neither the *Considerations* nor its author aroused much interest.[72] Languishing in London, he petitioned Lord Dartmouth, secretary of state for American affairs, for a position in one of the middle or northern colonies. Long residence in South Carolina, he claimed, had "so effected the state of his Nerves" that his return there would be fatal. Nevertheless, along with other councillors then in England, he was given the choice of returning or resigning his position. He resigned.[73] After the conquest of Charleston, however, he went back to South Carolina, and became a member of the military commandant's advisory council, the Board of Police, and an intendant of the city.[74] He also recommended to the ministry that civil government be reestablished as soon as possible and that, because of his experience, he be appointed governor. Neither event occurred; instead Leigh, who had been ill for some time, died in Charleston on September 15, 1781.[75]

The pathos and scandal in Leigh's career should not be allowed to obscure its historical significance. Clearly, his actions and, ultimately, his mere presence, helped to disenchant South Carolinians with imperial authorities and their policy. Eventually, through the circulation of pamphlets and by word of mouth, Leigh became notorious throughout the colonies. As a result, he contributed significantly to the growing American hostility toward the Vice-Admiralty Courts and to the increasing feeling that Great Britain and her servants were corrupt.

The obvious question, however, is how a man of Leigh's ability, to all intents and purposes firmly entrenched in local society, could have gotten himself into such a predicament. One plausible explanation might be that events beyond their control placed all Crown servants in untenable situations; another might stress Leigh's apparent immorality. Neither interpretation is quite adequate. Leigh was not merely a passive victim of forces beyond his control. Rather, as the pre-Revolutionary movement embroiled him in difficulty, he seems almost suicidally to have rushed to meet his fate. Nor was he entirely immoral. It is difficult to believe that Laurens and others would have trusted him initially if he had been an unmitigated scoundrel. Apart from his relationship with his sister-in-law—an aberration more deserving of the clinical compassion of a psychiatrist than condemnation by a historian—none of Leigh's actions could be termed iniquitous by an impartial observer. He did occasionally use poor judgment and in a few cases violated propriety—something to which he seemed oblivious. This quality of ethical obtuseness is indeed a key to explaining much of Leigh's behavior. Like his self-destructiveness, to which it was closely related, this trait manifested itself chiefly in Leigh's inability to protect an appropriate public image in a society where image and reputation mattered enormously. Being a perceptive man, he recognized that his difficulties, as well as those of other Crown officials, arose fundamentally from a lack of public support. Being something of an intellectual, he sought to resolve symbolically those dilemmas which he could not resolve in actuality. So when his actual power failed him, he loved to replay the scene on paper—a medium in which he had more control. In the process, of course, he hoped that his pamphlets would vindicate him, shame his detractors, and thereby regain for him the power which he believed he deserved to possess. However, the results of his efforts were exactly the opposite of what he intended.

These attempts at self-justification were more than the self-pitying afterthoughts of a discredited officeholder. Throughout the pre-Revolutionary controversy, Leigh struggled in his own tenacious way to understand the political culture of South Carolina and, in the light of the reverses he had suffered there, to understand himself. He could not help but broadcast the conclusion that he was a uniquely gifted bureaucratic and judicial operator. His presumption to a special legal insight into matters of Vice-Admiralty law which was denied to laymen, his belief that only his intelligence and sense of the dramatic could save the Council from further degradation, and his conviction that attacks upon himself were attempts to destroy the institutions which he served were not only defense mechanisms. They were also expressions of his pride as a placeman and the products of his sustained effort at political analysis and self-examination. His pride and intellectual determination thus drove him to accentuate the very presumptions about himself and about British authority which South Carolinians most detested and impelled him to equate their resulting hostility with a leveling process which he alone could diagnose and denounce.

Although his approach was hardly calculated to win applause in South Carolina, Leigh was correct in realizing that profound changes had occurred in the character of local politics during the preceding quarter of a century. What he did not realize was that the dominant position of the Commons House of Assembly was associated with the development of a particular climate of opinion in which his own political instincts were unreliable. His success, and that of the family in which he was brought up, had depended on the ability to impress a small number of individuals who possessed the power to grant or withhold preferment. Ability, good intentions, and loyalty to one's patron were qualities which enabled one to navigate this political world successfully. Leigh's apologia, then, condemned ingratitude and disloyalty to family and friend as the greatest of sins; purity in those areas, he seemed to think, excused admitted lapses in judgment. Where political power was controlled by small factional groups, such a defense was at least relevant and might have been effective.

In South Carolina it was worse than irrelevant. Effective political power depended less on imperial than upon local popular support, and for nearly a generation, though the pre-Revolutionary period accelerated the trend, South Carolinians had reserved their esteem for those politicians who appeared to put the public welfare above all else. Laurens, a product of the local political environment, understood this; Leigh, a product of a different system, never did. Consequently, when the tensions of the 1760s undercut the position of Crown officers, he had no effective way to protect himself. In fact, his attempts to defend himself instead of confounding his critics merely served to condemn him by his own words, for they revealed that he subscribed to a different set of political mores. Lest anyone should miss these implications, Laurens hammered the point home when he replied to the charge of family disloyalty. "As far as human Strength will assist me," he wrote, "I am never influenced in Favour of any Man contrary to the publick Good, from so poor a Consideration *only* as his *Alliance to me.*" These words could well serve as Leigh's political epitaph, for if, as he charged, Laurens was not at home in the technicalities of the law, Leigh was equally out of his element in the political atmosphere of pre-Revolutionary South Carolina.[76]

The point here is not to draw an invidious distinction between differing sets of political ethics, but rather to demonstrate that a difference did exist.[77] When rents began to appear in the fabric that bound royal officials and local leaders together into a coherent whole, it became clear that in many cases they spoke a different language. Thus attempts at communication often failed. Instead of resolving differences, moral considerations frequently accentuated them. Isolated and introspective, Leigh sensed more acutely than most of his contemporaries that this failure of communication had occurred. As a result, his writings depict the anguish of a misunderstood villain in a complex moral struggle and provide poignant, illuminating insight into facets of the personal and intellectual dilemma of many loyalists on the eve of the Revolution.

Author's Note (2008)

When they wrote this article in 1968, the authors focused on the quest for power in the Commons House of Assembly and unraveling the sexual scandal involving Leigh and his sister-in-law, Molly Bremar. But the authors overlooked a religious dimension to the dispute arising from Laurens's Pietism and Leigh's exploitation of Laurens's perceived religious vulnerability. That oversight has now been ably corrected in Samuel C. Smith, "Henry Laurens: Christian Pietist," *South Carolina Historical Magazine* (1999).

Notes

1. [Sir Egerton Leigh], *Considerations on Certain Political Transactions of the Province of South Carolina* (London, 1774), p. 2; entry of Aug. 31, 1774, in L. H. Butterfield, et al., eds., *The Diary and Autobiography of John Adams* (Cambridge, Mass., 1961), vol. 2, p. 118. The authors wish to thank Wylma Wates of the South Carolina Archives Department for calling their attention to the latter reference.

2. For standard treatments of this affair, see David D. Wallace, *The Life of Henry Laurens* (New York, 1915), pp. 137–49, and Oliver M. Dickerson, *The Navigation Acts and the American Revolution* (Philadelphia, 1951), pp. 224–31. Thomas C. Barrow, *Trade and Empire: The British Customs Service in Colonial America, 1660–1775* (Cambridge, Mass., 1967), pp. 206–10, 234–35 and Carl Ubbelohde, *The Vice-Admiralty Courts and the American Revolution* (Chapel Hill, N.C., 1960), pp. 107–14, provide brief accounts that anticipate some points which we emphasize.

3. H. Hale Bellot, "The Leighs in South Carolina," *Transactions of the Royal Historical Society,* 5th ser., 6 (1956), 175; Aug. 12, Nov. 6, 1754, Miscellaneous Records, KK, 76, 113, S.C. Archives Department, Columbia, S.C.; Governor William Henry Lyttelton to Board of Trade, Apr. 14, 1759, Transcripts of Records Relating to South Carolina in the British Public Record Office, vol. 28, p. 188, S.C. Archives. Hereafter these transcripts will be cited as Trans., S.C. Records.

4. It is not clear that at the time of his election Leigh held property in St. Peter's, a rural district relatively remote from Charleston. Indeed, on Jan. 24, 1755, he purchased the first real estate that he is known to have owned in South Carolina, two lots in Charleston, for which he paid £2,000 South Carolina currency. Less than one week later he was elected to the Assembly. It hardly seems a coincidence that the election law stipulated that a member of the Commons House must possess a freehold of 500 acres and 10 slaves or £1,000 worth of buildings, lands, or town lots. Two other men had been elected for the parish and failed to qualify; Leigh, who was elected unanimously, was therefore the third choice. In all probability, a relatively small number of voters turned to him because, as a resident of Charleston and a man of ability who was willing to serve, he represented an available candidate. See Charleston County Deeds, vol. PP, 236–37, on microfilm at S.C. Archives; Thomas Cooper and David McCord, eds., *The Statutes at Large of South Carolina* (Columbia, S.C., 1838), vol. 3, p. 137; Nov. 13, 1754, Jan. 8, Feb. 6, 7, 1755, South Carolina Commons Journals, vol. 30, Pt. 1, pp. 28–29, 60, 62, 216–18, 226, in S.C. Archives; Oct. 6, 1757, South Carolina Commons Journals, Colonial Office Group, Class 5, Piece 474, Public Record Office; and Jan. 11, 1760, South Carolina Council Journals, vol. 28, p. 154, S.C. Archives.

5. Nov. 3, 1755, Oct. 2, 1761, Jan. 31, 1765, Misc. Records, KK, 402, LL, 405, MM, 277.

6. Egerton Leigh, Memorial to Lord Dartmouth, Mar. 2, 1775, Dartmouth Papers, II, 1174, William Salt Library, Stafford, England. Although it is impossible to give a precise figure for the worth of each of Leigh's offices, a rough idea can be obtained from the fact that James Simpson, who replaced Leigh as attorney general in 1771, claimed to have received more than £2,000 sterling per year from a private practice worth £700, the attorney generalship, and the office of clerk of the Council. The vice-admiralty position was not considered lucrative. See James Simpson's case in Examinations in London: Memorials, Schedules of Losses, and Evidence, South Carolina Claimants, American

Loyalists, Audit Office Transcripts, vol. 54, p. 213, Manuscript Division, New York Public Library, New York, hereafter cited as Loyalists' Trans.; and Lieutenant Governor William Bull to Lord Hillsborough, Oct. 16, 1768, Trans., S.C. Records, vol. 32, p. 55.

7. In 1770 he added an additional 100 acres. See grants on May 21, 1757, Dec. 5, 1759, May 18, 1763, Nov. 9, 1770, Pre-Revolutionary Grants, vol. 8, pp. 4, 480, vol. 11, p. 62, vol. 21, p. 283, S.C. Archives; Sept. 30, 1758, July 2,1775, Sept. 9, 1757, July 27, 1761, Charleston County Deeds, TT, 338–339, SS, 52, 114, XX, 288–291, microfilm, S.C. Archives. See also M. Eugene Sirmans, "The South Carolina Royal Council, 1720–1763," *William and Mary Quarterly,* 3rd ser., 18 (1961), 373–92.

8. Bellot, "Leighs in South Carolina," *Trans. Royal Hist. Soc.,* 175; Joseph W. Barnwell, ed., "Correspondence of Henry Laurens," *South Carolina Historical and Genealogical Magazine,* 29 (1928): 103; the entry of Jan. 17, 1744/5, in James H. Easterby and Ruth Green, eds., *The Colonial Records of South Carolina: The Journals of the Commons House of Assembly, 1736–1750,* 5 (Columbia, S.C., 1955), 277.

9. See Laurens to Francis Bremar, Mar. 27, 1748, in Barnwell, ed., "Correspondence of Henry Laurens," *S.C. Hist. and Geneal. Mag.,* 31 (1930): 222, and will of Francis Bremar, May 16, 1760, Charleston County Wills, Works Progress Administration Transcripts, vol. 8, pp. 482–83, S.C. Archives. For Leigh as Laurens's lawyer, see Henry Laurens to Lachlan McIntosh, May 19, 1763, Laurens to Elias Ball, Oct. 5, 1765, and Laurens to Inglis and Hall, Dec. 12, 1767, Philip M. Hamer and George C. Rogers, eds., *The Papers of Henry Laurens* (Columbia, S.C., 1968–2003), vol. 3, pp. 454–55; vol. 5, pp. 19, 503–504. Hereafter cited as *Laurens Papers.*

10. *South Carolina Gazette* (Charleston), Dec. 3, 1772, Feb. 28, 1771; "Historical Notes," *S.C. Hist. and Geneal. Mag.,* 11 (1910), 133–34.

11. *South Carolina Gazette* (Charleston), Dec. 16, 1760; *South Carolina Gazette and Country Journal* (Charleston), Dec. 31, 1765.

12. Bull to Hillsborough, Aug. 7, 1771,Trans., S.C. Records, vol. 33, p. 80; Bellot, "Leighs in South Carolina," *T.R.H.S.,* 169–74; Lyttelton to Board of Trade, Apr. 14, 1759, Trans., S.C. Records, vol. 28, p. 188; Leigh, Memorial to Dartmouth, Mar. 2, 1775, Dartmouth Papers, II, 1174.

13. For his attendance in the House, see Feb. 7, 1755 to Oct. 13, 1759, South Carolina Commons Journals, vols. 30–33, passim. On the basis of the importance and amount of committee work which he performed, Leigh reached the second rank of leadership in the 1757–1758 session, Jack P. Greene, *The Quest for Power: The Lower Houses of Assembly in the Southern Royal Colonies, 1689–1776* (Chapel Hill, N.C., 1963), p. 481. For Leigh's most important committee assignments, see Mar. 5, 7, Apr. 11, 12, 1755, June 22, 1756, May 16, Dec. 8, 1758, Jan. 31, 1759, South Carolina Commons Journals, vol. 30, Pt. 1, pp. 293, 314, 449, 457; vol. 31, Pt. 1, p. 204; vol. 32, pp. 220 [*sic*], 38, 97–98.

14. For a listing, see entries for Leigh in the manuscript index to the Misc. Records.

15. Lyttelton to the Board of Trade, Apr. 14, 1759, Trans., S.C. Records, vol. 28, p. 188; Privy Council, June 26, 1759, Trans. S.C. Records, pp. 201–2; Jan. 11, 1760, South Carolina Council Journals, p. 154.

16. Laurens to Edwards Pierce, Mar. 31, 1773, *Laurens Papers,* vol. 2, p. 82; Laurens to William Fisher, Aug. 1, 1768, Letters and Papers Regarding the Ship *Ann,* Etting: Large Miscellaneous Manuscripts, 24, Historical Society of Pennsylvania, Philadelphia; Laurens to Isaac King, Apr. 3, May 7, 1764, *Laurens Papers,* vol. 4, pp. 268–70; vol. 5, pp. 180–84.

17. For an account of the effects of the crisis, see Robert M. Weir, *Colonial South Carolina: A History* (Columbia, 1997), pp 293–299. For Shinner's comments, see his report enclosed in Governor Lord Charles Montagu to the Board of Trade, May 6, 1766, Trans., S.C. Records, vol. 31, p. 134.

18. Laurens to John L. Gervais, Sept. 1, 1766, *Laurens Papers,* vol. 5, pp. 180–84; Leigh, Memorial to Dartmouth, Mar. 2, 1775, Dartmouth Papers, II, 1174.

19. June 24, 1766, South Carolina Commons Journals, vol. 37, Pt. 1, p. 175; Laurens to William Fisher, Aug. 1, 1768, Letters and Papers Regarding the Ship *Ann,* 24; Committee of Correspondence to Garth, July 2, 1766, Charles Garth Letter Book, 1766–1775, 2, S.C. Archives.

20. Garth to Committee of Correspondence, Sept. 26, 1766, Jan. 31, Mar. 12, 1767, Garth Letter Book, pp. 14, 25, 28.

21. *S.C. Gazette,* Mar. 23, 1767. For a brief biography of Moore—which omits his service in South Carolina—see Sir Lewis Namier and John Brooke, *The History of Parliament: The House of Commons, 1754–1790* (New York, 1964), vol. 3, pp. 160–61. For a more sympathetic treatment of Moore than ours, see Barrow, *Trade and Empire,* pp. 204–209; for a more hostile account, the South Carolina merchants' version of his activities, see *A Representation of Facts, Relative to the Conduct of Daniel Moore, Esquire; Collector of His Majesty's Customs at Charles-Town, in South Carolina* (Charleston, 1767).

22. *A Representation of Facts,* passim; Montagu to Lord Shelburne, Oct. 5, 1767, Trans., S.C. Records, vol. 31, p. 414; *S.C. Gazette,* Sept. 19, 1768.

23. "Case," Treasury Group, Class I, Piece 465, Photostats, Library of Congress.

24. Sir Egerton Leigh, *The Man Unmasked: or, The World Undeceived in the Author of a Late Pamphlet entitled "Extracts from the Proceedings of the High Court of Vice-Admiralty in Charlestown, South Carolina &c." with Suitable Remarks* (Charleston, 1769), p. 96; "Case," T. 1/465, Lib. of Cong. Photosts.

25. For complaints against Leigh, see Barrow, *Trade and Empire,* p. 318.

26. See Laurens to James Habersham, Sept. 5, 1767, *Laurens Papers,* vol. 5, pp. 292–99.

27. Laurens to James Habersham, Sept. 5, 1767, *Laurens Papers,* vol. 5, pp. 292–99.

28. Laurens to George Appleby, to James Habersham, May 24, 1768, Sept. 5, 1767, *Laurens Papers,* vol. 5, pp. 687–89.

29. Feb. 26, 1755, S.C. Commons Journals, vol. 30, Pt. I, pp. 249–50. Roupell was also an artist of considerable local renown. See Anna Wells Rutledge, "Artists in the Life of Charleston Through Colony and State to Reconstruction," *Transactions of the American Philosophical Society,* vol. 39, Pt. 2 (1949), 118–19; Carl Bridenbaugh, *Myths and Realities: Societies of the Colonial South* (Baton Rouge, La., 1952), p. 107.

30. George Roupell to Commissioners of the Customs, July 11, 1768, enclosed in Commissioners of the Customs in America to Lords Commissioners of Treasury, Aug. 25, 1768, T. 1/465, Lib. of Cong. Photosts.; May 12, 1768, Charleston County, Records of the Court of Common Pleas, 1763–1769, W.P.A. Trans., S.C. Archives, p. 244.

31. Transcripts of Proceedings in the Case of the *Ann,* T 1/465, 7, 14, 16, Lib. of Cong. Photosts.; Henry Laurens, *Extracts from Proceedings of the High Court of Admiralty,* 2d ed. (Charleston, 1769), passim; Henry Laurens, *Extracts from the Proceedings of the Court of Vice-Admiralty in Charles-Town, South Carolina* (Philadelphia, 1768), 9. Items in these sources pertaining to Laurens have been published in the *Laurens Papers.*

32. For citations to this correspondence, see Barrow, *Trade and Empire,* p. 318.

33. Trans. of Proc. of the *Ann,* T. 1/465, 10, 24–25, 28, Lib. of Cong. Photosts.

34. *S.C. Gazette,* July 11, 1768. Robert Wells, the publisher of the leading rival newspaper, *South Carolina and American General Gazette,* was marshall of the Vice-Admiralty Court. See Wells's case in Loyalists' Trans., vol. 56, p. 548.

35. Roupell to Commissioners of Customs, July 11,1768, enclosed in Commissioners of Customs in America to Lords Commissioners of Treasury, Aug. 25, 1768; T. 1/465, Lib. of Cong. Photosts.

36. Trans. of Proc. of the *Ann,* T. 1/465, 25–26, 28, Lib. of Cong. Photosts.; Laurens to William Fisher, Aug. 1, 1768, Letters and Papers Regarding the Ship *Ann, 24;* Leigh, *The Man Unmasked,* pp. 20–21, 27–28.

37. For Laurens's difficulties during the Cherokee War and the Stamp Act Crisis, see Wallace, *Life of Henry Laurens,* pp. 103–106, 116–20, and Laurens to James Habersham, Sept. 5, 1767, *Laurens Papers,* vol. 5, pp. 292–99.

38. Laurens to William Fisher, Aug. 1, 1768, Letters and Papers Regarding the Ship *Ann,* p. 24; Laurens to William Cowles & Co., to Ross and Mills, to James Habersham, June 7, 1768, Oct. 8, 14, 1767, *Laurens Papers,* vol. 5, pp. 718, 335–41, 364–67.

39. Laurens to William Cowles & Co. and William Freeman, Aug. 8, 1768, vol. 6, pp. 57–61; Wallace, *Life of Henry Laurens,* passim; Laurens, *Extracts,* 1st ed., passim; Laurens to William Fisher, Aug. 1, 1768, Letters and Papers Regarding the Ship *Ann,* p. 24.

40. Laurens, *Extracts,* 2d ed., passim; Commissioners of Customs in America to Lords Commissioners of Treasury, Aug. 25, 1768, and enclosure of George Roupell to Commissioners of Customs, July 11, 1768, T. 1/465, Lib. of Cong. Photosts.; Commissioners of Customs in America to Lords Commissioners of Treasury, Dec. 16, 1768, T. 1/465, Lib. of Cong. Photosts.; Bull to Hillsborough, Oct. 16, 1768, Trans., S.C. Records, vol. 32, p. 54; Leigh, *The Man Unmasked,* p. 100.

41. Bull to Hillsborough, Nov. 30, 1770, Trans., S.C. Records, vol. 32, p. 376; A. K. Gregorie and J. N. Frierson, eds., *Records of the Court of Chancery of South Carolina, 1671–1779* (Washington, D.C., 1950), p. 577 and passim.

42. Laurens to James Habersham, Sept. 5, 1767, *Laurens Papers,* vol. 5, pp. 92–99.

43. Mar. 16, 1768, Aug. 1, 1769, S.C. Commons Journals, vol. 37, Pt. 2, 588, vol. 38, Pt. 1, 102; Bellot, "Leighs in South Carolina," *T.R.H.S.,* p. 181; Laurens, *Extracts,* 2d ed., Appendix, pp. 20–22.

44. Henry A. M. Smith, "Charleston and Charleston Neck: The Original Grantees and the Settlements along the Ashley and Cooper Rivers," *S.C. Hist. and Geneal. Mag.,* 19 (1918): 59.

45. In Jan. 1768, before the pamphlet war with Laurens, the local lodge petitioned the Duke of Beaufort to appoint Leigh grand master; his official installation did not come until two years later. "Historical Notes," *S.C. Hist. and Geneal. Mag.,* 4 (1903): 313; *S.C. and American General Gazette,* Jan. 1, 1768; *S.C. Gazette,* Mar. 8, 1770.

46. Laurens to William Cowles & Co. and William Freeman, Aug. 8, 1768, *Laurens Papers,* vol. 6, pp. 57–61; Leigh, *The Man Unmasked,* pp. 70–71.

47. Leigh, *The Man Unmasked,* pp. 7–10, 40–41.

48. Leigh, *The Man Unmasked,* pp. 12–19.

49. Leigh, *The Man Unmasked,* pp. 43–44, 77–89, 100–101, 122–23.

50. Leigh, *The Man Unmasked,* pp. 19–25. The concept of a "ruling passion" was fairly common in eighteenth-century literature, but Leigh cited Laurence Sterne as the source of his own sophisticated version of the doctrine. Sterne's most famous work, and the one to which Leigh probably referred, was *The Life and Opinions of Tristram Shandy.*

For an introduction to Sterne and his use of Lockean psychology, see Albert C. Baugh, ed., *A Literary History of England* (New York, 1948), pp. 1022–26.

51. Leigh to [the Earl of Rochford], July 29, 1772, State Papers, Domestic, Class 37, Piece 9, 63, and Class 44, Piece 379, 384–385, Public Record Office; Leigh's patent as baronet indicated that he had made a sizeable contribution to the Crown which was a major factor in his receipt of the honor; the patent said nothing of his service in South Carolina but commended him for contributing a sum sufficient to support thirty troops in Ulster for three years, Leigh Family Papers, CR 162/576, Warwick Record Office, Warwick, England.

52. Although the girl changed her story several times and Leigh at first denied his complicity, he eventually confessed during a face-to-face confrontation with Laurens and offered to make a monetary settlement, an offer which Laurens did not accept. Henry Laurens to Leigh, to James Laurens, Jan. 30, 1773, Sept. 15, 1774, *Laurens Papers,* vol. 8, pp. 556–63, vol. 9, pp. 559–61. Historians have always chivalrously assumed that Leigh was the aggressor; nevertheless there is reason to suspect that the girl was something of a hellion in her own right. See Henry Laurens to James Laurens, postscript of Feb. 10, 1772 to Feb. 6, 1772 letter; *Laurens Papers,* vol. 8, p. 175.

53. *S.C. Gazette,* July 2, 1772, Oct. 22, 1772; Laurens to Leigh, to Edwards Pierce, Jan. 30, 1773, Mar. 31, 1773, *Laurens Papers,* vol. 8, pp. 556–63, 654–55.

54. Laurens to Leigh, Jan. 30, 1773, Leigh, *The Man Unmasked,* pp. 556–63.

55. Henry Laurens to John Laurens, Jan. 28, 1774, *Laurens Papers,* vol. 9, pp. 258–59. Bull, who had been a notary public and register of mesne conveyances until his disgrace, was apparently not related to Lieutenant Governor William Bull; the latter was a native of South Carolina, the former of England, *S.C. Gazette,* Feb. 9, 1769.

56. Henry Laurens to James Laurens, Oct. 5, 1772, *Laurens Papers,* vol. 8, pp. 490–96; Butterfield, *Diary and Autobiography of John Adams,* vol. 2, pp. 117–18.

57. Jackson Turner Main, *The Upper House in Revolutionary America, 1763–1788* (Madison, Wis., 1967), pp. 11–20. [Arthur Lee], *Answer to Considerations on Certain Political Transactions of the Province of South Carolina* (London, 1774), p. 60. On Leigh as a liability to the Crown by 1773, see also Marvin R. Zahniser, *Charles Cotesworth Pinckney* (Chapel Hill, N.C., 1967), p. 29.

58. Jack P. Greene, "Bridge to Revolution: The Wilkes fund Controversy in South Carolina, 1769–1775," *Journal of Southern History,* 29 (1963), 19–52.

59. S.C. Council to Bull, Aug. 23, 1773, C.O. 5/395, 117–20; Leigh's warrant for Powell's arrest, Aug. 31, 1773, Bull to Lord Dartmouth, Sept. 18, 1773, ibid., 151, 133–38.

60. S.C. Council to George III, Sept. 9, 1773, Leigh to Bull, Sept. 18, Oct. 16, 1773, ibid., 163, 179–82.

61. Sept. 8, 1773, S.C. Commons Journals, vol. 39, p. 88, Committee of Correspondence to Garth, Sept. 16, 1773, Garth Letter Book, 1766–1775, 153–54.

62. Henry Laurens to John Laurens, Nov. 19, 1773, *Laurens Papers,* vol. 9, pp. 152–54; Sept. 1, 1773, S.C. Upper House Journals, C.O. 5/478, 20; May 31, 1773, S.C. Council Journals, vol. 37, pp. 178–79; Leigh, Memorial to Dartmouth, Mar. 2, 1775, Dartmouth Papers, II, 1174.

63. James Simpson's case, Loyalists' Trans., LIV, 240; Laurens to Edwards Pierce, Dec. 6, 1773, *Laurens Papers,* vol. 9, pp. 193–94; *S.C. Gazette,* June 20, 1774.

64. Greene, "Bridge to Revolution," p. 45.

65. Laurens to Ralph Izard, Sept. 20, 1774, *Laurens Papers,* vol. 9, pp. 565–70.

66. For an account of this controversy, see M. Eugene Sirmans, *Colonial South Carolina: A Political History, 1663–1763* (Chapel Hill, N.C., 1966), pp. 301–309. The committee, after requesting more time to study the matter, was eventually discharged without making a final report. Nov. 25, 27, 1755, Apr. 22, 1756, S.C. Commons Journals, 31, Pt. 1, pp. 10, 15–16, 192.

67. Leigh, *Considerations,* pp. 18–20.

68. Leigh, *Considerations,* pp. 18–20; Ian R. Christie, *Wilkes, Wyvill, and Reform: The Parliamentary Reform Movement in British Politics, 1760–1785* (London, 1962), pp. 33–49; Leigh, *Considerations,* pp. 26–27.

69. Leigh, *Considerations,* pp. 3, 17, 30.

70. Leigh to Bull, Sept. 18, 1773, C.O. 5/395, 163.

71. Leigh, *Considerations,* p. 54.

72. Greene, "Bridge to Revolution," p. 48.

73. Leigh, Memorial to Dartmouth, Mar. 2, 1775, Dartmouth Papers, II, 1174; John Pownall to Leigh, May 16, 1775, Trans., S.C. Records, vol. 35, p. 114; Leigh to Dartmouth, June 26, 1775, Dartmouth Papers, 1339.

74. Feb. 20, 1781, Misc. Records, SS, 382–83; Miscellaneous Proceedings of the Board of Police, 1780–1781, C.O. 5/520, 62 ff.

75. Leigh to Hillsborough, Feb. 25, 1781,Trans., S.C. Records, vol. 36, p. 112; Mabel L. Webber, ed., "Death Notices from the *South Carolina and American General Gazette,* and its Continuation the *Royal Gazette,* May 1766–June 1782," S.C. *Hist. and Geneal. Mag.,* 17 (1916): 160.

76. Laurens, *Extracts,* 2d ed., Appendix, 33.

77. See also John Higham's suggestions that the Revolution be reinterpreted "as a problem in political ethics," in "Beyond Consensus: the Historian as Moral Critic," *American Historical Review,* 67 (1962), 623.

"I Have Deduced Your Rights"

Joseph Galloway's Concept of His Role, 1774–1775

Robert M. Calhoon

1

On September 28, 1774, Joseph Galloway proposed to the First Continental Congress his solution to the imperial crisis. His famous Plan of Union envisioned the creation of an American branch of the British Parliament possessing concurrent jurisdiction over all colonial legislation. Although the delegates debated the proposal and postponed further consideration by a narrow vote, Congress repudiated Galloway's cautious approach by endorsing the Suffolk Resolves, adopting non-importation, and allegedly expunging the Plan of Union from the Journal of Congress. Historians have rescued the Plan from oblivion, some fascinated by the intrinsic merit of its ideas on imperial reform and others intrigued with the light it throws on the perplexing problem of loyalist motivation.[1] Yet Galloway's writings of 1774 and 1775, including recently utilized letters described in the 2007 author's note, have not been fully utilized, and these sources remain the best historical account of his feelings and motives. His *Candid Examination of the Mutual Claims of Great Britain and the Colonies . . .*[2] not only contained the first published version of the Plan of Union and Galloway's arguments in its behalf, but also denounced the constitutional arguments of his critics, diagnosed their ethical and intellectual sins, and presented a truly candid view of his own injured pride and quest for distinction. When John Dickinson and Charles Thomson, his longtime political enemies, attacked the *Candid Examination,* Galloway responded with a bitter *Reply . . .*[3] which drew together brilliantly the tangled threads of his argument.

William H. Nelson and David L. Jacobson have shown that Galloway's chief concern in 1774–1775 was his consuming desire to exclude Dickinson from prominence.[4] At the heart of this mutual antagonism were their different assumptions about the province's interests and the ways of preserving colonial liberty. Dickinson opposed Galloway's scheme to make Pennsylvania into a royal colony and denounced successive British encroachments in the 1760s, because he sensed a growing and pervasive conspiracy to subvert colonial liberty.[5] As Speaker of the

Assembly from 1766 to 1774, Galloway became increasingly concerned that resistance against British policy would upset the delicate balance within Pennsylvania politics and jeopardize his own power.

In a curious way, competition with Dickinson may have stunted Galloway's own development as a whiggish defender of constitutional liberty in America. During a struggle, in 1760, with the proprietors over judicial tenure, he had defended the independence of the judiciary on broad, libertarian grounds.[6] In 1766 and 1770 he privately denounced British restrictions on colonial currency as inexcusable deprivations of liberty.[7] His breadth of vision contracted as he came to fear that British encroachments would keep Pennsylvania politics in turmoil and encourage the appetites of his own political rivals. He came to believe that his dominance was an essential prerequisite to the defense of Pennsylvania's interests.[8] His opposition to non-importation as well as his contempt for Dickinson's constitutional views alienated votes and led to the defeat of Galloway and his faction in Philadelphia in the Assembly election of 1770, forcing him to rely on his home county of Bucks for a seat in the Assembly and on assemblymen from outside of Philadelphia for his reelection as Speaker. These events vindicated his conviction that colonial resistance against British policy only served to feed the ambitions of dangerous men.[9]

The crisis of 1774 brought this struggle for preeminence to an abrupt conclusion. Dickinson dominated the meetings in Philadelphia during May and June which led to the calling of a Provincial Congress in July, and his *Essay on the Constitutional Power of Great Britain* strongly influenced the Congress's recommendations to the Assembly. Under Speaker Galloway's influence, the Assembly ignored the proposals advanced by the Congress, excluded Dickinson and his supporters from the delegation to the Continental Congress, and instructed those delegates to devise a "Plan" of reconciliation and to oppose any pronouncements "indecent or disrespectful to the Mother State."[10] Delegates to the Congress arriving in late August and early September 1774 found Galloway acting as a self-appointed chairman of local arrangements for the Congress while Pennsylvania seethed with rumors of Galloway's treachery and ambition. The erosion of Galloway's influence in provincial politics culminated in October when Philadelphia elected Dickinson to a seat in the Assembly, and the Assembly in turn removed Galloway as Speaker and named Dickinson a delegate to the Congress.[11]

Studies of these events by William Nelson and David Jacobson have properly concentrated on Galloway's statements and writings from July 1774, when he began to reveal his proposals for imperial reform, until April 1775, when he finally withdrew from the pre-Revolutionary debate. These sources provide a more accurate guide to his pre-Revolutionary motives than does his retrospective *Political and Historical Reflections on . . . the American Rebellion.*[12] His writings of 1774–1775 deserve reconsideration, not only because they depict his well-known ambition and haughtiness as well as the ingenuity and resourcefulness of his Plan, but also because they abound with implicit and explicit testimony about the role he was playing, the inner struggle he experienced as he perceived the collapse of his strategy, and the compulsion he then felt to salve his own ego and vindicate both the utility and validity of his proposals. Nelson touched briefly, and suggestively, on this problem when he hinted that Galloway's "disabling vanity" crippled his energetic, imaginative quest for reconciliation.[13] Surviving sources permit a reconstruction of Galloway's own comprehension of this experience. No writer has yet made extensive use of personal testimony in the *Candid Examination* and *Reply*. To use Galloway's polemical pamphlets as guides to his personality is, of course, risky, and some of the following analysis is, admittedly, speculative. What is not speculative is that the portrait of Galloway's motives in his pamphlets is corroborated by his surviving correspondence, several revealing quotations in John Adams's diary, and other sources.

Galloway's view of his own dilemma—his conception of his role and attempts to cope with the collapse of his political effectiveness—involved several elements. First, there was the structure of his famous imperial ideas, and next his persistent attempts to reconcile the disparate elements in his argument. Further, there were moral issues which the triumph of his enemies forced him to consider. Finally, the pattern of his introspection and intransigence, as it gradually developed, served to relate and connect all of these factors.

2

On September 8, 1774, Galloway sat on a committee of Congress listening to a debate on the sources of colonial liberty. Most involved in the discussion were four delegates: Richard Henry Lee and John Jay argued that the colonies were distinct political communities voluntarily associated with the British state, while John Rutledge and James Duane took the more limited position that the colonies were extensions of the British political system. At stake was the wording of the Congress's statement on colonial rights; Lee, Jay,[14] and others wanted to base the American cause on the natural law right of a people to constitute a government as well as on English common law precedents protecting the rights of the subject. Duane and Rutledge considered natural law a dangerous ground and pleaded that the English constitution alone would serve as the basis of colonial remonstrance.

Only after these differences had emerged did Galloway enter the debate— apparently speaking at much greater length than the others, he attempted to provide irrefutable support for Duane and Rutledge's position. Congress should not base its appeals on natural law, he argued, because the colonies had been from the earliest settlement politically organized societies rather than ones which had emerged from a state of nature. Therefore, only the constitutional history of England provided a credible explanation of colonial rights. "The Essence" of the constitution was the representation in Parliament of the proprietors of land in the realm and their consent to legislation binding the inhabitants of those lands. Because the first settlers in America occupied territory not so represented, no law of Parliament enacted since the establishment of the colonies necessarily bound the colonists. Even Lord North, Galloway concluded, would concede the validity of these arguments if he made an effort to inform himself of the history of the constitution. Strong language! Galloway quickly acknowledged its radical implications: "I am well aware that my Arguments tend to an Independency of the Colonies and militate against the Maxim that there must be some absolute Power to draw together all the Wills and strengths of the Empire."[15]

That admission represented the crux of Galloway's problem during his direct involvement in the pre-Revolutionary debate, from July 1774 to April 1775. Throughout that period he tried to sustain two distinct lines of argument containing the very contradictory implications he confessed to the committee of Congress. *Representation* was the key to the imperial problem; therefore, the exercise of Parliamentary jurisdiction over the colonies was a grievous anomaly which justified colonial opposition to the British policy. At the same time the *subordinate* status of the colonists within the Empire sharply circumscribed the permissible limits of colonial remonstrance. He felt confident that he alone could reconcile those two truths and in so doing promote the only possible solution to the imperial controversy. It is plausible to argue that Galloway stressed the need for some form of colonial representation in the councils of the Empire until October 1774 as a means of attracting support for his Plan of Union and that he lapsed into negative talk of subordination only after the delegates rejected his positive proposals. There was, of course, a distinct change in emphasis between the summer of 1774 and spring of 1775, but only of emphasis and not of substance. Galloway continued to insist throughout the 1774–1775 period that his doctrines of representation and subordination could be reconciled. His unpublished memorandum on the imperial constitutional problem, "Arguments on Both Sides . . . ," urged their compatibility. His statements in Congress and subsequent pamphlets dealt at length with both colonial rights and obligations. Perhaps the depth of his commitment to both doctrines was best illustrated when a friend in New York, Samuel Verplanck, sent him copies of polemical tory pamphlets, in all likelihood those of Samuel Seabury and Thomas Bradbury Chandler. After complimenting them for their insistence on colonial obedience, he complained that "they do not show the rights of the American Subject or even acknowledge that we do have any. They do not own that we have any Grievance and consequently nothing is pointed out as a Constitutional Remedy."[16]

Though withdrawn and secretive at the opening of Congress, Galloway was excited and sustained by his belief that "I stand here almost alone" in seeing both sides of the imperial dispute; "perhaps were I to remove to your great Capitol," London, he wrote to the English politician and colonial agent, Richard Jackson, "where the most important Matters are decided, I should not be less so." The margin for error in seeking to resolve the differences between Britain and the colonies, he told Jackson, was perilously small. Fundamental to the problem of colonial discontent was the burgeoning population of the colonies which would probably grow by tenfold in the coming century. It was inconceivable, he added,

that Parliament could continue to exercise unlimited jurisdiction over so populous and expanding a society."[17]

His *Candid Examination* elaborated on these dangers. The "circumstances"
of the colonies—their territorial extent, distance from Britain, and numerous
harbors and ports—encouraged colonial autonomy and should behoove Britain
to offer the colonies tempting inducements to remain within the Empire. More
pressing was his concern that "the genius" and "temper" of the Americans required
tactful handling for "no people in the world have higher notions of liberty."[18]
Therefore the inability of the colonists to share in the process of imperial lawmaking violated "Reason," "Common Sense," and "the Principles of the English
Government." "Is it unreasonable," he asked, "to expect . . . Discontent will not fill
the Breasts of Americans?" In retrospect, Galloway regretted that the British government had not begun constitutional reform of the Empire at the close of the
Seven Years' War by guaranteeing to the colonists "the same Rights and Privileges
. . . enjoyed by the Subjects in Britain." The ministry and Parliament should have
then seen the need for such a settlement if for no other reason than the difficulty
experienced in obtaining fiscal support from colonial assemblies during the War.
Similarly, he believed, the colonists had squandered their opportunities during
the previous decade by ridiculing the notion of colonial representation in Parliament which, while impractical, was a theoretically sound proposal deserving respectful consideration. Instead the colonists had poisoned future relations with
the Mother Country by "tracing American Rights up to Sources from which they
never came."

The dynamics of Britain's increasingly assertive policy and the growing intransigence of the colonists perplexed Galloway and instinctively he wished these new
forces would cease functioning until he could implement a solution. "Is it not
high Time," he asked Jackson, "that both Countries should retreat a little and take
other Ground seeing That which they are now upon is likely to prove dangerous and distressing to Both?" Even if he could persuade the colonists to seek conciliation, he warned Jackson, nothing could be accomplished unless Parliament
showed a willingness to modify its claims of unlimited supremacy: "I cannot find
that there is the least Disposition in the People of this Country to submit to the
parliamentary jurisdiction under the present System of Government and the
Share they hold in it."[19] That precarious balance—the necessity for simultaneous
"retreat" on both sides—entirely engrossed Galloway and helped account for his
withdrawn behavior at the outset of the Congress.

Galloway's confidence that he could effect reconciliation sprang from his assumption that scrupulous wording of the colonists' petition to the Crown could
induce the ministry to accept negotiation without appearing to force its hand. He
proposed to accomplish this feat by a studious appeal to the rights of Englishmen.
From the composition of the first Saxon Witan, feudal courts, and Parliaments
under Edward II, all proprietors of land had possessed an integral role in the
enactment of legislation binding the inhabitants of the realm. Only by an accident

of history were the inhabitants of the colonies left unrepresented. The first settlers had not permanently surrendered that right, but had merely accepted Parliamentary supervision from "extreme necessity." Therefore, he concluded, the constitutional solution was for Parliament to introduce some form of representation. Until this change was accomplished, British authority in America would remain valid only in theory, and would be in practice, "as absolute and despotic" as that of any continental monarch. In the meantime, he wanted Britain to hold its power in abeyance. As a practical matter, "Parliament ought not, *as the Colonies are at present circumstanced,* to bind them by its Legislative Authority." On this basis reconciliation consisted of prodding Britain gently to adopt restraint by having colonial demands clothed in language which would not offend British sensibilities. Any disinclination to obey Parliament, he warned, would imply disrespect of the very institution which had the power to make needed changes in the status of the colonies. However, he acknowledged, some implied colonial defiance was unavoidable. "Yet when that denial shall be accompanied with an express desire of establishing a political *Union* with the *Mother Country,*" he exulted, having discovered the goal of this tortuous maneuver, "such a denial does not carry with it any Thing unjust, offensive, or indelicate."[20]

His *Candid Examination* refined the techniques of reconciliation by demonstrating how statements of colonial rights could be embodied in the rhetoric of obedience. His suggested model petition to Parliament acknowledged the necessity of a supreme authority within every state before it pointed to the sacrifices and hazards endured by the colonists in settling a wilderness and increasing the "wealth and power" of Britain. He attributed the limitations of colonial liberty to historical accident: "by such settlement" the colonies had "lost the enjoyment of, though not the right to, some of the first and most excellent privileges of Englishmen," the representation of their lands in Parliament and capacity to "participate in the supreme legislative authority." By emphasizing the constitutional flaw in the structure of the Empire, his petition minimized the significance of specific colonial grievances regarding Parliamentary taxation, commercial policy, and interference with colonial self-government. Certainly, he conceded, those British policies had caused "great discontent . . . in the breasts of his Majesty's faithful American subjects"; however, the petition assured Britain that this discontent was chiefly regrettable because it eroded "that harmony which ought to subsist between the members of the same community." Finally, he insisted that the whole justification for colonial petition was the fact that only Parliament could remedy the situation. Colonial disunity and the absence of institutions representative of the colonies as a whole prevented any colonial contribution to the costs of imperial defense. Parliament possessed the power of restoring to the colonies a voice in Parliament and thereby enabling them to respond to the needs of the parent state.[21]

Galloway sought to enhance the attractiveness of this approach by projecting its future consequences. Legislative union with Britain would not only exempt the colonies from onerous Parliamentary restrictions, it would enable the colonies to contribute to the cost of the Empire without any loss of freedom. On these terms, reconciliation would produce lasting stability in the colonies by eliminating at one stroke existing colonial grievances and giving the colonies "the best of all political securities," a perpetual exemption from further British restrictions on trade and manufacturing. Critical to this stabilizing process was a new procedure, "a capacity of discharging with justice and punctuality all [colonial] duties to the [British] State." This solution aimed at the transformation of the British Empire by the "uniting of two great countries by the firmest hands of political freedom into one grand and illustrious Empire."[22]

Galloway's Plan of Union sought to reconcile the requirements of colonial liberty with the closer integration of the Empire. Its preamble spurned the notion that the colonies were autonomous communities within the Empire. Its purpose, "the establishment of a Political Union," was defined both as the repair of disunity among the colonies and the creation of a durable connection between them and the parent state. It conceded the impracticality of colonial representation in Parliament and sought Parliament's approval of a plan which would simultaneously consolidate the capacities of the Empire to meet common dangers, advance the "interest of both countries," and preserve the "rights and liberties of America."[23] To secure these ends, the Plan would have created a continental legislature, a "Grand Council," whose delegates would be chosen by provincial assemblies for three-year terms, and the assemblies would retain control over their internal affairs. The Plan would have enlarged the scope of royal authority through the creation of a "President General," appointed and serving at the pleasure of the Crown and vested with extensive administrative and executive power which he would exercise with the "advice and consent" of the Grand Council. He could withhold his assent from bills passed by the Council. All colonial legislation would require the approval of both Parliament and the Council.[24]

The closest equivalent to Galloway's Plan of Union was a proposal for an American parliament drafted in 1767 by William Smith, Jr., a New York Councillor and historian.[25] Both men were certainly familiar with Benjamin Franklin's Albany Plan for a union for the American colonies (1754) and revamped for their own purposes its recommendations for a continental assembly and royally appointed Governor General.[26] Franklin, in 1775, repudiated Galloway's Plan and argued that British policy since the Declaratory Act had so altered the imperial relationship as to make any extension of British administration in America undesirable. Galloway, for contrasting reasons, also recognized that colonial suspicion of British policy rendered the Albany Plan obsolete and for this reason called for a legislative union with the British Parliament.[27] That very innovation, however, provoked Franklin's acerbic comment, "when I consider the extreme corruption prevalent among all orders of men in this old, rotten state [he was then in England], and the glorious public virtue so predominant in our rising country, I cannot but apprehend more mischief than benefit from a closer union. . . . It seems like Mezentius' coupling and binding together the dead and the living."[28] Franklin's treatise on population may well have exercised a more pervasive influence on Galloway and Smith than did his Albany Plan. Both men were fascinated with the impact of burgeoning colonial population on American self-assertiveness and imperial relations.[29] In addition, both men devised their proposals in response to the pre-Revolutionary controversy as means of healing the breach in the Empire and both ultimately became loyalists. Smith indeed was excited when he heard rumors of Galloway's Plan, noting in July 1774 that "at Philadelphia a Plan is digesting for an American Constitution. I know not the Out lines of it. I hope it is for a Parliament and to meet here annually."[30]

Though Galloway's and Smith's plans contained similar proposals, they were based on quite different assumptions about constitutional doctrine and the nature of imperial politics. The two documents also differed on a fundamental issue. Smith's legislature would have bypassed Parliament and dealt directly with the Crown in matters of imperial finance; Galloway sought a legislative union in which the British Parliament and its American branch would share concurrent jurisdiction over colonial affairs. Smith prefaced his plan with an analysis of imperial relations which was far more pragmatic and flexible than Galloway's. Smith abhorred the use of abstract constitutional principles because these interfered with constructive discussion."[31] Where Galloway spoke sketchily in 1774 about an increased political stature for the colonists under the Plan of Union, Smith propounded an expansive view of the future of American politics. He envisioned a time when population growth and westward expansion would make the colonies Britain's equal; his imperial constitution was to be a practical step in adjusting imperial relations during a generation of change from subordination to parity.

Galloway conceived of the Plan of Union as an instrument for his own public vindication, whereas Smith shunned any open participation in the controversies of 1774–1775. He preferred to work quietly among acquaintances in New York. His letters to friends in the Second Continental Congress suggested elaborate and subtle ground rules governing any attempts to negotiate with Britain and put forward his plan for an American parliament as a basis for negotiation. However, unlike Galloway's approach to reconciliation, Smith's imperatives were entirely tactical and revealed a clinical sense of political communication: "feeling the pulse" of the ministry, proceeding "without a Word about Rights," and exercising exquisite tact and timing.[32] Galloway was much too concerned with questions of doctrine and with his own self-justification to bother with these questions of tactics and protocol. The two men, then, suggested similar proposals for imperial reform, but proceeded from very different assumptions about constitutional doctrine and the mechanics of reconciliation.

As Richard Koebner demonstrated, ideas about the nature of the Empire underwent a bewildering transformation in 1774–1775.[33] Writers as diverse as Richard Cartwright, Dean Tucker, John Adams, Thomas Jefferson, Edmund Burke, and George III sought to define the structure of the Empire, praised its benefits, and called for vigorous steps to preserve it. What they lacked was a meaningful vocabulary to describe the Empire's internal stresses. In seeking to articulate their respective diagnoses they endowed concepts like "power," "liberty," "rights," and "reconciliation" with a host of contrasting meanings. Koebner made passing reference to Galloway's Plan as "a new constructive solution."[34] Had he chosen to discuss Galloway in the detail he lavished on other writers, Koebner would certainly have found additional support for his view that imperial concepts in 1774–1775 were derived more from the initial presuppositions of their authors than from any consensus about the meaning of the term "British Empire."

Galloway's "grand and illustrious Empire" referred not to the familiar Empire of the past but rather to a future relationship which only the Plan of Union could bring into being. Created under the same pressures which inspired other equally novel imperial concepts on the eve of revolution, Galloway's view could easily have appeared overwhelmingly original to its author and only part of a cacophonous blur to his audience.

3

Galloway's reputation as a skilled theorist was established as early as 1897 by Moses Coit Tyler's *Literary History of the American Revolution.* Julian P. Boyd's study of the Plans of Union added substance to that view. Nelson's account astutely shifted the emphasis away from the Plan of Union and toward Galloway's conception of representation. "In perceiving that Parliament was a territorial assembly with no rightful claim to control lands which were not represented," Nelson concluded, "Galloway went to the heart, not of the political, but of the constitutional impasse between Britain and America."[35]

The gap between constitutional and political acumen merits further consideration, and Galloway's doctrine of subordination provides a key to his difficulties at reconciling theory and practice. His strictures on obedience rested on a series of distinct propositions which he never integrated into an effective argument. First, he endeavored to establish the inseparability of the authority of the Crown and Parliament. Further, he insisted on the necessity of a supreme authority within every state. Finally, he sought to prove that the colonies were, of necessity, integral parts of the British state. The logical connection between these propositions was clear enough, but they lacked the unifying purpose and ingenuity which he had brought to the problem of representation. So elaborate and didactic were his writings on these issues that he was never able to reconcile, in a straightforward manner, the colonial right to representation in the legislative processes of the Empire with the need for a single supreme source of power lodged in the hands of Parliament and the Crown. He could only plead that the contradiction would cease to exist once his Plan of Union became a reality. Long before he had reached that conclusion, his assumptions about subordination in his *Candid Examination* had spread confusion and distrust. "Mr. G[alloway] has spent (I think) his first 20 pages in laying a wrong foundation and the superstructure he has raised on it falls of itself," Ebenezer Hazard wrote to Silas Deane, sensing Galloway's vulnerability. "He has taken for granted a very principle part of the dispute, *viz.*, our being *within the Realm*—a monstrous proposition."[36]

Hazard, of course, distinguished between the British realm and the British Empire, a distinction which Galloway did not deny. The Plan of Union and its accompanying theory of representation acknowledged that the colonies possessed, by historical accident and present circumstances, a different relationship to Parliament than did the lands of the realm. What he insisted upon was that subordination was as important a bond of the Empire as the colonists' right to representation in imperial legislative processes. The subordination which Hazard considered monstrous was what Galloway sought to pacify and render innocuous by imperial reform.

The unpublished "Thoughts on Both Sides . . ." laid the initial foundation for Galloway's theory of subordination when he insisted that the colonies owed simultaneous obedience to both the Crown and Parliament. To refute the argument that colonial charters obligated the colonists to obey the Crown alone, he argued that charters assumed the first settlers in America to have been "Members" of the British state who "did implicitly agree and consent . . . to yield Obedience to the supreme Authority of the State." If the King could exempt the colonists from obedience to Parliament, Galloway argued, he could as easily "discharge the whole People of *Great Britain* from their Obedience" and thereby "dissolve the Constitution."[37] Colonial petitions to the Crown which ignored Parliament, he asserted in the *Candid Examination,* "involve the cause of America in an inextricable absurdity" by acknowledging the authority of the Crown but denying other equally inherent constitutional principles.[38]

No doctrine of political theory, he declared, was more "firmly established" than the necessity of a supreme authority within every state. That argument, he apparently came to realize, depended on more than the concurrent authority of the King and Parliament. He had to demonstrate that the political order of the colonies was subject to all manner of deadly misfortunes against which the supreme legislative authority of Parliament was the only antidote. Carefully arranged citations from Burlamaqui, Tully, Locke, and Acherley all identified the legislative power as the cement of society and obedience as the only alternative to political disintegration.[39] This characterization of Parliament's power as a solitary line of defense against chaos was, for Galloway, a comparatively forthright way of claiming that the colonies were in fact part of the British state. Either they were part of the British state, he reasoned, or they were "so many independent Communities, in a state of nature" and bound by no authority whatever.[40] In this condition, colonial governments fell under Samuel Pufendorf's stricture, "with regard to lawful bodies, . . . whatever rights and whatever power they have over their members are all defined and limited by the supreme power, and cannot be opposed to or prevail against it. For otherwise, were there a body not subject to limitation by the supreme civil power, there would be a state within a state."[41] Galloway found further doctrinal support in Locke's statement, *"whoever . . . enjoys any part of the Land"* within a state *"must take it with the Condition . . . of submitting to the Government of the Commonwealth."* [42] Finally, Galloway argued, the rights of the colonists carried "reciprocal" and unavoidable duties; "shall Americans have the right to withdraw from the performance of duties," he demanded "and the state be bound to continue *them* in the enjoyment of all their rights?" [43]

Galloway's purpose in explaining the meaning of subordination was, in part, to eliminate all alternatives to his Plan of Union as solutions to the imperial crisis. But these strictures only involved him in his most pointed exchange with his detractors, Dickinson and Thomson. They attacked the rigidity of his definition of subordination, which insisted that the colonies were either fully independent states like Hanover or France or else they remained "complete members of the [British] State." [44] Such an arbitrary definition of the bases for subordination, Dickinson and Thomson retorted, reduced the colonies to the level of "mere Corporations." [45] "I confess I do not understand what you mean by a 'mere corporation,'" Galloway replied. A corporation, he explained, was a respectable political entity, a dependent community within a sovereign state. Pufendorf insisted on the subordinate status of such communities with respect to the governing power. Indeed a subordinate community not bound by a supreme authority was "a *monster,* a thing *out* of nature." By focusing on the abnormality of autonomous subordinate communities, Galloway instinctively shifted the argument away from the primary issue—whether the colonies were in fact within the boundaries of the British state. [46]

Confident that he established the propriety of applying the term "corporation" to the status of the colonies, Galloway continued the discussion on his own terms. The natural characteristic of a subordinate community was the power to exercise local police power. [47] It simply did not follow, he lectured Dickinson and Thomson, that a community could expand local police power into full legislative authority. Now he was prepared to confront one of Dickinson's and Thomson's chief contentions: that the colonial assemblies were not subordinate because they exercised within their provinces jurisdiction as complete as that of Parliament within Great Britain. The Pennsylvania Assembly, he retorted, possessed no such unbridled authority. It could not enact laws repugnant to those of Britain; its laws had to conform as closely as possible to British law; none of its enactments could interfere in any way with the enforcement of Parliamentary laws. Surely, he concluded, a legislative body so circumscribed was scarcely supreme. On the contrary, colonial assemblies differed in no way from the units of English local governments, "corporations" like Bristol or the City of London. After all, he reminded his critics, both Bristol and London were represented in Parliament. Dickinson's and Thomson's claim that colonial assemblies were supreme within their respective provinces clarified their intentions, Galloway concluded, thanking his adversaries "for *blabbing this long concealed and most important secret"* and revealing for the first time "the cloven foot, ... the black scheme of Independence ... exhibited in all its horrid deformity."[48]

Virtually the only reference to "independence" in the pre-Revolutionary debate —at least prior to 1775—were in these exasperated accusations by Galloway and other critics of colonial resistance. Among the most important practical consequences of their writings was to raise the spectre of independence at the very time that the leaders of resistance were attempting to redefine Parliamentary supremacy in terms compatible with colonial autonomy.

Bernard Bailyn's *The Ideological Origins of the American Revolution* sets Galloway's constitutionalism in context.[49] His strictures on subordination restated what had been, until the 1760s, an orthodox view in the Anglo-American world. It was the English "Whig conception of a sovereign Parliament" which had been hammered out in the struggles of the seventeenth century, given classic form in Blackstone, and embodied most bluntly in the Declaratory Act. "How to qualify, undermine, or reinterpret this tenet of English political theory was the central intellectual problem that confronted the leaders of the American cause," Bailyn explained. "It is a classic instance of the creative adjustment of ideas to reality. For if in England the concept of sovereignty was not only logical but realistic, it was far from that in the colonies."[50] Dickinson's *Essay on the Constitutional Power of Great Britain* was one of the foremost efforts to accomplish this trick by devising separate spheres in which Parliamentary authority and colonial autonomy could operate. Dickinson's argument—which, it will be recalled, was drafted in a vain attempt to influence the Pennsylvania delegation to Congress later dominated by Galloway—argued that "the sovereignty over these colonies must be limited" and that "there must be ... a line" drawn clearly designating the limits of Parliamentary jurisdiction.[51]

In October 1774 Congress adopted this position in its Fourth Resolve which acknowledged Parliament's control over imperial commerce and reserved to the provincial assemblies "exclusive right of legislation ... in all cases of taxation and internal policy."[52] It was this solution to the problem of sovereignty which led Galloway to define most clearly his differences with Dickinson and Thomson; "you first took into your *learned* heads, philosopher-like, to conceive that the supreme legislative authority, which is indivisible to its nature, was like matter, divisible *ad infinitum*; and under this profound mistake, you began with splitting and dividing it, until by one slice after another, you have hacked and pared it away to less than an atom."[53]

4

Galloway's doctrines of representation and subordination and his contentious style of argument were a cumbersome apparatus which he carried proudly. But refusing to jettison arguments he could not convey effectively, he was progressively isolated by his erudition from the public discussion he longed to dominate.

"He is a man of integrity" and "improved understanding, but he is too fond of *system,*" Rev. John Vardill, a New York tory, said of Galloway in a letter to an English official in 1778, to which he added, "his natural warmth of temper, inflamed by the oppressions and indignities he has suffered, will render you cautious in trusting his representations."[54] This same rigidity in the structure of his ideas and fluid, volatile self-consciousness was already apparent in Galloway's writings in early 1775. Such was his resourcefulness that as his intellectual position became increasingly vulnerable and misunderstood, he turned his attention inward and contemplated with growing fascination his peculiar role as a critic of colonial resistance. "I . . . have laid before you the constitutional extent of parliamentary jurisdiction," he declared at the close of his *Candid Examination*: "I have . . . *deduced* your rights, . . . and explained your duties. I have pointed out the mode which . . . you ought to pursue for a restoration of those rights."[55] This didactic posture was the essence of his concept of his role; it drew together in his mind the complex threads of his arguments and set his whole endeavor in perspective.

That concept of his role was implicit in all of Galloway's conduct in 1774–1775. He assumed that situations should hold still and men stand attentive while he brought the power of his mind and the persuasion of his pen to bear on the problem. "Parliament ought not, as the colonies are at present circumstanced, to bind them by its Legislative Authority," he pleaded in July 1774, "both Countries should retreat a little and take other Ground."[56] All of his secretive preparation in August and September 1774 demonstrated—as Nelson adroitly concluded—that "Galloway conceived of the Continental Congress as a constitutional convention; indeed, as *his* constitutional convention."[57] As the delegates deviated from Galloway's scenario, he adapted his approach accordingly by enlarging his role and gambling everything on the hope that his brilliant speech in behalf of his Plan would compel his critics to accept his leadership or admit that their own motives were selfish and disruptive. He sought to shield himself from personal attack by identifying himself entirely with the manifest virtues and disinterestedness of his Plan.

The last thing he expected was that his enemies would oppose his Plan by ignoring its substantial provisions. During the final stages of the Congress, an unidentified Virginia delegate, almost certainly Patrick Henry, taunted Galloway that his Plan was "big with destruction to America" and challenged him to debate its merits. Desperate to get the Plan reconsidered by Congress, Galloway agreed on the condition that the debate be part of its proceedings. The clash never materialized, but Galloway was shocked to hear that the Virginia delegates were at the same time openly talking of their intention to have the Plan expunged from the Journal of Congress.[58] When Dickinson and Thomson chided him for refusing to debate with Henry about his Plan "when he had been for months haranguing and caballing about it,"[59] Galloway concluded that trickery and deceit were the only replies he would receive to his serious proposals. "Your assaults have not even ruffled its scarf-skin," he said of attacks on his Plan more in chagrin than triumph. His accusation that, "It stands like an impregnable bulwark in the path of your independence and you do not know how to remove it,"[60] did not conceal his disappointment that his enemies had not tried to "remove it," that they did not consider his Plan the central issue in the debate, and that they preferred to discuss British abuses which he overlooked and to impugn his dedication to colonial liberty.

At the heart of these tactics Galloway perceived the sin of "sophistry," the twisting of words about colonial rights without regard for the inherent limitations of colonial institutions, and the reinterpretation of colonial interests in terms of men's imaginations and ambitions. When Dickinson and Henry engaged in these practices, he conceded, they may have done so unwittingly, out of "perverseness," but they violated the ethical standards of "honour and candour" which should govern polemical debate and thereby forfeited the respect of "sensible and honest men." Techniques of boldness, clever construction of arguments, and ideological finesse, in his view, had become ends in themselves, blinding men to the fact that "sophistry" could not "render . . . 'supreme' and independent what is in its nature limited, subordinate, and dependent."[61]

This intellectual confusion explained to Galloway's satisfaction the success of the movement toward colonial resistance. Not content with their own disobedience, whig leaders felt compelled to spread their guilt more widely by stampeding into rebellion men "whose leisure and abilities will not suffer them to inquire into . . . fallacious doctrines."[62] A decade earlier he had used the same argument to explain why members of his own political faction joined the resistance to the Stamp Act. "Our Friends were inclined to unite with those Wretches," he had then written, "not seeing their Design of bringing us to an Act which would Crown all the Violent Measures they had . . . taken against the Power of Parliament."[63] Now in the light of his experience in the First Continental Congress and his inquiry into the morality of his opponents' conduct, Galloway believed he had isolated the source of disorder. His *Candid Examination* closed with a question calculated to unmask it: "are you *still* resolved," he asked of his readers, "to surrender up your reason to the miserable sophistry and jargon of designing men?"[64]

Galloway's diagnosis of whig "sophistry" marked the end of his attempt to playa meaningful role in the pre-Revolutionary debate. In May 1775, he asked to be removed as a delegate to the Second Continental Congress; and by June he considered himself "retired . . . from the distressing and ungrateful Drudgery of Public Life."[65] The superstructure of ideas he had constructed during the previous year was fraught with internal stresses. He had worked with tireless industry to resolve apparent contradictions in his doctrines of representation and subordination. He only could have succeeded if his audience had sympathized with his basic purposes: to "deduce" colonial rights single-handedly from arbitrarily chosen premises and then to neutralize colonial discontent with a Plan so ingenious and dramatic as to compel assent. That concept of his role, and the experiences from which it crystallized, comprised the moral and emotional basis for his subsequent loyalism.

Author's Note (1988)

In the original article I accepted Galloway's claim that his Plan of Union had been "expunged" from the Journal of the Continental Congress. For procedural reasons, the plan never became a part of the record of the Congress; see Paul H. Smith, ed., *Letters of Delegates to Congress* 1774–1789 (Washington, D.C., 1976), vol. 1, pp. 112–13, 116–17.

Author's Note (2007)

Between July and November 1774, as the charged political events related in this chapter unfolded, Galloway was caught up in another transatlantic legal controversy also charged with issues of rights, virtue, reciprocity, and civic and personal ethics. On July 1, 1774, he wrote to his brother-in-law Thomas Nickleson in Dorset, England, describing a legal struggle between Galloway and Abel James, Nickleson's legal agent in Pennsylvania, over the settlement of Galloway's father's estate, Trevose, in Bucks County, in which Galloway and Nickleson had entwined financial interests. After years of silence, Galloway now sought Nickleson's understanding by shifting blame for the tangled legal situation from himself to Abel James. The private dispute over land and the public one over imperial governance—both coming to a head in the summer and autumn of 1774—deserve to be reconstructed as the inner and outer arenas of Galloway's ambition and combativeness. "As to the unfortunate Dispute between the Mother Country and her Colonies," Galloway concluded the 1774 phase of this correspondence,

> I fear it is now arrived to such an Heigth that it will be with great difficulty accommodated. Nothing has been wanting on my Part to moderate the violent Temper of the warm & indiscreet People here, and bring about a Reconciliation between the two Countries upon Principles of Liberty and Government. But what can one or a few men do in so arduous a Task. You will no Doubt hear the Resolves of our Congress and their other Proceedings. I cannot say I approve of them, they are too warm & indiscreet and, in my Opinion, have not pursued the right Path to an Accommodation. All the violent Parts of them I strenuously opposed from Conscience & Judgment and because was convinced they must widen the Differences between us.

This explanation from a colonial politician to an English relative, written at the conclusion of a lengthy and tortuous account of the ongoing estate settlement and dated on the day after the tumultuous adjournment of the first Continental Congress, pinpointed, in both time and political reality, Galloway's disagreement with the Congress more precisely than other surviving sources. (See Galloway to Nickleson July 1, November 1, 1774, and June 4, 1779, Joseph Galloway Papers, Library of Congress.) When the Library of Congress acquired these letters, Mary Beth Norton called them to my attention although I did not examine them until 2006.

Notes

1. Julian P. Boyd, *Anglo-American Union: Joseph Galloway's Plans to Preserve the British Empire, 1774–1788* (Philadelphia, 1941); William H. Nelson, *The American Tory* (Oxford, 1961), pp. 47–69; Benjamin L. Newcomb, *Franklin and Galloway: A Political Partnership* (New Haven, 1972); David Jacobson, *John Dickinson and the Revolution in Pennsylvania, 1761–1776* (Berkeley and Los Angeles, 1965), chapter 5; Max Savelle, "Nationalism and Other Loyalties in the American Revolution," *American Historical Review,* 67 (1962): 910; Moses Coit Tyler, *Literary History of the American Revolution* (New York, 1897), vol. 1, pp. 369–83.

2. [Joseph Galloway], *A Candid Examination of the Mutual Claims of Great Britain, and the Colonies: with a plan of Accommodation, on constitutional principles* (New York, 1775).

3. [Joseph Galloway], *A Reply to an Address to the Author of a Pamphlet, entitled, "A Candid Examination," &c. By the Author of the Candid Examination* (New York, 1775).

4. Nelson, *The American Tory,* pp. 47–48, pp. 54–69; Jacobson, "Dickinson and Galloway," pp. 178–204, and *John Dickinson and the Revolution in Pennsylvania,* pp. 83–85.

5. See Bernard Bailyn, ed., *Pamphlets of the American Revolution, 1750–1776* (Cambridge, Mass., 1965), vol. 1, pp. 660–65, and Jacobson's articles, "John Dickinson's Fight against Royal Government, 1764," *William and Mary Quarterly,* 3rd. ser., 19 (1962): 64–85, and "The Puzzle of 'Pacificus,'" *Pennsylvania History,* 31 (1964): 406–18.

6. Bailyn, ed., *Pamphlets of the American Revolution,* vol. 1, pp. 249–72.

7. Galloway to Benjamin Franklin, January 13 and June 16, 1766, June 21, 1770, Jared Sparks, ed., *The Works of Benjamin Franklin* (Boston, 1836–1840), vol. 7, pp. 303–305, 321–25, 481–83.

8. On Galloway's political strength and tactics in the late-1760s, see Benjamin H. Newcomb, "Effects of the Stamp Act on Colonial Pennsylvania Politics," *William and Mary Quarterly,* 3rd. ser., 23 (1966): 257–72.

9. Jacobson, *John Dickinson and the Revolution in Pennsylvania,* pp. 66–69.

10. Jacobson, "Dickinson and Galloway," pp. 178–79; *Pennsylvania Archives,* 8 Series, vol. 8, p. 7100.

11. William Bradford to James Madison, August 1, 1774, William M. E. Rachal and William T. Hutchinson, eds., *The Papers of James Madison* (Chicago, 1962), vol. 1, pp. 117–19; Silas Deane to his wife, September 5–6, 1774, in Edmund C. Burnett, ed., *Letters of Members of the Continental Congress* (Washington, D.C., 1921–1936), vol. 1, p. 11; Jacobson, *John Dickinson and the Revolution in Pennsylvania,* pp. 80–81.

12. The only surviving copy of Galloway's speech to Congress of September 28, 1774, proposing the Plan of Union is the draft in his *Historical and Political Reflections on the Rise and Progress of the American Rebellion . . .* (London, 1780), pp. 41–44. John Adams's notes on Galloway's speech reveal, as Julian P. Boyd has demonstrated, that the 1780 version was heavily revised for its English readers and is not a reliable source for Galloway's ideas in 1774, see *Anglo-American Union,* pp. 35–36, and Lyman Butterfield, et al., eds., *The Diary and Autobiography of John Adams* (Cambridge, Mass., 1961), vol. 2, pp. 141–44. Merrill Jensen reprinted a striking passage from *Historical and Political Reflections* in *American Colonial Documents to 1776* (London, 1955), pp. 801–803, which depicted the motives of Galloway's enemies in Congress in terms similar to those he used in 1775; however, this passage places somewhat more emphasis on the "republican" character of

their beliefs and economic factors—"declining fortunes" and "debt to British merchants"—than his 1775 analysis of whig motives.

13. Nelson, *The American Tory,* p. 54.

14. When Galloway presented his Plan, Duane, Edward Rutledge, and Jay spoke in its
defense, provoking Patrick Henry's outburst to John Adams about his "horrid Opinion"
of "Galloway, Jay, and the Rutledges" and "their System," *Diary and Autobiography of
John Adams,* vol. 2, p. 151. Jay's support of Galloway's Plan raises a curious problem, for
in the committee on colonial rights and grievances he led the attack against the objections of John Rutledge, Duane, and Galloway who wanted to restrict Congress to the use
of English constitutional precedents. Congress, Jay insisted then, should "recur to the Law
of Nature" as well because "there is no Allegiance without Protection. And Emigrants
have a Right to erect what Government they please." (Adams, *Diary and Autobiography,*
p. 128).

15. Adams, *Diary and Autobiography,* pp. 129–30.

16. "Arguments on Both Sides in the Dispute Between Great Britain and her Colonies . . . ," *Archives of New Jersey,* vol. 10, pp. 483–92; Galloway to Verplanck, February 14,
1775, *Pennsylvania Magazine of History and Biography,* 21 (1897): 480–81.

17. Galloway to Richard Jackson, August 10, 1774 (a copied extract in Jackson's handwriting enclosed in Jackson to Lord Dartmouth, December 21, 1774), Dartmouth Papers,
II, 1031, William Salt Library, Stafford, England, printed in Jack P. Greene, ed., *A Documentary History of American Life,* vol. II, *Colonies to Nation, 1773–1789* (New York,
1967), pp. 239–41.

18. Galloway, *Candid Examination,* pp. 42–43.

19. Galloway to Jackson, August 10, 1774, Greene, ed., *Colonies to Nation,* pp. 239–41.

20. "Arguments on Both Sides . . ." *Archives of New Jersey,* vol. 10, pp. 483–92.

21. Galloway, *Candid Examination,* pp. 59–61.

22. Galloway, *Reply,* pp. 6–8.

23. The introductory resolution is printed in *Candid Examination,* 53, and another
version is "Resolutions intended to be offered by Mr. Galloway & seconded by J[ames]
D[uane] for Promoting a Plan of Union between G. B. & A.," with the notation, "But as
the Plan itself was rejected by the Congress; the Resolves became fruitless & were not
proposed," James Duane Papers, New York Historical Society.

24. Boyd, *Anglo-American Union,* pp. 112–14; Nelson, "The Last Hopes of the American Loyalists," *Canadian Historical Review,* 32 (1951): 40–42.

25. Robert M. Calhoon, ed., "William Smith Jr.'s Alternative to the American Revolution," *William and Mary Quarterly,* 3rd. ser., 22 (1965): 105–18.

26. Galloway, of course, must have known the Albany Plan well from his long association with Franklin, and Smith's father, William Smith, Sr., was a member of the committee at the Albany Congress which approved Franklin's proposal; see Leonard W.
Labaree, et al., eds., *The Papers of Benjamin Franklin* (New Haven, 1962), vol. 5, p. 376 n.
6, and pp. 417–18 n. 4.

27. One critic accused Galloway of plagiarizing Franklin (*Pennsylvania Journal,* April
5, 1775), and Galloway retorted that his Plan differed materially from Franklin's, especially in its provision for a "political union" with Great Britain (*Pennsylvania Gazette,*
April 26, 1775); for further discussion see Nelson, *The American Tory,* p. 60, n. 23,
Boyd, "Joseph Galloway's Plans of Union . . . ," *Pennsylvania Magazine of History and*

Biography, 64 (1940): 503, n. 34, and Labaree, et al., *The Papers of Benjamin Franklin,* vol. 5, pp. 417–18, n. 4.

28. Franklin to Galloway, February 25, 1775, in Samuel Eliot Morison, ed., *Sources and Documents Illustrating the American Revolution, 1774–1788* . . . (Oxford, 1923), pp. 137–39.

29. For documentation see Calhoon, ed., "William Smith's Alternative . . ." p. 117, n. 18.

30. Smith to Philip Schuyler, July 23, 1774, in William H. W. Sabine, ed., *Historical Memoirs from . . . 1763 to . . . 1776 of William Smith* . . . (New York, 1956), p. 190.

31. Calhoon, ed., "William Smith's Alternative . . .," p. 113.

32. Smith to Schuyler, May 16, 1775, and Smith to Lewis Morris, June 5,1775, in Sabine, ed., *Historical Memoirs,* pp. 224–25, 228–227c.

33. Richard Koebner, *Empire* (Cambridge, Eng., 1961), pp. 194–238.

34. Koebner, *Empire,* p. 209

35. Nelson, *The American Tory,* p. 59.

36. Ebenezer Hazard (in New York) to Silas Deane, April 7, 1775, *Connecticut Historical Society Collections,* 2 (1870): 211–13.

37. "Arguments on Both Sides . . ." pp. 478–81.

38. Galloway, *Candid Examination,* p. 26.

39. Galloway, *Candid Examination,* pp. 4–5.

40. Galloway, *Candid Examination,* p. 10.

41. Galloway, *Candid Examination,* pp. 29, 21–22; Samuel Pufendorf, *De Jure Naturae et Gentium Libri Octo,* C. H. and W. A. Oldfather, trans. *(Publications of the Carnegie Endowment for International Peace* [Oxford and London, 1934]), vol. 2, p. 996; on Pufendorf's utility to both sides in the pre-Revolutionary debate, see Leonard Krieger, *The Politics of Discretion: Pufendorf and the Acceptance of Natural Law* (London and Chicago, 1965). Galloway found in Pufendorf an explanation of the necessary limits placed on subordinate communities, and James Otis, Samuel Adams, and Alexander Hamilton cited his dictum that "colonies may be . . . planted in different ways. For either they remain a part of the state from which they were sent forth, or they are obligated to show respect to the mother state and to uphold its majesty . . . by a kind of unequal treaty, or, finally, they treat with it on equal terms and right." *(De Jure Naturae,* vol. 2, p. 1356; Krieger, *Politics of Discretion,* pp. 260–61, 302–3.)

42. Peter Laslett, ed., *John Locke's Two Treatises on Government* (Cambridge, Eng., 1960), p. 366; Galloway, *Candid Examination,* pp. 14–15.

43. Laslett, ed., *Two Treatises,* pp. 13, 24.

44. Laslett, ed., *Two Treatises,* p. 5.

45. *Pennsylvania Journal,* March 8, 1775.

46. Galloway, *Reply,* pp. 25–26.

47. Galloway's service in 1777–1778 as General William Howe's Superintendent General for Police in Philadelphia amplified his understanding of this idea. He strived with considerable administrative and political ingenuity to expand the office into a powerful executive position from which he might rally and dominate loyal sentiment and thereby demonstrate how benevolent, strong-minded colonial administration could—in conjunction with effective military measures—break the back of the Revolution. He viewed the police power of a provincial government as the cutting edge of imperial policy and

as a means of achieving the same kind of reconciliation he had first proposed in 1774. See John M. Coleman's study of Galloway's concept of his role in 1777–1779, "Joseph Galloway and the British Occupation of Philadelphia," *Pennsylvania History,* 30 (1963): 272, 274, 279–80, 288–93.

48. Galloway, *Reply,* pp. 26–27, 15–16, 4–5.

49. Bernard Bailyn, *The Ideological Origins of the American Revolution* (Cambridge, Mass., 1967), pp. 201–3.

50. Bailyn, *Ideological Origins,* p. 223; Galloway, *Reply,* p. 20.

51. *Pennsylvania Archives,* 2 Series, vol. 3, pp. 528, 594; Bailyn, *Ideological Origins,* p. 223.

52. W. C. Ford, ed., *Journals of the Continental Congress, 1774–1789* (Washington, 1904), vol. 1, p. 68.

53. Galloway, *Reply,* p. 20.

54. [Vardill] to [William Eden], April 11, 1778, quoted in Coleman, "Joseph Galloway and the British Occupation of Philadelphia," pp. 281–82.

55. Galloway, *Candid Examination,* p. 61.

56. See above note 19.

57. Nelson, *The American Tory,* p. 48.

58. Galloway, *Reply,* pp. 33–34.

59. *Pennsylvania Gazette,* March 8, 1775.

60. "To the Public," Galloway, "To the Public," April 26, 1775; Galloway, *Reply,* pp. 35–36.

61. Galloway, *Reply,* pp. 41–42, 3–4.

62. Galloway, *Reply,* pp. 24–25.

63. Galloway to William Franklin, November 14, 1765, Leonard W. Labaree, ed., *The Papers of Benjamin Franklin* (New Haven, 1959–), vol. 12, pp. 372–75; Newcomb, "Effects of the Stamp Act on Colonial Pennsylvania Politics," p. 269.

64. Galloway, *Candid Examination,* p. 62.

65. Galloway to Verplanck, June 24, 1775, *PMHB,* vol. 21, p. 483.

Six

"Unhinging Former Intimacies"

Robert Beverley's Perception of the
Pre-Revolutionary Controversy, 1761–1775

ROBERT M. CALHOON

1

Considering the enormous amount of scholarly writing that has been done on the causes of the American Revolution and the motives of men who supported and opposed colonial resistance, little is known of the dilemma of men who felt immobilized by doubt or uncertainty during the crisis of 1774–1775. The subject deserves attention, all the more now in light of Bernard Bailyn's pioneering analysis of the "interior view" of Revolutionary ideas, "the assumptions, beliefs, and ideas ... that lay behind the manifest events of the time."[1]

The plight of the uncommitted was recognized at the time, even by men who were themselves wholly committed to the Revolutionary cause. "I say, gentlemen, there are men among us who are not enemies to their country, who are friends to all America, ... [who] acknowledge that we are greatly aggrieved and oppressed," Henry Laurens told the South Carolina Provincial Congress on July 4, 1775, "but they cannot, they dare not, for many reasons, subscribe to the [non-importation] Association. ... Other men there are who are no less friendly to America ... but who think we have precipitated a measure which ought to have been delayed." Laurens refused to "anathemize" these "good men."[2] Such a man was Richard Wells, a Philadelphia moderate, who affirmed that the colonies could not submit to Parliamentary dictation and yet searched for a means of avoiding rash or violent resistance. "When an individual shall dare to step forth with his private opinion and offer to public notice on affairs of the utmost importance to his country, much does he risque in the attempt. ... Hard is the *middle* path to find." Yearning for political wisdom which he feared he did not possess, Wells continued, "*I contend with a zeal which convinces me that I am right* that ... our passions cannot always remain upon the stretch; we shall gently relax ... and heedlessly and gradually slide down the hill of opposition; our rulers will become tyrants; and from a country of happy freemen, we shall degenerate into a land of abject slaves."[3] The Reverend Jeremy Belknap of Dover, New Hampshire, an Old Light Congregationalist, refused to sign a non-importation "Covenant" in July 1774, "because tyranny in one shape is as odious to me as tyranny in another." The Covenant had been drafted in Boston and distributed from Portsmouth to the towns of New Hampshire "without any legal authority" from the people asked to sign it. "Here is no liberty of conscience nor right of private judgment." A year later Belknap was a member of a Committee of Safety and a militia chaplain, but the moment of crisis in 1774 found him immobilized.[4] An Anglican cleric in Phila-delphia, William Smith, preached a militia sermon in June 1775, condemning alike "passive submission" to Parliament and "licentious opposition" by ambitious fac-tions against British authority; when, however, the logic of his argument com-pelled him to prescribe an ethical course for men to follow during the crisis, Smith acknowledged and then evaded the issue: "To draw the line and say where sub-mission ends and resistance begins is not the province of ministers of Christ . . . Pulpit casuistry is too feeble to direct or controul here."[5]

Running through these pathetic, candid self-appraisals was a suspicion that political endeavor was neither a meaningful form of human activity nor an effec-tive means of achieving social change. This apolitical scepticism hardened as the pre-Revolutionary controversy grew in intensity and made the opponents of colonial resistance feel increasingly vulnerable and immobilized. Few of these crit-ics of the pre-Revolutionary movement left enough personal testimony to enable historians to explore the interrelationships between their attitudes. One who did was Robert Beverley, a Virginia planter who was neutral during the war. While nearly all of his contemporaries among the Virginia gentry received thorough training in local government and actively participated in resistance against British policies, Beverley avoided the duties of government throughout the pre-Revolu-tionary period and could not comprehend why his fellow Virginia aristocrats reacted so vigorously to British encroachments. He became a critic of colonial re-sistance in a colony where whig leaders achieved a remarkable unity. Though him-self a third generation planter-aristocrat, he refused to align himself with men of identical social and economic background. He felt ill at ease in political discus-sion, even within his own family, though he lived in a society which valued politi-cal discourse. Beverley's situation was, therefore, a paradox which he did not fully comprehend and which other men misunderstood.[6]

Beverley worried about what made him different from other men and tried to adjust his behavior toward conformity. However, he also valued his vantage point outside of politics and above its temptations and emotions. From this position he tried to join in the pre-Revolutionary debate, to point out flaws in whig reason-ing and tactics. At the same time, he refused to compromise his impartiality by joining in the activity of Virginia politics. To complicate his confused situation still more, many Virginians took offense at his apparently carping advice, and their hostility confirmed his worst suspicions about the corroding effect of politics upon such values as trust, tolerance, and good will. Thus he felt a simultaneous pull toward active participation in the pre-Revolutionary debate and aversion to its emotion and discord.

2

Beverley felt vaguely out of place when he returned to Virginia at the age of twenty-three in 1761 after spending ten formative years acquiring an English education. He described one of his first impressions as "an aversion to slavery: 'tis something so very contrary to humanity that I am really ashamed of my country ... and if I ever bid adieu to Virginia, it will be from that cause alone."[7] He sent detailed instructions to his coachmaker in London for a "post chariot, ... light green upon silver";[8] resolved to put his newly inherited estates on a sound footing and eliminate his debts and then return permanently to England, where "I solemnly aver I had much rather be an inhabitant ... upon £500 per annum than to blaze away here upon four times the sum."[9] Gradually he reconciled himself to settling permanently in Virginia, perhaps because of the weight of his debt to English merchants and his marriage two years later to Maria Carter, the daughter of Landon Carter of Sabine Hall.

He never felt at ease among the Carters, though by every external qualification he was fully their social equal. Perhaps he never had a chance; even before Beverley's marriage the family regarded him with suspicion, and Landon Carter heard warnings from his brother that Beverley was immature and irresponsible.[10] Beverley continued to abstain from the drudgery of work in local government in Virginia, assuming none of the posts of vestryman, justice of the peace, or member of the House of Burgesses expected of the planter elite, depriving himself of the opportunity to learn the vocabulary and concepts of political practice. His only recorded interest in public office before 1787 was to ask Landon Carter in 1772 to recommend him for a possible vacancy on the moribund royal Council.[11] Nothing came of his passing interest in a Council seat, and his disagreements with his father-in-law were enervating experiences, dissipating what little interest he had in political activity. At the close of one of their arguments, when Carter apparently tried to remain cordial, Beverley compulsively replied, "There was not the least need for apology in your last letter. There can be no real [trust?] if we must send every letter with professions and apologies that we would be thought sincere."[12]

As public discussion dealt increasingly with opposition to British policy, his sense of inadequacy heightened. During the tense month of August 1774, for example, he wrote to Carter, "... you put an improper construction on my words in making me say that I am resolved to carry my political opinions to the grave." "I meant to say," he explained, that the arguments he had heard in favor of resisting British authority had not *yet* changed his mind. "This is what I intended to say, and if I made use of other sentiments, it was a mistake." Pleading his open-mindedness, he insisted on his right to resist novel opinions as well as his duty to change his mind in the face of convincing evidence: "... it [is] the highest folly to be attached blindly to any particular notions or servilely to change opinions," he concluded in defense of his indecisive approach to political issues.[13]

Landon Carter was, of course, by 1774 a deeply embittered man, disappointed in his children and violently hostile toward his son, Robert Wormeley Carter; he would have been a difficult father-in-law for the most congenial young man. Carter's choice of insults, however, and Beverley's reactions to them reveal elements of the younger man's self-image. "Your comparison of your soil and my temper may possibly be applicable enough," he complained to Carter, "but I scarce know a man to whom this comparison may not be extended with equal propriety, for I find very few amongst us who are willing to sacrifice any opinions . . . to adopt others of a different complexion."[14]

Perhaps in an effort to make amends for his neglect of politics, he occasionally made random comments from the sidelines. At first these gestures did him no harm. In 1763 he labeled British restrictions on Virginia currency "a very genteel . . . method of repaying our *ridiculous* and overzealous loyalty in the course of the late war." During the Stamp Act crisis he wrote to Landon Carter, "It cannot be conceived that two millions of free born people will sink tamely into slavery, or give up part of their liberties without making some effort to preserve it." He even suggested expedients which the Burgesses might adopt—renewed remonstrance and then closing the courts—but seemed to sense how little these proposals compensated for his inactivity in the controversy. His letter to Carter ended plaintively, "I am afraid I have transgressed upon your patience, . . . however . . . I will make no further apology. . . . You may . . . spend a moment or two reading my nonsense, for 'tis possible it may create a smile to find that *I have become a politician.*"[15] He soon abandoned this hesitant endorsement of resistance against British measures, refused to subscribe to the non-importation association after the passage of the Townshend duties, and expressed anger when men accused him of a "sinister purpose" where he believed he had acted out of principle.[16] In 1771, when Carter snorted his disapproval of Lord Dunmore's appointment as governor, Beverley interjected his reasons for reserving judgment. "I do not think it absolutely necessary that every governor . . . should be excessively learned or profoundly wise." Instead he considered a "good heart" more important than intellect, and he proposed to take Dunmore's good sense and integrity for granted until he saw evidence to the contrary. Lord Botetourt, he recalled, had overcome in experience and achieved success in his performance as governor. "I . . . judge men," he concluded, "as I find them . . . I think it rather cruel to forbode otherwise."[17]

Beverley's insistence on judging men as he found them masked his lack of information on which to found a judgment. Behind a genuine attempt at detached thoughtfulness, he did not know how to think through political issues. Others might come to quick judgments about British intentions, he conceded, but he wanted to reflect longer. The purpose of prolonged contemplation, he implied, was a sense of inner satisfaction which he acquired from making independent judgments.

3

"At present the country is in a most unhappy state of anarchy and misrule," Beverley wrote to John Backhouse of Liverpool in July 1775; "all I can do is to remain . . . a sorrowful spectator of these tumultuous times."[18] He hoped he could remain a static observer on the fringe of Virginia's intense political activity and enjoy the tranquility he would find in neutrality. From that vantage point, however, he could not avoid making occasional comments on politics, and the hostility which these aroused spurred him to defend himself and extend his criticism of whig tactics. His aloofness and political naïveté, as well as his compulsiveness, tended to hide another side of his introspective personality—his acute curiosity about the consequences of emotionalism and agitation on the conduct of politically active Virginians in 1774–1775. "In the ardour of commotions," he observed, "the passions become so inflamed and the tempers so much prejudiced, that frequently measures of the most salutary nature are rejected as the effects of pusillanimity or treachery."[19] Beverley was not only isolated and immobilized by that turmoil, but he also understood how anxiety and stress[20] among Virginia's ruling elite could accelerate the pace of events and limit the options open to political leaders. Certainly he believed that his reason and judgment had revealed to him an atmosphere in which those rational tools were of little use. While that assessment may have been a subtle and even sophisticated one, Beverley himself was not the kind of facile thinker who could pursue the implications of this sobering insight. He preferred instead to make a virtue of indecision. "In all combustions of this kind," he predicted, "the impartial world will find errors and faults on both sides."[21]

Nothing soothed Beverley's anxiety more than finding equivalent injustice in both British and colonial conduct. At the outset of a long letter to William Fitzhugh in July 1775, he put the best possible face on colonial grievances. He acknowledged the colonies' exemption from British taxation. He conceded that the operation of courts as well as the penal provisions of the Coercive Acts infringed on the right of trial by jury in a defendant's own locality. He condemned the suspension of the New York Assembly in 1767."[22] But here his concession to the whig position ended. The Boston tea party, he feared, had fatally compromised the integrity of colonial principles. In discussing the tumult in Boston, he brooded over the excesses of both sides. Avoiding the obvious issue of authority versus disobedience, he weighed instead a variety of extenuating circumstances which suggested to him that both sides were wrong, yet each had some justification for its actions. Clearly, Boston had the right to oppose implementation of the Tea Act, but the violent destruction of the tea itself did not sound to him like a deed motivated by patriotism. Because many men there stood to lose money under the East India Company's monopoly, he queried Fitzhugh, "Let me ask how far the destruction of the tea was influenced by virtuous principles." The ministry, he cautioned, ought first to have asked for restitution for the tea before considering harsher penalties. Thus torn, he could only "lament that this unnatural civil war took rise from such a cause."[23]

However, because the crisis in Boston did exist and did involve Virginians, Beverley sought pretexts which would justify continued submission. Virginia could not complain too loudly about the treatment of Boston, he suggested incorrectly, because it had "beheld with silence and unconcern" the suspension of the New York Assembly in 1767 and thereby compromised its capacity to defend the preservation of Massachusetts' representative institutions. Nor, he added, could the colonies claim that the colonial charters protected their assemblies from arbitrary suspension. Charter rights seemed to him conditional on good behavior. Quickly retreating from such a positive statement, he doubted whether the destruction of the tea in itself merited so severe a penalty. Still, he went on, the people of Massachusetts had only themselves to blame because "their constitution . . . rests so entirely with the people that they are perpetually engaged in tumults and cabals."[24]

Patriot agitators and the emotional quality of their appeals alarmed Beverley much more than the underlying constitutional issues of the pre-Revolutionary crisis. Demagoguery provided him with a phenomenon he could analyze endlessly, pass judgment upon, and blame for all public disorder. The tone of patriot polemics explained to his satisfaction why a constitutional dispute had grown into an emotional contagion endangering his society. At the outset of the controversy each side, he believed, had nervously exaggerated its claims. "Extravagant encomiums" and "illiberal abuse" at once became the medium of discussion. Agitators quickly took advantage of the situation and perpetuated the use of emotional and ill-considered rhetoric. Caught in a trap of their own making, responsible colonial leaders could not retreat or compromise without arousing cries of cowardice or treachery. The tone of patriot propaganda also suggested several concrete consequences of the controversy. The functioning of the British constitution, Beverley explained, depended on men's restraint and willingness to forego personal advantage when they engaged in politics. The militant tone of patriot appeals suggested to him that "ambition, corruption, [and] faction" had seriously blemished the operation of the constitution in Virginia. Emotional rhetoric, moreover, foreclosed the possibility of reconciliation because it artificially inflated men's estimates of their own power and exaggerated the rightness of their position. Under its influence Beverley's acquaintances simply would not listen to his arguments about the true interest of the colonies. Finally, emotional whig arguments only needlessly antagonized British officials. Virginian attacks on Lord Dunmore illustrated this danger. Conceding that Dunmore was a bad governor and ignorant of the colony's interests and rights, Beverley argued that vilifying him served no useful purpose. "May it not be presumed . . . that he has met with some unmerited, illiberal treatment? If he has, resentment is natural to all men, and most probably he may be supposed to retaliate."[25]

The alacrity with which patriot agitators exploited their advantages—such as Dunmore's indiscretions—excited Beverley's curiosity about their motives. "I have long apprehended," he told Fitzhugh, "that we had some men amongst us who, from the beginning, have been artfully endeavouring to blow up the seeds of dissatisfaction that they might gradually and wickedly prepare the minds of men for a change of government." These militants, he suspected, had no concrete program. Instead they felt only a vague anticipation that a republic might be more congenial to their restless temperaments than the ordered society of a limited monarchy. Patriot leaders therefore recognized no debt to what Beverley considered the province's traditions of law enforcement, and their committees of safety in many instances have "tyrannized over the liberty of mankind, and trampled upon the very appearance of humanity and justice."[26] Still more suggestive about the motives of agitation, in Beverley's eyes, was the conduct of colonial printers in publishing anti-British tracts and their ambition to "flatter our prejudices and fascinate our understandings."[27] Typically, he came to no definite conclusions about the motives of agitators. Their conduct suggested to him their lack of appreciation of colonial political traditions, their inability to select concrete goals, and their willingness to undermine the liberties of their critics. Unable to proceed beyond these indefinite suggestions about their motives, he relied on the imagery of disease to satisfy his desire for explanation. He returned repeatedly to the "inflamed" condition of their minds and those of their converts. The printers' ambition to "fascinate our understandings" indicated, suggestively, the nature of the sickness.

The resort to emotional persuasion and the encouragement of intimidation made, in Beverley's eyes, the colonial defense of liberty ambiguous. Throughout the controversy that ambiguity made him feel more comfortable in his own precarious neutrality. Even when he tried to put the best possible face on the colonists' cause in a letter to an English merchant in September 1774, he underlined its ambiguity. "I profess myself strongly for moderate though not submissive measures," he explained. The colonists wanted "liberty, not licentiousness [nor] independence." If pushed too far they might try to develop their own manufacturing capacity, but such austerity would be unpleasant. "I would not have you infer from hence that this measure is the object of our choice," he cautioned his correspondent. "It is a step which cruelty, injustice, and necessity have driven us to." Quickly he qualified himself: "independence we desire not, as we are conscious it must be as serious to ourselves as to you, and must involve us in endless misery." In this light he reassured the merchant about the purposes of the non-importation association initiated by the First Continental Congress. It was not an act of defiance, but a safety valve, "a means of extricating many people from their present distresses."[28] Beverley's inability to take a resolute position on the validity of colonial grievances or the propriety of non-importation was rooted in his yearning for repose. "Little more is required," he declared, "to bring this dreadful dispute to a fortunate and honorable issue . . . than to consider ourselves as members of the British Empire."[29] Only tactics "of the negative cast," he warned Fitzhugh, could serve the cause of liberty.[30]

Throughout the year of crisis in Virginia, roughly between the summers of 1774 and 1775, he tried to find something constructive to say. When he did so he moved erratically from one suggestion to another, uncertain of his facts or their meaning to politically conscious Virginians. He praised the period of relative calm during Lord Botetourt's term as governor (1768–1770) and deduced from that example an argument for restraint in dealing with Britain. He dwelled on a host of dangers created by the controversy. As an alternative he proposed a scheme of negotiated reconciliation which seemed to him to go to the heart of the imperial problem. His compulsion to speak on these issues, if even to a small audience of other planters, occurred in fits and starts during his period of general avoidance of political activity. The process became all the more painful as his relations with Landon Carter continued to deteriorate. "I heard perhaps a pretended excuse from Blandfield [Beverley's estate] for its coolness to Sabine Hall," Carter wrote in his diary in August 1775. "It seems the conceited wise one attempted, in his trammelled way of condemning all measures publikly fallen upon to support our liberties."[31]

To Carter's astonishment Beverley saw no oppressive pattern in recent British policy and he separated Virginia's political interests in the controversy from those of other colonies. No British encroachment had occurred in Virginia, he declared, since 1770, when Parliament had partially repealed the Townshend duties. So restricted was his definition of a British encroachment that he saw no danger to Virginia's liberty in the Tea Act or Coercive Acts. Having disposed of more recent developments, he turned to consider Lord Botetourt's term as royal governor and depicted it as a happy interlude during which discontent evaporated. Citing two pieces of evidence, which seemed to him conclusive, he recalled Botetourt's speech announcing partial repeal of the Townshend duties and the Burgesses' conciliatory reply. He also called attention to the statue which the Burgesses purchased to honor Botetourt. These considerations, he concluded, "ought in some measure to have restrained our passion for laying aside government."[32] These suggestions revealed Beverley's scepticism about the cumulative dangers of British policies and about the durability of colonial unity. He therefore feared that colonial retaliation would jeopardize colonial interests, especially Virginia's, far more than a continuation of their present difficulties. Non-importation, for example, was particularly dangerous. British merchants, he warned, would not consider an embargo as a temporary delay in the payment of planter debts but as an absolute repudiation of those obligations; non-importation would not only destroy the planters' credit standing, it would needlessly ruin "nine-tenths of the persons engaged in this trade." Finally, it would not deprive the British treasury of needed revenues because Parliament had enacted the Tea Act "more . . . as a precedent" than as a revenue measure.[33]

As an alternative to these precipitate actions, Beverley proposed a plan of negotiated reconciliation which constituted his most forthright contribution to the pre-Revolutionary debate and the furthermost extent of his reluctant participation in it. In the summer of 1774 he had presented a version of his plan to a meeting of freeholders in Essex County. The colonies, he urged, should send a delegation of prominent colonists with mercantile experience to London, which would reiterate colonial opposition to Parliamentary taxation but temper that stand with the offer of an annual contribution to the cost of imperial defense. The negotiators should reaffirm colonial sympathy for the plight of Boston and request repeal of the Coercive Acts. If the ministry did not respond sympathetically to these suggestions, they should appeal directly to the British electorate.[34] The Essex freeholders declined to endorse Beverley's proposals; in Landon Carter's view they found them "too round about and too passive for people infringed in their common right."[35] Beverley's hopes declined even more when the First Continental Congress showed no more interest in reconciliation. Congress's action was all the more tragic for Beverley because he felt "fully persuaded that the ministry and nation . . . are cordially disposed to accommodate the matter." Britain, he argued, had made a meaningful gesture by proposing Lord North's plan of conciliation. Conceding the unpopularity of North's proposals, he characteristically declared, "I do not by any means approve it, but am sincerely concerned it was not made use of for the purpose of opening a negotiation."[36]

4

The failure of the colonies to seek reconciliation rendered meaningless Beverley's sole concrete suggestion. His halting retreat into isolation left a terminal moraine of warnings about the consequences of independence, but primarily he nursed personal grievances against men who had ostracized him. Acknowledging his ignorance of what colonial leaders were actually doing, he felt that his disregard of tactical considerations gave him a clearer vision of larger problems. "Take it from me," he told Fitzhugh, "though [I am] *no adept in politicks,* as my present character will plainly evince, . . . America can enjoy no solid or even tolerable advantages from an independence."[37] The colonies, he asserted, could only prosper in close commercial relationship with Britain; they needed British protection from European powers; they possessed neither the technical skills nor resources to wage war against Britain. The disunity of the colonies, their proliferation of political systems, religious groups, and ways of life all undermined their apparent unity. "It is true indeed that there seems to be a union of sorts at present, but . . . only in appearance. Ambition, resentment, and interest have united us for a moment." But inevitable disagreements about taxes, the autonomy of the states, the powers of the central government, and the conduct of foreign policy would surely tear apart any American union. In the face of these perils, negotiations with the British ministry seemed a mild ordeal. Regretting the unwillingness of the House of Burgesses to seek reconciliation, Beverley condemned the representatives for jeopardizing the safety of their constituents. Had the responsibility been his, Beverley declared, "I would scrupulously have kept the claims and grievances of the people in view, and would in an ingenuous and declaratory stile have laid them before the Crown." Nothing more complicated seemed necessary. "These [grievances] would have been attended to, and no exception could have been made to the propriety or legality of the petition."[38]

As his hopes for negotiation and restraint crumbled, Beverley could only ponder his own position. The hostility with which other planters regarded his neutrality and criticism of whig tactics caused him unrelenting pain. "I want only to vindicate myself in the estimate of my friends," he told Fitzhugh, "from the cruel suspicion of being unfriendly to my country." He encountered that suspicion in what seemed to him bizarre forms. Men suspected him of seeking special favors from Governor Dunmore, he complained, and even of aspiring to a position in the royal government. All he desired, he replied, was to be left alone to tend his plantations and enjoy the companionship of his family. That privacy was, for Beverley, his "constitutional liberty." Though resisting bitterness, he occasionally burst out in resentment before lapsing into despondency. "You seem surprised," he told Fitzhugh, "that I should conceive I have been ill-treated by my quondam friends. But I tell you I have been, and by some nearly allied to me—or mine." He wished his tormentors well in their political ambition but questioned whether they would find inner satisfaction. What hurt him was not their disagreement with his views, but their inability to separate personal regard from public differences. "It is astonishing," he complained, "that men cannot differ in political opinions without unhinging their former intimacies." In his complete withdrawal from the issues of the pre-Revolutionary debate, he could define his feelings about events only in terms of the damage men had done to his self-esteem. Tolerance and relaxed discussion had always been an essential feature of gentry society, he reflected. Men had an obligation to state their views candidly and temperately. In his limited participation in political discussion he believed he had always done so.

The apprehension he felt, but could not fully express, impelled him in July 1775 to state in conceptual terms his perception of what had happened to political discourse: "I do not esteem a man a jot the less for differing with me in opinion; 'til of late it was common to do so. But by some strange metamorphosis or other, this contrariety of opinions is denied." *"Some strange metamorphosis or other"*—this comment came close to expressing the essence of his view of the Revolution. Because he perceived no difference between ordinary discussion and intense political strife, he could not realize that for his contemporaries the pre-Revolutionary debate had passed the stage of a conversation between gentlemen. Driven by events he profoundly misunderstood, he tried to acquiesce gracefully. "I have found the torrent strong, and therefore shall not oppose it," he wrote, concluding his apologia to Fitzhugh. "The die is cast; 1 must await the event with melancholy concern." To the end he kept his fundamental commitment clearly in view. "I have always endeavored to avoid any side but that of reason and justice," he wrote in a perceptive summary of his conduct. "I have ever disliked the idea of being thought a party man."[39]

Appendix: Robert Beverley to William Fitzhugh, July 20, 1775

My Dear Sir,[40]

I received your very kind Letter and return You my warmest Thanks for it, as it conveys Sentiments I shall ever remember. In these Times of civil Dissensions there is no Virtue more rare or uncommon than a Spirit of *true* Christianity; otherwise a Difference of Opinion on the Part of the Minority would never [ever?] draw down the Vengeance or Persecution of the Majority upon every Man who, perhaps unfortunately for himself, cannot relinquish his own Opinions to adopt others which he cannot from Principle approve. I think I may venture to affirm I have never yet met with a Virginian or scarce even a Foreigner who does not deny any Right to be vested in Parliament to tax America, to remove us out of our own Vicinage for Tryal[41] or in any Instance to burthen us with arbitrary or oppressive Laws or Regulations. The few People who think like me are persuaded we ought to consider ourselves as Members of the British Empire, that we should endeavour to ease the Nation of Part of the Interest of a Debt mostly incurred by entering into a War for our Protection and Support,[42] that the Quantity of this Aid together with the Mode of raising it ought to be left entirely to the Direction of our constitutional Representatives, who ought to exert themselves to the utmost to assist the parent State upon every honourable Occasion. When I tell You these are my real Sentiments, that they are Sentiments formed upon the most mature Reflection, improved by the Arguments of Men of Probity and Ability, and confirmed by the Writings of Authors of Merit and Discernment of all Parties, it appears astonishing how any Man can consider me as a Traitor or indeed in any other Light than that of a true Patriot. Compare these Opinions with your own expressed in your Letter and You will find how very nearly they assimilate with yours. I do not wish to animadvert on your Conduct because it may differ from mine, but only to vindicate myself in the Estimation of my Friends from the cruel Suspicion of being unfriendly to my Country; but I cannot help observing that You surprise me much when You tell me that at the Beginning of this Dispute you relied upon the Opinions of Men whose Abilities You thought superior to your own. I never could take up Opinions by Wholesale, let who would advance them, because a Man must be possessed of Integrity and Knowledge, both natural and acquired, before I can venture to build my Faith implicitly on him. He must not be ambitious, artful, or malicious because if he is so, his Judgment will be biassed and his Abilities will render him the more dangerous Adviser. For these several Reasons, in all Disputes of this important Nature, I always conceived it the Duty of every Man to inform himself fully of the Ground on which it began and the Machinations by which designing Men on both Sides of the Water proposed to carry it on. This I endeavoured to sift out minutely and without Prejudice and this I verily believe I have amply discovered in this Investigation, having found a Self-Interest and want of Candour on both Sides. I could never fully approve of the Conduct of either or give into the extravagant Encomiums I have heard on one Side or applaud the illiberal Abuse thrown out on the other. I could have wished the Commencement of our Opposition had a more honorable Foundation than the Destruction of the Tea at Boston because Injustice can never be palliated, let it come from what Quarter it will. I never could think so violent a Transaction was the Effect of Patriotism, and think it is proved beyond a Doubt that it was committed from the Resentment arising from the Impossibility there would be of smuggling to Advantage provided the East-India Company were allowed to export Tea under that Act of Parliament. They had acquiesced under the Tax by importing in the Course of 2 Years into the Town of Boston 2000 Chests for which they paid this Duty,[43] and upon the Rumour of the Companies sending their Tea, several Merchants, particularly at Boston, expressly directed their Correspondents not to ship them any, provided the Company persevered in sending theirs. Some of these private Orders had directed so much as 60 Chests. Considering the Matter in this Light, and I verily believe it is the only true Light in which it can be considered, let me ask how far the Destruction of the Tea was influenced by virtuous Principles and with what Propriety could America applaud their Conduct when some few Years before, She beheld with Silence and Unconcern the Legislature of New York suspended because they would not submit to an arbitrary and oppressive Act of Parliament for billiting the Soldiers.[44] I say we sat silent and unconcerned at this scandalous Encroachment upon the Liberties of America and in a Moment took Fire upon the Report of an Injury offered to Boston. This then being the true state of the Matter, I shall ingenously confess to You that I think the Punishment inflicted upon the Bostonians at large for the Transgression of a Part highly unjust and oppressive. A Compensation ought first to have been demanded of the Town, which being denied would perhaps have rendered this rigorous Proceeding more excuseable, and in all human Probability had an Indemnification been required at first this unhappy Dispute might have been happily adjusted. Thus therefore I must lament that this unnatural civil War took its Rise from such a Cause. I cannot agree with some People whom I have heard insist that the Charter of a Colony cannot be revoked. These Charters were granted with an Expectation that People living under their Protection should demean themselves as dutiful and loyal Subjects, and as long as they should continue to do so, they were to live in the quiet Enjoyment of their Privileges, but so soon as they should endeavour to throw off all necessary Restraint and commit unjustifiable or lawless Outrages they would certainly deserve Chastisement and such a Government as should be able to bridle their licentious spirit. I do not apply this to the People of Massachusetts Bay because I do not think the Destruction of the Tea was sufficient to authorize so flagrant an Innovation. But for my own Part, I should rejoice at exchanging the Constitution of the Massachusetts Government for any other possessed with greater Governmental Powers, for theirs rests so entirely with the People that they are perpetually engaged in Tumults and Cabals, and I believe it to be absolutely impossible to live upon tolerable Terms with any Governour who wishes to enforce a due Observance of the Laws. I have long apprehended that we have some Men amongst us who, from the Beginning, have been artfully endeavouring to blow up the Seeds of Dissatisfaction that they might gradually and wickedly prepare the Minds of Men for a Change of Government, under the Masque of Virtue and the Parade of being Defenders of public Liberty. You will remember I told You these were my Suspicions some time since. They have since increased, and I verily believe will in a few Months be fully confirmed. Abler Heads than mine have dreaded it, and perhaps when it is too late the patriotic Party will be convinced of the Truth of such Conjectures. I do not set myself up as a finished Statesman, but without being a Conjurer, I think I can discern that a Republick will suit the ambitious and tyrannical Temper of some People much better than the quiet and regular Authority of a limited Monarchy. I see so many Beauties and so great a display of political Wisdom in our Constitution that I cannot look upon any Attempt to subvert it with Patience. I will acknowledge Great Britain hath made some Encroachments upon it and in many Instances hath not exercised that Benignity towards us which Children have a Right to expect from a Parent, but then there hath been little or no Addition to these Encroachments since 1768. Lord Bottetourt's Statue and the Address of the House of Burgesses to that Governour are subsequent to the Tea Act, and ought in some Measure to have restrained our Passion for laying aside Government.[45] I declare to You once more my Veneration for our Constitution and my steady Resolution of exerting myself in Defence of it, but then You will observe when I make this Sacrifice it must be done to preserve it entire, not mutilated or in Part, but possessed of all its Beauties and Blessings, unimpaired by Ambition, Corruption, or Faction. These are my Sentiments upon this important Subject. They are Sentiments formed upon Reflection and the happy Enjoyment of Freedom in its Purity, until June 1, 1772.[46] I am fully persuaded the Ministry and Nation at large are cordially disposed to accomodate this matter. They have made the first Advances, particularly in Lord North's Plan being introduced into the Congress, signed by Grey Cooper, Secretary to the Treasury.[47] I know very well this Plan hath been universally objected to as incompatible with a Reconcilement. I do not by any means approve it, but am sincerely concerned it was not made use of for the Purpose of opening a Negotiation. Had this been done I firmly believe every just Claim would have been allowed, and therefore I cannot applaud any Persons who would omit any Opportunity of accomodating this Dispute. Matters have been precipitated. Our own Powers have been multiplied extravagantly and great Pains used to prepare us for a Change of Government. Time alone will convince us of the Propriety of our Measures and the Integrity of our L- [Leaders?]. Misfortunes will come fast enough upon us. The Southern Colonies, from the Peculiarity and Unhappiness of their Situation, will fall easy Victims upon the first Introduction of a military Force; for if we shall be considered in a State of Rebellion, every Method to subdue us will be deemed honorable and the Emancipation of our Slaves be perhaps the first Declaration, the Consequences of which you will allow to be immediately fatal.[48] For these Reasons therefore I have never approved any Attempt to take up Arms, fully persuaded it was never the Duty or Policy of this feeble Country to tempt Danger and involve itself in such disastrous Calamities. All we could do in Defence of the common Cause was of the negative Cast. The withholding our Commerce during a Continuance of these Disputes must be a prevailing Sort of Argument and in the end prove safe and effectual. But when the Temper of the Time becomes so inflamed and the Judgment of Mankind so much fascinated, it is almost impossible and upon many Occasions extremely dangerous to point out the true Interests of the Country. History furnishes many Examples of this Kind, and my Knowledge of my own Country induces me to think this Reflection somewhat applicable. Very few amongst us have expressed a sufficient Attention at the Commencement of this Dispute to our real Constitution. Shutting up the Courts of Justice was a dangerous Step and has contributed in a great Measure to the Introduction of Anarchy and Oppression. We have seen the Magistrates, the legal Officers of the Public, succeeded by a new Institution,[49] which in many Instances hath tyrannised over the Liberties of Mankind, and trampled upon the very appearance of Humanity and Justice. To these succeeds another Institution,[50] as fond of exercising lawless Power and as little careful of keeping within the Line of our Constitution. It appears to me wonderful in Struggles of this Sort that there can be any Occasion for Tyranny when contending for Freedom or the smallest Necessity for inquisitorial Powers when *we are opposing the Catholick Religion.*[51] The Way to preserve Liberty is by exercising the Privileges of Freedom, not by introducing the Terrors of Torture or the Spirit of Persecution. They appear to me to be natural Enemies of each other, but by a strange Perversion of Nature and Reason *now* constantly attendant on each other. The Appointment of the first Congress I approved most heartily because it seemed as if we had been denied the Rights of Legislation and of laying our Grievances at the Feet of the Throne. I then fondly thought the Minds of Men were as fondly disposed to a Reconcilement as my own, and that we were to make no external Claims. The Delegates from this Country[52] were in some Measure instructed and that gave them additional weight with me.[53] How far they answered the Expectation of the Publick or what Steps they took to bring on an Accomodation, I do not take upon me to say; but certain it is, I do not think their Proceedings unexceptionable or absolutely confined within the Limits or Design of their Appointment. Ever since the Publication of their Resolves, I have *heard* of Anarchy, ill-Blood, and Oppression. I therefore became totally indifferent as to another Meeting of the same kind, and was much surprised when I found this second Choice made with unlimited Powers and a House of Burgesses declaring they were not competent as to a Redress of the Grievances of People. I may venture to assure you as a Friend to me and the common Rights of Mankind that as a Representative of the People and attached to our excellent Constitution, I never would have made such a formal and deliberate Surrender of my Trust and Dignity into the Hands of any second Estate. I would scrupulously have kept the Claims and Grievances of the People in View and would in an ingenuous and declaratory Stile have laid them before the Crown. I should have chearfully embraced the Offer made by Government of meeting in a constitutional Way and with Spirit, Firmness, and Candour would have assirted our Claims. These would have been attended to and no Exception could have been made to the Propriety or Legality of the Petition. This would have brought on a Reconciliation, and our Liberties would have been established upon an honorable and permanent Basis. The other Assemblies had the same Opportunities and would have derived the same glorious Advantages. You may be assured I am far from wishing for a Defection of any particular Colony as to a Demand of the Confirmation of our just Rights and Privileges. The Crown and People of Great Britain I must suppose do not wish to deprive us of these valuable Blessings. A Ministry hath been mistaken but does it follow from thence that upon any Misunderstanding we should wantonly involve ourselves and our Friends—for Friends I must esteem Great Britain, and valuable ones too—in misfortunes of the most lamentable Kind purely that we may speak a dictatorial Language or idly suppose they mean to reduce us to a State of Slavery? Take it from me, though *no Adept in Politicks,* as my present Character will plainly evince, that America can enjoy no solid or even tolerable Advantages from an Independence on Great Britain. We are, notwithstanding our Gasconades, in the Southern Colonies extremely feeble and ill-qualified for Opposition. We are calculated for a great commercial People. We may rise, grow rich, and be happy under the fostering Protection of Great Britain. But, without her parental Aid, must become Victims to the first foreign Invader. We have neither Arms, Ammunition, or Ships to protect our Commerce. We have no Resources to conduct War and no Artisans to carry on Manufactures or improve us in the Arts of Life. We are an infant Country, unconnected in Interest and naturally disunited by Inclination. Our Forms of Government differ egregiously, but our religious Tenets still more so. Our Modes of Life vary, and our Articles of Commerce interfere prodigiously. Nor are we naturally more disjointed in Situation than in Temper. It is true indeed there seems to be a Sort of Union at present, but I am afraid it is only in Appearance. Ambition, Resentment, and Interest may have united us for a Moment but be assured, when Interests shall interfere and a Dispute shall arise concerning Superiority, a Code of Laws, and all the Concomitants of a new Government, that that Union will soon be converted into Envy, Malevolence, and Faction, and most probably will introduce a greater Degree of Opposition than even now prevails against the Mother Country. History is full of such Examples, and what has happened once may and probably will happen again. Considering therefore our Ideas of Independence in this serious Light I think it absurdly ridiculous and highly criminal in any Man, or Set of Men, to widen a Breach which can be so easily and so happily closed. Such however I do suspect there are, and such I do say deserve the Execrations of Mankind. Their Projects are chimerical but must, if adopted, ultimately end in our Ruin. I give you my honest Word that there is not a Man in America who would more chearfully and resolutely enter into an Opposition against our

King than I should, could I see any thing which could convince me he intended
to lay aside his Character of Chief Magistrate and stalk forth as the Tyrant of his
People.[54] But until I find that to be the case—and I believe I never shall—I shall
think my Allegiance due to him and him alone. I do not pretend, nay, I cannot
applaud the Conduct of our Governour. In publick life it may be weak, capricious,
and ill-advised. In private it may be very reprehensible. But be it what it will, as a
Man we have nothing to do with it, and I will venture to affirm to You his Example is not so brilliant as to tempt me to set him down as a Model. I am much
removed from the Scene of Action, nor have I seen more than one of your Members since the Adjournment of the House. He and I agreed pretty well in Sentiments and Conjectures, but I think he gives too much into the common Opinion
that is as to the malicious designs of Lord Dunmore. That he [Dunmore] is not
friendly disposed towards the Country, I am afraid, may be too well presumed.
But may it not be presumed also that he has met with some unmerited, illiberal
Treatment? If he has, Resentment is natural to all Men, and most probably he may
be supposed to retaliate. I never had any intimacy with Lord Dunmore. I never
saw an Instance of his ill-Behaviour, but yet I do not say that he is incapable of
behaving ill. If I am to believe every Story propagated to his disadvantage, I must
think him a Villain and a Blackguard of no common Cast; but still to be consistent, I must and will make allowances for Exaggeration. Envy is a prevailing
Vice and a Vice productive of almost all the others. Therefore every thing we hear
ought not to be credited, nor ought our Opinions to be formed on current Reports. I know it has been suggested that I have paid Court to Lord Dunmore, and
that I want a Place. It is very difficult for a Man so to conduct himself, as to be
exempt from Obloquy, and to undertake it is a task too difficult for me. I am conscious of the Rectitude of my own Intentions, and, let the Temper of the Times
be even more dangerous than they are, my Conscience shall be my Guide. If that
acquits me, I shall be happy, although I end my Life on a Gibbet. To You, as my
Friend, I will impart any thing, and to You I will declare ingenuously that I neither directly or indirectly have solicited the smiles of Lord Dunmore or any other
Governour. I have an ample Fortune, and can be happy in the enjoyment of that,
and an endearing Family. I ask no further Favour of my Country than the quiet
Possession of it, and think I have so conducted myself, both in publick and private Life, as justly to be entitled to it. I want no Post of Profit, and if any honorable
one should be conferred on me I presume I have a Right to accept it, although I
have not the smallest Reason to expect it. Nor do I deem myself either a Sage, a
Fool, or Villain. I envy no Man the good things of this Life, or the Pageantry of
ministerial or popular Honors. I never solicited the Great nor ever will court the
People. Retirement suits me extremely well, and in that humble Walk I shall be
content to end my Days in Peace and the enjoyment of my constitutional Liberty,
free from Faction on one Side and Corruption on the other. You seem surprised
that I should conceive I have been ill-treated by my quondam Friends. I tell You
expressly that I have and by some nearly allied to me—or mine. They may be

happy in their Positions and carry them with them, if they can *conscientiously,* to the other World. In this World I shall never court their Acquaintance. It is very astonishing that Men cannot differ in political Opinions without unhinging their former Intimacies. It is certainly a Right inherent in all free Countries, and it seems Virginia is looked upon as such an one, for every Man to speak his Sentiments with Decency and Candour. I am not conscious of having violated this Rule, and therefore think my *Friends* have transgressed the Bounds of Justice. I declare to God I do not esteem a Man a Jot the less for differing from me in Opinion; until of late it was common to do so, but by some strange Metamorphosis or other, this Contrariety of Opinions is denied, and it would seem as if the World was drawing to an End, that being one of the distinguishing Characteristicks of the last Day. I set out at first, that Opposition was just; but have always since October at least disagreed as to the Mode of Opposition. I have found the Torrent strong, and therefore shall not oppose it, but whenever I see any thing I can approve, I shall cordially accede thereto. In the mean time as the Die is cast, I must wait the Event with melancholy Concern. I may hereafter appear what I at this Moment hope I am, an Honest Man. Having perused this long Scroll you will be able to determine whether my Principles are bad, or whether I am mistaken in my political Creed. I have greedily sought after Information, and shall ever hold myself open to Conviction; but the Conviction I shall willingly submit to is that of sound Sense and Argument, not Force or the prevailing Fashion of the Times. I am extremely and affectionately obliged to You for your Concern upon Account of the Side *I have taken* in this dispute. I always endeavoured to avoid any Side but that of Reason and Justice. I have ever disliked the Idea of being thought a Party-Man, and declare I do not think in this Instance I can be justly called one. If I do deserve to be thought violently attached to any Party, I acknowledge myself rivitted to the reconciling one, if such an one there can be found. One thing I can seriously assure You is that I am attached to You in the strictest Sense of Friendship however we may differ in Politicks, and am with my best Wishes for the Prosperity of You and Your's.

Your &c . . .

[Robert Beverley]

Notes

1. Bernard Bailyn, *The Ideological Origins of the American Revolution* (Cambridge, Mass., 1967), p. vi; on the theme of indecision and ambivalence during the pre-Revolutionary crisis, see Wallace Brown, *The King's Friends: The Composition and Motives of the American Loyalist Claimants* (Providence, R.I., 1966), pp. 251–52; William H. Nelson, *The American Tory* (Oxford, 1961), chap. vi; Alan Heimert, *Religion and the American Mind from the Great Awakening to the Revolution* (Cambridge, Mass., 1966), chap. viii; Leonard Woods Labaree, *Conservatism in Early American History* (New York, 1948), pp. 156–66; Sydney V. James, "The Impact of the American Revolution on Quakers' Ideas about Their Sect," *William and Mary Quarterly,* 3rd ser., 19 (1962), 360–82.

2. David D. Wallace, *The Life of Henry Laurens* (New York, 1915), pp. 207–12; cf. *The Works of John Witherspoon* (Edinburgh, 1805), vol. 7, pp. 103–104.

3. [Richard Wells], *A Few Political Reflections*... (Philadelphia, 1774), pp. 26, 59–60, and *The Middle Line*... (Philadelphia, 1775), p. 3.

4. *Proceedings of the Massachusetts Historical Society,* Second ser. (1885–1886), vol. 2, pp. 481–86.

5. William Smith, *Sermon on the Present Situation of American Affairs*... (Philadelphia, 1775), p. 19.

6. Robert M. Calhoon, ed., "'A Sorrowful Spectator of These Tumultuous Times': Robert Beverley Describes the Coming of the Revolution," *Virginia Magazine of History and Biography,* 73 (1965), 41–42.

7. Beverley to Edward Athawes, July 11, 1761, Robert Beverley Letterbook, 1761–1793, Library of Congress.

8. Beverley to Page, Nov. 10, 1761, Beverley Letterbook, Library of Congress.

9. Beverley to Edward Athawes, March 3, [1762], Beverley Letterbook; on Beverley's indebtedness and his comparatively successful efforts "eventually to surmount his financial difficulties," see Emory G. Evans, "Planter Indebtedness and the Coming of the Revolution in Virginia," *William and Mary Quarterly,* 3rd ser., 19 (1962): 521, and on his property holdings during the 1790s, see Jackson T. Main, "The One Hundred," *William and Mary Quarterly,* 3rd ser., 11 (1954): 369.

10. Charles Carter to Landon Carter, Jan. 4, 1763, Sabine Hall Collection, Alderman Library, University of Virginia.

11. Jack P. Greene, ed., *The Diary of Colonel Landon Carter of Sabine Hall,* 1752–1778 (Charlottesville, Va., 1965), vol. 2, p. 704.

12. Robert Beverley-Landon Carter Correspondence, Dec. 23, 1771, Colonial Williamsburg, Sabine Hall Collection.

13. Beverley to Carter, Aug. 28, 1774, Robert Beverley-Landon Carter Correspondence, typescript, Research Department, Colonial Williamsburg, Inc., p. 38.

14. Beverley-Carter Correspondence, p. 43; on Landon Carter's relationships with his children, see Jack P. Greene's introduction to the *Diary of Landon Carter,* vol. 1, pp. 52–57.

15. Calhoon, ed., "'A Sorrowful Spectator ... ,'" p. 46 n. 9; Beverley to Carter, Oct. 9, 1765, Beverley-Carter Correspondence, pp. 9–10.

16. Beverley to Carter (fragment), Oct. 7, 1770, Beverley-Carter Correspondence, p. 21.

17. Beverley to Carter, Dec. 23, 1771, Sabine Hall Collection.

18. Calhoon, ed., "'A Sorrowful Spectator ... ,'" p. 42.

19. Beverley to Samuel Athawes, [n.d. ca. June 1775], Beverley Letterbook.

20. Gordon S. Wood, "Rhetoric and Reality in the American Revolution," *William and Mary Quarterly,* 3rd ser., 23 (1966): 27–30.

21. Beverley to Samuel Athawes, [ca. June, 1775], Beverley Letterbook.

22. Beverley to William Fitzhugh, July 20, 1775, Calhoon, ed., "'A Sorrowful Spectator ... ,'" pp. 45–46, 48; the significance of this letter is discussed on pp. 42–45, "'A Sorrowful Spectator. ... '"

23. Calhoon, ed., "'A Sorrowful Spectator ... ,'" pp. 47–48.

24. Calhoon, ed., "'A Sorrowful Spectator ... ,'" p. 48; on Virginia's reaction to the suspension of the New York Assembly, see "'A Sorrowful Spectator ... ,'" n. 11.

25. Calhoon, ed., "'A Sorrowful Spectator ... ,'" pp. 47–49, 53.

26. Calhoon, ed., "'A Sorrowful Spectator ... ,'" p. 50.

27. Beverley to John Backhouse, Aug. 10, 1775, Beverley Letterbook.

28. Beverley to ?, Sept. 6, 1774, Beverley Letterbook.

29. Beverley to Samuel Athawes, June 6, 1775, Beverley Letterbook.

30. Calhoon, ed., "'A Sorrowful Spectator . . . ,'" p. 50.

31. Greene, ed., *The Diary of Landon Carter,* vol. 2, pp. 933–34.

32. Calhoon, ed., "'A Sorrowful Spectator . . . ,'" p. 49; Beverley misunderstood the Burgesses' response to Botetourt, see n. 12, "'A Sorrowful Spectator. . . .'"

33. Beverley to Carter, June 18 and Aug. 28, 1774, Beverley-Carter Correspondence, pp. 35–36, 38–43.

34. Beverley-Carter Correspondence, pp. 46–47.

35. Carter's marginal notation, Beverley-Carter Correspondence, p. 48.

36. Calhoon, ed., "'A Sorrowful Spectator . . . ,'" p. 49.

37. Calhoon, ed., "'A Sorrowful Spectator . . . ,'" p. 52.

38. Calhoon, ed., "'A Sorrowful Spectator . . . ,'" p. 51.

39. Calhoon, ed., "'A Sorrowful Spectator . . . ,'" pp. 53–55; on Beverley's experience after 1775, see Calhoon, ed., "'A Sorrowful Spectator . . . ,'" p. 45 n. 10. See also "American Nationalism and Other Loyalties in the Southern Colonies, 1763–1775," *Journal of Southern History,* 34 (1968): 50–75 and Robert M. Calhoon, review of William Eddis, *Letters from America,* Aubrey C. Land, ed., *Studies in Burke and his Time,* 13 (1971–72): 2168–71.

40. Calhoon, ed. "A Sorrowful Spectator . . . ," 55.

41. Beverley referred here to the provisions of the Administration of Justice Act, 1774, providing for the transportation of certain offenders in Massachusetts to Britain or other colonies for trial (see *English Historical Documents: American Colonial Documents to 1776,* Merrill Jensen, ed. [London, 1955], p. 784, and compare the wording in Jefferson's *Summary View,* in *Papers of Thomas Jefferson,* Julian P. Boyd, ed. [Princeton, 1950–2006], vol. 1, pp. 128–29).

42. Few Virginians would have agreed with Beverley that British protection during the Seven Years' War obligated the colonies to acquiesce to British policy after the war. His father-in-law put it forcefully: "[The British] talk of the Protection given to the Colonies. I will first . . . ask what sort of Protection that is which demands a Slavery in return. The Colonists, had this been the alternative, either to submit to the scalping knives of the Indians sharpened by the French or the chains of . . . . , could not have made a moments hesitation in the choice. The one must certainly end in death; but then it would have ended their misery also in a few days; but the other: a whole lifetime of misery!" (Landon Carter to a correspondent in London, November 30, 1765, Sabine Hall Collection, Alderman Library, University of Virginia). Indeed Beverley himself felt the same way in 1763 when he wrote irritably of British criticism of Virginia's currency laws as "a very genteel . . . method of repaying our *ridiculous* and overzealous Loyalty in the Course of the late War" (Beverley to John Bland, May 5, 1763, Beverley letter book).

43. Beverley's estimate of 2,000 chests of tea was reasonably accurate; Oliver M. Dickerson has set the exact figure of chests of tea imported into Boston from 1771 to 1773 at 1,643 chests (*The Navigation Acts and the American Revolution* [Philadelphia, 1951], p. 101).

44. This apparently referred to the Act of Parliament of 1767 suspending the New York Assembly if it refused to enact quartering legislation. That Virginians "beheld" the suspension "with Silence and Unconcern" was debatable; see, for example, *Virginia Gazette* (Purdie and Dixon), July 21, 1768.

45. The House of Burgesses did thank Botetourt for his address announcing the partial repeal of the Townshend duties, but the House's reaction scarcely suggested any confidence in British intentions. The Burgesses warned, "We will not suffer our present Hopes, arising from the pleasing Prospect your Lordship hath so kindly . . . displayed to us, to be dashed by the bitter Reflection that any future Administration will entertain a wish to depart from that Plan" (*The Journals of the House of Burgesses of Virginia, 1766–1769,* John P. Kennedy, ed. [Richmond, 1906], p. 233). The statue of Botetourt, to which Beverley referred, signified the governor's personal popularity rather than any acceptance of British policy (*Virginia Gazette* [Purdie and Dixon], July 25, 1771).

46. The significance of this date is not clear; perhaps he alluded to the burning of the *Gaspee* on June 9, 1772.

47. On Lord North's plan for reconciliation, see Weldon A. Brown, *Empire or Independence: A Study of the Failure of Reconciliation, 1774–1783* (University, La., 1941), pp. 35–37; on Grey Cooper, secretary to the treasury under Lord North, see Dora Mae Clark, *The Rise of the British Treasury* (New Haven, 1960), p. 178.

48. Beverley's fear that the South would bear the brunt of the war supports John R. Alden's view that a southern regional consciousness began to develop during the Revolutionary period (*The First South* [Baton Rouge, 1961], esp. pp. 29–30). Beverley anticipated Lord Dunmore's proclamation offering freedom to slaves who joined the British side (Benjamin Quarles, "Lord Dunmore as Liberator," *William and Mary Quarterly,* 3rd ser., 15 [1958]: 494–507).

49. That is, the Associations in Virginia.

50. The county committees of safety in Virginia (*The Committees of Safety of Westmoreland and Fincastle: Proceedings of the County Committees, 1774–1776,* Richard B. Harwell, ed. [Richmond, 1956]).

51. An indirect allusion to the anti-Catholic colonial antagonism of the Quebec Act, 1774.

52. Virginia.

53. Jefferson wrote these instructions, *Papers of Thomas Jefferson,* vol. 1, pp. 141–43.

54. For other views of George III, see Stella Duff, "The Case against the King: The *Virginia Gazettes* Indict George III," *William and Mary Quarterly,* 3rd ser., 6 (1949): 383–97.

The Uses of Reason in Political Upheaval

ROBERT M. CALHOON

The search for accommodation reflected the ordeal of men who wanted to find practical ways of reconciling colonial liberty with the maintenance of British authority. As events swept past them, they tried to adjust their thinking to the rapidly changing conditions and to gauge the dynamics of the imperial controversy in order to find standards of analysis and conduct that they and their fellow men could use in a dispute in which both sides seemed to be wrong, misguided, or lost.[1]

The threatening polarization of British policy and colonial response provoked and fueled the search for accommodation. "Affairs are now brought to a crisis," wrote Edward Burd, of Pennsylvania, in July 1774, in a typical discovery of this fact. "The Parliament of Great Britain claim and have endeavored to enforce the right of taxing America," while the colonists deny "that such a right exists and [are] determined to oppose the execution of it to blood. If they both persist in a determined resolution of this kind, wretched will be the situation of us both." Repeatedly these diagnoses of British and colonial folly sprang from the sense of helplessness and foreboding each man felt. The entire range of advantages that accrued to the colonists from their "connection with Great Britain," including the British legal and religious heritage, a supply of British products, the protection of the fleet and army, and the role of the Crown as mediator of colonial disputes, had "sheltered" the colonies from the "machinations of all the powers of Europe," declared another Pennsylvanian; "no wonder, therefore, we look forward with horror to those convulsions which must attend ([for] ages hence) our separation from that country." But it was equally unthinkable, the writer continued, to acquiesce further to British directives. The colonists had to find a way to weather "the storm of British vengeance and tyranny." Britain's insistence on its power to tax the colonists, wrote Richard Wells, in June 1774, was "so unjust, so unnatural, and absurd that ... every American ... must unite in opposing it," but "to oppose force to force is what the heart of every American must revolt at." The real danger was that "the base profligacy of a ministry abandoned to every principle of virtue and raging for despotism" would "tempt" the colonists and British brothers "to sheave sword into each other's bowels." There must be, Wells pleaded, "surer, safer ways to end the controversy." The alternatives of submission and rebellion repeatedly provoked an unstable mixture of urgent alarm and bewilderment. "What are we to do! Tamely to give up our rights and suffer to be taxed at the will of persons at such a distance . . . is to consent to be slaves. . . . How dreadful the thought of a contest with the parent country," the Reverend Andrew Eliot sadly declared. A considerable feat of imagination was needed to conceive of a resolution of the imperial impasse that would escape the twin evils of submission and bloody conflict. "May the cloud which hangs over Great Britain and the colonies," declared the proposer of a toast at a Philadelphia banquet for Congressional delegates, in September 1774, "burst *only* on the heads of the present ministry." Few sober men thought the explosion could be so neatly deflected.[2]

The looming poles of submission and rebellion raised discomforting questions about the mentality of the British ministry and the colonists' capacity to respond intelligently to hostile British policies. "I am not a malcontent," declared Eliot, "but . . . I see nothing but little, mean, sinister views in those who have direction of your public affairs." Their stubborn legalistic view of the colonies, Eliot feared, would only ignite the passions of volatile men, whose rash actions, in turn, would provoke even harsher British reactions. "There are men with you and men with us," he shuddered, "who regard no consequence if they can gratify their passions." Lenient, mild, healing measures alone, he stressed, would disarm the rash and impetuous. As the controversy moved toward its conclusion, the men of accommodation increasingly realized that only colonial exertion could guide British policy back into reasonable channels. Americans must avoid "abject servility" and "unbecoming petulancy" in order to disarm hostile British intentions, advised a Philadelphian in January 1775. "We must have the strictest guard on our passions," urged Richard Wells, in order to keep the initiative and respond to British provocations with calm deliberation. Governor Tryon, of New York, understood the moderate dilemma. "The American friends of government," he explained in August 1775, "consider themselves between Scylla and Charybdis, that is the head of Parliamentary taxation and the tyranny of their present [Revolutionary] masters; would the first principle be put out of the way, his Majesty would probably see America put on a less determined complexion."[3]

The search for a viable alternative to the awful choice between submission and Revolutionary tyranny began with an evaluation of the location and function of reason in politics. For the rationalist clergy of New England, reason meant many things: it was the opposite of evangelical enthusiasm and pietistic fervor; it motivated restraint and self-discipline and thereby encouraged the spread and practice of true religion; most important, reason taught the rationalist clergy that men were not fundamentally sinful in their nature. Elements of this intellectual position permeated widely the search for accommodation in the pre-Revolutionary debate.

The strongest imperative behind this search for reason was the need to locate and localize the human evil manifested by British policy and colonial disobedience.

Both the colonies and mother country were victims of "the grand enemy of mankind," who uses "every opportunity to raise up heats and animosities, to stir up depraved passions . . . to do his destructive work. . . . The heads and rulers of societies are men of like passions and infirmities with their subjects." Above all, the rationalist clergy stressed, evil circulated through society and tempted men, rather than springing internally from their very natures. George III was therefore "a prince, whose goodness of soul and unsuspecting heart, unfortunately for his people, have unwarily betrayed him into the ensnaring measures of designing men." On this assumption that rulers were good men and subject to external temptation the rationalist search for accommodation built its case for restraint and prudence. Rulers, the Reverend John Tucker declared, had the same interests in the welfare of the community as the people; "they are both parts of the same body, their true interests are interwoven, and their happiness inseparable." This mutuality of interests made resistance to tyranny a formalized and restricted activity. The people had a right and a duty to oppose tyranny, the Reverend Gad Hitchcock announced in 1774, but only as a means of appealing to the ruler's prudence and good sense. Given the opportunity of responding to the protests of the community, any ruler would prefer to base his power on "the surest foundation," the esteem and respect of the people. Self-interest alone assured the success of remonstrance. By institutionalizing resistance in this way and making it a means of communication with the ruler, the rationalists acted on their assumption that men were basically good and reasonable.[4]

An additional justification for applying reason to the imperial controversy was the need for a workable program of action. Only positive, identifiable deeds could break down the polarization of political hostility and stem the rising tide of blind emotion. "Such is the violence of our disputing parties, that whoever differs from either is immediately stigmatized as a *Whig* or a *Tory*," both "terms of disgrace," a Massachusetts "Moderate Man" announced. "To moderate these party heats, to draw that zeal into a channel where it would really be serviceable, is the duty of every member of the community." This channeling of human energy, Eliot believed, required the utmost discrimination. "Perhaps," he suggested, "it might be as well not to dispute in such strong terms the legal right of Parliament. This is a point that cannot easily be settled, and had therefore best be touched very gently." There were other ways of exerting political muscle, Jeremy Belknap agreed. Britain could not understand that "force could not generate submission," nor could the colonists sense that "resistance could not enervate force." Neither could respect the other's "strengths and resources" because each side perceived only the other's weaknesses and folly. The task of reasonable men was to find an alternative strategy that did not pit British force against colonial recalcitrance. Paine Wingate, of New Hampshire, wanted the colonists to "press on" in the controversy with Britain but to use "healing" measures as a means of securing "the restoration of our invaded rights." Nonimportation, he suggested, would enable Britain to estimate the annual value of colonial trade to the mother country; the colonies should seize the initiative by making an estimate of their own and then proposing it as the basis for computing a voluntary colonial contribution toward the cost of running the Empire. Any conciliatory gesture, Wingate felt, would delay the impending collision. "Time," he assured, "performs miracles. If we could only while away the time" for as much as a year, circumstances might change and new possibilities arise. "If we would not be so needlessly irritating" to the British, "I doubt not our deliverance will come."[5]

No matter how concrete and forceful, programs for securing accommodation crumbled in the face of growing intransigence on both sides and were reduced to pleas for time and the arrival of unforeseen good fortune. "Does not that man deserve to be heard with candour," asked "A Philadelphian," "who desires not to counteract the general sentiments of his countrymen, but thinks it a duty . . . to guard against an evil which may . . . destroy the hope of every virtuous patriot . . . , [for] lasting and happy union . . . between the mother country and her colonies?" Nathaniel Peaslee Sargeant, of Haverhill, Massachusetts, wanted the colonists to turn Lord North's peace proposal of 1775 to their own advantage by accepting it as a basis for negotiation. North had proposed the repeal of tea duties if the colonies would agree to a perpetual contribution to the British Treasury. Sargeant eagerly examined the possible colonial responses to this proposal. By praising it, the colonists could make North a political hero in England and give him a freer hand to pursue reconciliation. If they rejected the plan, North would be able to point to the "apparent fairness" of the proposals as a means of uniting British opinion against the Americans. A still more delicate maneuver, Sargeant envisioned, would be an offer to contribute to the British a sum slightly less than the cost of colonial defense rather than a vague proposal to pay some undesignated amount in lieu of taxes. Such a shrewd tactic would serve to "embarrass him in his policy with safety to ourselves." The essential aim, Sargeant explained, was to make Lord North appear to exact concessions from America, while in fact the colonies were giving up very little and gaining, in the bargain, a perpetual exemption from parliamentary taxation. But to humiliate him by wrecking his peace initiative would, in actuality, free North to coerce the colonists. "He, as a politician, ought to keep his arm extended over us. The honor of government likewise requires . . . that it might appear . . . they compelled us to take their terms. I think he clearly proves in his *speech* that a people may with dignity recede from some of their claims. . . . If we don't get all we asked for *before,* won't such an accommodation secure to us something worth all our trouble and expense?"[6]

For all its ingenuity, the search for accommodation failed to find a way of utilizing reason to solve the pre-Revolutionary crisis; but as the advocates of accommodation wrestled with this problem, they sought for a secure point of departure in their thinking—an ultimate source of moral and political authority. They found this source of authority by locating the central elements of their anxiety. "The Americans are no idiots," J. J. Zubly wrote in a public appeal to Lord Dartmouth.

"Oppression will make wise men mad, but oppressors in the end frequently find they are not wise men; *there may be resources even in despair* sufficient to render any set of men strong enough" to resist tyranny. The ominous prospect that "we must either submit to *slavery* or defend our liberties by our own sword," the Reverend Simeon Howard complained, was all the more painful because "everything belonging to the present state [of affairs] is uncertain and fluctuating." For the Reverend David Hall, a Congregationalist clergyman, "the disputes between the nation and her colonies" made the early 1770s "an evil, dark, and doubtful day," not because colonial liberty was in jeopardy but because God was displeased with his people. Andrew Eliot could only pray that, "amidst all the fears, dangers, and anxieties" of "the present troubles," he would grow more deeply committed to serving his "heavenly Father."[7]

A sense of humility and skepticism about the righteousness of political judgments, the advocates of accommodation believed, was the first obligation of men facing difficult political decisions. "We would fain obey our superiors, yet we cannot think of giving up our . . . rights," declared J. J. Zubly in a now familiar reiteration of the apparent alternatives available in 1775. "We would express duty, respect, and obedience to the king as supreme, and yet we wish not to strengthen the hands of tyranny nor call oppression lawful." In this "delicate situation," Zubly asserted, coming to the crux of the problem, men should heed the scriptural injunction "'so speak ye, and so do, as they that shall be judged by the law of liberty.'" That liberty was the freedom given to believers to act as moral men, not in fear of punishment or under coercion from other men but, rather, in the confidence that God alone, on the day of judgment, would weigh the deeds of men and in the meantime would guide but not dictate how they should behave. This expectation of final judgment should "make us act with prudence, justice, and moderation." The Christian law of liberty, Zubly explained, meant that conscience alone governed men in dealings with their political rulers; it forbade men from giving unquestioning obedience to their government; it condemned arbitrary uses of governmental power; it assured rulers and ruled alike that God would ultimately judge their actions and intentions. Because the purpose of Christianity was to "regulate our desires and restrain our passions" by teaching men humility, the most valuable benefit derived from the law of liberty was the extraordinary self-consciousness it implanted in men. God will not judge a man from "external appearance" or even by his "own opinion of himself" but, rather, "by his inward reality . . . ; God judges men according to their invisible spring," their innermost instincts and desires. "Let me entreat you, gentlemen," Zubly implored the Georgia Assembly in early 1775, "think coolly and act deliberately; rash counsels are seldom good ones. Ministerial rashness and American rashness can only be productive of untoward compounds. . . . Let neither the frowns of tyranny nor the pleasure of popularity sway you from what you clearly apprehend just and right. . . . Endeavour to act like freemen, like loyal subjects, like real Christians, and you will '. . . be judged by the law of liberty.' Act conscientiously, and with a view to God, then commit your ways to God, leave the event with God, and you will have great reason to hope that the event will be just, honourable, and happy."[8]

That hope, Zubly knew, was a slender one. But it was also the only possible one men could properly embrace. "Never let us lose . . . sight that our interest lies in a perpetual connection with our mother country," he told the Georgia Assembly in the spring of 1775; rather, "let us convince our enemies that the struggles of America have not their rise in a desire of independency, . . . that to the wish of a perpetual connection" we add only "that we may be virtuous and free." By the time he had prepared the sermon for publication in September 1775, he noted, "a British ministry . . . [had] wasted British blood and treasure to alienate America and Great Britain; the breach is growing wider and wider." The only moral he could draw was the urgent need to find some grounds for reconciliation. The quest for accommodation had to seek continually for finer distinctions between the righteous defense of liberty and immoral recklessness. Simeon Howard constructed a lengthy catalogue of tests to distinguish between the two kinds of resistance. Any governmental action that made men timid and complacent was oppressive and required vigorous and outspoken denunciation. The happiness of future generations was the responsibility of the living. Men could recognize in themselves the quality of "truest fortitude" when their political conduct merited "the favor of God" by its discipline, vitality, and concern for the good of the community. Candor, sincerity, and idealism distinguished good from evil in political struggles. "*Designedly* to spread false alarms, to fill the minds of people with groundless prejudices against their rulers, . . . to stir up faction and encourage opposition to *good* government are things highly criminal," Howard concluded; "but to show people their real danger, point out the source of it, and exhort them to such exertions as are necessary to avoid it are acts of benevolence." With this kind of aesthetic judgment about the ugliness of selfish political ambition and the beauty of controlled protest by the whole community, the rationalist clergy pronounced the duty of Christian men in the last stages of the pre-Revolutionary controversy.[9]

In the final analysis, the quest for accommodation reflected a peculiar perception of the function of politics in American society. Acts of organized resistance and protest against British policy and authority, these men believed, varied widely in propriety and legitimacy; invariably, however, resistance was closely related to some form of political enthusiasm, rivalry, or maneuver. "Our own provincial politics," New York moderate John Jones wrote to James Duane in December 1775, is "a subject . . . I never troubled my head with, till it was connected with the general interests of America in the present unhappy and deplorable contest." The practice of his friends in the Livingston faction of distributing militia posts only to their own political supporters almost turned Jones speechless with "honest rage" provoked by "Whig and Tory" alike. "Would to heaven," he exclaimed, "I could throw a veil over this nakedness of my countrymen." For many colonists, the pre-Revolutionary debate thrust politics into their experience for the first time and upset the equilibrium of their values. An obscure New Englander named Gill "contemplated the scenes of oppressions, hardships, and miseries" caused by the "struggles of many with the rod of arbitrary power." The whole enterprise seemed to him misguided because of the "ignorance of multitudes" and their lack of a "clear gospel vision." Political alignments of all kinds, he lamented, channeled "the pride, the extreme selfishness, the narrowness, and bigotry of the human heart"; these, he explained, "are the sources of my apprehension." The intensity of pre-Revolutionary protest disturbed him most because it substituted "a fiery zeal and a cold charity" for the example of "the meek and lowly Jesus." Gill felt torn by this "apprehension" because he respected "the cause," which some call "liberty" and others decry as "anarchy or rebellion or faction." The colonists, he conceded, had a duty to preserve their rights against the "ravages of tyranny," but he was still disturbed by "unwarrantable measures" and "low means" used in that defense of liberty. On balance, he concluded, only a "fool" would expect "large bodies of men (as are at this day engaged in the controversy)" to make only "wise speeches, wise determinations, and wise actions." "Errors of judgment" and "imprudence of conduct" were inevitable, if lamentable, and brought the whole cause of liberty into disrepute. If Gill's ambivalence makes his openness and candor difficult to recognize, it also underlines the dilemma: "I can live on as friendly terms with an Episcopalian as a Congregationalist; a Tory (as they're called) as a Whig; a disciple of . . . Arminius as of Calvin. Yet in my heart I am inclined to the doctrines of Calvin, the principles of true Whigism, and the model of the Congregational Churches."[10]

"True Whigism"! The term implied a conscious intellectual and emotional effort to return to a pure source of political values and to refurbish a once proud historical orthodoxy. "I am a Whig of the old stamp," William Smith, Jr., said at a Christmas Day dinner in 1777 during a discussion of the virtues and hazards of republican government; "no roundhead," he explained, referring to Puritan insurgents in the English civil wars, but rather more like "one of King William's Whigs, for liberty and the constitution."[11] When the advocates of accommodation appealed to the English whig tradition of liberty and constitutional government, they were striving to occupy a position of detachment from which they could study the prevailing tumult. William Samuel Johnson, of Connecticut, had struggled to maintain just such a balance between his commitment to colonial liberty and his preference for order and civility. As a member of the Stamp Act Congress in 1765, he had drafted the key document that labeled all parliamentary taxation—both internal taxes like the Stamp Act and external revenue-producing duties on trade—denials of the "reasonable measure of civil liberty" belonging to the colonists as "freemen and British subjects." Accordingly he strongly opposed the Townshend duties. "The principle on which they are founded, alone, is worth contesting," he declared, because "a tax of a penny is equally a tax as one of a pound; if they have a constitutional right to impose the first they may the last."

He served as Connecticut's colonial agent in London from 1766 to 1771 and during that period became increasingly adamant in his insistence that even token parliamentary taxation would destroy colonial liberty. Johnson could not move from that position to the slightly more advanced one of advocating resistance against British encroachments. A devout Anglican, he was the son of the Reverend Samuel Johnson, the president of King's College in New York City and the most prominent colonial Anglican clergyman until his death in 1772. But more than filial obedience constrained him. "The ill-advised measures that have been taken with respect to the colonies have weakened the connection between the two countries but have not yet broken it; a little wisdom and a little shrewdness might yet set all right again," he wrote, expressing his deep yearning for a peaceful resolution of the conflict between British authority and colonial rights. Johnson had no illusions. "In every light the prospect is melancholy," he wrote in July 1774. "Will no hand be stretched forth to prevent these two countries, perhaps the finest in the universe, from . . . injuring each other?" Despite his close connections with the leaders of the pre-Revolutionary movement in Connecticut, Johnson withdrew into isolation in 1775 and, like Daniel Dulany, became a neutral because he was "convinced that I could not join in war against England and much less . . . against my own country."[12]

Carl Becker noted a similar "preciseness, . . . awareness of small matters, . . . [and] rigidity" in the personality of another of these introspective accommodating loyalists, Peter Van Schaack, "that made it [difficult] for him to associate with others in a common cause." As late as spring 1774, Van Schaack, a New York lawyer, believed that the colonies should prepare for war with Britain unless Parliament renounced any right to tax America. Only dire consequences, he predicted, would "compel" the British to alter their colonial policy. By early 1775, however, the colonists were not simply defending their rights; rather, they had recklessly accused the British of "a design of subverting the constitution and enslaving America." British violations of colonial liberty were still a serious matter, he believed, but did not yet amount to systematic tyranny. Colonial resistance, on the other hand, had taken on an ominous quality: "The present situation of affairs—committees, remonstrances, addresses to the people, pretending dangers of impending slavery . . . —cannot fail to remind us of those unhappy times which blackened the annals of English history [referring to the English civil wars of the 1640s]. May God avert similar calamities."[13] Retiring to his country home at Kinderhook in January 1776, Van Schaack read and reread John Locke's *Two Treatises on Government* and wrote this private statement of political conscience. Dealing firmly and deliberately with many of the conflicting truths and values sensed by the advocates of accommodation, it deserves to be quoted here at length:

> The only foundation of all legitimate governments is certainly a compact
> between the rulers and the people, containing mutual conditions, and equally
> obligatory on both the contracting parties. No question can, therefore exist,

at this enlightened day, about the lawfulness of resistance, in cases of gross and palpable infractions on the part of the governing power. It is impossible, however, clearly to ascertain every case which shall effect a dissolution of this contract; for these, though always tacitly implied, are never expressly declared, in any form of government.

As a man is bound by the sacred ties of conscience, to yield obedience to every act of the legislature so long as the government exists, so, on the other hand, he owes it to the cause of liberty, to resist the invasion of those rights, which, being inherent and inalienable, could not be surrendered at the institution of the civil society of which he is a member. In times of civil commotions, therefore, an investigation of those rights, which will necessarily infer an inquiry into the nature of government, becomes the indispensable duty of every man. . . .

Our reasonings must resolve into one or the other of the following three grounds, and our right of resistance must be founded upon either the first or third of them; for either, first, we owe no obedience to any acts of Parliament; or, secondly, we are bound by all acts to which British subjects in Great Britain would, if passed with respect to them, owe obedience; or, thirdly, we are subordinate in a certain degree, or, in other words, certain acts may be valid in Britain which are not so here.

Upon the first point I am exceedingly clear in my mind, for I consider the Colonies as members of the British empire, and subordinate to the Parliament. But, with regard to the second and third, I am not so clear. The necessity of a supreme power in every state strikes me very forcibly; at the same time, I foresee the destructive consequences of a right in Parliament to bind us in all cases whatsoever. To obviate the ill effects of either extreme, some middle way should be found out, by which the benefits to the empire should be secured arising from the doctrine of a supreme power, while the abuses of that power to the prejudice of the colonists should be guarded against; and this, I hope, will be the happy effect of the present struggle. . . . I cannot see any principle of regard for my country which will authorize me in taking up arms, as absolute dependence and independence are two extremes which I would avoid; for, should we succeed in the latter, we shall still be in a sea of uncertainty, and have to fight among ourselves for that constitution we aim at.

There are many very weighty reasons besides the above to restrain a man from taking up arms, but some of them are of too delicate a nature to be put upon paper; however, it may be proper to mention what does not restrain *me*. It is not from apprehension of the consequences should America be subdued, or the hopes of any favor from government, both which I disclaim; nor is it from any disparagement of the cause my countrymen are engaged in, or a desire of obstructing the present measures. . . . It is a question of morality and religion in which a man cannot conscientiously take an active part without being convinced in his own mind of the justice of the cause; . . . whatever disagreeable consequences may follow from dissenting from the general voice, yet I cannot but remember that I am to render an account of my conduct before a more awful tribunal, where no man can be justified who stands accused by his own conscience of taking part in measures which, through the distress and bloodshed of his fellow-creatures, may precipitate his country into ruin.[14]

Author's Note (2009)

This chapter as it appeared in *The Loyalists in Revolutionary America, 1760–1781* included testimony from moderate loyalists, such as William Samuel Johnson, William Smith, Jr., Peter Van Schaack, and John J. Zubly, as well as deeply conflicted patriots, such as Andrew Eliot, Nathaniel Peaslee Sargeant, Richard Wells, Edward Burd, and the obscure Massachusetts man known only to history as Mr. Gill ("inclined to the doctrines of Calvin, the principles of true Whigism, and the model of the Congregational Churches" and willing "to live on friendly terms with an Episcopalian, a Tory [as they're called] as a Whig") Whether ambivalent, loyalist leaning, or patriots, these men articulated fears and anxieties permeating Revolutionary political culture.

Unpublished portions of the Ebenezer Parkman diary at the American Antiquarian Society provide a fuller picture and more complex explanation of ambivalent political moderation in the Revolutionary crisis. Parkman was a Congregationalist minister in Westborough, Massachusetts, and a cautious New Light—wary of controversy. When George Whitefield first preached in Massachusetts in 1741, Parkman and his wife, Hannah, journeyed to Marlborough to hear him, and in a letter to Jonathan Edwards, Parkman prayed that "the minds of all men, of ministers especially, might be opened to behold the glorious work of God and the Grace of our Lord Jesus Christ more universally experience everywhere!" But when Whitefield converts, "youth particularly," became active in Westborough, Parkman worried that these "lads and young women" needed to be "guarded" from "all snares and delusions, vain presumptions black despair." Thereafter Parkman's silence on the subject of Whitefield and his absence from the great revivalist's services did not go unnoticed, although he did decline to participate in organized ministerial criticism of the famous itinerant. And when Eunice Andrews, a New Light convert from John Cleaveland's separatist church in the Chebacco neighborhood of Ipswich, and her husband sought communicant status in Parkman's church, Parkman resisted, citing the "Disorders and Irregularitys" that the couple brought with them from Chebacco and Eunice's indiscreet suspicion as to whether "Mr. P[arkman] has a spark of Grace in him, for I could never see any."

Although the dispute with Mrs. Andrews and her husband, George, was formally resolved in 1764 through a neighboring minister's mediation, Mrs. Andrews's access to "transient" communion when she visited Westborough was impeded by her dislike of Parkman and by the aggrieved feelings a handful of Parkman's sympathetic parishioners held against her. Finally, in January 1768 Parkman orchestrated a compromise by which Eunice was acknowledged to be a "professing Christian" but, in a slap at "Disorders" in "Chebacco or elsewhere," she was classified as a "Professor" of the faith "in general and not as a Member of one particular Church or another." After four years of acrimony, community and ministerial pressure had forced Parkman to compromise and to acknowledge the rising tide of New Light sentiment on which the Andrewses relied in their public spat with Parkman.

The Andrews affair overlapped with the Stamp Act crisis during which Parkman privately deplored mob destruction of Hutchinson's house ("a melancholy Occurrence! Much to be Deplored") and the Townshend duties crisis and the dispatch of British troops to Boston. Of the Boston Massacre, he noted in his diary, "Sad Accounts of Tumults in Boston—a number killed by the Regulars."

Thus troubles in his church in the long aftermath of the Great Awakening from 1741 through 1768 constrained Parkman's clerical autonomy to respond to public events as he saw them. Parkman stalked out of a town meeting on July 4, 1774, to consider a covenant against British incursions on Massachusetts, refusing to counsel or encourage the gathered townspeople: "I conceived it was not *safe* for me to do it, Safe either *for men* or *for them*," considering Governor Thomas Gage's threat to arrest the circulators or signees of the covenant. Almost two months later "great Disquietment . . . at [his] not Signing something or other" convinced him that "rather than have a Hubbub and unroar," he should sign the controversial document. Just four days earlier, Parkman had resolved to stay just a step ahead of public opinion and "willingly, heartily promote what ever is lawful, constitutional, and consistent with Wisdom and prudence under our unhappy Circumstances." That pledge was not as evasive as it now sounds; in it Parkman drew the same principled line as many other nervous colonists stunned by the severity of the Coercive Acts. It served him well. When Westborough militiamen went to Cambridge after April 19, 1775, he could publicly pray that "abundant Grace be given to prepare and qualifie you for the most Memorable Action—Not in Rebellion, not in Transgression, but in just and unavoidable Defence of our invaluable Rights, Laws, Libertys, and Privileges." On August 25, 1776, Parkman did read the Declaration of Independence from the pulpit, but he could not go as far as his Northborough colleague, the Reverend Peter Whitney, who also lectured on the document and participated in "other Great Doings . . . on that occasion."[15]

Notes

1. For an introduction to the study of moderate loyalist thought, see Calhoon, "'Unhinging Former Intimacies,'" 246–48, and Calhoon, review of William Eddis's *Letters from America,* ed. Aubrey C. Land, *Studies in Burke and His Time* 13 (Winter 1971–72): 2168–71. Two studies of British attempts at reconciliation throw considerable light on the frustration of colonial attempts: Weldon A. Brown, *Empire or Independence* (University, La.: Louisiana State University Press, 1941), and Herbert A. Meistrich, "Lord Drummond and Reconciliation," *Proceedings of the New Jersey Historical Society* 80 (October 1963): 256–77. For corrections and amplification, see Milton M. Klein, "Failure of a Mission: The Drummond Mission of 1775," *Huntington Library Quarterly* 35 (August 1972): 343–80. Michael G. Kammen, "Intellectuals, Political Leadership, and Revolution," *New England Quarterly* 41 (December 1968): 583–93, raises important questions about the social roots of ambivalence and moderation on the eve of the Revolution.

2. Edward Burd to E. Shippen, July 14, 1774, Lewis Burd Walker, ed., *The Burd Papers . . . 1763–1828* (n.p., 1899), 67; *Pennsylvania Gazette,* May 18, 1774; [Richard Wells], *A Few Political Reflections . . .* (Philadelphia, 1774), 3–4; Andrew Eliot to Thomas Hollis, September 27, 1768, December 25, 1769, *Collections of the Massachusetts Historical Society,* 4th ser., (1858): vol. 4, pp. 423, 445–46; *Pennsylvania Packet,* September 19, 1774; "Letters of Thomas Wharton, 1773–1783," *Pennsylvania Magazine of History and Biography* 33 (October 1904): 437–40, 446–47.

3. Eliot to Blackburne, December 15, 1767, Andrew Eliot Papers; *Pennsylvania Ledger,* January 28, 1775; [Wells], *A Few Political Reflections,* 18; Tryon to Dartmouth, August 7, 1775, Additional Manuscripts, 38650, 9 pp. 1–2, British Museum, London; Thomas Combe to Rockingham, February 5 and November 5, 1774, Rockingham Papers, R 1, nos. 1480 and 1529, Sheffield City Library, Sheffield, England.

4. Jeremy Belknap, *A Sermon on Military Duty . . .* (Salem, N.H., 1773), 6; [Wells], *A Few Political Reflections,* 36; John Tucker, *A Sermon Preached . . . before His Excellency Thomas Hutchinson . . . May 29, 1771* (Boston: Printed by Richard Draper, 1771), 21; Gad Hitchcock, *A Sermon Preached before His Excellency Thomas Gage . . . May 25, 1774 . . .* (Boston: Printed by Edes & Gill, 1774), 24; Daniel Shute, *A Sermon Preached before His Excellency Francis Bernard . . . May 25, 1768 . . .* (Boston: Printed by Richard Draper, 1768), 60.

5. *Massachusetts Gazette and Boston Weekly News-Letter,* February 2, 1775; Clifford K. Shipton, *Sibley's Harvard Graduates* 10 (1958): 151; Jeremy Belknap, Extracts and Remarks on the Correspondence of J[ohn] W[entworth] and T[homas] W. W[aldron], Jeremy Belknap Papers, Massachusetts Historical Society; Wingate to Timothy Pickering, April 28, 1775; Charles E. L. Wingate, *The Life and Letters of Paine Wingate* (Medford, Mass.: Mercury Publishing Co., 1930), 1:59–162; fourteen members of the New York Assembly to Gage, May 5, 1775, Colonial Office Papers, 5th ser., Public Record Office, London, 92:168–69.

6. *Pennsylvania Gazette,* September 7, 1774; "Jeremy Belknap's Reasons against Subscribing the Covenant, June 28, 1774," *Proceedings of the Massachusetts Historical Society,* 2nd ser. (Boston: Massachusetts Historical Society, 1886), 2:484–486; Nathaniel Peaslee Sargeant to Thomas Cushing, May 22, 1775, Robert Treat Paine Papers, Massachusetts Historical Society.

7. J. J. Zubly, *The Law of Liberty* . . . (Philadelphia, 1774), vi–vii; Simeon Howard, *A Sermon Preached before the Ancient and Honorable Artillery Company* . . . *June 7, 1773* . . . (Boston, 1773), 38; Diary of Reverend David Hall, April 5, 1770, Massachusetts Historical Society; Andrew Eliot to John Eliot, May 4 and August 1, 1775, Andrew Eliot Papers; see also the letters of Isaac Smith, Jr., in *Proceedings of the Massachusetts Historical Society* 59 (1925): 117–138; John Eliot to Jeremy Belknap, February 18, 1775, *Collections of the Massachusetts Historical Society,* 6th ser., (1890): vol. 4, pp. 83–84; and Jeremy Belknap, *A Prayer,* June 26, 1774, Jeremy Belknap Papers.

8. Zubly, *Law of Liberty,* 11, 18–19, 25–26. The Reverend John Joachim Zubly, a Swiss immigrant, was a Presbyterian clergyman in Georgia; see Marjorie Daniel, "John J. Zubly . . ." *Georgia Historical Quarterly* 19 (March 1935): 1–16.

9. Zubly, *Law of Liberty,* 24–25; Howard, *Sermon before Artillery Company,* 30–36.

10. Jones to James Duane, December 7 and July 13, 1775, James Duane Papers, New York Historical Society, New York; Gill to Rev. Mr. Hawley, August 18, 1770, S. P. Savage Papers, Massachusetts Historical Society.

11. Quoted in L. S. F. Upton, *The Loyal Whig: William Smith of New York & Quebec* (Toronto: University of Toronto Press, 1969), title page and p. 110.

12. Edmund S. and Helen M. Morgan, *The Stamp Act Crisis: Prologue to Revolution* (Chapel Hill: University of North Carolina Press, 1953), 149; William A. Benton, *Whig Loyalism: An Aspect of Political Ideology in the American Revolutionary Era* (Teaneck, N.J.: Fairleigh Dickinson University Press, 1969), 93, 160; Michael G. Kammen, *Rope of Sand: The Colonial Agents, British Politics, and the American Revolution* (Ithaca, N.Y.: Cornell University Press, 1968), 163. Johnson to Thomas Pownall, November 3, 1772; to Richard Jackson, August 3, 1774; and to Sally Johnson, November 21, 1774, William Samuel Johnson Papers, Connecticut Historical Society.

13. Carl Becker, "John Jay and Peter Van Schaack," *Everyman His Own Historian* (New York: F. S. Crofts, 1935), 288; Benton, *Whig Loyalism,* 134; Van Schaack to ?, January 3, 1775; and to [William Laight], September 2, 1774, Peter Van Schaack Papers, Columbia University Library, New York; and Van Schaack to John Maunsell, May 7, 1775, Henry C. Van Schaack, *The Life of Peter Van Schaack* . . . (New York: D. Appleton, 1842), 37–39.

14. Ibid., 54–58. "Inalienable" in the second paragraph is spelled "unalienable" in the published version of this document.

15. Ross W. Beales, Jr., "'The present Torrent of Liberty is irresistible': From Revival to Revolution in Westborough, Massachusetts," Liberty University Conference on Awakenings and Revivals in American History, Lynchburg, Va., April 18, 2009.

2
Action

The Character and Coherence of the Loyalist Press

Janice Potter-MacKinnon
and Robert M. Calhoon

1. "Subservient to the Intentions of Government": The Nature and Dilemma of the Loyalist Press

The loyalists' use of the press—like almost everything else they did—eludes precise definition. Strictly speaking, the term *loyalist press* refers to manifestly pro-British, anti-whig newspapers published during the crises of 1774 to 1776 and still more appropriately to newspapers published in British-held garrison towns from 1776 through 1783. These papers abounded with anonymous opinion essays which perpetuated a tradition of support of British authority and colonial subordination in the press during the entire pre-Revolutionary controversy. Both as a *journalistic enterprise* during the War for Independence and as a *polemical form* throughout the Revolutionary era, the loyalist press is a unique source of insight into the behavior, expectations, and anguish of the American loyalists.

One way to gauge the quality and thrust of pre-Revolutionary loyalist newspaper polemics is to survey the most celebrated of the series of essays appearing under the same pseudonyms. The "Dougliad" essays in the *New-York Gazette and Weekly Mercury* in 1770—written in response to Alexander McDougal's sensational broadside 'To the Betrayed Inhabitants of . . . New York'—were a full-scale indictment of licentiousness, turmoil, and the Cromwellian antecedents of the doings of the New York Sons of Liberty.[1] Two years earlier the same paper carried numerous installments of the "Whip for the American Whig" by Myles Cooper and other high Anglicans, a series that scourged colonial society for its hostility to Anglicanism and to constituted authority.[2] Another Anglican clergyman, Henry Caner, writing anonymously as "Chronus" in the *Massachusetts Gazette and Boston Weekly News-Letter* in 1771–72, set forth a comprehensive rationale for protecting colonial liberty by the "wise and prudent use of the privileges and advantages we enjoy."[3] In 1769 William Henry Drayton and William Wragg wrote a barrage of letters to the *South-Carolina Gazette* condemning the non-importation movement—Drayton noting that its coercive machinery institutionalized popular opposition in a new and destabilizing way and Wragg denouncing coercion and intimidation as a gross violation of traditional political conscience among the South Carolina elite.[4] The famous "First Citizen"–"Antilon" exchange in the *Maryland Gazette* in 1773 between Charles Carroll and Daniel Dulany, though ostensibly concerned with the powers of the Maryland proprietary governor, grew into a dispute over the meaning of the British constitution, the sources of imperial authority, and the historical roots of colonial liberty.[5]

Surpassing all other loyalist newspaper polemicists was Jonathan Sewall, who published five series of essays between 1763 and 1775. Writing as "J" in the *Boston Evening-Post* in 1763, he replied to attacks on the Bernard administration by James Otis and Oxenbridge Thacher with an argument that, Carol Berkin explains, "espoused liberty, then redefined it in its most conservative form . . . ; endorsed the vigilance of the citizen against tyranny, but reversed the direction from which that tyranny threatened society." As "Philanthrop" in 1766–67 he used the same arguments to deflect the criticism heaped on Governor Bernard during the Stamp Act crisis, and under the same pseudonym in 1770–71 he refuted Samuel Adams's attempt to retry the Boston Massacre trials in the Boston press. As "Philalethes" in 1773 in the *Massachusetts Gazette and Boston Weekly News-Letter*, he sought to stem the torrent of abuse being heaped on Governor Hutchinson, and as "Phileirene" in 1775, he examined in detail the sources and impetus of the Revolutionary contagion.[6]

Finally, John Adams's and Daniel Leonard's climactic duel as "Novanglus" and "Massachusettensis" in the *Boston Gazette and Country Journal* and *Massachusetts Gazette and Boston Post-Boy and Advertiser* in 1774–75 raised what Bernard Mason calls "antithetical models of society," a tory model of "order and imperial stability" and a whig model in which the "key ingredients" were "liberty and innovation."[7]

While these major series of anti-whig polemics made a thorough case for dutiful submission and restraint by the colonists, scores of individual anonymous essays elaborated on the loyalist argument in the pre-Revolutionary debate and reflected the range and seriousness of the impediments to a unified colonial opposition against British policy. Some of these articles appeared originally or were reprinted in newspapers closely identified with the whig position while most filled the columns of identifiably pro-British or "tory" papers: the *New-York Gazette and Weekly Mercury* and the two *Massachusetts Gazettes* already mentioned; the *Georgia Gazette*, the *South-Carolina and American General Gazette*, *Rivington's New-York Gazetteer*, the *Boston Evening-Post*, the *Boston Chronicle*, the Boston *Censor*, and the *New Hampshire Gazette*.[8]

Beginning with the seminal research of Stephen Botein, scholars now emphasize that colonial printers sought to perform a nonpolitical service of opening their columns to all shades of opinion, a role that became increasingly untenable during the early 1770s. As late as July 1774, James Rivington declared that "the printer of a newspaper ought to be neutral in all cases where his own press is employed" and publish all materials submitted to him, "whether of the Whig or Tory flavour." Rivington's perilous neutrality collapsed when a crowd of seventy-five horsemen under Isaac Sears vandalized his press on May 10, and wrecked it completely on November 23, 1775.[9] Hugh Gaine, printer of the *New-York Mercury,* was the classic example of a colonial printer driven against every professional instinct toward a partisan role in the Revolution. Throughout the pre-Revolutionary controversy he gave balanced, objective accounts of political upheaval and published anonymous essays on both sides that were decent and moderate in tone.[10]

Rivington's sympathies undoubtedly lay with the British while Gaine, like many loyalists from the middle colonies, felt equally torn between his sympathy for colonial rights and his aversion to rebellion and violence; the important point is that neither became a partisan of the British cause until the outbreak of war and royal occupation of New York City made neutrality impossible. For a short time in September and October 1776, Gaine tried to print a paper in Newark, New Jersey, in a territory controlled by the patriots while allowing Gen. William Howe's secretary, Ambrose Serle, to manage the *New-York Mercury.* Financial losses in Newark and patriot suspicion forced him to abandon this arrangement, take refuge in New York City, and make the *Mercury* into an avowedly loyalist newspaper.[11] Rivington, who had gone to England in early 1776, returned in September 1777 and resumed publication of his paper on October 4. In his second issue he candidly and accurately affirmed his willingness to make the *Gazette* "subservient to the intentions of government—the restoration of peace, order, and happiness through the continent—by recalling the infatuated multitude to the use of their reason and understanding and by convincing them how grossly they have been imposed upon by the misrepresentations and false glosses of their leaders in sedition and rebellion."[12]

In addition to *Rivington's Gazette* and Gaine's *New-York Mercury,* ten other loyalist newspapers appeared in towns occupied by the British between 1776 and 1783. These included the *Royal American Gazette* in New York City from 1777 to 1783; the *Newport Gazette* in Rhode Island from 1777 to 1779; the *Pennsylvania Evening Post, Pennsylvania Ledger,* and *Royal Pennsylvania Gazette* in Philadelphia for varying parts of the British occupation of Philadelphia from October 1777 to May 1778; the *South-Carolina and American General Gazette, The Royal Gazette,* and the *Royal South-Carolina Gazette* during the British occupation of Charleston in 1780–82; the *Royal Georgia Gazette* in occupied Savannah from 1779–82; and the *East Florida Gazette* in St. Augustine in 1783–84.[13] The newspapers provided a necessary semblance of normality in towns under British military and administrative control. They spurred the economy by carrying advertisements and other information vital to merchants, artisans, and consumers; trumpeted British military successes; published the numerous official announcements for British commanders and civilian administrators; and provided a forum in which loyalists could lambast their patriot enemies, prod the British government to meet the needs of the King's friends, and explore the ramifications of their self-pitying and often paranoid view of recent history.[14]

The intrusion of Revolutionary politics into the workings of the press and the volatile public impact of political news and opinion in the newspapers together constitute a previously little-understood dimension of the political culture of Revolutionary America. Modern scholarship has explored the editing, coverage, management, and social role of loyalist newspapers.[15] Little systematic attention, however, has been paid to the intellectual and ideological content and character of the great mass of signed and anonymous opinion essays in the newspapers that opposed the Revolutionary movement and vindicated British authority over the colonies. This essay attempts such an appraisal.

2. "Disaffection, Petulance, Ingratitude, and Disloyalty": The Themes of Loyalist Polemical Journalism

In the sixteenth of his "Massachusettensis" letters, Daniel Leonard declared, with bitter sarcasm, "some idolaters have attributed to the congress the collected wisdom of the continent." It was an astute observation. The decision of the First Continental Congress to impose a trade boycott enforced by local committees, coupled with its resolution for a second Congress to assemble in May 1775, significantly altered the nature of the Congress. By setting these events in motion, the Congress shifted from a gathering of representatives of the colonial assemblies into an active guardian of American liberty and authoritative spokesman for American interests. Those functions required Congress to interpret the meaning of fast-moving events and respond with appropriate boldness and vigor to British actions. "The collected wisdom of the continent" exactly expressed Congress's new status, and Leonard's grasp of that political reality enhances the credibility and interpretive value of the remainder of the concluding paragraph in the sixteenth "Massachusettensis" letter. "It is as near the truth to say," he continued, "that every particle of disaffection, petulance, ingratitude, and disloyalty that for ten years past have been scattered through the continent, were united and consolidated in them [the Congress]."[16]

Disaffection, petulance, ingratitude, and *disloyalty* were terms that came easily to Leonard's pen. To the casual reader of tory diatribes against whig ideology and politics they are nearly synonymous words. At face value, certainly, they are overlapping terms which collectively describe several facets of colonial remonstrance and resistance. But when examined in the context of eighteenth-century usage, each word connotes values and beliefs that distinguish it from the others. *Disaffection* meant filling otherwise faithful subjects with discontent and described the understandable reaction of people to inconsistent, abusive government; it was therefore a process by which a people's natural affections and kindliness were eroded or subverted and replaced with malignant, persistent resentment against constituted authority. *Petulance* depicted a range of personality traits associated with immaturity: saucy, perverse, immodest, pert, insolent behavior. The word suggested too a more deeply engrained trait: wantonness—an undisciplined, animal quest for sensual gratification. In the hands of loyalist polemicists, petulance was an unwillingness, even refusal, to admit objective reality when it clashed with men's desires for domination over others and with their craving for freedom from all restraint. *Ingratitude* was an indisposition to acknowledge benefits received from a government, a patron, or a family. Gratitude implied the existence of interests that knitted groups of men together and provided a rational basis for social cooperation and political acquiescence. Identifying interests as useful, desirable, and beneficial social arrangements, the idea of ingratitude presupposed that men were capable of knowing whence their livelihood, security, and prosperity came and of knowing too that posing deeper questions about human nature and destiny was a dangerous, delusive, and futile activity to pursue. *Disloyalty* was the fatal, irreversible act of rebellion against legitimate authority, the inevitably violent exposure of the vicious animal appetites which, implanted in human nature, were barely restrained by the conventions and habits of civilization and the laws and authority of legally established institutions."[17]

Instead of being merely overlapping, redundant synonyms, Leonard's four terms of abuse conveyed distinct perceptions of politics, morality, and human nature. *Disaffection* was a malignant process; *petulance* a perverted reaction to the truth; *ingratitude* a denial of rational self-interest; and *disloyalty* an ugly and destructive action. Applying these broader meanings to the analysis of anti-whig, anti-Revolutionary, and pro-British opinion essays in the press of the Revolutionary era reveals something of the coherence of loyalist ideology. These terms were not rigorous, precise ideas in the loyalists' minds—indeed their cumulative adversities prevented them from ever developing a mature, stable system of thought—but they do provide a new and significant point of access into the interior of loyalist newspaper writing.

Most whigs found their disillusionment with Britain a painful experience and agreed that disaffection was a protracted process in which intellectual and ideological leadership played a critical role in weaning the populace from its accustomed allegiance to the British crown. In contrast to the loyalists, however, the whigs placed disaffection in the historical context of a struggle for political and religious liberty stretching from the eighteenth century back to the Middle Ages. Recent British encroachments on colonial liberty represented to them an aberration from that long historical movement—a tragic, benumbing reminder that even prominent, august institutions and statesmen were capricious and corruptible.[18] Disaffection arose, according to the loyalist press, from the central problem of social control in a free society. "Man is a social Animal . . . whose wants, whose natural powers of Reason, and whose capacity of improving those powers . . . demonstrate," wrote Jonathan Sewall in the first of his "Philanthrop" exchanges with Samuel Adams in 1771, "that he was made for social life." His reason, his need for companionship, and his ability to find safety in numbers dictated that man sacrifice "part of that unlimited freedom of action . . . to which he was born . . ." to obtain and enjoy "the more valuable blessings and benefits of *society*." That realization of their own rationality and sociability implanted in human beings a moral obligation to "promote the general good" and a realization that "the public good and his own are so intimately connected and interwoven together that whatever is inconsistent with the *former* is equally incompatible with the *latter*." For that reason, the preservation and maintenance of the public peace were a subject's "principle" responsibility and concern.[19]

Meeting the duty confronted the good citizen with every variety of political guile, aggression, and evil. As "dissentions and divisions" arose around him, the good citizen had to "endeavour, within his proper sphere, to keep up in the minds of all about him an inviolable respect for the *laws*" and "a rational submission to those in *authority*." Expressed in these terms, obedience and acquiescence to authority required a high degree of self-consciousness and intellectuality. When individuals knew of error and abuse in government, they had a higher moral duty to restrain themselves from uttering harsh criticism lest they promote a general clamor, dishearten and discourage those entrusted with public office, and jeopardize "that *essential subordination* upon which the well being and happiness of the whole *absolutely depends*."[20]

Disaffection therefore sprang from a single-minded tendency to see in particular political abuses evidence "that *all* in authority are traitorously combined in plotting the *slavery*, misery, and ruin of the society." The subject had a moral duty to assume the "*integrity of intention*" of public officials even when they exhibited their "*human fallibility*." After all, public officials had to meet the most exacting tests of virtue over long periods of time, operate according to legal and administrative procedures, endure without complaint a constant barrage of abuse, invective, and intimidation, and exhibit superior ability and blameless private conduct. They therefore deserved respect and deference from thoughtful, reflective subjects. "Arraigning, accusing, and condemning those in the most important stations," Sewall warned, would only "weaken the pillars of the state."[21]

Thus in 1771 Sewall reacted bitterly to the abuse heaped on himself and on acting governor Thomas Hutchinson following the Boston Massacre. By 1775 the cruel, judgmental outlook of the people had brought government to the verge of collapse and threatened to destroy the future stability of the colonial society. "If we look back upon the conduct of the Colonies for some years past, we may find many critical junctures where a prudent silence or a dutiful and rational remonstrance" would have exacted concessions from the British and cleared the atmosphere of rancor and crisis which harmed colonial society. Congress, Sewall complained, should therefore proceed with "extreme caution" so that everyone in the colonies would be "thoroughly convinced that we have truth, justice, reason, and equity for our foundation" before assaulting Parliament and the Crown with hasty, ill-considered, patently erroneous grievances. Once again, he lamented, very few men had enough sophistication and toughness to perceive that tact, discretion, and patience were the foremost defenses for colonial liberty. "Such is the unhappy frailty of the human mind that we are in general less attentive to the calls of reason and prudence than the suggestions of passion, prejudice, and vicious habits."[22]

To counteract the infatuation that gripped the public mind, Daniel Leonard declared, involved telling people with painful bluntness that their conduct was dangerous and self-destructive. Was it unduly censorious to accuse the "leading whigs" of deliberately misleading their unwary contemporaries? Leonard asked; "Whoever has been conversant with the history of man, must know that it abounds with such instances. The same game, and with the same success, has been played in all ages, and all countries." The "game" was to enflame—to politicize—the "bulk of the people" who had neither the "inclination or opportunity" to inform themselves about public life but who carried within themselves "a latent spark" of outrage and animal energy "capable of being kindled into a flame." The manipulation of that human weakness, Leonard insisted, "has always been the employment of the disaffected. They begin by reminding the people of the elevated rank they hold in the universe, as men; that all men by nature are equal; that kings are but the ministers of the people; that their authority is delegated to them by the people for their good, and they have a right to resume it, and place it in other hands, or keep it themselves whenever it is made use of to oppress them. . . . Thus the seeds of sedition are usually sown, and the people are led to sacrifice real liberty to licentiousness which gradually ripens into rebellion and civil war."[23]

The shameless dishonesty and diabolical cunning of the agitator therefore combined with the emotional immaturity and suggestability of his audience to create a powerful dynamic propelling society toward anarchy. "If you are so hurried along with the tide of general fanaticism which runs so strong at this day as to believe those *pretended* grievances, which are held up to the public view, to have any *real* foundation," Sewall declared, "you will perhaps think that nothing but a malignant party spirit . . . can stimulate me to thus arraign and condemn the proceedings of the Continental Congress." There was, he insisted, a legitimate human basis for his intransigence "when I see your fears alarmed, your tempers irritated, and passions inflamed, without any just cause, by men, the sole motives of whose conduct are envy, malice, or ambition, I think myself justifiable in attempting to expose the errors and defeat the inimical designs of such men."[24]

Once functioning in tandem, "the minds of the multitude" and their "crafty deceivers" communicated through language almost perfectly suited for conspiracy and sedition. Once men's "passions are engaged, . . . their reason is lulled into a perfectly stupid lethargy, and then mere sounds govern their judgments. The words king, parliament, ministers, governors, mandamus councillors, revenue, tea &c. carry the idea of slavery with them, while with as little color or reason the words congress, charter, patriots, delegates, charter councillors, independence, coffee, &c. carry with them all the powers of necromancy [i.e., magic] to conjure down the spirit of tyranny."[25] "Citizens," it appeared, "have been deluded by the cry of Liberty." Virtually mesmerized by such slogans, the mob committed numerous "violences" in the name of liberty and engaged in ritualistic and bizarre behavior—

they marched around a field to a liberty pole, where some of their members harangued the rest, and then they elected committees to undertake the most trivial tasks.[26] "Are there not many among them whose case we may lament," wondered one supposedly bewildered observer, "who at some seasons appeared frantic, superstitious and in some degree idolators by their veneration for a tree and the number 92 . . . [and] their sacrifice on the annual solemnity or feast of dedication of the juice of lemons, wine &c. which, with the temper and behaviour of the votaries, appear to have some resemblance of the ancient Bacchanalia?"[27]

Disaffection, then, was like a poison infused into the populace to erode their reason, benevolence, and loyalty, and to evoke, instead, their passions, malignity, and licentiousness. Such baser instincts, which many loyalists believed lurked beneath the surface of mankind's rationality and kindliness, should be curbed by individual self-restraint and by the authority of the institutions of church and state. When, however, these barriers were broken down by unscrupulous intriguers who aroused the public by appeals to its passions, the less noble and more irrational side of human nature was exposed. The loyalist assumption that a small cabal of designing, crafty, and self-interested men had played upon weaknesses in human nature to bring out men's baser instincts and in this way to infuse disaffection into the populace was basic to their interpretation of the Revolution. Americans were rebelling, according to many loyalists, not because of concrete and well-founded grievances but because of the concerted designs of a well-organized and disaffected minority to subvert the authority of legally established institutions and undermine America's allegiance to the Mother Country.

For the loyalists petulance was an attribute of human depravity—conclusive evidence that most people were unfit for political responsibility; only subordination of subjects to their rulers and the maintenance of social hierarchy protected society from the perverse childishness of the disobedient and restive. Whig ideology, on the other hand, rested on a far more comprehensive inquiry into human nature. Only a people imbued with a sense of a social covenant and determined to regulate the exercise of power through constitutional means, whig ideology contended, could guard against the greed and aggression that were intrinsic to human nature.[28]

The loyalists' judgmental rhetoric betrayed their exasperation with the public's tolerance of disorder and disrespect for authority. "Wake up my friends," an anonymous loyalist exhorted his readers, "act like men, like free men, like reasonable creatures. . . . See and judge and act for yourselves." "Truth," he proclaimed, "delights in free enquiry"; therefore, he was appealing to the colonists to read and consider both the patriot and loyalist points of view.[29] Daniel Leonard also pleaded with his readers to "divest" themselves of "prejudice" and to "hear and weigh everything that is fairly adduced on either side of the question with equal attention and care."[30] Similar attempts to persuade the public to reflect dispassionately on both interpretations of the Anglo-American crisis were made by other loyalists. The Boston *Censor,* for instance, asserted that "truths" were arrived at by "compar[ing] discordant opinions,"[31] and an unknown New York loyalist proclaimed, "The ears of a genuine son of liberty are ever open to all doctrines; it is his glory to hear them, examine them, to adopt them if they are true, to confute them if they are false. . . ."[32] Yet loyalists themselves seemed to sense the futility of their endeavors to convince the public and their opponents of the need for an open and dispassionate discussion of Anglo-American issues.

The touchstone of patriot resistance, various loyalist writers declared, was its petulant refusal to listen to or tolerate criticism. A Massachusetts loyalist denounced the Worcester Resolves for advocating that loyal Americans refrain from subscribing to loyalist newspapers like the *Massachusetts Gazette* and likened the patriots to the Catholics who supposedly kept their parishioners in "total heathenish ignorance" so that they could be more easily controlled.[33]

Jonathan Sewall denounced the patriots as a "set of *enthusiastical* persons, who seem to think they have a right to tyrannize over their fellow creatures, and to threaten, insult and abuse everybody that cannot think and speak with them upon the state of our public affairs."[34] The perverse unwillingness of the patriots to tolerate other points of view was also condemned by Myles Cooper, who asked rhetorically, "Can they be friends to liberty, who will not allow any to think or speak differently from themselves, without danger? Will they compel the society to act according to their arbitrary decisions, and yet tell us we are free?"[35] Such intolerance and abusiveness, Daniel Leonard declared, was the product of "an illiberal, bigoted, arbitrary, malevolent disposition."[36] "Whoever contradicts a prevailing humour," explained the author of a prolonged reply to Dickinson's *Farmer's Letters,* "draws upon him the clamor of the multitude. The voice of a modest and impartial enquirer is often drowned in the popular cry. Wild enthusiastical rant, disconnected and unintelligible declamation which only serve to heat the world without instructing it, pass upon the world for truth and solid reasoning."[37]

The patriots' use of intimidation and coercion to silence those whose views were incompatible with their own, the loyalists alleged, opened the door to various excesses and naive ideas about the possibility of imposing virtue on a people. A taste of coercive power over their fellow men so intoxicated the people that they lost the sense of purpose and discrimination that had dignified the parliamentary leaders in their opposition during the early stages of the English civil war:

> Treating all men as mortal foes,
> Who dare their high behests oppose.
> Stark raving mad with party rage,
> With coward arms, those foes engage.
> . . . Dares the poor man impartial be,
> He's doomed to want and infamy . . .
> Sees all he loves a sacrifice,
> If he dares publish, ought—but lies.

> ... Alas, vain men, how blind, how weak;
> Is this the liberty we seek?
> Alas, by nobler motives led
> A Hampden fell, a Sydney bled.[38]

As the loyalists tried to analyze the perverse, petulant, abusive tide of American behavior, they perceived a new kind of revolutionary justice operating according to its own rules and imposing its own exalted standards of public virtue. The patriots did not appreciate the impossibility of imposing a new morality on their fellow men because they were blinded to the monstrous evil of intimidation and coercion. "You vainly imagined to force . . . belief [in] the treasonable articles of your absurd creed," Sewall complained, "by extorted *confessions, acknowledgements, recantations,* and *submissions*." How could the patriots be so gullible, Sewall demanded to know, as to place any credence in extorted, coerced conversions to their cause. Only "inebriated and intoxicated devotees of rapine and licentiousness" could be so deluded and irrational "as to suppose that any promises, declarations, and engagements thus extorted can be binding upon those unhappy victims to popular frenzy."[39] "Union," another loyalist argued, "can then only be right when the principles upon which it is founded are so." These principles involved "bring[ing] us over by argument and conviction not terror." "It is from such a temper alone that a permanent union can be formed."[40]

In addition to being associated with an obstinate and aggressive intolerance of dissenting views, petulance was related to the apparent churlishness and undisciplined character of the colonists. One of the most thoughtful considerations of the latter manifestation of petulant behavior was the high-Anglican series "A Whip for the American Whig." Only a powerful, conservative church that was closely allied with the government, the "Whip" argued, could inculcate enough respect for authority and decorum in public affairs to prevent liberty from degenerating into licentiousness and to restrain the passionate enthusiasts from trampling on the rights of the reasonable, dutiful subjects. "Religion is so confessedly advantageous to society that every reasonable man must endeavor to advance it," Myles Cooper posited, if only from the selfish motive of "increasing the happiness of the community of which he is a member." Reason and self-interest might incline some people to practice "honesty and obedience of government," but, for most men, the "sallies of ambition" and "the unresisted desire of unlimited freedom" could only be inhibited by the prospect of "future rewards" for "virtue" and "punishment of vice." By training people in self-discipline and reinforcing continually men's moral duty to respect and obey legitimate authority, religious teaching established "that *order* and *harmony* so requisite to the just motion in the springs of every political system."[41]

Deeply imbued with enlightenment ideas about equilibrium among theoretical political orders, the "Whip" series saw the Church of England and the British Crown subtly using each other—the church receiving protection and sponsorship, the Crown enjoying a gentle, non-coercive way of influencing its subjects. "This prerogative [by which the King was head of the Church] tends . . . to create a reverence and veneration for the prince as head of two bodies united, as defender of . . . religious as well as civil privileges: a reverence extremely well adapted to engage his subjects to a ready and cheerful obedience."[42]

The incessant campaign of vilification against the Anglican church—characterized by its "abusive" criticisms, "Slander," "Invective," and "Billingsgate"[43]—and the misrepresentation of its role as a handmaiden of authority, the "Whip" authors argued, undermined public respect for both religion and government. By persistently and abusively attacking the established Church of England, "The American Whig" was in fact "endeavouring to prejudice the cause of Christianity and to bring its ministers into disgrace."[44] Besides leveling a blow at Protestantism in casting "the most odius reflections on the Reformation,"[45] Livingston and Smith, by attacking the established church which was "so interwoven" with the constitution of the British state "that the one must be bent and torn to pieces with the other," were attempting to "inflame the passions of the populace and so root their prejudice that they become, in a great measure, invincible."[46]

Petulance was therefore a mixture of impatient irrationality and limited but dangerous cunning. The Tryon County magistrates and grand jurors, on March 16, 1775, denounced "the artifices used by violent and designing men to practise on the easy credulity of the good people."[47] "These inconsiderate people," complained "Bellisarius," "have made themselves idols, viz. Liberty Trees, Newspapers, and Congresses, which by blindly worshipping, have so engrossed their minds, that they neglect their honest professions and spend all of their time" in "taverns where they talk politicks, get drunk, damn King, Ministers, and Taxes and vow they will follow any measures proposed to them by these demagogues, however, repugnant to religion, reason, and common sense."[48] To some loyalists, the impulse behind petulant opposition to all restraint was narrow self-interest: "smuggling merchants" who, "finding themselves too closely watched," conspired to subvert all British authority in America. Resistance was clearly directed by "unprincipled, factious, designing men whose interest it has been to keep alive the coals of sedition."[49] "Every measure of the cabal" against enforcement of the Tea Act "is an undoubted proof that not your liberties but their private interest is the object," declared "Popicola" in the *Norwich Packet:* "They have too richly experienced the fruits from a contraband trade . . . to relinquish them to others without a struggle. To Liberty they can pretend no friendship. Every Step they have hitherto taken has been introductive of the most fatal tyranny, a tyranny of so high a nature as not to permit a fellow citizen even to think differently from them without danger."[50] "O poor *degenerate* children!," lamented two New York loyalists. "Such destroyers of liberty itself are a disgrace to their mother, if she is the goddess of liberty. For doth not liberty herself allow every man to enjoy his own sentiments."[51]

Conniving, avaricious politicians fed upon each other's weaknesses. "A New York Freeholder" commended the Athenian statute drafted by Solon that imposed

banishment or forfeiture of property on any citizen who stood aloof from a controversy that divided society into two fiercely antagonistic factions. "Designing,
passionate, or selfish persons," this writer explained, "are generally the promoters
of faction in every state whereas men of real merit and judgment are naturally
averse to tumults and fly from the boisterous haunts of discord." "Temperate, discreet colonists," "America's Real Friend" lamented, "have been too indolent; whilst
restless spirits [have] . . . led the inconsiderate into the deep gulphs of sedition,
where they lost virtue, loyalty, and good manners."[52]

Petulance was most dangerous because it perverted natural communication
between parent state and subordinate colonists. "Far from exciting our gratitude
or satisfying our uneasiness and discontent," Isaac Wilkins declared in the New
York Assembly, the repeal of the Stamp Act "has only emboldened us to make further encroachments upon [British] authority. We foolishly attribute this gentle
conduct towards us to fear and to a consciousness of her inability to compel us to
submission." Colonial antagonism and hostility to Britain, Wilkins complained,
displaced normal relations with the colonists' "kind and indulgent mother . . .
whose arms are open to receive all such of her children as will return to their
duty." Only "detestable parricides" would stab a mother's "bosom" simply to gratify the desire of "Ungrateful brethren" in Boston. The only way to secure redress
of grievances from a firm and loving parent was to argue the undue exercise of
power, not the illegitimacy of superior authority.[53] To the Anglican rector Henry
Caner, the American opposition to British measures was marked by a childlike
peevishness. Some American liberties had been "infringed," he admitted, but "will
it therefore follow that like froward children we should peevishly throw away
the rest, because some things have been taken away?" Instead, he advised that
the colonists adopt attitudes of "peace and submission, union and harmony"
to prevent "all blessings from being taken away."[54] Another observer castigated
the unruly and licentious methods adopted by the patriots in the dispute with
Britain when he asserted, "Sirs, is mobs, bullying, riots, treasons, rebellions &c.
the only effectual method for you to prosecute, to obtain his Majesty's and parliament's favour?"[55] Insolence and wantonness described the Continental Congress's approach to the Anglo-American dispute, according to an unknown loyalist
who contended that instead of pursuing "wise and prudent" courses of action, the
Congress adopted "rude, insolent and absurd resolves" and "wantonly" altered the
"constitution."[56] The colonists made fools of themselves when they "gravely assert
that [the British] people long famed for wisdom and love of liberty" would spend
"a thousand years in compounding and rearing up a constitution out of the
materials of the different simple forms of government" and in the end "select
nothing but the tyrannical forms of each." Too much of the history of England
had gone into the making of the constitution that the colonists now found
oppressive and too much blood had been spilled in defending it against domestic and foreign tyrants for colonial diatribes to weaken British resolve to maintain

Parliamentary supremacy. "Arguing from the abuse" of Parliamentary and royal power "rather than from the use" of those "things," the colonists would only forfeit any right to be taken seriously as commentators on British constitutionalism.[57]

To some loyalist writers, the Bostonians, who appeared to be spearheading the American opposition to Britain, epitomized the petulance characteristic of the patriots. Several loyalists criticized their intolerance and desires for domination over others. Peter Oliver in his "Address" to the Massachusetts militia depicted other Americans' attitudes toward Massachusetts as follows: "*the Massachusetts have a different interest from the rest of the Continent; they are a set of brave, hardy dogs; and are always encroaching upon their neighbours.*"[58] The Anglican authors of "A Whip for the American Whig" reminded their readers that it was the people of Massachusetts who hanged the "poor, harmless, inoffensive Quakers," while another defender of the Anglican church recounted the history of seventeenth-century Puritan bigotry.[59] The New England clergy, in the opinion of "Bellisarius," were "the instigators and abettors of every persecution and conspiracy."[60] A Quaker in Massachusetts itself shared the same view of the intolerance of his fellow colonists: "we tell thee friends we esteem George [III] a good sort of a Man ... he is willing every Man should worship God according to his Conscience ... which the town of Boston is not."[61] The "insidious" actions of the First Continental Congress, which were comparable to those of the "Spanish Inquisition," were, in the eyes of one loyalist, "borrowed from the seditious Bostonians."[62] The wantonness and self-righteousness associated with the Massachusetts capital was suggested by a group of New York freeholders who spoke of the "rebellious Saints at Boston."[63] A Massachusetts loyalist satirized the insolent and immodest behavior of the Bostonians by contriving a conversation in which a "high Patriotic Bostonian" was made to say "do not we in Boston live at the fountainhead of political knowledge and are we not to be believed?" In light of such patriot self-perceptions, the author concluded that it was dangerous to speak unless one were unalterably opposed to Britain and that the liberty of the press was for patriots only.[64] In describing the endeavors of the "cunning" and "zealous" patriots in the late 1760s to arouse the passions of the multitude, "Z.T." of Massachusetts paused "to consider the part acted by the town of Boston." "Their spirited resolves and instructions, polemical writings and ... practices, and their undue influence and example must have had some effect," he reasoned. "Did not the inhabitants of that town on all occasions keep up such a perpetual din to people from the country about politics, that they were even confounded with the clamour of it?," he began. "They so abounded with politicians, or the echoes of them," he continued, "that in all companies, the poor countryman must hear them display their oratory or vociferations, whether they would or not." Besides being assertive and rabble-rousing, the Bostonians were cunning and intolerant: "if anyone did offer to oppose them in their extravagant flights and invectives ... he might depend upon being ill treated; and called a d——g sl——ve, t——ry, or f——l; and it was also very difficult for a countryman to find where he might set in quiet to drink some-thing . . . for there are those who are more ready to stir up sedition or slander than to stir a bowl of punch; by which practices the weaker sort are misled, and the less credulous abused."[65]

Petulance, associated with insolent, pert, and undisciplined behavior, a child-ish unwillingness to consider seriously the reasoned arguments of critics, and an aggressive intolerance of dissenting views, was regarded as being a fatal weakness of the patriots. It led them, according to loyalists, to ignore the best long-term interests of the colonies in a reconciliation with the Mother Country which re-quired mature, prudent, discreet, and dutiful representations of colonial griev-ances to a supposedly just Mother Country, and to persevere in the belligerent, irresponsible, and shortsighted courses of action that were aggravating the dis-pute with Britain.[66] And to many loyalists, it was this kind of insolent, provoca-tive, and uncompromising behavior on the part of the patriots that was largely responsible for the crisis in Anglo-American relations. After discussing at length the high-handed, unrestrained and intolerant patriot methods, "Z.T." stated "that it may be justly concluded that such proceedings were greatly instrumental to our present distresses."[67] Henry Caner also believed that if "our affairs . . . are not so eligible now it is manifestly owing to the improper conduct of our officious patriots. . . ."[68] The Boston Port Bill, in the opinion of "A New York Freeholder," was the result of American "provocation."[69] Daniel Leonard was distressed at the measures adopted by the Continental Congress, which he felt would "irritate and enrage the inhabitants of the two countries, against each other, beyond a possi-bility of reconciliation"; however, the tone of the resolves could be explained to some extent by the fact that "some of the most influential of the members were the very persons that had been the *wilful* cause of the evils they were expected to remedy."[70] And a group of loyalists in White Plains, New York, declared, "our dis-approbation of many hot and furious proceedings against the measures taken by the mother country, as, in our opinion, they will rather tend to ruin this once happy continent, than remove grievances."[71]

Moreover, the patriots' attempts to intimidate or coerce those who held opposing views convinced many loyalists that, while mouthing shibboleths about liberty, the patriots were in fact infringing the most basic civil freedoms of Ameri-cans. This conviction led several loyalist writers to conclude that the most sub-stantive threat to their freedom emanated not from Britain but from the patriot congresses, committees, and mobs in their midst. As early as November 1773, Myles Cooper advised his readers that "while we are watchful against external attacks upon our freedom, let us be on our guard, lest we become enslaved by . . . tyrants within."[72] "Take heed," another loyalist warned, "that while the words tyranny and oppression are bandied about, and fixed on Britain, you are not unawares enthralled at home."[73] After denouncing the tyrannical implications of the First Continental Congress's Association, one loyalist declared, "I shall not dare to think or act, but I shall be in danger of being held up as an enemy to my country. . . . Am I to be a slave? I will then be a slave to a King and a Parliament."[74]

The charge of ingratitude touched a sensitive nerve in whig consciousness. The Revolutionary generation had become increasingly enmeshed in its dependence on British consumer goods, capital, and credit. The price of this economic Anglicization, Marc Egnal and Joseph A. Ernst argue persuasively, was periodic liquidity crises and the erosion of colonial mercantile independence in the marketplace.[75] Against this background of provincialism and uncertainty, many colonists groped toward a reassessment of the benefits they enjoyed as subjects of the Empire. Loyalist writers to the press, in contrast, boldly seized the issue of colonial self-interest in imperialism and made it their own. Ingratitude for the benefits of the Empire weakened the fabric of colonial subordination, the loyalist press argued, because men ignored their own best interests, misunderstood the reciprocal benefits that colonists and the British nation received from the imperial connection, and lacked the patience and sophistication to engineer a reconciliation of the imperial controversy which would preserve American liberty without destroying the Empire. Concerned with economic interests, with the preservation of stability and harmony in society, and a pragmatic approach in dealings with imperial authority, the denunciation of patriot ingratitude was grounded in reason and experience.

"It is impossible to review the advantages we derive from our connection with Great Britain," "A Philadelphian" declared, "without wishing it to be perpetual. We are formed by her laws and religion: we are clothed by her manufacturers and protected by her fleets and armies. Her kings are the umpires of our disputes, and the center of our union. In a word, the Island of Britain is the fortress in which we are sheltered from the machinations of all the powers of Europe." Here was the classic loyalist view of the nature of the Empire which portrayed Britain as a dynamic culture from which law, religion, military security, and political authority flowed irresistibly to weaker, far-flung colonial societies. The colonists, this writer maintained, were instinctively anxious and insecure about their own ability to survive in a world of powerful assertive European nations. It was therefore axiomatic that a "review" of imperial benefits would strengthen people's identification with the Empire: "no wonder . . . we look forward with horror to those conclusions which must attend ([for] ages hence) our separation from that country."[76]

The stabilizing effect of the British tie was emphasized by Isaac Wilkins, who argued, "Shall we not derive strength, protection and stability from that oak around which we have so long twined ourselves and under the shadow of whose branches, we have so long flourished in security"; it is "our interest" and "our duty" to "cultivate the closest and most intimate union with her [Britain]."[77] Other loyalists stressed the security and freedom guaranteed to the colonists by the British constitution. To Henry Caner, the English constitution was "most perfect," most "favourable to Liberty," and a constitution under which "the subject enjoys more liberty, is more secure in his property, and in the enjoyment of every valuable blessing and Privilege than the subject of any other nation under Heaven." Similarly, a group of loyalist Associators joined together "to declare our firm and indissoluble attachment to our most gracious Sovereign George the third . . . and with grateful hearts to acknowledge that we are indebted to his paternal care for the preservation of our lives and fortunes."[78] In the opinion of another loyalist, the unity, harmony, and vitality of the various colonies depended on the maintenance of the British tie. "The superintendence and mediation of Great Britain seems to be necessary to balance . . . the different interests of the several plantations and colonies, and to direct, command and govern the operations and powers of *each* for the benefit and defence of *All.*" Furthermore, he contended, "protected by her navy and armies, we shall rise with fresh vigour and strength, and see her free and well balanced constitution gradually communicated to us. In a state of separation, on the contrary, ages may pass, and rivers of blood be shed before any regular form of government could be adopted and fixed on a firm basis."[79] An important factor in colonial economic growth and prosperity, declared "Rusticus," was Britain's "readiness to increase our industry and protect us from foreign injuries. . . . Surely some returns of gratitude, such as become a free and liberal people are justly due for favours received."[80]

Though mutual interest and obligation knit the Empire together, the relationship of the colonies to their parent state depended upon British restraint in the use of imperial authority and colonial passivity in responding to British measures. "Eugenio" felt unable to conceive of the Empire in terms other than those of "a parent and her children. . . . I look upon it as the duty of Great Britain," he declared, "to give her colonies that countenance and protection to which as children they are certainly entitled, . . . not only defense of person and property against our common enemies abroad, but [also] the preservation of our essential rights and liberties." He counted on "mutual forebearance" to compensate for "any little appearances of severity on one side or petulancy on the other." The need for such familial goodwill was imperative: "I can easily foresee that unnumbered calamities must burst upon these American colonies unless present difficulties between them and the parent land be speedily adjusted." If the British abridged colonial rights, then colonial self-interest required an added measure of toleration and acquiescence; conversely, the British needed to allow their headstrong children a healthy latitude in coping with the requirements of imperial policy.[81]

The colonists' ingratitude—their unwillingness to recognize the past, present, and future benefits derived from the imperial tie—led them, according to loyalists, to countenance a rebellion that was totally unnatural. The adjective *unnatural,* used frequently by loyalists to describe the Revolution, reflected their belief that the colonies and Britain were naturally tied to each other by the bonds of culture, history, and mutual interest. Severing such a beneficial and deeply rooted link was contrary to the dictates of both reason and colonial self-interest. Because of the "infatuated blindness"[82] of the colonists to their "true interest" and their ingratitude for past British aid and benevolence to the colonies, the patriots could assert what appeared to loyalists to be totally inconsistent with reason and history: that Britain was no longer the mother who "nourished, protected and established us," but had become a tyrant.[83] That such a perception of Britain was totally irreconcilable with common sense and history was asserted forcefully by Daniel Leonard: "Are we to take up arms and make war against our parent, lest that parent, contrary to the experience of a century and a half, contrary to her own genius, inclination, affection and interest, should treat us or our posterity as bastards, and not as sons, and instead of protecting, should enslave us."[84]

The debate in Philadelphia in the spring of 1776 over the alternatives of independence and reconciliation matched the infectious radicalism of Thomas Paine's *Common Sense* against Provost William Smith's deft, adroit advocacy of delay, caution, and patience as bulwarks of colonial liberty. "I am bold to declare and hope yet to make it evident to every honest man," Smith asserted, "that the true interest of America lies in reconciliation with Great Britain upon constitutional principles, and . . . upon no other terms." Smith's bold pronouncement was at once aggressive and flexible. Inclusion in the Empire was not merely a negative restraint, he explained, it was also a source of insight, capability, and strategy for the colonists. "We [have] considered our connection with Great Britain as our chief happiness" because under it "we flourished, grew rich and populous. . . . Let us then act the part of skillful physicians and wisely adapt the remedy to the evil."[85]

Smith realized that there was a broad coalition of moderates in Pennsylvania who feared the social disruption that would accompany independence and civil war. The Pennsylvania social order—with its numerous ethnic and religious factions and its divided political elite—was more than any other colony susceptible to this argument. "The world has already seen numberless instances of fine-spun political theories which, like the quackeries of mountebank doctors, are to cure all the political evils to which human nature is liable," Smith observed. Sweeping programs of political purification, he went on, invariably ran afoul of a "thousand little passions and interests" which protected people from the arbitrary whims of ambitious rulers and agitators. Independence won through armed rebellion, he warned, would produce "every convulsion attendant upon revolutions and innovations in government untimely attempted or finally defeated: the loss of trade for want of protection, the consequent decay of husbandry, bloodshed and desolation, . . . an exchange of the easy and flourishing condition of farmers and merchants for a life at best of hardy poverty as soldiers or hunters." Smith saw the society and economy of the middle colonies as rich, expansive, and rewarding while the political system governing the province was brittle, inexperienced, and vulnerable. While "agriculture and commerce have hitherto been the happy employments by which these middle colonies have risen in wealth and importance," all of these attainments could be lost if the British ceased protecting the colonies from the grasping designs of other European powers. Even a successful revolt against the Mother Country would leave the Americans discredited in the eyes of mankind as a "faithless people," and an abortive rebellion would disrupt the fragile infrastructure of trade, credit, and the honoring of civil obligations. "To see America reduced to such a situation may be the choice of adventurers who have nothing to lose or of men exalted by the present confusions into lucrative offices which they can hold no longer than the continuation of the public calamities," Smith declared. It was not only the bloodshed and dislocation of a civil war that alarmed him, but the emergence into leadership positions of new men hungry for recognition and impatient with the pace of advancement under imperial rule. Surely the "great and valuable people in *America,* who by honest industry have acquired a competency and have experienced a happy life," would do everything in their power to avoid an abrupt shift in leadership and power.[86]

The trouble with this conservative calculation, Smith acknowledged, was that "the people generally judge aright [only] when the whole truth is plainly laid before them, but through inattention in some and fondness for novelty in others" only "one side" in the imperial controversy was receiving wide circulation and appreciation. Politicians abused the privilege of addressing a public audience when, like the advocates of independence, "they exaggerate or conceal facts, . . . state but one side of a question, . . . warp the judgment [of their audience] by partial representation, . . . give railing for reason, invectives for arguments, and . . . urge the people into hasty resolutions by addressing [men's] passions rather than [their] sober reason."[87] Reconciliation, therefore, required a calm, dispassionate citizenry capable of hearing all of the arguments on both sides of the imperial dispute and secure enough to resist being stampeded into precipitous action. Smith conceded that independence could be legitimately declared if the whole community became "convinced by better arguments than declamations and abuse of things venerable and ancient that future connection with *Great Britain* is neither possible nor safe."[88] For all practical purposes, he argued, the colonists had already declared de facto independence by preparing to resist British coercion and by asserting broad claims of colonial liberty. "It is our duty to continue this resistance till Great Britain is convinced (as she must soon be) of her fatal policy and open her arms to reconciliation." Resolute but not offensive, united and eschewing factional agitation, the colonists, Smith argued, could secure redress without resorting to violence or rebellion. "Upon such a footing we may again be happy. Our husbandmen, our mechanicks, our artificers will flourish. Our language, our laws, our manners being the same as those of the nation with which we are again to be connected." It was an appealing formula. Political calm would restore a flourishing economy; an easing of imperial tensions would enable British culture to continue to serve as a stabilizing force in the diverse society of the middle colonies. Having shown firmness and patience in dealing with British encroachments, the imperial "connection will become more natural and we shall more easily guard against foreign innovations." "*Pennsylvania,*" Smith concluded, making his point unmistakably clear, "has much to lose in this contest and much to hope from a proper settlement of it."[89]

Loyalist writers stressed that colonial ingratitude was a self-inflicted wound that deprived the Americans of the leadership of some of their most courageous and unselfish fellow citizens. "Does not that man deserve to be heard with candour," asked "A Philadelphian," "who desires not to counteract the general sentiments of his countrymen but thinks it a duty incumbent upon him to endeavor to guard against an evil which may have a tendency to destroy the hope of every virtuous patriot—a hope of our united efforts may be a means to a redress of grievances [and] that the lasting and happy union may be restored between the Mother Country and her Colonies?" By identifying liberty and happiness with the maintenance of political calm and unity, the loyalists were able to depict ingratitude as a cast of mind into which people slipped when they tired of the burden of supporting a common public consensus—a middle position enjoying the widest possible support. The emotional gratification of fracturing that consensus by abusing individuals was, lamentably, very strong.[90] "Such is the violence of our disputing parties," wrote "A Moderate Man," that "whoever differs from either is immediately stigmatized as a *whig* or a *tory*, . . . terms of disgrace according as they are applied by these parties to each other." Many of those who suffer such vituperation "are really pursuing that which appears to them for the interest of the community." What was remarkable about this persecution of the innocent moderates, "A Moderate Man" explained, was a new self-consciousness and sense of political purpose which the experience instilled into the personalities of apolitical novices: "to moderate these party heats, to draw that zeal into a channel where it would really be serviceable, is the duty of every member of the community," he concluded; only when "mutual forbearance, amity, and love" replace "hard words" can "any society" become "quiet and happy."[91]

To execute this kind of political therapy, urged "A Farmer" in the *Pennsylvania Packet*, " let us equally shun the benumbing stillness of *overweening sloth* and the feverish activity of ill-formed zeal which busies itself in maintaining little, mean, and narrow opinions."[92] The most self-conscious newspaper advocacy of a fresh mental outlook in the pursuit of reconciliation appeared in a series of essays by Richard Wells in the *Packet* in the summer of 1774. "The more 1 consider the importance of the present controversy," he declared, "the more I am convinced of the need of wisdom in our councils. . . . Reason must command our forces. . . . The sparkling ideas of a warm imagination are too apt to soar into the regions of danger and, without providing a proper retreat, involve the bold adventurer in unthought of perplexities." Resisting Parliamentary violations of the colonists' constitutional rights, Wells insisted, required rigorous self-control and disciplined use of imagination. "I *contend with a zeal which convinces me that I am right* that we must not pass by the present temper of the times" for a time of crisis was precisely the moment when a high sense of responsibility could offset men's rashness and mindless aggression. "Our passions cannot always remain upon the stretch;

[soon] we shall gently relax from the severity of strict right and heedlessly and gradually slide down the hill of [mere negative] opposition [allowing] our rulers [to] become tyrants and from a country of happy freemen, we shall degenerate into a land of abject slaves."[93]

Pleading for a cautious, deliberate response to British encroachments, Wells advocated a circuitous strategy in which the Americans would ask the King to instruct his governors to recommend to the assemblies the gathering of a continental congress to draft *an American Bill of Rights.* Colonial negotiators could then carry this document to London and bargain for British approval of a "legal and firm contract." Such a process would recognize that the Empire was an amalgam of many activities, motives, and purposes: "'tis offensive [and] defensive, connected [and] independent, a mixture of rivalry and friendship, a greater [entity] subordinate to the lesser, and yet all bound together by one interest and affection." By conceiving of the Empire as a source of vast material benefits to the colonists, the advocates of reconciliation pointed within the social order itself for insights and wisdom to guide their fellow citizens in confrontation with British power.[94]

Confronted with an apparently brutish and immoral British regime, the whigs looked deeply into their collective selves as the final crises of 1774–76 crashed around them. Externally, they assumed a posture of defiant disobedience. As they prepared for defensive, hopefully peaceful, resistance to the Coercive Acts, they discovered their ability to decentralize resistance through local committees of inspection and correspondence and also how to entrust direction of the common cause to a continental congress. Surprised and emboldened by these discoveries, the leaders of resistance scarcely realized how much they had accelerated the pace of events leading toward independence and war.[95] A few years earlier, a unified movement for national independence would have been inconceivable; to the loyalists watching, the spectacle was incomprehensible and outrageous.

Overt, deliberate, violent disobedience to constituted authority, the loyalist polemicists declared, was rebellion—the ultimate outrage against God and society. "Rebellion is the most atrocious offence that can be perpetrated by man," exhorted Daniel Leonard; "it dissolves the social band, annihilates the security resulting from law and government; introduces fraud, violence, rapine, murder, sacrilege and the long trail of evils, that riot uncontrouled in a state of nature."[96] In one of the most cogent and informative loyalist newspaper polemics, "Plain English" in February 1775 depicted the threshold of rebellion in a listing of twenty-nine specific acts of aggression against "people, who from a sense of their duty to the King and a reverence for his laws, have behaved quietly and peaceably." "Barbarous cruelties, insults, and indignities, . . . disgraceful even for savages to have committed," composed his profile of "lawless mobs and riots." "Plain English" perceived clearly that the abuse and intimidation of known allies of the Crown and of all officials who refused to renounce the legitimacy of the Coercive Acts radically changed the framework of politics in Massachusetts. The assertion of the will of the people and the physical power that large numbers of people could exert created a new atmosphere of fear and terror in the province. "Last August a mob in Berkshire forced the justices of the court of common pleas from their seats and shut up the court house," the enumeration began; "they also drove David Ingersoll, Esq. from his house and damaged the same. . . . Col. [Thomas] Gilbert of Freetown, a firm friend to government, in August last, being at Dartmouth, was attacked at midnight by a mob of about an hundred but by his bravery [and] with the assistance of the family where he lodged, they were beat off." "Mr. [Jonathan] Sewall, his Majesty's attorney general for this province was obliged to repair to Boston for refuge; his elegant house at Cambridge was attacked by a mob, his windows broke, but they were beat off by the gallant behaviour and bravery of some of the young gentlemen of his family."

Rebellion, "Plain English" sensed, was more than the seizure of power through physical coercion and violence. Random, spontaneous acts of aggression created an aura of their own—unintended and unanticipated by the perpetrators of such conduct—which corroded the structure of civility and acquiescence to authority that were essential to civil government. Daniel Leonard was not only forced to evacuate his fine house in Taunton, but also compelled to watch as the mob fired bullets into the empty structure as a ghoulish gesture of their determination to destroy every vestige of support for the Crown. Vandals cut hair from the mane and tail of Timothy Ruggle's fine horse. At Worcester a crowd of 5,000 required thirty judges, sheriffs, and lawyers to walk bareheaded between two columns of armed men and then signify their compliance with the closing of the courts in defiance of the Coercive Acts. It was the mobs' insistence on symbolic victories that revealed to "Plain English" their design of destroying the symbols of authority and self-respect held by men of accomplishment and social standing in the community. "Daniel Dunbar of Halifax, an ensign of militia there," this account explained, "had his [regimental] colours demanded by the mob, some of the selectmen being the chief actors; he refused; they broke into his house, took him out, forced him upon a rail and was held on it by his hands and legs and tossed up with violence." When Dunbar "resisted" being put "on the rail, they seized him by his private parts to drag him on it, then beat him and after keeping him two or three hours in such abuses, he was forced to give his colours up to save his life."[97]

In the extreme form of rebellion, political disobedience was a mania compounded from the guilt and desperation of evil leaders. "Your officers, my countrymen!," Peter Oliver appealed to Massachusetts militiamen in January 1776, "have taken great pains to sooth and flatter you, that you may not quit your posts and forsake *them* until they have accomplished their ambitious and desperate schemes. Your leaders know that they have plunged themselves into the bowels of the most wanton and unnatural rebellion that ever existed; they think that by engaging large numbers to partake in their guilt that they shall appear formidable, and that by so numerous an appearance the hand of justice will not dare to arrest them." That desperate gamble, that willingness to plunge society into chaos without any consideration of the consequences, generated powerful destructive energies. In what would be a preview of his full-scale history of the Revolution, Oliver narrated the "origin and progress of the publick disorders which . . . terminated in a most unnatural and ungrateful rebellion." By systematically engaging in smuggling, a group of merchants had accustomed themselves to "defrauding King," "injuring and publickly ruining" their fellow subjects, and "by degrees" abandoning every pretense to virtue and responsibility. In the pursuit of illegal gain, the smugglers enlisted as an ally James Otis, Jr., who through oratory and radicalism "swore he would set the province in a flame if he died in the attempt." But the flame that Otis ignited and fanned, because it originated in compulsive ambition and vindictiveness, was the "sort of flame that consumes not only a man's property but also [his] understanding." To offset the "popular commotions" aroused by an attack on the authority of Parliament, Otis felt "it was necessary to enlist a *black regiment*" of clergymen to cast an aura of religiosity on these turbulent and vicious actions. What had started as an opposition to the acts of trade became a torrent of perverted moral outrage: "the press roared out its libels; the sacred desk . . . sounded the trumpet of sedition and rebellion. . . . Libertinism, riot, and robbery soon became the effects of this sort of public spirit; houses were plundered and demolished; persons were beat, abused, tarred and feathered; courts of justice were insulted; the pillars of justice were destroyed; and no way to escape the torrent of savage barbarity but by paying obeisance to the sovereign mandates of a mob." In this macabre setting, the drama could lead only to death and desolation. "Garretts were crowded with patriots; mechanicks and lawyers, porters and clergymen huddled promiscuously into them; their decisions were oracular, and from thence poured out their midnight reveries: . . . to form an independent empire" in which "all the friends of licentiousness were to be reimbursed out of the estates of the friends to government."[98]

Rebelliousness, the loyalists concluded, was therefore an irreversible contagion sustained by the desperation of its fomenters and the fear and ignorance of its growing circle of adherents. Once they employed violence and deceit, the patriots could not hope to control and regulate the behavior of their own supporters; the most ambitious and most cowardly among them would always succumb to the temptation to commit fresh outrages. The career of Nathanael Greene, "A British American" in Charleston wrote in May 1781, illustrated perfectly the way in which "political phrenzy" elevated the most "infamous" men to positions of profit and power. Greene's avarice had been whetted by speculation in Rhode Island paper currency; his ambition ignited when he inveigled his way into Washington's favor early in the war. His early attachment to the dignified and upright Washington was further evidence of his unscrupulous behavior. Washington, at the outset of the war, was known to have doubts about the wisdom of independence. Greene must have known that Washington's heart was not wholly committed to the patriot cause and must have planned to consign "Washington to oblivion" and take his place. "Did you indeed expect Washington would resign?," "British American" demanded. "Is it possible ambition had so totally obliterated humanity that"—unlike Washington—"you could look forward to the redoubled calamities of war and ruin of your country without emotion? Recent experience answers you could. . . . The deliberate murders committed in cold blood, under your influence and direction in the Carolinas in the space of two months, exceed the number ever committed in any one war recorded in the history of Europe. . . . Entrusted with a separate command, . . . your vanity has been partly gratified, . . . and the peaceable inhabitants of America now feel, what they might have long expected, from such a commander as you are."[99]

Disobedience and rebellion, the loyalist press maintained, dissolved the delicate network of social relationships that held human aggression under control and enabled people to live in peace and security. By drawing large numbers of people into lawless behavior and by creating large geographical areas where no law or constituted authority functioned, warfare accelerated and magnified this process of social disintegration and moral abandon. Among the most vivid documents illustrating these conditions and expressing this point of view was the narrative of Levi Smith, a South Carolina loyalist militia officer, which told of his capture and imprisonment by the patriots in the South Carolina backcountry during May and June 1781. Disobedience and rebellion generated rampant falsehood, Smith complained; "our enemies have been indefatigable in propagating and screaming accounts of every circumstance by which they feel themselves aggrieved or improperly treated by our government" while "a uniform silence prevails on our side under the hardest usage, . . . although we have had by far the greatest reason to complain." Loyalist prisoners of the patriots, Smith testified, had received "the most cruel treatment" from their captors, and these "shocking" atrocities should be made known to the whole world. Sceptical readers of his narrative, Smith suggested, could consult numerous loyalist refugees and British soldiers—several identified by name—who had been eyewitnesses to the outrages he had seen.

Smith's story was a grisly one. Upon capture he had been stripped to his undershirt and forced to run for a mile ahead of his mounted captors. When he collapsed, the patriot soldiers beat him with the flat edges of their swords. Once confined in Francis Marion's camp, he arranged to be exchanged for Samuel Cooper, a patriot held by Lord Rawdon. Cooper's brother, William, one of Smith's captors, initiated the exchange. For the next few days he was treated leniently, even allowed to go fishing with a single guard and visit his wife and children while awaiting the prisoner exchange to be completed. Then on the afternoon of May 14, the patriots captured a British outpost and confined their new loyalist and British prisoners, along with Smith, in a mill house. The American commander, Col. Francis Lee, then ordered the hanging of a young loyalist militia officer named Fulker who was accused of turning a sick woman from her house and thereby causing her death. Next the Americans condemned two loyalist militiamen to death. For carrying intelligence to the British army, Priv. John Jackson "was hurried off, stripped, and tied up [by the neck] about dark, and left hanging all night . . . while Fulker's body, which had been cut down to make room for him, lay naked under the gallows." The following day a militiaman named Hugh Maskelly, charged with various forms of collaboration with the British, was led off to the gallows with "only an old dirty shirt tied round him," executed "without the slightest trial or hearing." To his horror, Smith discovered that he was next on Francis Lee's execution list. Demanding to know the charges against him, Smith was charged with having had a part in the burning of the tavern of a Mrs. McCord, whom Smith knew as "a person of notorious disaffection to the British cause." Protesting he had known nothing of the burning until two hours after it occurred, Smith convinced several Continental officers standing nearby that he deserved a trial. Nevertheless, "I was now made ready for execution. The old dirty hunting shirt was taken from Maskelly's body and wrapped around mine." Fearing that Rawdon would retaliate by executing his brother, Samuel, William Cooper got a message to General Marion who arrived at the improvised gallows in time to save Smith's life.

Greene then ordered Smith put in irons. While waiting further disposition of their cases, the loyalist captives in Greene's camp underwent a further ordeal. John McCord, the son of the woman whose tavern had been burned by the patriots, arrived in the camp with a group of loyalist prisoners in chains. These prisoners brought harrowing rumors. A few days earlier, their reports contended, McCord had taken fourteen loyalist militiamen prisoner and handcuffed them in seven pairs. Marching these prisoners to Greene's headquarters and fearful of being overtaken by pursuing patriots, McCord had ordered two of his subordinates to shoot the prisoners in cold blood. "All . . . died except one Joseph Cooper. . . . The person who was handcuffed with him was named Conrad Millar and was shot first. The murderer . . . loaded his piece again" and "with great deliberation took sight at Cooper, who moved his head on one side when he perceived him drawing the trigger. . . . The bullet passed through the right side of his neck and he fell; upon which one of the guard run his sword through his neck to make sure of dispatching him and observed he had never seen a son of a bitch bleed so much in his life." Miraculously, Cooper did not die from these wounds. He dragged his dead companion and himself under a shade tree. The next day, the "stench" of Millar's body attracted the attention of two women in the neighborhood. They returned with a knife, cut off Millar's arm below the elbow, and moved Cooper to a house where his handcuff could be broken off and his wounds treated. (Some of these details Smith learned later when both he and Cooper were safely in Charleston.) News of this atrocity filled Greene's camp and so terrorized many loyalists that, fearful of the same fate, they enlisted in the rebel cause to escape captivity. Smith, however, refused to renounce his British allegiance. By this time Greene was in possession of captured documents showing that, prior to his capture, Smith had provided the British with military intelligence. "He asked me if I did not deserve death, as I was American born. I told him that the province had been conquered and that I had, of course, become a British subject." Apparently taking account of Smith's previous mistreatment, Greene paroled him to a nearby plantation to regain his health, and Smith—with some moral qualms—took the chance to escape and, still clad in Hugh Maskelly's bloody shirt, found safety with Lord Rawdon's force which was marching to relieve Fort Ninety Six.[100]

Rebellion, in these gruesome terms, was the natural, predictable outgrowth of all of the political opportunism, social degeneracy, and perverted communalism that had precipitated the upheaval. It fused all of these symptoms into a single fatal malady. The process of disaffection climaxed in a state of rebellion where the whole network of social relations and the traditional authority of institutions of church and state, which restrained passions and inculcated morality, were undermined to unleash the thinly veiled depravity of mankind. Released from the restraints of law and morality and aroused by a cabal of cunning and aggressive intriguers, the passions of the populace knew no bounds. Atrocities took place, often without the knowledge of the Revolutionary leaders themselves, which were unimaginable in a civilized community. For Daniel Leonard this descent into barbarity was what rebellion meant: "a state of war, of all against all . . . [where] might overcomes right; [and] innocence itself has no security."[101] America had been led down the fatal road to rebellion, in the opinion of the loyalist press, by a minority of crafty and aggressive patriots who displayed an incomprehensible ignorance of the best long-term interests of the colonies and an obstinate refusal to take account of the reasoned appeals of critics. They had plunged the colonies into an irrational, unjustifiable, and self-destructive war against a Mother Country whose benevolence, protection, and aid to the colonies, and whose commitment to constitutional liberty, should have evoked Americans' gratitude rather than their disloyalty. Calm, dispassionate colonists who tried desperately to warn their fellow Americans of the dangerous route that they were embarking upon were, loyalist writers contended, intimidated, coerced, and silenced by patriots who would brook no opposition. As was often the case, Daniel Leonard summarized succinctly the loyalist view of the Revolution when he proclaimed, "the annals of the world have not yet been deformed with a single instance of so unnatural, so causeless, so wanton, so wicked a rebellion."[102]

3. "To Make Blind Eyes Blinder and the Deceived People [to] Imagine Vain Things": The Ultimate Moral Indictment of the Revolution

The corpus of loyalist essays in the press of the Revolutionary era depicts the psychic turmoil wrought by a radical change in the political culture. As old patterns of acquiescence collapsed, as new standards of political morality came to dominate public affairs, and as the pace and tempo of events accelerated, the loyalists' sense of identity, probity, and composure came under severe stress. Internalizing a political culture that was rapidly disappearing and assigning themselves a new role as agents of virtue and reason in a world gone mad, the writers of the loyalist press illustrate the intimate connection between the human spirit and the larger culture of values, expectations, and behavioral norms within which people live. Convinced that the dominant culture of their society no longer motivated people to adopt proper conduct, they sought to "revitalize" it—to make it satisfying and coherent once again. They tried to understand the plight of a strife-ridden and war-torn political order by rethinking and recasting their own deepest yearnings and aspirations in a manner that would harmonize once again their inner and outer worlds.[103]

Simply recognizing the disparity between their own perception of the truth and the motivations and impulses of the patriots liberated the loyalist writers from uncertainty and apprehension. An open letter to "Peyton Randolph" by "Grotius" in January 1775 gained momentum and accusatory power as it identified the tension: "how then, sir, could you thus attempt to make blind eyes blinder, to make the mad Americans rage, and the deceived people imagine vain things. How could you thus set yourselves and take counsel against the Lord's anointed—stimulating the inhabitants of this continent to wage war with their parents and rebel against their lawful sovereign after declaring yourselves his most *loyal subjects* and avowing an *affection and regard for your fellow-subjects*?" "Grotius's" dialectic between morality and disobedience was so taut and highly charged that his argument fairly leaped from assumption to prescription: "surely you could not suppose" that the Continental Association was "a healing measure, tending to an accommodation of our unhappy differences. You must know your preamble was calculated to blind the reason and enflame the passions of Americans, and your association an open act of hostility which could not fail to sharpen the resentments of an affronted, powerful nation, jealous of their rights and tender of their honour."

It was this insensitivity to the known and natural predispositions of British national sentiment that represented for "Grotius" the clearest evidence that the patriots were ignoring the most obvious moral and political realities: "Englishmen, Sir, can never submit to [the] despotism" of illegal committeemen; "an Englishman cannot tamely look on and see bread snatched by ruffians from his children's mouths—it is too much for human nature to bear—it will drive men to desperation, and must surely be productive of confusion and bloodshed." By the grossness and barbarity of their behavior, "Grotius" explained, the patriots would goad humane British rulers to unleash the severe retribution at the hand of a long-suffering, almost infinitely patient, parent finally driven to impose discipline. "It is strange indeed," he concluded incredulously "that wise men should hit upon treason and rebellion as a means of *pacifying* an *offended sovereign;* upon *violence* and *robbery* as the preservatives of *civil liberty.*" Reason and elementary political judgment indicated that just the opposite was true; "how much more certainly would the tendency of a gentle, peaceable, orderly conduct have been to obtain these desirable ends."[104]

By adopting a system of moral absolutism, the loyalist press maintained, the patriots dehumanized the British—forgetting the human feelings that ingratitude and rebellion aroused in the minds and hearts of British rulers. When the New

York Constitutional Convention, in early 1777, castigated Britain for its coercion and abuse of colonial Americans who had a long record of loyalty and service to the Empire, "Integer," in Gaine's *New-York Mercury,* seized the polemical initiative. Incredulously, he quoted the convention's characterization of "the inhabitants of Britain" as a "nation and people bound to us by the strongest ties; a people by whose side we have fought and bled; whose power we have contributed to raise, who owe much of their wealth to our industry, and whose grandeur has been augmented by our exertions." "Gentle reader," retorted "Integer," "here is a great deal of matter in a few words. . . . 'Bound to us by the strongest ties'; I suppose the Convention meant by saying this to give us a proof of their great strength in having burst those ties asunder. . . . 'Whose power we have contributed to raise'; that is, Great Britain had no power till after she had drained herself of people in order to strengthen us, that we might strengthen her." By making their own ego the center of their political culture, "Integer" explained, the New York patriots had "totally inverted . . . the order of things" in claiming that the British had reduced them to being "*miserable slaves.*" "All of us know," "Integer" scornfully declared, "what wretches, what Israelites in bondage, we have hiterto been till our good representatives . . . undertook our deliverance. Nobody could possess his farm or dispose of his merchandise; nobody lived in peace or security. Nobody could even say that he had life or property before we were under the direction of our Congresses, Conventions, and watchful committees."[105]

Imbibing unnatural and untried doctrines about their obligations as subjects, the loyalists contended, the patriots became victims of their own desperation. "It was the universal and professed maxim" at the outbreak of hostilities with Britain, wrote the Reverend J. J. Zubly under the pseudonym "Helvetius" in the *Royal Georgia Gazette* in 1780, that "*if we succeed we will be called a revolution and deemed a rebellion if we miscarry.*" This "neck or nothing" frame of mind anesthetized the patriots from the pain of anticipating the "ruin and destruction . . . coming on apace." "Helvetius" had even heard South Carolina patriots say, "we must not look to the consequences," as though the very possibility of defeat and punishment, seriously considered, would be enough to unnerve the radicals. "Upon no other principle than the prospect of success, and that success would abolish the criminality of the means," he concluded, "would men that have any regard for their lives engage in any desperate action." The rebellion not only ignored the truth and gloried in violence, injustice, and irresponsibility, it necessarily converted truth into falsehood and good into evil: "upon this plan . . . men must place perjury in the room of a lawful oath, to murder must be no crime; rapine and violence hold the place of equity and justice, nor can any design be too dark or any action too villainous for men that expect to succeed in wickedness." By this circular morality, the Revolution became a self-justifying endeavor in which "success will sanctify . . . all the measures made use of to obtain it."[106]

Bound together by their desperate flight from reality, by an abandonment of traditional moral norms, and by the perversion of the truth, the revolutionaries had plunged their society into a moral and social morass. "Before the interruption of regal government [in South Carolina], plenty, affluence, and increasing prosperity seemed to combine to render the people happy, while poverty, wretchedness, and ruin characterize the era of democratick oppression," wrote "Drusus" in the *South-Carolina and American General Gazette* early in British reoccupation of the province. Yet pacification and submission to British authority was not yet complete. "Can any man be so absurd as to imagine that the inhabitants of this country were subjects to Congress?" If Congress could not provide protection and military security for the people living under British occupation, how could it claim allegiance?, "Drusus" demanded. In theoretical terms, no confederation even existed until the Articles of Confederation were ratified. In practical terms, the disintegration of the insurrectionary administration in South Carolina was ample evidence of Congress's artificiality and illegitimacy. "If . . . this MIGHTY STATE [i.e., South Carolina from 1775 to 1780] in possession of *legislative authority*" and an "*executive*" inflicting "vengeance and confiscation against the refractory and, exercizing arbitrary and despotick power in violation of every principle of the constitution, could not prevent its DISSOLUTION, can it be reasonably supposed . . . that Congress, aided by a few republican enthusiasts in this province will be able to reestablish its independency and participation in the union?"[107]

In their quest for a coherent understanding of the Revolution—for a reasonable way of dealing with capricious, illogical events—the writers of the loyalist press commented astutely on Revolutionary behavior. They noted, as we have seen, the symbiotic union of moderation and radicalism in whig rhetoric: a defense of the existing social order that magnified to fantastic dimensions the evil potential of British policy and heightened the moral drama of colonial opposition. The resulting tension within American society was excruciating, and the loyalists noted the release of guilt and desperation into every political transaction. Aware that this emotional energy needed to be channeled and conserved, some patriot leaders advocated Spartan discipline, and others struggled to construct and operate constitutional government. Unable to appreciate those corrective, self-denying measures by the revolutionaries, some of the most thoughtful and knowledgeable loyalist polemicists believed that they alone lived in a world of discipline and constraint. "There are bounds to all human power," "Helvetius" declared in the *Royal Georgia Gazette;* "the doctrine of nonresistance has long and deservedly been exploded, but its opposite, like some powerful and dangerous medicine, ought to be handled with the utmost caution, lest it become a dangerous weapon in the hands of a madman." The history of modern Europe, explained Zubly—who chose the name "Helvetius" because he was a Swiss emigrant—showed that civility and maturity were the mark of people who did not resist every injustice or jealously guard every scrap of power. "The Swiss never revolted," and ever since the height of the Roman Empire they "pleaded, petitioned, and appealed" against imperial encroachments but "suffered" with grim dignity rather than "taking up arms or revolting." The Spanish Netherlands, "Helvetius" continued, did revolt against Phillip II, goaded to violence by the Duke of Alva's barbarous suppression of the Dutch Protestants; in marked contrast with the American revolutionaries who casually printed millions of dollars of worthless currency and boasted of their national greatness, the Dutch were tenacious, humble, and soft-spoken. Even courage and genuine patriotism, "Helvetius" concluded with a final example, did not guarantee success to a people fighting for their freedom. The Corsicans had fought bravely for more than forty years against their Genoese overlords only to have "the French, like true politicians, after weakening both parties at last make a conquest of it for themselves"—inflicting cruel atrocities on the Corsican patriots. The lesson of history was clear: "intestine commotions and civil wars are productive of such infinite mischiefs that humanity shudders at their approach, and very great evils and just complaints grow foul and unworthy of the resentment they might otherwise deliver, where the evils produced by an intestine war for redress are thrown into the opposite scale of the balance."[108]

"Helvetius" skillfully arranged a series of quotations from Emmerich de Vattel's treatise on international law. This humane and rational commentary on the limitations of military power as an agent of change placed extremely narrow limits on the meaning of a just war. Vattel observed that while legitimate national interests were at stake in many wars, the passions and aggressiveness of particular rulers were more intimate causes of conflict. He underscored—in the passages "Helvetius" quoted—the futility of war as a means of achieving social change; war itself settled nothing, it only compelled a defeated nation to submit to negotiation. If peace settlements depended on "exact and punctual" compliance by all parties, no war would ever end short of the utter desolation and annihilation of the losing side. Because warfare itself spawned so much incidental injustice, a war was never an instrument of justice. The civilized way to end a war, Vattel insisted, was for both sides to strike an imperfect bargain and "extinguish differences by the most equitable" feasible arrangements. On the basis of these terms, the concessions proposed by the Carlisle Commission in 1778 conceded virtually every American claim short of independence. "Is it a just and lawful plea against generous offers of peace," he demanded, "that they cannot be accepted because those to whom they were made" are allied to France? Is fear of insulting an opportunistic ally a valid reason to perpetuate a dreadful war?

Ultimately, the unity of the moral order—which the Revolution had so savagely torn—depended not on history or philosophy but on God's final judgment. Looking forward to that vindication, "Helvetius" defined the Revolution in much of its complexity: "The penalty due to obstinate rebellion in this life is a trifle not to be mentioned with what you must expect when all of the ghosts of the slain, every drop of innocent blood you spilt, every act of violence you concurred in or committed, all the confederates of your crime whom you have forced or seduced, every injured widow's groan and every orphan's tear whom you have ruined, the spoils of the honest and innocent whom you have robbed, every friendly warning which you rejected, will at once arise in judgment against you and render you as completely miserable as you have rendered yourselves distinguishedly wicked."[109] No single sentence in all of the loyalist press dealt so comprehensively with the nature and impact of the Revolution. In a single spacious and ominous image, Zubly juxtaposed the innocence, agony, spiritual and physical isolation, virtue, and brutalization of the loyalists with the destructive force and inner nature of revolution: the self-justifying use of violence, the way coercion expanded outward until it overwhelmed even the weak and helpless, and the patriots' determination to pay any price—moral or material—to ensure the permanence of their new regime.

The loyalist press did not enunciate a fully developed alternative ideology or a coherent political code, nor did it refute very cleverly the novel and untested features of patriot constitutionalism and mission. But it did articulate a profound sense of moral estrangement from the values that the revolutionaries claimed for themselves and that permeated their republicanism. Loyalist pamphleteers, Leslie F. S. Upton argued, failed to confront the colonists with "the conventional wisdom" of Georgian political orthodoxy.[110] Writers to the loyalist press operated at the more elemental level of moral self-vindication. They internalized their perceptions of upheaval and vented the anguish they felt as innocent victims of a cruel and unnatural rebellion.

Notes

1. Patricia U. Bonomi, *A Factious People: Politics and Society in Colonial New York* (New York, 1971), pp. 270–71; *New-York Gazette and Weekly Mercury,* Apr. 9–June 25, 1770, hereafter cited as *New-York Mercury.*

2. Robert M. Calhoon, *The Loyalists in Revolutionary America, 1760–1781* (New York, 1973), pp. 255–56; see also "Popicola," *Rivingto's New-York Gazetteer,* Nov. 18, Dec. 2 and 23, 1773 (for the various titles of this newspaper, see Timothy M. Barnes, "Loyalist Newspapers of the American Revolution: A Bibliography," *Proceedings of the American Antiquarian Society* 83 [1974]: 227), hereafter cited as *Rivington's Gazetteer* for the years 1773–75 and *Rivington's Gazette* thereafter.

3. Catherine B. Mayo, ed., "Additions to . . . Hutchinson's History of Massachusetts Bay," *Proceedings of the American Antiquarian Society* 59 (1949): 42; "Chronus," *Massachusetts Gazette and Boston Weekly News-Letter,* Jan. 23, 1772, hereafter cited as *Boston Weekly News-Letter.*

4. Robert M. Weir, ed., *The Letters of Freeman, Etc.: Essays on the Nonimportation Movement in South Carolina Collected by William Henry Drayton* (Columbia, S.C., 1977), pp. 53–57, 86–95, essays by Drayton and Wragg from the *South-Carolina Gazette* dated Oct. 26 and Nov. 16, 1769.

5. Peter S. Onuf, ed., *Maryland and the Empire, 1773: The Antilon-First Citizen Letters* (Baltimore, 1974), pp. 3–39.

6. For a convenient listing of Sewall's letters to the press except for the "Phileirene" letters and an analysis of his ideas, see Ann Gorman Condon, "Marching to a Different Drummer: The Political Philosophy of the American Loyalists," in Esmond Wright, ed., *Red, White, and True Blue: The Loyalists in the Revolution* (New York, 1976), pp. 1–18,

175–77 and Carol Berkin, *Jonathan Sewall: Odyssey of an American Loyalist* (New York, 1974), pp. 31–34, 37–43, 87–89, 97–100 and "Jonathan Sewall: One Tory's Conception of the Press," paper read at the St. Augustine Conference on American Loyalism, St. Augustine, Fla., Feb. 8, 1975.

7. Bernard Mason, ed., *The American Colonial Crisis: The Daniel Leonard-John Adams Letters to the Press, 1774–1775* (New York, 1972), pp. ix–xix.

8. Stephen Botein, "'Meer Mechanics' and an Open Press: The Business and Political Strategies of Colonial American Printers," *Perspectives in American History* 9 (1975): 215–17; Timothy M. Barnes, "The Loyalist Press in the American Revolution, 1765–1781" (Ph.D. diss., University of New Mexico, 1970), chaps. 1–8; Janice Potter, *The Liberty We Seek: Loyalist Ideology in Colonial New York and Massachusetts* (Cambridge, Mass., 1983); Larry R. Gerlach, *Prologue to Independence: New Jersey in the Coming of the American Revolution* (New Brunswick, N.J., 1976), pp. 236–39, 335–36; S. F. Roach, "The *Georgia Gazette* and the Stamp Act: A Reconsideration" and C. Ashley Ellefson, "The Stamp Act in Georgia," *Georgia HistoricalQuarterly* 55 (1971): 471–91 and 46 (1962): 1–19; John E. Alden, "John Mein: Scourge of Patriots," *Publications of the Colonial Society of Massachusetts* 34 (1937–42): 571–99; and Sidney Kobre, *The Development of the Colonial Newspaper* (Pittsburgh, 1944), p. 148. For loyalist essays printed in newspapers closely identified with the whig position, see for example "Pacificus," *Pennsylvania Chronicle,* July 25, 1768; "A Barbadian," *Pennsylvania Chronicle,* Aug. 1 and 8, 1768; "Machiavel," *Pennsylvania Chronicle,* Aug. 15, 22, and 29, 1768; "Country Farmer," *Pennsylvania Chronicle,* Aug. 22, 1768; "Anticentinel," *Pennsylvania Journal,* June 16 and Sept. 29, 1768; and "Anatomist," *Pennsylvania Journal,* Sept. 8, 25, and 29, and Oct. 13, 1768.

9. Botein, "'Meer Mechanics,' and an Open Press," pp. 217–19, and Leroy Hewlett, "James Rivington: Tory Printer," in David Kaser, ed., *Books in America's Past* (Charlottesville, 1966), pp. 172–76.

10. Anne Y. Zimmer, "Hugh Gaine, Loyalist Printer," paper read at the St. Augustine Conference on American Loyalism.

11. Zimmer, "Hugh Gaine, Loyalist Printer," and Barnes, "Loyalist Newspapers . . . a Bibliography," pp. 225–26.

12. *Rivington's Gazette,* Oct. 11, 1777; quoted in William F. Stierer, "Losers in the War of Words: The Loyalist Press in the American Revolution," paper read at the St. Augustine Conference on American Loyalism; Botein, "'Meer Mechanics' and an Open Press," pp. 217–19.

13. Stierer, "Losers in the War of Words"; Ralph Adams Brown, "The *Newport Gazette*: A Tory News Sheet," *Rhode Island History* 13 (1954–55): 11–21, 97–108 and "The *Pennsylvania Ledger*: Tory News Sheet," *Pennsylvania History* 9 (1942): 161–75.

14. Timothy M. Barnes, "Occupational Allegiance and Political Neutralism: Loyalist Printers during the Revolutionary War," paper read at the Pacific Coast Branch of the American Historical Association, Aug. 13, 1977; John M. Coleman, "Joseph Galloway and the British Occupation of Philadelphia," *Pennsylvania History* 30 (1963): 289–94; George S. McCowen, *The British Occupation of Charleston, 1780–1782* (Columbia, S.C., 1972), pp. 24–42.

15. The participants in the session on "The Loyalist Press" at the St. Augustine Conference on American Loyalism, Feb. 6–8, 1975, generously assisted the authors of this paper. Carol Berkin, William Stierer, Anne Y. Zimmer gave us copies of their papers and Stephen Lucas discussed his findings with us in conversations and correspondence.

Timothy M. Barnes, a commentator at the conference, placed at our disposal his extensive collection of photocopies of the loyalist press and answered innumerable questions.

16. *Massachusetts Gazette, and the Boston Post-Boy and Advertiser,* Mar. 27, 1775, hereafter cited as *Boston Post-Boy Advertiser;* for the prescience of Leonard's observation on the First Continental Congress see David Ammerman, *In the Common Cause: American Response to the Coercive Acts of 1774* (Charlottesville, 1974), chaps. 6 and 8.

17. See "disaffection," "petulance," "ingratitude," and "disloyalty" in *Dr. Johnson's Dictionary* and the *Oxford English Dictionary.*

18. The classic analysis of disaffection from the whig point of view was John Adams, "Dissertation on the Canon and the Feudal Law" (1765), *The Works of John Adams* (Boston, 1851), 3: 447–64.

19. *Boston Evening-Post,* Jan. 14, 1771.

20. *Boston Evening-Post,* Jan. 14, 1771.

21. *Boston Evening-Post,* Jan. 14, 1771; see also. "A Suffolk Yeoman," *Boston Weekly News-Letter,* Dec. 29, 1774; "Philo Patria," *Boston Weekly News-Letter,* Dec. 22, 1774; "C.," *Boston Weekly News-Letter,* Feb. 16, 1775; "Mercator," *Rivington's Gazetteer,* Aug. 11, 1774; "Major Benjamin Floyd and a great number of others," *Rivington's Gazetteer,* Apr. 6, 1775; "An Answer to the Declaration of the General Congress," *Pennsylvania Evening Post,* Mar. 25, 1778.

22. *Boston Weekly News-Letter,* Apr. 6, 1775; for an exhaustive historical argument that the 1692 Charter did not fetter in any way the authority of the Crown in Massachusetts, see "A.Z.," *Boston Weekly News-Letter,* Mar. 2, 1775, and also the major pro-administration arguments in the controversy over the removal of the General Court from Boston by "Verus," "Aequitas," and "Chronus," *Boston Weekly News-Letter,* May 16, July 18, 1771 and Jan. 2, 1772.

23. *Boston Post-Boy Advertiser,* Dec. 26, 1774.

24. *Boston Weekly News-Letter,* Mar. 30, 1775; see also "A.B.C.," *Boston Evening-Post,* Sept. 20, 1773; "Protector Oliver," *Rivington's Gazetteer,* Feb. 9, 1775.

25. "Plain Heart," *Boston Weekly News-Letter,* Feb. 16, 1775.

26. "Anti-Licentiousness," *Rivington's Gazetteer,* Apr. 20, 1775.

27. "Z.T.," *Boston Evening-Post,* May 15, 1769.

28. Bernard Bailyn, *The Ideological Origins of the American Revolution* (Cambridge, Mass., 1967), pp. 55–60.

29. "Plain Heart," *Boston Weekly News-Letter,* Mar. 2, Feb. 16, 1775.

30. *Boston Post-Boy Advertiser,* Dec. 12, 1774, Feb. 20, 1775.

31. [Boston] *Censor,* Nov. 30, 1771.

32. "T.W.," *Rivington's Gazetteer,* Dec. 15, 1774; see also "Conciliator," *Boston Post-Boy Advertiser,* Feb. 6–13, 1775; "A Farmer," *Rivington's Gazetteer,* Dec. 2, 1773.

33. "Plain Heart," *Boston Weekly News-Letter,* Mar. 2, 1775; "A Card," *Rivington's Gazetteer,* Mar. 9, 1775, called the Revolutionaries "Protestant Jesuits"; see also "Yeoman," *Boston Weekly News-Letter,* Dec. 10, 1772.

34. "Phileirene," *Boston Weekly News-Letter,* Feb. 9, 1775.

35. "Popicola," *Rivington's Gazetteer,* Dec. 2, 1773.

36. *Boston Post-Boy Advertiser,* Feb. 20, 1775.

37. "Letters . . . which contain a compleat Answer to the Farmer's," *Boston Evening-Post,* Feb. 6, 1769.

38. *Rivington's Gazetteer,* Dec. 8, 1774.

39. *Boston Weekly News-Letter,* Jan. 12, 1775.

40. "Agrippa," *Rivington's Gazetteer,* Mar. 30, 1775.

41. "A Whip for the American Whig," No. 22, *New-York Mercury,* Sept. 5, 1768.

42. "A Whip for the American Whig," No. 32, Nov. 14, 1768.

43. "A Whip for the American Whig," No. 2, Apr. 11, 1768.

44. "A Whip for the American Whig," No. 19, Aug. 15, 1768.

45. "A Whip for the American Whig," No. 14, July 4, 1768.

46. "A Whip for the American Whig," No. 21, Aug. 29, 1768.

47. *Rivington's Gazetteer,* Apr. 6, 1775.

48. *Rivington's Gazetteer,* Mar. 9, 1775.

49. "Phileirene," Mar. 2, 1775, and Jan. 12, 1775, *Boston Weekly News-Letter;* see also [Samuel Seabury], "The Congress Canvassed," *Salem Gazette,* Jan. 13, 1775.

50. *Norwich Packet,* Nov. 25–Dec. 2, 1773.

51. John Grou and John Peters in *Rivington's Gazetteer,* Sept. 2, 1774; see also "An Answer to the Declaration," *Pennsylvania Evening Post,* Feb. 24, 1778.

52. "A New York Freeholder," *New-York Mercury,* Oct. 10, 1774; "America's Real Friend," *Rivington's Gazetteer,* Feb. 16, 1775.

53. "America's Real Friend," *Rivington's Gazetteer,* Apr. 6, 1775.

54. "Chronus," *Boston Post-Boy Advertiser,* Dec. 2, 1771.

55. "John Herbert," *Boston Evening-Post,* Mar. 13, 1769.

56. "A Freeholder of Essex and a Real Lover of Liberty," *Rivington's Gazetteer,* Jan. 5, 1775.

57. "Cato," "To the People of Pennsylvania, VII," *Pennsylvania Gazette,* Apr. 10, 1776; see also "An Answer to the Declaration," *Pennsylvania Evening Post,* Feb. 17, 1778.

58. [Peter Oliver], "An Address to the Soldiers of Massachusetts Bay who are now in Arms against the Laws of their Country," *Boston Weekly News-Letter,* Jan. 11, 1776.

59. *New-York Mercury,* Apr. 25, 1768; see also "Anatomist III," *New-York Journal,* Oct. 13, 1768, and "A Dissenter," *Boston Evening-Post,* January 11, 1773.

60. "Bellisarius,"*Rivington's Gazetteer,* Mar. 9, 1775.

61. "A Letter from a Quaker," *Boston Evening-Post,* Jan. 25, 1773.

62. "America's Real Friend," *Rivington's Gazetteer,* Feb. 16, 1775.

63. "Major Benjamin Floyd and a great number of others," *Rivington's Gazetteer,* Apr. 6, 1775.

64. "Dialogue Between a high Patriotic Bostonian and a plain honest countryman," *Boston Weekly News-Letter,* Jan. 14, 1773.

65. "Z.T.," *Boston Evening-Post,* May 15, 1769.

66. "Juba," *Rivington's Gazetteer,* Sept. 2, 1774.

67. "Z.T.," *Boston Evening-Post,* May 15, 1769.

68. "Chronus," *Boston Post-Boy Advertiser,* Jan. 6, 1772.

69. "A New York Freeholder," *New-York Mercury,* Sept. 26, 1774.

70. *Boston Post-Boy Advertiser,* Mar. 27, 1775.

71. "Subscribers, Freeholders, and Inhabitants of White Plains in the County of Westchester," *Rivington's Gazetteer,* Jan. 12, 1775; see also "A Freeholder of Essex and a Real Lover of Liberty," *Rivington's Gazetteer,* Jan. 5, 1775.

72. "Popicola," *Rivington's Gazetteer,* Nov. 18, 1773.

73. "Philo-Libertas," *Rivington's Gazetteer*, Oct. 18, 1774.

74. "A Freeholder of Essex and a Real Lover of Liberty," *Rivington's Gazetteer*, Jan. 5, 1775; see also "Declaration of the Grand Jury and Magistrates of Tryon County," *Rivington's Gazetteer*, Apr. 6, 1775; "Anti-Licentiousness," *Rivington's Gazetteer*, Apr. 20, 1775; "Phileirene," *Boston Weekly News-Letter*, Jan. 12, 1775; "X.," *Boston Weekly News-Letter*, June 16, 1774.

75. Marc Egnal and Joseph A. Ernst, "An Economic Interpretation of the American Revolution," *William and Mary Quarterly*, 3rd ser., 29 (1972): 3–32.

76. *Pennsylvania Gazette*, May 18, 1774.

77. Isaac Wilkins, "Speech to the New York General Assembly," *Rivington's Gazetteer*, Apr. 6, 1775; see also [Joseph Galloway], "A West County Farmer," *Pennsylvania Gazette*, June 16, 1768.

78. "Chronus," *Boston Post-Boy Advertiser*, Dec. 2, 1771; "Form of an Association in Cortlandt's Manor," *Rivington's Gazetteer*, Feb. 16, 1775; see also "Philanthrop," *Boston Evening-Post*, Jan. 14, 1771; "A New York Freeholder," *New-York Mercury*, Sept. 12, 1774.

79. "Extract of a Letter from London," *Rivington's Gazetteer*, Feb. 16, 1775.

80. "Rusticus," *Pennsylvania Packet*, Jan. 2, 1775; see also "Rusticus," *New-York Mercury*, Jan. 16, 1775; "An Account between Great Britain and her Colonies," *New-York Mercury*, June 6, 1774; "Phileirene," *Boston Weekly News-Letter*, Jan. 26, 1775; "Mr. Cruger's Speech in Answer to Lord North," *Rivington's Gazetteer*, July 13, 1775.

81. *Pennsylvania Ledger*, Jan. 28, 1775; see also "Masschusettensis," *Boston Post-Boy Advertiser*, Jan. 2, 1775; "Phileirene," *Boston Weekly News-Letter*, Jan. 26, 1775; "Isaac Wilkins's Speech," *Rivington's Gazetteer*, Apr. 6, 1775; "Form of an Association in Cortlandt's Manor," *Rivington's Gazetteer*, Feb. 16, 1775.

82. "Phileirene," *Boston Weekly News-Letter*, Jan. 26, 1775.

83. "Isaac Wilkins's Speech," *Rivington's Gazetteer*, Apr. 6, 1775.

84. "Massachusettensis," *Boston Post-Boy Advertiser*, Mar. 20, 1775.

85. "Cato," "Letter to the People of Pa., II," *Pennsylvania Gazette*, Mar. 13, 1776.

86. "Rationalis," *Pennsylvania Gazette*, Feb. 28, 1776.

87. "Cato," "To the People VIII," *Pennsylvania Gazette*, Apr. 24, 1776.

88. "Cato," "To the People III," *Pennsylvania Gazette*, Mar. 20, 1776.

89. "Cato," "To the People IV," *Pennsylvania Gazette*, Mar. 27, 1776; on Smith's use of the press, see Don R. Byrnes, "The Pre-Revolutionary Career of Provost William Smith, 1751–1778" (Ph.D. diss., Tulane University, 1969); on Smith's emphasis on social pluralism and instability in Pennsylvania, see Stephen Lucas, "Between Protest and Revolution: The Ideology of Reconciliation and the Popular Debate over Independence," paper read at the St. Augustine Conference on American Loyalism, and *Portents of Rebellion: Rhetoric and Revolution in Philadelphia, 1765–76* (Philadelphia, 1976), chap. 7.

90. *Pennysylvania Gazette*, Sept. 7, 1774.

91. *Boston Weekly News-Letter*, Feb. 2, 1775.

92. *Pennsylvania Packet*, Feb. 27, 1775.

93. *Pennsylvania Packet*, June 22, 1774; see also "Anti-Tormentor," *Pennsylvania Packet*, Nov. 21, 1774.

94. *Pennsylvania Packet*, July 20, 1774; see also "Amor Patnae," *Boston Weekly News-Letter*, Jan. 19, 1769; "A Plan of Reconciliation," *Rivington's Gazetteer*, Nov. 2, 1775; "Isaac Wilkins's Speech," *Rivington's Gazetteer*, Apr. 6, 1775.

95. Pauline Maier, *From Resistance to Revolution: Colonial Radicals and the Development of American Opposition to Britain, 1765–1776* (New York, 1972); chap. 9 treats the interior of these tactics and perceptions while Ammerman, *In the Common Cause,* examines their external thrust and impact.

96. *Boston Post-Boy Advertiser,* Feb. 6, 1775; see also "Chaubullagungamuggensis," *Rivington's Gazetteer,* Sept. 22, 1774 ("I cannot but consider the present opposition to Parliament as resistance of lawful authority and the beginning of a rebellion") and "Tranquillus," *Pennsylvania Gazette,* Sept. 7, 1774.

97. *Boston Weekly News-Letter,* Feb. 23, 1775; *Rivington's Gazetteer,* Mar. 9, 1775.

98. *Boston Weekly News-Letter,* Jan. 11, 1776.

99. [South Carolina] *Royal Gazette,* May 30–June 2, 1781; see also "Drusus," *South-Carolina and American General Gazette,* Aug. 2, 9, 1780 and in [S.C.] *Royal Gazette,* May 2–5, 1781.

100. [S.C.] *Royal Gazette,* Apr. 13–17, 1782.

101. *Boston Post-Boy Advertiser,* Feb. 6, 1775.

102. *Boston Post-Boy Advertiser,* Mar. 20, 1775.

103. See Anthony F. C. Wallace, "Revitalization Movements," *American Anthropologist* 58 (1956): 264–81; Clifford Geertz, "Thick Description: Toward an Interpretive Theory of Culture," in *The Interpretation of Cultures: Selected Essays* (New York, 1973), chap. 1; Peter Berger and Stanley Pullberg, "Reification and the Sociological Critique of Consciousness," *History and Theory* 4 (1965): 196–211; and George Grant, *Lament for a Nation: The Defeat of Canadian Nationalism* (Toronto, 1965).

104. *Boston Post-Boy Advertiser,* Jan. 30, 1775; for a similar diagnosis of British sensibilities, see "Scotus Americanus," *South-Carolina Royal Gazette,* June 8, 1780 and "Planter," *South-Carolina Royal Gazette,* Dec. 19, 1780.

105. *New-York Mercury,* Mar. 3, 1777.

106. *Royal Georgia Gazette,* July 27, 1780; "Helvetius" was the Reverend J. J. Zubly, a Presbyterian clergyman who frequently referred to his Swiss origins and whose diary (Georgia Historical Society, Savannah) bore an acrostic which spelled "Helvetius." Zubly was a classic case of a "whig-loyalist" who vigorously defended colonial liberty before 1775 and reluctantly became a loyalist in 1776; see Calhoon, *Loyalists in Revolutionary America,* pp. 180–82 and Bailyn, *Ideological Origins,* pp. 169, 181–82, and 217.

107. *South-Carolina and American General Gazette,* July 20, Aug. 2, 1780.

108. *Royal Georgia Gazette,* Aug. 3, 1780; see also "An Address to the People of this Country by an American Loyalist," *South-Carolina Royal Gazette,* Dec. 25, 1780.

109. *Royal Georgia Gazette,* Sept. 28, 1780; see also *Royal Georgia Gazette,* July 27, Aug. 31, Sept. 7, and Oct. 12, 1780; to appreciate Zubly's skillful use of Vattel, cf. James Turner Johnson, *Ideology, Reason, and the Limitation of War: Religious and Secular Concepts, 1200–1740* (Princeton, N.J., 1975), pp. 240–53.

110. Leslie F. S. Upton, "The Dilemma of the Loyalist Pamphleteers," *Studies in Burke and His Time* 18 (1977): 71–84.

Nine

Loyalist Discourse and the Moderation of the American Revolution

Timothy M. Barnes and
Robert M. Calhoon

Some loyalists were drawn to hydrological metaphors. "I discern the goddess, but on the other side of the river," William Smith, Jr., said of American independence; "most men are for plunging in to embrace her. I am for going over in a boat, distrusting my power to swim the stream." Jonathan Boucher observed in 1776 that "civil broils are the luxuriant offspring of the best formed governments, as hurricanes are of the best climates. The multitude will ever be wrought on by public speaking" because "in America, literally and truly, all power flows from the people." In the garrison town of Boston, John Wiswall despaired that only "the God who stilleth the raging of the sea, the noise of the waves, and the madness of the people" could "restore peace, order, and government to this distracted continent" because America was "too free and happy" ever "to be contented with its happiness."[1]

These images graphically underscored the geography of Britain's North American empire and highlighted the contours of the loyalist mind. Rivers, coastal waters, and port towns constituted a great arc from Quebec on the St. Lawrence River to St. Augustine in East Florida and Pensacola in the Gulf of Mexico and along the Atlantic coast towns like Boston and Newport with natural harbors and New York, Philadelphia, Wilmington, Charleston, and Savannah, on inland river basins—all entry points for British naval and military forces into the rebellious interior. In the experience of British officials and their loyalist allies, these waterways connected the continent to the Atlantic Ocean and ultimately to the British Isles. A seaborne empire guaranteed Britain's ability to enrich the colonies through trade, stabilize them with political administration, and, if need be, discipline and subordinate them by military force.

The language of geographic connection resonates with historians more strongly today than a generation ago. From the late 1940s until the 1980s, British historians assumed that Walpolean stability dominated the life of the British nation throughout the eighteenth century. During the same era, historians of early America regarded the Atlantic as a protective barrier between the British Isles and North America. Recent British scholarship, however, has discovered that, from 1688 until well into the nineteenth century, the very idea of British civilization itself was problematic. The Hanoverian succession, the whig supremacy, and the union of Scotland and England, historians now appreciate, were fragile achievements. Culture wars between Anglican orthodoxy and Protestant dissent, between popular radicalism and an uneasy political establishment, between English and Scots peoples, and between the English government and rival Irish-Protestant and Irish-Catholic elites posed a far greater threat to national stability and cohesion than historians realized during the half century following Sir Lewis Namier's delineation of "the structure of politics" in Hanoverian England.[2] And if Britain was still a nation in the making, the rebellious American colonies, by the same token, may have been simply an overseas extension of incomplete Anglicization rather than a maturing society slipping the leash of imperial control.

If the concept of a British nation was problematic, could it be that the supposedly myopic American loyalists were acutely aware of the fragility of British culture and national identity? Did the loyalists correctly regard the American Revolution as a dangerous laceration of young, still-tender social linkages binding the British Isles and the larger Britannic world? William Eddis, the Maryland loyalist and proprietary official, wrote of British maritime regions as wholesome and mature and the land as bestial and diseased:

> Seagirt Britannia! mistress of the Isles
> Where faith and liberty united reign;
> Around whose fertile shores glad Nature smiles,
> And Ceres crowns with gifts the industrious swain! . . .
>
> Now through the land dissention stalks confest;
> With foul distrust, and hatred in her train;
> The dire infection runs from breast to breast,
> And statesmen plan—and patriots plead in vain!
>
> All gracious Heaven, avert the impending storm,
> Bid every jealous, jarring faction cease;
> Let Sweet content resume her lovely form,
> And o'er the land diffuse perpetual peace:
>
> And, when again our colours are unfurl'd,
> May Britons nobly join one common cause!
> With rapid conquests strike the wondering world,
> In firm support of Liberty and Laws.[3]

Eddis used poetic form to construct a model of empire in which cosmopolitan core values and provincial dysfunctionality existed in troubled equilibrium—the center trying to radiate healing power outward, the peripheries exhibiting vices resistant to correction by reason and tradition. Though loyalist rhetoric often appears superficially blemished with partisanship and rage, historians have gradually come to appreciate that loyalists were uniquely positioned to perceive the concrete reality of the Revolution as it exploded in specific situations and affected the lives of individuals and communities.

A sea change in historiography since the 1980s, as well as the availability of a large mass of underutilized loyalist evidence, such as Eddis's poem, enables historians to organize loyalist discourse into a complex narrative. Such a complex loyalist narrative serves several functions. It provides a more detailed account of the course of events triggered by American independence; it identifies actors and actions that, though integral to the Revolution, have not been invested with explanatory force by the interpretive questions historians have asked; and finally a complex narrative recognizes that, because neither patriot nor loyalist actors knew which side was going to prevail, a huge imponderable of uncertainty beclouded their rhetorical world.[4]

Loyalist communities in British garrison towns during the War for Independence engaged in extensive debate, discussion, and polemicism. New York from 1776 to 1783, Philadelphia in 1777–78, Newport from 1776 to 1778, Norfolk in 1775–76, Savannah from 1778 to 1782, Charleston from 1780 to 1782, and Wilmington, North Carolina, for most of 1781, as well as St. Augustine and Pensacola in British East and West Florida and Quebec and Montreal in Canada constituted the urban interface between imperial authority and Revolutionary resistance.[5] These garrison towns were military outposts under martial law (except for Savannah where civil administration was reinstituted in 1779) and, at the same time, refuges for loyalists and neutralists whose careers and family ties kept them there during the war, as well as for refugees driven from their former homes in patriot-occupied territory. Garrison towns were also potential showcases for British pacification and the setting for efforts to reconcile colonists to the likely military suppression of the Revolution. Every garrison town published one or more newspapers, subsidized by the British but edited by loyalist printers and filled with writings by loyalist inhabitants. Some of these writings—and much of the judgmental comment on the garrison towns by patriots in the Revolutionary hinterland—depicted the garrison towns as pathological societies, rent with violence, anger, desperation, and corruption.

But amid these dark images, loyalist discourse in the garrison towns suggests an alternative interpretation: that these towns were functional, Anglo-American communities where people lived, worked, loved, hated, produced, consumed, and, sometimes, died and where colonial-imperial cultural and political interaction continued after 1776. Loyalist discourse in the garrison towns not only conveys a better understanding of the political ideas of the loyalists, but it also resonates with the loyalist discovery of the power of language to make their world whole and coherent during a time of turmoil and dislocation.

The Political Culture of the Garrison Towns

The political culture of the garrison towns—the assumptions, expectations, beliefs, fears, antagonisms, and moral sensibilities of these urban loyalists—had an explicit outer shell and an implicit, interior, alternative set of meanings. First, from 1776 to 1778, the stark inconceivability of independence and the apparent madness of armed rebellion dominated garrison town loyalist discourse. Second, from late 1778 through 1783, a more nuanced sense of political reality surfaced among garrison town loyalists. Radical ideas seemed to sustain the rebel cause in spite of military adversity; the unnatural alliance with France flew in the face of Protestant realism; and the loyalists' repeated and futile calls for reconciliation between the colonies and Great Britain completed the steep learning curve of their political education. Some lessons took. The patriots' effort to create a stable, functioning, republican regime moderated their revolution. Likewise the loyalists' struggle to sustain morale, conduct trade, administer local government, and advise British military commanders mobilized men and women of differing temperament and tolerance for ideological polarization. Just as tory and patriot partisanship fed each other, there was also a silent seepage of moderation into and out of the garrison towns.

The nervous exhilaration of loyalists in New York and Newport immediately following British occupation of those towns in the autumn of 1776 was symptomatic of the emotional fluidity of the garrison town community. They chortled over satirical advertisements extolling "Congress-dollars as a particularly cheap form of papering for the walls of houses, . . . kindling fires, lighting pipes, shaving, and still more ignoble purposes."[6] Confident of a quick British military victory, they did not regard the outbreak of hostilities as a serious long-term threat to the imperial bond. They lamented the fact that matters had come to this, but they believed it was foolish to imagine that an untrained rebel army could offer any threat to the greatest military and naval power in the world. Consequently, within the garrison towns there was no serious discussion of issues raised by the war. Instead the perceived futility of the Revolution became a source of humor, characterized by taunts, ridicule, and mockery—a diversion from the increasing rigors and suffering of garrison life. Officers of the Continental Line were laughed at as "low-bred . . . oyster picklers and plough-joggers," upstarts who found it "easier to be commanders of armies than masters of tailor and shoemaker shops." One garrison town resident remarked that "it had been better you had stayed behind your counters, rolling your eyes, and cheating friends and neighbors, than to take the field." The soldiers that these officers commanded were nothing more than the "scum of hell," chiefly "transported convicts."[7] Loyalists supposed that these hopelessly ignorant and unrefined people could never pose a serious threat to the Empire.

In the fall of 1776, faced with the advance of the British army under the command of General Sir William Howe, Congress fled the Philadelphia capital for the safety of Baltimore. Garrison town dwellers quickly dubbed it "the Flying Congress" and challenged "these governors of the Western World . . . to tell us where they are, and from what region they issue . . . their mandates to bind people." Before 1778 Congress's whereabouts was a nearly continual source of mocking entertainment, when, fearing another attack on Philadelphia, Congress fled again, this time to York, Pennsylvania. Seen from within the loyalist enclaves, the whole display confirmed the view that the rebellion, although still in existence during the winter of 1776–77, was "diminishing considerably" and was nothing more than the flimsy work of a cowardly "intoxicated rabble" in Congress.[8] The diplomacy of this peripatetic Congress was summed up by one "observer" who reported that when American diplomats in France were presented to the queen, she shouted, "My God! . . . these are no better than the mob." The whole idea of a potential Franco-American alliance, which had been an early aim of Congress, seemed so absurd to loyalist writers that it became a great joke: "A Rebel Deputy [Benjamin Franklin], from a Rebel Mob [Congress], solicits in the Court of a despotic Prince, and begs Assistance for Rebellion!, begs of a Monarch to convince his subjects, who labor under heavy . . . taxes that rebellion . . . [ought] to be encouraged."[9]

By the end of the campaign of 1776–77, Washington had retreated from Long Island, out of New York City, and across New Jersey, yet only a few former patriots had come into the British lines and received a pardon in return for an oath of allegiance. More ominous still, patriot military resistance continued. This potentially dangerous opposition prompted little concern within the towns, however, let alone a public debate on military policy. Instead loyalists dismissed the Revolution and trivialized it with more jokes. Revolutionary leaders, they said, kept up resistance only by persuading Americans that the British victories of 1776–77 were actually losses. One loyalist commented sarcastically that Washington's retreat from "Long Island was a sad thing for us" as patriots took "the advantage [by] intimidating the British with a display of unparalleled Agility [in] . . . dancing off by the quick Step." The same writer noted that, in the spring of 1777, the British "met with the mishap of destroying 10,000 barrels of salt beef bound for the Continental Army." As a result of the seizure, Continental soldiers in the next campaign would be able to avoid the dangers of indigestion. It was a "vast Advantage!" A vegetarian army "will escape the gout, . . . will be lighter, and in better running order than before, if [that were] possible. Alas! We must endeavor to be comforted; and [next year] when we have taken Philadelphia, we shall beg . . . you to sympathize in our Misfortune." After this anticipated Philadelphia "loss" for the British, the prediction was made that the patriots would immediately "perceive the benefit [of] living in the [Appalachian] Mountains" with charming views, the freedom of a "goat, and full as sweet," and release from the "unsatisfactory pleasures of this world, [and] . . . the vile shackles of vain fashion."[10]

John Sullivan, the patriot general at Providence, Rhode Island, dismissed his militia in late 1776 and then, early the next year, sent out calls for it to form again in the spring. At the nearby garrison at Newport, the loyalists could not contain their amusement at this evidence of uncommitted revolutionaries and bungled military planning. The towns that the British army occupied during the war became crude places, not far above military encampments, and until 1778 produced a coarseness unmatched anywhere during the Revolution. One writer taunted the patriots at Providence with the story that Sullivan had blamed the failure of his militiamen on their returning home to attend to the emotional and physical needs of "their involuntarily ravished spouses." These lovers were apparently at home "earnestly unit[ing] and join[ing] together . . . for the Cause." From his constant calls, it was abundantly clear to loyalist detractors that General Sullivan believed enough time had passed to "restore tranquillity to a breast torn . . . by [the] . . . rape [of a] spouse and sister too." This failure of the Revolution to fill the ranks of the militia could be easily solved, according to these garrison town wits: transvestite patriot women would make up the difference. The loyalist writer who adopted the pseudonym, "C. C.," suggested that "the ladies of Providence, . . . vestals of a fishing-town," were to join the militia, "shave their heads, and let their beards grow." When these lady-soldiers were interested in sex, they could signal the local men with the word "liberty emblazoned on their chests."[11]

The fictive vestal angels of Providence were not the only women in the garrison towns whose lives were turned upside down by the Revolution. In Philadelphia a network of Quaker women took refuge from warfare and strife by sharing poetry, prose, and correspondence exploring issues of life and death, friendship and duty, family and affection, integrity and peaceable behavior. Sometime during the War for Independence, probably during the British occupation of Philadelphia from September 1777 to May 1778, Milcah Martha Moore carefully inscribed 126 pieces of prose and poetry into a commonplace book that then circulated among her circle of Quaker kinswomen and friends. "The Revolution created all kinds of hardships and anxieties for many Philadelphia Quakers," Karin A. Wulf explains in her introduction to Moore's commonplace book; "loyalism," she explains, "was the result of complicated negotiation among a common sense of obligation and attachment to England and the king, genuine aggrievement at British policies and particular British politicians, and a commitment to pacifism."[12] The triad of obligation, aggrievement, and pacifism was the prism through which these female Quakers perceived their world.

One of the most explicitly political poems in Moore's compilation, composed by a close friend, Hannah Griffitts, in January 1776, reacted immediately to the publication of Thomas Paine's *Common Sense:*

> A deeper wound at freedom, ne're was made,
> than by this Oliverian display'd.
> Orders confounded,—dignities, thrown down,
> Charters degraded equal with the Crown,
> The impartial press, most partially maintain'd

> Freedom infring'd & conscience is restrain'd,
> The moderate man is held to publick View,
> "The Friend of Tyranny & Foe to you."

Associating Paine with Oliver Cromwell, defending privileged "orders," caring about "dignities," and regarding Paine's rhetoric as a deep "wound" in the body politic of "freedom," all bespoke conservative Quaker aversion to political discord and upheaval, as well as their attachment to the Pennsylvania Charter, to "conscience," and to moderation as guardians of liberty.

> Our Representatives,—the people's choice
> are held contemptuous by this daring voice
> persons are seiz'd and posts monopoliz'd
> And all our Form of government dispis'd.

Griffitts's attack on Paine's *Common Sense* continued, emphasizing the way the seizure of power by the Pennsylvania radicals represented a violation of the web of Pennsylvania's proprietary system of government:

> Then from this "Specimen of Rule" beware,
> Behold the Serpent & avoid his Snare.
> 'Tis not in names [like Paine or Timothy Matlack]
>   our present Danger lies,
> Sixty, as well as one, can tyrannize.[13]

The diffuse nature of the radical regime—unknown upstarts without reputation or standing in the community—frightened and offended genteel Quakers.

Moore's commonplace book was more than an elegy for the old order of proprietary government that the Revolution was sweeping away. While much of the poetry and prose that she collected dated from the 1760s and 1770s and was familial and private, some pieces echoed explicitly and all contrasted implicitly with the centrifugal forces roiling outward from a sacred center of Quaker discipleship and spirituality. One of the last dated entries, Griffitts's "To a Parent on the Death of a Child who Died at Phila[delphi]a 26th Ap[ri]l, 1778," asked grieving, peace-loving parents and Friends to reflect on the martial character of human existence:

> Lovely Infant, well releas'd
> Center'd in thy sacred Rest
> Safe from ev'ry dangerous Snare,
> That surrounds the Sons of Care,
> Favour'd child, exempt from Pain
> Or the Warfare to sustain
> Life's rough warfare on a soil
> Lost with Ease & won with Toil.

Realities like the British occupation of Philadelphia, the persecution of Quakers by the Continental Congress, and the poisonous atmosphere in the garrison towns lay barely concealed in the poem's final lines:

> Favour'd is your child to know
> His Release from Scenes of Woe;
> Scenes that not your fondest Care,
> Could secure from Dangers here
> Cease your Tears & let him rise
> To Heaven, a spotless Sacrifice.[14]

Martha Moore's commonplace book was a product of garrison town culture. The months of hard work Moore put into constructing the book corresponded with the British occupation of Philadelphia and the Continental Congress's imprisonment in Winchester, Virginia, of twenty prominent Pennsylvania Quaker leaders arrested just before the arrival of British troops. The mixture of political apprehension and private anxiety pervading the commonplace book corresponds exactly with the plight of Quaker women in the Philadelphia garrison town.[15] While these women were, strictly speaking, neutralists rather loyalists, their political and personal travail alienated them from the Revolution and drew their sympathies toward the British side. The psychic effort invested in maintaining their political purity was a measure of just how intensely politicized the garrison towns became during the War for Independence.

Loyalist discourse revealed not only the shattered emotional equilibrium of the garrison town inhabitants but also their intuitive reliance on the sinews of power in an embattled empire. What appeared to the loyalists as naive, amateur, and crude contrasted in their minds with the capability of imperial power and institutions. Nevertheless the new world of licentiousness and rebellion that surrounded them mocked those conventional reassurances and threw the writers of garrison town loyalist polemics back on their own experience and resources. Their political culture in flux, the garrison town loyalists were about to become more assertive as well as more troubled communities.

Loyalist Extremism

The failure of Great Britain to crush the rebellion militarily galled many garrison town loyalists and provoked harsh, judgmental attacks against the patriots and British commanders. In late 1777 a British army of seven thousand soldiers under the command of General John Burgoyne surrendered at Saratoga, New York, and began a long period of humiliating detention in America. The Saratoga defeat and the train of British diplomatic disasters that followed in 1778 ended the period during which garrison town loyalists believed that the patriots deserved nothing but mocking insults. As a result of Saratoga, France entered the war in early 1778 in support of the Revolution, and in April Congress rejected Parliament's offer of negotiations carried to America and headed by the Earl of Carlisle. Because of these catastrophes, the garrison towns now came to understand the Revolution in a new way that dramatically reshaped their attitudes toward the revolutionaries. Gone was the notion that the Revolution was to be dismissed and that the rebellious Americans were ridiculous people whose only value was to provide diversion for town dwellers. In the minds of urban loyalists, the Revolution, in the space of a few months, had turned into a deadly serious business. This new thinking produced an explosion of loyalist extremism, marked immediately by a fury directed at the recent American alliance with France and at the American rejection of the Carlisle Commission. Both of these crushing diplomatic setbacks for the loyalists occurred during the seven months after Burgoyne's surrender at Saratoga.

British military policy after this catastrophe was designed to shift the role of the army away from General Howe's aim of using it to slowly force the patriots to end the war through negotiation. The policy, after Saratoga, was to destroy the Continental Line. The garrison loyalists certainly approved of this, but they wanted to move beyond using the army as a military weapon. Instead they wanted the military to serve as an engine of vengeance to avenge their post-Saratoga humiliations. According to loyalist insiders, the failure of Howe's original policy of patient application of military power had caused a brief flurry of frustrated threats from the garrison towns during the winter of 1776–77. These threats charged that "TWENTY-FIVE THOUSAND MEN . . . [had] lost their lives" as a result of the patriot rejection of Howe's offers of "peace and pardon." This carnage, however, would pale in comparison with the fearsome calamities that would befall the rebellion for its failure to seek peace. In the future, private dwellings would be targeted, the "country filled with horror, bloodshed, and slaughter," and "thousands of widows and ten thousands of fatherless children" made "destitute."[16] Threats like these prepared the garrison mind for the bloody plans that would come from the towns after 1778.

In 1776 and 1777, garrison town society had been willing to tolerate much suffering in its midst on the assumption that this suffering would soon come to an end when British military superiority was applied with full force. After the Saratoga disaster, when it became clear that the rebellion would not be quickly defeated, garrison dwellers gained a new appreciation of their miserable condition. Leading loyalists now publicly acknowledged that they had long "grieved for the misery" of ordinary town dwellers but were no longer going to keep silent. These suffering people had been "torn from their families and . . . possessions, . . . [and had] wandered about . . . with aching hearts, and hungry bellies."[17] Loyalist spokesmen within the towns believed they now deserved to be avenged with "unexampled carnage and devastation."[18] Garrison leaders rallied ordinary townspeople against a new patriot foe.

The post-Saratoga characterizations of Revolutionary leadership by garrison town loyalists were distinctly different from those of the previous two years. Loyalist writers now vilified their opponents as murderous creatures deserving of particularly vicious retaliation. Theater audiences in Philadelphia watched a worn and fatigued Saratoga army march across the stage to accept surrender terms, only to have two of its officers murdered by a "rebel Colonel." In the next scene, several soldiers from Burgoyne's army were brutally hanged by the Boston town council. Such graphic characterizations horrified audiences and marked a new intransigence in the garrison towns' attitude toward the Revolutionary enemy. The two years of fruitless military dithering and diplomatic failure from 1776 to 1778 took on a new meaning for the garrisons when the terms of reconciliation offered by the Carlisle Commission were summarily rejected by Congress in what appeared a conscious attempt to insult Parliament. Loyalists viewed Carlisle's terms as exceedingly generous, and they were outraged by Congress's rejection of them. This was the turning point for almost all garrison loyalists who were given to anger. It was almost as if the rebellion began for them, at least as a serious threat to loyalism, with this astonishing piece of American diplomacy in which the Continental Congress seemingly went "off the hinges." Loyalist refugees, who had been persecuted by the patriots, now "despaired of ever seeing [the] country reclaimed by" Howe's policy of "lenity and the mild hand of forbearance."[19]

Howe's leniency earned him the unremitting hatred of the garrison town loyalists, who now swept aside reconciliation as nothing more than the work of "philosophers in the[ir] closets." The sword, they claimed, was the only means by which Americans could now be reminded of their proper loyalty. "For their ingratitude," British weaponry would be "unsheathed and fall upon them . . . with redoubled vengeance," and the army would be completely "justified in desolating" the countryside.[20] Loyalists wanted to make clear to the revolutionaries that the offers of peace from Britain were not forwarded "through a sense of her inability to conquer." Loyalists also understood that their anger would not destroy the Revolution immediately, but they hoped the military could punish American arrogance in the short term, leaving "farms . . . desolate[ed]" and wives and children exposed to an approaching winter.[21] Failing an immediate renunciation of independence by the Continental Congress, one loyalist writer proposed, "positive orders should immediately be given to his Majesty's ships . . . to sink every privateer in the service of the . . . Rebels, WITHOUT SAVING A MAN."[22]

Some garrison town writers hoped to raise the stakes even further. Whole colonies that refused to take up arms against the rebellion, and even individual rebellious towns within predominantly loyal provinces, should be singled out and "lay[ed] waste." According to a Pennsylvania essayist, this was a policy that the army had long been "able to execute," had it not been for Howe's "mistaken lenity" during the battles around New York City in 1776.[23] Although garrison town loyalists believed that the regular army, headquartered in New York under the new British commander, General Sir Henry Clinton, might be able to develop and carry out such a plan, they frankly admitted that support for draconian measures did not originate with the "polish[ed]" or "prudent" part of the population and that it would be best executed by those driven by a desire for revenge.[24]

According to loyalist writers, Clinton's army was at a disadvantage, for it tended to be far too gentle in its application of force. An irregular loyalist band, which would fight a "partizan war," would be much more effective "in distributing halters, prisons, [and] banishments." There would be nothing more powerful in crushing the rebellion, the loyalists claimed, than a "large body of men, well armed, and fully determined" to right the individual injuries done to them, "or perish in the attempt."[25] Loyalists acknowledged that this kind of guerrilla service was not for the regular soldier and would attract men driven by a desire to retaliate against personal enemies in the Revolutionary camp. Such soldiers would not have the temperament for long and disciplined action; instead they would be best employed moving into a province and, in one burst of rage, crushing the rebellion with "fear and terror." The most ominous element of this bloody plan was that angry loyalist civilians would accompany these militia units "and point out where the rod should be applied." In this way armed loyalists who knew "every inch of the country . . . would dislodge the rebel militia from their lurking holes, disarm the disaffected, [and] put arms into the hands of the well-affected."[26] The acknowledged model for this design was Colonel John Butler, who had used similar methods on the New York frontier. The rebellion, garrison town loyalists confidently predicted, would be quickly exterminated if more Butler-like "hell hounds" could be formed into units with the single objective of going after patriot civilians.[27]

As a result of their bitter post-Saratoga frustration, garrison town communities not only struck out at patriots, but also turned inward and brutalized themselves by angrily denouncing fellow townspeople for their lack of loyalty. The original call for garrison loyalists to form themselves into vengeful militias had been designed to promote an extremism that would take away the ground occupied by the less committed within the towns. Increased loyalist radicalism, it was hoped, would purge the garrison towns of malingering neutralists, strengthen the movement, and cause it to surge into dominance. Proponents of the plan believed this demand for extremism would create a military "ardour" among quiet townspeople and refugees. The plan would ferret out and remove the dangerous middle, those "white-washed rebels" and "lukewarm friends" of loyalism. The willingness of garrison town dwellers to join the "chosen bands" was to be a litmus test of enthusiastic loyalty. "Apostate" town dwellers who refused would be branded as "worse than rebels" and "a burden on" the loyalist community. Hardline loyalist writers were especially vitriolic in attacking moderates who presumed to speak for the "great majority" of garrison town residents but in reality shrank "from danger" or simply tried to "avoid . . . trouble." According to garrison extremists, what loyalism needed after 1778 was the "disinterested . . . virtue" and enthusiasm of the patriots, the passion of a Tom Paine. The problem, according to these loyalist enthusiasts, lay with the "many among us who would . . . reap the fruits without the trouble of cultivating the vineyard, and who would . . . ridicule every scheme attempted with trouble or difficulty."[28]

Under particular suspicion "were the lower classes of Refugees." If they refused to support extreme measures, "it will be hinted that they have taken refuge here, not so much out of principles of loyalty, as to avoid the burdens . . . of the rebel governments; and that mean selfishness and pusilanimity are at the bottom of their conduct."[29] These people, the militants demanded, should be driven out no matter how painful the consequences in the short term. Emerging from this purge would be a purified and resurgent loyalism that would force moderate loyalists in the garrison towns to commit themselves unreservedly to the British cause or else seek refuge elsewhere.

The language of loyalist extremism echoed the anger and frustration that had come to define garrison town culture. Even more revealingly, this charged and emotive discourse identifies the moment in the garrison towns when loyalists envisioned partisan conflict rescuing the conventional military struggle from the hands of indecisive professional soldiers. Loyalist writers indulged in extremist rhetoric because they wanted to purify the British cause and cleanse their society of opportunism, greed, laxity, and inertia. Loyalist discourse in 1776–78 was a mirror opposite of the patriots' rage *militaire*.

The Emergence of Pragmatic Moderation

It was not until the spring of 1780 that both Savannah and Charleston were in British hands. Consequently a significant number of people in those two cities were former patriots who had come to terms with the British victories, switched sides, and were now nominally loyalist. For the minority of constant southern loyalists whose watchword became deceit, this easy accommodation was far too painless. They were furious that the British commanders in the South were repeating the same mistakes made around New York City in 1776 by granting pardons to any patriot who would take an oath of allegiance rather than unleashing the British army to inflict "Misery and Slaughter." These angry southern loyalists, who had suffered for five years at the hands of the revolutionaries, argued that newly reformed patriots would neither act with gratitude for their generous pardons nor respect new oaths to the king. When former patriots took oaths of allegiance to the Crown, they mocked "god and man, by publickly owning themselves the King's subjects, and privately . . . praying (if they pray at all) for his enemies." If the garrison town loyalists of the South had something to fear, many felt it was not the British army's inability to subdue patriots outside the city lines, but those within towns "who have obtained or begged for protection." Far from being "our loyal fellow subjects," these trimmers were our "secret and worst enemies" and, thus, should not find protection within British lines. "At no other door can we let in among us" people of questionable loyalty to the Crown, one South Carolina writer fumed, "unless we act as idiots, and mean to endanger our own safety."[30]

As fewer and fewer loyalists in the garrison towns in the South remained wedded to sentiments of vengeance, however, this fanatical extremism quickly spent itself. Whether from war weariness or from an appreciation of the personal ambiguities produced by the rapidly changing fortunes of the war in the South or from the increasing viciousness of military action in the interior of the provinces, the garrison town presses in Charleston and Savannah favored gentler plans to resolve the problems of allegiance. Although it may have outraged loyalists, the garrison town administration in Charleston and Crown officials in Georgia (where the British restored civil government) had allowed "known and professed enemies to remain . . . unmolested, to walk at liberty, and enjoy their possessions." Seven months after the British captured Charleston, former patriots were strong enough to avoid being labeled as a defeated party and were referred to only as a "declining party."[31] The loyalists of Charleston and Savannah, even more than their brothers and sisters to the north, were never able to turn their garrisons into pure loyalist strongholds. Instead these towns remained an uneasy mix of patriots, former patriots, and long-time loyalists.

Revolutionaries who remained publicly visible long after the British seizure of these towns felt comfortable enough to irritate loyalist officials by being ready "on all ocassions," the writer who called himself "Scriblerus" complained, "to exclaim against the present course of publick proceedings, grumble . . . at every little disappointment, and . . . attribute . . . the cause of all their difficulties to the [British] management" of the city. Even revolutionaries who had served in provincial assemblies, individuals who had "been active in raising a patriot military in the first commencement of . . . the Revolution" and who held "their commissions in the rebel army long after the surrender of Charleston," and who even now openly refused to "return to their allegiance," felt comfortable enough to live in these loyalist enclaves and bold enough to argue with their former enemies on the streets.[32]

In this confused situation, what urban loyalists in the South wanted above all was not extermination or exile of former patriots and allegiance switchers, but simple clarity—something that had become nearly impossible in Charleston and Savannah. During the first year after the British recaptured these cities, leading garrison town dwellers spent their energies distinguishing between loyal "PEOPLE AT LARGE," the truly contrite patriots, unpunished hypocrites, and outright enemies. If fine distinctions of allegiance could be publicly drawn among garrison dwellers of a wide variety of loyalties, living together would certainly seem less chaotic, and harmony, under the aegis of the Crown, might be realized.[33] The first step toward living in some peace within these diverse towns of the South was the development of brief loyalist histories of the Revolution. Such narratives were, in fact, the first attempts since 1776 by southern loyalists to interpret the Revolution and provide an accounting of past behavior of people of all allegiances.[34] The hope was not that these accounts would put a stop to discrimination altogether. Instead, by drawing ever finer distinctions among garrison town dwellers, "indiscriminate censures" of former patriots could cease.[35] Distinctions based on careful analysis of past behavior would provide orderly relations among people.

In enclosed garrison towns, where any face-to-face encounter could become confrontational, clear distinctions were crucial. "We see a person [on the street] perfectly at large, and apparently as much at his ease as his neighbor; we form a connection, and perhaps enter into plans and business with him; . . . we . . . involve ourselves, though very innocently, . . . merely because we trusted a person we did not know, and who does not stand . . . [identified] in the community, by anything that might excite our caution." These allegiance-switching trimmers could be identified readily in the towns by the "contemptuous, haughty air and look of disdain [they] bestow . . . on the friends of government." They were the "disorderly, idle and suspicious" types that anyone could see throughout the garrison. Future problems for trusting or naive loyalists could be solved by drawing "some line . . . between . . . [former patriots] and those whom . . . [they] must call, Loyal Subjects."[36]

The commingling of loyalists and acquiescent former patriots in Savannah and Charleston changed loyalist discourse in the South. Anger and outrage did not dissipate, but the quest for precise gradations of past loyal and rebellious behavior moderated loyalist discourse all the same. The loyalists in Charleston and Savannah learned that in chaotic, enclosed urban settings only a managed and moderate belligerency could both give voice to their antagonisms and protect their interests.

Polemical Origins of Loyalist Moderation

Like the tincture of moderation that appeared in loyalist discourse in the southern garrison towns, an authentically moderate viewpoint began to emerge shortly after 1778 in New York. Like Charleston and Savannah, garrison town residents in New York moderated their loyalism. Their anger toward the patriots had abated and, moreover, they were embarrassed by the truculence of a handful of tories seeking scapegoats for the military disaster at Saratoga. As a result a new moderation characterized writings in the loyalist press in 1778. From then until the end of the war, the garrison town loyalists increasingly came to understand that frustration over the inability of British superiority to strike a decisive blow was counterproductive and that loyalists' demands for aggressive military action only inflamed the garrison town public.

This bunker mentality became most pronounced during the spring and summer of 1778, when the loyalists focused their attention on the no-man's land separating the garrison towns from the patriot-held countryside. The war became a desperate struggle for food and fuel. After the disappointment of Saratoga and the realization that loyalist deprivation in the garrison towns was nowhere near an end, military authority broke down completely in border areas as armed loyalist bands moved into them and on their own admission "committed . . . horrid plunder," which in turn prompted patriot retaliation that "butchered [loyalist] citizens."[37] But vengeful zealotry lacked the capacity to become the cement of community. The majority of garrison town loyalists were passive supporters of the kind of British rule that had existed in America before 1776. They had no new program with which to confront independence, and they believed they did not have to explain their steady behavior. By nature they were contented and wanted to remain so; they were those who had felt most comfortable occupying the moderate middle ground in the pre-Revolutionary debate. William Smith, Jr., a moderate patriot until 1776, who had cast his lot with the British in 1778, published in 1780 his *Candid Retrospect on the American War examined by Whig Principles,* which included a revealing passage from his 1776 diary, "thoughts as a rule for my own conduct at this melancholy hour of approaching distress."[38] Extremists bemoaned the fact that for American loyalists there was no corresponding institution to the Continental Line, which so effectively indoctrinated thousands of potential patriots. Loyalist enthusiasts particularly regretted that those in the garrison had "not been compelled to take up arms, or go over to the other party, as has been the case among the rebels."[39] Moderate loyalists were uncomfortable with so stark a depiction of their alternatives.

Increasingly after 1778, moderate garrison town exiles concluded that the hatreds produced by the war were not only contaminating the middle ground within the garrison town, but were also pushing the whole of American society to the brink of anarchy. This frightening possibility energized the moderates and brought an end to their three years of passivity in the midst of ever-increasing demands for bloodshed. It also confirmed in them their belief that moderation was the only way to confront the possibility of complete social breakdown. As a result a furious debate occurred within the garrison community. On the one side were those who never recovered from their post-Saratoga hatred and who continued till the end of the war to advocate plans for bloody reprisal. Against this group were pitted the newly energized moderates. The extremists shouted for the garrison to "awake and rouse . . . out of your lethargy" and take up arms as guerrilla fighters. It was better to band together, fight, and "die in the attempt, than to . . . perish" by inactivity. Nothing galled the extremists so much as the indignity of hearing lectures from fellow loyalists about "Moderation, Reconciliation, and Unity."[40] Moderate writers responded to the extremists by urging that they join others in "waiting patiently the result of Parliamentary deliberations" on the Saratoga crisis and, most of all, in "guard[ing] against either extremes of despondence or rashness."[41]

When it became clear to the extremists that the majority of garrison loyalists were not to be pushed out of their natural moderation, they leveled all manner of charges at moderate garrison town dwellers for their lack of zeal. They especially targeted men of property for not bestirring themselves in the war effort and for caring only about "posts of honour or preferment." Some tory enthusiasts flatly charged that key loyalists had been corrupted into their moderation with regular government payments that allowed them distance from "the calamities of others."[42] In a grotesque moral reversal, one writer circulated the idea that it was the members of the lower classes who lacked enthusiasm and that those who had sacrificed the most for loyalism were the few who had "been driven from the lap of ease, elegance and plenty to the rude level of mean artifice." According to this writer, "Plebeians" were "not to be pitied" and, in fact, were surely doing damage to the war effort with their "profligate and lazy" ways.[43] Failing all else, some New York extremists purposefully confused moderation with a lack of courage, charging that at least in the New York garrison, no one deserved the title of loyalist. The city was simply populated with "dastardly" people within the lines, who "passed under that name" but refused to serve the British cause. They had "neither the courage to come out in favor of rebellion" nor the courage to oppose it. No taunting would propel the majority of the "cowardly . . . friends of government" from the middle ground—not a threat to their property, not the experience of persecution, not even the urging of extremists to join the ranks of the bitter and vengeful.[44] The moderates responded that "true fortitude and courage consists in patience and prudence," not in passion or in rashness. As one moderate wrote, "All men are not soldiers, . . . and, among the loyalists, all are not adventurers," a code word for terrorists.[45]

The failure of the small group of extremists to whip a majority of their fellow townspeople into a military rage was the defining moment for wartime loyalism. The moderate course of the movement from 1778 to 1783 was now determined. The threat of a catastrophic social and political breakdown was what had moved the moderate loyalist majority out of their passivity into the public arena. Moderates did not see themselves engaged in some kind of glorious cause. Instead they entered the garrison town debate to put a stop to the plans of vengeance and to prevent what they believed would be genuine "public calamities."[46] Buoyed by their achievement of stopping extremist recruitment, they set to work, in moderate language that was neither insulting nor patronizing, to lay out the dangers they saw ahead for Revolutionary America. For the next six years they provided a constant reminder to all Americans that there were moderate paths even in the midst of revolution. In doing so, they provided the only source of moderate criticism of radical revolutionary change. In the process of dealing with key moderate issues—the dangers of republican government, the radical alliance with France, and the possibility of reconciliation and a return to a civil society—they offered the first cogent defense of British wartime policies since 1775.

Loyalist Moderation

Garrison loyalists based their most fundamental political beliefs on eighteenth-century Enlightenment science, the principles of which they regarded as near universally held. They coupled these principles, which proclaimed a benign order in nature, with the British tradition of moderate political order that had been achieved in the half century since Charles II had been restored to the throne in 1660. It was a tradition of moderate order that had come about by resolving the conflict between Parliament and the Crown in favor of Parliament, but without the radical alternative of destroying the British authority. Like their Enlightenment soul mates in Britain, American loyalists used rational argument to support their own concepts of political moderation and stability. This type of rational argumentation had gained favor among Anglo-American thinkers in a powerful reaction to the chaos of the English civil wars that had preceded the Restoration. When moderate garrison town loyalists applied reason to the comparison of the new state constitutions with the received tradition of British order and with scientific principles, they were immediately struck by the radical character of the constitutions. The untried nature of these constitutions, they contended, would nearly institutionalize in America the turmoil that Britain had spent half a century overcoming.

The Moderate Loyalist Critique of Revolutionary Radicalism

The garrison loyalists had entered the wartime debate not primarily to advance human progress but to head off the frightening possibility of anarchy. Consequently they never understood the radical constitutional experiments of the revolutionaries as anything other than a mad gamble. The Revolution risked the "beautiful and desirable ... blessing of domestic quiet," to "new fangled systems, and untried novelties" that were almost always "false and imperfect."[47] Garrison town moderates aimed to warn all Americans of the radical and dangerous state governments that seemed to the loyalists to reject both the wisdom of recent British political tradition and the best theory and practice of the Enlightenment. As good Enlightenment thinkers, loyalist advocates applied reason to the "laws of nature" that governed politics and came to an understanding of political principles that the revolutionaries could no more change "than we can change the laws of gravity ... which ... regulate the universe."[48] Not only did moderate loyalists think of themselves as heirs of European intellectual tradition, they knew also the lessons of past republics. In their view, Revolutionary America revealed its true extremism when it cobbled together ideas that were "without model—without parallel," ideas that on every occasion in the past had resulted in the destruction of liberty and happiness.

According to the moderate loyalists, British experience had resulted in a mixed government, the "most perfect ever invented," with a division of power "into three branches; each of which could control the others," thereby suppressing the "tyranny of one" or the "mischiefs of popular confusion."[49] In Revolutionary America, however, the case was wholly different. "The Congress have found means to unite ... in themselves," moderate loyalist writers alleged, "the power of King, Lords and Commons," making Congress "absolute, paramount, and unrestrained."[50] Tyranny and confusion spawned the radicalism of a confused democracy that "no man of common sense would support." Republics were dangerous, but republics gone to democracy were headed toward catastrophe. A democratic government in America would be condemned to "perpetual dissension and discord," with every election an opportunity for "ambition [and] faction."[51] Accordingly, loyalist writers warned, civil society would be destroyed in America and replaced with "a constant succession" of revolutions by those out of power, revolutions that would come "as the seasons" and would bring "Murder, Desolation and Misery."[52]

The Moderate Loyalist Critique of Revolutionary State Constitutions

Though modeled on Enlightenment principles of balance, the state constitutions drafted by twelve of the thirteen original states in 1776–77 deeply alarmed loyalist critics, who found it impossible to believe that power could be safely lodged within a single democratic part of society. As the moderates saw it, the belief that the people would act virtuously was preposterous in light of history. The 1776 state constitution of Pennsylvania was one of the most radically democratic to come out of the Revolution. When that constitution reached New York City, loyalist polemicists seized upon its dangerous disregard of British precedents. Under the Pennsylvania model, moderate loyalists claimed, the "rude, envious and illiterate spirit of the peasantry, will predominate, . . . the Rich, the Artificer and the Merchant will live unhappy," and "merit[orious] people will be discouraged" from participating in public life.[53] In making these charges, loyalist commentators did not engage in mockery, ridicule, or extreme statements. Perhaps with half an eye to someday living under these new constitutions, they aimed to provide blunt but genuinely instructive advice. When moderate loyalist commentators warned Americans of the dangers of republics, they conceded to the revolutionaries that a virtuous and tranquil republic could be maintained in small face-to-face societies. However, this kind of a republic had nothing to do with large American states like Pennsylvania, which in the future might stretch to the Pacific. The population of such a state would be in the millions and would produce, from "the interior districts, . . . a host of lawgivers that would pour their delegates into her senate. The government will then be that of a mob."[54]

According to moderate loyalists, even if large republican societies could somehow produce a virtuous citizenry, this achievement would never be enough by itself to prevent the ill effects of what the American states seemed determined to achieve—power immoderately lodged solely in the legislature. An all-powerful legislature of poor "rustics from the woods beyond the Ohio, [who] can boast of nothing but their honesty," would bring down a republic as fast as any tyrant. Garrison town moderates believed there were no values strong enough to serve as a barrier against the timeless desire to redistribute wealth. "The Poor," the moderate polemicists warned from experience, "never will want to devour the Rich, if it can be done with impunity." An all-powerful republican "legislature of beggars" would invariably be thieves, and the rich will be "envied and robbed, and [their] opulence distributed as the property of the public."[55]

The inherent problem of "criminal avidity" in a legislature, the moderates explained in a school-masterly way, could be overcome by placing the rich in a separate "House of Patricians, [a] nobly educated . . . Roman Senate," with its members possessing characteristics of "dignity, grandeur, . . . majesty, [and] a sense of honor." An upper house with these attributes would curb the worst behavior of the representatives of the poor and was the republic's only chance for long-term success. Although some moderate loyalists granted that education, dignity, and honor might occasionally surface in republican legislatures, they believed such traits were "commonly found only in men of birth, rank, and education. Several ages must roll over our heads before such characters come from the Mississippi."[56]

The inescapable problem for the moderate loyalists was that the state constitutions reflected the crisis conditions in which they were written. They were potentially dangerous wartime documents that did not follow past experience or wise principle. They were designed by all-powerful democratic legislatures for the purpose of efficiently conducting a war, a purpose for which they were admirably suited. Constitution writing by a representative assembly was a wonderful means to secure "the power of the multitude for constant and quick exertions" on the battlefield.[57] It was, however, a terrible way to write fundamental law. The garrison town moderates asked whether the authors ought not to give "some consideration . . . to the future." They warned that governments "founded in war and finding their internal balance in the principle of their founding" would "fall unbalanced into discord and confusion," with "ambitious . . . armed" ex-soldiers making their own law. These popular military governments were understandable but dangerous; their drafters had intentionally generated an "unrelenting" and "inextinguishable rage" among the people in order to create a potent military force out of untrained civilians—a frenzy incompatible with freedom. In the midst of war, revolutionary leaders would have to make an excruciatingly difficult, and possibly irreversible, choice between the power of military "rage" and the "liberty" they sought.[58]

Fundamental constitutional questions like these, moderate loyalists contended, could not be answered by regularly elected legislators. Writing in *Rivington's Gazette* in 1780, "An American Loyalist" advised the patriots that when a completely new foundation for government was contemplated, the people would have to deliberate on that issue alone.[59] Though probably unaware that Massachusetts had already adopted this approach by electing a constitutional convention in 1779 after voters rejected a constitution drafted by the legislature, the writer recognized that formalizing the process of constitution writing was essential to healing the wounds in the body politic caused by severing the imperial connection.

The Moderate Loyalist Critique of Republicanism

The garrison town moderates also tried to alert Americans to a timeless republican problem—that republics were always in danger of becoming marked by either the rigidity of tyranny or the confusion of democracy. As difficult as life was in the garrison for almost everyone, it was the refugees who suffered most and who saw the garrison as a model of liberty in contrast to the extremes of Revolutionary tyranny experienced by them when they lived outside the lines. It was these people who constantly warned that the Revolution could be a vicious and illiberal affair. They published in the garrison press simple pieces that were almost certainly the result of personal experience. In these pieces the refugees spun out their hopes of moderating extremes of the Revolution. They noted again and again that in Revolutionary America, no man could "speak, or write, or eat, or drink what he pleases." According to the refugees, the "plague of [government by] committees" was worse than "the inquisition" when "all comforts of life" were "destroyed" by their "low and illiberal tyranny." Civilians were forced into the patriot militia and into battle because "wives, children, and possessions were hostages for their . . . good behavior." If they refused to be enthusiastic in their service, they were met with a "jealous eye" kept over them by the "violent partisans" of rebellion. Anyone whose patriotism was suspect had "a tyrant at his door, watching over him with the utmost suspicion."[60]

Some perplexed garrison observers went beyond these cautionary stories and began to consult their libraries to try to find a rational explanation of why, despite such warnings, ordinary Americans who supported the patriot cause believed their "rights and liberties" were "preserved and secure" under the new governments. They found their answer in what they saw as Congress's skillful use of the radical political theories of Machiavelli. Following Machiavelli's ideas, Congress had given the appearance of sincere devotion to the highest ideals of liberty and virtue, using fast days "and days of public humiliation" to disguise their real purposes. At the same time that Congress proclaimed these ideals, the loyalists charged, it was effectively destroying those who disagreed with them by "tarring and feathering, riding men on rails by mobs, chaining men together by dozens and driving them like cattle to distant provinces, [and] shooting them in swamps."[61] Garrison town loyalists believed this eighteenth-century revival of Machiavellianism was too much of a match for the moderate "dictates of truth, the lessons of experience and history, the remonstrances of conscience, and duty to mankind." Yet despite their understanding that they confronted a formidable foe from a position of weakness, moderate loyalists maintained that quiet argument and moderate discussion would be sufficient to expose to ordinary Americans the extremism of the Revolution.[62]

Such didacticism, coming as it did from the morally and culturally tainted environment of the garrison towns, had, in patriot eyes, no moral standing whatever. The Reverend John Witherspoon, delegate to Congress from New Jersey, was the self-appointed monitor of garrison town doings. When the Continental Congress returned to Philadelphia in May 1778, following the British evacuation of the city, the loyalist printer Benjamin Towne approached delegates asking for news and contributions to his newspaper, the *Philadelphia Evening Post.* Witherspoon refused to cooperate unless Towne first publicly apologized for his collaboration with the British during the recent occupation. Out of either naïveté or servility, Towne asked Witherspoon to compose a suitable apology for him. When Towne saw the mea culpa that Witherspoon composed, he realized his blunder in entrusting the rehabilitation of his public image to the moralistic and judgmental Scottish cleric. Towne refused to sign it without substantial deletions. Witherspoon thereupon circulated the original document in Philadelphia and sent copies to the printers of other patriot newspapers, one of which, Fishkill's *New York Packet,* published it in October 1778. Witherspoon then composed a wholly unsolicited and spurious recantation for another notorious loyalist printer, New York's James Rivington, whose *Gazette* was a bastion of journalistic support for the British cause.[63]

Witherspoon's mock loyalist recantations portrayed Towne and Rivington as case studies of the way the imperial regime recruited its American lackeys and the way metropolitan British culture clothed such operatives with a pathetic veneer of cosmopolitan learning. "I hope the public will consider," Witherspoon had Towne plead, "that I have always been a timorous man, . . . a coward from my youth, so that I cannot fight—my belly is so big that I cannot run—and I am so great a lover of eating and drinking that I cannot starve." Witherspoon's intent was to drive home the point that the failure to cultivate moral self-consciousness left men prey to corruption and manipulation by sinister political forces. "A man that has run the gauntlet of creditors, duns, and bailiffs, for years in England and has been cudgelled, kicked, and pissed upon in America," as Witherspoon's Towne shamelessly described himself, "is in no danger of loving his reason . . . so long as there is the least prospect of saving his life." To clinch his argument for the moral debasement of garrison town printers, Witherspoon drew upon a vocabulary of degradation that he knew intimately—that of anti-Scottish stereotypes. "I can assure your mightinesses," he had Rivington implore American whig leaders, "that I am as great a coward as King James VI of Scotland, who could never see a naked sword without trembling, having been, it was said, frightened in his mother's belly, when the fierce barons of that country came in and killed David Rizzio in her presence"—referring to Mary Queen of Scots and her Italian lover. Presenting Rivington as someone who would pander to any public prejudice, Witherspoon had the printer invoke the opinion of the sixteenth-century Scottish historian George Buchanan that "the Scot is by nature zealous" to the point of unpredictable instability.[64]

Witherspoon's heavy-handed satire obscured the fact that moderate garrison town loyalists were also uncomfortable with the hegemonic swagger of British imperial policy and administration. Beginning in 1779 the garrison moderates proposed, as a middle course between independent and dependent status, a British role in America that would be something akin to a "superintendent" in a semi-independent state. According to the moderates, Britain's function under this system would be to mitigate many of the potentially critical constitutional problems—such as the "animosity and discord" among the states over control of western lands—that were keenly observed by garrison town observers. The loyalist moderates outlined a new theory of empire stressing Britain's historic moderating role in intercolonial disputes over land and boundaries. Loyalist realpolitik, for example, questioned whether the Revolutionary regime could function as a sovereign nation when separatist Vermont sat poised between the other American states and Quebec was ready to strike its own deal with the British.[65] Another loyalist critic of Revolutionary constitutionalism noted that "the minds of the inhabitants . . . differ so widely . . . that no particular system can be framed . . . to suit the inclinations of the whole."[66] Once Britain departed from North America, these writers predicted, angry contention between the states over western lands would turn to "scenes of bloody discord for ages," but if the imperial connection could remain intact as the American populace moved westward, then the imperial bond would rescue America from its territorial predicament and render her "noble, independent, and great."[67]

The Moderate Loyalist Critique of the French Alliance

Integral to understanding the loyalists' view of themselves as moderates who rightly rejected the radical ideas of the revolutionaries was the relationship of Catholicism to the traditional British forms of maintaining civil peace. The great achievement of British politics in the late seventeenth and early eighteenth centuries was settling the vexing question of a predictable succession to the throne. This question involved problems of political stability and turned on a fear of dangerous civil turmoil stemming from the ambitions to power of James II. This king's zeal for absolute power, backed by the French Catholic tyrant Louis XIV, had been halted when James II fled in the face of the Glorious Revolution in 1688. From that moment onward, English men and women throughout the Atlantic basin had linked an aberrant and dangerous tyranny with the all-but-Catholic Stuarts, who were willing to countenance French Catholic influence in the British nation. Out of this experience, both the British and the Americans associated Catholicism and France with the dreadful consequences of deadly fights for the throne and threats of a return to absolutism.

British political stability, guaranteed by the Protestant succession to the throne, was a seventy-five-year-old tradition by the time of the American Revolution, yet the threat to that stability was still fresh enough in the historical memory of garrison town dwellers. They thought of Catholic influence in America, through the alliance with France, not only as a national betrayal, but also as an introduction of Jacobite despotism, which the Glorious Revolution had averted in England. Consequently, when news reached the garrison town dwellers that fellow Anglo-Americans had allied with Catholic France, it was met with horror and all the memories of national catastrophe.[68] "Fe! Fe!" chided one garrison town polemicist, "are ye really the offspring of Old England?" The French alliance, "half sheep, half monkey,"[69] linked America "to a nation, which, from their souls they abhor," a nation from which they differed in "manners, customs, policy, religion, everything."[70] To garrison town writers, the alliance was as unconscionable as the horrors of the St. Bartholomew's Day massacre of thousands of French Protestants, an event still fresh in the cultural memory of the numerous descendants of Huguenots in New York and Charleston.[71] As a writer in *Rivington's Gazette* exclaimed, "it could not even be imagined what would have been the feelings [of] our forefathers," who understood the full meaning of religious peace, if they knew their "children would have entered into a league with the avowed, the severest enemy of their Faith."[72] This was the ultimate act of extremism, and it confirmed even for moderate loyalists the radically sinister nature of the Revolution.

So menacing was the French alliance that virtually all commentary on public issues in the garrison towns after the spring of 1778 made it a topic of discussion. Believing that the alliance, "the blackest . . . in the annals of infamy," would be properly greeted by "the people in general . . . with the horror and detestation it alone deserves," the moderates hoped it would "act more powerfully than fleets and armies, in the good work of restoring America to the parental arms of Great Britain."[73] They believed the radically unconventional nature of the alliance could be exposed by focusing on its religious and political dimensions, and they understood that what had energized the early years of the Revolution was the ability of the patriots to characterize themselves as a "virtuous, religious people, particularly attached to the Protestant faith."[74] The moderates countered that the French alliance, coupled with the religious toleration that had come with the disestablishment of the Anglican Church, threatened to put an end to a stable and virtuous American government, which had been solidly based on Protestantism. Toleration of Catholicism, according to the moderates, would result in the destruction of morality, the onset of corruption, and a repetition of the political and religious bloodshed of the seventeenth century. Eventually, they argued, Catholicism would end toleration, an established American Catholicism would crush the Anglican church, which, since the Glorious Revolution, had been so successful a custodian of the British political-religious settlement.[75]

In the moderates' view, there was no "Popish country in the world, where the Protestant religion is tolerated," since "the particular genius of Popery [was] to insinuate itself into all countries, and use every possible means of propagating its doctrines, wherever it gains a footing." What then could America expect, by embracing Catholicism, than rounds of absolute tyranny and the kind of violent resistance that had preceded 1688 in Britain. Moderates insisted that if the revolutionaries thought they could obtain the benefits of the French alliance and insulate themselves from the ill consequences of embracing Catholicism, they were terribly mistaken. Garrison town loyalists said America's British ancestors knew from long experience the malignant effects of this religion. Americans should take heed, they warned, for "circumstances less threatening" than an alliance with France had "frequently roused our ancestors against the encroachments of popery" in Britain and America.[76]

To the garrison town moderates, Revolutionary Americans seemed to be recklessly abandoning the hard-won seventeenth-century guarantees of religious liberty for Protestants and to be naive about impending Catholic influence. In New York state, according to some garrison observers, "Popery [was] now as much established by law . . . as any other religion; So that . . . [the] Governor and all [the] rulers may be Papists, and [there] may be a Mass House in every corner" of the country.[77] Rumors spread in the garrison towns that, along with several thousand rosary beads, "shoals of priests under every possible disguise" were being put into America by the French. All Americans knew that Puritan New England, with its "antipathy to popery," had long been vigilant concerning the dangers of Catholicism. In the past it had been a vigilance "border[ing] on enthusiasm." Now, after the French alliance, many in the garrison towns claimed that patriots in New England had declared "a wish to see a popish priest seated in every county."[78] In the garrison towns, the threat of Catholicism evoked images of chaos so powerful that those who passed along such stories were forced to comfort their fellow townspeople that nothing of the sort could occur behind the king's lines. One garrison town resident assured his readers that the French Catholic priests they saw on the streets of New York would, like prisoners on parole, be immediately jailed and deported if they were ever so bold as to say a mass.[79]

According to loyalist writers, the French Catholic threat to social and political order in the Anglo-American empire also extended to matters of territorial security for the new and fragile confederation. Garrison town papers published anonymous essays, some probably written by former royal officials, containing biting criticisms of the French alliance. These attempts at instructing untried American foreign policy makers in Congress assumed a naïveté among Revolutionary diplomats and expressed fear that France had maneuvered Congress into untenable positions that put both America and Britain at risk. In particular jeopardy, according to loyalists, were the goals of the Revolution—liberty and independence. The loyalists warned that France would not selflessly come to the aid of America, would not lend money and offer a navy without some promise of reward that would ultimately compromise American independence. These loyalists cautioned that the national policy of France, like that of all nations, was to "seize upon every opportunity" in seeking to protect its own national interests. France would be an "ambitious ally, interested . . . in conquest in America and [would] seek her own ends without regard to truth."[80]

Loyalists held that naive belief in French sincerity was an embarrassment—a reflection on America's, or, for that matter, on Britain's, capacity for "credulous virtue."[81] American commerce would not be enough to satisfy the French, and the price of American credulity might have to be paid with diminished independence. Some claimed that untried American diplomats might have already ceded a portion of American territory to France in a secret addendum to the published treaty. One garrison town writer claimed to have it on "good authority" that some "of the warmest independents themselves . . . confess[ed] their apprehensions that their country is sold to the French Kings."[82] Garrison town commentators called attention to the "solemn ceremony" by Silas Deane, "delivering the turf and twig to French Minister to Congress," in a "ritual . . . never made use of on any other occasion than the transferring of real estate."[83] According to this loyalist, the cession of American sovereignty would soon be accompanied by the disastrous presence of a French army. France would never withdraw and would use its new influence in all of North America to garner control of trade by exploiting the "differences between the northern and southern ports." At that point European naval powers would be forced to react to correct the balance of power. Belgium, Sweden, Denmark, and Russia would not tolerate a preponderance of French power and would reply with force in order to repartition America, with "Britain doubtless" having "her share."[84]

Thus, the loyalists argued, the cause of liberty would be no better served by the French alliance than by the winning of American independence. The loyalists believed it was extremely important that the Confederation Congress move cautiously. France had a long history as "the greatest enemy of . . . civil liberty," and Louis XVI had no better a record than his predecessors as a patron of freedom. However much military power France might provide, the alliance was a bad bargain for liberty. America was foolishly attempting to end a relationship with a British nation that had long been the "scourge of despotism" and "the guardian of injured freedom." Replacing this relationship—founded on a common passion for liberty—with reliance on a country whose citizens were "mere engines of [the king's] power," often "neither fed nor clothed, as if they were [not] part of the human race"—was the work of ill-trained or ignorant diplomats desperately in need of moderate guidance.[85]

The Moderate Loyalists and Reconciliation

American loyalists never had the power to control or even to influence the British wartime policies of reconciliation, but they did have fleeting opportunities to create a spirit of reconciliation among warring Americans. It was a mark of the failure of garrison loyalism that it did not begin the difficult process of moderating the hatreds of war and creating a spirit of reconciliation until three years into the conflict, and then only after the British effort, under the Earl of Carlisle, had been rejected by Congress. The Carlisle Commission had been empowered to concede virtually complete colonial autonomy short of independence. After Congress rejected the offer, the North ministry refused to sweeten the pot by defining in more explicit terms the kind of autonomy Britain was willing to grant her rebellious colonies. The garrison town press contended that the Carlisle plan had been killed off in 1779 when Virginia, in an "excess of madness" and "violence," had spread false reports that Norfolk had been burned by the British, a rumor that turned "the multitude" against the peace terms and overawed "all men of moderation." Garrison town loyalists blamed rumors of the burning of Norfolk on Virginia planters "jealous of the town's becoming the metropolis of the colony." In fact a land and naval force of 1,800 men commanded by Major General Edward Matthew and Commodore Sir George Collier descended on nearby Portsmouth and Suffolk on May 8, destroying more than one hundred vessels, burning Suffolk, and inflicting a major economic disaster on the Americans.[86]

While the moderate loyalists were not heartened by this military success, they did not despair of a negotiated solution to the conflict. Plunging into the work of creating an environment within which reconciliation might still succeed, they shaped a three-pronged attack: first, convincing an angry post-Carlisle garrison of the wisdom of moderating their own hatreds and prejudices and seeking to mollify patriot hostilities; second, encouraging mutual forgiveness; and finally, after the American victory at Yorktown, trying to persuade the patriots to reject triumphalism. Convinced that the winter halt in campaigning in late 1778 would be the "most favourable interval," a moment when "divine providence might intercede,"[87] the moderate loyalists maintained over the next four years that the conditions for reconciliation were palpably close: The "golden period is now come. . . . Military arrests, arbitrary imprisonments, suppression of trial by jury . . . introduction of foreign troops and the toleration of the Roman Catholic religion" must induce "people to begin to think" about peace.[88] In this sense, loyalist discourse on reconciliation was the new wine of conflict resolution in the old bottles of garrison town loyalist resentment.

Reconciliation and the Calming of Garrison Town Hatred

After Congress rejected the British peace offer, conditions went from bad to worse. Moderate loyalist writers complained that irregular military units of both patriots and loyalists committed "horrid plunder," which widened the "breach and increased our animosities."[89] In this environment it took a concerted effort to continue to believe in the possibility of reconciliation. In their frantic work to revive the peace process and maintain their optimism, the moderates gave an unrecognizable interpretation to these unprecedented acts of viciousness, arguing that nothing was "more certain than that this [plundering] was done in direct violation of the express orders of Government and the British Commissioners." Moderates were also certain "that Congress did not authorize nor approve of it on their part." As the war ground on through the late 1770s, garrison town writers made even greater efforts to reduce bitterness, observing that "friends have fallen out, and their dispute" has been "carried to extremes." They now characterized the war as little more than an unpleasant interlude in a long relationship, conflict brought on not by powerful and complex constitutional issues but by ordinary human passion that had concealed the "separate faults from . . . both sides." When this emotional intransigence subsided, the moderates maintained, both "will clearly see their errors," and with "generosity and candour," reconciliation would occur naturally.[90]

These moderate loyalist appeals were the first efforts within the towns to undo the damage of 1778 and to renew the possibilities for peace. The moderates were attempting to change the tone of garrison thinking and writing about the patriot movement—from mocking and angry demands for retribution against civilians to moderation and a kindly style. They invoked "the language of expostulation," or earnest remonstration. The moderates frankly admitted that, in the past, few garrison writers had "preserved their temper, or refrained from asperity of language." The aim after the defeat at Saratoga and the failure of the British peace effort had been "abuse and triumph over their adversaries." Such behavior, they contended, was the very kind of behavior that "destroyed men of moderate spirits and reconciling principles" and ended hope for accommodation.[91] Now the moderates wanted to make it clear to the patriots that garrison town loyalism had changed. It no longer meant "defam[ing] the character of any[one], or industriously lay[ing] traps [to] catch . . . unwary . . . brethren." Trying to live down their past and avoiding insults had only kindled "resentment" and made reconciliation more difficult,[92] the moderates hoped that there were too many bonds of "blood" and "religion" between American and Britain for reconciliation to fail. America, they argued, was irreversibly joined to "the only free nation in the world" in an Anglo-American mission to "prevent the human race from being debased and rendered miserable" by French tyranny and Catholic intrigue. Garrison town publicists maintained that a powerful common ground existed between loyalists and patriots, people of "virtue and enlarged minds" who "sincerely wish well to their country" and were therefore capable of reconciliation.[93]

Reconciliation as Mutual Forgiveness

Moderate loyalists hoped that the period after the Carlisle Commission might be the crucial turning point for peace. The perspective from within the garrisons showed a decline in the demands for a war of vengeance and suggested that reconciliation might now be a real possibility. Accordingly they began to explore recent, as well as the more distant, history for examples of how moderate people had behaved in political crisis. Coupled with the new spirit of reconciliation, garrison town loyalists drew encouragement from the return to Congress, in early 1779, of the well-known moderate revolutionary John Dickinson. It was a signal that reconciliation, if properly encouraged, might be at hand. Although Dickinson had been a prominent leader in the movement against British taxation and other forms of imperial centralization in the 1760s, he had refused to vote for independence in July 1776 and later in that year had retired from public life. Now, in 1779 the loyalist advocates of reconciliation seized Dickinson's eleventh-hour opposition to independence. He became a role model for moderate loyalists who looked for signs that among the patriots were "wise and good men who had oppose[d] the storm" and who had tried to "dissuade their country from lunging . . . into . . . misfortunes."[94] Dickinson's arrival in Congress was a call to action for loyalist moderates.[95]

Garrison town loyalists also turned to the writings of British moderates who had survived the English civil wars of the 1640s and had eventually helped reconcile the warring Puritans and Royalists. Their hero was Sir William Davenant, the London theatrical producer and royalist, who had returned to England from exile in the 1650s to lead the regicide Puritans back to an accommodation with a much moderated and less authoritarian monarchy. Moderate loyalists believed Davenant spoke to their situation when he said not to "despair of the Public," for despair was "the last thing that should enter into the heart of wise and honest men." Loyalists echoed Davenant's words that "though they see their country miserably rent asunder by faction, in appearance deaf to terms of reconciliation, yet good men ought not to be disheartened." Instead moderates should, following Davenant's example, wait for "the proper time . . . to exercise their industry," the moment "when both parties maybe willing to hear reason."[96]

In addition to Dickinson and Davenant, loyalist advocates of reconciliation drew on the testimony of New England loyalists. Having inhabited the very center of the Revolutionary cauldron, the New England loyalists had special cachet as analysts of upheaval. One posited the idea that there were "three sorts of men" in Revolutionary America. First, there were a large number of ordinary people who were quietly loyal to the Crown. Second, a small number of extremists, "REBELS AT HEART," included "men of desperate fortunes and republican principles, who have projected this dreadful crisis, at once to gratify the restless propensity of their natures, and to raise fortunes to themselves out of the general . . . ruins of their country, [and finally] the bulk of the people—'PRACTICAL REBELS,'" driven neither by ideology nor by narrow self-interest, who were open to reason.[97] Moderate loyalists in the garrison town contended that the third group, the practical revolutionaries, were potential peacemakers who, with the right encouragement, might persuade "Congress" to "make peace and let us be what we were in . . . 1763."[98] What the garrison town moderates could not understand was why the practical revolutionaries had not already seen the handwriting on the wall, why they had been "so much agitated, and worked up to such a degree of heat," in 1776 that they had been "incapable" of rationally "examining matters"[99] or why, in 1778, they had remained silent about the Carlisle Commission peace terms.[100] Nor could they solve the "perfect riddle" of why practical supporters of the Revolution had avoided service in the Continental Army but were willing to "risque their lives" as militia men whenever the British army had appeared.[101] The only explanation that made any sense was that practical revolutionaries had simply fallen victim to "custom and habit."[102] That conjecture was, in reality, highly perceptive; custom and habit were deeply ingrained political traits in eighteenth-century America and were central to the cautious revolutionary motivation of many patriots.

Above all, moderate loyalist writers stressed the importance of reconciliation based on forgiveness. They knew that substituting compassion for condemnation and retaliation would not be easy, but they were determined to try. Before the post-1778 viciousness that marked loyalist and patriot attitudes, garrison town residents hoped that time might "gradually extinguish" in the minds of the Revolutionaries "the throbbings of revenge for the . . . loss of a part of your family . . . slain in the field" or for "the loss of friends."[103] Late in the war, however, the issue of forgiveness had become far more difficult than just hoping for time to do its work.[104] The great barrier now was that Americans of both sides, and the British too, had come to believe that "forgiveness, in any process of time" was "an impossible thing." As the writer noted, "The sons of America as well as those of England" had bled, and "the graves of men are to be seen in every county . . . which was the seat of the war."[105] Coming forward to solve this intractable problem were garrison town refugee clergy, almost certainly Anglicans from New England. In gentle essays addressed "to the People of this Country," they used reason and scripture to "reduce the temperature" and to bring about a spirit of mercy. They presented themselves as loyalists who regarded patriots as brethren who had long since been forgiven for their part in the carnage of war and as people who "anxiously" wished for the day when patriots and loyalists could "embrace as friends."[106]

Seeking to assuage such anxiety, moderate loyalist clergymen assured moderate patriots that British law would distinguish between overt acts of rebellion and the conduct of thousands of colonists caught up in the Revolution. Above all, these churchmen pointed to the sin of pride, which had kept the largest number of patriots from reconciling with their loyalist brethren. The scriptural prodigal son, whose pride stood in the way of his being restored to the love of his father, became the model for this projected reconciliation. If patriots were to set aside their pride and reclaim their allegiance, they could be assured that loyalists, despite their own sufferings, would never exhibit the anger and jealousy shown by the profligate's older brother.[107]

Loyalist clergy knew from experience that there were many patriots who feared that changing sides would subject them to "the scorn and contempt of those, who all along [had] been steady in their . . . loyalty." Thus loyalist advocacy of reconciliation sought to recruit not only wavering revolutionaries but also angry garrison town loyalists in reciprocal reconciliation. Loyalist clergy praised garrison town residents for their "undeviating virtue" throughout the long years of controversy and war, for "passing through . . . contagious folly untainted," and, in the eventuality of a future royal victory, for never allowing their honor to be "soiled by . . . a wayward and untimely triumph" over reconciled former revolutionaries.[108]

Reconciliation and the Problem of Patriot Triumphalism

The reconciliation efforts of moderate loyalists hinged on the revolutionaries' willingness to eschew triumphalism. While they recognized that Americans who had supported the Revolution would naturally want to celebrate their victory, garrison town writers stressed the importance of not allowing celebration to spill over into mean-spirited denigration of those who had sided with Great Britain. In a fictive dialogue between a hot-tempered swaggering patriot man and a thoughtful conciliatory patriot woman, the author—speaking through the female character—warned the man that exaltation and gloating would drive out of the new nation "men of distinguished rank, . . . remarkable for honour and integrity." It was just these kinds of people, the feminine voice emphasized, "who might be particularly useful" during the transition from war to peace.[109]

Most loyalists loved stability and included themselves among "those who are not given to change." A dialogue in May 1783 between "Philocles, a Gentleman" living outside New York City, and "Constantia," his "friend" in the garrison town, explored the character of those loyalists who faced the prospect of exile from their native land. Constantia stressed that such loyalists had been faithful to the king "out of principle," "conscience," and "honour"—traits that would also make them "dependable supporters of the new Government." But if they were driven into exile, Constantia warned, these wealthy and talented people, "under British protection" and inhabiting "a flourishing colony in our vicinity" could "prove a . . . scourge to the United States." Philocles countered by noting that British colonial policy prior to 1776 had denied the colonists some of the "benefits" of the British constitution and had drawn an "ignominious distinction between Britons and Americans." "Does it become an American," he asked, "to feel an attachment to that government?" Eventually, however, Constantia wore Philocles down, and he finally conceded that the patriot regime in New York should conciliate the "thousands of useful, wealthy citizens" who had remained loyal to the Crown during the war.[110]

At this late stage of the war, the authors of these loyalist dialogues had no reason to create strawmen who could be easily pushed aside. They had their characters ask tough questions in order to better prepare the remaining loyalists for what they would confront after the departure of the British army. For example, one loyalist author's patriot character asked whether victorious Americans should be expected to sympathize with those who had cooperated with "the fleets and armies" that had "destroyed, depopulated, and ravaged our" country. In just "what light . . . must those men appear, who in so great . . . a cause, would unite with" the enemy?[111] These were brutal questions, and moderate characters in these dialogues could only hope "that Providence" would give the "powers of government . . . the wisdom to conciliate" the hatreds engendered by war. If these bodies could restore these "respectable [loyalist] characters" to their property, it would exhibit "to the world a generosity that will subdue all hearts."[112] As the war drew to a close, garrison town loyalists realized that if moderation, charity, and brotherly love did not come to the triumphant patriots soon, the new nation would reap bitter consequences. These loyalists warned Americans of all persuasions that if an unforgiving spirit continued after a formal peace, there was "every reason to fear, that the calamities of war have not yet sufficiently humbled us, and prepared our minds for peace, and the Almighty may still have greater punishments in store."[113]

The American loyalists wanted the victors to know that one of the preconditions of postwar political and social stability had been the presence of the British army in the garrison towns as a deterrent of patriot atrocities. If, after the army departed, patriot Americans had not rid the country of its "mutual enmity, piques, suspicions" and "rancor," there would be one "massacre after another" until "we must be a ruined people." Seven years of war, the loyalists claimed, had brought about a moral collapse as people on both sides had become selfish, irrational, and vicious. In this morally eroded condition, Americans had been "hurried on . . . to perpetrate the greatest enormities without remorse." The most advanced garrison town thinking at the end of the war implored Americans to "calm our passions, forget our animosity," abandon "passion," "phrenzy," and "civil rage," and return to the values of moderation in human relations.[114]

This call to civic maturity was the culmination of a process of identity formation that had taken place over the preceding three years. As early as 1779, the garrison town press had called attention to the issue of corrupt "speculators and monopolists" in the Continental Army's Commissary Department—a problem epitomized by a Presbyterian "parson, not many leagues from" New York City, who had apparently been known to the garrison town community as a man who had not been "worth a groat when the rebellion began" but "was put into the Commissary department" and now had "an estate of £25,000."[115] The garrison town loyalists prized their character as a people above petty thievery whose fellowship had been forged in sacrifice and suffering. In the loyalist mind, it was this sense of shared community that differentiated the garrison town loyalists from what they saw as a criminal element among so many patriots. Forged in the cauldron of shared hardships and indignities, the loyalists' moral courage had been tempered by "insults, . . . persecution, bonds, imprisonments, confiscation, and death." It was a litany that loyalist writers recited again and again. Despite having felt the sting of undeserved poverty and having "literally FORSAKEN ALL" because of their "steady adherence to duty and conscience," they had sustained themselves, according to the garrison town ethos, by their willingness to give "aid and affectionate assistance" to the least fortunate among their brethren.[116]

There was a genuine belief in the garrison towns that this kind of mutual assistance and fellow feeling, if it spread, might reverse the moral decay in America. According to loyalist writers, the collective spirit of the garrison towns reflected a "luster on human nature" and offered national atonement for the "atrocious crimes" committed by the patriots during their war for independence. Moderates believed the war had been unprecedented among "civilized nations" in its viciousness and had been accompanied by a moral breakdown caused by the extraordinary animosity with which the conflict had been conducted on both sides. According to a writer in the *New York Mercury*, civilized nations tempered the horrors of war with the "same principles and knowledge" that refined and improved "manners in social life." Not so in this war in which both sides had pursued the conflict with such "relentless rancour" that soldiers had aimed to "destroy and exterminate" regions and whole groups of people. Moderate loyalist publicists believed that moral regeneration depended on leadership from garrison town loyalists who had joined in colonial remonstrances before independence but had also witnessed the horrors of the rebellion and could evoke sympathy in every American.[117]

John Joachim Zubly, a Swiss-born Presbyterian minister in Savannah, almost perfectly met these leadership specifications. A "Whig Loyalist" who had staunchly defended colonial liberty until 1775 and thereafter forthrightly condemned the cause of American independence, Zubly's 1769 pamphlet, *An Humble Enquiry into the Nature of the Dependency of the American Colonies,* had reversed the logic of parliamentary supremacy. Zubly argued that parliamentary power derived from the British constitution, rather than from Parliament's presumptions to being the sole arbiter of British constitutionalism. The same pamphlet distinguished between the terms "kingdom" and "empire" by emphasizing that the rigors of royal authority lessened as one moved outward from the British Isles into British North America.[118] Zubly's 1775 sermon *The Law of Liberty* drew a delicate distinction between "duty, respect, and obedience to the King" and the "wish not to strengthen the hands of tyranny nor call oppression lawful." The only way to satisfy both demands was to adhere to the biblical "law of liberty," which entailed being guided politically by God who did not judge a man according to his "external appearance" or even by "his own opinion of himself," but rather by "his inward reality." "Let me entreat you, gentlemen," Zubly implored the Georgia Commons House of Assembly, to "think coolly and act rationally," for "rash counsels are seldom good ones. . . . Let neither the frowns of tyranny nor the pleasure of popularity sway you from what you clearly apprehend just and right. . . . Let us convince our enemies that the struggles of America have not their rise in a desire of independency." "The wish of a perpetual connection," Zubly added, was the only way "that we may be virtuous and free."[119]

The Revolution, Zubly sadly concluded by 1777, did not enable Georgians to be virtuous and free.[120] Arrested in July 1776 for refusing to swear allegiance to the Revolutionary regime in Georgia and driven into exile in 1777 in South Carolina's Black Swamp, where he preached to slaves, Zubly "resolved," by God's "grace, . . . to watch against every notion of revenge and to commit all . . . unto him that judgeth righteously." "Tho I do not mean to deny myself justice," he held, "I would guard against passion, revenge, & hatred; if restored to my congregation, I pray that I may be more diligent & more faithful especially toward Children."[121] Returning to Georgia in 1778 when the British reoccupied portions of the colony, Zubly sought to walk the narrow path between passion and humility. In 1780 he published in the *Royal Georgia Gazette* a powerful series of essays signed "Helvetius," recommending Swiss history to Americans as a model for understanding patient, nonviolent, disciplined defense of liberty against invading tyrants.[122]

While that uncompromising moral denunciation does not sound moderate or conciliating, it echoed the tensions Zubly had felt for nearly a decade between his love of colonial liberty, on the one hand, and his aversion to arrogance, vengefulness, and mindless zeal, on the other. Isolated in the Savannah garrison town and unaware of like-minded loyalist moderates in New York City, Zubly reached back into his continental humanist education and recalled Montaigne—what a recent scholar calls Montaigne's "ethics of yielding." It was a phrase Zubly would have cherished. The French wars of religion had convinced Montaigne's generation of humanists—as well as eighteenth-century continental Protestants like Zubly—that bravery, courage, and intransigence, admirable though they might sometimes be as discrete human actions, needed to be subordinated to tradition, custom, patience, and respect for authority, which were the sinews of a stable society. For Montaigne, healing conservation ethically transcended political advocacy. Zubly's diatribe against Georgia patriots bearing arms in the interior was in reality a passionate, if frustrated, attempt to communicate with people he had once known well and whose better selves he now sought to awaken.[123]

Reconciliation and the Garrison Town Endgame

Despite a significant number of garrison town loyalists who believed that the defeat of the British army at Yorktown in October 1781 was just a Saratoga-like setback, most knew soon enough that the new British commander in chief, Sir Guy Carleton, had begun organizing a withdrawal from the remaining garrisons at Savannah, Charleston, and New York. It was quite clear that the loyalists must soon leave the towns or stay and seek reconciliation with the patriots on very different terms from what they had imagined. This change of circumstances was a demanding test of the genuineness and flexibility of the loyalists' commitment to moderate measures. Yorktown presented them with a form of reconciliation that had been unthinkable a few months earlier. Loyalist town dwellers wanted patriots to appreciate and sympathize with the "cruel dilemma" they had faced early in the war. Just as their original allegiance had not been seasonal, their willingness now to seek accommodation with a patriot victory was not driven by opportunism. Their loyalty had come from an honest and examined commitment to moderate principles founded on simple decency. Their choice was "either taking up arms against their rightful sovereign, in . . . direct opposition to the dictates of conscience," or "sacrificing their whole property—a sacrifice which was made by thousands."[124]

Spokesmen for the New York garrison town community came to believe, after Yorktown and the fall of the North ministry, that they could communicate their moral identity and humanity to their patriot contemporaries as the material of peacemaking. Starting with the English takeover from the Dutch in 1664, New York had been a constitutional experiment in the making—intermingling elements of a Dutch outpost, an Anglo-American province, a counterrevolutionary garrison town encircled by a Revolutionary state government, and by 1782, an amalgamation of these several political cultures.[125] The Revolution's endgame played itself out according to this accumulated mixture of unwritten rules and constrained by these divergent tendencies. In 1767 William Smith had described an imperial constitution operating in New York as an "adventitious state," and in 1776 Peter Van Schaack called the Hudson Valley the one place in America where "some middle way" between unbridled imperial authority and unjustifiable rebellion could be "found out."[126] The question posed by "The New York Freeholder" in 1782, "whether America is likely to be happier and more flourishing by independency or by constitutional union with Great Britain?" was a "moral" consideration that hinged, in large part, on how to make the best use of the "activity and enterprising spirit of the Americans."[127]

The garrison town moderates were, therefore, sensitive about the question of their motivation. The period after Yorktown was one of abrupt transition, and explanations of why garrison town residents had maintained or adopted a new allegiance fluctuated wildly between aggressive apologies and passive requests for pardon. In their helpless new position, some vigorously objected to any "insinuation that something else other than true patriotism" had "influenced" their allegiance. Despite the evacuation of Charleston and Savannah in 1782, some New York loyalists boldly told the patriots that their motivation was rooted in anticipation of "miseries . . . which will probably terminate in the ruin of the country." More moderate and less aggressive apologies from the northern garrison towns portrayed loyalist motivation as coming "more from a supposition, that America would not be able to vindicate her independence" and "establish her just rights," and not from a "belief that she was wrong in the attempt."[128]

While garrison town writers in the South used similarly moderate language, their tone adhered consistently to the spirit of the trimmer. In Charleston or Savannah, the explanation for loyalist behavior was not founded on anti-Revolutionary principles, matters of conscience, or sense of duty. The loyalists of the South plainly and unapologetically wanted patriots to know that they had shallowly slipped away from patriotism into loyalism after the British conquests of Savannah and Charleston out of sheer necessity because they could "not have done otherwise." The patriot reconquest of most of Georgia and South Carolina in 1781, as well as British evacuation of Savannah and Charleston in December 1782, rendered those provinces "conquered" lands in which any effort to halt British withdrawal was totally "ineffectual."[129] In explaining their switch of allegiance from Britain to America, South Carolina loyalists reminded patriots that their cause had been in similar disarray after the capture of Charleston and that Governor John Rutledge had even advised his closest friends to submit to the British. In like manner, garrison town loyalists in the South unashamedly justified their submission to the British with the rhetorical question, "What [else] were [we] to do?"[130]

Responding to such loyalist discomfiture in the period after Yorktown, garrison town newspapers made imaginative use of a genre that had been employed infrequently during the war years, publishing dialogues between fictitious people of opposite but moderate views who extended to each other remarkable generosity.[131] This genre repeated the gentle moderation that had begun after 1778 in all garrison towns. What garrison town dwellers most wanted to know was what treatment they could anticipate from their recent enemies. The dialogues answered these questions by advocating gentle treatment of loyalists seeking reintegration into American society.

In imagined meetings between old acquaintances—between a loyalist uncle and his patriot nephew, for example, or a conciliatory patriot woman and an enthusiastic patriot man—garrison town residents explored their futures and asserted their potential value to the new republic.[132] In these dialogues, former enemies greeted each other with simple and sympathetic explanations of how the war had occurred. One old garrison loyalist met a former friend and longtime patriot outside the lines and immediately defused the awkwardness by blaming "the great ones in England" for a war they had brought on by their "dissipation, debauchery, and irreligion." As the dialogue progressed, the loyalist and the patriot agreed that the worst condition of war was the "separation of friends connected by the nearest ties."[133] The message to both sides was that after Yorktown, in areas immediately adjoining garrison towns, former patriot and loyalist friends had taken the first steps to normalize their lives.

By the spring of 1782, the military's offensive operations had been stopped across America, and loyalists in the garrison at New York recognized in these conversations that some of their fellows apparently "came and went as much as they wanted" in patriot-controlled areas. Still, the garrison dialogues offered a warning to loyalists: in these first encounters, garrison people were assured that they were perfectly safe, that aggressive patriots "never came near," but that loyalists should make their initial visit outside the towns "with those of their [own] way."[134] Nevertheless, with the formal end to the war still more than a year away, loyalists were being given confidence by the moderate garrison press and were moving outside the lines to take the first steps in the process of rebuilding their communities.

Elevating Rationality over Aggrievement

The values of moderate loyalism reflected the fact that most loyalists in the garrison were ordinary people, and their conciliatory values were the simple ones they had customarily associated with their lives before they had been convulsed by war. Their ideology after 1775 had been controlled by the course of the war, and their ultimate arrival, after 1778, at a position of moderation was a yearning for the "days of peace and tranquillity, . . . security, protection, and safety" that existed before the conflict had destroyed their lives.[135] One garrison dweller in New York expressed the modest hope that, in the future, no one would "make him afraid" any longer. In the first two years of the war, moderate loyalists had every reason to believe that the rebellion could be easily suppressed and the Continental Army overwhelmed with British military might. The first taste of warfare around New York City in 1776, loyalists now recalled, had shocked them, and by 1778 many believed the nature of the war and the frightening demands for ever-greater levels of bloodshed made it too awful to continue. "How deplorable . . . are the scenes of war," one loyalist wrote, "families, houses, friends, property, life" and "civil communities" on both sides obliterated. The only solution was for patriots and loyalists to "detest and resist" warfare.[136] The social dynamics of revolutionary war, as Judith L. Van Buskirk has recently written, made New York patriots and loyalists into "generous enemies. . . . While some city residents found no reason to stay, others banked on their unoffending, quiet lives under British occupation to spare them from any American backlash." The discourse of moderation in the garrison town press undergirded that calculation, that "banking" on reciprocal patriot moderation.[137]

Like ships in the night, loyalist and patriot moderates unknowingly approached each other along parallel paths of ideological engagement. Few patriots read the garrison town press, and the loyalists paid little attention to the complex and difficult constitutional development of the confederation. But in spite of living in different political and ideological worlds, when moderates on both sides reflected on the course of events, they reached similar conclusions. Ever since the first Revolutionary committees of safety had begun grilling persons suspected of disaffection from the whig cause in late 1774, the political culture of the new regime had regarded the disaffected as potentially useful members of the new order who should be reintegrated into American society at the lowest legal, military, and social cost. Beginning in 1777, court systems in the new states recognized the right of individuals to enjoy a decent interval between the collapse of royal authority and the creation of durable Revolutionary regimes during which to settle on their allegiance. Legislatures imposed loosely worded oaths of allegiance as inexpensive ways to bind the apprehensive and the ambivalent to the new regime. Commanders of the Continental Army discovered the political value of playing for time as a way of persuading the large neutralist segment of the white population to tilt toward the Americans and away from the British. And when the government of George III finally acknowledged American independence in a treaty that sought to protect the interests of the king's loyal followers, patriot leaders came forward and took the heat of public outrage to argue that leniency toward the defeated loyalists was a first test of the maturity and civic responsibility of the new nation.[138]

Did these two forms of Anglo-American political moderation actually miss each other and fail to connect? On a cognitive level, they did. But in that more diffuse realm of knowing and being that we call political culture, middle ground emerged in 1783 and 1784. The revolutionaries lowered the cost of their victory by enacting severely punitive legislation but then enforcing it sporadically and loosely.[139] Confiscation of loyalist property and continued banishment of loyalist exiles reflected public hostility during the first years of independence, but by the end of 1783 a strong movement had developed within most states to honor the letter and spirit of the loyalist provisions of the Treaty of Paris.[140] Cosmopolitanism became a way of healing the social wounds of the Revolution. "How wise was the policy of Augustus," Alexander Hamilton exclaimed in his defense of loyalist property rights and civil liberties in his Phocion letters of 1784:

> After conquering his enemies, . . . [he] ordered the papers . . . of Brutus, . . . which would have disclosed all his secret associates, . . . to be burnt. He would not know his enemies, that they might cease to hate when they had

nothing to fear. How laudable was the example of Elizabeth, who, when she was transferred from prison to the throne, ... dismissed her resentment [and] buried all offences in oblivion. ... The reigns of these two sovereigns are among the most illustrious in history. Their moderation gave a stability to their government that nothing else could have effected.[141]

Hamilton's pseudonym, "Phocion," was inspired by an Athenian statesman who had made peace with Macedonia.

The same moderation toward the loyalists that Hamilton embraced as an act of civility and statecraft, animated Aedanus Burke, the suspicious localist and states rights' republican from South Carolina. His pseudonym in the campaign against retribution was "Ithuriel," based on the observant angel in Milton's *Paradise Lost*. It was Ithuriel who discovered Satan, disguised as a toad, waiting to tempt the unwary with "vain hopes, vain aimes, inordinate desires / blown up with high conceits, ingendering pride." Postwar prosecution of the loyalists, Burke warned, would have "the same pernicious effects on the multitude that private scandal and defamation has on an innocent individual. It breaks the spirit and generous pride which is the best guardian of public liberty and private honor."[142] The self-important, abusive South Carolina legislators who sought to make civic vengeance an instrument of the state thus became the targets of Burke's well-cultivated Irish moral outrage.[143] Burke, Hamilton, and the garrison loyalists shared an eighteenth-century distaste for partisan hostility, and they understood that moderating partisanship was a precondition of stabilizing a revolutionary situation.

Loyalists and patriots came to understand, in their own ways, that moderation was a logical response to a revolutionary situation and an ethical response to the choices both parties faced as the war moved toward its conclusion. That loyalists devised a moderate counterrevolutionary political ethic in the pressure-cooker circumstances of the garrison towns testified to the presence of prudence and constraint in the Augustan political culture that they sought to perpetuate in America. The garrison towns appeared to their patriot critics to have been pathological communities, and that impression has been confirmed in the historical record by polemical garrison town newspaper essays in the loyalist press. But intermixed with the anger, violence, and shrill polemicism of the garrison towns was also an understanding of the quality Barbara Tuchman calls "folly" in human affairs.[144] Precisely because garrison town loyalism was foolish, it was also instructive—to historians and also to the loyalists themselves. Josiah Tucker, the scourge of Augustan political complacency and economic wishful thinking, foresaw in 1775 exactly what the loyalists learned by the early 1780s. He argued that the American colonies were too unruly and uncivilized to be worth much as British possessions. Better to let them go and live in their own chaotic way, Tucker proposed. There would be time in the future, he predicted, to establish lucrative economic ties with independent American states. Such a strategy, he insisted, was preferable to holding them by force of arms. The fundamental cause of colonial discontent, he thundered to Lord North's ministry, was

> deep laid in the natural constitution of things. *Three thousand miles of ocean between you and them.* . . . You have indeed winged ministers of vengeance who carry bolts in their pounces to the remotest verge of the sea. But there a power steps in that limits the arrogance of the raging passions and furious elements and says, 'so far shalt thou go and no farther.' Who are you that [you] should fret and rage and bite the chains of nature? *Nothing else worse happens to you than does to all nations who have extensive empire.* . . . In large bodies, the circulation of power must be less vigorous at the extremities.[145]

Tucker articulated what a handful of British imperial officials and colonial politicians knew by 1775 (and what the garrison town moderates appreciated by 1780): that the slackening of imperial authority in American port cities, even when backed by military force, was a palpable reality. Loyalist discourse in the garrison towns, situated from a British imperial perspective at "the remotest verge of the sea," confirmed Tucker's shrewd understanding that "the arrogance of raging passions" was a blunt instrument of imperial control. The price the loyalists paid for that bit of wisdom was their struggle to conduct their discourse in a way that elevated rationality over aggrievement.

Notes

1. Robert M. Calhoon, *The Loyalists in Revolutionary America, 1760–1781* (New York: Harcourt Brace Jovanovich, 1973), 232, 258, 506.

2. Linda Colley, *Britons: Forging a Nation, 1707–1832* (New Haven, Conn.: Yale University Press, 1992), and *Lewis Namier* (New York: St. Martin's Press, 1989), 56–60; T. H. Breen, "Ideology and Nationalism on the Eve of the American Revolution: Revisions *Once More* in Need of Revising," *Journal of American History* 84 (June 1997): 13–22; H. T. Dickinson, *The Politics of the People in Eighteenth-Century Britain* (London: St. Martin's Press, 1995), 1–8; and Thomas Bartlett, *The Fall and Rise of the Irish Nation: The Catholic Question, 1960–1830* (Savage, Md.: Barnes and Noble, 1992).

3. William Eddis, *Letters from America,* ed. Aubrey Land (Cambridge, Mass.: Harvard University Press, 1969), 71–72.

4. Robert J. Berkhofer, Jr., *Beyond the Great Story: History as Text and Discourse* (Cambridge, Mass.: Harvard University Press, 1995), 26–27.

5. Calhoon, *Revolutionary America: An Interpretive Overview* (New York: Harcourt Brace Jovanovich, 1976), 143–47. The best studies of particular garrison towns are Elaine F. Crane, *A Dependent People: Newport, Rhode Island, in the Revolutionary Era* (New York: Fordham University Press, 1985); Robert Ernst, "Andrew Eliot, Forgotten Loyalist," *New York History* 57 (July 1976): 285–320; Milton M. Klein and Ronald W. Howard, eds., *The Twilight of British Rule in Revolutionary America: The Letterbook of General James Robertson, 1780–1783* (Cooperstown: New York State Historical Association, 1983); Joseph M. Coleman, "Joseph Galloway and the British Occupation of Philadelphia," *Pennsylvania History* 30 (July 1963): 272–93; Jacob E. Cooke, "Tench Coxe: Tory Merchant," *Pennsylvania Magazine of History and Biography* 96 (January 1972): 48–81;

George Smith McGowan, *The British Occupation of Charleston, 1780–1782* (Columbia: University of South Carolina Press, 1972); Patrick J. Furlong, "Civilian-Military Conflict and the Restoration of the Royal Province of Georgia, 1778–1782," *Journal of Southern History* 38 (August 1972): 415–19; Keith Mason, "A Loyalist's Journey: James Parker's Response to the Revolutionary Crisis," *Virginia Magazine of History and Biography* 102 (April 1994): 139–66; and Gregory D. Massey, "The British Expedition to Wilmington, January–November, 1781," *North Carolina Historical Review* 66 (October 1989): 387–411.

6. "Wanted. By a gentleman, fond of curiosities, who is shortly going to England, a Parcel of Continental Notes, with which he intends to paper some rooms," *New York Gazette and Weekly Mercury,* October 28, 1776, paraphrased in Moses Coit Tyler, *The Literary History of the American Revolution, 1763–1783* (New York: G. P. Putnam's Sons, 1897), 2:63.

7. "Veritas," *Royal American Gazette,* December 17, 1778; G.G., *Newport Gazette,* January 23, 1777; "Letter from Philadelphia," *Royal American Gazette,* March 6, 1777.

8. "A.A.," *Newport Gazette,* April 10, 1777, February 12, 1778.

9. "A.A.," *Newport Gazette,* April 10, 1777.

10. Ibid. Satirical trivializing of the Revolution, as a loyalist writer astutely observed in 1780, testified to the potent novelty of republicanism and popular politics: "Had it not been for liberty poles, associations, committees of correspondence, committees and congresses (all rebellious and illegal meetings) which were at first laughed at and despised by the magistrates, we never should have had this rebellion," "Anglo-Americanus," *Rivington's Gazette,* August 19, 1780.

11. "C.C.," *Newport Gazette,* January 20, 1777.

12. Catherine Blecki and Karin A. Wulf, eds., *Milcah Martha Moore's Book: A Commonplace Book from Revolutionary America* (University Park: Pennsylvania State University Press, 1997), 41.

13. Ibid., 255–56.

14. Ibid., 312–13.

15. Judith L. Van Buskirk, "They Didn't Join the Band: Disaffected Women in Revolutionary Philadelphia," *Pennsylvania History* 62 (Summer 1995): 306–29; Arthur J. Mekeel, *The Relation of the Quakers to the American Revolution* (Washington, D.C.: University Press of America, 1979), chap. 10; and Calhoon, *Loyalists in Revolutionary America,* 387–90.

16. "Americanus," *Royal American Gazette,* January 17, 1777.

17. "Pacificus," *Royal American Gazette,* September 29, 1778.

18. [James Robertson], *Royal Pennsylvania Gazette,* May 12, 1778.

19. "A Loyal Refugee," *Royal American Gazette,* April 10, 1777; "Answer to the Queries sent from the Country," *Rivington's Gazette,* September 19, 1778; "Scotus Americanus," *Royal American Gazette,* December 10, 1778.

20. "Scotus Americanus," *Royal American Gazette,* December 10, 1778.

21. "Pacificus," *Royal American Gazette,* October 13, 1778.

22. "A Friend to Peace and the British Constitution," *Royal Pennsylvania Gazette,* April 28, 1778.

23. Ibid.

24. "Pacificus," *Royal American Gazette,* September 29, 1778.

25. "Scotus Americanus," *Royal American Gazette*, December 10, 1778; "Committee Man," *Royal Pennsylvania Gazette*, December 17, 1778; "Pacificus," *Royal American Gazette*, January 21, 1779.

26. "Committee Man," *Royal Pennsylvania Gazette*, January 21, 1778.

27. "Letter to James Robertson," *Royal American Gazette*, September 24, 1778.

28. Ibid.

29. "A Real Loyalist," *Rivington's Gazette*, June 3, 1780.

30. "Scotus Americanus," *Royal South Carolina Gazette*, June 8, 1780.

31. *South Carolina and American General Gazette*, December 6, 1780.

32. "Scriblerus," *South Carolina and American General Gazette*, July 26, 1780.

33. "Drusus, Letter #3," *South Carolina and American General Gazette*, August 9, 1780.

34. Ibid.

35. Ibid.

36. "A Correspondent," *South Carolina and American General Gazette*, January 24, 1781; *Royal Georgia Gazette*, March 15, 1781.

37. "The New York Freeholder, #5," *Rivington's Gazette*, July 13, 1782; "Modestus," *Rivington's Gazette*, November 14, 1778.

38. L. F. S. Upton, *The Loyal Whig: William Smith of New York & Quebec* (Toronto: University of Toronto Press, 1969), 126; Calhoon, *Loyalists in Revolutionary America*, 104.

39. "Drusus, Letter # 3," *South Carolina and American General Gazette*, August 9, 1780

40. "A Loyal Refugee," *Rivington's Gazette*, April 11, 1778; "Integer," *New York Mercury*, March 24, 1777.

41. "A Loyal American," *Rivington's Gazette*, December 19, 1778; "Scotus Americanus," *Rivington's Gazette*, December 26, 1778; "A Loyal Refugee," *Rivington's Gazette*, April 11, 1778; "A Refugee," *Rivington's Gazette*, February 2, 1780.

42. "A Refugee," *Rivington's Gazette*, February 2, 1780.

43. "Scotus Americanus," *Rivington's Gazette*, December 19, 1778.

44. Ibid.

45. "A Loyal American," *Rivington's Gazette*, December 19, 1778.

46. "A New York Exile," *Rivington's Gazette*, January 6, 1779.

47. "Pacificus," *Royal American Gazette*, October 13, 1778; "Dialogue," *Royal Pennsylvania Gazette*, March 31, 1778; "Veridicus," *South Carolina and American General Gazette*, January 31, 1781.

48. "Papinian," *New York Mercury*, August 2, 1779 (supplement).

49. "Aristides," *Rivington's Gazette*, October 7, 1778.

50. "Papinian," *New York Mercury*, August 2, 1779 (supplement); "Aristides," *Rivington's Gazette*, October 7, 1778.

51. "Aristides," *Rivington's Gazette*, October 7, 1778.

52. "A.A.," *Newport Gazette*, April 10, 1777.

53. "Remarks . . . ," *New York Mercury*, October 12, 1778.

54. Ibid.

55. Ibid.

56. Ibid.

57. Ibid.

58. "C.D.," *Rivington's Gazette,* November 9, 1782.

59. "An American Loyalist," *Rivington's Gazette,* October 21, 1780.

60. "A Dialogue," *Royal Pennsylvania Gazette,* March 31, 1778; "Florus," *Rivington's Gazette,* April 7, 1779; "Clarendon," *New York Mercury,* June 7, 1779; [Benjamin Towne], *Pennsylvania Ledger,* February 4, 1778.

61. [Benjamin Towne], *Pennsylvania Ledger,* February 4, 1778.

62. "Papinian," *New York Mercury,* June 14, 1779.

63. Robert M. Calhoon and Timothy M. Barnes, "John Witherspoon and Loyalist Recantation," *American Presbyterians: The Journal of Presbyterian History* 63, no. 3 (1985): 273–84.

64. Calhoon and Barnes, "John Witherspoon and Loyalist Recantation," in *The Loyalist Perception,* 189–90. See chapter 14 below.

65. Upton, *The Loyal Whig,* 130–35.

66. Mary Beth Norton, ed. "John Randolph's 'Plan of Accommodations,'" *William and Mary Quarterly,* 3rd ser., 28 (January 1971): 108.

67. "Papinian," *New York Mercury,* August 2, 1779 (supplement); "C.D.," *Rivington's Gazette,* November 9, 1782.

68. "Papinian," *New York Mercury,* August 2, 1779 (supplement).

69. "Epistle to the American People," *Rivington's Gazette,* October 10, 1778.

70. Ibid.

71. Jon Butler, *The Huguenots in America: A Refugee People in New World Society* (Cambridge, Mass.: Harvard University Press, 1983), 120–43, 194–98.

72. "Edgar," *Rivington's Gazette,* October 10, 1778.

73. "Epistle to the American People," *Rivington's Gazette,* October 17, 1778, and "Edgar," *Rivington's Gazette,* October 10, 1778.

74. "Epistle to the American People," *Rivington's Gazette,* October 10, 1778.

75. Ibid.

76. "Papinian," *New York Mercury,* August 2, 1779 (supplement).

77. "A New York Exile," *Rivington's Gazette,* January 6, 1779.

78. "Papinian," *New York Mercury,* August 2, 1779 (supplement); "Epistle to the American People," *Rivington's Gazette,* October 14, 1779.

79. "Papinian," *New York Mercury,* August 2, 1779 (supplement).

80. "An American Loyalist," *Rivington's Gazette,* October 7, 1780.

81. Ibid.

82. "An American Freeman," *Rivington's Gazette,* August 22, 1778; "Britannicus," *Rivington's Gazette,* January 2, 1779; "Epistle to the American People," *Rivington's Gazette,* October 14, 1778.

83. "Epistle to the American People," *Rivington's Gazette,* October 14, 1778.

84. "An American Loyalist," *Rivington's Gazette,* October 21, 1780; "A New York Freeman, *Royal Pennsylvania Gazette,* August 3, 1782; "Aristides," *Royal South Carolina Gazette,* October 7, 1778.

85. "A New York Exile," *Rivington's Gazette,* January 6, 1779; "Epistle to the People of America," *Rivington's Gazette,* October 14, 1778; "An American Loyalist," *Rivington's Gazette,* October 7, 14, 21, 1780.

86. "A Friend to America and to Peace," *Rivington's Gazette,* September 8, 1781.

87. "Pacificus," *Royal American Gazette,* October 13, 1778.

88. "An American Loyalist," *Rivington's Gazette,* October 7, 1780.

89. "The New York Freeholder, #5," *Rivington's Gazette*, July 13, 1782.

90. Ibid., and "The New York Freeholder, #3," *Rivington's Gazette*, June 29, 1782.

91. "Pacificus," *Royal American Gazette*, October 8, 1778; "The New York Freeholder, #1," *Rivington's Gazette*, June 15, 1782.

92. "The New York Freeholder, #1," *Rivington's Gazette*, June 15, 1782.

93. "Mentor," *Rivington's Gazette*, September 23, 1778; "The New York Freeholder, #1 and #2," *Rivington's Gazette*, June 15, 22, 1782.

94. "Florus," *Rivington's Gazette*, March 6, 1779.

95. On the kind of moderation that the garrison town loyalists detected in Dickinson, see Stanley Johannesen, "John Dickinson and the American Revolution," *Historical Reflections* 2 (Summer 1975): 29–49.

96. "The New York Freeholder, #5," *Rivington's Gazette*, July 13, 20, 1782.

97. "An American Loyalist," *Rivington's Gazette*, October 14, 21, 1780.

98. Ibid., October 21, 1780.

99. "The New York Freeholder, #5," *Rivington's Gazette*, July 13, 1782.

100. "An American Loyalist," *Rivington's Gazette*, October 14, 1780.

101. Ibid., October 21, 1780.

102. Ibid., October 14, 21, 1780.

103. "Pacificus," *Royal American Gazette*, October 13, 1778.

104. "C.D.," *Rivington's Gazette*, November 9, 1782.

105. Ibid.

106. "The New York Freeholder," *Rivington's Gazette*, June 15, 1782.

107. "An American Loyalist," *Rivington's Gazette*, October 14, 21, 1780.

108. Ibid., October 21, 1780.

109. "A Dialogue, between a Gentleman from without the Lines, and a Lady within Them, His Friend," *Rivington's Gazette*, May 10, 1783.

110. Ibid.

111. Ibid.

112. Ibid.

113. "A New York Exile," *Rivington's Gazette*, January 6, 1779; "Candid," *Rivington's Gazette*, June 25, 1783.

114. "Queries," *Rivington's Gazette*, June 25, 1783.

115. "Papinian," *New York Mercury*, July 19, 1779.

116. Ibid., July 19, 1779.

117. Ibid., April 26, 1779.

118. Bernard Bailyn, *The Ideological Origins of the American Revolution* (Cambridge: Harvard University Press, 1967), 169, 181, 217.

119. Calhoon, *Loyalists in Revolutionary America*, 180–82.

120. John J. Zubly, "To the GRAND JURY at the County of Chatham, State of Georgia," October 8, 1777, in Randall M. Miller, *"A Warm & Zealous Spirit": John J. Zubly and the American Revolution: A Selection of His Writings* (Macon, Ga.: Mercer University Press, 1982), 166–70.

121. Lilla Mills Hawes, ed., *The Journal of the Reverend John Joachim Zubly, A.M, D.D., March 5, 1770 through June 22, 1781* (Savannah: Georgia Historical Society, 1989), xiii–xiv, 64–65.

122. "Helvetius #6," *Royal Georgia Gazette*, September 28, 1780, conveniently reprinted in Miller, ed., *"A Warm & Zealous Spirit,"* 191–96.

123. David Quint, *Montaigne and the Quality of Mercy: Ethical and Political Themes in the Essais* (Princeton: Princeton University Press, 1998), 102–44.

124. "The New York Freeholder, #5," *Rivington's Gazette,* July 13, 1782; "A Dialogue," *Rivington's Gazette,* May 10, 1783.

125. Daniel J. Hulsebosch, *Constituting Empire: New York and the Transformation of Constitutionalism in the Atlantic World, 1664–1830* (Chapel Hill: University of North Carolina Press, 2005), 157–69.

126. Calhoon, *Loyalists in Revolutionary America,* 95 and 186.

127. "The New York Freeholder, #s 1 and 7," *Rivington's Gazette,* June 15 and July 27, 1782.

128. "To the Printer of the Royal Gazette," *Rivington's Gazette,* November 20, 1782.

129. "Carolina Loyalist," *Royal South Carolina Gazette,* December 5, 1781; "A Suffering Loyalist," *Royal South Carolina Gazette,* July 13, 1782.

130. "A Suffering Loyalist," *Royal South Carolina Gazette,* July 13, 1782. For an interpretation of Rutledge's advice, see Robert M. Weir, "'The Violent Spirit,' the Reestablishment of Order, and the Continuity of Leadership in Post-Revolutionary South Carolina," in *"The Last of American Freemen": Studies in the Political Culture of the Colonial and Revolutionary South* (Macon, Ga.: Mercer University Press, 1986), 133–58.

131. The same idea occurred to Thomas Hutchinson in 1768 when he wrote "A Dialogue between a European and an American Englishman," as a private memorandum. In this document both sides of Hutchinson's persona conducted the kind of candid, restrained debate that he despaired of having with his contemporaries in pre-Revolutionary Boston. See Bernard Bailyn, ed., "A Dialogue between an American and a European Englishman, (1768)," *Perspectives in American History* 9 (1975): 343–410, and Calhoon, *Loyalists in Revolutionary America,* 55–57.

132. "A Dialogue," *Rivington's Gazette,* May 10, 1783; "To the Printer of the Royal Gazette," *Rivington's Gazette,* November 20, 1782.

133. "To the Printer of the Royal Gazette," *Rivington's Gazette,* November 20, 1782.

134. Ibid.

135. "Benevolus," *New York Mercury,* October 7, 1776; "Veridicus," *Royal South Carolina Gazette,* January 31, 1781.

136. "Veridicus," *Royal South Carolina Gazette,* January 31, 1781.

137. Judith L. Van Buskirk, *Generous Enemies: Patriots and Loyalists in Revolutionary New York* (Philadelphia: University of Pennsylvania Press, 2002), 7, 157.

138. Robert M. Calhoon, "The Reintegration of the Loyalists and the Disaffected," in *The American Revolution: Its Character and Limits,* ed. Jack P. Greene (New York: New York University Press, 1987), 51–74.

139. Albert S. Tillson, Jr., "The Maintenance of Revolutionary Consensus: Treatment of Tories in Southwestern Virginia," in *Loyalists and Community in North America,* ed. Robert M. Calhoon, Timothy M. Barnes, and George A. Rawlyk (Westport, Conn.: Greenwood Press, 1994), 45–53; Joseph S. Tiedemann, "Patriots, Loyalists, and Conflict Resolution, 1783–1787," in *Loyalists and Community in North America,* 57–88; David E. Maas, "The Massachusetts Loyalists and the Problem of Amnesty, 1775–1790," in *Loyalists and Community in North America,* 65–74; Norman K. Risjord, *Chesapeake Politics, 1781–1800* (New York: Columbia University Press, 1978); Jeffrey J. Crow, "What Price Loyalism? The Case of John Cruden, Commissioner of Confiscated Estates," *North*

Carolina Historical Review 58 (July 1981): 215–33; and Robert M. Weir, "The Violent Spirit," in "*The Last of American Freemen*," 133–58.

140. Roberta Tansman Jacobs, "The Treaty and the Tories: The Ideological Reaction to the Return of the Loyalists, 1783–1787" (Ph.D. diss., Cornell University, 1974), 116–68.

141. "A Letter from Phocion to the Considerate Citizens of New York," in *The Papers of Alexander Hamilton*, ed. Harold C. Syrett (New York: Columbia University Press, 1962), 3:496. Hamilton articulated unwritten protocols in post-Revolutionary New York for a tacitly negotiated reintegration of the loyalists into civil society. See Joseph S. Tiedemann, "Patriots, Loyalists, and Conflict Resolution in New York, 1783–1787," in Calhoon, Barnes, and Rawlyk, *Loyalists and Community in North America*, 75–78.

142. John C. Meleny, *The Public Life of Aedanus Burke: Revolutionary Republican in Post-Revolutionary South Carolina* (Columbia: University of South Carolina Press, 1991), 59–61.

143. Robert M. Calhoon, "Aedanus Burke and Thomas Burke: Revolutionary Conservatism in the Carolinas," in *The Meaning of South Carolina History: Essays in Honor of George C. Rogers*, ed. David R. Chesnutt and Clyde N. Wilson (Columbia: University of South Carolina Press, 1991), 59–61.

144. Barbara W. Tuchman, *The March of Folly: From Troy to Vietnam* (New York: Alfred A. Knopf, 1984). Tuchman defined folly as the "pursuit of policy contrary to self-interest" and applied the concept explicitly to the British political and military policies in America (3, 127–231).

145. Josiah Tucker, "A Letter to Edmund Burke," in *Josiah Tucker: A Selection from his Economic and Political Writings*, ed. Robert Livingston Schuyler (New York: Columbia University Press, 1931), 391; see also J. G. A. Pocock, "Josiah Tucker on Burke, Locke, and Price: A Study in the Varieties of Eighteenth-Century Conservatism," in *Virtue, Commerce, and History* (New York: Cambridge University Press, 1985), 186–91.

Civil, Revolutionary, or Partisan

The Loyalists and the Nature of the War for Independence

ROBERT M. CALHOON

The loyalists are a perplexing element in the history of the War for Independence. Piers Mackesy considers loyalist writings and documents about the war to be "a nightmare world" of fantasy, contradiction, and venom.[1] The loyalists were, nonetheless, the most immediate victims of the war and among the closest eye-witnesses of the struggle, so they cannot be ignored.[2] The loyalists were, to be sure, not an identifiable segment of the population during the war. In the more sparsely settled parts of the middle and southern colonies much of the population was inclined to acquiesce to whatever regime could maintain order and security. In this context, John Shy suggests, the British and patriots were competing for the allegiance and respect of a sizable, uncommitted segment of the population which was loyalist, neutral, inoffensive, or disaffected, depending on an observer's immediate perspective. John Shy has called on historians to think of the war as a "process which entangled large numbers of people for a long period of time in experiences of remarkable intensity."[3] To do so for the loyalists—to define the loyalists' military role, to appreciate their perception of military reality, and to assess their weight as military assets and liabilities—requires that we examine the ways in which the war worked upon, and interacted with, American society, British and American political systems, and the personalities of the participants. Seeking to place loyalists in a broad social context, historians have used the terms "civil," "partisan," and "revolutionary" to define the kinds of social conflicts which generated and fueled the War for Independence.[4] Civil war implies two conventional armies arising within the same populace; partisan war refers to the resort to decentralized, guerrilla fighting by at least one side; and revolutionary wars are grand upheavals against existing institutions.

This chapter will show how useful these terms can be in examining the factual record of loyalist military activity, especially in the first half of the war. However, another concept, "internal war," must be used if one is to see the later stages of the war through loyalist eyes and to understand the psychological impact which the war had on those loyalists who brooded over the military dilemma confronting them and the British.

From Lexington and Concord in April 1775, to the British occupation of New York City and much of New Jersey in the autumn and winter of 1776, and onward into the Howe and Burgoyne offensives of 1777, the advent of war in America was a ragged, chaotic affair. No simple formula can account for the nearly 10,000 loyalists who bore arms during the first half of the war.[5] There were roughly five categories of impulses that drew loyalists to arms. In the first place, some loyalists in arms simply represented Britain's natural assets in America (recently arrived British emigrants, those tied by interest to the British army in New York City or in Albany, or to the Indian Superintendents); second, other loyalists entered the fray in moments of rage, confusion, or fear; third, still others believed themselves to be strategically situated to unleash terrible vengeance on the rebels and acted from a combination of calculation and impulse; fourth, others responded to the need for organized pacification and reconciliation by supporters of the Crown; and fifth, a few groups of armed loyalists were agrarian radicals in conflict with aristocratic patriot elites. Clearly these categories overlap, dissolve into one another, and describe shifting behavior in different circumstances. In light of recent scholarship these are the principal dynamics of loyalist military involvement; we must, therefore, first examine the way in which each of these factors surfaced and interacted with one another.

During the critical early months of the Revolution in 1775 and 1776, British officials and loyalist leaders conceptualized boldly about the role which the loyal populace should play in quelling rebellion. At no other time during the war did initiatives in support of British authority occur so freely and spontaneously. While General Thomas Gage did not place a high priority on exploiting weaknesses in whig control of American territory, he responded positively to every opportunity for preliminary implementation of coordinated, widespread counterrevolutionary activity. He instructed John Stuart and Guy Johnson, Indian Superintendents for the southern and northern tribes, respectively, to place friendly Indian tribes in a posture of readiness to support British military efforts. He permitted Lieutenant Colonel Allen McLean, who on his own initiative had secured authorization to recruit recent Scottish immigrants, to operate from a base in Boston and to send covert agents to New York and the Carolinas. In North Carolina, Governor Josiah Martin, a former British officer, generated widespread opposition within the province to the work of the whig leaders. Then he planned a rising of loyalist partisans in the backcountry in early 1776 which would march to Wilmington to rendezvous with British regulars. Independent of Martin's appeals for a quick invasion of North Carolina, the ministry decided that such a move would be an effective means to checkmate the contagion. In May 1775, Gage dispatched part of the regiment at St. Augustine in East Florida to Virginia in order to assist Governor Dunmore in suppressing rebellion. These troops, plus a handful of Virginia loyalists and runaway slaves, occupied the towns of Gosport and Norfolk where from September 1775, until forced to evacuate in January 1776, Dunmore jeopardized the final transit of power in Virginia. At Dunmore's suggestion John

Connolly, British governor at Fort Pitt, journeyed to Boston to present to Gage a plan for a massive tory uprising in the upper Ohio valley and around Fort Detroit. Gage alerted General Guy Carleton in Canada and Guy Johnson in the Mohawk Valley to coordinate their movements with Connolly's.[6]

None of these risky, imaginative schemes functioned as their planners intended. Connolly was arrested on his way from Boston to Fort Pitt. The North Carolina loyalists arose prematurely, before the arrival of British troops was yet imminent, and were defeated decisively at the Battle of Moore's Creek. In spite of John Stuart's best efforts to manipulate events on the southern frontier, the Cherokees in the summer of 1776 sought to capitalize on the opportunity posed by the start of hostilities to drive white settlers from their lands. The Indians went to war before the arrival of British troops could divert patriot militia from a campaign of extermination.

Carleton, for his part, took firm charge of British dealings with the Iroquois during the summer and autumn of 1775. He vetoed Guy Johnson's plan for immediate Indian reprisals against rebel militia around Fort Ticonderoga; probably played a role in the dismissal of Daniel Claus, longtime Indian Superintendent for Quebec; and appointed Colonel John Butler, an aggressive, blustering, western New York landowner, to be acting Indian Superintendent when Guy Johnson, Claus, and Mohawk leader Joseph Brant sailed for England to lobby for a more substantial role in quelling the rebellion. Carleton's fear that premature Indian uprising would jeopardize Quebec's defense was sensible, but that admirable caution was offset by his inability to conduct Indian diplomacy. His jealousy of Claus and Johnson and his reliance on the heavy-handed John Butler deprived the British of a capacity to negotiate effectively with the Iroquois in late 1775. This was the very time when American representatives successfully were luring elements of the Iroquois confederacy into neutrality. Butler's jealousy of Brant and his refusal to treat Mohawk loyalists as equals significantly reduced British power. In July and August of 1777, when Indians and white loyalists made up half of Barry St. Leger's force that was besieging Fort Stanwix (in conjunction with Burgoyne's movement into the upper Hudson Valley), the Indians were so underfed, poorly supplied, and unsupervised that the 500 Seneca and Mohawk warriors in the offensive added little strength to the British strike force. When the siege on Fort Stanwix failed, retreating Indians plundered and assaulted their British and white loyalist compatriots.[7] The failure of these initiatives and preliminary maneuvers made them look clumsy and bizarre. Certainly they point up the truth that irregular warfare is at best only a supplement to, and not a substitute for, conventional military operations. But these British efforts also indicated a willingness to see the armed rebellion as a geopolitical process and to experiment with appropriate ways of dealing with an unprecedented military challenge. Even these military setbacks did not stifle irrepressible loyalist activity in the backcountry.

The divisions in American society which Martin, Connolly, McLean, Carleton, Dunmore and numerous obscure loyal subjects sought to exploit in 1775 represented some of Britain's natural assets at the outset of the war. The events of 1775–1776 demonstrated how rapidly those assets could be expended. The early months of the war also revealed how quickly new sources of instability within Revolutionary society tended to develop under the pressures of war and how difficult it was for either the British or the loyalists to respond with the right degree of speed and sensitivity to these opportunities.

Vermont provides a vivid example. Loyalist strength there fluctuated erratically. The allies of the Crown in the New Hampshire Grants region, New York land speculators, were driven from the region in 1775 by the insurgent movement led by Ethan and Ira Allen. Amid chaotic conditions in 1776, especially the absence of an institutional structure of committees, courts, and militia which could manage the suppression of disaffection, mobs harried and threatened some prominent Yankee settlers who had economic or political ties to the departed New York speculators. To the victims who tried to remain inoffensive these attacks seemed capricious and spontaneous. In fright, anger, or confusion some fled to Canada and many enlisted in loyalist regiments, particularly the Queen's Loyal Rangers under the command of John Peters. When Burgoyne's invasion passed through Castleton, Vermont, in July 1777, local loyalists recruited 400 local residents to help clear a road for the British force. After Saratoga, however, Vermont's prosecution of the leaders of this treasonable conduct was strikingly mild and confiscated property was resold to patriot members of the same families of convicted loyalists. The strongest political drive in the region, the desire for autonomy from New York, precluded internal bloodletting. Later in the war the Allens' abortive negotiations with the British for a separate peace cast them into alliance with the large minority of covert loyalists in the state.[8]

The mere presence of large numbers of persons disaffected from the Revolution reflected and aggravated social instability which inhibited either side from exploiting its best opportunities. New Jersey was the classic case of Britain's inability to translate military predominance into political advantage. The Revolutionary regime disintegrated in that province as the British occupied New Jersey after the seizure of New York City in the autumn and early winter of 1776. Nearly 2,500 New Jersey volunteers drawn from a pool of some 13,000 loyalist sympathizers provided ample manpower to pacify a conquered province, and the advent of war snapped the already attenuated lines of community between the two factions of Dutch Reformed inhabitants, one reluctantly favoring independence and the other cautiously opposing it. Yet even in this promising setting, pacification proved impossible. Plundering by Hessian and British troops and numerous acts of personal vengeance and cruelty by armed loyalists mocked British pretensions to be protecting the King's friends in the middle colonies. Even after the British were forced to retreat to isolated beachheads at Amboy and New Brunswick, turmoil in New Jersey at first presented the British command in New York City with the opportunity to make inroads and then pulled the mirage-like advantages away. The community of Jersey exiles in New York City continually

undermined the British commanders by their penchant for unauthorized terrorist activities.[9]

Garrison towns like New York City gave the British secure bases and havens
for loyalist refugees. Garrison towns also were unstable, abnormal communities
filled with violent, rootless men. St. Augustine in East Florida and Pensacola in
West Florida were refuges for more than 15,000 loyalists driven from the southern colonies. In order to organize these bloated wartime communities the British
distributed lavish new land grants and assured refugees that British rule in the
Floridas would be perpetual. In East Florida large numbers enlisted into a loyalist provincial corps, the East Florida Rangers, which became a pawn in a vicious
power struggle between Colonel Alexander Prevost and Governor Patrick Tonyn.
Tonyn appointed the irrepressible South Carolina backcountry partisan, Thomas
Brown, commander of the Rangers. First used to patrol the border between East
Florida and Georgia, the Rangers increasingly carried out raids into Georgia to
steal cattle and slaves.

Ambitious to recapture Georgia on his own initiative and constantly fearful
that rebel militia and regulars would swoop down on St. Augustine, Tonyn expected Prevost to function as a subordinate. Tonyn also tried to undercut Indian
Superintendent John Stuart's careful management of the Creeks and Choctaws.
The impetuous governor expected Stuart to arrange massive Indian support for
the reconquest of Georgia and for the periodic reinforcement of St. Augustine. He
could not comprehend Stuart's view that Indian support was a precious commodity that required careful bargaining and prudent use. For his part, Thomas
Brown knew that there were thousands of potential loyalists still living in the
Georgia and South Carolina backcountry and in pockets of the lowcountry as
well. With Tonyn's support he committed the Rangers to a dangerous role as
spearhead of the reconquest of the backcountry. Tonyn's and Brown's efforts to
instill energy, purpose, and zeal into the loyalist exile community in East Florida
were just the sort of energetic civil-military policy so badly lacking elsewhere in
America in 1776–77, but these efforts came at a high price. Incursions into Georgia, attempts to use Indians as shock troops, and the resort to savage, irregular
warfare awakened the dispirited and chaotic Revolutionary governments of South
Carolina and Georgia to the magnitude of the threat which the war posed for
their society.[10]

The most thorough and competent effort to pacify Revolutionary America
and to reinstitute British authority was, of course, Joseph Galloway's administration as Superintendent of Police and of Exports and Imports in occupied
Philadelphia from his appointment in December 1777, until British evacuation
the following June. Galloway successfully expanded a subordinate job in the military bureaucracy into that of a powerful administrative overseer of British policy
in the city. Since his flight to refuge in New York City in December 1776, Galloway
had labored to persuade Howe to move against Philadelphia. He even arranged
for pilots familiar with the Delaware River to rendezvous with the British attack

force. He was upset to learn that one of these men was caught and summarily hanged when Howe decided on the less risky and longer Chesapeake route to southeastern Pennsylvania.

Disdainful of Howe's languid movement into the city, Galloway assumed the role of civilian overlord of the region as soon as British troops landed at Head of Elk. He appointed a large staff of assistants and undertook systematic collection of intelligence, certification of loyalists, exposure of suspected rebel sympathizers, acquisition of food, establishment of hospital administration, and the issuance of regulations on curfews, garbage collection, tavern licenses, relief for the poor, and other local government functions. At his own expense he organized two companies of loyalist refugees and directed a number of guerrilla agents and spies who exhibited great discipline and loyalty. Reestablishing civil government in all but name was for Galloway one essential precondition for reconciliation; the other was constitutional reform along the lines of his 1774 Plan of Union.[11]

Bitterly disappointed by Howe's failure to move aggressively, Galloway in 1779 was the star witness in a Parliamentary inquiry into Howe's conduct of the war. His ludicrous assertion that 80 percent of the population was loyal to the Crown has tended to discredit his assessment of the war. Actually Howe and Galloway shared many of the same assumptions about the nature of the war and of the requirements for pacification. Howe believed that the mass of the population would begin to adhere to the Crown as soon as they saw the Continental Army forced to retreat from centers of population and unable to resist the steady, methodical occupation of territory by British regulars. Galloway predicted that if the loyalist majority of the population was given an opportunity to support pacification, they would respond in large numbers, provided that they were cajoled, coaxed, and assured of safety and security. Howe's and Galloway's views on the disposition of loyalist strength and mechanics of pacification differed in emphasis and tone, but not in substance. This may explain why the two men worked together reasonably well during the occupation of Philadelphia in spite of strong mutual antagonism. The real cause of conflict was Howe's disinclination to nourish Galloway's self-importance and the General's deeply bred aversion to zeal and personal singlemindedness.

That urbane quality of mind prevented Howe from sensing that the middle colonies contained many pockets of desperate men willing to risk their safety and security to vent their hostility toward the Revolutionary regime. In the Hudson Valley and on the eastern shore of Maryland these groups were populist rebels hostile to social hierarchy and anxious to disperse political power much more widely than prevailing whig oligarchs in New York and Maryland would tolerate.

In the Hudson Valley, where tenant unrest had smoldered for a decade, tenants on Livingston Manor, the baronial holdings of the great whig family of that name, seized the opportunity in 1775 to petition for redress of their own grievances. Some four hundred tenants took up arms for the King in 1776; the militia was riddled with disaffection. Finally in 1777, news of Burgoyne's offensive

triggered a premature uprising which was crushed swiftly by militia loyal to Liv-
ingstons.[12] On Maryland's Eastern Shore the war accentuated sharp economic
and social grievances in a region where the Revolutionary regime lacked the institutions and lines of direct political control and influence. Some slaves in the
region responded to Lord Dunmore's appeal to blacks to abandon their masters;
the first three slaves caught attempting to flee to the British were publicly hanged,
decapitated, and quartered. White loyalists were more numerous and more difficult to handle. Local committees of observation and the state Council of Safety
lacked the practical power or the political strength to impose severe penalties
on avowed British sympathizers. Thirty-four percent of Eastern Shore residents
indicted for political offenses during the Revolution were landless, and popular
pressure forced judges and juries to deal mildly with them. The militia was para-
lyzed by demands that officers be locally elected instead of centrally appointed. In
salt riots groups of armed men summarily appropriated scarce supplies of that
commodity from wealthy whig merchants. In numerous instances whig officials
were beaten, cursed, and otherwise abused with impunity.[13]

These isolated cases of violent, lower-class loyalist insurgency did not constitute a real threat to the success of the Revolution, but they manifested an important characteristic of the social order: the presence of a sizable minority of
groups who, in William H. Nelson's apt phrase, "felt weak and threatened" and
"had interests they felt needed protection from an American majority."[14] These
included pacifist and pietist groups, Mohawk Valley Indian and white settlers
alike who looked to the Indian Superintendent for the northern tribes for leadership and protection, and newcomers to the southern backcountry. The presence
and attitudes of these groups did not mean that Britain could have won the war
if she had only tapped this asset; it does mean that Britain's strongest resource
could be mobilized only at a price which the Mother Country could not afford to
pay—the dispatch of enough troops to occupy the large regions where fearful,
insecure subjects of the Crown resided and thereby to overcome the sense of
weakness which immobilized these defensive people. This confused ebb and flow
of loyalist military initiatives helps to define more precisely the nature of the partisan, civil, and revolutionary aspects of the war. Partisan war is irregular war
which often involves terror inflicted by informal bands of insurgents. Partisan
war occurs when the military and political institutions of one or more of the contending sides have ceased to function in part of the contested territory of the war.
A leadership vacuum is created to be filled by men uninhibited by prudence, humanity, or obedience to duly constituted superiors. Irregular war does not replace
conventional main force combat, but it occurs on the periphery of conventional
combat in areas where neither side can restore stable administration with the use
of regular troops. Although it occurs on the periphery of conventional operations,
irregular war is destabilizing in that it empowers a relatively small number of men
to upset the balance of power previously established between the contending parties. Brant's and Butler's campaigns in the Mohawk and Wyoming valleys were

exercises in partisan war. If the loyalist resistance movements in the North and South Carolina backcountry and the Connolly conspiracy in 1775 could have been supported promptly by British offensive operations, partisan war would have been much more widespread.

Civil wars are protracted hostilities between irreconcilably antagonistic segments of society within the same country who intend to exclude one another from political power and social advantage and to extirpate one another's beliefs and principles. By several standards the War for Independence was a civil war. Nineteen thousand loyalists bore arms at one time or another. But civil war was often important as a potential, rather than as an actual, condition. When individual loyalists beseeched the British to concentrate force in a given region—the Delaware Valley, around the Chesapeake Bay, the Hudson Valley, the Ohio Valley, southeastern Pennsylvania—in order to release the energies of numerous loyalist inhabitants,[15] these self-appointed strategic advisors were really saying that civil war was an imminent possibility. Such a war, they reasoned, would be based upon rival loyal and rebel zones of control. It would occur as soon as the British took the necessary risks and expended sufficient manpower and resources to establish secure zones on the colonial map where loyalist and passive adherents to the Crown could reside.

A revolutionary war is the hardest to define because, strictly speaking, the term applies to a society in the midst of a radical redistribution of wealth and opportunity or to a society shifting abruptly from one life style to another—conditions which did not entirely pertain to the case of the American Revolution. The rejection of British authority and the advent of republican government aroused strong passions which approximated those of a revolutionary war. Moreover, the volatile mixture of civil and partisan war which occurred spasmodically during the War for Independence made that conflict potentially revolutionary because it raised the spectre of a descent into barbarism.[16]

From such a perspective the War for Independence was partisan on its periphery, civil only when Britain threatened to gain secure control over a large territorial area, and revolutionary in discontinuous moments when the prospect of American victory portended social changes which were terrifying to cohesive and self-conscious loyalist and neutralist constituencies. This provisional model[17] does not rigidly separate civil, partisan, and revolutionary warfare. Residents of the Mohawk Valley, for example, felt that they were involved in a continuous civil war,[18] but only the period of the St. Leger offensive conforms to a precise definition of civil war: two rival, conventional armies faced one another and Britain nearly gained regional dominance. Mohawk depredations against pro-American Oneida villages during this period, however, marked the threshold of partisan warfare by Mohawk warriors and by Butler's raiders against patriot white settlers and Indians alike.

That very kind of difficulty, however, has impelled political theorists like Harry Eckstein to develop the model of "internal war" to deal with the whole range of conflicts including social revolution, struggles for national liberation, wars of secession, and internal conflicts which accompany political modernization—"any resort to violence within a political order to change its constitution, rulers, or policies." Our understanding of such conflicts is incomplete, Eckstein contends, because historians have focused on the specific "precipitants" of internal war and have neglected the "general disorientive social processes" which predisposed a society to slide into violent conflict. Internal war, moreover, becomes unavoidable only when the established government retains enough power to sustain itself in power long after it has ceased to command respect and acquiescence. In this way the concept of internal war encompasses both the "obstacle" thrown up by the old order and the mobilization of popular support needed to overcome those obstacles.[19] Loyalist writings about the last half of the War for Independence dealt with increasing urgency and cogency with the problem of internal war and with the sources of counterrevolutionary activity which lay hidden in the recesses of the social order.

These loyalist writings on the nature of the war may not be accurate objective accounts of military realists, but they reveal the harsh impact of the war on the human spirit and imagination, especially on people suddenly convinced that they were victims of both American cruelty and British incompetence. Conceiving of the war as an instrument of punishment was to recognize the immense complexity of the military dilemma facing the British and the loyalists. Colonel Robert Gray, South Carolina loyalist provincial officer, former whig, and backcountry native, recognized a yearning for order and fear of social disintegration in occupied South Carolina in the summer of 1780. "The conquest of the province was complete," he wrote; "the loyal . . . inhabitants, . . . one third" of the population "and . . . by no means the wealthiest, readily took up arms to maintain the British government and others enrolled themselves in the [loyalist] militia, partly because they believed the war to be at an end in the southern provinces and partly to ingratiate themselves with the conquerors. They fondly hoped they would enjoy a respite from the calamities of war and that the restoration of the King's government would restore to them the happiness they enjoyed before the war began. With these views [prevailing] on both sides, the Whigs and Tories seemed to vie with each other in giving proof of the sincerity of their submission" to British authority "and a most profound calm succeeded."[20]

Far from being an advantage to the British, this state of stability was quicksand. Rebels who took an oath of submission returned to their farms and commerce in Charleston revived. Caught up in this economic bustle, people were outraged by the British army's confiscation of horses, cattle and supplies. The sudden prominence of loyalists in the civil and military establishment afflicted former whig officials with "pangs of disappointed ambition." When notorious rebels were captured, "ignorant" British officers paroled them to their plantations and in a few days they broke parole and sought revenge on the loyalist militiamen who had assisted in their capture. In this fluid situation, which oscillated unpredictably between benumbed submission and furious retaliation, the loyalist militia lost their cohesion as fighting units—"officers not able to inspire their followers with the confidence necessary for soldiers" and British regulars contemptuous "of a militia among a people differing so much in custom and manners from themselves." The destruction of Ferguson's loyalist force at Kings Mountain and the increasingly brutal treatment of loyalists captured in the South Carolina backcountry combined to shatter the tenuous control which the Crown enjoyed in the province. "The unfortunate Loyalist on the frontiers found the fury of the whole war let loose upon him. He was no longer safe to sleep in his house. He hid himself in the swamps." Because the British refused to impose execution on rebel insurgents captured by frontier loyalists, Gray believed, many a loyalist was forced into collaboration with the rebels in order to be "safe to go to sleep without ... having his throat cut before morning." Other loyalists simply resorted to the brutal guerrilla tactics familiar to survivors of the Cherokee War—ambush, summary execution of helpless captives, decapitation of victims. "In short, the whole province resembled a piece of patch work" in which "the inhabitants of every settlement ... united in sentiment" took up "arms for the side it liked best" and made "continual inroads into one another's settlements."[21]

Both their keen perception of the strengths and weaknesses of the Revolutionary social order and their fixation upon the use of conventional and irregular violence to undermine that order induced the loyalists during the last half of the war to conceive of the conflict as an instrument of punishment, vengeance, and retribution and as a technique of social control. The Revolutionary social order, however, evaded punishment. Understandably frustrated and angered, the loyalists who dealt with the military situation became increasingly petulant and meddlesome. As a result their fundamental concern with the war as punishment has been neglected. Central to their viewpoint was the assumption that in 1778–1779 the Revolution was about to collapse and their belief that deft, purposeful British pressure could bring this process to fruition: "the rebel currency is tottering on the very brink of annihilation, if not allowed to recover; ... the people in general are becoming indifferent if not averse" to a government which has brought them only distress and regimentation; "the enthusiasm which at first enabled the Americans without funds, arrangements, or visible resources to act with such success is now lost in disgust and disappointment ... and in place of that general union and concert which then prevailed there now remains only a faction and a very limited and artificial army, neither of which are of the people." These were the conclusions which leading loyalist refugees in New York City asked Major Patrick Ferguson to convey to General Clinton in November 1779.[22] Taking seriously loyalist testimony about stress in Revolutionary society does not mean that pre-Revolutionary social antagonisms played a significant part in the causal pattern of the Revolution. Such testimony does suggest that the War for Independence was a sufficiently strong disruptive force to trigger or to exacerbate tensions in society which, while generally held in check, deeply alarmed Revolutionary leaders and impinged on the capacity of their political institutions to function effectively.[23]

The erosion of popular support for the Revolution and the artificial nature of the rebel regime, Ferguson told Clinton, provided the keys for a successful British prosecution of the war. Once the rebels realized that they could not drive the British from Georgia and once the fickle French fleet departed American waters, Britain would be free to undertake a campaign of retribution "distressing the countryside," seizing and punishing rebel leaders, and "living off of plunder." At this point Washington would have to do battle or suffer humiliating retreat, the currency would collapse, Congress would forfeit all capacity to punish deserters, and the people would "see no end of their fruitless sufferings." This scenario required Britain to employ "the only common, justifiable . . . modes of coercion, . . . destroying their resources," confiscating the property of anyone who impeded the suppression of the rebellion.

Joseph Galloway's trusted subordinate, Isaac Ogden, made much the same assessment a year earlier. "The rebellion hangs by a slender thread," he assured Galloway in November 1778. The great majority of Americans were "heartily tired of the war and groan under the yoke of tyranny." John Butler's raids in the Mohawk and Wyoming valleys so disrupted the provisions trade that men were desperate for peace, and now Butler stood ready to support Clinton in a major offensive anywhere in the middle colonies. "In this situation what is necessary to crush the rebellion, . . . [is] only one vigorous campaign, properly conducted. I mean by . . . a man of *judgment, spirit,* and *enterprise.*"[24]

Ogden and Ferguson both acknowledged that the rebellion was an authentic social movement. This implied that Congress and the Army, initially at least, had been "of the people" and that "enthusiasm" had for a time taken the place of money, bureaucracy, and leadership. Until British actions dramatically demonstrated the futility of resistance to large segments of the populace, both men conceded, the movement would not die, and to this extent they were acknowledging its indigenous social roots. Ogden and Ferguson further seemed to sense that the rebellion's indigenous character provided the key to its suppression. By carrying the war to the whole society, by using plunder and destruction as psychological weapons, in short, by threatening to precipitate complete social chaos, Britain could convert dispirited rebels into desperate and disillusioned advocates of peace and submission. John Goodrich of Virginia proposed to Clinton a pincer attack on Williamsburg, "the metropolis of infamy," from the James and York rivers. "I know the genesus of the Virginians," he explained; "an example of devastation would have a good effect, the minds of the people struck with a panic would expect the whole country to share the same fate. Offer rewards for bringing to justice the active rebels, let them be proportioned to their rank and consequence . . . make proper examples, countenance and protect the inoffensive and honest farmers. This done, every rebel will suspect his neighbor, all confidence will cease, the guilty in crowds will retire to the back country without a possibility of removing provisions for their subsistence, hunger will make them desperate and open their eyes, they will fall on their destructive leaders, peace and submission, of course, must follow."[25]

Anticipating in November 1780, just such an imminent British invasion of Virginia, John Connolly explained to Clinton how the upper Ohio Valley could be reclaimed for the Crown by manipulating critical features in the social organiza-tion of the region.[26] The population which had burgeoned in the years 1767–1776, he reported, consisted of "adventurers allured by the prospect of an idle life" and former tenant farmers from the northern neck of Virginia "whose increase in children and desire to be independent" motivated them to become squatters in a frontier where "civil authority" was too weak to restrain their land grabbing con-duct. Overnight the region changed from a "rude wilderness" into a "sociable and tolerably well cultivated settlement." In order to protect their own interest in western lands, Virginia Revolutionary leaders encouraged settlers in the region to join in the rebellion in 1775 and "royal authority" gave way "to a confused democ-racy." Predictably the rebel leaders in this unstable setting overplayed a strong hand by imposing harsh taxation and militia fines. Alienated by these measures "the great majority" of settlers, who are "valuable loyalists," "would be ready to shed their blood in support of the former constitution, yet, under their present embarrassments, their services are totally lost and we can expect nothing but their empty good wishes." With the loyalist majority entirely cowed, nothing stood in the way of rebel conquest of the Illinois territory. This would threaten Detroit and Niagara, cut off communications with Canada, and trigger new and more pow-erful raids down the Mississippi against West Florida.[27]

Connolly emphasized the desperate quality of the situation because it contained the key to a miraculous British recovery in the west: "from the description given, your excellency will perceive that many of the people—dispersed over that exten-sive country—are unencumbered with families and their attendant cares, [or by ownership] of fixed property, accustomed to an erratic life, and ready for every adventure wearing the face of poverty. Abandoned to the influence of designing men, their constitutional courage and hardiness have been prostituted to the basest purposes and their arms opposed to their sovereign and their own proper inter-ests. Policy requires that this unprovoked ill-humor should be turned from its present channel and directed to a proper object of resentment." By dramatically increasing the trade of the Ohio Valley with Montreal and Detroit, Britain could give its loyal allies in the regions a compelling motive "to support that power from which they derived such striking benefits." Simultaneously, Britain should mobi-lize the Spanish-hating southern tribes for a massive assault on New Orleans. Once in control of the Ohio and Mississippi valleys, Britain could invade western Pennsylvania and occupy Fort Pitt. All of this, Connolly admitted to Clinton, might seem an undertaking of "too considerable a magnitude," but he urged the general to trust him. "I feel myself so firmly convinced of the practicability of what I have advanced that I would stake my salvation upon a favorable outcome."[28]

The loyalists' determination from 1778 through 1781 to use warfare in order to scourge and punish American society for its sins of ingratitude and disobedience was the same kind of curious mixture of political sagacity and moral absolutism which characterized whig ideology. The loyalist conception of military reality was a caricatured mirror image of the Spirit of '76.

Notes

1. Piers Mackesy, *The War for America, 1775–1783* (London, 1964), pp. 253, 511.

2. See for example Robert M. Calhoon, *The Loyalists in Revolutionary America, 1760–1781* (New York, 1973), chapters 6, 26.

3. John Shy, "The American Revolution: The Military Conflict as a Revolutionary War," in Stephen G. Kurtz and James H. Hutson, eds., *Essays on the American Revolution* (Chapel Hill, 1973), pp. 124, 139–40.

4. Sidney George Fisher, *Struggle for American Independence* (Philadelphia, 1908); Russell F. Weigley, *The Partisan War: The South Carolina Campaigns of 1780–1782* (Columbia, S.C., 1970); Shy, "The American Revolution . . . as a Revolutionary War."

5. On the numbers of loyalists in arms see Paul H. Smith, "The American Loyalists: Notes on their Organization and Numerical Strength," *William and Mary Quarterly*, 25 (April, 1968): 259–77.

6. Calhoon, *The Loyalists in Revolutionary America*, pp. 439–42, 462–64, 552–55.

7. Barbara Graymont, *The Iroquois and the American Revolution* (Syracuse, N.Y., 1972), chapters 5 and 6; James H. O'Donnell III, *Southern Indians in the American Revolution* (Knoxville, 1973), chapter 2.

8. Hamilton V. Bail, ed., "A Letter to George Germain about Vermont," *Vermont History*, 34 (October, 1966): 226–34.

9. Paul H. Smith, "The New Jersey Loyalists and the British 'Provincial' Corps in the War for Independence," *New Jersey History*, 87 (Summer, 1969): 69–78; Ira Gruber, *The Howe Brothers and the American Revolution* (New York, 1972), pp. 146–54; Adrian C. Leiby, *The Revolutionary War in the Hackensack Valley: The Jersey Dutch and the Neutral Ground* (New Brunswick, N.Y., 1962).

10. See especially Tonyn to Germain, October 30, 1776, and Tonyn to Prevost, January 13, 1777, reprinted in Edgar L. Pennington, "East Florida in the American Revolution," *Florida Historical Quarterly*, 9 (1930): 29–31, 33–34 and Tonyn to Howe, February 24, 1778, Headquarters Papers of the British Army in North America, document no. 962, Colonial Williamsburg Microfilm, Williamsburg, Virginia.

11. John M. Coleman, "Joseph Galloway and the British Administration of Philadelphia," *Pennsylvania History*, 30 (July, 1963): 272–300; John E. Ferling, "Joseph Galloway's Military Advice: A Loyalist's View of the American Revolution," *Pennsylvania Magazine of History and Biography*, 98 (April, 1974): 171–88; for a very different role of loyalists in pacification, see the Minutes of the Board of Associated Loyalists, January to July 1781, Henry Clinton Papers, William L. Clements Library, Ann Arbor, Michigan.

12. Staughton Lynd, *Class Conflict, Slavery, and the United States Constitution* (Indianapolis, 1967), pp. 68–77.

13. Ronald Hoffman, *A Spirit of Dissension: Economics, Politics, and the Revolution in Maryland* (Baltimore, 1973), pp. 184–95, 227–39.

14. William H. Nelson, *The American Tory* (Oxford, 1961), p. 91.

15. Several are described in George W. Kyte, "Some Plans for a Loyalist Stronghold in the Middle Colonies," *Pennsylvania History,* 16 (July, 1949): 177–90; other loyalist proposals in the Clinton Papers include George Chalmers to Clinton, September 12, 1778; Moses Kirkland to Clinton, October 13, 1778; Neil Jameison to Clinton, December 11, 1778; Christopher Sower narrative, December 13, 1778; West Jersey petitioners to Clinton, ca. 1778; George Chalmers to Clinton, July 26, 1779; Board of Associated Loyalists to Clinton, July 20, 1781; Harden Burnley to Clinton, September 17, 1781; Hector MacAlester to Clinton, n.d.

16. Richard Maxwell Brown, "The Violent Origins of South Carolina Extremism," in *Strain of Violence: Historical Studies of American Violence and Vigilantism* (New York, 1975), chapter 3; Graymont, *The Iroquois and the American Revolution,* chapter 7; Patrick J. Furlong, "Civilian-Military Conflict and the Restoration of the Royal Province of Georgia, 1778–1782," *Journal of Southern History,* 38 (August, 1972): 415–42.

17. For a variant of this model, see Calhoon, *The Loyalists in Revolutionary America,* pp. 502–506.

18. David C. Skaggs suggested this difficulty to me.

19. Harry Eckstein, "On the Etiology of Internal Wars," *History and Theory,* 4 (1954–1955): 133–63.

20. The entire foregoing paragraph is based on "Colonial Robert Gray's Observations of the War in the Carolinas," *South Carolina Historical and Genealogical Magazine,* 11 (July, 1910): 153; much the same view can be found in an anonymous letter to Lord Rawdon, n.d., ca. 1781, Clinton Papers.

21. "Colonial Gray's Observations," pp. 139–159; Brown, *Strain of Violence,* pp. 75–81.

22. Patrick Ferguson to Clinton, November 22, 1779, Clinton Papers; see also Ferguson to Clinton, November 25, 1779; "Cursory Observations on the Present Situation of the Refugees and the Means of Rendering them More Effectually Beneficial," anonymous New York Loyalist to Tryon, November 1, 1775; and Samuel Hake to Clinton, n.d. and January 25, 1782, all in the Clinton Papers.

23. See Shy, "The American Revolution . . . as a Revolutionary War" and Jack P. Greene, "The Social Origins of the American Revolution: An Evaluation and an Interpretation," *Political Science Quarterly,* 88 (March, 1973), 1–22.

24. Isaac Ogden to Joseph Galloway, November 22, 1778, Balch Collection, New York Public Library.

25. John Goodrich to Clinton, November 2, 1778, Clinton Papers.

26. John Connolly to Clinton, November 25, 1780, Clinton Papers; see also Connolly to Clinton, April 20, 1781, Clinton Papers.

27. Connolly to Clinton, November 22, 1780.

28. Connolly to Clinton, November 22, 1780.

Eleven

The Floridas, the Western Frontier, and Vermont

Thoughts on the Hinterland Loyalists

ROBERT M. CALHOON

Study of the American Revolution has focused on the motivations and ideologies of participants in the struggle and on the organization of eighteenth-century American society. Both lines of inquiry have finally begun—belatedly and inadequately—to shape an understanding of the loyalists. Because we know that the pre-Revolutionary controversy was an intense, collective experience of self-appraisal for Americans, we can understand how it compelled defenders of British rule to renounce republicanism and why it persuaded them that imperial authority was a stabilizing factor in society and in their own lives. Furthermore, a growing body of research on loyalist groups and communities seems to confirm William H. Nelson's conjecture that the loyalist rank and file comprised cultural minorities who felt threatened by the rest of American society.[1]

These broad conclusions about the dynamics of the pre-Revolutionary debate and the structure of loyalist groupings during the War for Independence overlap but do not entirely coincide with another classification of loyalist motivation: an instinctive, unarticulated, but persistent expectation by loyalists living in the hinterland of Revolutionary America that British military, administrative, and diplomatic power ought to come to their protection and make the frontier the base for counterrevolutionary activity. There is little evidence of this sort of loyalist thought in traditional literary sources (pamphlets, correspondence, records of formal political activity); however, we can extrapolate evidence from the patterns of behavior of people in the hinterland, from concepts of empire which prevailed during the quarter century prior to the War for Independence, from notions of the nature of the empire held by British officials and loyalists on the frontier, and from recent scholarship on the actual level of British military, administrative, and diplomatic capability during the War for Independence.

For many settlers, the hinterland of Revolutionary America—that is, East and West Florida, the southern backcountry, the Ohio Valley, western New York and the Mohawk Valley, and Vermont—was a setting where British power and authority could be most readily exercised, indeed, that the British possessed a special talent for maximizing their assets and manipulating events to their advantage in this vast crescent of territory. What no one realized at the time was that British capability in this hinterland of colonial America was both expanding and retracting on the eve of the War for Independence. This flux in conditions deprived British adherents there of the ability to predict events and make reliable estimates. The strenuous, and in some ways highly sophisticated, efforts by loyalists and British officials on the periphery of Revolutionary America to defeat the whigs were motivated by a partial, inadequate comprehension of the flux in imperial capability.

The first and most important source of this confusion was the conduct of the British army and civil officials in 1775–76. Gage instructed John Stuart, British Superintendent for Indian affairs in the South, and Guy Johnson, his counterpart in the North, to guard against any rebel attempts to subvert the loyalty of the Indians to the Crown. Neither Stuart nor Johnson saw any value in precipitate Indian attacks on whig settlements, and both urged the Indians to adopt a defensive posture until the deployment of British regulars in adjacent provinces. In North Carolina, Governor Josiah Martin encouraged the formation of a large loyalist force which would march to Wilmington and there rendezvous with British regulars arriving by sea. In Virginia, Governor Dunmore secured British regulars from St. Augustine, invited slaves to escape and to take up arms under his banner, and, with a handful of Virginia loyalists, temporarily threatened the security of the Revolutionary regime and delayed for several months the transit of power. From Boston, Lieutenant Colonel Allen McLean, who had secured authority to enlist loyalist soldiers, sent recruiting agents to New York and North Carolina. Gage himself authorized John Connolly, British governor at Fort Pitt, to direct a loyalist uprising in the upper Ohio Valley and arranged with Guy Carleton in Quebec and Guy Johnson in the Mohawk Valley to coordinate their activities with Connolly's. Of course, none of these plans succeeded. Connolly was arrested on his way back to Fort Pitt. The North Carolina rising occurred before British troops reached the mouth of the Cape Fear River, and the North Carolina whigs were able to defeat the loyalists at the Battle of Moore's Creek. Despite John Stuart's best efforts to manipulate events, the Cherokees prematurely seized the opportunity to repel white settlers from their lands; they were defeated and their villages and crops destroyed by Virginia and North and South Carolina militia. In failure, these initiatives look clumsy and bizarre, and certainly they suggest that irregular warfare is not a substitute for conventional military operations. But even these setbacks did not stifle irrepressible loyalist activity in the backcountry.[2]

As the war progressed, the most favorable laboratory for such experimentation was the Mohawk Valley in New York. There, Sir William Johnson, Indian Superintendent for the Northern Tribes, had won for the Iroquois over the preceding quarter century valuable territorial guarantees and protection from illegal white encroachment on Indian land, in return for military and political loyalty. When Johnson died in 1774, he left a magnificent network of alliances among elements of the Iroquois confederacy, local white settlers indebted to Johnson for loans and favors, wealthy western New York landowners like John Butler, and British officials

in Quebec who were strategically located to oversee and direct counterrevolutionary efforts in the area and coordinate them with Burgoyne's projected invasion of
New York. These interests loyal to the Crown were, in fact, a delicate network of
relationships, ill designed to stand the severe stresses generated by the Revolution.
Sir William's successor as Indian Superintendent was his nephew, Guy Johnson,
who in 1776 was trapped in New York City en route from a trip to England. Acting Superintendent Colonel John Butler was suspicious of the Johnsons and their
close Mohawk ally, Joseph Brant. The maneuvering for advantage and leadership
between Butler and Brant almost certainly prevented Brant from organizing in
late 1776 and early 1777 a small, disciplined insurgent force of trusted Indian warriors and white loyalists to attack whig settlements in New York State and, in
effect, to serve as the cutting edge for Burgoyne's invasion. Brutal Mohawk depredations against the pro-American Oneidas in the summer of 1777 shattered what
was left of Iroquois unity. Burgoyne's defeat and the failure of Barry St. Leger's
offensive into the Mohawk Valley in the summer of 1777 helped ignite a savage
and debilitating civil war in the region, which did not materially affect the course
of the war but which wrecked Iroquois society and mocked British pretensions
to protect and defend its loyal subjects from the vengeance and violence of the
rebels.[3]

Despite overwhelming political and military disasters, the loyalists in Vermont
remained a potent and indestructible element during the Revolution. Most of the
leadership for supporters of the Crown in the New Hampshire Grants (as the territory was called until 1777) were New York land speculators, who fled the region
in 1775 when they lost control of the machinery of county government to insurgent Yankee settlers led by Ethan and Ira Allen. The instability of the Allens' insurgent regime, the precarious military security of the region in 1776 and 1777, and
the immaturity and malleability of political institutions in Vermont all tended to
influence inhabitants of the area to adopt supple political allegiances. Yankee settlers like Sylvanus Ewarts and Justus Sherwood filled the void in leadership just
prior to Burgoyne's brief occupation of Castleton, Vermont, in July 1777. Ewarts
recruited some 400 local residents to build a road for Burgoyne's force to use. The
majority of these volunteers changed their allegiances with chameleon-like adaptability and led Burgoyne to assume that Colonel Frederick Baum, his Hessian
subordinate, could expect a friendly reception when he led a foray into southern
Vermont to seize a cache of rebel arms in August 1777. Instead, Baum stumbled
into a defeat at the Battle of Bennington, in part because he believed that shirt-
sleeved insurgents approaching his rear must be local loyalists coming to his
support.

While the Vermont loyalists evaporated as a military factor, they retained extensive influence in the state, and much of the property confiscated by the new state
government in 1777 was resold at reasonable terms to close relatives of accused
loyalists. When New York blocked Vermont's bid for recognition by the Continental Congress as an independent state, the Allens began the now famous "Haldimand

negotiations" with the British to secure recognition of Vermont's independence in return for the state's repudiation of the American cause—a course of events which forced the Allens into alliance with covert loyalists in the state.[4]

Several factors weighed heavily in inducing the Vermont loyalists first to oppose the Allens and then to endure the vicissitudes of war while waiting for British authority to be reasserted. One was the seemingly capricious nature of local hostilities, which singled out some individual Yankee settlers with Yorker connections, labeling them tories and turning the rage of the community against them. Zadock Wright, John Peters, and Sylvanus Ewarts were all prominent Yankee settlers with close family ties to the Revolutionary leadership of Vermont. For reasons of both temperment and calculation, they tried to remain neutral in 1775–76, found themselves labeled tories by seemingly uncontrollable currents of opinion, and took up arms for the British from considerations of revenge, confusion, and desperation. More significantly, the strongest political force in the region was a desire for autonomy—a goal incompatible with internal bloodletting—so that the Allens maintained discreet alliances with covert loyalists and drew on this support during the Haldimand negotiations. At the core of this accommodation between the Allens and Vermont loyalists was the widespread expectation that Britain possessed sufficient leverage in Revolutionary America through its control of Quebec to checkmate rebel dominance in New England through prudent concessions to Vermont separatism. Joshua Locke, Yankee loyalist from Vermont, wrote to Lord George Germain in 1781 explaining the special character of Vermont loyalism. In Vermont, as anywhere else, Locke assumed, the legal security of landed property was the most immediate obligation of government to the subject. When the Revolution began, the ownership of a large amount of land in "the Green mountains" was disputed by New York and New Hampshire claimants, and some Yankee settlers even took the law into their own hands. "But I never understood . . . that they ever disputed his majesty's prorogative to shift any part of his subjects from the jurisdiction of one province to another . . . the fee of the land onely [sic] is what they have been contending for." The Revolution vastly complicated—but did not fundamentally alter—that situation: "They declared themselves an independent state free from both king and Congress as they could obtain fee of their lands from neither." Locke noted that the kind of proclamation which General Henry Clinton had issued in South Carolina promising protection to persons who laid down their arms and took an oath of allegiance "strikes these people [loyalists in Vermont] with horror"; if New York should accept the same terms, the Crown might validate Yorker land claims in the region and thereby invalidate the claims of Yankee loyalists and neutralists in Vermont. "But if such a thing as granting to those people pardons confirming them in the title of their lands and forming them into a separate province could be settled" in England, the entire population could be induced to declare their loyalty to the King. Locke argued that landowners concerned about the legal security of their titles were "in the center" of the colonial social order: "I need not mention the advantage it

would be to the British arms to have those people in favor of government." Moreover, if Britain neglected the Vermont loyalists, the region would become "a recep-
tical for the sum of rebellion and a refuge for a numerous banditti" which would
be most expensive to eradicate in the years after the Revolution—assuming it was
suppressed by the British.[5] Locke's commentary was astute and not entirely inac-
curate. Vermont, like other fringe areas of Revolutionary America, was particularly prone to violence and crime and especially fearful of the breakdown of law
and order; the loyalists utilized this asset to the maximum in securing an accommodation with the Allen regime. At least some Vermont loyalists expected that
Britain acting unilaterally could use this lever to swing the entire populace back
to British allegiance.

East Florida, and in some respects West Florida as well, represented the nexus
of command, that is, the location where leadership, civilian support, supply, manpower, relatively secure fortification, and proximity to theaters of conflict all
coincided. The loyalists who fled to St. Augustine and Pensacola had good reason
to expect the protection of a powerful military force. Lord Dunmore had secured
reinforcements from St. Augustine in 1775. John Stuart, Superintendent for Indian
affairs in the South, transferred his headquarters to St. Augustine in 1775 and
moved it again to Pensacola in 1777. In Governor Patrick Tonyn of East Florida
and Governor Peter Chester of West Florida, the British had officials who were
intent on galvanizing these elements of military power.

Tonyn empowered Thomas Brown, the irrepressible Georgia backcountry
tory partisan, to enlist loyalist exiles into the East Florida Rangers, which operated initially as a defensive force along the East Florida-Georgia frontier. Together,
Tonyn and Brown set about undercutting John Stuart's careful management of
the Creeks and Cherokees. Impatient for a general Indian uprising to strengthen
the province's security and undermine the Revolutionary regime in Georgia,
Tonyn and Brown thought of Indian uprisings as a torrent of violent power which
they could turn on at their discretion. The knowledgeable and experienced Stuart knew that Indian support was a finite, perishable resource; the Cherokee War
of 1776, which Stuart had tried to prevent, had decimated the villages and crops
of that tribe in the Carolinas. The Creeks feared similar whig reprisals and were
increasingly leery, first of Tonyn's demand that they march in force to the defense
of St. Augustine in the spring of 1778 and then of his appeal that they raise
hundreds of warriors for the British invasion of Georgia in December 1778 and
January 1779.[6] Tonyn further believed that bloody, irregular warfare along the
Georgia-East Florida border would "distress . . . our deluded neighbors" and
induce them "to return to their allegiance." By repeatedly sending raiding parties
into Georgia to steal livestock, he provided the British garrison with fresh meat.
"This, my lord, is not a very honorable method of making war," Tonyn wrote
colonial Secretary George Germain, "but . . . it is the only one left for supplying
this town and garrison with fresh provisions as the Georgians would not allow the
cattle . . . to be drove hence. Besides, my lord, the love of plunder engages many

daring fellows . . . to oppose the rebels . . . instead of joining with . . . them." "Regular troops," Tonyn added in a revealing aside, "are not well calculated for such moroding services."[7] Frederick George Mulcaster, wealthy East Florida landowner and surveyor-general, scoffed at Tonyn's faith in the combativeness of the populace. Of the 300 adult white males in the vicinity of St. Augustine, 200 were well-to-do government officials, merchants, or planters, while the remainder were overseers, cattlemen, fishermen, and "persons who live as they can. . . . It is from this class of hunters &c. that recruits can be raised; . . . as the price of workmanship is high, their wages support them too well to be easily tempted," but "some shift[ing]" for themselves "might be got." Money alone would not suffice, Mulcaster warned, but promises of land grants would bring East Florida pioneers to the King's standard: "the rage which these people have for that article might have some effect."[8]

Peter Chester in West Florida had fewer assets at his disposal. The province was vulnerable to rebel and Spanish attack. Although the population doubled during the War for Independence because Dartmouth had declared West Florida an asylum for loyalists driven from other colonies, the resulting influx of 2,000 to 2,500 people weakened as much as it strengthened royal administration. The young colony lacked an internal system of political and judicial institutions, kinship patterns, and traditions strong enough to bind its inhabitants into a community. Reckless land speculation along the Mississippi Valley had spread population into regions vulnerable to Spanish attack and had scattered the manpower resources of the province.[9] Maryland loyalist James Chalmers wrote Lord Rawdon that without "sugar to stimulate the avidity of planters or wheat to incite the industry of the inhabitants," West Florida was a languishing and dispirited province with "no vestiges of that youthful colonial ardor" which had sustained other newly established British colonies.[10] When the rebel James Willing led a daring raid down the Mississippi River into West Florida in 1778, for example, he exacted from settlers around Natchez a pledge to remain neutral in the war and to desist from aiding the British, and throughout the province news of the Willing raid caused panic and confusion. The exploitation of this fertile, plentiful territory with its strategic location for commerce had preempted the energies of the populace.[11] In spite of their lack of interest in the pre-Revolutionary controversy (apart from a mild remonstrance against the Stamp Act) and their ostensible support of the Crown in the war, the loyalist sentiments of the inhabitants were not particularly fervent. In West Florida, J. Barton Starr found official scepticism about the commitment of the populace to the British cause. "I find the inhabitants in general self-interested and without public spirit, whose minds are attached only to gain and their private concerns," declared General John Campbell. "In short, nothing can be had from them . . . but at an enormous extravagant price, and personal service on general principles of national defense is too generous and exalted for their conceptions." William Dunbar believed that half of the inhabitants secretly sympathized with the American cause and that, as a result, the others felt immobilized and fearful of making any zealous efforts in the support of British authority. Though the inhabitants fought bravely during the Spanish attack on Pensacola in 1781, that response to Spanish attack does not refute evidence of ambivalence and even indifference early in the war. Yet these liabilities of institutional immaturity, public apathy, and strategic insecurity were a hidden source of short-term advantage. If British West Florida was vulnerable to Spanish attack, Spanish Louisiana felt equally threatened by an expansionist British province. By mutually adroit diplomacy, Chester and Spanish Governor Bernardo de Gálvez tried to avoid conflict until Spanish entry into the war in 1779. Following the Willing raid, Chester moved vigorously and resourcefully to shore up the province's defenses and to instill a greater sense of urgency in the populace, but despite these efforts, the province fell to Spain in 1781.[12]

In the end, therefore, British strength and capability in the hinterland of Revolutionary America fell far short of the loyalists' ideal expectation of a vast, pervasive source of counterrevolutionary strength on which they would rely and to which they could contribute. The southern Indians, whom Stuart had so assiduously cultivated, were a highly perishable asset of negligible value by the time the reconquest of Georgia occurred. Iroquois effectiveness was negated by the internecine strife between the Brants and the Butlers and by the havoc wrought within the fabric of Iroquois life by the ravages of war. The Floridas did not significantly enhance the strength of the British invasion of the South prior to 1779–81. The promising start in the Haldimand negotiations did not checkmate rebel control of New England and adjacent New York State. The weaknesses and fragility of loyalists' expectations should not obscure the importance and intelligence of their position. It should prompt historians to treat loyalist ideas as an integral part of the larger history of ideas in the British Empire.

Loyalists' expectations about imperial vitality did not function as a self-conscious ingredient in their intellectual lives. If any terms characterize loyalist outlook during the War for Independence, they are *confusion, uncertainty, apprehension*. As Paul H. Smith wrote of many loyalists in arms, the Revolution was "too large an event for most persons to comprehend in its entirety" and it was therefore "perceived in terms of immediate, commonplace issues. . . . For many, the issue of their allegiance was never perceived as a matter upon which they might exercise some meaningful choice."[13] Loyalist expectations about the nature of the Empire were simply one element—albeit crucial and unique—in the milieu of doubt, confusion, and limited experience surrounding these people. Without endowing loyalist notions about the processes of empire with more formality than they deserve, it is nonetheless important to consider the ways in which hinterland loyalist expectations were a *system* of ideas, impressions, and beliefs, and the relationship of this intellectual experience to the larger ferment of thought occurring during the eighteenth century.[14]

The Empire in the eighteenth century generated a large body of in-house treatises by men within or near the imperial bureaucracy, each seeking to define the genius of the Empire, identify the sources of its vitality, and prescribe ways in which it could conduct men's energies into constructive channels. Franklin, Thomas Whately, Thomas Hutchinson, and William Smith, Jr., were only a few of the most important of those men who devoted a considerable share of their busy time during the 1760s and 1770s to this enterprise. While many of these theories and proposals had little immediate effect on policy, they all focused on those features of imperial administration which were in the greatest danger of malfunction, and sought to reconcile and bind together the traditional and the novel, the healthy and the sick, the routine and the unexpected elements of imperial development. It is no wonder that theories of empire were so rapidly consumed and supplanted. Franklin wanted British territory and institutions in America to be spacious enough to contain and encourage a population explosion; Pownall wanted mutual commercial prosperity to replace legal authority as the cement of empire; William Knox and Whately wanted the undisciplined ways of colonial assemblies to give way to order, system, and direction from Whitehall; Hutchinson and Smith—in very different ways—sensed the psychic damage to American politics by the abrupt intrusion of royal authority into colonial life. Loyalist expectation of British vigor on the hinterland was a further stage in this search for a workable theory of empire.

The key to this concept was *predictability*. British conduct affecting the loyalists should be utterly predictable, and to ensure against malfunctions of imperial policy and execution, loyalists should make their own needs and expectations painfully obvious. Self-consciousness and a literal view of political processes pervade two bodies of published sources familiar to students of Florida history: the first of these is Joseph B. Lockey's documentary history of the transition in East Florida from British to Spanish rule, and the second is the 1784 loyalist pamphlet, *The Case of the Inhabitants of East-Florida. . . .*[15] These documents seem at first glance to have dubious value for the study of ideas. Written after British defeat and after news that the Floridas were to be returned to Spanish rule, they reflect the special pleading of men desperately, cravenly seeking favors from the Crown. Tirelessly, and tiresomely, they complain of the cruel fate visited on the East Florida loyalists by the fortunes of war and diplomacy. "The principle part of the original planters," Tonyn wrote to Secretary of State for Home Affairs Thomas Townshend in May 1783, "after having expended large sums of money began to feel themselves in comfortable circumstances. . . . They were happy in the full enjoyment of their native rights and privileges under his Majesty's auspices. . . . Amidst a general revolt" they "stood firm." Then came 12,000 loyalist exiles confident of royal protection. "This consideration . . . induced them liberally to lay out the wrecks of their fortunes in building Houses and forming Settlements . . . they were ambitious of this province ever remaining characterized for loyalty."[16] Yet these heavy-handed, melodramatic documents are the quintessential expression of the loyalist perception of political reality. East Florida loyalist spokesmen and Tonyn, who had a flair for translating their sentiments into the prose of official correspondence, did not invent new modes of expression, new assumptions about the nature of politics, and new rhetorical devices in 1783. These documents and characteristics of language represent an experience stretching back to 1775.

With ill-disguised attempts at subtlety and indirection, *The Case of the Inhabitants* argued deductively that as subjects they had during the course of the war no choice but "to hazard life, fortune, and all that is dear" in support of the Crown and to acquiesce willingly in the terms of peace including the cession of Florida; that, having lost all, their shattered lives could be restored in no other way than from the generosity of the British nation, and, therefore, Britain had no choice but to assume the cost of their resettlement and full compensation for the land, possessions, and slaves they had lost. The burden of responsibility for affirmative action was entirely on Britain; the East Florida loyalists had simply accepted their duty to fight against the American rebels and then to acquiesce in the peace settlement which returned Florida to Spain. They were nothing but pawns in a world where allegiance placed absolute obligations to obedience and acquiescence on subjects and where rulers axiomatically protected the interests of their faithful supporters. "To admit a contrary idea," the document declared, "would be to assert that Great Britain hath lost all public faith": that she punished the innocent, disregarded justice, and forfeited her reputation for "probity, justice, and good faith," and "untied the strongest bonds that unites civil society.... That language may suit our northern neighbors," it concluded pointedly, but not the inhabitants of East Florida who have known Britain's "kindness and fostering hand." Belying the notion that allegiance required unquestioning acquiescence, it concluded, "and therefore we must now *as yet* complain."[17]

This helpless, immobile position provoked more than self-pity; it also prompted the East Florida loyalists to recall the whole range of emotions which had been brought forth by their experience and bad fortune. "Abandoned by that sovereign for whose cause we have sacrificed everything that is dear in life," a group of them wrote to the king of Spain in October 1784, "and deserted by that Country for which we fought and many of us freely bled," and "left to our fate bereft of our slaves by our inveterate Countrymen.... We ... are Reduced to the dreadful alternative of returning to our Homes, to receive insult worse than Death to Men of Spirit, or to run the hazard of being Murdered in Cold blood, to go to the inhospitable Regions of Nova Scotia, or take refuge on the Barren Rocks of the Bahamas where poverty and wretchedness stares us in the face Or do we do what our Spirit cannot brook ... renounce our Country."[18] This remarkable version of history depicted the Empire as a place of opportunity and protection for venturesome men, where venturesomeness bred a "spirit" which made humiliation and a lack of options a galling fate. War had consumed economic opportunity and the terms of the peace had denied its replenishment. A certain naïveté and unconcern for political power permeated these remarks. Tonyn underscored this attitude: "I am confident," he wrote to Secretary of State Townshend, "that our gracious sovereign will make liberal allowances for human frailties and that you will represent in the most favorable light spirited men laboring under difficulties and misfortunes which a steady adherence to the duty they owe their King and Country has accumulated upon them." They are "unacquainted with the great engines by which government is upheld," and therefore "have been led to think of themselves as agrieved because [they are] unfortunate."[19] The antidote, which Tonyn prescribed for this benumbed state of the "principle inhabitants" of the province, was a still more apolitical faith in royal beneficence: "nothing can give me greater pleasure than to find that you gentlemen—whom I have ever represented as well affected rather than [as] harbouring murmur and discontent in your present calamitous circumstances—[will] submit yourselves to the measures of government and rely upon the benignity of our sovereign, the justice of the nation, and the wisdom of His Majesty's ministers for a suitable provision to be made for you."[20] In April 1781, when the East Florida assembly renewed its contribution to the support of the Empire, Speaker William Brown wrote in just such a tone of calculating innocence to Tonyn, "we hope the present smallness of our quota may not be considered as a measure of our loyalty to the most benificent prince in the world or our attachment to our bountiful mother country."[21]

But there were centrifugal forces at work in the province Tonyn acknowledged in a superbly analytical letter to General Guy Carleton, which wrought havoc with these civilized and gentlemanly British standards of conduct. Tonyn reported that he could not dismantle his administration until the treaty with Spain was finally ratified, and in the interim "an abandoned set of men" in the Georgia and East Florida backcountry had "committed several daring robberies and will certainly attempt to ravage this country and insult government in its feeble, disabled condition. . . . In this stage of impotence the settlements will be exposed and the Negroes plundered . . . and when His Majesty's daily bounties to the refugees cease . . . they will become exceedingly clamorous and impatient, and the worst is to be expected from the lower sort. In addition to these evils, the licentious, disbanded soldiers who have discovered intentions of rapine and plunder are most to be dreaded." The logic of the situation was inescapable: "this ever loyal province, given up to accommodate the peace of the Empire, and the inhabitants thereby losing their pleasant abodes and property have, Sir, a just claim for every assistance and compensation which can be extended to them and indulgence in their choice of destinations to any part of His Majesty's Dominions."[22] Only by adequate resettlement and compensation could the Empire be true to its own best standards: a place where acquisitive, venturesome men could depend upon British reliability and predictability and receive, in addition to economic opportunity, just reward for risks and sacrifices in the service of the Crown.

Notes

1. See Robert M. Calhoon, *The Loyalists in Revolutionary America, 1760–1781* (New York, 1973), pp. 431–35, 502–506, 559–65.

2. Paul H. Smith, *Loyalists and Redcoats: A Study in British Revolutionary Policy* (Chapel Hill, N.C., 1964), chap. 2; Richard O. Curry, "Loyalism in Western Virginia," *West Virginia History* 14 (April 1953): 265–74; James H. O'Donnell, *Southern Indians in the American Revolution* (Knoxville, Tenn., 1973), chap. 2; Robert L. Ganyard, "North Carolina during the American Revolution: The First Phase, 1774–1777" (Ph.D. diss., Duke University, 1962), pp. 120–48.

3. Barbara Graymont, *The Iroquois in the American Revolution* (Syracuse, N.Y., 1972), passim.

4. Chilton Williamson, *Vermont in Quandary, 1763–1825* (Montpelier, Vt., 1941), passim; Gwilym R. Roberts, "An Unknown Vermonter: Sylvanus Ewarts, Governor Chittenden's Tory Brother-in-Law," *Vermont History* 29 (April 1961): 92–102; Hamilton V. Bail, "Zadock Wright: That 'Devilish' Tory of Hartland," *Vermont History* 36 (Autumn 1968): 186–203.

5. Hamilton V. Bail, "A Letter to Lord Germain about Vermont," *Vermont History* 34 (October 1966): 226–34.

6. O'Donnell, *Southern Indians in the American Revolution,* pp. 32–34, 70; Gary D. Olson, "Thomas Brown, Loyalist Partisan, and the Revolutionary War in Georgia, 1777–1782," *Georgia Historical Quarterly* 54 (Spring-Summer 1970): 1–19, 183–207.

7. Tonyn to Germain, October 18, 1776, quoted in Edgar L. Pennington, "Florida in the American Revolution, 1775–1778," *Florida Historical Quarterly* 9 (1930): 29–31.

8. Mulcaster to Clinton, n.d. [ca. 1776], Henry Clinton Papers, William L. Clements Library, University of Michigan, Ann Arbor.

9. Cecil Johnson, "Expansion in West Florida," *Mississippi Valley Historical Review* 20 (March 1934): 481–96.

10. Chalmers to Rawdon, May 21, 1779, Henry Clinton Papers.

11. Kathryn T. Abbey, "Peter Chester's Defense of the Mississippi after the Willing Raid," *Mississippi Valley Historical Review* 22 (June 1935): 17–32.

12. J. Barton Starr, *Tories, Dons, and Rebels: The American Revolution in West Florida,* (Gainesville: University Presses of Florida, 1976), pp. 118, 147.

13. Smith, "The American Loyalists: Notes on their Organization and Numerical Strength," *William and Mary Quarterly* 25 (April 1968): 259, 270.

14. Greene, "An Uneasy Connection: An Analysis of the Preconditions of the American Revolution," in *Essays on the American Revolution,* ed. Stephen G. Kurtz and James H. Hutson (Chapel Hill, N.C., 1973), pp. 32–80; Shy, "Thomas Pownall, Henry Ellis, and the Spectrum of Possibilities, 1763–1775," in *Anglo-American Politics, 1675–1775,* ed. Olson and Brown (New Brunswick, N.J., 1970), pp. 155–86.

15. Lockey, ed., *East Florida, 1783–1785* (Berkeley, Calif., 1949); *The Case of the Inhabitants of East-Florida, with an Appendix Containing Papers by Which All the Facts Stated in the Case, Are Supported* (St. Augustine, 1784).

16. Lockey, *East Florida,* p. 97.

17. *The Case of the Inhabitants of East-Florida, with An Appendix,* p. 14.

18. Lockey, *East Florida,* pp. 301–303.

19. Lockey, *East Florida,* pp. 96–99.

20. Lockey, *East Florida,* p. 117.

21. *The Case of the Inhabitants of East-Florida, with An Appendix,* p. 29.

22. Lockey, *East Florida,* pp. 154–56.

Twelve

Loyalism and Patriotism at Askance

Community, Conspiracy, and Conflict on the Southern Frontier

ROBERT S. DAVIS

[The king] has excited domestic insurrections amongst us, and has endeavored to bring on the inhabitants of our frontiers, the merciless Indian savages. . . .

Thomas Jefferson,
Declaration of Independence

The losers in a conflict are faced with whether to cut their losses or to gamble at continuing the conflict hoping that they will somehow "snatch victory from the jaws of defeat."

Daniel Kahneman

1.

On the morning of February 14, 1779, some six hundred of the king's loyal Americans, popularly known as loyalists, or tories, camped along cane-choked, swampy, flooded Kettle Creek in Wilkes County on the then northwest frontier of Georgia. Their local guides prepared to lead them to sympathizers in the Wrightsborough Quaker settlement and, from there, to the protection of regular British troops who had occupied nearby Augusta during the previous two weeks. The redcoats the Americans sought had themselves come to Georgia from New York on a mission to rendezvous with thousands of frontier Carolinians. British leaders in London imagined that this army's arrival would begin a counterrevolution wherein the Americans would restore to the Crown all of the colonies south of Maryland and perhaps beyond. Advocates of this grand scheme, now called the "Southern Strategy," wanted to believe it would change history.[1]

What ensued at Kettle Creek that morning would come to figure prominently in the folklore of the South as one of the few patriot victories in Georgia, a state otherwise seldom remembered as having any Revolutionary War heritage.[2] The battle resulted in little loss of life for either side: twenty dead identified as loyalists and at least four of the attacking militiamen killed and three men mortally wounded. It failed to affect the outcome of the invasion of Georgia in 1778–79, and it helped to relegate the overall campaign to obscurity. The battle itself, conversely, would achieve notoriety in American and British histories of the Revolution from the 1780s to the present as an incidental event outside of the mainstream of the war and of uncertain importance.[3]

What happened, and to a degree what failed to happen, that morning in that unknown pasture actually had special significance on many levels. Kettle Creek showed, for example, how military actions can result from and better represent major social and political currents than the strategies of war. An anonymous writer in 1780 noted the error in trying to understand the American Revolution as a whole by looking at such events in purely military terms:

> Most of these actions would in other wars be considered as skirmishes of little account, and scarcely worthy of a detailed narrative. But these small actions are as capable as any of displaying conduct. The operations of war being spread over the vast continent, . . . it is by such skirmishes that the fate of America must be decided. They are therefore as important as battles in which a hundred thousand men are drawn up on each side.[4]

At Kettle Creek the British Southern Strategy failed as it would fail repeatedly to the end of the war, in part, because in such specific clashes of arms it revealed itself as a historical but misguided use of military force to address social issues such as economic ambitions, politics, class, religion, and race. Loyalists in this particular fight demonstrated that what remained of the "king's men" largely consisted of desperate and cowering members of what historian Linda Colley described, speaking of all of America, as a coalition of polyethnic minorities who sought protection for themselves more than the opportunity to die for an already failed cause. The "thousands" of loyal frontiersmen actually turned out to be hundreds of men who mainly disappeared into the canebrakes and woods in the face of violent opposition from their neighbors. His Majesty's struggle in America had become a foreign occupation that desperately tried to achieve victory without any clear definition of what victory meant or how to achieve it. Had the significance of this battle been fully understood in 1779, the events of 1775 and 1776 could have been interpreted in ways that would have avoided the fighting in the South in 1780 and 1781 and thus saved thousands of lives. This situation places the American struggle for independence in the same category as modern revolutionary conflicts.[5]

The issues that turned into armed conflict as part of an American civil war that morning on Kettle Creek represent much more, including a sometimes violent social struggle on the southern frontier that began before and that would continue after the American Revolution, a war that the British colonel Robert Gray rightly noted consisted of a patchwork of settlements each fighting for its own cause. A long-standing general political struggle between the individual colonial governments—oriented toward the coastal planters—and the families who settled in the backcountry masked the clash of cultures of different groups on the frontier. In the months before the war officially broke out, for example, thousands of southern frontiersmen appeared to have actively and very publicly come forward in support of the king's cause. In 1774 hundreds of backcountry Georgians, including such later whig (rebel) leaders at Kettle Creek as John Dooly and Elijah Clarke, signed petitions in support of royal rule. They specifically opposed the actions of the coastal-oriented rebels as threatening the protection the British provided frontier families from Indian attack. Royal Governor Josiah Martin of North Carolina arranged a similar petition drive in his colony. In South Carolina thousands of frontiersmen who opposed the Revolution refused, en masse, to sign the rebels' Continental Association. Overall at least 2,500 loyalists throughout the Carolinas took up arms and marched against the Revolution in 1775 and 1776. Leaders in London would base their hopes upon these men and their neighbors starting a civil war that would restore the colonies to the Crown.[6]

The true number of frontiersmen opposed to the rebellion in its early years in the South, however, proved deceptive because it was more representative of the people of the backcountry coming together to express common concerns rather than loyalty to the colonial system. Most of these people could, and would, be won over to any political cause that contributed to their own ongoing struggle for greater self-determination. A restoration of the situation to what it had been held little interest for these people. Consequently the backcountry loyalists who rose up for the king in the early years of the war suffered defeat at the hands of greater numbers of their neighbors at the Battle of Moore's Creek Bridge in North Carolina and in the Snow campaign of South Carolina. Scotsman Baika Harvey, a new arrival to the Kettle Creek–Wrightsborough area, watched the failure of the efforts of the king's men:

> the Americans are Smart Industrious hardy people & fears Nothing . . . I am Just Returned from the Back parts where I seed Eight Thousand men in arms all with Riffeld Barrill guns which they can hit the Bigness of a Dollar between Two & Three hundreds yards Distance the Little Boys not Bigger than my self has all their Guns & marches with their Fathers & all their Cry is Liberty or Death Dear Godfather tell all my Country people not to come here for the Americans will kill them Like Dear in the Woods & they will never see them they can lie on their Backs & Load & fire & every time they draws sight at anything they are sure to kill or Creple & they Run in the Woods like Horses I seed the Liberty Boys take Between Two & Three hundred Torreys & one Liberty man would take & Drive four or five before him Just as shepards do the sheep in our Cuntry & they have taken all their arms from them and put the head men in gaile.[7]

Leaders of the loyalists, men such as the Englishman Thomas Brown, went into exile and there advocated an invasion of the South by British troops that would result in the uprising that ended at Kettle Creek. Historian William H. Nelson argues that after 1776, however, only two populations of the king's supporters of any significance remained: one along the frontier from Georgia to New York and the other in the mid-Atlantic ports. He added that these Americans lived in areas that suffered most from the economic interests of the far wealthier neighboring

areas and least from any British policies. These two groups were also only mar-
ginally influenced by the transatlantic trade, which motivated other Americans
to support the Revolution. Scholars of the Revolution now know that the British
ministry sought to win a war that needed popular support in a land where the
loyalists were outnumbered by three to one. An estimated one hundred thousand
Americans actively served in the whig war effort. The thirty thousand of their
neighbors who took up arms for the king's cause, had they been treated as a serious military force, might just have balanced that opposition when added to the
numbers in the king's regular army, Indian allies, self-emancipated slaves, and
German auxiliaries. Critics note, however, that this number of armed loyalists only
comes to one-third of the number who, at the end of the war, moved to British
territories rather than remain in the new country. Among Americans opposed to
living in the new United States, two-thirds were willing to risk an uncertain future
in unknown lands but would not fight for the king's cause.[8]

British leaders had reasons for failing to accept the true situation in America
that originated in an appreciation of how they stood to lose the war. By 1778 they
realized that intimidation had failed. The men of Washington's army could now
match them in battle prowess, although victories still largely eluded them. Great
Britain lacked the military and financial resources to continue the war as it had
been fought, especially now with France as an ally of the American rebels and
with other European nations threatening to take advantage of the situation. The
fixed battles that the redcoats still won now came at the cost of encouraging more
political, guerrilla, and social resistance in a populist backlash against the use of
formal military force at home and abroad against people of English descent. The
situation mirrored the brief, bloody, and failed British occupation of Manila in
the 1760s, which had demonstrated, according to historian Fred Anderson, that
"armed force could conquer lands and peoples, but only voluntary cooperation
could maintain imperial control. Wherever the conquered withheld their consent, the empire's sway extended only as far as the range of its guns."[9] The British
general Charles O'Hara similarly observed during the American Revolution "how
impossible must it prove to conquer a Country, where repeated success cannot
ensure permanent advantages, and the most trifling check to our Arms acts like
an Electric Fire, by rousing at the same moment every Man upon the vast Continent to persevere upon the most distant dawn of hope."[10]

From the earliest days of the fighting, the British strategists had a nebulous
plan for incorporating American support to somehow achieve victory. They called
for seizing the ports to use as bases from which the military could control the
coasts. The army could then establish fortified outposts in the interior from which
to recruit and draft the people into provincial and militia units, something very
close to the strategy used later by the occupying forces in Vietnam and Iraq. Lord
George Germain, 1st Viscount Sackville and the secretary of state for America,
served as the chief administrator for the British war effort. He grew desperate
enough to try such a plan and William Knox, his undersecretary and a powerful

influence upon him, prepared the details for such a campaign. A Protestant Irishman, Knox had been the provost in Georgia and had spent years in that colony building large and highly profitable plantations that he still owned. Later he moved to London where he served as colonial agent for that colony and still later in many influential positions within the British bureaucracy of state. Throughout the war Knox diligently served as one of those bureaucrats described by historian Robert M. Calhoon:

> These men had worked for years to master the intricacies of imperial administration and formulate new and tough colonial policies. . . . The result of all of these developments was a new colonial policy—on which several high ranking ministers staked their careers—prepared by a shadowy group of sub-ministerial advisors and directed by harassed nervous men possessing neither the time nor the temperament to listen to colonial opinion or to reflect upon the long-range impact of British policy on the health of the empire.[11]

Knox specifically and very publicly promoted a number of reconciliation schemes that included forming an American aristocracy with its own representation in Parliament. With the passage of the Declaration of Independence, he still saw an opportunity to replace the old colonialism with a new Anglo relationship that proved visionary in that it represented a connection very similar to what would successfully exist between the two nations in the future. Historians have credited the Southern Strategy to various southern loyalists, but a plan by this undersecretary, in his own handwriting, for the invasion of Georgia matches that actual campaign as it unfolded in almost every detail.[12]

William Knox chose Georgia as the target for reasons beyond his own self-interest. It had a small and politically divided population with an inept state government that had fractured into partisanship of greater menace to itself than to the king, and geographically it stood as a bridge between the thousands of loyalists believed to still be found on the Carolina frontier, the still larger numbers of Indian warriors supported by the king's agents, and the loyal populations of East Florida, West Florida, and Louisiana. A similar accident of location had led to the creation of Georgia in 1733 as a military buffer between British South Carolina and then neighboring provinces of France and Spain as well as a hoped for (but never realized) source of exotic products from a Mediterranean environment. The colony also began as a government financed experiment, with a nonprofit board of trustees established to solve the social problems of England's middle-class Protestant majority. From these beginnings through the American Revolution, circumstances often created opportunities for societal experiments in Georgia, alternatives to the philosophy of the Enlightenment of the type that Knox sometimes argued for in his writings. In 1774 the thirteenth colony's eighteen thousand white and fifteen thousand black inhabitants had the same community-oriented and often loyalist society as South Carolina did. Georgia failed to send a delegation for the whole colony to the First Continental Congress, and it had the highest percentage of loyalists in its population of the thirteen colonies.[13]

As with the advocates of the Southern Strategy, however, British planners such as Knox misunderstood the cultural and historical reality of Georgia. Historian Andrew C. Lannen has documented that, from its beginnings, individuals and very different communities in this colony had fought almost continuously for local authority and against rule imposed from abroad. This conflict mirrored the ambitions of Americans in the later stages of the Revolution. The dissension within the new state government represented a continuation of the struggle for local authority rather than any desire for a return to authoritarian rule. After the British conquered the state and reduced it to colonial status, one of the restored provincial assembly's last acts before its dissolution would be to establish, on paper, local government in the colony's farthest backcountry.[14]

Germain and Knox saw that the war would be decided by Americans but mistakenly believed, to the point of obsession, that at least half the colonial population still supported the king's cause. In 1777 His Majesty's troops tried to rally the population's support in frontier Pennsylvania and New York. The subsequent defeat of British regulars at Saratoga by the professional American army, however, obscured the significance of the serious defeats that the loyalists suffered at the hands of their neighbors in that campaign.[15] Despite these setbacks, the British government would cling to this belief in their desperation to win the South with invasions of Georgia in 1778, South Carolina in 1780, and North Carolina in 1781. These attempts to mobilize the backcountry people to the king's cause that started with the Kettle Creek campaign continued almost to the end of the war. Lord Cornwallis made his invasion of Virginia, en route to his disastrous defeat at Yorktown, while still pursuing a hope of finding what proved to be illusionary legions of Americans. British historian Richard Holmes has compared this strategy to the attempt two centuries later by the United States to "Vietnamize" its war in Southeast Asia. In both instances, and as with the American support for the White Russians in the Russian Revolution, soldiers who had become seen as invaders tried to build a popular consensus around groups outside of and in opposition to the local mainstream with the effect of further alienating the general population to the benefit of the rebellion. The king's soldiers became foreign peacekeepers in an alien land without peace as they tried to indigenize the war. They even became a part of a hopelessly flawed effort at restoring colonial government in Georgia; today that would be called "nation building." Ultimately they only further succeeded in uniting Americans of many groups and of different interests in ways that the rebel leaders had failed to do on their own. What remained of the king's "good Americans" came to appear as collaborators with an invading foreign army.[16]

Unfortunately for the thousands of men, women, and children who suffered in the last years of the war, such a conflict usually ends only when the invading nation finally depletes its resources and is forced to abandon its adventure. Leaders who could have ended it proclaim that the war has turned one metaphorical corner after another while ignoring how many times they have returned to the same place. "Staying the course" for "100 years" or as "long as necessary" to achieve "peace with honor" exists more in desperate bravado, and as ideas for modern novels like *1984*, than in reality, but national security and popular prejudices can provide an excuse to continue the fight after the chances for victory have fallen to nil. Holmes has pointed out that the king's government went so far as to adopt the tactic of warning the public that, if America won independence, Ireland would attempt the same at a time when it was more an occupied and exploited foreign land than any other British possession was. Such alarmist rhetoric resembles the modern "domino effect" hysteria associated with concerns about new leftists and Muslim fundamentalist governments. In the American Revolution the majority of Britons viewed religious freedom as a great internal and national threat, especially when applied to easing civil restrictions on members of the Holy Roman Church in Ireland or elsewhere in the Empire. British historian Robert Harvey argued that rejection of Catholics had been and would continue as an internal struggle in Great Britain for decades. On top of the challenges faced waging a war of foreign occupation, the nation was still dealing with religious-based resistance at home as well as abroad, and progress on one front could be cancelled by failure on the other. A 1778 act innocently intended to drum up badly needed support for the American war by granting some political recognition for Catholics, for example, brought about the famous Gordon Riot in London in 1780, the worst public violence in the city's history. This massive civil disobedience undermined the concurrent British victories in South Carolina and compelled the ministry to tie down troops in the south of England to assure the public that the country had protection from invasion by Catholic France. Those regiments might have otherwise been sent to America to follow up on the military successes there. Thomas Jefferson, the author of the humanist Declaration of Independence, also proposed an act establishing religious freedom in Virginia, thus feeding popular British fears that its Protestant faith was under siege by Papists and their allies. The situation became particularly partisan when Catholic France and Spain openly joined the war against Great Britain after the British defeat at Saratoga in 1777. Using the prospect of an independent Papist Ireland on Protestant England's borders—with Roman Catholics freely able to promote their faith in Britain—supporters of continuing the war could play on widespread fears. American supporters of the Revolution also questioned the necessity of an alliance with Roman Catholic France. Had they not served, hardly a decade earlier, with their British kinsmen in finishing a century of French-supported Indian wars on the frontier? In a situation repeated in later conflicts, the British home government thus used the support of minorities to sustain its political and military ambitions abroad while using the fear of a minority in the home country to try to maintain popular support for the war. Parliamentary treatment of Ireland, however, actually improved in response to the American rebellion; a nonmilitary revolution subsequently helped to keep the entire island in the United Kingdom into the twentieth century.[17]

Not everyone failed to understand the situation in America. Charles Carroll of Carrollton, a Maryland signer of the Declaration of Independence, correctly predicted at least as early as March 29, 1776, that the British army, however often victorious, could only succeed in holding the ground where it stood. Carroll believed that Great Britain must be "an immense loser" in America because war fails as a weapon in subduing the human spirit. Frederick Howard, the 5th Earl of Carlisle wrote similar words to his wife as early as 1778 while heading an official peace commission sent by Parliament to the Americans, words that would find echoes in many modern conflicts:

> The leaders on the enemy's side are too powerful; the common people hate us in their hearts, notwithstanding all that is said of their secret attachment to the mother country. I cannot give you a better proof of their unanimity against us than in our last march; in the whole country there was not found one single man capable of bearing arms at home; they left their dwellings unprotected, and after having cut all of the ropes of the wells had fled to Gen. Washington. Formerly, when things went better for us, there was an appearance of friendship by their coming in for pardons, that might have deceived even those who had been the most acquainted with them. But no sooner our situation was in the least altered for the worse, but these friends were the first to fire on us, and many were taken with the pardons in our [sic, their] pockets. Beat Gen. Washington, drive away Monsr. d'Estaing, and we should have friends enough in the country; but in our present condition the only friends we have, or are likely to have, are those who are absolutely ruined for us [that is, those afraid, from experience, to express their loyalty openly], and in such distress [that is, as refugees protected and supported at British expense] I leave you to judge what possible use they can be to us.[18]

2

On March 8, 1778, Lord Germain sent to General Sir Henry Clinton, British commander in North America and son of the former colonial governor of New York, a lengthy and detailed set of instructions on how to conduct the operations in the Western Hemisphere of what had become a world war. The entry of France into the conflict postponed the start of the year's campaign until the winter. Clinton then had to start a new march to try to find and defeat Washington's army while defending his base at New York and returning six hundred marines to Halifax. This list, of what historian William B. Willcox came to describe as "a collection of strategic fossils," only began with those basics. By the end of the year, Clinton also had to dispatch five thousand men under Major General James Grant to capture the island of St. Lucia and thirteen hundred reinforcements under Brigadier General John Campbell of Strachur to British Pensacola in West Florida to protect that isolated colony. Sir Henry again tried to resign, and he certainly protested these orders: "You have but one army. 'Tis a good one; it has never been affronted. You may want it. You ought to have kept it together, nursed it, cherished it. By the present arrangement I wish one half of it may not be under ground by Christmas and the rest reduced to an ignominious fight to avoid still greater disgrace."[19]

The instructions from Germain also included orders for the invasion of Georgia. Clinton selected Scotsman and lieutenant colonel Archibald Campbell to command the campaign for reasons that now appear almost inexplicable. Campbell only learned of the existence of this expedition that he would be ordered to take to a place about which he knew nothing on the night before its fleet sailed from New York in November and long after news of it had leaked to George Washington and the Continental Congress. John Fauchereau Grimké, an officer serving in a whig invasion of Florida in mid-May 1778, learned most of the details of the plan. Trained as an engineer, Campbell had little experience in command; and coming from Britain's rising and ambitious professional classes, he would have suffered the disdain of officers like Sir Henry who owed their rank to being in the aristocracy. The Scotsman claimed that jealousies among other officers caused Clinton to decline to promote him to brigadier general, a rank commensurate with his responsibilities and which would have garnered more respect from the Americans.[20]

This expedition appeared, like its leader, hardly credible for the mission it undertook. Lieutenant Colonel Campbell's force consisted of only some three thousand men in a collection of units of northern and southern loyalists, with German battalions and two battalions of his own Seventy-first Fraser's Scots Highlander Infantry Regiment. The British government had proclaimed the latter to be made up of elite and martial "Highlanders," but at least some Irishmen and impressed Englishmen from the dregs of society and of questionable physical qualities filled its ranks. Although this regiment would see more combat by the time of Yorktown than any other British unit and would almost cease to exist, when Campbell commanded it in 1778, the Seventy-first had little firsthand war experience. The fleet transporting this army also proved to have serious shortcomings, including mismanagement (that appeared suspiciously like sabotage) made worse by the foul weather.[21]

Sir Henry Clinton may have simply divided his limited forces as best he could to meet Germain's many and unrealistic demands, but he may also have dispatched the highest ranking officer he could afford to lose, with the troops that the British army least needed, on what he regarded as a strategic mistake imposed upon him by a micromanaging superior thousands of miles away in London. He himself had led an expedition to reach the southern loyalists in 1775–76 that had given the rebels morale-boosting victories at Charleston, South Carolina, and over the loyalists who did rally from the backcountry. To try to implement so many plans simultaneously, he felt, would only incite more Americans against the king's cause and make those who did come forward liable to retaliation at the hands of their rebel neighbors.[22] That Clinton entrusted one of the most critical roles in the

Georgia campaign, the covert recruitment of the loyalists, to someone vaguely referred to as "Boyd" (a man whom he may have never met) leads to further questions about the general's faith in the expedition's chances for success.[23]

The inexperienced Archibald Campbell, however, successfully led his untested command to Georgia. His troops defeated a professional American army and captured the colonial capital of Savannah on December 29, 1778. He then linked up with troops from neighboring East Florida and boasted, after then overrunning the rest of Georgia, of being the first officer to tear a star and stripe from the rebel flag. Campbell used his commission as the royal civil governor of Georgia to receive oaths of allegiance from almost 1,800 men, the largest part of the male population of military age, whom he hastily organized into a colonial militia.[24]

Most of these men, however, quickly returned to the whig cause or fled once Campbell and his troops moved on. The experience with the Wilkes County frontier in early February 1779 proved typical. A Mr. Freeman, a delegation of Quakers from Wrightsborough, and a group of Baptists arrived in the British camp at Augusta to offer the surrender of the settlements in that last area of Georgia. Campbell sent then Captains John Hamilton and Dugald Campbell with their loyalist horsemen through the Kettle Creek–Wilkes County frontier to receive the voluntary submissions of the population and to find Boyd and his loyalists. Captains Hamilton and Campbell, reportedly working in conjunction with Daniel McGirth's bandits, forced the submission of these last outposts before being surrounded and nearly forced to surrender by enemy militiamen under Andrew Pickens and John Dooly at Robert Carr's fort, near Kettle Creek. Hamilton later told a British historian that "although many of the people came in to take the oath of allegiance, the professions of a considerable number were not to be depended upon; and that some came in only for the purpose of gaining information on his strength and future designs."[25]

Lieutenant Colonel Archibald Campbell could have predicted such results. His superiors in New York had assured him of a reinforcement of six thousand Carolinians, as well as significant numbers of Indian allies; in a memoir he wrote of how his expectations steadily declined. By the time his troops had penetrated the backcountry and captured Augusta, the planned place of rendezvous with Boyd on January 31, 1779, Campbell had lowered his expectations to one thousand Americans coming to his standard. Although reports arrived in Georgia that thousands of loyalists had gathered on the Saluda River in South Carolina, Boyd's uprising actually numbered, on its best day, only some five hundred to eight hundred men of questionable value to fulfilling British aspirations. In Great Britain a report arrived that this uprising had consisted of only three hundred fifty men![26]

During the early hours of February 14, 1779, Campbell had his troops evacuate Augusta and the Georgia backcountry. Plans to make a surprise attack against the growing numbers of American troops across the Savannah River fell apart as his command increasingly risked being cut off from their base near the coast. Backcountry Americans, "Crackers" as he called them, who had joined his expedition frequently engaged in plundering that alerted the enemy of any movements made by Campbell's troops. On February 3, three hundred Charleston militia and twenty Continentals under General William Moultrie stopped a diversionary raid by two hundred British regulars at Beaufort, South Carolina. Outposts that Campbell had set up to protect his route back to Savannah began to fall to whig horsemen. These small victories illustrated to all the small size of the British expeditionary force and demonstrated that the redcoats could be beaten. Campbell's troops at Augusta increasingly looked as though they would be the next Saratoga. Campbell had no news of Boyd, and his army had also run out of rum, a dangerous circumstance in any eighteenth-century military that included even Indian war parties; consequences ranged from soldiers refusing to fight to armed violence against officers. Upon returning to Savannah, the British soldiers reportedly threatened mutiny and assaulted General Augustin Prévost when he failed to supply the almost required allotment of drink.[27]

Campbell thus lived the scenario envisioned by the Earl of Carlisle in 1778. Shortly afterward the lieutenant colonel learned that Boyd and many of his officers had been killed at Kettle Creek on the same morning that he had evacuated Augusta. Captain Hamilton rescued the fewer than three hundred survivors of the battle from Wrightsborough, where they had found refuge. The few Georgians still willing to take up muskets for the British cause subsequently suffered crushing defeats at the hands of the Georgia and South Carolina militia. Of the promised Cherokee and Creek Indian allies, only some six hundred warriors came to Georgia, and they largely went home after clashing with the same militiamen who had dealt an end to Boyd's expedition at Kettle Creek. On March 3, 1779, the king's regular troops did attack and destroy an American army that had camped at Briar Creek, Georgia, in preparation for an attempt to retake Savannah, but yet another British success in a fixed formal battle that brought the king's cause no closer to victory could hardly have justified the risks of the invasion of Georgia. To add insult to injury, the redcoats found oaths of loyalty to the king issued by Campbell in the pockets of dead and captured Americans.[28]

General Augustin Prévost, the British commander in Georgia, despite constantly seeking the favor of his superiors, still dared to inform them that what little loyalist support had existed in the South had been eliminated by acts of terrorism committed against the cooperating Americans by their neighbors. He warned that the only success to be found in the region would come at the hands of the regular British army. Sir Henry Clinton concurred and wrote that any benefit from American support, specifically in the Georgia campaign, had cost more than its value. The British navy, army, and engineers that served so well in formal battle proved of limited use in fighting a guerrilla war waged on land and water. By contrast, the insurgents survived and were strengthened by booty taken in their raids on fixed camps, supply trains, and outposts; deserters from the enemy army also supplied the new American army with badly needed training and helped to fill rebel ranks from drill sergeants to generals.[29]

The Southern Strategy lived on, however, despite the rebels having acquired by 1779 all of what have become—as demonstrated in modern times in such places as Vietnam, Afghanistan, and Iraq—the classic ingredients for a successful rebellion: a widespread view of the occupying army as foreign invader, effective weapons for use by individual resistance fighters, and foreign support. Germain reinstated Governor Sir James Wright and his colonial government in Georgia, however. Historian Edward F. De Lancey would argue a century later that had the British (Knox's) plans for this campaign been followed and the war kept in South Carolina, William Knox's goal of saving at least one of the thirteen colonies could have been implemented and would have had a profound effect on the further settlement of North America. "But," he wrote, "to the misfortunes of America and injury of Great Britain, a strange kind of fatality was evident in all proceedings during the continuance of the American Revolution."[30] In 1779, while the king's army continued to seek the rumored legions of loyalist soldiers, Pickens, Dooly, Clarke, and other rebel leaders used small bands of riflemen to defeat loyalists, Indians, and redcoats. Such Americans, far from rallying to the king's standard, confined the area of restored colonial rule to scarcely more than the range of British muskets and bayonets. Wright had hardly returned to his former province when he wrote that weak loyalist support necessitated a continued rule by the military.[31]

Ignoring the lessons of the failed Burgoyne campaign in the North in 1777 and of Campbell's experience in Georgia in 1779, Sir Henry Clinton used almost all of his available forces in 1780 in an attempt to make the Southern Strategy work with a temporary, concentrated increase in resources. He laid siege to Charleston, South Carolina, and the city surrendered with almost all the regular American troops in the South on May 12, 1780, avenging his failure to take it years earlier. Soon after, Clinton returned to New York with most of his army, leaving Lord Cornwallis with the responsibility for finding the still undiscovered way to win the war. The red-coated soldiers defeated yet another American army in a formal battle near Camden, South Carolina, on August 16. Efforts by rebel leaders Andrew Williamson and Elijah Clarke to wage a guerrilla war largely failed. Thomas Sumter made the most classic and usually fatal mistake that a partisan leader could make when he concentrated all of the remaining guerrilla groups, some one thousand men, at Blackstocks, South Carolina, on November 20, 1780, for an attack on the enemy outpost at Ninety Six. The resulting battle ended as an American tactical victory. British commander Banastre Tarleton, leading the regulars of the Seventy-first Regiment and the Americans of his own legion, however, rightly considered it a great strategic success for the king's cause as it resulted in the dispersal and discrediting of the remaining rebel resistance in the South. Historian John E. Ferling makes a compelling argument that, overall, during the winter of 1780–81 the rebel cause reached a near fatal low.[32]

Such rebel missteps, however, failed to provide the British cause with what it needed most, a clear plan to achieve victory. The army successfully overran all of

Georgia and most of South Carolina, while organizing militias as Campbell had done, but it still failed to create a credible native American military force for reclaiming the rebellious colonies. By the end of 1780, the British had revisited the February 1779 experience in Georgia, but on a larger scale. The Americans who had initially joined the rebels but now found themselves legally compelled to serve in the king's militia proved to be of little military value. The formal loyalist provincial units in the South, otherwise unable to replace casualties and deserters, had to disobey orders and enlist prisoners of war to fill their declining ranks. Before learning of the total destruction of his corps of nine hundred provincials and militia by an equal number of frontier riflemen at King's Mountain, South Carolina, in 1780, Lord Charles Cornwallis wrote despondently of his Americans. Despite the facts that they had been well trained in the use of the musket and bayonet and that they outnumbered Washington's army, they proved to be "dastardly and pusillanimous"; arming his militia, in essence, amounted to giving weapons to the rebels. A year later he warned Germain that the backcountry of no colony could be held. Historians later noted that most of the men responsible for the destruction of the loyalists at King's Mountain had traveled hundreds of miles from today's Tennessee, on their own initiative and leaving their families vulnerable to Indian attack, for the opportunity to kill the Americans who served voluntarily as provincials and the men conscripted into the colonial militia. A South Carolinian wrote, "The greatest cause of the Militia not turning out so well as was perhaps expected was the atrocious cruelties exercised upon them whenever they fell into the hands of the Rebel Militia, cruelties so great that they exceed all belief and were they to be mentioned in England would be generally rejected as the exaggerations of a heated fancy."[33]

The British needed but had failed to seek a means of winning what today would be called the "hearts and minds of the rebels." Two centuries later, in remembering Vietnam, poet Adrienne Rich unintentionally described the situation in the American Revolution: "A patriot [true loyalist] is not a weapon. A patriot is one who wrestles for the soul of her country / as she wrestles for her own being, for the soul of his country /. . . / as he wrestles for his own being. A patriot is a citizen trying to wake / from the burnt-out dream of innocence."[34] Germain saw using existing American support only as a tool for ending the war—by subjugation rather than by reconciliation. The men charged with carrying out the Southern Strategy also failed to consider winning Americans over to their cause despite Knox's recommendations. Even officers such as Banastre Tarleton and Patrick Ferguson, men who commanded loyalists, argued for a fire-and-sword policy. Some discontented American leaders, such as Colonel John Thomas of Georgia, did come forward. A successful local colonial official, he had, with great personal doubts, openly joined the rebellion after the arrival of the news of the battles of Concord and Lexington only to undergo arrest when he decided to return to his original allegiance by 1778. Thomas would suffer a severe wound and later imprisonment for fighting for the king in 1779. Lieutenant Colonel James Ingram of

Richmond County similarly made an impassioned plea to his fellow Georgians to resist the British in January 1779, on the eve of the patriot success at the battle of Burke County jail but before he, like Benedict Arnold, became a defeatist and an equally dedicated loyalist officer.[35] Redcoat officers, however, showed contempt for the likes of Thomas Brown, John Thomas, James Ingram, Boyd of Kettle Creek, John Moore, John Spurgeon, and Henry Sharp, men who risked and sometimes gave their lives to lead their fellow "good Americans" in a war to save colonial America for the king. The army's leadership made only minimal efforts, at the least expense possible, to recruit Americans. The survivors of the Kettle Creek campaign who reached the king's army received nothing more in compensation for their sacrifices than Archibald Campbell taking them drinking, an expense that His Majesty's auditors later disallowed. He had no authority to pay them. The thirty thousand loyalists who did bear arms by the war's end became martyrs to the shortsightedness of Germain and the king's military.[36]

General Sir Henry Clinton made these matters worse before leaving for New York from his temporary southern campaign by ordering almost all men in Georgia and South Carolina to serve in the restored colonial militia, including the rebels who had surrendered and received paroles. By this action, he inadvertently allowed the latter, including men like Andrew Pickens, to feel released to return to the war and to resume leading the resistance. At that same time, loyalist leaders such as Thomas Brown and Sir James Wright called for the strongest measures to be taken, as punishment and intimidation, against the former whigs. Lord Charles Cornwallis, commanding His Majesty's forces in the South, did not object to such a policy. He felt more comfortable with building fortified outposts, conducting marches, and fighting formal fixed battles than in establishing civil governments or implementing populist peacemaking schemes. Cornwallis pursued a hope for victory centered around destroying the formal military structure of the rebels and, with it, possibly their hopes for their revolution's success. The American generals Nathanael Greene and Daniel Morgan thwarted even those questionable aspirations. Beyond failing to reach out to or pacify the population, the actions of Cornwallis, Clinton, and others all contributed to reigniting the fighting. Outposts set up as bases for completing the pacification of Georgia and South Carolina became besieged refuges where British and loyalist troops, with their families, awaited surrender/evacuation (as at Augusta) or rescue/evacuation (as at Ninety Six). These remaining loyal Americans came to call for the removal of the British army. The campaigns in South Carolina, according to historian Henry Lumpkin, resulted in an estimated 1,200 dead and wounded British and loyalist soldiers with another 1,286 men taken prisoner. Their enemy's losses, however, were only 497 killed and wounded, with another 320 men taken as prisoners. In the end the only achievements of these campaigns were to give South Carolina the distinction of having more Revolutionary War battlefields than any other state and to have left Georgia, overall, the state most thoroughly devastated by the Revolution, suffering more loss of property than it would during the Civil War (1861–65).[37]

Each half of the tepid partnership of necessity between loyalist and redcoat had mistakenly believed that the other would somehow find a way to undermine a broad-based, well-organized, and often violently ruthless independence-oriented native rebellion that now only had to refuse to surrender in order to succeed. Had the regular American armies been thoroughly defeated, the Continental Congress bankrupted, and the French government compelled to abandon its support of the American cause, the mere thirty thousand British and German soldiers would still have had to occupy almost every town, county, and state in America to subdue a population of some 2.5 million Americans, almost all of whom had joined in some form of resistance, if not open rebellion, against the king. A temporary increase of military force, as in 1777 and 1780, could give an initial appearance of success but failed to address the reasons the British war effort continued to fail. Historian Richard Holmes argues that, as late as 1778, months before the loyalist catastrophe at the battle of Kettle Creek, the British no longer had a viable long game plan in America.[38]

Some loyalists foresaw the outcome of the war before many British leaders did. Native Englishman and American explorer William Lee, for example, came to Georgia in 1780 as he had heard that it had been pacified. He discovered a reality so very different that he had to abandon his wife and newborn child to flee for his life. Similarly the seaman Samuel Kelly would find British-occupied Charleston a deforested wasteland of abandoned houses and ruins rather than the beautiful city he remembered as a child. He blamed the change not only on the direct violence of the war but also on the degrading effects of the presence of the military in a defensive siege posture and the accommodation of the refugees.[39]

3

On March 11, 1779, a disenchanted Archibald Campbell left the South and his doomed regiment forever to marry and to find other venues for his considerable ambitions.[40] Why did he fail to find the thousands of American recruits he had been assured awaited only his arrival to march to the king's standard? Frontiersmen, like the "Over the Mountain men" at the battle of King's Mountain, left few expressions of their ideals or motivations, but the political issues affecting backcountry residents sometimes surface by implication. During the last years of the French and Indian War, Great Britain had made allies of the Americans in their mutual conflict but especially in the backcountry. That century of warfare had represented an earlier and more striking example of a European nation (France) supporting the original ethnic minority groups on the frontier (different Indian nations and their white allies) in a heroic but doomed struggle against the much greater Protestant American majority. It had been on the battlefields of that war that George Washington, Benjamin Franklin, Andrew Pickens, and other colonials had first seen the weaknesses of the king's regular military establishment and something of the power of what they could accomplish for themselves in their own environment.[41]

With the peace that followed, the relationship between Great Britain and America as a whole fluctuated between mutual indifference and that of master and fractious subjects. Usually more conflict existed within individual colonies than anger at the home country. As late as 1780, when James Simpson reviewed the loyalist situation in Georgia and South Carolina, he concluded that the people of the backcountry would support the king because the rebels largely came from the coastal society, the frontierman's traditional enemy.[42] Before the Revolution the colonies suffered violent internal unrest, which contributed to the group conflict of the later war. During the North Carolina Regulator rebellion of 1764 to 1771, for example, as many as six thousand frontiersmen rose up against corrupt local governments with connections to the coastal elite.[43] South Carolina's great colonial conflict of the same name (1767–71) involved vigilante backcountry communities suppressing bands of thieves while pressuring the colonial government to establish and finance rule of law on the frontier. (Although two-thirds or more of the total population of South Carolina lived in the backcountry, the lowcountry port of Charleston had the colony's only court and local government.)[44]

In North Carolina the word "Regulator" came to mean anyone who opposed the American Revolution although early historian David Ramsey wrote that veterans of the South Carolina Regulator rebellion became whigs. To many frontiersmen the later Revolution did appear as only a continuation of their struggle against political domination by the coastal elite. John Ashe, for example, by both suppressing the North Carolina Regulators in 1771 and later becoming a major general of the Revolution only seemed to confirm that impression. Some members of the minority communities did serve in the Regulator struggles, but only to fight for the goals, ideals, and traditions of their respective ethnocentric settlements.[45]

Historian Jack Greene saw these struggles as part of the ambitions of the frontier's majority population for "improvements" that included a hierarchical social structure that sought unrestricted commercialization and exploitation of slaves, Indians, and other minorities.[46] People of the backcountry sought change to create opportunities beyond limitations set by the old colonial system. The British government had done little for the people of the backcountry beyond protecting the rights and privileges of enclosed ethnic minority communities. Although the issues of tea and taxes in Boston would hardly have affected these people, the majority had to wonder, after reading the accounts in the colonial gazettes, about loyalty to a distant government that sent troops to kill dissenting Americans in coastal cities instead of to the frontier to protect settlements from Indian attacks. Contrary to the images left by observers such as William Bartram, Charles Woodmason, William Mylne, and others, many of the people of the backcountry had ambitions beyond being ignorant wandering herdsmen living in a wilderness. The history of the family of Colonel John Dooly, the commander of the Georgians at Kettle Creek, represents the rising aspirations of a growing class of ambitious "professional" frontier entrepreneurs. Dooly's father, Patrick, likely began in America as a butcher in Philadelphia, one of the European emigrants to the backcountry from mercantile/merchant urban backgrounds. In Virginia and later in South Carolina, Patrick, his growing family, and his few slaves developed tracts of land of a few hundred acres each that, prior to 1774, the king had allowed to be granted virtually for free. Although he did serve in the militia, his movements seemed to follow the peace with the Indians as it moved across the British colonies with the conclusion of the French and Indian War in 1763. Patrick would sell his lands to later arrivals before repeating the process of land development on newer frontiers until his death in 1768. He had a blacksmith or wheelwright shop. He owned books, which suggests that he worked as a teacher and/or minister. Patrick Dooly's son John continued the same pattern of upward mobility, but his lands totaled thousands of acres and he owned more slaves than his father. He supplemented his income by becoming a surveyor and a merchant. In 1773, at the height of the prosperity that followed the end of the South Carolina Regulator rebellion, John sold much of his property and borrowed large sums of money for a new real estate venture on the frontier of what would become Wilkes County, Georgia. He died in 1780 at the hands of loyalists, or at least by someone he had crossed in his frequently questionable dealings. His younger brother George, after avenging the deaths of at least three brothers that had occurred during the American Revolution, would move on to Kentucky, where he would receive grants for tens of thousands of acres and own more slaves. Upon his death in 1821, his slave children were emancipated and given part of his estate.[47]

The rebels (or whigs), in contrast to British colonial leaders, recognized the menace and the potential of ambitious men like the Doolys and worked to obtain their support. They effectively used propaganda, persecution, and promotion to win over merchants, millers, and blacksmiths—the local backcountry leaders who could then influence their neighbors. Whig currency in Georgia and elsewhere carried a depiction of a frontier rifleman, and the revolutionaries initially reached out to those who would later become prominent loyalists, men such as Moses Kirkland, John Thomas, Daniel McGirth, Thomas Waters, and others. Important men who did not actively work against the Revolution, such as Jonas Bedford and George Galphin, went undisturbed. The fact that each colony had a centralized government in a coastal capital aided the revolutionaries, who, in the main, lived in those same cities and who could rally local support there over such issues such as trade and taxes. In any revolution, controlling the government, newspapers, speech, and ministry proves a great boon in gaining recruits, silencing opposition, and intimidating those individuals not committed to either cause. In America almost all government was centered in the coastal cities, where the rebels also drew their greatest support and which they quickly controlled, facilitating the rule of entire colonies.[48] With shifts in power during the war, few men could have been clearly categorized as loyalist or whig for all of 1775 to 1783 but restoration of British control came too late to regain any real authority.[49]

The whigs also addressed backcountry concerns about the Indians. A widespread war of terror had gone on between the two notoriously violent frontier cultures for decades with only periods of ceasefire interspersed between relentless campaigns of what today is termed "ethnic cleansing." This conflict had manifestations that went beyond the well-known clashes over land, game, cattle, and horses; even the physical size and appearance of the Indian warriors intimidated and awed the frontiersmen. A chain of forts essentially marked the white frontier from Canada to Florida and thus displayed the fear of the backcountry families. On Raeburn's Creek, the home of many of the loyalists who later marched to Georgia, more than thirty people reportedly died in Cherokee attacks in 1759 and 1760.[50]

The Kettle Creek area, because of its proximity to the major Creek Indian trading path, also had a bloody past that well represented the most desperate of such life-and-death conflict on the western borderlands. It had been first settled as the Brandon settlement by a few white families from Virginia that critics called rogues led by "pretending Quaker" Edmund Gray in the late 1750s. Resettled in 1774 as part of the Ceded Lands (what became Wilkes County), it was evacuated that same year when Creek attacks on two families and the rout of the local militia terrorized the new settlers. They returned, only to face assaults from their Indian neighbors every year from 1776 to the end of the American Revolution. The Kettle Creek families would "fort up" at Robert Carr's fort at the fork on nearby Beaverdam Creek until an Indian raiding party of eleven warriors entered that refuge in the spring of 1779 and burned the buildings. The Creeks killed illiterate Captain Robert Carr, probably a veteran of the battle of Kettle Creek, although his family escaped in their nightshirts. The relatively well-off Carrs left behind almost everything that they owned: horses, cattle, beds, pewter, tableware, basic clothes, a silk hat, and a cardinal cloak. Local people subsequently would move to Robert McNabb's fort on Kettle Creek for safety, but Indian raiders destroyed it in 1778 and again in 1781 before killing McNabb and his men in an ambush on January 3, 1782, when the fort again came under siege. Seven months before the battle of Kettle Creek, the South Carolina militiamen who would fight there had also come to the aid of Colonel John Dooly and his Wilkes County militiamen against the Indians, and they would do so many times in the years that followed. A faction in Wilkes County sought to make war with the neighboring Creeks and to end the business of the white men who traded with the Indians as a means to force a peace while acquiring Creek lands.[51]

When the Cherokees attacked the frontier in 1776, southerners launched multistate, coordinated expeditions that devastated the villages in that nation. Many of the frontiersmen who had previously marched with the loyalists joined in that campaign and would remain figuratively and literally in the rebel camp afterward. Whether British Indian agent John Stuart primarily tried to keep the peace or to organize Indians to attack the frontier remains a matter for debate, but white frontiersmen by 1776 believed that the king's agents encouraged these most feared enemies to make war on the backcountry. Training, weapons, and organization needed for fighting the Indians subsequently served the frontiersmen in their later battles against the loyalists and British regulars in the American Revolution.[52]

By 1779 Elijah Clarke, John Dooly, and Andrew Pickens, the whig commanders at Kettle Creek, had all led men in battle against the Indians, and all three had participated in the 1776 campaign. Meeting today's definition of "warlords," these dedicated soldiers had thus proven themselves and could inspire, persuade, and lead very different men. By the time of the battle of Kettle Creek, Elijah Clarke had been wounded at least twice in the war, fighting Cherokees in Georgia in 1776 and in battle against Thomas Brown's loyalist provincials in Florida in 1778. John Dooly had lost a brother to an Indian attack in 1777 and had tried to hold a Creek Indian delegation hostage for satisfaction for that death. Pickens would come to spend time, as a prisoner of the British, in the same jail at Ninety Six, South Carolina, that had held the condemned loyalists captured at Kettle Creek.[53]

By 1779 such men and the thousands of their neighbors who followed them had already defined the Revolution as their local interests against any opposition. Before the war began, the backcountry had moved economically from what historian Margaret Ellen Newell described as dependency to independence, a change that she attributes to bringing about the American Revolution in New England.[54] Conversely British leaders had failed to realize that, in the backcountry, how best to continue the political, economic, and social progress that the people had been making for themselves since the 1760s mattered more than which government ruled. Reasons for the Southern Strategy's failure include the misidentification by Germain, Knox, Kirkland and other planners of the coincidental American Revolution as a rebellion against "government" and in support of "anarchy" rather than as a phase in a widespread social evolution toward self-determination. A better British plan would have embraced those aspirations, but a mindset that failed to recruit people for its cause would hardly have understood and taken advantage of their ambitions. American rule, however, would in time open more land for development, expand slavery, and bring about the type of local government with an effective and honest civil authority sought by the Regulators. As if to memorialize the changes that began during and continued after the war, the settlers around Kettle Creek established a Presbyterian church just north of the battlefield that they named "Liberty." Clarke, Dooly, and Pickens would become notables in the new order, and Georgia would name counties for all three. Counties in three states honor the memory of Andrew Pickens. Their sons would have important political careers in state capitals established after the war on what often had been British-dominated Indian lands during the Revolution.[55]

This frontier empowerment did have a negative side as well. Many Americans who had sacrificed for the Revolution found the new country as alien, restrictive, and hostile as did their loyalist counterparts. Undetermined numbers of such disenchanted whigs would also seek and find their own independence by joining in the postwar emigration to British, French, Spanish, and later Mexican territories, in some instances protecting those provinces from acquisition by the United States and, at other times, aiding in such mergers. Some of the Americans who remained would answer Herman Husband's call to resist the new national government in the Whiskey Rebellion. Patriots and other backcountry leaders, prominent men such as John Sevier, George Rogers Clark, and Thomas Sumter, would come to conspire against or outside of the interests of the country they had risked so much to help found. Elijah Clarke of Kettle Creek fame, for example, would lead his followers in private campaigns against Spanish East Florida and in an unsuccessful effort to found an independent republic on the Oconee Indian frontier in opposition to the policies of then President George Washington and his new government.[56]

4

Why then did anyone risk so much to support the king's cause as to find himself hundreds of miles from home, in hostile territory, on Kettle Creek on the morning of February 14, 1779? Aside from the grand ambitions of the British leaders, the events that led to Kettle Creek and similar battles share a lost history found only by understanding the collective consciousness of settlements on Raeburn Creek, South Carolina, and in Tryon County, North Carolina, from where most of the Kettle Creek tories hailed. Arthur Dobbs, later colonial governor of North Carolina, wrote as early as the 1720s that Great Britain had been fighting and losing what modern observers could call "a cold war" with its own American subjects for the control of the colonies, but especially for the vast unrealized wealth of the frontier, for more than a century. He urged Britain to regain its authority over its New World holdings with a chain of strategic forts that would control the orderly development of the backcountry as well as manage relations and trade with the Indians.[57]

Dobbs's advice went unheeded. Inherent dangers and the sparseness of the frontier population instead led to the creation of independent, self-supporting societal islands. Individual colonial governments created townships by setting aside reserves for specific ethnic and cultural groups, offering these groups exclusive areas as inducements to develop the best lands in the backcountry. At the same time, the British government did little in the way of controlling the settlement of the American frontier beyond enforcing its usual policy of the toleration of such minorities, people who then and during American Revolution naturally supported a system viewed by them as benevolent and to which they owed so much. Robert Harvey has argued that the king's government even became a guardian of Indians and slaves.[58]

The exclusive but very different minority groups in the backcountry belonged to what historians Wallace Brown and Robert M. Calhoon defined as clusters of "cultural minorities," settlements of societal fringe groups that Calhoon specifically identified as religious pacifists, white men who traded with the Indians, unassimilated ethnic minorities, and small farmers—"thousands of previously obscure men" caught during the subsequent American Revolution "in the machinery of internal security."[59] Robert V. Hine in his book on community on the frontier (appropriately subtitled "Separate but Not Alone"), argued that mainstream society demanded conformity and unity due to the inherently dangerous challenges on a frontier, but the larger an isolated minority community became, the longer it remained separate and the more it struggled internally, in peace or in war, to cling to its traditions under any set of circumstances. Oppression of minority communities has a long tradition in American history, from the religious persecutions in early New England and Virginia to silencing dissent directed at popular wars in the twentieth and twenty-first centuries. In the South the pro-Confederate majority took action against minority opposition communities from 1862 through 1865 by deeming such persons "tories," the Revolutionary War derogatory term for pro-British Americans.[60]

Communities of such loyalists, as rebels in their own right, would stand together to resist the tyranny of the majority of the backcountry's population despite having internal ethnic, religious, and sometimes racial differences as great as those separating them from the mainstream of frontier society. They sought to protect their personal freedom to choose to live differently and within their own culture, much as their countrymen in the majority fought for self-determination for the frontier as a whole. Colonial frontier social rebel and pacifist Herman Husband inspired and became a unifying thread between these socially besieged peoples on the North Carolina frontier. He had studied the political writings of Benjamin Franklin and the methods used in the resistance to the Stamp Act. Husband's personal journey of self-fulfillment went beyond leadership roles in the libertarian movements of the Regulator, American, and Whiskey rebellions to include a concurrent exploration of all religions he encountered. He became the spokesman, spiritual leader, and moral conscience of the North Carolina Regulators in the 1760s. His nonviolent role in that particular political dissension became so controversial that his North Carolina Quaker meeting disowned him. After that struggle failed, he fled the province for Pennsylvania.[61]

Within this resistance movement, historian Marjoleine Kars found a nucleus of discontent seeded among independent, highly moralistic, closed communities largely drawn from the Quakers and the Separatist or New Light Baptists. Both groups were active in the Raeburn Creek area, and each had significant ties to Herman Husband's followers in North Carolina. Such congregations must have already appeared as heretical cults to mainstream old school Presbyterians such as Andrew Pickens, a church elder, and to the other traditional American religions. Raeburn Creek's Quakers of the Bush River Meeting included former members of Husband's Cane Creek Meeting such as the parents of James Lindley, a loyalist later hanged after his capture at the battle of Kettle Creek. This meeting, however, existed so far outside of the Quaker mainstream that it had unspecified difficulties in fulfilling the standards for recognition by the Yearly Meeting of Discipline for the South.[62]

Leaders such as Husband had the power to motivate followers for a cause but especially within communities whose members already believed that they faced threats from the malevolent outside forces of the "world,"—the perceived evils practiced by the greater population beyond their immediate settlement. Different ministers of the new highly emotional revision of the traditional Baptist religion inspired the faithful in much the same way in their congregations, and among black as well as white converts. This new faith, thus, would benefit and grow by becoming the common faith of all peoples on the frontier. Following the colonial militia's dispersal of the North Carolina Regulators, the Baptists fled to Raeburn Creek and founded a church there. They likely contributed to what one visitor mentioned, without further explanation, as that congregation's "peculiarities." The rebellion of South Carolina Regulators had targeted as enemies to society an almost identical Separatist Baptist community on Fair Forest Creek that cohabited with Indians and with whites who lived as Indians. A writer in the whig *Gazette of the State of South Carolina* likely referred to such people when describing the later Kettle Creek loyalists as deluded by Boyd and, perhaps, a number of persons who came among them from North Carolina on a variety of pretences. David Fanning of Raeburn Creek, the famed loyalist partisan, would recruit whole regiments from those of Husband's Regulators who had remained in North Carolina.[63]

Raeburn Creek did become a center of loyalist activity.[64] Moses Kirkland, one of the major architects of the Southern Strategy, lived there when he served as a major leader among the South Carolina Regulators; prominent loyalist Richard Pearis lived nearby. The Cunningham brothers, Robert and Patrick, known to be among the king's friends, held leadership roles in this community, as did their cousin, the famous partisan William "Bloody Bill" Cunningham. On, or near, Raeburn Creek lived a James and a John Boyd, as well as Aquila Hall, James Lindley (father of Hall's son-in-law), Samuel Clegg (a likely relation to Boyd), and other men who would be important at the battle of Kettle Creek. The previously mentioned David Fanning led men from Raeburn Creek to aid the Cherokees in their frontier raids in 1776 and in attacks against the whigs along the Savannah River in 1778. (He missed the Kettle Creek campaign, however, as he was busy escaping from the jail at Ninety Six, South Carolina, where he had been confined as an enemy of the state.)[65]

Details about these people of Raeburn Creek document that they lived as a political culture outside of the mainstream, and were a prime example of an insular colonial community that remained loyalist. The residents included "white savages," white men who lived as Indians and who were feared more than anyone else by the majority of frontiersmen. During the Snow campaign, militia supporting the Revolution occupied the settlement. In a famous clash of arms, whigs seized loyalist James Lindley's fort on Raeburn Creek in July 1776 to prevent a loyalist uprising. They then successfully held off a siege by 88 Cherokees, 102 white men living as Indians, and other loyalists. Leaders in this settlement, like many of their followers, were often born in Britain or, at the least, outside the southern frontier. Historian Robert Barnwell noted that backcountry loyalism, outside of the militant Scots-Irish from Virginia, rested with Germans, Quakers, and recent immigrants. Boyd reportedly hailed from Ireland, as did William Cunningham and some of the other Raeburn Creek loyalists. Thomas Rogers, supposedly one of the some twenty men captured at Lindley's fort and nearly hanged for his role in the same, also came from Ireland. Joseph Cartwright described Aquila Hall as "one Campbell," likely a descriptive term for a tory Lowland Scotsman. By contrast, Elijah Clarke in North Carolina, John Dooly in Virginia, Andrew Pickens in South Carolina, and many other rebel leaders had spent all, or almost all, of their lives on the American frontier. (Many whig leaders also hailed from Europe, but few—if any—whole whig communities consisted largely of European immigrants.)[66]

Loyalists from settlements on Raeburn Creek, South Carolina, and from Tryon County, North Carolina, both of which had ties to the pacifist Husband's spiritual and political leadership, heard and answered the king's call. They would camp at Kettle Creek, Georgia, on February 14, 1779, en route to sympathizers in the nearby Wrightsborough, Georgia, community that also had ties to Husband. Joseph Maddock and other future leaders of that township had moved from what later became Delaware to Orange County, North Carolina, in the 1750s, but they never completely assimilated into their new meeting. In a dispute over the disowning of a certain female member, later Wrightsborough leaders risked being disowned themselves by supporting Husband's views in this matter; North Carolina Regulators met at Maddock's mill.[67]

During those troubles Maddock created the Wrightsborough community in far-off Georgia around his core following, although this isolated meeting also drew members from many colonies. He named it for the settlement's patron, royal governor James Wright. The Society of Friends (Quakers) had a deep tradition of social and political activism that inspired many of Thomas Paine's passages in his provocative *Common Sense* even though traditional Quaker principles of pacifism ruled out such extreme measures as revolution and violence in self-defense.[68] Maddock, however, quietly allowed non-Quakers to settle in his township and to erect a fort. Not holding Quaker principles of nonviolence and nonmilitarism, these other families from backcountry North Carolina provided armed defenders for the settlement. They included some of Husband's Regulators, such as Isaac Jackson. Maddock thus created an exclusive ethnic pacifist community whose radical politics could influence a significantly larger, surrounding militant population, a situation that likely mirrored what also existed at Raeburn Creek, South Carolina, and in Tryon County, North Carolina.[69]

Aside from accepting the need for sympathetic armed neighbors, the Quakers of Wrightsborough did try to coexist peacefully with the nearby Creeks. Their three town squares bore the names Maddock, McGillivray, and Galphin. Lachlan McGillivray and George Galphin likely used their considerable influence to help Wrightsborough maintain peaceful relations with the Indians. These two

British-born white men made their fortunes by trading with the Indians, and each had fathered mixed white/Creek children. (Galphin also sired children by white and slave women.) During the American Revolution the pacifist George Galphin risked his property and his life to maintain the peace, contrary to the ambitions of some Georgians, as an Indian commissioner for the Continental Congress. South Carolinians remembered that he, like later bandit Daniel McGirth, had been a "moderator," one of the backcountry leaders who sought compromise during their Regulator struggles. False rumors survived for generations that he and his racially diverse sons became bloodthirsty loyalist bandits.[70] The backcountry settlers of lesser means who feared Indian attack must have looked askance at both Galphin's lifestyle and his extensive and thriving entrepreneurial speculations in frontier land, timber, livestock, and slavery, as well as his trade with the Indians and his and McGillivray's township of emigrants from northern Ireland. He must have appeared to be trying to take over and remake the southern frontier into his own agricultural corporation with his children of various races as the middle management and on his principles of pacifism and racial harmony. McGillivray's mixed-blood son Alexander worked as an agent for the British and would become the great leader of the Creek nation. White Indian-fighting frontiersmen must have held the Wrightsborough Quakers as suspect by association for their very public acknowledgment of these prominent white men who traded with the Indians and who openly cohabited with nonwhites.[71]

The communities of Friends became centers of controversy on race in another way. With their prohibition on owning human beings, Quakers must have been a radical minority anywhere on the frontier. Wrightsborough always prohibited that institution among its meeting's members and the Bush River (Raeburn Creek) Quaker Meeting purged its membership of anyone who failed to free his or her slaves. Mainstream frontiersmen, however, saw human bondage as a means of economic advancement, and militiamen wanted captured African Americans and Indians treated as spoils of war. Up-and-coming men of means and slave owners, men such as Andrew Pickens and John Dooly, had little fear of abolitionists, although groups to end slavery in the colonies existed in Great Britain by the 1760s and a London court accepted arguments in the 1772 Somerset case that slaves had the legal right to unobstructed self-emancipation. Americans recognized the potential consequences of this decision in the British colonies; slave owners must have had concerns about the threat to slavery by opposition groups. Minority communities on the frontier also became notorious for protecting runaway slaves, especially those settlements with members of mixed races.[72]

Another settlement on Georgia's border with the Indians gained a similar reputation as a loyalist center and as a refuge for McGirth's mixed race bandit gang. It too opposed slavery in conflict with prevailing colonial society of the South. America's prewar religious enthusiasm had largely excluded emancipation but, as with society as a whole, some of the Quaker communities and other fringe elements had proven to be exceptional. Matthew Moore, likely an Irish-born member of the Scots-Irish Queensborough Township created by Galphin and McGillivray, founded one of Georgia's first Separatist Baptist congregations on Big Buckhead Creek (in today's Burke and Jenkins counties). A loyalist who would die during the war, Moore rallied his congregation for the king's cause behind the leadership of Henry Sharp, his brother-in-law and a deacon in his church. Sharp had clashed with Georgia's officials continually since his arrival from Virginia in the 1760s. His struggles preceded the American Revolution. Colonial juries found him guilty of various violations of the colony's civil law. For trading with the Indians without a license, he received a public lashing. Despite routinely conveying hundreds of acres of land to almost anyone else for little more than the asking, Governor Wright and his council turned down all of Sharp's requests for land grants, no doubt because of his reputation as a troublemaker.[73]

After 1775, when the majority of the population joined the Revolution, Sharp continued resistance against his society in general, a traditional practice in socially radical Georgia. In 1777 Moore persuaded Sharp to emancipate George Liele to minister to black Baptists. The congregation had been so inspired by this slave's preaching that they had ordained him. As the first black Baptist minister, and with the support of George Galphin, Liele would go on to form at least two congregations on the Savannah River. Georgia law, reflecting the fear of violent slave revolts, prohibited such assemblages. Rebel authorities, most likely due to his emancipation of Liele, regarded Sharp as a danger and had him imprisoned on a ship to prevent his release by court order or by his congregation. Free after (or because of) Campbell's capture of Savannah, Sharp led successful guerrilla attacks against the whigs until he suffered a mortal wound on March 30, 1779, in a battle that also took the life of Major John Spurgeon of South Carolina, the man who had tried unsuccessfully to rally the loyalists during the battle of Kettle Creek.[74]

It would hardly surprise students of the American Civil War (1861–65) and the modern civil rights struggles (1954–68) that the American Revolution in the South involved conflict between communities over race, religion, and foreign nativity. All three of the most divisive struggles in the United States would become inseparable from these same social problems because they exposed contradictions between the nation's worst realities and the widely proclaimed ideals so famously expressed in the Declaration of Independence, a document that highlights these impasses by also being the great starting point of propaganda against loyal Americans. The equality of all men and of all Americans proclaimed by Thomas Paine, Thomas Jefferson, and other founding fathers often failed to include toleration of those holding minority opinions before, during, or after the Revolution. Many of those loyalists suffered and even died for practicing those principles and at the hands of patriot neighbors who would claim to be fighting for the same rights denied them by Great Britain.[75]

The fact that loyalist communities often consisted of immigrant families of significantly different religions and/or attitudes than the much greater numbers of their American-born neighbors aided in this "Americanization" of the Revolution by changing the war from just being against a foreign occupation to including resident alien collaborators as enemies of the state. Contempt for foreign-born persons and religious prejudice became powerful tools to gain support for the revolution in the backcountry by making already suspect minority communities that failed to support the rebellion its victims. The Highland Scots of North Carolina, for example, had largely been royalists in Europe, and their American neighbors generally viewed them with suspicion. With the coming of the Revolution, this mistrust evolved into a violent civil war that culminated in the whig victory over fourteen hundred Highlanders and two hundred former North Carolina Regulators at the Battle of Moore's Creek Bridge, North Carolina, on February 27, 1776.[76] The German community of the Broad and Saluda fork in South Carolina also remained predominately loyalist. Historian Peter N. Moore has written about nearby poor, immigrant, ethnically distinct, nonslaveholding loyalists in the Waxhaws community in the Catawba Valley, on the border between North and South Carolina. This Scots-Irish "Blackjack" settlement found itself "suspect, excluded, and vulnerable." It suffered abuse from mainstream neighbors who "crushed dissent and heightened fear and hatred of difference." Like the Irish communities, some Germans, the Quakers, and the escaped slaves, the members of this settlement had been victims of intolerance elsewhere, at least as individuals, before seeking freedom and liberty on the British colonial frontier. They felt, like many members of the Wrightsborough community, compelled to go to the British army for protection, and likely some of them did so by following Boyd in 1779.[77]

5

During the American Revolution, loyalists found themselves regarded as common criminals, or relegated to an even worse status, rather than as prisoners of conscience. George Washington, later credited for his personal sacrifices that guaranteed a united nation, demanded at Yorktown that the loyalists be surrendered to civil authorities for prosecution rather than receive the status of prisoners of war.[78] At least seven men went to the gallows for their participation in the battle of Kettle Creek. Southern rebels, however, claimed that they only punished men for civil crimes committed before the war. James Cannon, a guard of the South Carolinians taken at Kettle Creek, stated that in the end his superiors only hanged the most violent offenders, including James Lindley, Samuel Clegg, and John "Rogue" Anderson. The latter may have been a notorious pre–Revolutionary War thief. Aquila Hall, another of the men executed, went to the gallows specifically on the charge of having committed a murder in North Carolina.[79] He allegedly acknowledged the justice of his sentence.[80]

Loyalists defined as "criminals" credibly fit historian Crane Brinton's definition of victims of "dual sovereignty." Each side, by claiming governmental legitimacy, could then define the actions of the other as crimes against public law and against humanity. The British first made that distinction with the arrest of Ebenezer Smith Platt, a Georgia civilian, for sedition early in the war. Under the authority of government, for example, any American could condone, as legal impressment, what his neighbors condemned as pillaging. Raeburn Creek's loyalists included active members of both North and South Carolina's Regulator rebellions, men from communities that already had seen resistance to corrupt civil authority or, at best, a provincial government that ignored brigands, as a moral and a religious cause above and beyond opposition to an unjust system. Violation of state laws that worked against traditional royal authority would thus hardly appear as criminal acts to persons openly loyal to what had been established British colonial rule of law. Escaped slaves, "white savages," and other persons could also see what others defined as "lawlessness" as necessary and excusable self-defense from an unjust society.[81]

The general population could, however, identify enough men of dubious reputations and motivations with tories to impute similar reputations to all those who supported the British. Beginning at least as early as 1739, for example, frontiersmen in the upcountry Welsh Tract community of South Carolina, had continually petitioned the colonial government to take action against the racially mixed, propertyless families in their midst. Following the opening of the new lands after the Cherokee War of 1759, South Carolina's backcountry had become a magnet for men who lived on society's fringes and outside of any law. Southerners had, for years, been labeling frontier bandits as "Scoffelites," after Joseph Coffel (or Scovel), a notorious rustler, chicken thief, and militia colonel who had opposed the South Carolina Regulators. (Patriot William Moultrie described him as a stupid, ignorant, noisy blockhead.) Friend and foe came to apply that term to all South Carolina loyalists, as well as to white men who lived as if they were Indians and to the self-emancipated African Americans. In 1778 some 350 frontiersmen, reportedly drawn from remnants of French-German Palatine settlers in South Carolina and referred to as "Scoffelites," marched to British East Florida, taking horses and whatever else they needed from farms and collecting recruits along their route.[82] During the war members of the colonial elite commanded men popularly seen as society's dregs because too few other men would enlist in the king's service. English-born gentleman Thomas Brown, for example, one of the up-and-coming men on the frontier before the war, recruited a battalion of young men from Georgia and South Carolina that he freely admitted had close associations with the white frontiersmen's traditional Indian enemies and some of whom had been identified as Scoffelites. Even British officers called Brown's men bandits. Loyalist Daniel McGirth, a member of a prominent whig family, led a mixed band of white, Indian, and black raiders who used rape as a weapon of terror. With an extensive organization that crossed political boundaries, he used voter fraud and manipulated the legal situation to pioneer true organized crime in America. In the last days of the Revolution, Georgia's restored colonial government would call on McGirth for help when no one else would come to its defense. He then used his new commission to perpetuate further robberies and violence, damaging the little respect the government had left.[83] During the American Revolution, such men

as Daniel McGirth could try to use the status of pro-British partisans—or the war
as a whole—as a cover for criminal activities. Frontiersmen could understand punishing such people as felons rather than as political dissenters. Claims that the king's
men were seizing horses, arms, supplies, and prominent frontier whig leaders,
as in the Kettle Creek campaign, compelled many men to join the militia under
Pickens and Dooly simply to protect themselves or their personal property—
outside any social, political, or military argument. Many British officers did want
to use the loyalists and Indians as instruments of terror and enforced submission,
all the more so when the majority of Americans already held these people under
suspicion and in contempt. The British major Patrick Ferguson suggested offering a confiscated rebel farm to every man who would join in such a campaign as
a means to lure to the king's cause propertyless European emigrants who made
up so much of the whig's professional military.[84]

The whigs, while calling the loyalists criminals and traitors, hypocritically
excused any of their own questionable actions in the rebellion as necessary self-
defense against the invading and occupying British army and, later, against "trai-
torous" tory bandits. They used this excuse even as they opposed the king's laws
under which they had once proudly identified themselves as dutiful subjects. The
rebels actively recruited troops of young frontiersmen without property, popularly called "Crackers," who survived by stealing cattle and hunting deer. Although
lacking discipline, by virtue of being single and having nothing to protect, they
also had little reason to desert or to fear retribution for their acts of violence
and robbery. Their descendants have come at times to remember such wholesale
killers as Robert Sallett, the "white savage" Patrick Carr, and such plunderers as
former Wrightsborough Quaker Josiah Dunn and George Dooly (John's brother)
as heroes. While John Dooly and his men risked their lives fighting for the Revolution against loyalists at the battle of Kettle Creek, whig horsemen under
Leonard Marbury robbed the families of some of those same Georgia militiamen for having, days earlier and under duress, taken an oath of allegiance to
the king.[85]

Racial prejudice, while being used as a weapon to drum up popular support
against loyalists, was often surmounted by whigs when it came to their own men.
Thomas Sumter, for example, once lived as an Indian, and he spoke fluent Cherokee. Dempsey Tyner, either an Indian, African American, dark-skinned Caucasian,
or of some mixed racial identity, and likely a relation to loyalist agent Harris Tyner,
served under Pickens repeatedly as a scout and spy, against Indians and at the battle of Kettle Creek. (Dempsey would also serve at the battle of King's Mountain
as a member of the loyalist militia.) The slave Austin Dabney would earn emancipation for his services fighting under Elijah Clarke in Augusta in 1781 or 1782.[86]

The similarities between both sides highlights that this civil war within the
Revolutionary War went beyond issues of individuals to larger movements between competitive communities; the more powerful and numerous came to seek
political independence from Great Britain, and the minorities sought to retain

the king's protection of their freedom to be different. Rachel N. Klein, William H. Nelson, and others historians argue against using such issues as race, reputation, ideology, class, background, and economics to categorize political motivations *of the individual* (emphasis mine), especially as the fortunes of war pushed many people, often reluctantly, into both camps at different times.[87] Modern sociologist Daniel J. Levinson wrote, however, that refusing to participate in the "patriotism" of the majority makes already existing "out groups" more ethnocentric and more of an anathema to the general public. A cycle begins that makes each side less willing to compromise to the point that the majority must "liquidate" the minority to prevent an undermining of the greater group's increasing and unquestioned unity of purpose, according to sociologist Arnold Mindell. (Within closed minority groups, dissension also steadily disappears in times of crisis.) Levinson described "liquidation" as subordinating and segregating, but in a civil war it could also encompass the worst of what has come to be termed "ethnic cleansing." In the American Revolution, as in the South during Reconstruction (1865–76) and in so many later conflicts, the resident opposition majority recognized that the enemy occupation forces, however powerful, have to fail if their local support disappears by means of intimidation. Animosity toward the British grew to where men who failed to join in the oppression of their loyalist neighbors could themselves become suspect and victims of the mainstream. Historian Robert M. Weir wrote that the Regulator struggle brought home to South Carolinians the fact that those leaders who failed to act against the perceived public enemy risked losing authority. Similarly whig leaders who tried to end the atrocities against the loyalists, or tried to defend them, compromised their respect and control. They could even be regarded as the enemy. Whatever reasons motivated the initial violence, retaliation followed and later still more revenge, giving all groups greater motivation to act without restraint or humanity. Historian Michael Stephenson has pointed out that colonial wars especially inspire such suppression and the executions of collaborators by their neighbors in the resistance. British historian Richard Holmes referred to the civil war element of the American Revolution as a society sinking into "fanaticarchy."[88] By the end of the Revolution, partisan murder did become so common in the Deep South that cynics called the killing of unarmed prisoners, usually men who dared to openly support the king's cause, as releasing the victim through the granting of a "Georgia parole."[89]

Whig leaders like Andrew Pickens and Tarleton Brown also refused to forgive the loyalists for being the cause, if unintended, of the British invasions and the resulting years of conflict. Men such as Andrew Jackson would go so far as to blame the tories, rather than circumstances of disease, heat stroke, or anything else, for the deaths of family members during the war. Even Americans who had preferred a return to colonial rule came to blame the presence of the king's army for inciting violence against them and their families. During the last years of the war, Brown and men like him persecuted the king's followers to the point of meeting today's definition of genocide.[90]

Many loyalists, however, wanted to live, remain in America, and save their property from theft by partisans or state confiscation. When they acted accordingly, they became something of a living eulogy for British aspirations in what had been the thirteen colonies. Their numbers included men such as the local leaders who met with Boyd at Wrightsborough in January 1779 but who ended the war actually claiming land bounties either as whig refugees who had served in other states or under the category of citizens who had peacefully remained politically neutral in Georgia after August 20, 1781. A suspicious similarity exists between the names of men on the rosters of Thomas Brown's loyalist Carolina Rangers and some of the recipients of these land certificates for Revolutionary War service or at least neutrality. (Two-thirds of the men who received bounty land grants in Georgia did so only as citizens.) William Lee returned to Georgia and became an elected local official in Augusta.[91]

Many dedicated loyalists did remain in or returned to America. Claims for property losses filed with the British government after the war provide biographical information on some of those men. Jonas Bedford, for example, a New Jersey son of English-born parents, had been wounded thirteen times as a militia officer in the French and Indian War in the 1750s. He had helped to raise a company to suppress the North Carolina Regulators in the 1760s, and he subsequently received colonial commissions as a militia officer and a justice of the peace. Refusing to take any active role in the war until 1780, when threats from bandits to burn his home caused him to abandon his wife and eight children, Bedford then joined the loyalists at King's Mountain, just before the battle, as a private and later served in John Moore's (of Kettle Creek fame) troop and in Brown's Carolina Rangers. He narrowly escaped execution by vengeful whigs during the war and would flee to Georgia, East Florida, and England. Nonetheless, in 1823 he died peacefully as a free man of property at his home in backcountry North Carolina.[92] The notorious South Carolina tory raider Daniel McGirth also found ways to remain in Georgia after the war, usually as a free man and a felon, until his death in 1804. Prominent North Carolina loyalist Colonel John Hamilton lived in Norfolk, Virginia, as a British consul from 1790 until the opening of the War of 1812. His past did not prevent important Americans such as Stephen Decatur from being his house guest and, likely as at least an acquaintance, his former nemesis in the Kettle Creek campaign, then Congressman Andrew Pickens. One loyalist community that remained in Abbeville District, South Carolina, after the war would found the New Britain community on Indian lands in Tennessee in 1806. Despite their community's past, they were led by a man named George Washington Morgan.[93]

Many loyalists, including survivors of Kettle Creek, succeeded so well at staying in the United States that they and their descendants helped in major ways to create the new country. The heritage of some of the communities that survived the American Revolution to, or almost to, the present day can be heard in places that still bear such ethnic American names as "Irish Buffalo Creek" and "Dutch Buffalo Creek" and in the varied accents spoken in Raleigh, the North Carolina

state capital that sprang up on the frontier. Ironically the descendants of those opposed to the creation of the new country would include an exceptional number
of the greatest political voices the Old North State has produced. Such families
often come to remember their Revolutionary War ancestors as rebels and patriots.
By having chosen to remain as loyal subjects to King George III until they reluctantly abandoned that cause in order to survive and by remaining in America to
build the modern United States, their forebears actually do, in a broader but more
accurate sense, count as both.[94]

6

Americans who had been denied the liberty to refuse to commit treason against
their lawful monarch committed social and political rebellion against the new
United States. They left their homes on Raeburn Creek, South Carolina, and in
Tryon County, North Carolina, to join the British army in Georgia in early 1779.
In making this effort, they demonstrated the strengths and weaknesses of determined but diverse minority communities working together in rebellion against
the majority frontier society.

Their journey actually began in 1778. That year Robert Cunningham, a leader
of the Raeburn Creek community, reported to Thomas Brown that thousands of
men in South Carolina were prepared to march to British East Florida and had
stockpiled two years' worth of corn for such a journey. Brown, a prominent
English-born planter then commanding a loyalist provincial battalion, had been
tortured in Augusta, Georgia, for rallying support against the rebellion in 1775.
He subsequently moved to St. Augustine. Now he sent his agents John York and
Harris Tyner into the backcountry to bring these thousands of men to the defense
of East Florida. York has been described as a white man who lived as an Indian
and Tyner counted as a "free person of color," that is, he was probably of mixed
European, Indian, and/or African blood. When the rebellion cut off American
trade with any British possession, troops from East Florida launched repeated
cattle-rustling raids to feed a population that had swelled with the addition of
seven thousand refugees from Georgia and the Carolinas. The whigs responded
with counterraids and invasions of their own that were encouraged by reports of
support in the province for the Revolution. Antiloyalist legislation in all of the
Deep South's new state governments further pressured at least politically neutral
frontiersmen to answer Brown's call as a minimal means of finding a refuge that
might remain in the British Empire should the United States win independence.
Partisan fighter David Fanning of Raeburn Creek first joined one group of men
led by John York at Raeburn Creek and then another with Colonel Ambrose Mills
from the Tryon County area of North Carolina, but both groups turned back in
the face of whig opposition. Another group of these backcountry loyalists, some
three hundred fifty men under John Murphy and Benjamin Gregory, succeeded
in reaching East Florida in April 1778. Friend and foe alike called them Scoffelites.
Along their route they lived off the land as bandits. The king's forces rescued them

from the island and swamp where they had sought refuge from the rebels for a week. An observer noted upon their arrival that they rode good horses, wore red bands in their hats as identification, and each carried a rifle.[95] Initially they served under Lieutenant Colonel Jacques Marcus Prévost, a Swiss officer in the British army and brother of General Prévost. Three hundred and twenty-eight of their number gave up their rags and moccasins for uniforms of green riding waistcoats trimmed in black and other more formal attire. They became a professionally drilled provincial unit of two forty-man troops of rifle dragoons and four forty-five-man companies of infantry armed with a combination of rifles and Brown Bess muskets. As the South Carolina Royalists, they were then placed under the command of their former neighbors Lieutenant Colonel Joseph Robinson and Major Evan McLaurin. The latter, a Scottish-born frontier merchant who had been serving as a quartermaster in East Florida, had secretly made return trips to the backcountry for the British.[96]

Men like Aquila Hall of Raeburn Creek (he became an ensign in the new unit) might have joined the military in hopes of, if captured, being treated as a prisoner of war instead of being prosecuted for past criminal acts. They found themselves starving with the rest of the colony's growing and increasingly hungry population. Many of them now talked of deserting and returning home to South Carolina to take their chances with their neighbors. Some of their number did desert to the enemy army that summer. Boyd, however, represented men guilty of hardly more than refusing to join in a rebellion fostered by people who already held them in deep suspicion and had been their oppressors. Instead of joining the provincials or going home, he must have left St. Augustine to find help for the loyalist settlements in the Carolina backcountry in late 1778. This loyalist traveled to British-occupied New York, a city whose capture the king's ministers had once believed would somehow win the war for them. By late 1778, it had become virtually the only safe area left for the king's soldiers, civilians, and refugees in the thirteen former colonies, but its environment had steadily deteriorated as a result of being besieged, undersupplied, and overcrowded. There Boyd found support for taking the war to the South if only because the military and civilians had become despondent for any other means of victory. By being in the right place at the right moment, he became the critical element in implementing the Southern Strategy that Moses Kirkland, his former neighbor in South Carolina, had been promoting for years on an odyssey across Revolutionary America. The ideas of Kirkland and other southern loyalist leaders to use a British invasion to spark a civilian uprising coincided with the plan for an invasion of Georgia that William Knox had urged upon Lord George Germain, secretary of state for America, in London.[97]

Returning to the South with Campbell's successful invasion force and likely among the loyalists who traveled on the ship owned by loyalist John Hamilton, Boyd only left the British army at Savannah on or after January 10, 1779. By then Campbell's men had been reinforced by troops from East Florida under General

Augustin Prévost. Ensign Aquila Hall accompanied them and now joined the mission to reach the loyalists in the backcountry. Within days and probably with the help of men from McGirth's bandits and Sharp's Big Buckhead community, Boyd proceeded as far as the quasi-Quaker community Wrightsborough, where he held a meeting on January 24 with Joseph Maddock and other prominent members of the settlement. He sought guides to lead him safely to the South Carolina frontier. They all likely knew one another from having attended meetings almost a decade earlier at Maddock's Mill in North Carolina in support of Herman Husband and his North Carolina Regulator movement. Shortly afterward and back in South Carolina, Boyd almost certainly used the services of "white Indians" and other frontiersmen from Thomas Brown's rangers to take him on the last leg of his journey, back to his home at Raeburn Creek. Sympathetic and influential neighbors, including William "Bloody Bill" Cunningham, Thomas Fletchall, Zachariah Gibbes, Christopher Neally, and John Spurgeon helped him gather men to march to Georgia. He reached further, likely through his community's connections to Herman Husband and his North Carolina Regulators, so that he finally began his march with some 700 men, including 250 to 350 North Carolinians under John Moore and Nicholas Welsh. With drums beating, fifes playing, and flags waving, the men of this hastily formed regiment secured isolated outposts such as Fort Independence and the station at Broadmouth Creek; seized personal property that they needed; and captured enemy leaders along the South Carolina Indian frontier as they moved south. In all of these actions, they could claim that they acted legally on behalf of their sovereign. Having obtained enough men to have filled the requirements of an open commission as a colonel in the provincials (like the commission given by Campbell to John Hamilton), Boyd had—in only a matter of days and with hardly more than a proclamation—put together a regiment of men from diverse communities for the king's cause and marched them through hundreds of miles of territory made hostile by whigs and by people who, beyond any politics, regarded Boyd and his followers as dangerous men and bandits.[98]

Independent settlements of social malcontents on a sparsely settled frontier could organize a regiment as they were used to defending themselves from Indians, bandits, Regulators, or whigs. They should have had greater problems coming together that quickly in a time and place when communications traveled only as fast as a horse. The proclamation declaring John Boyd, John Spurgeon, and their followers enemies of the state would, for example, be issued by South Carolina governor John Rutledge months after the loyalists had reached Kettle Creek. Boyd's success had to have depended upon networked communities of men, although of different backgrounds, ready to follow an inspiring man of their own beliefs. To identify him as the leader, however misses the point. Men like him—and Clarke, Dooly, and Pickens on the other side—become the creations of their followers, becoming messiahlike figures who served to channel the group's most important but often unrealistic expectations. Boyd became only a reflection of their own aspirations, delusions, prejudices, and misinformation. His men essentially followed their own shadow. Historian Crane Brinton wrote that such groups recruit men such as Boyd, Nat Turner, and John Brown—otherwise realistic, practical members of the community—to lead them in grand but delusional, fatalistic schemes; they become "unfettered by common sense" while they gain "enough of the prophet's fire to hold followers." Brinton summed up such leaders as being transformed by their closed groups into persons more determined, dedicated, reckless, and fanatical than the members of the community as a whole, as "Machiavellians in the service of the Beautiful and the Good."[99]

The success and failure of Boyd matches Brinton's model. Almost nothing credible about his background, including his given name, survives. Any prominence he had must have been confined to within his own closed community.[100] As a resident of the Raeburn Creek settlement, "there great Colo. Boyd," as Dooly described him, may still have been a previous acquaintance of Andrew Pickens and possibly of John Dooly, but his one moment of importance came when he convinced—and became convinced by—his like-minded neighbors to leave their families to make a perilous journey in a desperate effort to rendezvous with the British army. His belief in their cause became a legend through his alleged final words, wherein he blamed the failure of his mission only upon his being mortally wounded early in the battle. He proudly proclaimed that he died for his king and his country. Whatever his religious background, he wanted none of the devout Presbyterian Andrew Pickens's "damned rebel" prayers. Reportedly, when the colonel confronted Boyd's widow with news of her husband's death and returned her husband's watch and other personal belongings, she angrily refuted the news as a rebel lie.[101]

If the widow made such a retort, she spoke for her entire community as much as for her late husband. In such an environment, the political commitment of the women had to be as strong as the men's and, as the basis of the community, must have been as important. On the frontier, observers such as Charles Woodmason, William Mylne, and Louis Milfort described the women as the industrious base of settlement while their husbands lived like wild vagabonds. The leaving of wives and children behind to keep communities alive had deep roots. Frontiersmen, like the famous Daniel Boone of North Carolina and Kentucky, would abandon their often large families for years at a time before the Revolution. Colonial Americans, as reflected in the claims filed by loyalists and the requests for pensions by widows of whigs, such as Margaret Strozier of Kettle Creek, considered land and business as the realm of the husband while the household goods belonged to the wife in practice and in law. Each side believed, often mistakenly, that while the soldiers of the other camp might execute or imprison men, the enemy would avoid harming noncombatants and might leave alone property that supported the basis of any community, its women and children.[102]

While the dedicated can remain committed to a cause to the end, the commitment among the average members evaporates the farther they travel from their enclosed group and the more they are forced to confront reality outside the range of the dissenting voices of their community.[103] The North Carolinians under John Moore that set out to join Boyd early in the march illustrated this. They tried to raid the house of the whig colonel John Thomas. One young man, together with a household of women and small children, drove them off. Boyd's combined force failed to cross the Savannah River at Cherokee Ford when a whig lieutenant with only a handful of men, a swivel gun, a blockhouse, and sheer bluff obstructed their passage. The loyalists then had to cross the river into Georgia on rafts at the mouth of Vann's Creek (today's Van Creek). A small force of militia suffered a severe defeat while challenging that crossing. Thirteen of these whigs, including two captains, were captured; their defeat likely owed more to the jungle in which the fight took place than to the military prowess of their enemy. Boyd alleged that he had suffered about one hundred casualties in this skirmish, but the greater loss likely consisted of loyalists who had come to have serious doubts about this venture and used the confusion to slip away and return home. He still had an advantage in that most of his whig neighbors who could have stopped him had already marched to the Savannah River, opposite Augusta, to block any attempt by the British troops there to enter the backcountry. With his superior numbers, he should have been able to march quickly and successfully through any remaining opposition to Augusta by a circuitous route through Wilkes County, but delays and detours at Cherokee Ford and Vann's Creek exposed the fragility of his regiment's unity and guaranteed that he would, at the least, arrive too late to achieve his goal.[104]

The events of this uprising told and foretold much. The men who followed Boyd, voluntarily or under threat, must have noticed that at almost every step of their march armed frontier Americans, sometimes by the dozens, rose up to stop them as if pursuing a hostile Indian war party. The moment of truth about this uprising and the true nature of the support for the king's cause came to a head at swampy Kettle Creek on the morning of February 14, 1779. Boyd made his headquarters in a cowpen on or adjoining a narrow, highly defensible hilltop on the north and east side of a bend in the creek, where the path to Wrightsborough passed. This tory leader, who had traveled thousands of miles and faced innumerable obstacles, spent that last morning getting his prisoners and most of his men and horses across the flooded channels of the cane-choked creek. He allowed dissidents to leave, and he ordered the spare horses released. With the last of his followers, he waited atop present-day War Hill as the last of his men butchered a cow. They would have to join their comrades camped across the creek before marching on to find succor from the sympathetic settlers in Wrightsborough and then travel on to the British troops whom they still believed waited for them one day away. (Campbell actually had given up on Boyd and had withdrawn with his troops from Augusta only hours before.) Captain John Hamilton might have arrived with his horsemen as reinforcements. The loyalists knew that various groups of militiamen had pursued them since they had begun their march, but they apparently had ceased to care. They had skirmished with Pickens's men the evening before, but from where they now camped, they must have had ample reasons to hope for success.[105]

This moment had significance beyond anything that the men in the coming battle might have appreciated. A frontier cowpen stood at the battlefield site, one of the many facts about this campaign of at least symbolic importance. More than merely a split rail pen, a cowpen usually included cabins, riflemen armed to hunt game, and crops, and it was surrounded by a broad meadow that made any assault a dangerous proposition. It served as a small farm with the qualities of a fort. Andrew Pickens, in the first battle fought in South Carolina during the American Revolution, had successfully used such a compound as a defensive position at Ninety Six against the loyalists in 1775. As a backcountry settlement consisted of only a few buildings, at best, such places would take on special importance beyond any military value during the war. These enclosures could be used as make-shift prisons, as they would for the men in the battle of Kettle Creek. The Burke County jail, a similarly isolated log building or buildings on the Georgia frontier, and the tiny village of Ninety Six in South Carolina provide classic examples of perceived political control through occupation of the symbols of government. These places hardly existed as more than names on a map, but both sides expended considerable effort to "hold" these locations. Some cowpens, in the years after the war, would evolve into towns, such as George Galphin's famous colonial ranch that became Louisville, an early state capital of Georgia. It became a symbol of the history, progress, and potential of the frontier as it passed into the more settled world that followed.[106]

Rifles and swivel guns used that day at the battle of Kettle Creek have also been underappreciated as symbols and tools of change on the frontier. Revolutionaries traditionally need weapons "of the people" to counter the well-equipped and highly trained military of their enemy. An effective tool for use in hunting and in warfare with the Indians, the rifle democratized violence by giving America's early revolutionaries a practical means for individual action, much as the AK-47 and the improvised explosive device would do for partisans in modern wars. Although more accurate in legend than in reality, it encouraged the user to take careful aim at an individual target and thus worked effectively without requiring disciplined, drilled soldiers. It actually went against formal tactics of the time as it could not carry a bayonet, the instrument of mass terror that worked with the smoothbore musket's use of grouped, if not well-aimed, fire. British small arms and artillery had the same shortcomings in their day as tanks, helicopters, and bombers in modern times, that of being so broad and indiscriminate that they became symbols of indifferent authority and the ruthless use of power. Such tools often prove less than useless against the individual "freedom fighters" / terrorists by encouraging widespread resentment against the invader. In time the rebel veterans of Kettle Creek and their comrades proved that the rifle could win against the disciplined use of the bayonet and smoothbore musket at South Carolina battles such as Cowpens and King's Mountain. At the major battle of Blackstocks in 1780, the militiamen of Wilkes County used their ability to load while lying on the ground, described by Baika Harvey in 1775, against loyalist dragoons and the (by then) battle-experienced survivors of the Seventy-first Infantry Regiment. One man with such a weapon could have a decisive effect on a battle by killing or just breaking the will, by means of fear, of a leader such as Boyd who held his group together by personal charisma. Individual militiamen used rifles to kill Sharp, Spurgeon, Ferguson, and so many others, ending the last hope of the men who followed these tory leaders.[107] Similarly the swivel gun demonstrated a frontier commitment to the Revolution. These small wheelless cannons, used at Kettle Creek and elsewhere, were taken from ships or made in the frontier's early blacksmith shops and iron furnaces. Swivel guns had little use in combat against Indians or individual men, however they were highly effective against massed men and fortifications.[108]

At the cowpens at Kettle Creek on the morning of February 14, 1779, the very personal nature of the political, social, and ethnic conflict on this frontier war revealed itself. Ordered to check their rifles and to advance, the exhausted militiamen continued on with little more than faith in Andrew Pickens, John Dooly, and Elijah Clarke. Pickens's advance guard, however, disobeyed orders and fired at the enemy sentries, allowing Boyd personally to arrange a successful ambush of some 200 South Carolinians advancing in the main column. At the same time, Dooly and Clarke struggled to lead their 140 Georgians through the maze of channels in the swamps adjoining the creek. Three of those riflemen emerged behind the enemy lines and successfully fired on Boyd, inflicting mortal wounds. Whig militiamen then attacked from all directions, with rifles and swivel guns as the "battle" became a struggle between almost identical individuals representing different communities.[109]

The loyalists still significantly outnumbered their attackers and defended a strong position. They could easily have withdrawn from the fight intact and continued on to Wrightsborough and Augusta. Pickens and Dooly had unknowingly assaulted only the loyalists camped at the cowpens on the east side of the creek. Most of Boyd's men had settled on high ground to the south and west of the marshy waters. The loyalist captain Christopher Neally, alone, brought up 150 of his men once the fighting had begun.[110]

Boyd's regiment, however, disintegrated in the face of determined opposition. Its leader had fallen and Lieutenant Colonel John Moore of North Carolina, the second-in-command, took the opportunity to disappear as his men went in search of him. Major John Spurgeon, the third-in-command, tried to rally the men who remained, but the whig lieutenant colonel Elijah Clarke led his 50 Georgians in a successful charge against that position as Captain Richard Pollard attacked Captain James Lindley's loyalist company and captured Lindley. Dooly would marvel that he, Pickens, and Clarke survived a rain of rifle fire while leading their men on horseback from the front, although the latter did lose his horse in that charge and a Captain James Little, who had survived Cherokee Ford, Vann's Creek, and other battles of the Revolution, nearly died from his wound.[111] Upon learning of the battle of Kettle Creek later that day, the loyalists guarding the prisoners taken in the earlier fighting surrendered to their captives. Spurgeon and 270 of his men, however, would successfully escape to Wrightsborough, and from there they would be escorted to the British army by Captain John Hamilton and his horsemen. Campbell sent to Savannah for clothes for these men. Nicholas Welsh would claim that he and Moore had started with 270 men in North Carolina of whom only 90 reached the British army in Georgia. With only 20 of their comrades killed and 22 taken prisoner in the battle, the balance of the estimated 500 to 600 loyalists in the camps on Kettle Creek that morning must have chosen simply to leave and return to their homes in the Carolinas. The men who reached Archibald Campbell and the British army would be formed into the Royal South Carolina Volunteers (which subsequently became the Second Battalion of the South Carolina Royalists Regiment under Lieutenant Colonel Evan McLaurin) and into the North Carolina Royal Volunteers under Lieutenant Colonel John Moore. Both units all but ceased to exist by the summer of 1779 due to casualties and desertions. The few men who remained would have a brief moment of glory when they found themselves in the worst of the fighting at Savannah on October 9, 1779. They received no recognition for their part with the other British forces in driving off an attack by a combined American and French force, one of the largest victories of the war.[112]

Decades later Andrew Pickens wrote of Kettle Creek as "the severest check & chastisement, the tories ever received in South Carolina or Georgia."[113] That claim seems exaggerated considering the size of the defeats that John Moore and the loyalists later sustained. Pickens would be correct, however, if he meant that Kettle Creek demonstrated conclusively that the king's followers could achieve little militarily without, and sometimes even with, the regular British army. Any effective loyalist support of military value that had been on the frontier in 1775 and 1776 had almost ceased to exist by February 14, 1779.[114]

British leaders Archibald Campbell, Lord Cornwallis, and Robert Gray would leave memoirs and papers to explain why this campaign and those that followed failed for want of loyalist allies, while whigs Andrew Pickens and Tarleton Brown would write partisan reminiscences that would encourage a contempt for and misunderstanding of the Americans who did risk, or came under suspicion of having risked, their lives and property for the cause of British colonial America. A historical voice with which the loyalists could themselves explain their beliefs and actions, however, largely disappeared with their defeat to be replaced by generations of antitory propaganda and later, during the civil rights movement and the war protests of the 1960s and 1970s, by condescending views of the king's followers as merely people who held a different opinion.[115] Historians must continue to seek the story of these special rebels by studying their communities and their actions as individuals at places like Kettle Creek.

The men who lost that battle and so many others that followed had been a part of a secular movement with nonsecular roots. Their faith had been strong within their communities and had been kept alive by Boyd—while he still lived—despite tremendous difficulties of time and distance. In the end, however, hard realities persuaded them to give up and return to their homes or to find refuge elsewhere. While historians have written about the creation of communities of exiles of the king's friends after the war, the Revolution also often resulted in the destruction of many such exclusive groups in America. Historian Hugh McCall, likely one of Pickens's Kettle Creek veterans, so wrote about the end of Boyd's following: "Dispirited by the loss of their leader, and sore under the lashes of the Americans, the enemy fled from the scene of action; their army exploded, and some of the fragments fled to Florida, some to the Creek [Indian] nation, some found their way to the Cherokees, some returned to their homes and submitted to the mercy of the American government."[116]

The tory settlements that survived ceased to have any importance after the war and the withdrawal of the British. A visitor to the Raeburn Creek Quaker Meeting in 1792, for example, found it a poor congregation whose meeting house had a dirt floor. Wrightsborough gradually faded completely out of existence.[117] The British government continued its liberal policy of protecting and encouraging diverse ethnic communities in its remaining colonial possessions, including those formed by the loyalist refuges. Linda Colley has pointed out that, overall, the number of Americans who would leave the new United States for British possessions, almost all of whom qualified as members of various ethnic minorities, comes to more than five times the number of persons who abandoned France after its revolution, an example of how an empire "so often assumed now to be necessarily racist in operation and ethos, could sometimes be conspicuously poly-ethnic in quality and policy, because it had to be."[118] Among the Kettle Creek loyalists, John Hamilton, Robert Alexander, Christopher Neally, John Murphy, Zachariah Gibbes, Nicholas Welsh, William Payne, William Young, and others lived to move to distant lands and file claims with the British government for their respective property losses. William Knox, the designer of the southern loyalist strategy, lost his land in Georgia to confiscation. Most of the slaves he had transferred to Jamaica died in hurricanes. Virtually bankrupt, he replaced his deceased friend, Sir James Wright, as attorney for the loyalist claimants. After years of petitioning, he received less than half of his claim and a relatively small pension. Like the loyalists whose cause he had championed, he had long before lost his position and credibility in the British government. Despite his efforts, whatever he and his fellow "good Americans" received must have fallen far short of just compensation for their sufferings and for what they left behind.[119]

Overall, however, the white loyalists did better than did their Indian and African American allies. The British abandoned the former and most of the latter. The self-emancipated slaves left behind in the South formed isolated free communities that state militias later destroyed.[120] An estimated five thousand Georgia slaves, close to one-third of the total slave population, fled to the British army, but from all of the thirteen colonies, the king's government took only three thousand slaves to freedom, largely to Nova Scotia and, later, to Sierra Leone. They failed to prosper in the latter place, and by 1800 they had begun a series of unsuccessful rebellions against British rule, led in part by Henry Washington, one of George Washington's former slaves.[121]

The king's followers who abandoned the United States forever, or for a time, have been documented, but those Americans so alienated also included unknown numbers of embittered individuals who had supported the Revolution. Poet Adrienne Rich, in calling to all sides in the Vietnam conflict two centuries later, could also have written to survivors of America's war for political independence about how any birth is accompanied by pain: "to remember her true country, remember his suffering land: remember / that blessing and cursing are born as twins and separated at birth to meet again in mourning / that the internal emi-grant is the most *homesick* of all women and of all men / that every flag that flies today is a cry of pain."[122]

Many individuals and communities in the South had reasons to believe that their sacrifices had been wasted or, at the least, settled nothing. The Southern Strategy continued in a mutated form as part of British ambitions for the Ameri-can frontier. It finally came to an end at the Battle of New Orleans on January 8, 1815, when the often disappointed United States regulars, joined by militiamen, crackers, Choctaw Indians, freedmen, pirates, Frenchmen, and mixtures of seem-ingly every other group in the country's western lands defeated the red-coated armies of King George III one last time. This victory guaranteed the claim of the United States to the vast Louisiana Territory and West Florida. Conquering the frontier was subsumed by the ambition to extend the United States from the Atlantic to the Pacific to fulfill its "Manifest Destiny." It also called up numerous ghosts of the American Revolution. Andrew Jackson, the successful commanding general and architect of the victory, carried emotional and physical scars of the original Southern Strategy. A product of the economic, racial, and social complexi-ties of the frontier, he would become an icon of entrepreneurial and political empowerment in the West. The ideas of what came to be known as "Jacksonian democracy" would include practical innovations that have come to be greater and more successful contributions to people having control of their government and lives than the Declaration of Independence or anything called for by the Enlightenment. A week after Jackson's great victory, in the liberal frontier state of Georgia, another British army occupied St. Mary's, the home of the by-then de-ceased bandit terrorist Daniel McGirth and on the centuries-old invasion route to and from East Florida. The news that the War of 1812 had ended caused the withdrawal of these soldiers before they could continue on to attempt a repeat of Archibald Campbell's success at Savannah more than thirty-six years earlier. Great Britain and the independent United States would now move to form the very alliance that William Knox had publicly called for all of those many years earlier. This Anglo-American unity, sometimes formally acknowledged and at other times less officially carried out by policy, still continues to this day through many adventures in many lands and among very different peoples.

Notes

Kahneman quoted from an interview with John Ydstie, January 7, 2007, on the National Public Radio program *Weekend Edition Sunday.*

1. For the military events and planning of the Southern Strategy, see John Shy, "British Strategy for Pacifying the Southern Colonies, 1778–1781" in *The Southern Experience in the American Revolution,* ed. Jeffrey J. Crow and Larry E. Tise (Chapel Hill: University of North Carolina Press, 1978), 155–73, and Richard S. Dukes, "Anatomy of a Failure: British Military Policy in the Southern Campaign of the American Revolution, 1775–1781" (Ph.D. diss., University of South Carolina, 1993).

2. Robert S. Davis, "Georgia History and the American Revolution," *Georgia Social Science Journal* 10 (Spring 1979): 172–81.

3. Robert S. Davis, "Change and Remembrance: How Promoting the Kettle Creek Battlefield Went from the Means to Becoming an End in Itself," *Journal of the Georgia Association of Historians* 24 (2003): 61–79. Historian Hugh McCall gave much higher casualty figures in his 1816 history: seventy loyalists killed and seventy-five wounded, while the whigs suffered nine men killed and some twenty men wounded. The higher numbers were likely supplied by Andrew Pickens, from memory, decades after the battle. Hugh McCall, *The History of Georgia,* 2 vols. (Savannah, Ga.: Seymour & Williams, 1811–16), 2:201–3; Andrew Pickens to Henry Lee, August 28, 1811, Thomas Sumter Papers, 1 VV 107, Lyman C. Draper Collection, State Historical Society of Wisconsin, Madison (hereafter cited as the Draper Collection).

4. Quotation from *The Annual Register, or, A View of the History, Politics, and Literature for the Year 1781* (London: J. Dodsley, 1781), 83. Donald B. Chidsey used the battle of Kettle Creek to make the same point in his book *The War in the South: The Carolinas and Georgia in the American Revolution; An Informal History* (New York: Crown, 1969), 9–12.

5. Linda Colley, *Captives* (New York: Pantheon Books, 2002), 236.

6. "Colonel Robert Gray's Observations on the War in Carolina," *South Carolina Historical and Genealogical Magazine* 11 (July 1910): 153; Carole Watterson Troxler, "The Migration of Carolina and Georgia Loyalists to Nova Scotia and New Brunswick" (Ph.D. diss., University of North Carolina, 1974), 8–17; Robert M. Calhoon, *The Loyalists in Revolutionary America, 1760–1781* (New York: Harcourt Brace Jovanovich, 1973), 439, 448–57; Wallace Brown, *The Good Americans: The Loyalists in the American Revolution* (New York: Morrow, 1969), 98.

7. Baika Harvey to Thomas Baika, December 30, 1775, Orkney Island Archives, Scotland. The different versions of the petitions in support of Wright appear in Robert S. Davis, comp., *Georgia Citizens and Soldiers of the American Revolution* (Easley, S.C.: Southern Historical Press, 1979), 11–19. Harvey would have had a hard time distinguishing one group of Americans from the other. Whigs would sometimes wear white paper and the loyalists green twigs/pine knots in their hats as political identification. Thomas Young, "Memoirs of Major Thomas Young," *South Carolina Magazine of Ancestral Research* 4 (Summer 1976): 183; William Speer to John A. Speer, December 9, 1869, copy in the possession of the author. General Augustin Prévost wrote that loyalists identified themselves with either a red cross or pine twigs in their hats. Prévost talk to the Creeks, March 13, 1779, Colonial Office Papers 5/80, folio 240, National Archives of the United Kingdom, London.

8. William H. Nelson, *The American Tory* (Oxford, U.K.: Clarendon Press, 1961), 87; Brown, *The Good Americans*, 111–12, 122; Clyde R. Ferguson, "Carolina and Georgia Patriot and Loyalist Militia in Action, 1778–1783," in Crow and Tise, *The Southern Experience in the American Revolution*, 174–76.

9. Fred Anderson, *The War That Made America: A Short History of the French and Indian War* (New York: Viking, 2005), 227.

10. Quoted in Michael Stephenson, *Patriot Battles: How the War of Independence Was Fought* (New York: HarperCollins, 2007), 313–14.

11. Edward J. Cashin, *Governor Henry Ellis and the Transformation of British North America* (Athens: University of Georgia Press, 1994), 217–19; Calhoon, *The Loyalists in Revolutionary America*, 35–36.

12. Leland J. Bellot, *William Knox: The Life and Thought of an Eighteenth-Century Imperialist* (Austin: University of Texas Press, 1977), 39–40, 143–44, 155–57, 163–65.

13. Heard Robertson, *Loyalism in Revolutionary Georgia* (Atlanta: Georgia Commission for the National Bicentennial Celebration, 1978), 3, 19.

14. For a discussion of authority and society in colonial Georgia, see Andrew C. Lannen, "Liberty and Authority in Colonial Georgia, 1717–1776" (Ph.D. diss., Louisiana State University and Agricultural and Mechanical College, 2002).

15. Richard A. Ketchum, "England's Vietnam: The American Revolution," *American Heritage Magazine* 22 (June 1971): 8–9, and Ketchum, *Saratoga: Turning Point of America's Revolutionary War* (New York: H. Holt, 1997), 70–71, 80–81, 108–9, 111, 239, 252–54, 315–16.

16. Robert Harvey, *"A Few Bloody Noses": The Realities and Mythologies of the American Revolution* (Woodstock, N.Y.: Overlook Press, 2002), 81, 252–54, 315–16, 427; Nicholas Rogers, *Crowds, Culture, and Politics in Georgian Britain* (Oxford, U.K.: Clarendon Press, 1998), 152–75; Hugh Bicheno, *Rebels & Redcoats: The American Revolutionary War* (New York: HarperCollins, 2004), 255. Yorktown thus joined Saratoga, Kettle Creek, King's Mountain, Cowpens, and Guilford Courthouse on the long list of military engagements to which the loyalist strategy contributed, at least in part, to the overall defeat of the king's cause in America. Richard Holmes's remarks come from *Rebels and Redcoats,* his 2005 BBC documentary, but cannot be found in the series's companion volume by Bicheno, *Rebels & Redcoats.* For discussions of the justification of comparing the American Revolution to Vietnam, see Stephenson, *Patriot Battles,* xviii–xxi, 19, 298, and Robert M. Calhoon, *Revolutionary America: An Interpretive Overview* (New York: Harcourt Brace Jovanovich, 1976), 108.

17. Ian R. Christie and Benjamin W. Labaree, *Empire or Independence, 1760–1776: A British-American Dialogue on the Coming of the American Revolution* (New York: Norton, 1976), 4–5, 43; Stanley Weintraub, *Iron Tears: America's Battle for Freedom, Britain's Quagmire, 1775–1783* (New York: Free Press, 2005), 223–39, 242–44; Maurice R. O'Connell, *Irish Politics and Social Conflict in the Age of the American Revolution* (Philadelphia: University of Pennsylvania Press, 1965), 146, 150, 190, 394–96; Reginald Coupland, *The American Revolution and the British Empire* (New York: Russell & Russell, 1965), 85–128.

18. Lord Carlisle to Lady Carlisle, July 21, 1778, in Historical Manuscripts Commission, comp., *The Manuscripts of the Earl of Carlisle Preserved at Castle Howard* (London, 1897), 356–57. The Carroll quote comes from Ketchum, *Saratoga,* 10–11.

19. George Germain to Sir Henry Clinton, March 8, 1778, in Kenneth Gordon Davies, ed., *Documents of the American Revolution, 1770–1783*, 21 vols. (Dublin, Ire.: Irish University Press, 1973–1983), 15:58–59; Sir Henry Clinton to H. F. C. Pelham-Clinton, 2nd Duke of Newcastle, July 27, 1778, Ne C 2648, Newcastle Collection, Manuscripts and Special Collections, University of Nottingham, Nottingham, United Kingdom.

20. Robert S. Davis, "The British Invasion of Georgia," *Atlanta Historical Journal* 24 (Winter 1980): 1–8; Barnet Schecter, *The Battle for New York: The City at the Heart of the American Revolution* (New York: Walker & Company, 2002), 306–7; Stephenson, *Patriot Battles*, 67; John Fauchereau Grimké, "Journal of the Campaign to the Southward," *South Carolina Historical and Genealogical Magazine* 12 (April 1911): 63–64; Archibald Campbell, *Journal of an Expedition against the Rebels of Georgia in North America*, ed. Colin Campbell (Darien, Ga.: Ashantilly Press, 1981), x–xi, 4–7, 103n12.

21. Campbell, *Journal*, 9–10, 104n20; Davis, "The British Invasion of Georgia," 14–15; *Newcastle Journal or General Advertiser* (Newcastle-upon-Tyne, England), February 10, 1776, p. 2, col. 2; Ed Brumby, historian of the Seventy-first Regiment, to author, September 2, 2002; Stephenson, *Patriot Battles*, 328–31, 336–39. For a history of the Seventy-first Regiment, see J. Ralph Harper, *The Fraser Highlanders* (Montreal: Society of the Montreal Military & Maritime Museum, 1979).

22. William B. Willcox, *Portrait of a General: Sir Henry Clinton in the War of Independence* (New York: Knopf, 1964), 320–22; Shy, *A People Numerous and Armed*, rev. ed. (Ann Arbor: University of Michigan Press, 1990), 203–4; Paul H. Smith, *Loyalists and Redcoats: A Study in British Revolutionary Policy* (Chapel Hill: University of North Carolina Press, 1964), 93, 102, 202; R. Arthur Bowler, *Logistics and the Failure of the British Army in America, 1775–1783* (Princeton, N.J.: Princeton University Press, 1975), 245. For negative views of Clinton and his major associates, see Alexander Rose, *Washington's Spies: The Story of America's First Spy Ring* (New York: Bantam Books, 2006), 323n108; Robert S. Lambert, *South Carolina Loyalists in the American Revolution* (Columbia: University of South Carolina Press, 1987), 98–100; and the references in Thomas Jones, *History of New York during the Revolutionary War*, ed. Edward F. De Lancey, 2 vols. (New York: Printed for the New-York Historical Society, 1879).

23. Boyd was so little known that he appears in only one surviving record relating to these events before the battle at Kettle Creek, the deposition of William Millen of January 28, 1779, now in the Miscellaneous Papers, 1776–1789, War of Revolution, Military Collection, North Carolina State Archives, Raleigh. The Clinton Papers in the William L. Clements Library and those in the National Archives of the United Kingdom omit any reference to Boyd.

24. For the military events of the British invasion of Georgia, see David K. Wilson, *The Southern Strategy: Britain's Conquest of South Carolina and Georgia, 1775–1780* (Columbia: University of South Carolina Press, 2005).

25. Charles Stedman, *The History of the Origin, Progress, and Termination of the American War*, 2 vols. (Dublin, Ire.: Printed for Messrs. P. Wogan, P. Byrne, 1794), 2:119; Campbell, *Journal*, 122; McCall, *History of Georgia*, 2:192. For John Hamilton's background, see Carole Watterson Troxler, "John Hamilton" in *Dictionary of North Carolina Biography*, ed. William S. Powell, 6 vols. (Chapel Hill: University of North Carolina Press, 1979–96), 3:16–17, and Robert S. Davis, "Biography: Colonel John Hamilton of the Royal North Carolina Regiment," *Southern Campaigns of the American Revolution* 3 (May

2006): 32–34; available online at http://www.southerncampaign.org/newsletter/v3n5.pdf (accessed July 20, 2009).

26. Campbell, *Journal*, 6, 61–65, 76; *Royal Georgia Gazette* (Savannah), February 11, 1779; "Case of the Loyalists," *Political Magazine* 4 (April 1783): 266; Stephenson, *Patriot Battles*, 67–68, 130n196.

27. Campbell, *Journal*, 91–93, 99; *South Carolina & American General Gazette* (Charleston), March 11, 1779. In July 1779 John Dooly wrote to General Benjamin Lincoln from Augusta asking for medicines and two hogsheads of rum to relieve the sufferings of his men. Dooly to Lincoln, July 27, 1779, in Michael J. O'Brien, "The Doolys of Georgia," *Journal of the American Irish Historical Society* 26 (1927): facing page 178.

28. Revolutionary War pension claim of William Smith, SC S 4855, *Revolutionary War Pension and Bounty Land Warrant Application Files, 1800–1900* (National Archives microfilm M804, roll 755); Gregory Palmer, *Biographical Sketches of Loyalists of the American Revolution* (Westport, Conn.: Meckler, 1984), 918; Bicheno, *Rebels & Redcoats*, 181; Ferguson, "Carolina and Georgia Patriot and Loyalist Militia," 178–83; Robert S. Davis, *Georgians in the Revolution* (Easley, S.C.: Southern Historical Press, 1986), 13–16, 20, 108–11. For the Battle of Briar Creek, see Joshua Howard, "'Things Here Wear a Melancholy Appearance': The American Defeat at Briar Creek," *Georgia Historical Quarterly* 88 (Winter 2004): 477–98.

29. John E. Ferling, *Almost a Miracle: The American Victory in the War of Independence* (New York: Oxford University Press, 2007), 386, 416.

30. Bellot, *William Knox*, 168, 181–82; Jones, *History of New York during the Revolutionary War*, 1:290–91. For more on the possibility of Georgia remaining a part of the British Empire as part of a peace proposal, see Kenneth Coleman, *The American Revolution in Georgia* (Athens: University of Georgia Press, 1958), 144, 167.

31. Bellot, *William Knox*, 168; Nelson, *The American Tory*, 91–92.

32. Weintraub, *Iron Tears*, 240–41; Robert D. Bass, *The Green Dragoon: The Lives of Banastre Tarleton and Mary Robinson* (New York: Holt, 1957), 118–24, 445, and Bass, *Gamecock: The Life and Campaigns of General Thomas Sumter* (New York: Holt, Rinehart and Winston, 1961), 103–11; Ferling, *Almost a Miracle*, 415–28, 435–443, 468–75.

33. Robert S. Davis, "The Invisible Soldiers: The Georgia Militia at the Siege of Savannah," *Atlanta Historical Journal* 25 (Winter 1991): 32, 60n27; Davis, "Lord Montagu's Mission to Charleston in 1781: American POWs for the King's Cause in Jamaica," *South Carolina Historical Magazine* 84 (April 1983): 92, 94; Franklin and Mary Wickwire, *Cornwallis: The American Adventure* (Boston: Houghton Mifflin, 1970), 221; Weintraub, *Iron Tears*, 277; Bicheno, *Rebels & Redcoats*, 232; "Character of Lord Rawdon, character of Lieut. Col. Doyle &c.," Georgia Papers, Chambers Collection, New York Public Library.

34. Adrienne Rich, "An Atlas of the Difficult World," in *An Atlas of the Difficult World: Poems, 1988–1991* (New York: W. W. Norton, 1991), sect. 11, p. 23.

35. Davis, *Georgians in the Revolution*, 103–4; Dorothy Jeter Barnum and George Ely Russell, "James Johnson alias Ingram: A Southern Odyssey," *National Genealogical Society Quarterly* 76 (March 1988): 8–9.

36. Stephenson, *Patriot Battles*, 55–62; Davis, *Georgians in the Revolution*, 24n49; Bellot, *William Knox*, 142, 144; Shy, *A People Numerous and Armed*, 186–90. That the king's auditors hounded Campbell and, after his death, his heirs for years over such accounts and his claim to pay as a brigadier general resulted in his writing and his family keeping his memoir of the Georgia campaign. Campbell, *Journal*, 87, 103n12.

37. Willcox, *Portrait of a General,* 321; Dukes, "Anatomy of a Failure," 169–71, 295–99; Lambert, *South Carolina Loyalists,* 90, 98–103.

38. Richard Holmes's remarks come from his 2005 BBC documentary, *Rebels and Redcoats.*

39. Davis, *Georgians in the Revolution,* 215, 224; Samuel Kelly, *Samuel Kelly, an Eighteenth Century Seaman,* ed. Crosbie Garstin (New York: Frederick A. Stokes Company, 1925), 51.

40. Campbell went on to a highly successful career in Jamaica and India. Robert S. Davis, "Portrait of a Governor," *Atlanta Historical Journal* 26 (Spring 1982): 45–48.

41. For the issues of the French and Indian War, see Anderson, *The War That Made America.*

42. Gordon Burns Smith, *Morningstars of Liberty: The Revolutionary War in Georgia, 1775–1783* (Milledgeville, Ga.: Boyd Publishing, 2006), 183–84.

43. For the history of the North Carolina Regulators, see Marjoleine Kars, *Breaking Loose Together: The Regulator Rebellion in Pre-Revolutionary North Carolina* (Chapel Hill: University of North Carolina Press, 2002).

44. For the history of the South Carolina Regulators, see Richard Maxwell Brown, *The South Carolina Regulators* (Cambridge, Mass.: Belknap Press of Harvard University Press, 1963).

45. Martha F. Franklin, "The Quaker Settlement of Wrightsborough" (master's thesis, Georgia Southern College, 1984), 30; Rachel N. Klein, *Unification of a Slave State: The Rise of the Planter Class in the South Carolina Backcountry, 1760–1808* (Chapel Hill: University of North Carolina Press, 1990), 95.

46. Jack P. Greene, "Independence, Improvement and Authority: Toward a Framework for Understanding the Histories of the Southern Backcountry during the Era of the American Revolution," in *An Uncivil War: The Southern Backcountry during the American Revolution,* ed. Ronald Hoffman, Thad W. Tate, and Peter J. Albert (Charlottesville: University Press of Virginia, 1985), 17–20. For a general discussion of frontier social conflict in the colonial period, see Eric Hinderaker and Peter C. Mancall, *At the Edge of Empire: The Backcountry in British North America* (Baltimore: Johns Hopkins University Press, 2003), and William R. Nester, *The Frontier War for American Independence* (Mechanicsburg, Pa.: Stackpole Books, 2004).

47. For the Dooly family, see chapter 13. For examples of other such families, see Robert W. Ramsey, *Carolina Cradle: Settlement of the Northwest Carolina Frontier, 1747–1762* (Chapel Hill: University of North Carolina Press, 1964). Members of the Maverick family could stand as representatives for thousands of such families. They had been fighting in that struggle since the earliest days of the Massachusetts Bay Colony to the extent that by the time the family had crossed the continent, they had given their name as "a synonym for independent eccentricity in America." David H. Ficher, *Albion's Seed: Four British Folkways in America* (New York: Oxford University Press, 1989), 785.

48. Brian Crozier, *A Theory of Conflict* (New York: Scribe, 1975), 104.

49. Brown, *The Good Americans,* 96, 126–46; Rachel N. Klein, "Frontier Planters and the American Revolution: The South Carolina Backcountry, 1775–1782," in Hoffman et al., *An Uncivil War,* 40–50.

50. Jesse Hogan Motes III and Margaret Peckham Motes, comps., *Laurens and Newberry Counties South Carolina: Saluda and Little Rivers Settlements, 1749–1775* (Greenville, S.C.: Southern Historical Press, 1994), 13–22.

51. Alex M. Hitz, "The Earliest Settlements in Wilkes County," *Georgia Historical Quarterly* 40 (Winter 1956): 260–80; Robert S. Davis, *Thomas Ansley and the American Revolution in Georgia* (Red Springs, N.C.: Ansley Reunion Press, 1981), 11–12; Louise Frederick Hays, comp., "Indian Depredations 1787–1825," five volumes of unpublished typescripts (Works Projects Administration, 1939), Georgia Archives, Morrow, 2: 749–50, 758–62, 963–65; Andrew Williamson to James Bowie, October 14, 1778, James Bowie Papers, New York Public Library; Robert S. Davis, "George Galphin and the Creek Congress of 1777," *Proceedings and Papers of the Georgia Association of Historians* 3 (1982): 23.

52. For an in-depth study of these tactics, see John Grenier, *The First Way of War: American War Making on the Frontier, 1607–1814* (Cambridge: Cambridge University Press, 2005).

53. For biographical information on Clarke, Dooly, and Pickens, see Richard L. Blanco, ed., *The American Revolution, 1775–1783: An Encyclopedia* (New York: Garland, 1993), 322–24, 480–81, 1299–1300.

54. See Margaret E. Newell, *From Dependency to Independence: Economic Revolution in Colonial New England* (Ithaca, N.Y.: Cornell University Press, 1998).

55. Eliza Bowen, *Chronicles of Wilkes County, Georgia,* ed. Mary B. Warren (Danielsville, Ga.: Heritage Papers, 1978), 148–49; George Howe, *History of the Presbyterian Church in South Carolina,* 2 vols. (Columbia, S.C.: Duffie & Chapman, 1870), 1:659.

56. E. Merton Coulter, "Elijah Clarke's Foreign Intrigues and the 'Trans-Oconee Republic,'" *Mississippi Valley Historical Review* 10 (extra number, November 1921): 260–79.

57. Arthur Dobbs, "A Scheme to Increase the Colonies and Commerce of Britain," Cholmondeley Houghton 84, pp. 18–19, Ms No. 68, University Libraries, Cambridge, England.

58. Robert M. Weir, *Colonial South Carolina: A History* (Millwood, N.Y.: KTO Press, 1983), 111–12, 208–9, and Weir, *"The Last of American Freemen": Studies in the Political Culture of the Colonial and Revolutionary South* (Macon, Ga.: Mercer University Press, 1986), 118; Franklin, "The Quaker Settlement of Wrightsborough," 25; Harvey, "A Few Bloody Noses," 6; Edward J. Cashin, *Lachlan McGillivray, Indian Trader* (Athens: University of Georgia Press, 1992), 235.

59. Robert M. Calhoon, *The Loyalist Perception and Other Essays* (Columbia: University of South Carolina Press, 1989), 11; Brown, *The Good Americans,* 46. For the diversity of the backcountry, see David Colin Cross, Steven D. Smith, Martha A. Zierden, and Richard D. Brooks, eds., *The Southern Colonial Backcountry: Interdisciplinary Perspectives on Frontier Community* (Knoxville: University of Tennessee Press, 1998); Robert W. Ramsey, *Carolina Cradle;* and George Lloyd Johnson, Jr., *The Frontier in the Colonial South: South Carolina Backcountry, 1736–1800* (Westport, Conn.: Greenwood Press, 1997).

60. Robert V. Hine, *Community on the American Frontier: Separate but Not Alone* (Norman: University of Oklahoma Press, 1980), 176–78; "Tories," *Atlanta Southern Confederacy,* June 28, 1862.

61. During his long life, Husband would continually stir up rebellions that he avoided physically participating in due to his pacifist principles. As an exile from the South, Husband would support the American Revolution, but he opposed the United States Constitution and he helped to organize the Whiskey Rebellion. See Mark H. Jones, "Herman Husband: Millenarian, Carolina Regulator, and Whiskey Rebel" (Ph.D. diss., Northern Illinois University, 1982).

62. Kars, *Breaking Loose Together,* 135; Robert S. Davis, *Quaker Records in Georgia: Wrightsborough, 1772–1793, Friendsborough, 1775–1777* (Augusta, Ga.: Augusta Genealogical Society, 1986), 15. For examples of political loyalties and other attitudes about religion in the frontier Welsh Tract area of South Carolina, see Johnson, *The Frontier in the Colonial South,* 130. The whigs, however, had an effective Quaker spy among these communities, Adam Reep. "Adam Reep: A Hero of the Revolution," *Atlanta Constitution,* January 24, 1898.

63. Mary E. Lazenby, *Herman Husband, a Story of His Life* (Washington, D.C.: Old Neighborhoods Press, 1940), 121; Leah Townsend, *South Carolina Baptists, 1670–1805* (Florence, S.C.: Florence Printing Company, 1935), 166–67; Seth B. Hinshaw and Mary Edith Hinshaw, *Carolina Quakers: Our Heritage, Our Hope* (Greensboro, N.C.: privately printed, 1972), 19; George W. Paschal, *History of North Carolina Baptists,* 2 vols. (Raleigh: The General Board, North Carolina Baptist State Convention, 1930–55), 1:392; Jones, "Herman Husband," 83–91, 94, 101–6, 110–11; Klein, "Frontier Planters," 51–67; *Gazette of the State of South Carolina* (Charleston), April 14, 1779. The history of the Bush River meeting can be found in Willard Heiss, *Quakers in the South Carolina Backcountry* (Indianapolis: Indiana Quaker Records, 1969).

64. Robert W. Barnwell, "Loyalism in South Carolina, 1765–1785" (Ph.D. diss., Duke University, 1941), 128, 131. Archibald Campbell remembered Boyd as bringing his loyalists from Red Creek, South Carolina. Campbell, *Journal,* 58. No such place exists in the upcountry but, in Campbell's native Gaelic, "Red Creek" would be "Raeburn," the name of a waterway in present day Laurens County, South Carolina. For the early settlers of today's Rabon Creek (also Raburns, Raeburn, Rayborn, and Reborns Creek), see the COM Index to land grants at the South Carolina Department of Archives and History, Columbia. The name first appears with John Turk's request for land in 1753. Turk, formerly of Augusta County, Virginia, had been living there as early as 1749. No records have been found that support the claim that it received its name from an early settler named "Ray Burns." Motes and Motes, *Laurens and Newberry Counties,* 5, 233; [no title], *Names in South Carolina* 27 (Winter 1971): 8. For some of the lists of loyalists that include men from Raeburn Creek, see: "List of Prisoners, Ninety Six Jail, 1779," *South Carolina Magazine of Ancestral Research* 5 (Fall 1977): 195–98; "Tories Murdered in the South Carolina Upcountry in the Revolution," *South Carolina Magazine of Ancestral Research* 9 (Summer 1981): 123–27; Peter Wilson Coldham, *American Migrations, 1765–1799* (Baltimore: Genealogical Publishing Company, 2000), 655; *Gazette of the State of South Carolina,* December 24, 1779; Murtie June Clark, *Loyalists in the Southern Campaign,* 3 vols. (Baltimore: Genealogical Publishing Company, 1979), 3:412–18; Bobby G. Moss, *Roster of the Loyalists in the Battle of Kings Mountain* (Blacksburg, S.C.: Scotia-Hibernia, 1998) and Moss, *Roster of the Loyalists in the Siege of Fort Ninety Six* (Blacksburg, S.C.: Scotia-Hibernia, 1999).

65. Lambert, *South Carolina Loyalists,* 51, 53, 71; Barnwell, "Loyalism in South Carolina," 129; Clyde R. Ferguson, "General Andrew Pickens" (Ph.D. diss., Duke University, 1960), 18; Troxler, "The Migration of Carolina and Georgia Loyalists," 242–43; Brown, *The South Carolina Regulators,* 128–29; Revolutionary War pension claim of John Brown, SC S17848, *Revolutionary War Pension and Bounty Land Warrant Application Files, 1800–1900* (National Archives microfilm M804, roll 370); David Fanning, *The Narrative of Col. David Fanning,* ed. Lindley S. Butler (Davidson, N.C.: Briarpatch Press, 1981), 4–5, 19; John Hairr, *Colonel David Fanning: The Adventures of a Carolina Loyalist* (Erwin,

N.C.: Averasboro Press, 2000), 16, 54. Boyd reportedly came from the area that became Newberry County, near Raeburn Creek. Francis Pickens to J. H. Marshal, May 12, 1858, Thomas Sumter Papers, 16 VV 356, Draper Collection. Robert O. DeMond wrote that Boyd came from the Lower Yadkin Valley of Anson County, North Carolina. Surviving records fail to support that claim although Mordecai Miller, in his 1832 Revolutionary War pension claim, stated that Boyd and Moore came from Lincoln County, North Carolina, a fact true of Moore but likely a misunderstanding with regard to Boyd. Robert O. DeMond, *The Loyalists in North Carolina during the Revolution* (Durham, N.C.: Duke University Press, 1940), 105; Revolutionary War pension claim of Mordecai Miller, SC S 16972, *Revolutionary War Pension and Bounty Land Warrant Application Files, 1800–1900* (National Archives Microfilm M804, roll 1729).

66. Lambert, *South Carolina Loyalists*, 51–53, 71; "Col. David Fanning," unidentified newspaper clipping in the possession of Linda Roholt of Bellevue, Washington, D.C.; Barnwell, "Loyalism in South Carolina," 141–42; Palmer, *Biographical Sketches of Loyalists*, 742; deposition of Joseph Cartwright, September 1, 1779, North Carolina Papers, 1 KK 108, Draper Collection; Brown, *The Good Americans*, 46–47. Thomas Rogers may have meant that he was in the attack on Lindley's fort and later was also among the some twenty loyalists captured at the battle of Kettle Creek, of which five of the South Carolinians went to the gallows. Rogers wrote that two or three of the men [eventually?] captured after the battle at Lindsey's fort were hanged. Barnwell, "Loyalism in South Carolina," 166–67.

67. Minutes of the Cane Creek Monthly Meeting (1760–1900), 29–30, 32–33, 38–39, 47, Friends Historical Collection, Hege Library, Guilford College, Greensboro, N.C.; Jones, "Herman Husband," 84–88, 104–5, 107, 110, 116–18.

68. Rose, *Washington's Spies*, 156–58.

69. Davis, *Quaker Records*, 157–67; John Guy Jackson, Jr., *My Search for John Stephen Jackson: His Ancestors and His Descendants* (Greenville, S.C.: Southern Historical Press, 2006), 7-1 through 7-4.

70. Davis, *Quaker Records*, 26; Cashin, *Lachlan McGillivray*, 72, 235; "George Galphin," *Jacksonville* (Alabama) *Republican*, June 1, 1852, p. 2, col. 3–4; Alick Cornels to Creek Headmen, June 14, 1793, in Louise F. Hays, ed., "Creek Indian Letters, Talks, and Treaties" (typescript, Atlanta: Georgia Department of Archives and History, 1939), pt. 1, p. 323; Davis, "George Galphin and the Creek Congress of 1777," 14–16, 24–25. Early Creek historian Thomas Woodward wrote of Galphin that "of the five varieties of the human family; he raised children from three, and no doubt would have gone the whole hog, but the Malay and the Mongol were out of his reach." Thomas Woodward, *Woodward's Reminiscences of the Creek, or Muscogee Indians* (Montgomery, Ala.: Berrett & Wimbish, 1859), 91–92.

71. For the ambiguous views held by southern frontiersmen about the Indians, see Joshua Piker, "Colonists and Creeks: Rethinking the Pre-Revolutionary Southern Backcountry," *Journal of Southern History* 70 (August 2004): 503–40, and for the background of the whites who traded with the Indians of the southern frontier, see Amos J. Wright, *The McGillivray and McIntosh Traders on the Old Southwest Frontier, 1716–1815* (Montgomery, Ala.: NewSouth Books, 2001), and Theresa M. Hicks and Wes Taukchiray, *South Carolina Indians, Indian Traders, and Other Ethnic Connections: Beginning in 1670* (Spartanburg, S.C.: The Reprint Company, 1998). Alexander McGillivray is covered in Melissa A. Stock, "Sovereign or Suzerain: Alexander McGillivray's Argument for Creek

Independence after the Treaty of Paris of 1783," *Georgia Historical Quarterly* 92 (Summer 2008): 149–76.

72. Klein, "Frontier Planters," 67–68; Alfred W. Blumrosen, *Slave Nation: How Slavery United the Colonies and Sparked the American Revolution* (Naperville, Ill.: Sourcebooks, 2005), 1–17, 24, 142; Stephen B. Weeks, *Southern Quakers and Slavery: A Study in Institutional History* (Baltimore: Johns Hopkins Press, 1896), 180–81; John B. O'Neall and John A. Chapman, *The Annals of Newberry* (Newberry, S.C.: Aull & Houseal, 1892), 33; Franklin, "The Quaker Settlement of Wrightsborough," 23; Johnson, *The Frontier in the Colonial South*, 121. For issues of slavery, see Robert Olwell, *Masters, Slaves & Subjects: The Culture of Power in the South Carolina Low Country, 1740–1790* (Ithaca, N.Y.: Cornell University Press, 1998).

73. Mary Louise Clifford, *From Slavery to Freetown: Black Loyalists after the American Revolution* (Jefferson, N.C.: McFarland, 1999), 17; Davis, *Georgians in the Revolution*, 108–11. The origins of Matthew Moore's Big Buckhead Creek Baptists and any ties that they had to Herman Husband and the Separatist Baptists of the Regulators remain undiscovered.

74. Robert S. Davis, "The Other Side of the Coin: Georgia Baptists Who Fought for the King," *Viewpoints in Georgia Baptist History* 7 (1980): 47–58; Allen D. Candler, comp., *The Colonial Records of the State of Georgia*, 39 vols. (Atlanta, 1907–41), 10:697; 11:85; Elizabeth Evans Kilbourne, *Savannah, Georgia, Newspaper Clippings (Georgia Gazette)*, 5 vols. (Savannah, Ga.: privately printed, 1999–2003), 1:226–27, 380; Loris D. Cofer, *Queensborough: Or, The Irish Town and Its Citizens* (Louisville, Ga.: privately printed, 1977), 56. White attitudes concerning slavery find discussion in W. Robert Higgins, "The Ambivalence of Freedom: Whites, Blacks, and the Coming of the American Revolution in the South," in *The Revolutionary War in the South: Power, Conflict, and Leadership: Essays in Honor of John Richard Alden*, ed, W. Robert Higgins (Durham, N.C.: Duke University Press, 1979), 43–63. Biographical information on John Spurgeon appears in Coldham, *American Migrations*, 656, and Davis, *Georgians in the Revolution*, 110–11, 117n74.

75. For the Declaration of Independence as a propaganda tool, see Carl L. Becker, *The Declaration of Independence: A Study in the History of Political Ideas* (New York: Harcourt, Brace, 1922).

76. Lambert, *South Carolina Loyalists*, 48–49; Wayne E. Lee, *Crowds and Soldiers in Revolutionary North Carolina: The Culture of Violence in Riot and War* (Gainesville: University Press of Florida, 2001), 171; Calhoon, *The Loyalists in Revolutionary America*, 439–46; A. Roger Ekirch, "Whig Authority and Public Order in Backcountry North Carolina," in Hoffman et al., *An Uncivil War*, 99–106. Bobby G. Moss identifies many of the loyalists at Moore's Creek Bridge in *Roster of Loyalists at the Battle of Moore's Creek Bridge* (Blacksburg, S.C.: Scotia-Hibernia, 1992). Many of these Scotsmen must have been among the 1,400 men who eventually served in John Hamilton's Royal North Carolina Regiment.

77. Klein, "Frontier Planters," 46; Peter N. Moore, "This World of Toil and Strife: Land, Labor, and the Making of an American Community, 1750–1805" (Ph.D. diss., University of Georgia, 2001), 59–61, 112–14, 132, 137.

78. Daniel J. Levinson, "The Study of Ethnocentric Ideology," in T. W. Adorno et al., *The Authoritarian Personality* (New York: Harper, 1950), 146–47, 150; Wickwire and Wickwire, *Cornwallis*, 386.

79. Robert S. Davis, "The Loyalist Trials at Ninety Six in 1779," *South Carolina Historical Magazine* 80 (April 1979): 172–81; "Colonel David Fanning," unidentified newspaper clipping in the possession of Linda Roholt of Bellevue, Washington; Davis, *Georgians in the American Revolution,* 16; Motes and Motes, *Laurens and Newberry Counties,* 6–7, 17–19; claim of James Cannon, SC S 32166, *Revolutionary War Pension and Bounty Land Warrant Application Files, 1800–1900* (National Archives Microfilm M804, roll 464); Brown, *The South Carolina Regulators,* 29, 36–37. In August 1779 nine men were sentenced to die for treason in Wilkes County; seven received reprieves. The records do not indicate if these men were connected with the battle of Kettle Creek. Allen D. Candler, comp., *The Revolutionary Records of the State of Georgia,* 3 vols. (Atlanta, 1908), 2: 177–79; Grace G. Davidson, comp., *Early Records of Georgia Wilkes County,* 2 vols. (Macon, Ga.: J. W. Burke Company, 1933), 2:2–12. For the officially sanctioned hangings of loyalists in South Carolina, see Barnwell, "Loyalism in South Carolina," 166–73.

80. According to legend, Aquila Hall betrayed a fort to the Indians, resulting in the deaths of the families inside. This story may be a garbled account of the attack by the loyalists and Cherokees upon Lindley's fort in 1775. During the march to Kettle Creek, Hall made threats to coerce reluctant neighbors to join Boyd's band. He apparently fell into rebel hands after reaching the British army and returning to his provincial commission of ensign in the South Carolina Royalists. Deposition of Samuel Beckham et al., June 1, 1812, Joseph Bevan Collection, Georgia Historical Society Library, Savannah; deposition of Joseph Cartwright, September 1, 1779, North Carolina Papers, 1 KK 108, Draper Collection; Clark, *Loyalists,* 3:415; McCall, *History of Georgia,* 2:205. That Hall may have been hanged for his part in the attack on Lindley's fort is supported by a statement by Thomas Rogers that two or three men were [eventually?] hanged for their role in that battle and by a 1769 deed that mentions John Anderson and cites Aquila Hall as a witness and James Lindley, a justice of the peace, as the notary, showing that these three men, later hanged after being captured at Kettle Creek, knew each other before the war. Barnwell, "Loyalism in South Carolina," 166–67; Motes and Motes, *Laurens and Newberry Counties,* 167.

81. Crane Brinton, *The Anatomy of Revolution,* rev. and expanded ed. (New York: Vintage, 1965), 133–34, 161–67; Robert S. Davis, "A Georgian and a New Country: Ebenezer Platt's Imprisonment in Newgate for Treason in 'The Year of the Hangman,' 1777," *Georgia Historical Quarterly* 64 (Spring 2000): 106–15; Nancy Gentile Ford, *Issues of War and Peace* (Westport, Conn.: Greenwood Press, 2002), 21.

82. Klein, *Unification of a Slave State,* 73; Klein, "Frontier Planters," 55–59; Smith, *Morningstars of Liberty,* 103–4; Barnwell, "Loyalism in South Carolina," 137.

83. Johnson, *The Frontier in the Colonial South,* 115, 121; Gordon Burns Smith, *History of the Georgia Militia, 1783–1861,* 5 vols. (Milledgeville, Ga.: Boyd Publishing, 2000), 3:84–90; Edward J. Cashin, *The King's Ranger: Thomas Brown and the American Revolution on the Southern Frontier* (Athens: University of Georgia Press, 1989), 48–49, 98; Campbell, *Journal,* 48; McCall, *History of Georgia,* 2:192, 202–3; Klein, "Frontier Planters," 60–66.

84. John Shy, *A People Numerous and Armed,* 187; Charles Woodmason, *The Carolina Backcountry on the Eve of the Revolution: The Journal and Other Writings of Charles Woodmason, Anglican Itinerant,* ed. Richard J. Hooker (Chapel Hill: University of North Carolina Press, 1953), 181, 207–8, 242; Nelson, *The American Tory,* 7; Calhoon, *The Loyalists*

in Revolutionary America, 453–54; Troxler, "The Migration of Carolina and Georgia Loyalists," 9; Davis, *Georgians in the Revolution,* 113–14.

85. Smith, *History of the Georgia Militia,* 4:68n5, 103; Leslie Hall, *Land & Allegiance in Revolutionary Georgia* (Athens: University of Georgia Press, 2001), 153; Davis, "The Invisible Soldiers," 25–26; Campbell, *Journal,* 127n183. The molested Georgians had previously taken oaths before Captain John Hamilton, the British representative, before escaping to join Colonel John Dooly just before the battle of Kettle Creek. Dooly to Samuel Elbert, February 16, 1779, Miscellaneous Manuscripts Collection, Manuscripts Division, Library of Congress.

86. Robert S. Davis, "The Mysteries of Tyner, Tennessee," *Chattanooga Regional Historical Journal* 9 (July 2006): 33–44; Blanco, *The American Revolution,* 127. Popular legend credited Dabney with earning his freedom as a substitute for his master at the battle of Kettle Creek.

87. M. Scott Peck, *The Different Drum: Community-Making and Peace* (New York: Simon and Schuster, 1987), 70–73; Brinton, *The Anatomy of Revolution,* 190–97.

88. Jerome J. Nadelhaft, *The Disorders of War: The Revolution in South Carolina* (Orono: University of Maine at Orono Press, 1981), 51, 55–60; Arnold Mindell, *Sitting in the Fire: Large Group Transformation Using Conflict and Diversity* (Portland, Ore.: Lao Tse Press, 1995), 21–23, 33, 228; Levinson, "The Study of Ethnocentric Ideology," 107, 146–47, 150; Weir, *"The Last of American Freemen,"* 148–49; Stephenson, *Patriot Battles,* 19; Klein, "Frontier Planters," 87; Lambert, *South Carolina Loyalists,* 296–98. The Richard Holmes quote comes from the 2005 BBC documentary *Rebels and Redcoats.*

89. Robert S. Davis, "A Georgia Loyalist's Perspective of the American Revolution," *Georgia Historical Quarterly* 81 (Spring 1997): 119, 119n3, 138.

90. Edmund S. Morgan, *The Genuine Article: A Historian Looks at Early America* (New York: W. W. Norton, 2004), 147–49; Tarleton Brown, *Memoirs of Tarleton Brown* (1862; repr., Barnwell, S.C.: Barnwell County Museum and Historical Board, 1999), 9–10; Robert M. Weir, "'The Violent Spirit': The Reestablishment of Order, and the Continuity of Leadership in Post-Revolutionary South Carolina," in Hoffman et al., *An Uncivil War,* 72–91.

91. Alex M. Hitz, "Georgia Bounty Land Grants," *Georgia Historical Quarterly* 38 (September 1954): 337–38, 341; Davis, *Georgians in the Revolution,* 215. Owen Fluker represents a relevant example of this type of frontiersman. He fought at Kettle Creek under Dooly, likely to protect his nearby farm. The state of Georgia took no legal action against him as a loyalist but did allow him a land grant for peacefully remaining in Georgia during the last eleven months of the war. After his death an informant prevented his heirs from receiving a grant of land in Georgia's land lotteries for his Revolutionary War service on the grounds that Fluker had been a "tory." Like hundreds of his neighbors, he had probably only been compelled to serve in the restored colonial militia. Bowen, *Chronicles of Wilkes County,* 19; Robert S. Davis, *The Georgia Black Book: Morbid, Macabre, and Sometimes Disgusting Records of Genealogical Value* (Greenville, S.C.; Southern Historical Press, 1982), 42.

92. Carolyn Murphree Backstrom, "Mercy Raymond Bedford of North Carolina, Patriot," *Mayflower Quarterly* 44 (August 1978): 80–82; Wallace Brown, *The King's Friends: The Composition and Motives of the American Loyalist Claimants* (Providence, R.I.: Brown University Press, 1965), 103–4; Davis, *Georgians in the Revolution,* 40; Palmer, *Biographical Sketches of Loyalists,* 57. Curiously the lives of Jonas Bedford, Richard Pearis, and

other southern loyalists could have been the model for the fictional whig Benjamin Martin in *The Patriot*, a motion picture made in 2000 that ignored the conflicts between Americans in the South to blame atrocities in the Revolutionary War solely upon the occupying British army.

93. Calhoon, *The Loyalist Perception*, 195–210; Bettye J. Broyles, *History of Rhea County, Tennessee* (Dayton, Tenn.: Rhea County Historical and Genealogical Society, 1991), 327.

94. For examples of the lives made by frontier loyalists, see Lambert, *South Carolina Loyalists*, 71.

95. Wilbur H. Siebert, *Loyalists in East Florida, 1774 to 1785*, 2 vols. (Deland: Florida State Historical Society, 1929), 2:349; Siebert, *East Florida as a Refuge of Southern Loyalists, 1774–1785* (Worcester, Mass.: American Antiquarian Society, 1928), 10–11; Lambert, *South Carolina Loyalists*, 70–72; Klein, *Unification of a Slave State*, 95; Smith, *Morningstars of Liberty*, 103–4; Cashin, *The King's Ranger*, 75; S. D. H——u to ?, January 16, 1779, in William L. Stone, comp., *Letters of Brunswick and Hessian Officers during the American Revolution* (Albany, N.Y.: J. Munsell's Sons, 1891), 238. The historian Heard Robertson found no evidence that Joseph Coffel had anything to do with this 1778 march of loyalists. He believed that they received the name "Scoffelites" simply as an inflammatory and derogatory term for any backcountry bandits much as the word "tory" (from the Irish words for "pursued" and "bandit") came to be a negative descriptive for any loyalist. Heard Robertson, unpublished biography of Thomas Brown, chap. 6, p. 13, in the possession of Thomas H. Robertson of Augusta.

96. S. D. H——u to ?, January 16, 1779, in Stone, *Letters of Brunswick and Hessian Officers*, 238; Martha Condray Searcy, *The Georgia-Florida Contest in the American Revolution, 1776–1778* (University: University of Alabama Press, 1985), 132, 248n34; Barnwell, "Loyalism in South Carolina," 185–87, 321; Palmer, *Biographical Sketches of Loyalists*, 564; Clark, *Loyalists in the Southern Campaign*, 1:48; Walter B. Edgar, *Partisans and Redcoats: The Southern Conflict That Turned the Tide of the American Revolution* (New York: Morrow, 2001), 72–73.

97. Grimké, "Journal of the Campaign to the Southward," 65, 130, 191. For Moses Kirkland's role in promoting the Southern Strategy, see Cashin, *The King's Ranger*, and for the situation in New York, see Schecter, *The Battle for New York*.

98. Davis, *Georgians in the Revolution*, 13–17; Davis, *Quaker Records*, 61; Palmer, *Biographical Sketches of Loyalists*, 918; David Schenck, *North Carolina 1780–'81* (Raleigh, N.C. Edwards & Broughton, 1889), 52–53; Memorial of John Hamilton, Audit Office Papers A. O. 13/119/421, National Archives of the United Kingdom, Kew.

99. Clark, *Loyalists*, 3: 431; *South Carolina and American General Gazette*, November 19, 1779; Brinton, *The Anatomy of Revolution*, 157–58.

100. William Millen swore that he met with a loyalist leader, representing Archibald Campbell, named James Boyd in Wrightsborough. William Millen deposition, January 28, 1779. Zachariah Gibbes, however, would identify his leader at Kettle Creek as Colonel John Boyd. A John Boyd appeared on a 1779 list of South Carolina loyalist outlaws that also included John Spurgeon, Boyd's major at Kettle Creek. Coldham, *American Migrations*, 656, 689; Clark, *Loyalists*, 3:431. Millen or Gibbes may have been mistaken, although both a John and a James Boyd lived on Raeburn Creek. A James Boyd settled on the South Carolina frontier by 1744 and a James Boyd left a will in 1784 wherein he bequeathed his Raeburn Creek plantation to his son Samuel; a John Boyd petitioned for

land in that area in 1753. National Society of the Colonial Dames, comp., *The Register Book for the Parish Prince Frederick Winyaw* (Baltimore: Williams & Wilkins, 1916), 51, 95–96, 98; Willie Pauline Young, comp., *Abstracts of Old Ninety Six & Abbeville Districts Wills & Bonds* (1950; repr., Greenville, S.C.: Southern Historical Press, 1977), 33. If two Boyds participated in the Kettle Creek campaign, a John Boyd who served as a colonel and a James Boyd (a father or older brother of John who was allowed to remain in South Carolina after the American Revolution?), then William Millen would have been correct in stating that he met James Boyd at Wrightsborough, where James would have been likely trying to influence old friends, and Zachariah Gibbes would also be right in stating that the loyalists had John Boyd as their commander.

101. Davis, *Georgians in the Revolution*, 11, 13, 20, 57n3; Francis Pickens to J. H. Marshal, May 12, 1858, Thomas Sumter Papers, 16 VV 356, Draper Collection; Motes and Motes, *Laurens and Newberry Counties*, 259; Robert S. Davis and Kenneth H. Thomas, *Kettle Creek: The Battle of the Cane Brakes* (Atlanta: Georgia Dept. of Natural Resources, Historic Preservation Section, 1975), 60. Moses Kirkland, formerly of Raeburn Creek, attempted a similar mission to the British headquarters in Boston in 1775, but the whigs intercepted him at sea. Calhoon, *The Loyalists in Revolutionary America*, 456. No record appears in Archibald Campbell's accounts of his advancing Boyd any funds although passing mentions of this loyalist emissary appear in Campbell's memoirs.

102. Mary Beth Norton, "Eighteenth-Century American Women in Peace and War: The Case of the Loyalists," *William and Mary Quarterly*, 3rd ser., 33 (July 1976): 396, 398; Cynthia A. Kierner, *Southern Women in Revolution, 1776–1800* (Columbia: University of South Carolina Press, 1998), xxv. Examples of loyalists leaving their families for the safety of the British lines can be found in Davis, *Georgians in the Revolution*, 94, 224, and Davis, *Georgia Citizens and Soldiers*, 80, 167. For a description of the typical backcountry family, see Woodmason, *The Carolina Backcountry*, 39; and for women of the backcountry, see Kierner, *Southern Women in Revolution*.

103. Blanco, *The American Revolution*, 480–81; M. Scott Peck, *The Different Drum*, 70–73; Brinton, *The Anatomy of Revolution*, 190–97.

104. Davis, *Georgians in the Revolution*, 13–16.

105. Davis, "The British Invasion of Georgia," 11; Campbell, *Journal*, 59–60; Memorial of John Hamilton, Audit Office Papers A. O. 13/119/421, National Archives of the United Kingdom, Kew.

106. John H. Logan, *A History of the Upper Country of South Carolina: From the Earliest Periods to the Close of the War of Independence*, 2 vols. (Charleston, S.C.: S. G. Courtenay & Company, 1859), 1:152–53; John Bartram, "Diary of a Journey through the Carolinas, Georgia, and Florida," ed. Francis Harper, in *Transactions of the American Philosophical Society*, new ser., 38 (1942), pt. 1, p. 26; Ferguson, "General Andrew Pickens," 24–26; Davis, "The Loyalist Trials at Ninety Six in 1779," 174, and Davis, *Georgians in the Revolution*, 97–118, 139, 161–62. For Ninety Six, South Carolina, see Marvin Cann, *Old Ninety Six in the South Carolina Backcountry, 1700–1781* (Troy, S.C.: Sleepy Creek Publishing, 1996); Robert K. Dunkerly and Erik K. Williams, *Old Ninety Six: A History and Guide* (Charleston, S.C.: History Press, 2006); and Robert D. Bass, *Ninety Six: The Struggle for the Back Country* (Lexington, S.C.: Sandlapper, 1978). For more on cowpens, see Richard D. Brooks, Mark D. Groover, and Samuel C. Smith, *Living on the Edge: The Archaeology of Cattle Raisers in the South Carolina Backcountry* (Columbia, S.C.: Savannah River Archaeological Research Program, 2000).

107. Lilla M. Hawes, comp., "The Papers of James Jackson, 1781–1793," *Georgia Historical Society Collections* 11 (Savannah, 1955), 17–18; Lyman C. Draper, *King's Mountain and Its Heroes: History of the Battle of King's Mountain, October 7th, 1780, and the Events Which Led to It* (Cincinnati: P. G. Thomson, 1881), 252–54, 258, 272, 314. The same account in Thomas U. P. Charlton, *The Life of Major General James Jackson* (Augusta, Ga.: Printed by G. F. Randolph, 1809), 21, has the men from Wilkes County using their reloading ability at the battle of Cowpens. The rifle and the smoothbore musket/bayonet in the American Revolution are discussed in Henry Lumpkin, *From Savannah to Yorktown: The American Revolution in the South* (Columbia: University of South Carolina Press, 1981), 135–42.

108. William Lake found a cannon ball, likely from a swivel gun, at the Kettle Creek battlefield. He donated it to a World War II scrap-metal drive. Davis and Thomas, *Kettle Creek*, 53. For a technical description of a swivel gun, see Stephenie Ambrose Tubbs and Clay Straus Jenkinson, *The Lewis and Clark Companion: An Encyclopedic Guide to the Voyage of Discovery* (New York: Henry Holt, 2003), 287.

109. Moore, "This World of Toil and Strife," 136.

110. Davis, *Georgians in the Revolution*, 13–19.

111. John Dooly to Elbert, February 16, 1779, Misc. Mss. 174, Yale University Libraries, New Haven; Pickens to Lee, August 28, 1811, Thomas Sumter Papers, 1 VV 107, Draper Collection. The effect of the rifle was partially countered by the skill of some of the era's surgeons. Captain Little survived Kettle Creek and other battles and lived to see 1807. Francis Carlisle and John Harris of Pickens's command received severe wounds in the battle of Kettle Creek but would live to be old men. Harris had a bullet in his skull that passed through his eye. They, and others, owed their lives to the surgical skills of a Thomas (?) Langdon. In a war that cost the lives of 25 percent of its wounded, Langdon's surgery appears extraordinary. Davis, *Georgians in the Revolution*, 23, 23n43; Stephenson, *Patriot Battles*, 162–64; Bobby G. Moss, *Roster of South Carolina Patriots of the American Revolution* (Baltimore: Genealogical Publishing Company, 1985), 552.

112. Davis, *Georgians in the Revolution*, 20. Evan McLaurin eventually gave up his commission as his battalion faded out of existence in 1780. He died in Charleston in July 1782 while trying to raise another loyalist corps. Barnwell, "Loyalism in South Carolina," 322–25; Palmer, *Biographical Sketches of Loyalists*, 564.

113. Pickens to Lee, August 18, 1811, Thomas Sumter Papers, 1 VV pp. 107[1]–107[7], Draper Collection.

114. For another discussion of numbers, community, and loyalties, see Carole W. Troxler, *Pyle's Defeat: Deception at the Racepath* (Graham, N.C.: Alamance County Historical Association, 2001). John Moore would go on to lead units that served without distinction in the loyalist defeats at Ramsour's Mill, King's Mountain, and Hammond's Store before whigs finally captured and hanged him in 1783. Draper, *King's Mountain*, 298.

115. Morgan, *The Genuine Article*, 147–55; Tarleton Brown, *Memoirs of Tarleton Brown* (1862; repr., Barnwell, S.C.: Barnwell County Museum and Historical Board, 1999), 9–10; Robert M. Weir, "'The Violent Spirit': The Reestablishment of Order, and the Continuity of Leadership in Post-Revolutionary South Carolina," in Hoffman et al., *An Uncivil War*, 72–91; Davis, "A Georgia Loyalist's Perspective," 119, 119n3, 138; Wickwire and Wickwire, *Cornwallis*, 386. Summaries of traditional views of southern loyalists appear

in Draper, *King's Mountain,* 75, 238–42, and James Potter Collins, *A Revolutionary Soldier* (Clinton, La.: Feliciana Democrat, 1859), 23.

116. Brinton, *The Anatomy of Revolution,* 190–97; McCall, *History of Georgia,* 2:203. Henry Williams's journeys represent the broad travels of these loyalists. He survived the defeat at Moore's Creek, North Carolina, near his home to move, with his brothers, to Wilkes County, Georgia. When the British overran much of the South in 1780, he stayed in his new home and became a major in Colonel Waters's loyalist militia regiment before Waters's defeat at Hammond's Store, South Carolina. After the war he too went into exile. Troxler, "The Migration of Carolina and Georgia Loyalists," 5–6, 236.

117. Thomas Scattergood, *Journal of the Life and Religious Labors of Thomas Scattergood* (Philadelphia: C. Gilpin, 1874), 103–4; Pearl Baker, *The Story of Wrightsboro* (Thomson, Ga.: The Foundation, 1965), chap. 9 [unpaginated].

118. Colley, *Captives,* 236.

119. Bellot, *William Knox,* 185–205. Robert DeMond in *The Loyalists in North Carolina during the American Revolution,* 59–60, argued for identifying members of the loyalist communities by comparing property confiscation documents to other sources such as contemporary land records. Loyalist confiscation records have appeared in print in R. J. Taylor, Jr., Foundation, *An Index to Georgia Colonial Conveyances and Confiscated Lands Records* (Atlanta: R. J. Taylor, Jr., Foundation, 1981), and Albert B. Pruitt, *Abstracts of Sales of Confiscated Loyalists' Land and Property in North Carolina* (n.p., 1989).

120. Olwell, *Masters, Slaves, and Subjects,* 277–79; Lambert, *South Carolina Loyalists,* 259–85; Davis, *Georgians in the Revolution,* 40; Coldham, *American Migrations,* 674, 683, 720, 751; Palmer, *Biographical Sketches of Loyalists,* 196, 312, 639, 644, 676, 957; Blanco, *The American Revolution,* 126–28; Davis, *Georgia Citizens and Soldiers,* 32.

121. Clifford, *From Slavery to Freetown,* 59, 192–210; Simon Schama, *Rough Crossings: Britain, the Slaves, and the American Revolution* (New York: Ecco, 2006), 97, 124–25, 257–422. For more on former slaves in America, Nova Scotia, and Sierra Leone, see Cassandra Pybus, *Epic Journeys: Runaway Slaves of the American Revolution and Their Global Quest for Liberty* (Boston: Beacon Press, 2006). African American minister George Liele did escape to Jamaica, as a servant of Raeburn Creek loyalist Moses Kirkland. While reestablishing his ministry on that island, Liele even worked for Governor Archibald Campbell, the conqueror of Georgia who had given a provincial commission to Henry Sharp, Liele's rebellious former master. Liele kept Sharp's bloody glove as a memento. Davis, *Georgians in the Revolution,* 109–11.

122. Rich, "An Atlas of the Difficult World," sect. 11, p. 23.

Thirteen

The Man Who Would Have Been

John Dooly, Ambition, and Politics on the Southern Frontier

ROBERT S. DAVIS

Early in the twentieth century, Georgia historian Otis Ashmore wrote that "of the many heroic men who illustrated that stormy period of the Revolution in Georgia that 'tried men's souls' none deserves a more grateful remembrance by posterity than Col. John Dooly."[1] Ashmore's subsequent entry, however, failed to meet that need because, before the bicentennial of the American Revolution, almost all of the source material on Colonel John Dooly and Georgia's other Revolutionary War figures, patriot and loyalist, came from Hugh McCall's partly autobiographical *The History of Georgia* (1811–16). Collectively what McCall wrote about the colonel formed a heroic tale of a martyred battlefield leader and patriot in the struggle for American independence who lost a brother in an Indian attack, led his forces to victory over the tories at the battle of Kettle Creek, and, finally, died as a martyr to the American cause in his own home.[2] Hugh McCall gave literature its first Georgia folk hero but within a simplistic context that remains in the popular mind today, wherein all supporters of the Revolution (the rebels, whigs, or patriots) appear as heroes and all of the war's American opponents (the loyalists or tories) as villains.[3]

Dooly's story, however, would rise above such lore as described by historian Hugh Bicheno as "propaganda not merely triumphing over historical substance, but virtually obliterating it."[4] Research on the American Revolution since Ashmore's time has moved from examining only the major military events of that war to looking at the world in which the conflict occurred and to a more sophisticated appreciation of its personalities. Dooly's life, for example, illustrates how Dooly and his neighbors of all political persuasions had been moving for greater control of their frontier world in a struggle that occurred before, during, and after the American Revolution. He emerges in that context as a man of motives and actions more complex than McCall's simplistic although basically accurate account. When other "great white fathers" of the Revolution too often still appear only as icons, a reappraisal of John Dooly's historical persona provides important insights into his times. He comes across in the records now as obsessively ambitious, even opportunistic, in a world undergoing tremendous change and as a man who lost literally everything he had gambling on a future as fraught with risks as with potential.[5]

John Dooly's role in those events began with his father, Patrick. Everything known about Patrick Dooly's life parallels that of the archetypical southern Scots-Irish frontiersman portrayed in works such as David Hackett Fischer's *Albion's Seed: Four British Folkways in America* and James Webb's *Born Fighting: How the Scots-Irish Shaped America*.[6] Likely a native Irishman, he appears in Frederick County, Virginia, records as early as 1755. Patrick moved to the South Carolina frontier sometime between August 2, 1764, and July 2, 1765, according to land grant records, likely in search of unclaimed land to develop for sale to later settlers and to find security from conflicts with the Indians. Subsequent deeds show that he had a wife named Anne and that he could at least sign his name.[7] A few years later John Dooly traveled the hundreds of miles from the Ninety Six District on the western frontier to Charleston, the seat of government in South Carolina, to go through the legal formalities to settle his father's insignificant estate. The probate records prove that both Patrick and Anne had died by December 6, 1768, because on that date John received all of his father's property as the nearest male relative under the laws of primogeniture then in effect. The household inventory listed a slave woman, a female slave child, books, household goods, and the remains of a small wheelwright, or blacksmithing, operation. John sold off the estate's only other asset, Patrick's last tracts of land. Other records document that Patrick had four other sons and, at least, one daughter who lived to adulthood.[8]

The implied age of John's own oldest known son, also named John, suggests that John Sr. married in about 1765 although he does not appear in the surviving public records until June 2, 1767, when he first applies for a grant. Those dates imply that he was born in 1746. Patrick and John Dooly would share an interest in land development but, as proved true more often with later leaders of the Revolution than with its opponents, the father and son would follow significantly different lives, the latter with ambitions beyond the comfortable status quo of what would later be called a Jeffersonian small farmer.[9] By means unknown, John acquired an education and, on February 3, 1768, secured a commission as deputy surveyor. The colony of South Carolina employed him in 1771, probably as a participant in the expedition to help the colony's surveyor, Ephraim Mitchell, locate and mark the boundary with North Carolina. Within a few years Dooly became a merchant and a land developer successful far beyond anything his father had achieved.[10] John married Dianna Mitchell, who was probably related to the many Mitchells who were South Carolina surveyors, including deputy surveyors John and Thomas Mitchell. The latter also became the first husband of John Dooly's sister Elizabeth. John and Dianna Dooly's growing family eventually included at least two sons, John Mitchell and Thomas, and a daughter, Susannah. By 1773 John Sr. had made his brothers Thomas and George his protégés, with Thomas also becoming a deputy surveyor.[11]

General descriptions of the lives of such backcountry people as the Doolys survive but often suffer from being highly prejudiced. English-born Charles Woodmason, for example, described the people of the southern frontier as living lives little different than those of their open-range livestock. In 1774 Scotsman William Mylne wrote less passionately. He lived alone in the woods on a rented farm on Steven's Creek, in South Carolina (near Dooly-owned land) but also close to Augusta. Mylne's house consisted of a sixteen-by-twenty-foot enclosure made from stacked pine logs and covered with a clapboard roof. When not keeping snakes and the resident cat from eating his chickens, he subsisted by hunting and fishing. His stout and well-made male neighbors lived off the wilderness Indian-style and by following their livestock, while the women planted a wide variety of grains, vegetables, and fruits as well as doing the spinning and weaving. Mylne wrote of how the colorfully dressed and largely Baptist backcountry people raised tobacco that they took to distant cities, such as Charleston and Savannah, to sell. The tobacco leaves would be shipped on to Europe and then returned for purchase by the original growers as snuff. Frontier people could barter for goods from local merchants like John Dooly, but they found the prices in such stores to be too high.[12]

The appearance of Separatist Baptists, a new Protestant religion that Anglican minister Charles Woodmason regarded with great disdain, on the southern frontier represented one of many important changes on the frontier. Sanders Walker, one of the appraisers of Patrick Dooly's estate, had been a Baptist minister in South Carolina since 1767. He and his fellow locally ordained clergymen created their own revolution, filling a long-standing need for ministers in the backcountry that traditional faiths had failed to meet because they required a long process of formal ordination. Religious leadership has always played a significant role in social political movements of all types. The Church of England's Reverend Woodmason, for example, would help to lead the South Carolina Regulators. The highly emotional style of Baptist ministers such as Walker would allow the Baptists simultaneously to gain strength from and to feed the political fervor in both camps during the American Revolution, as well as to continue to flourish regardless of which side won.[13]

The South Carolina Regulator rebellion that broke out in the late 1760s, almost literally at John Dooly's door in the Ninety Six settlement, serves as an even greater example of what historian Jack P. Greene described as the people of the southern frontier desiring "improvement" in the form of courthouses, schools, towns, and an environment conducive to trade and investment. Thousands of frontiersmen participated in the Regulator rebellion, a political and social movement to demand from South Carolina's government (what historian Hugh Bicheno termed the "Tidewater Rats" and "wealthy coastal slavocrats" with a "pseudo-aristocratic social structure") the right to the rule of law in the backcountry. Woodmason denounced what he viewed as a morally uninhibited culture in frontier South Carolina, but he also saw the growth of its population as dynamic (he claimed that ninety-four out of every one hundred brides in ceremonies he performed were obviously pregnant) and observed that its economy grew as fast. Its struggle became an economic revolution as opportunities grew so fast so as to outstrip any limitations placed on them. Historian Margaret E. Newell would claim this same type of change in New England, from dependency to independence, caused the American Revolution.[14]

The name Dooly, like the names of thousands of the participants in the South Carolina Regulator rebellion, appears in none of the surviving records, including the list of pardons granted to 120 of the movement's leaders. Being a merchant, land speculator, and surveyor, however, he benefited in many ways from the success of the Regulators, as did the millers and blacksmiths who assumed leadership roles in the backcountry. Civil affairs on the South Carolina frontier had been so confused that Dooly's father, Patrick, once received a grant of land that appears in various colonial records as being in three different counties, none of which had a courthouse or any other form of local government. Previously John Dooly had to travel the hundreds of miles to Charleston to file or answer court suits. In 1771, for example, he had to go to the provincial capital to defend himself in a suit over a debt based on a document to which his name had been crudely forged in 1769. In another instance, Dooly took William Thomson to court over debts due for a long list of trade goods in 1771. The latter apparently finally paid up with land. Soon after, however, Thomson filed a civil suit for damages against Dooly for having "beat bruise wound & evilly entreat him so that his life was greatly despaired" with "swords & staves." Dooly countered that Thomson had repeatedly threatened his life. Such incidents proved that further progress on the frontier, for him and other ambitious men of the new and growing middle class of the backcountry, required meaningful civil government.[15]

John Dooly's own opportunity to take a public leadership role came later and in Georgia. In January 1772, after the peace and security of the new courts brought about a rise in property values on the South Carolina frontier, he mortgaged 2,050 acres of his lands to Charles Pinckney, a prominent Charlestonian. With his new capital, Dooly could finance a major investment. Four months later he petitioned to secure land across the Savannah River in St. Paul Parish near Augusta, on the then western frontier of colonial Georgia, but as a resident of South Carolina. He also obtained a commission as a Georgia deputy surveyor and had by then acquired seven slaves.[16] Dooly shortly afterward abandoned these beginnings for another prospect. George Galphin and other Georgia and South Carolina traders had tried to compel the Cherokee Indians to trade a large tract of land to pay for growing debts allegedly owed to them. In 1773 the royal governor of Georgia, James Wright, preempted this plan and persuaded the Creek and Cherokee nations jointly to give up what he named the "Ceded Lands," some 1.5 million acres that would greatly expand the northwest border of St. Paul Parish. The Indians received a cancellation of their debts, which Wright intended to pay by selling the new lands, a plan that benefited from the British government at the same time ending all of the free headright land grants in America. The additional territory, in theory, would significantly add to Georgia's colonial population and militia numbers by being limited exclusively to one-hundred-acre tracts sold only to non-Georgians with the means to afford the land. Ceded Lands sales would also finance a company of rangers, who would serve as a form of civil protection from bandits, an inducement that settlers familiar with the pre-Regulator days of South Carolina would particularly appreciate.[17]

Families did arrive from other colonies but rules and restrictions gave way to land speculation, as usually happens in such situations. Some Georgia residents, such as Martin Jollie and Thomas Waters, now claimed other provinces as their homes. To improve disappointing land sales, legal technicalities were found so that the amount of land allowed to each claimant increased dramatically, and essentially unlimited acreage could go to a single person through the purchase of the recorded claims of other individuals. Britons, such as the Englishman Thomas Brown and the Scotsman William Manson, brought whole settlements of their countrymen to the area as indentured servants and, as did Governor Wright and members of his council, claimed large tracts of land, under special circumstances, in fringe territory that might have been considered within the old provincial boundaries, but which had been largely abandoned to the Indians years before. As Wright and the other large entrepreneurs, Georgia residents or otherwise, paid for these lands—lands that would benefit from their proximity to the adjoining Ceded Lands—they technically sidestepped the ban on headright land grants. However, what they paid also went to the colonial treasury, failing to pay directly for any of the costs of the new territory.[18]

In the new Ceded Lands, John Dooly built a cabin on Fishing Creek, which he later abandoned, before claiming 500 acres that included an island and the 200 acres of "Lee's Old Place," also called Leesburg, at the mouth of Soap Creek on the Savannah River. Thomas Lee of South Carolina had obtained a warrant of survey for this land on the indeterminate edge of what was the Georgia Indian frontier in 1759, but he had never obtained a formal grant. Overall, Dooly, now identifying himself as a resident of South Carolina, would make payments on two tracts of 250 acres each and would purchase William Campbell's claim for another 250 acres. Dooly, like most of his neighbors, borrowed money from Lieutenant Thomas Waters of the rangers to make the initial payment on his acquisitions. He also obtained loans from Savannah merchants to pay for further improvements, and he may have raised still more funds by selling three of his slaves.[19] Dooly thus set out to create a plantation similar to the much larger venture begun by Waters, his new neighbor on the Savannah River. Thomas Waters, a native Englishman, had been a resident of Georgia and South Carolina since at least 1760, when he had worked for a previous company of rangers as a quartermaster.[20]

This opening of the Ceded Lands came during, and became part of, a transitional period in local government on the Georgia frontier that, like the Regulator rebellion, predated the American Revolution. Naturalist William Bartram passed through the area at the time, twice, and would write a description of it that reads like a biblical prophecy of its coming troubles:

> The day's progress was agreeably entertaining, from the novelty and variety of objects and views; the wild country now almost depopulated, vast forests, expansive plains and detached groves; then chains of hills whose gravelly, dry, barren summits present detached piles of rocks, which delude and flatter the hopes and expectations of the solitary traveller, full sure of hospitable habitations; heaps of white, gnawed bones of the ancient buffaloe, elk and deer, indiscriminately mixed with those of men, half grown over with moss, altogether exhibit scenes of uncultivated nature, on reflection, perhaps, rather disagreeable to a mind of delicate feelings and sensibility, since some of these objects recognize past transactions and events, perhaps not altogether reconcilable to justice and humanity.[21]

In 1768 Governor James Wright avoided the troubles of the South Carolina frontier by siding with the backcountry people in a successful political campaign to have the colonial assembly establish courts at Augusta and at Halifax. Georgia's backcountry also had, for several years, sent representatives, such as Leonard Claiborne and Edward Barnard, men who lived on the frontier and had fortunes tied to its future, to the colonial assembly. When raiding parties of disaffected Creeks protested the loss of the Ceded Lands in 1773–74 by attacking settlements there and defeating the St. Paul's Parish militia, Wright negotiated with Emistisiguo, a pro-British Indian leader, to end the crisis. The Creek headman bluntly complained of how Indian agent John Stuart, Governor Wright, and other British leaders used him to act against the best interests of his people, but he had also risen to power from humble beginnings because of British support. Wright had even commissioned him as commander and head warrior of the Creeks on September 6, 1768. Emistisiguo reciprocated by giving the king's officials a lifetime commitment of loyalty—and made good on it, even to the extent of arranging for the assassinations of the leaders of the raids on the Ceded Lands settlements and of other Creeks.[22]

The backcountry people of Georgia repaid the now Sir James Wright for his support later in 1774. In the face of the largely coastal opposition to British policies, a delegation from the frontier that included Dooly tried to present Georgia's provincial congress with a letter protesting the increasingly public political discontent that was growing in the colony. These backcountry men argued that Georgia had no connection with troubles over taxation, tea, or Boston and that the province depended upon the king's protection from the neighboring tribes of Indians. Representatives of the growing whig movement, meeting at Tondee's tavern in the province's capital of Savannah, refused to receive the delegation. As a result, John Dooly, Elijah Clarke, George Wells, Barnard Heard, and many others who would later become whig leaders joined hundreds of their neighbors in exercising their rights as Englishmen to sign and publish petitions in support of British rule in the colony's newspaper, the *Georgia Gazette*.[23]

Future circumstances would prove that the frontiersmen acted, as their protest implied, primarily out of their own interests.[24] As John Dooly and his neighbors knew from the colonial gazettes, while the British army could shoot Americans in Massachusetts, it could not be found on the frontier protecting them from the Indians.[25] The whigs also had much to offer to the frontiersmen, starting with local control of their own affairs. John Dooly already served as a colonel, with Stephen Heard as lieutenant colonel, and Barnard Heard as major in a vigilante militia created by him and his neighbors.[26] The rebels in Georgia divided the province into districts, in this instance, each with a justice of the peace court, political committee, and a militia company. John Dooly served as captain of his local company, with his brother Thomas as a first lieutenant. The former also obtained the positions of justice of the peace and deputy surveyor; and he likely served on his local Chatham District's political committee. While held as a prisoner, before fleeing to British warships on February 11, 1776, Georgia colonial governor Sir James Wright saw how support for the rebellion had shifted. He suffered the indignity of the "western" riflemen who guarded him firing into his house and endangering his family. As those same ships threatened Savannah, Dooly marched his company for four days from the Ceded Lands to reach the threatened town to serve on behalf of the rebels, at least for pay.[27] Sixty of his neighbors under Jacob Coleson also marched to South Carolina to help in putting down a counterrevolution by the supporters of the king. In response to Cherokee raids during the summer of 1776, Dooly and his company, as part of an expedition under Major Samuel Jack, destroyed two villages. Virginia and both of the Carolinas contributed thousands of men to simultaneous campaigns that wrecked that Indian nation. Jack's force, however, demonstrated that even Georgia, with its comparatively small population, could provide a effort uniting the southern frontiersmen, whig and loyalist.[28]

Only the dependency upon the British government for protection from the Indians remained to hold the backcountry to the king's cause by 1776, and even that issue faded away as men who followed leaders such as John Dooly proved capable of protecting themselves against enemies whom they came to believe, rightly or wrongly, the king's agents encouraged. Far from being a mob, the men of the backcountry had decades of experience in military organization and discipline. Even Patrick Dooly in Virginia in the 1760s had been a member of the militia. Andrew Pickens, John Dooly's later ally, had served in the French and Indian War alongside British regulars whose cruelty he found appalling. A surviving record shows that Pickens later kept careful accounts, as public property, of items captured in the battle of Kettle Creek in 1779. A formal morning report of Dooly's militia regiment in that same year shows that it had a sophisticated organization that included quartermasters, musicians, boatmen, blacksmiths, cow drivers, butchers, wagon masters, and deputy commissaries. Even his later subordinate, the illiterate Lieutenant Colonel Elijah Clarke, had his routine orders placed in writing.[29]

These militia commanders, however, depended upon more than organization and experience. Men committed to a cause had to believe in their leaders. Kinsmen of Colonel Benjamin Few of Richmond County, in writing about him, described the kind of charisma that these leaders, whig and loyalist, must have possessed to keep their followers together:

> Benjamin the eldest was bred to the farm, he was in person about 5 feet 10 inches in height, stout, & a muscular and powerful man, bold, bluff, kind-hearted, and magnanimous tempered . . . but Uncle Ben (our family appellation) fell into the Soldier's habits, was frolicsome & bolstering and often drank too much inebriating liquor—Still he was one of the most popular men who ever bore the name—his Soldiers almost idolized him.[30]

In February 1779, however, an unknown Georgian offered another opinion of this same Benjamin Few and his men:

> A villainous tribe of plunderers, under the celebrated horse thief Captain Few finding their cause desperate, have left the Georgians a lasting impression of rebellious authority, by ravaging the country for 30 miles above Augusta, without regard for age or sex, the widow or the orphan cries. Not satisfied with rapine they have dragged forth the peaceable inhabitants like slaves to war, and worse than the heathen savages of the wilderness, murdered in cold blood a Mr. ——— who refused to join them in their infamy.[31]

Captain Few, however, represented more than just the men who in another age would have been called "warlords." His father had posted a bond to help Herman Husband, the leader of the North Carolina's Regulators, and colonial officials hanged his brother James for participating in the same frontier resistance. A younger sibling, William, would rise so far above his backcountry origins that he would go from being a major under Benjamin to signing the United States Constitution for Georgia and becoming one of the founders of the United States Senate.[32]

The whigs recognized the ambitions of such men in ways that the British government failed to understand, and they would work to win over and support leaders like the Fews with money, munitions, commissions, and salt. In 1778, and during the years that followed, Dooly and his neighbors, as a project of the Revolution, erected a string of forts to provide protection from Indian attack. Absalom Chappell remembered the extensive efforts made by the backcountry people to build defenses:

> By their own voluntary labor the people of each neighborhood, when numerous enough, built what was dignified as a fort, a strong wooden stockade or blockhouse, entrenched, loop-holed, and surmounted with look-outs at the angles. Within this rude extemporized fortress ground enough was enclosed to allow room for huts or tents for the surrounding families when they should take refuge therein—a thing which continually occurred; and,

indeed, it was often the case, that the fort became a permanent home for |the women and children, while the men spent days in scouring the country, and tilling with their slaves, lands within convenient reach; at night betaking themselves to the stronghold for the society and protection of their families, as well as for their own safety.[33]

These forts provided only temporary refuge, however. A Mrs. Newton later told Jeremiah Evarts that "when her door was shut, she dared not open it, for fear of seeing Indians; and when it was open, she dared not shut it, for fear Indians would approach unseen. The settlers could not live all the while in forts, because they must gain subsistence from the land, and they could not live all the while on their farms without imminent danger."[34]

The Continental Congress provided Georgia with further support in the form of five regiments of full-time continental soldiers, as well as ships and artillery batteries, for the defense of the province. Georgia had such a small and politically divided population, the majority of whom avoided committing to either side, that recruits for this brigade had to be found elsewhere. John Dooly obtained a commission as a captain in the new Regiment of Horse. With his brothers Captain Thomas Dooly and Second Lieutenant George Dooly, as well as brother-in-law First Lieutenant Thomas Mitchell, all of the Third Georgia Continental Regiment, he traveled to Virginia to find men for the Georgia service. They took with them four hundred pounds that John had borrowed from Peter Perkins, but which he never paid back. In Guilford County, North Carolina, and Pittsylvania County, Virginia, he and his relations succeeded in enlisting ninety-seven men, by illegally signing on deserters from the local military. Upon returning to Georgia, John went to Savannah to collect bounty money, while his brother Thomas took the company to a post on the frontier.

The consequences of making a commitment in the American Revolution now affected John Dooly in a most personal way. On July 22, 1777, Thomas Dooly, with twenty-one men in two companies, set out to return to the post after having recovered some horses stolen by Creek war parties led by Emistisiguo. Some two miles from Skull Shoals on the Oconee River, fifty Indians launched an ambush. Thomas Dooly fell with a wound to his Achilles tendon. Unable to move, he cried out in vain to his fleeing comrades not to leave him to suffer death at the hands of the Indians.

This attack, which ended Thomas Dooly's life, came as part of a massive campaign by British Indian superintendent John Stuart to disrupt the efforts of the Irish-born Indian trader George Galphin, a former ally of Governor Wright and a moderate leader in the South Carolina Regulator rebellion who had reluctantly agreed to serve as Indian commissioner for the whigs in the South. Galphin worked to move the Indians to a neutral position. John Dooly inadvertently played into Stuart's plans, however, when he seized a Creek peace delegation on a visit to the Indian commissioner. Dooly announced that he would hold them as hostages until he had satisfaction for his brother's death. With great effort, Galphin and the Georgia authorities compelled Dooly to release the delegation and, later, to surrender a fort where he and his supporters had barricaded themselves. The commissioner then persuaded the Creek delegates that they were being protected from a plot to murder them by Emistisiguo and other British agents. As the headman had arranged such assassinations for the British before the war, the story had credibility. The delegates, upon returning home, led a war party that would have killed Emistisiguo and Stuart's agent David Taitt but for the physical intervention of rising Creek leader Alexander McGillivray. After various delays, Captain Dooly stood trial in Savannah and then resigned his commission. He must have believed that while the new government authorities could not or would not move against Indians, they could deal effectively with him.[35]

Dooly's problems came at a time when his neighbors debated related issues. Dr. George Wells, the protégé of the populist Georgia politician Button Gwinnett, organized a clique in the Ceded Lands that petitioned the American commander of the southern forces to invade and seize the Creek lands. Both Wells and Gwinnett were viewed as perennial failures and misfits, the type of characters who often lead, if not create, radical factions in revolutions. Wells led a petition drive to have the Continental Congress remove Georgia's continental commander, Lachlan McIntosh, whom he accused of being incompetent, a "murderer" (in a duel with Gwinnett where both men had been wounded), and related by blood to pro-British Indian leaders.

Dooly had every reason to have supported, or even assumed a leadership position in, Wells's movement. Nonetheless he, Clarke, and other whig leaders in the Ceded Lands did not sign Wells's petition. John Coleman, formerly of Virginia and a wealthy leader in the Ceded Lands, also opposed the petition and even wrote to McIntosh complaining that "Gentlemen of Abilities, who's Characters are well Established, are the only persons objected to, to govern and manage in State affairs with us. The Consiquence [sic] of which I fear, we too soon will see to our sorrow."[36]

Within a year John Dooly did make a comeback. Progress in local government moved quickly in the new state of Georgia, and he took advantage of it. He sought both bounty land to build a mill and bounty certificates for the military service of himself and his deceased brother. What had been the Ceded Lands became, under Georgia's constitution of 1777, Wilkes County, the state's first county. Dooly served as its representative in the new one-house state legislature, which eventually gave him and fellow legislator John Coleman turns on the Executive Council that supervised the actions of the governor. Coleman and Dooly received orders from the council to qualify Thomas Waters and Isaac Herbert as justices of the peace in Wilkes County. For reasons not given, they instead gave the commissions to Edward Keating and Jacob Coleson, an action that the council ordered suspended. No further information on this matter appears in the Executive Council minutes, but a few months later, Thomas Waters appeared before the council to take an oath under the act for the expulsion of enemies from the state. John and

George Dooly made payments to the state for grants of new land in 1778. With the death of Coleman from disease in the summer of 1778, John Dooly rose to command his county's militia, and he led his neighbors against Creek raiders that same summer and won a victory against the Indians at Newsome's Ponds. At almost the same time, John Dooly also became the county's first sheriff and, as such, had suspected loyalists arrested, searched, and confined in chains. In late December the local electorate voted him colonel, with battle-scarred veteran officer Elijah Clarke as his lieutenant colonel and Burwell Smith as major. Smith, a former Virginian, had received an appointment to Thomas Dooly's command in the Georgia Continentals following Thomas's death. The fortunes of Clarke, a former North Carolina frontiersman of the most modest means, had been on the rise during the Revolution because of Clarke's abilities as an almost fatally courageous leader in battle. The loyalist aristocracy would have understood Elizabeth Lichtenstein Johnston as referring to men like him when she wrote of Georgia's revolutionaries, "everywhere the scum rose to the top."[37]

For John Dooly success as a popularly elected leader came at a price. That December, a British land and naval force captured Savannah. Redcoats overran Georgia, except for Wilkes County, and occupied nearby Augusta by the end of January 1779. Fourteen hundred Georgians, a large portion of the state's population, came forward to sign oaths accepting British protection and acknowledging an obligation to serve in the king's militia. A man named Freeman and a party of Baptists from Wilkes County, arrived at Augusta to offer the surrender of Wilkes County's forts and civilians. Eighty loyalist horsemen under the Scottish captains John Hamilton and Dugald Campbell then set out to receive those submissions. As he later related to a British writer, however, Hamilton discovered that "although many of the people came in to take the oath of allegiance, the professions of a considerable number were not to be depended upon; and that some came in only for the purpose of gaining information on his strength and future designs. In various quarters, he met with opposition and all their places of strength held out until they were reduced. The reduction of most of these was not, however, a work of great difficulty, as they consisted only of stockade forts, calculated for defense against the Indians."[38]

John Dooly, now a militia colonel without a state and a sheriff guilty of prosecuting the king's most loyal subjects, faced a particular problem in finding allies in South Carolina. During the previous summer's Indian troubles, 546 South Carolina militiamen had come to Wilkes County's aid under Brigadier General Andrew Williamson, originally an illiterate cattle driver who had risen to wealth and prominence at Ninety Six before the war. The South Carolinians failed to discover any hostile Creeks, or even Dooly and his Georgia militiamen; they only found local people overcharging them for provisions. Williamson had written to his subordinates that John Dooly could not be trusted and recommended avoiding any future dealings with him. Now Dooly needed help from those same men.[39]

Having withdrawn to South Carolina by early February, John Dooly made an appeal to Andrew Pickens, colonel of the Upper Ninety Six Regiment and Williamson's longtime subordinate. Pickens and his command were guarding the Carolina frontier against the Cherokees while Williamson and the rest of the brigade tried to block the British forces at Augusta from entering South Carolina. Pickens brought two hundred men to Dooly's aid, but once in Georgia, he insisted upon and received command of all of their forces. Together they pursued the horsemen of Hamilton and Campbell across Wilkes County, northeast to southwest, from Thomas Waters's plantation near the mouth of the Broad River to Heard's Fort in the center of the county. They finally caught up with and besieged their prey at Robert Carr's fort, near the Little River on the southern border and the last outpost in Wilkes County that the horsemen intended to visit.

After an attempt to entrap the loyalists between the fort and his men failed, Andrew Pickens had the fort's water supply cut off as he prepared to use a burning wagon and even cannons to force the besieged into surrendering. He then received news that hundreds, perhaps thousands, of loyalists from North and South Carolina were en route to Georgia with the clear intention of joining the British army in Augusta. Pickens chose to give up the siege of Carr's fort and withdrew his forces on the night of February 12, having achieved little more than the capture of the loyalists' horses, baggage, and a brace of pistols belonging to Hamilton.[40]

The South Carolinian made the decision to try to intercept the new threat despite the fact that, in doing so, he gave up a certain victory in the hope of finding and defeating an enemy force much larger in numbers than his own. His ad hoc command had suffered casualties, and he withdrew so quickly that his dead received little more consideration than being covered with leaves. Pickens also abandoned any advantage he might have held if the approaching enemy force passed near Carr's fort en route to join sympathizers at the nearby Wrightsborough settlement. Dooly had a deposition taken by justice of the peace Stephen Heard, wherein a William Millen had described a meeting with a loyalist leader identified as James Boyd when Boyd had recently been at Wrightsborough seeking guides to South Carolina. The loyalist leader had carried a proclamation from the British commander now in Augusta that called for Americans to join the king's army. Dooly must have understood that the redcoats at Augusta expected the arrival of Boyd with a significant force of loyalists from the Carolinas, guided during the last of their journey by the horsemen under Hamilton and Campbell. He also knew that to follow Pickens in returning to South Carolina to try to intercept the otherwise largely unknown enemy would risk a great deal.

The combined whig command of Pickens and Dooly tried to pursue the loyalists in South Carolina and then back in Wilkes County before rendezvousing with the survivors of the battle of Vann's Creek, men of the two state militias who had clashed with Boyd's oncoming force with disastrous results on February 10. The original militiamen found themselves back at Robert Carr's fort two nights after having left it and after what must have been an exhausting march. Boyd and his ad hoc regiment of some six hundred North and South Carolina loyalists, however, now camped at a cowpen, or small farm, in a meadow on swampy Kettle Creek, less than a mile from Carr's fort and hardly much further from Wrightsborough, on Sunday morning, February 14. Pickens then ordered a complicated attack through thick canebrakes, creeks, and woods with his combined force of only three hundred forty men. Unbeknownst to Pickens, the loyalists, numbering some six hundred, had largely crossed the creek and had camped on high ground with the flooded creek between them and the approaching militiamen. They knew that they were being pursued and had a capable leader in the now Colonel Boyd, a man reportedly known to Pickens and quite possibly also a previous acquaintance of Dooly's. Pickens sent Dooly and Clarke to lead columns through the woods and swamps to cross the creek in order to assault the farm on the flanks and cut off the enemy's retreat. When Pickens directed his own men up a narrow path to attack the cowpen and the hill in the center, Boyd launched an ambush with those of his men who were butchering a cow and had yet to cross the creek. Dooly would write that only the hand of Providence saved him, Clarke, and Pickens, as they exposed themselves, on horseback, during the entire fight at Kettle Creek and that their enemy seemed to fire two hundred shots at them in less than half a minute.

By the time that the battle of Kettle Creek had ended, however, Pickens's usual good luck had held. Many of the loyalists, having come along only under threats and intimidation, had already deserted or had decided to escape to their homes at the first opportunity, even before the battle began. Three of Dooly's riflemen found themselves behind the lines, and they mortally wounded Boyd. Elijah Clarke, despite having a horse shot out from under him, led a successful charge against the loyalists who tried to come to Boyd's rescue from across the creek. Unable to find John Moore of North Carolina, their second in command, most of the king's men fled, either back to the Carolinas or to sympathizers in the nearby settlement of Wrightsborough. Two hundred seventy loyalists would later be rescued by Captains Hamilton and Campbell from Wrightsborough. By the afternoon Pickens, Dooly, and Clarke had won an overwhelming victory.[41]

A month later George Galphin received warning of an approaching pro-British Indian invasion of seven hundred warriors under David Taitt and Emistisiguo. This force of Indians and loyalists burned Folsom's fort and other outposts along the Ogeechee River in then western Wilkes County. South Carolina militiamen again came to the rescue. The Indians under Alexander McGillivray met defeat at Rocky Comfort Creek on March 29 at the hands of militiamen under Colonel Leroy Hammond of South Carolina and Colonel Benjamin Few of Georgia. The battle resulted in the deaths of nine Indians, including two headmen, and three loyalists who had accompanied them. The three Indians and three "white savages" (white men who lived as Indians) captured included Emistisiguo's son. The next day Pickens and Dooly led their men against Emistisiguo himself. Three Indians were reportedly killed at the head of the Ogeechee River. In the face of such opposition, most of Taitt's followers deserted. Only seventy warriors remained with him when he reached Savannah. The men of the Georgia militia paraded the scalps of the dead warriors in Augusta although they released Emistisiguo's son as a peace gesture. Pickens and Williamson now had high praise for Dooly and specifically for the intelligence obtained from his network of scouts.[42]

Such victories by the militia reversed the overall military situation. The British army had already withdrawn from Augusta just hours before Boyd met defeat. Georgians who had taken the king's oaths disappeared, and the redcoats found themselves unable to control much more than the ground that the regular army occupied. These professional soldiers from the fortified garrisons in New York and East Florida had won and would continue to win the fixed formal battles only to eventually lose the war to a widespread popular resistance that won by keeping the insurgency going indefinitely. British leaders had been led to believe that thousands of average frontiersmen remained loyal and willing to die for the king's cause in a campaign of "Americanizing" the war. The hundreds of men who did turn out under leaders like Boyd, however, actually came from socially isolated frontier communities of Quakers, Baptists, bandits, ex–North Carolina Regulators, Irish emigrants, Palatines, white men who lived as if they were Indians, Indians, freed/self-emancipated blacks, and others perennially outside the mainstream of colonial frontier society. These "loyalists" acted more like refugees trying to find protection under what had come to be seen as a foreign army of occupation than like combatants committed to serve the king. The survivors of Kettle Creek and those of Taitt's warriors who reached Savannah proved to be of little military value to the king's forces, and they certainly failed to justify the costs and losses that the British cause had suffered invading Georgia.[43]

The pathetically small turnout represented a hard reality for the king's cause. The frontier population had its own agenda above and beyond whoever won the formal war known as the American Revolution. The number of settlers who supported the king's cause and the population of the apolitical, most of whom opposed the war in general, likely matched John Adams's famous claim that one-third of Americans opposed independence and one-third were indifferent to the struggle's outcome.[44] However, even prominent men of the Georgia frontier who had been royal officials or otherwise invested in colonial America, men such as native John Thomas, Englishman Thomas Waters, Englishman James Grierson, Scotsman Thomas Manson, and Irishman George Galphin, could be persuaded to be neutral under American rule, to be what came to be called "Pet Tories," or even, as in the case of Galphin, to help in ways such as working to keep peace with the Indians.[45] Ardent loyalist leaders could be made examples of by torture and humiliation (like English-born Thomas Brown); effectively silenced by exile (like Brown, Irishman James Boyd, and the royal governor Sir James Wright); arrested (like Quaker Joseph Maddock); or killed (like Boyd and several of his lieutenants) without anyone coming to their aid.[46]

In the spring of 1779, restored British rule in America represented a dead cause, and John Dooly became the symbol of that fact to anyone in Wilkes County. In what then remained of whig Georgia, he would simultaneously hold the state's most important positions in the military, government, and judiciary, a situation unique in Georgia's history. As the highest ranking officer left in the state militia, he became the colonel commandant. Refuge elected officials, after false starts, finally created an extralegal executive council at Augusta to act as a civil government and with Dooly as a member. Faced with mortal threats from external enemies, the new council also appointed Dooly as state's attorney to prosecute, in capital cases of treason, the most active local British collaborators. At a court held at Jacob McClendon's house in August 1779, Dooly so prosecuted several of his neighbors. Nine of these "tories" were condemned to die for treason, but the ad hoc state government granted reprieves to all but two of them.[47] (North and South Carolina also held trials that condemned and hanged seven participants of Boyd's uprising as civil criminals.) Historian Robert M. Weir wrote that the Regulator rebellion had brought home to South Carolinians that those leaders who failed to act against the perceived public enemy risked losing authority. John Dooly determined to avoid that mistake.[48]

With an opposition army so close at hand, such actions would hardly have been tolerated by the general public if the new order failed to offer more than various forms of suppression of dissent. Georgia's first state government, unlike the old colonial regimes in the two Carolinas, embraced, encouraged, and benefited from the progressive movement on the frontier. It continued, for example, the efforts begun by the South Carolina Regulators and by Governor Wright's reforms to bring rule of law to the backcountry. Courts had been held in Wilkes County as early as 1778, with John Dooly as at least a plaintiff. In 1780 the county had a permanent courthouse in Washington, a town laid out specifically as the county seat and with Dooly as one of its original commissioners.[49] At the same time, John Dooly and his neighbors affirmed that in the new order they, when cooperating, could do almost anything that they wanted to do in their own affairs. Dooly, Pickens, Williamson, and their comrades had thwarted both their enemy's plans to create a counterrevolution and invasions by Indian war parties. The expensive and increasingly mercenary continental and state military establishments, by contrast, had often failed the frontiersmen.[50]

The situation in Wilkes County remained grave, however. Much of Georgia had become a no man's land between the opposing armies, much like South Carolina's frontier had been before the Regulators, where guerrillas and apolitical gangs acted as destructive brigands who took advantage of the lack of civil law. Seeking to protect the frontier loyalists, Augustin Prévost, the British brigadier general in Savannah, wrote to Williamson in early April 1779 requesting a truce for the northwest frontier, which he declined to refer to as "Wilkes County." Governor John Rutledge of South Carolina adamantly declined the offer. Williamson did send sixty men to bolster Dooly's command and to discourage the people of

Wilkes County from moving to the safety of North Carolina and Virginia. Major Burwell Smith arrived in the camp of General Benjamin Lincoln, commander of the Southern Department, to present John Dooly's pleas for money for the Georgia militia. The general ordered $8,295.70 to be advanced to Smith to cover the expenses of Dooly's men from January 1 to March 1, 1779, and another $1,000 to be advanced to Dooly, although he demanded that notarized vouchers justifying the disbursement of the money be sent back.[51]

Georgia's frontier still knew no peace. By July, Indians had killed three people and scalped two others alive on the Wilkes County frontier. Sixty men left behind under Colonel Few and Lieutenant Colonel Clarke, however, killed and scalped seven of the enemy, wounded two others, and took two prisoners. Hardly a week later, however, General McIntosh wrote from the Georgia frontier that "the few Militia in this area to stick yet to their Integrity & have not Joined the Enemy or Shamefully left us altogether to ourselves do not exceed Six hundred men, are much scattered & chiefly pinned up in little Forts to Secure their Families from the Savages to whom they are exposed & harass them continually, Loath to Leave them upon any Emergency, are now almost tired out & despairing to see any effective assistance come to them, are Selling off, and leaving us also."[52] The situation for Georgia's loyalists, many of whom would become refugees behind the British lines, proved hardly any different. An anonymous writer observed in that same summer of 1779 that "the whole country within twenty-five miles of Savannah has been plundered and every man almost who had submitted to, and received protection of government, either killed or taken prisoners, and the few that have escaped that fate, have been obliged to submit to such terms as the rebels pleased to subscribe."[53]

Facing such a grim situation, John Dooly committed himself to using the new frontier self-empowerment to drive the British from Georgia and thus end any hopes of returning the South to colonial rule. He left Elijah Clarke to defend the frontier while he and Burwell Smith led a series of campaigns against an army that they did not perceive as liberators who had come to rescue them from "anarchy" and that now appeared, even to loyalists, as a foreign occupation force. In March 1779 Dooly marched with his militiamen to the mouth of Briar Creek, in Burke County, Georgia, the rallying point for the Georgia, South Carolina, and North Carolina forces preparing to retake Savannah. Dooly's men arrived on March 4, the day after the American camp there had been attacked by the British regulars. The American forces had been thoroughly defeated with more than 150 men killed, 173 men captured, and more than half of the 800 soldiers who escaped deserting. Dooly had the dead buried and then returned to Wilkes County, having learned a lesson on the consequences of facing a professionally trained army in formal battle.[54]

The following June, when most of the British forces in the South invaded South Carolina, Lincoln asked the Georgians to launch their own diversionary campaign against occupied Savannah. Colonel Benjamin Few of the Georgia militia had written to Lincoln about his success in finding sympathy for the American cause in the territory between Augusta and Savannah during a raid in May. Dooly gathered four hundred Georgia militiamen at Augusta and sent a request to Lincoln for supplies, arms, medicine, and money, even though he had failed, as Lincoln noted, to send receipts for the funds already advanced to him. After an angry exchange of letters, Dooly did eventually send the vouchers, but along with new bills for the services of his men that amounted to thirty thousand dollars.

Everything went wrong in this subsequent Burke County campaign because of John Dooly's failure to obtain any cooperation. Colonels John Twiggs and John Baker of the state's militia ignored his call and went on their own raid, alerting the Savannah garrison to its vulnerability. George Wells refused to recognize Georgia's makeshift government and Dooly's authority. Wells had been elected as the first colonel of the Wilkes County militia, and although he had been a very active officer in 1777, he lost his position in a subsequent reorganization and election under the new state constitution. He would later win election as colonel of another newly created battalion in neighboring Richmond County in 1778. Whether he or Dooly actually held senior rank depended on whom one asked, with no impartial authority available to decide that now critical issue. Dooly had Wells court-martialed. Most of the British forces in South Carolina returned to Savannah before the militia in Augusta could finally march. Despite this news, Dooly insisted on taking those militiamen who had not fallen sick in the meantime into the military "no man's land" of Burke County that June. During that time supplies from Lincoln finally arrived in Augusta, but civilians there seized even this succor and absconded with it to Wilkes County. Lincoln also failed to win a leave for John Dooly's brother Robert serving in the South Carolina continentals to visit John and their surviving brothers George and William in Augusta. It would have been the first time they had all been together since the war had begun. Whatever Dooly's campaign could have been, he and his men accomplished nothing more than a cattle rustling raid that frightened the governor, Sir James Wright, now restored to power in British-occupied Savannah, and resulted in the death of at least one loyalist, an action that may have later led to Dooly's own demise.[55]

Finally, in September, Benjamin Lincoln's army united with America's French allies in a campaign to retake all of Georgia. For frontiersmen, the uniformed professional French army and fleet, its vast artillery, and the sea of tents provided an inspiring spectacle that the frontiersmen never forgot and that must have seemed to guarantee the success of their cause. Loyalists and neutrals across Georgia now joined in the Revolution as an outcome in the favor of United States seemed assured.

The campaign should have been a turning point of the war more decisive than the siege of Yorktown two years later. The professional British army, however, could hardly have been in a better position. Redcoats stranded in South Carolina succeeded in reaching the Savannah garrison, concentrating behind extensive fortifications and batteries that the engineers and slave labor erected almost overnight.

Within the town, the British army, with its white, black, and red allies, had ample supplies of cattle and stores. The besiegers, by contrast, suffered from hunger, disease, and exposure while engaged in grueling but ineffective trench warfare. As part of an ad hoc brigade under General Lachlan McIntosh, Dooly and his men participated in the disastrous Franco-American attack upon the British lines on October 9, 1779. The Georgia militia and Andrew Williamson's brigade traveled half a mile across a swamp and into a barrage of musket and artillery fire as a British band serenaded them with "Come to Maypole, Merry Farmers All." The bullets that fell around them often came from guns aimed at them by Georgia loyalists. Dooly and the militiamen retreated under fire. Elsewhere on the battlefield, the French army and the American continentals took huge losses, being repulsed largely by North and South Carolinians loyal to the king—including survivors of Kettle Creek. The allied forces suffered the second highest casualties of either side in a single battle of the American Revolution, even without counting the many Americans who had already tried to desert from the militia and the war. Immediately afterward the allies lifted the siege and began to withdraw. Sick and discouraged, Colonel Dooly returned home with his men.[56]

The aftermath of these failures came to visit Dooly with a vengeance. Georgia's northern frontier had joined the Revolution earlier and had been a partner in the new state's government. With the British capturing Savannah and overrunning the coastal counties, the western backcountry had now become the state. Elections in December 1779 restored the constitutional state government. The electorate, however, disenchanted with a council populated by refugees of occupied Georgia as well as with the failures of the war, voted in new leadership from the radical antiestablishment party of the late Button Gwinnett. George Wells and other members of Gwinnett's faction had previously campaigned against the council to which Dooly belonged, even to the point of forming their own competing government. Wells now became governor, but he quickly followed the example of Gwinnett and died at the hands of a political opponent, in this instance in a duel with James Jackson, who later became governor. John Twiggs had been leading a guerrilla war and various raids into Burke County for several months while avoiding anything to do with Dooly or the Supreme Executive Council. He now served in the House and on the Executive Council of the newly elected government. New governor George Walton managed to have General Lachlan McIntosh, long treated as an enemy of the state by the Gwinnett/Wells faction and Walton's former friend, removed from his command in Georgia.[57]

Initially the new political leadership did try to cooperate with John Dooly. They approved his requests for more men and forts, and they allowed him to sell slaves captured at Savannah to raise money for the militia. The question of Thomas Lee's claim to Leesburg reemerged, however. Georgia's original state government had ordered Dooly evicted from the Lee property, but various circumstances, including Indian raids that Dooly led his militiamen against, kept the orders from being carried out before the British army captured Savannah and the state government disappeared. Exactly one year after the battle of Kettle Creek, the new government aided Thomas Lee in his suit to reclaim the land that Dooly had borrowed so heavily against to improve, and it even ordered Elijah Clarke to evict the Dooly family, by force, if necessary. The members of the governor's council stayed that order temporarily when they learned that Lee had never received a grant for the land in question, but they also ordered Dooly and Burwell Smith to answer for their past confiscation of cattle and supplies for use by the military.[58]

The resurrected state government did not last long enough to see its mandates carried out. A chain of events began that would solve Dooly's problems with the new leaders but, typically, in a way that boded still worse for him. In the spring of 1780, a massively reinforced British army laid siege to Charleston. Brigadier General Williamson sent a combined force of Georgia and South Carolina militia under Colonels Twiggs and Pickens, respectively, against Savannah. The general, after conferring with Georgia governor Nathan Bronson, now prepared to gather all of the free militia of the two states, perhaps as many as one thousand men, for a major diversionary attack against Savannah in an attempt to end the siege of the South Carolina capital. Before that could happen, however, General Sir Henry Clinton and the British forced the surrender of General Benjamin Lincoln, the continental American army of the South, and Charleston.[59] Now the people of the backcountry had to face the king's army and its allies alone. Williamson convened a meeting of militia leaders in Augusta to decide what should be done. Dooly and Clarke argued for carrying on a guerrilla war, even without the regular American army, against the British lines around Charleston and Savannah. The general promised to consult with them further after he addressed his own men. Despite Williamson's pleas to continue the war, however, his South Carolina militiamen compelled him to surrender with them. They all became prisoners of war on parole. John Dooly held a similar meeting at his home at Leesburg soon after and with the same result, except that thirty men under Elijah Clarke, Burwell Smith, and Sanders Walker, the Baptist minister whom Dooly had chosen as regimental chaplain, decided to continue the war as guerrillas in South Carolina. Stephen Heard, now the governor, and the remnants of the state government moved to Heard's Fort in Wilkes County and then disbanded.

William Manson, a Scotsman whose foreign settlement project in the Ceded Lands had finally failed because of the Revolution, then came to Wilkes County and accepted the surrender of John Dooly and four hundred Georgia militiamen on a ridge outside the town of Washington in late June 1780. Manson acted on behalf of Thomas Brown, the commander of loyalist provincials and Indians, who now occupied Augusta. Brown, an Englishman, had been tortured at the hands of a whig mob and later would suffer various wounds in battle for the king's cause. He too originally came to Georgia to create a Ceded Lands settlement, but his Brownsborough had shared the same fate as Manson's Friendsborough.[60]

Even then John Dooly and the frontier would not find peace. His creditors from before and during the war pressed him for payment.[61] Georgia now became the only American state ever completely reduced to colony status, but the new and restored leadership had little interest in reconciliation. They chose instead to divide the frontiersmen by politics in ways that had never existed before. The colonial assembly, for example, included Dooly in its attempt to disqualify former rebels from again holding any public office. On June 3, 1780, General Sir Henry Clinton revoked almost all of the paroles, thereby freeing Dooly, Pickens, and others to return to the American cause without violating their oaths and, likely, to die in battle against the king's army. Two months later men who had not joined the restored colonial militia could have their property confiscated. Loyalist leaders believed that Dooly and other men on parole wanted just such an opportunity to return to the war. These concerns seemed justified when, in September 1780, Elijah Clarke led Georgia and South Carolina guerrillas in attacking and nearly capturing Brown and the loyalist and Indian garrison in Augusta. Rescued and reinforced by South Carolina loyalist provincials, the long suffering tories and Indians then began a campaign of retaliation as they went from being the oppressed to the avenged, starting with the executions of men captured during Clarke's attack. From John Dooly's home, Lieutenant Colonel John Harris Cruger announced the arrival of his loyalist force in the Ceded Lands. He dispatched colonial militia under Thomas Waters and others to destroy the forts, courthouse, and settlements of Wilkes County. Wright reported that at least one hundred homes were destroyed. Families believed to have supported the Revolution either went into exile with Elijah Clarke or their men became prisoners confined in Augusta.[62] Sanders Walker, at the least, risked his reputation with both sides to seek a truce. Elijah Clarke's request to Britain's General Lord Charles Cornwallis for a cessation of hostilities went unanswered.[63]

Completely credible information has not survived, but John Dooly, having few options, seemed to have been preparing to return to the rebellion. Before he could do so, however, someone arrived at his home and killed him, quite likely in revenge for some of his complicated actions earlier in the war. His killer might have blamed Dooly for surrendering, for Clarke's attack on Augusta, for actions he took against backcountry dissenters who incidentally might have been loyalists, for some action the obsessively ambitious frontiersman had taken unrelated to the war, or for some combination of these reasons. John Dooly may have died because of all that he represented more than the life he had lived.[64]

Loyalist and British leaders learned too late that, through atrocities such as the killing of John Dooly, they created rather than suppressed a widespread uprising. Clarke's "followers" had consisted of relatively few men, and most of them appeared to have been apolitical bandits who had been challenging authority even before the war. As a loyalist wrote, "Clarke's party is said to have consisted of men, whose restless dispositions, or whose crimes prevented their living in any country where even the resemblance of government was maintained, and therefore taking themselves to the vacant lands on the frontiers; living without any control; they made inroads upon the industrious inhabitants of the back settlements, and have frequently involved the Province in wars with the Indians."[65] Many other members of his party, as with Boyd's men at Kettle Creek, came along only because of threats to their lives and property. Even Pickens and Williamson had refused to cooperate with him. Royal Lieutenant Governor John Graham took a census of Wilkes County and came away anything but encouraged. He found that of 723 men, only 255 could be compelled to serve in the loyalist militia and at least 411 had—at least at that time—joined the rebels. Residents of Wilkes County forced into the royal militia must have included men who had fought under Dooly at Kettle Creek as whigs and who would now serve the king as "loyalists." Reportedly 150 of the men still in the royal militia were subsequently killed, while serving on assignment in South Carolina under Colonel Thomas Waters, at the battle of Hammond's Store in December 1780. In a bizarre twist of fate, they fell near the homes of the Raeburn Creek loyalists who had been defeated more than a year earlier in Wilkes County at the battle of Kettle Creek.[66]

If British leaders had deliberately encouraged an uprising to eliminate the king's unrepentant American enemies, that strategy backfired spectacularly. The American military in the South would make a decisive comeback under General Nathanael Greene. Over the next two years his professional army, in cooperation with partisans, would drive the British from the South and create the string of events that directly resulted in the decisive American victory at Yorktown. Elijah Clarke, James Jackson, John Twiggs, and other Georgians played significant roles in those battles and campaigns. The former Wilkes County militiamen who had served under John Dooly, for example, participated in the major victory at King's Mountain and played critical roles in the American success at the battle of Cowpens. Emistisiguo's fate also became intertwined with those final battles of the Revolution. He led warriors in attacks against the settlers in present day Kentucky and Tennessee who had come to the aid of the Americans at King's Mountain and in Wilkes County. On June 24, 1782, in his final act for his British patrons, he died in hand-to-hand combat with General Anthony Wayne while leading a Creek war party and loyalists in a desperate but successful effort to break through the American lines to the garrison at Savannah, even as the king's cause stood as all but lost. The Creek headman thus joined John Dooly and so many others in failing to survive the war. The Americans left the Indian corpses unburied, open to the predation of the forest animals.[67]

The British evacuated Savannah and Georgia on July 11, 1782, and the entire South during the following months, leaving the Indians and the Americans to their fate. In one of its last acts, the restored colonial Georgia assembly, on paper, gave the Ceded Lands courts and separate political representation through the formation of two new parishes. Had such ideas been included in the original Southern Strategy, colonial officials would have provided the people of the backcountry an alternative to the corrupt, incompetent, and bitterly divided state governments and that would have incorporated rather than threatened the progress the frontiersmen had achieved themselves since the 1760s. The outcome of the war in the South, and even the future of the country as a whole, might have been very different. Even as a symbolic expression, however, this offer of local government in the Georgia backcountry was far too little and much too late to do anything but demonstrate that civil progress on the American frontier was a much greater revolution than the formal war with which it briefly coexisted. True revolutions begin as conservative rebellions against change, become radical as men like George Wells prey upon public fears, and end up conservative as change achieves an accommodation with reality. Elijah Clarke's desire late in life to abandon the pressures of the settled society he had helped to build in Georgia for Kentucky and the uninhibited frontier world in which he had lived most of his life would seem to prove this sequence of events as a true rebellion. Dooly and his neighbors, however, actually belonged to a greater and more consistent movement that began before the war and progressed even as their world shifted westward until, as Frederick Jackson Turner famously observed in 1893, the American frontier ceased to exist.[68]

In the latter part of the Revolution, George Dooly led a company that took repeated revenge for the deaths of his brothers Thomas, John, and Robert in the American cause.[69] Little else came from John Dooly's participation in the American Revolution. Had he lived, he might have had a successful postwar career in the military and in politics, as did Andrew Pickens and Elijah Clarke. The latter would rise to the rank of major general and would fight to obtain Creek lands for Georgia, inside and outside of the restraints of the official government authority, much as he had acted against the British colonial government. For his services and sacrifices in the Revolution, Clarke received large tracts of land and the confiscated property of Thomas Waters. He would also set up his son John's successful public career, which would eventually include the governorship of Georgia.[70] Even Thomas Lee lived a long life.[71] If Dooly's reputation as a patriot suffered for having surrendered, as did Andrew Williamson's, and he lost his property in Georgia to his creditors, he could still have moved with his brother George and his sister Elizabeth Dooly Mitchell Bibb to the Kentucky frontier and, like them, started a new life.[72]

John Dooly's problems survived his death. The restored state government granted land, in recognition of his military service, to his minors but also ordered Elijah Clarke to evict Dooly's widow and orphans from the two-hundred-acre Leesburg plantation in response to Thomas Lee's claims. Present day Elijah Clarke State Park in Lincoln County (which was created in 1796 out of Wilkes County and named for Benjamin Lincoln) reportedly encompasses the plantation, which includes John Dooly's burial place somewhere near the "Dooly Spring." Even Thomas Waters from his exile in England joined the creditors making claims against Dooly's estate,[73] and John's last surviving son, John Mitchell Dooly, and his daughter, Susannah, were left without anything from their father. The young Dooly, who had only rags to wear, would study law as a young man and rise to prominence as a judge and politician. He too would have the distinction of becoming a legend in the state but as a civilian in the new United States. He likely used his own considerable influence as a judge and politician, along with the notoriety created by McCall's history of his father, to persuade the Georgia legislature to create a county named for Colonel John Dooly in 1821. This honor, however, came years after being bestowed upon the memories of Elijah Clarke, John Twiggs, Button Gwinnett, James Jackson, and many other of his father's contemporaries. Ironically, considering the career of its namesake, Dooly County suffered several Creek attacks in its early years. Even the honor of having a county named for John Dooly dimmed when, in 1840, a novelist portrayed a fictional Dooly family as loyalists. Judge Dooly's widow viewed this work as an insult to the memory of her father-in-law and his brothers. An old veteran, consulted on the matter, said of John Dooly: "Why truly he was a real Liberty man I know it as well as I know anything; for he saved my father's life once . . . [but] he was the only one in his family who was not [a loyalist] his brothers were tories."[74]

Some latter-day Shakespeare could have found the ironies in John Dooly's story excellent material for a sophisticated historical tragedy built around ambition, commitment, coincidence, consequence, and fate. The colonel did see great battles, but more important, his story serves as a way to chronicle the dramatic changes during his lifetime; the world he lived in was transformed from an almost natural state of anarchy to a self-governing society under a rule of law that transcended misleading and simplistic divisions of patriot and loyalist. As the price of democracy, the electorate both gave and took from him; and as his ambitions became so tangled in political events, he faced a dire future regardless of whether the American or the British cause succeeded. In true Shakespearean fashion, Dooly's personal actions, successful or failed, ultimately cost him everything. His life's story forms not a patriotic eulogy but a human and realistic biography of a multidimensional man who lived in complicated times. As such, Colonel John Dooly's life must stand for many lives of that age that, like the American Revolution itself, yield far more to critical study than simplistic tales of heroes and villains.

Notes

The author acknowledges the help provided by Deanna Slappey, Richard Smallwood, Karen Walker, and Jess Shelander in the preparation of this article.

1. Otis Ashmore, "Colonel John Dooly" in *Men of Mark in Georgia*, ed. William J. Northen, 6 vols. (Atlanta: 1907–12), 1:54. An earlier version of this article appeared as Robert S. Davis, "A Frontier for Pioneer Revolutionaries: John Dooly and the Beginnings of Popular Democracy in Original Wilkes County," *Georgia Historical Quarterly* 60 (Fall 2006): 315–49.

2. Hugh McCall, *The History of Georgia*, 2 vols. (Savannah, Ga.: Seymour & Williams, 1811–16), 2:85–86, 193–204, 306.

3. As late as 1950, Edith Duncan Johnston wrote a history of her prominent Houstoun and Johnston ancestors, *The Houstouns of Georgia*, without any mention of their loyalism. Until their memoirs were recently reprinted, loyalists William Lee and Elizabeth

Lichtenstein Johnston had no biographical information at the Georgia Department of Archives and History. Many of Georgia's loyalist families remained in the state or returned after the Revolution, although to have ancestors who fought for the king became a scandal that sometimes resulted in duels. See, for example, Catharine Haynes Fort, *Memoirs of the Fort and Fannin Families* (Chattanooga, Tenn.: Press of Macgowan & Cooke, 1903), 17, and Jonathan Dean Sarris, "'Hellish Deeds . . . in a Christian Land': Southern Mountain Communities at War, 1861–1865" (Ph.D. diss., University of Georgia, 1998), 34.

4. Hugh Bicheno, *Rebels & Redcoats: The American Revolutionary War* (New York: HarperCollins, 2004), xxv.

5. The land given up in 1773 in northwest colonial Georgia was known as the "Ceded Lands of St. Paul Parish" until it became Wilkes County under the state constitution of 1777. It is roughly modern-day Wilkes and surrounding counties. Alex M. Hitz, "The Earliest Settlements in Wilkes County," *Georgia Historical Quarterly* 40 (September 1956): 260–80. The *Georgia Historical Quarterly* is hereafter cited as *GHQ*.

6. David Hackett Fischer, *Albion's Seed: Four British Folkways in America* (New York: Oxford University Press, 1989); James Webb, *Born Fighting: How the Scots-Irish Shaped America* (New York: Broadway Books, 2004).

7. Peggy Shomo Joyner, comp., *Abstracts of Virginia's Northern Neck Warrants & Surveys*, 5 vols. (Portsmouth, Va.: privately printed, 1985–95), 2:6, 17, 21, 74; Amelia C. Gilreath, comp., *Frederick County, Virginia: Deed Books: 17 and 18, 1775–1780 and Early Troop Records 1755–1761* (Nokesville, Va.: privately printed, 1993), 198; Gertrude E. Gray, comp., *Virginia Northern Neck Land Grants*, 5 vols. (Baltimore: Genealogical Publishing Company, 1993–95), 2:160, 220, 222; Lloyd DeWitt Bockstruck, comp., *Virginia's Colonial Soldiers* (Baltimore: Genealogical Publishing Company, 1988), 348; Ge Lee Corley Hendrix, comp., *Edgefield County South Carolina Abstracts of Deed Books 1–12, 1786–1796* (Greenville, S.C.: Southern Historical Press, 1985), 50, 106; Patrick Dooly, COM Index, South Carolina Department of Archives and History (hereafter SCDAH). A Patrick Dooly appears as a butcher in the 1747 papers of the estate of Richard Harrison of Philadelphia, Pennsylvania, Logan Papers, vol. 21, p. 9, Historical Society of Pennsylvania, Philadelphia (hereafter HSP). The first biographical sketch of John Dooly has him as the son of Irish parents and born in Wilkes County, North Carolina, around 1735–1740. Adiel Sherwood, *A Gazetteer of the State of Georgia* (Philadelphia: Printed by J. W. Martin and W. K. Boden, 1829), 198. The reference to Wilkes County, North Carolina, may have actually been a confused reference to John Dooly's son John or his younger son, born circa 1771, John Mitchell. The sketch has details that can be confirmed, such as Dooly's ownership of the Egypt plantation and having a brother George. John Mitchell Dooly (d. 1827; John Dooly's son) or J. M. Dooly's widow may have been the source for the information. Legends among the descendants of Patrick Dooly have him as a trader and/or missionary to the Indians and a former British officer. No record of his role in any such activities has turned up. Madge Pettit (Dooly genealogist) to author, June 12, 1983; Madge Pettit, *Families of Genery's Gap Alabama* (Bowie, Md.: Heritage Books, 1986), 34. Other frontiersmen did lead lives that unconventional; see, for example, William Lee's memoirs in Robert S. Davis, comp., *Georgians in the Revolution* (Easley, S.C.: Southern Historical Press, 1986), 215–28.

8. Brent Holcomb, comp., *Probate Records of South Carolina*, 3 vols. (Easley, S.C.: Southern Historical Press, 1977–79), 3:65; South Carolina Colonial Inventory Book Y

(1769–71), p. 89, SCDAH; Marylynn Salmon, *Women and the Law of Property in Early America* (Chapel Hill: University of North Carolina Press, 1986), 142; John Dooly to Benjamin Lincoln, June 27, 1779, in Michael O'Brien, "The Doolys of Georgia," *Journal of the American Irish Historical Society* 26 (1927): facing page 178; will of George Dooley, October 9, 1821, Will Book H, p. 144, Office of the Superior Court, Lincoln County courthouse, Stanford, Kentucky; Clara A. Langley, comp., *South Carolina Deed Abstracts, 1719–1772*, 4 vols. (Easley, S.C.: Southern Historical Press, 1983–84), 4:194, 282.

9. For a discussion of leaders in the period of the American Revolution and their relationships with their respective fathers, see Robert M. Weir, "Rebelliousness: Personality Development in the American Revolution in the Southern Colonies," in *The Southern Experience in the American Revolution*, ed. Jeffrey J. Crow and Larry E. Tise (Chapel Hill: University of North Carolina Press, 1978), 25–54.

10. John Dooley, James Dooly, and John Dooly, COM index, and Common's House Journal, 1771, pp. 545, SCDAH; *South Carolina Gazette* (Charleston), June 20, 1774; Charles S. Davis, "The Journal of William Moultrie While a Commissioner on the North and South Carolina Boundary Survey, 1772," *Journal of Southern History* 8 (November 1942): 551; Katie-Prince Ward Esker, *South Carolina Memorials, 1731–1776*, 2 vols. (Cottonport, La.: Polyanthos, 1973–77), 1:1; Jesse Hogan Motes III and Margaret Peckham Motes, comps., *South Carolina Memorials: Abstracts of Land Titles, Volume 1, 1774–1776* (Greenville, S.C.: Southern Historical Press, 1996), 390; and Motes and Motes, *Laurens and Newberry Counties South Carolina: Saluda and Little River Settlements, 1749–1775* (Greenville, S.C.: Southern Historical Press, 1994), 45, 47, 49–51, 53–54, 57–58, 61–63, 67, 72–73, 88–89, 107–8, 113, 116, 153, 177, 179. Aside from using words like "Injun" for "Indian" and "skail" for "scale," in his several surviving letters, John Dooly wrote in a more sophisticated hand than did John Rutledge, the prominent lowcountry lawyer of the Middle Temple of London and later governor of South Carolina. Rutledge was a man Dooly knew from his legal dealings.

11. Wilkes County Court Minutes (1787–92), April 12, 1787, microfilm drawer 17, box 40, and Lincoln County Deed Book H (1812–16), 61–63, microfilm drawer 71, box 13, Georgia Archives, Morrow (hereafter GAr); George Dooley will. That two (John and Thomas) of the three known sons of John Dooly who lived to adulthood died young and that his third son (John Mitchell) left no issue after many years of chronic illness suggest the effects of a less celebrated aspect of frontier life. The Reverend Charles Woodmason claimed that 90 percent of the population on the frontier had venereal disease. Woodmason, *The Carolina Backcountry on the Eve of the Revolution: The Journal and Other Writings of Charles Woodmason, Anglican Itinerant*, ed. Richard J. Hooker (Chapel Hill: University of North Carolina Press, 1953), 100.

12. William Mylne, *Travels in the Colonies in 1773–1775*, ed. Ted Ruddock (Athens: University of Georgia Press, 1990), 25–33. For Reverend Woodmason's account, see the previous note, and for other accounts of life in this area and time, see George Hanger, *The Life, Adventures, and Opinions of Col. George Hanger*, 2 vols. (London, 1801), 2:398–406; Robert S. Davis, "Letters from St. Paul Parish," *Richmond County History* 10 (Summer 1978): 19–35; Edward J. Cashin, comp., *A Wilderness Still the Cradle of Nature: Frontier Georgia: A Documentary History* (Savannah: Library of Georgia, 1994); Robert S. Davis, "A Georgia Loyalist's Perspective on the American Revolution: The Letters of Dr. Thomas Taylor, 1776–1782," *GHQ* 81 (Spring 1997): 118–38; S. D. H——u to ?, January 16, 1779, in William L. Stone, comp., *Letters of Brunswick and Hessian Officers during the American*

Revolution (Albany, N.Y.: J. Munsell's Sons, 1891), 236–37; and William Bartram, *The Travels of William Bartram: Naturalist's Edition,* ed. Francis Harper (New Haven, Conn.: Yale University Press, 1958).

13. David Benedict, *A General History of the Baptist Denomination in America,* 2 vols. (Boston: Printed by Lincoln & Edmands, 1813), 2:392–93; J. R. Huddlestun and Charles O. Walker, *From Heretics to Heroes: A Study of Religious Groups in Georgia with Primary Emphasis on the Baptists* (Jasper, Ga.: Pickens Tech Press, 1976), 24–42; Patrick Dooly estate, Charlestown Inventory Book Y, p. 89, SCDAH.

14. See Jack P. Greene, "Independence, Improvement and Authority: Toward a Framework for Understanding the Histories of the Southern Backcountry during the Era of the American Revolution," in *An Uncivil War: The Southern Backcountry during the American Revolution,* ed. Ronald Hoffman, Thad W. Tate, and Peter J. Albert (Charlottesville: University Press of Virginia, 1985), 3–36, and Eric Hinderaker and Peter C. Mancall, *At the Edge of Empire: The Backcountry in British North America* (Baltimore: Johns Hopkins University Press, 2003). The Hugh Bicheno quotes come from his *Rebels & Redcoats,* 154, 159, and 188.

15. Joseph Israel vs. "John Dooley," 1771, 0151 002 090A 0040A 00, John Dooly vs. William Thomson, 1771, 0150 002 095A 0302A 00 and Thomson vs. Dooly, 1772, 0151 002 092A 0053A 00, Judgment Rolls, SCDAH; Langley, comp., *South Carolina Deed Abstracts,* 4:194. For Patrick Dooly's land grants, see Patrick Dooly, COM Index. William Thomson had been one of the significant leaders on the South Carolina frontier who, with George Galphin, Richard Richardson, and Daniel McGirth, had worked to negotiate a peace between the Regulators and the colonial government. He would also be a leader in the American Revolution. Richard Maxwell Brown, *The South Carolina Regulators* (Cambridge, Mass.: Belknap Press of Harvard University Press, 1963), 94–95, 206.

16. Charleston Mesne Conveyances Book E-4, pp. 247–50, SCDAH; Mary B. Warren, comp., *Georgia Governor and Council Journals 1772–1773* (Athens, Ga.: Heritage Papers, 1994), 138; George White, comp., *Historical Collections of Georgia* (New York: Pudney & Russell, 1854), 40.

17. Hitz, "The Earliest Settlements," 261–65; Robert S. Davis, *The Wilkes County Papers, 1773–1833* (Easley, S.C.: Southern Historical Press, 1979), 10, 46; J. Russell Snapp, *John Stuart and the Struggle for Empire on the Southern Frontier* (Baton Rouge: Louisiana State University Press, 1996), 121, 126–27, 132–36, 139–42.

18. Robert S. Davis, *Quaker Records in Georgia* (Augusta, Ga.: Augusta Genealogical Society, 1985) 14, 177.

19. Receipts, 1775, William and Edward Telfair & Company Collection, Special Collections, William R. Perkins Library, Duke University; Warren, *Georgia Governor and Council Journals 1772–1773,* 138, 166, 167, 169, 174; Grace G. Davidson, comp., *Early Records of Georgia Wilkes County,* 2 vols. (Macon, Ga.: J. W. Burke Company, 1933), 1:8, 12, 18; Michael Martin Farmer, comp., *Wilkes County, Georgia Deed Books A-VV, 1784–1806* (Dallas: Farmer Genealogy Company, 1996), 397; Hitz, "The Earliest Settlements," 261–63.

20. Davis, *The Wilkes County Papers,* 25; James M. Johnson, *Militiamen, Rangers, and Redcoats: The Military in Georgia, 1754–1776* (Macon, Ga.: Mercer University Press, 1992), 93. Thomas Dooly, John's brother, worked for Waters as a deputy surveyor in South Carolina in 1773. Motes and Motes, *South Carolina Memorials,* 266.

21. Bartram, *The Travels of William Bartram,* 204.

22. Davis, *The Wilkes County Papers,* 32–35, 216n2; Allen D. Candler, comp., *The Colonial Records of the State of Georgia,* 39 vols. (Atlanta, 1907–41), 14:524, 527–28, 545–46; Colonial Commission Book B-1 (1754–1776), p. 160, GAr.

23. Davis, *The Wilkes County Papers,* 26, and, Davis, comp., *Georgia Citizens and Soldiers of the American Revolution* (Easley, S.C.: Southern Historical Press, 1979), 16, 19; Mylne, *Travels in the Colonies,* 46.

24. Rachel N. Klein, "Frontier Planters and the American Revolution: The South Carolina Backcountry, 1775–1782," in Hoffman et al., *An Uncivil War,* 49.

25. For an example of the effect of the news of Concord and Lexington on the Georgia frontier, see the experience of Col. John Thomas as recorded in Joseph W. Barnwell, "Bernard Elliott's Recruiting Journal, 1775," *South Carolina Historical Magazine* 17 (July 1916): 97.

26. Revolutionary War pension claims of Evan Haines, Ga. W 8897, and John Cloud, S 30935, *Revolutionary War Pension and Bounty Land Warrant Application Files, 1800–1900* (Microfilm M804, rolls 1154 and 582), Records of the Veterans Administration Record Group 15, National Archives and Records Administration, Washington (hereafter NARA); William Downs to the Council of Safety, November 11, 775, Telamon Cuyler Collection, Hargrett Rare Books and Manuscripts Library, University of Georgia Libraries, Athens. The Heards had, like Waters, served in the Georgia frontier rangers in the 1760s and had been drawn back by the opening of the Ceded Lands. Robert S. Davis, "Georgia's Colonial Rangers," *Historical Society of the Georgia National Guard Journal* 8 (Spring/Summer 2001): 11–14.

27. John D—— file, File II Names, Record Group 4-2-46, GAr; "Georgia Colonial Records," *Georgia Genealogical Magazine,* no. 15 (January 1965): 912; Allen D. Candler, comp., *The Revolutionary Records of the State of Georgia,* 3 vols. (Atlanta: Franklin-Turner Company, 1908), 1:72; Farmer, *Wilkes County, Georgia Deed Books,* 283; "Reminiscences of Dr. William Read," in *Documentary History of the American Revolution,* comp. Robert W. Gibbes, 3 vols. (New York: D. Appleton, 1853–1857), 2:252. The David Avant Collection, GAr, has a copy of the minutes of a 1775 justice of the peace court in St. George Parish.

28. Gordon Burns Smith, *Morningstars of Liberty: The Revolutionary War in Georgia, 1775–1783* (Milledgeville, Ga.: Boyd Publishing, 2006), 43; Revolutionary War pension claim of John Cloud, S 30935 (Microfilm M804, roll 582, NARA); *South Carolina and American General Gazette* (Charleston), August 21, 1776. Because the British did not support these Indian raids, Emistisiguo kept the Creeks out of those attacks. John Stuart to George Germain, August 23, 1776, Colonial Office Papers CO 5/229, pt. ii, National Archives of the United Kingdom, Kew. If Dooly did serve in the campaign against the Cherokees in 1776, he officered with later Georgia leaders of the Revolution such as John Twiggs and Leonard Marbury. McCall, *History of Georgia,* 2:87.

29. Gilreath, *Frederick County, Virginia,* 198; Bockstruck, *Virginia's Colonial Soldiers,* 348; Morning Report, June 30, 1779, Keith Read Collection, MS 921, no. 7:11, Hargrett Rare Book and Manuscripts Library, University of Georgia Libraries; Andrew Pickens to John Irwine, March 12, 1779 in Gibbes, *Documentary History of the American Revolution,* 2:109; Clyde R. Ferguson, "Functions of the Partisan-Militia in the South during the American Revolution," in *The Revolutionary War in the South: Power, Conflict, and Leadership,* ed. W. Robert Higgins (Durham, N.C.: Duke University Press, 1979), 239–57; original orders, Revolutionary War pension claim of Richard Heard, Ga. W 4229

(Microfilm M804, roll 1242, NARA). For examples of the organization of the colonial southern militia, see Gordon Burns Smith, *History of the Georgia Militia, 1783–1861,* 4 vols. (Milledgeville, Ga.: Boyd Publishing, 2000), 1:49–70, and James B. Whisker, *The American Colonial Militia,* 5 vols. (Lewiston, N.Y.: E. Mellen Press, 1997), 5:154–55, 167–68, 170.

30. I. A. Few to Mary Few, May 25, 1837, quoted in Florence Knight Fruth, *Some Descendants of Richard Few of Chester County, Pennsylvania, and Allied Lines, 1682–1976* (Beaver Falls, Pa.: privately printed, 1977), 49.

31. *Royal Georgia Gazette* (Savannah), February 11, 1779. Benjamin Few arrested several of Georgia's frontier loyalists. He almost disappeared from public service after his defeat in the battle of Long Cane, South Carolina, in 1781. Court Minutes, April 1779, in Davis, *The Wilkes County Papers,* 52; Davis, *Georgians in the Revolution,* 102.

32. Fruth, *Some Descendants of Richard Few,* 56–63, 75–96.

33. Absalom H. Chappell, *Miscellanies of Georgia* (Atlanta: J. F. Meegan, 1874), 8. For other descriptions of Wilkes County forts, see Davis, *Georgia Citizens and Soldiers,* 158–67.

34. Quoted in diary of Jeremiah Evarts, entry of April 26, 1822, National Anthropological Archives, Smithsonian Institution, Washington, D.C.

35. Robert S. Davis, "George Galphin and the Creek Congress of 1777," *Proceedings and Papers of the Georgia Association of Historians* 3 (1982): 13–29; Mary Bondurant Warren, *Revolutionary Memoirs and Muster Rolls* (Athens, Ga.: Heritage Papers, 1994), 79, 169; John Dooly to John Adam Treutlen, September 26, 1777, HSP; David Haley to David W. Haley, March 19, 1839, Acquisition 706, Manuscript Section, Tennessee State Library and Archives, Nashville; Revolutionary War pension claim of John Watkins, R11190, (Microfilm M804, roll 2505, NARA). Both Galphin and Stuart died before the end of the American Revolution. Davis, "George Galphin," 23.

36. Warren, *Georgia Governor and Council Journals 1772–1773,* 150, 167, 168, 174; "Vertias," *South Carolina and American General Gazette* (Charleston), October 16, 1777; Edward J. Cashin, *The King's Ranger: Thomas Brown and the American Revolution on the Southern Frontier* (Athens: University of Georgia Press, 1989), 15, 47, 54, 67; Davis, "George Galphin," 15; and Davis, *Georgia Citizens and Soldiers,* 22–28. For the controversies around McIntosh, see Harvey H. Jackson, *Lachlan McIntosh and the Politics of Revolutionary Georgia* (Athens: University of Georgia Press, 1979), and for Gwinnett's background, see Richard L. Blanco, ed., *The American Revolution, 1775–1783: An Encyclopedia* (New York: Garland, 1993), 713–14.

37. Elizabeth Lichtenstein Johnston, *Recollections of a Georgia Loyalist* (New York: M. F. Mansfield, 1901), 45; petition of John Dooly to John Adam Treutlen, September 26, 1777, HSP; grant fees paid, 1775 and 1778, Georgia Surveyor General Department, Record Group 3, GAr; Margaret Godley, comp., "Minutes of the Executive Council, May 7 through October 14, 1777," *GHQ* 33 (December 1949): 327–28; 34 (March 1950): 108; Candler, *The Revolutionary Records,* 2:28, 137; Revolutionary War pension files of Benjamin Thompson, Ga. S 32016, Joshua Ford, Ga. S 3368, Jesse Hooper, Ga. S 1913, Charles Gent, Ga. S 1903, and John Bynum, Ga. S 3111 (Microfilm M804, rolls 443, 1001, 1061, 1322, and 2373, NARA).

38. Charles Stedman, *The History of the Origin, Progress, and Termination of the American War,* 2 vols. (Dublin, Ire.: Printed for Messrs. P. Wogan, P. Byrne, 1794), 2:119; *New York Gazette and Weekly Mercury,* March 29, 1779; Davis, *The Wilkes County Papers,*

28. For Hamilton's biography, see Robert S. Davis, "Biography: Colonel John Hamilton of the Royal North Carolina Regiment," *Southern Campaigns of the American Revolution* 3 (May 2006): 32–34; available online at http://www.southerncampaign.org/newsletter/ v3n5.pdf (accessed July 20, 2009).

39. Andrew Williamson to James Bowie, October 14, 1778, James Bowie Papers, New York Public Library. Williamson's relations with Dooly, however, may have been complicated by the repeated recruitment of men from Wilkes County by the South Carolina militia, despite the risk of Indian attack that removing such men from Georgia could cause. Ironically the recruitment of Georgia frontiersmen for South Carolina included, in 1775, enlisting men for a campaign against the loyalists of Raeburn Creek, South Carolina. Members of that same community would later be defeated by Dooly at the battle of Kettle Creek, Georgia. Revolutionary War pension claim of John Cloud, S 30935, (Microfilm M804, roll 582, NARA).

40. Davis, *Georgians in the Revolution,* 14–17. The pistols, later used by Pickens at the battles of Kettle Creek and Cowpens, can be seen today in the Pickens County Museum of Art and History, Pickens, South Carolina.

41. John Dooly to Samuel Elbert, February 16, 1779, Misc. Mss. 174, Yale University Libraries, New Haven; Andrew Pickens to Henry Lee, August 28, 1811, Thomas Sumter Papers, 1 VV 107, Lyman C. Draper Collection, State Historical Society of Wisconsin, Madison (hereafter cited as the Draper Collection); Davis, *Georgians in the Revolution,* 3–24.

42. *South Carolina and American General Gazette* (Charleston), April 9, 1779; McCall, *History of Georgia,* 2:409–10, 471–72; Clyde R. Ferguson, "General Andrew Pickens" (Ph.D. diss., Duke University, 1960), 66–69; Smith, *Morningstars of Liberty,* 148–49; C. F. W. Coker, ed., "The Journal of John Graham, South Carolina Militia, 1779," *Military Collector & Historian* 19 (Summer 1967): 39, 41; Charles C. Jones, Jr., ed., "The Autobiography of Col. William Few," *Magazine of American History* 7 (November 1881): 349; Revolutionary War pension files of Henry Anglin, Ga. S 31521, Samuel Hammond, SC S 21807, and John Smith, Ga. / SC R 9769 (Microfilm M804, rolls 66, 1176, 2219, NARA). Veteran George Robuck remembered the battle under Few and Hammond that resulted in Major Ross's death occurred at Galphin's cowpens. Revolutionary War pension file of George Robuck, SC S 9467 (Microfilm M804, roll 2069, NARA).

43. Wallace Brown, *The Good Americans: The Loyalists in the American Revolution* (New York: Morrow, 1969), 46; Robert M. Calhoon, *The Loyalist Perception and Other Essays* (Columbia: University of South Carolina Press, 1989), 11, 154–58, 168; Klein, "Frontier Planters and the American Revolution," 46; John Shy, *A People Numerous and Armed,* rev. ed. (Ann Arbor: University of Michigan Press, 1990), 231–32. For newspaper accounts of the campaigns of the Americans against the British and the king's allies, many of which are abstracts of letters from Andrew Williamson to Benjamin Lincoln, see Mary B. Warren, comp., *Georgia Governor and Council Journals, 1778–1779: Savannah under Siege* (Athens, Ga.: Heritage Papers, 2007).

44. Heard Robertson, "A Revised or Loyalist Perspective of Augusta during the American Revolution," *Richmond County History* 1 (Summer 1969): 5–23.

45. For the politics and backgrounds of these men, see Cashin, *The King's Ranger.*

46. Davis, *The Wilkes County Papers,* 30–32.

47. Davidson, *Early Records of Georgia,* 2:2–12; Candler, *The Revolutionary Records,* 2:177–79.

48. Robert S. Davis, "The Loyalist Trials at Ninety Six in 1779," *South Carolina Historical Magazine* 80 (April 1979): 172–81; Robert M. Weir, "The Last of American Freemen" in *"The Last of American Freemen": Studies in the Political Culture of the Colonial and Revolutionary South* (Macon, Ga.: Mercer University Press, 1986), 148–49; Robert M. Weir, "'The Violent Spirit': The Reestablishment of Order, and the Continuity of Leadership in Post-Revolutionary South Carolina," in Hoffman et al., *An Uncivil War*, 72–91.

49. Wilkes County Court Minutes (1778–1780), microfilm drawer 45, roll 29, GAr; Eliza A. Bowen, *Chronicles of Wilkes County, Georgia from Washington's Newspapers, 1889–1898*, ed. Mary B. Warren (Danielsville, Ga.: Heritage Papers, 1978), 41.

50. For the decline of patriotism as a motive for service in the Continental Army, see Michael Stephenson, *Patriot Battles: How the War of Independence Was Fought* (New York: HarperCollins, 2007).

51. Andrew Williamson to Benjamin Lincoln, April 9, 1779, Benjamin Lincoln Manuscripts, Special Collections, Perkins Library, Duke University, Durham; John Rutledge to Lincoln, April 11, 1779, Lincoln to Dooly, April 14, 1779 (Lincoln letterbook), Benjamin Lincoln Papers, Massachusetts Historical Society, Boston; Benjamin Lincoln Warrant Book, p. 65, New York Public Library.

52. Dooly to Lincoln, July 25, 1779, Lloyd W. Smith Collection, Morristown National Historical Site, Morristown, New Jersey; Warren, *Georgia Governor and Council Journals, 1778–1779*, 215; Lachlan McIntosh to Lincoln, August 4, 1779, William L. Clements Library, University of Michigan, Ann Arbor.

53. Quotation in *Remembrancer: Or Impartial Repository of Public Events* 8 (1780): 304.

54. Revolutionary War pension claims of Benjamin Thompson, Ga. S 32016, and Moses Perkins, Ga. S 3677 (Microfilm M804, rolls 1912 and 2373, NARA).

55. "Extract of a Letter from Charleston, May 29, 1779," *Pennsylvania Gazette* (Philadelphia), July 7, 1779; Godley, comp., "Minutes of the Executive Council," 34:106, 123; Robert S. Davis, "Colonel Dooly's Campaign of 1779," *Huntington Library Quarterly* 46 (Winter 1984): 65–71; Smith, *Morningstars of Liberty*, 156; Davis, *Georgia Citizens and Soldiers*, 99; Joseph Clay to Benjamin Lincoln, October 18, 1779, in Georgia Historical Society, *Collections* (Savannah, 1913), 8:151–53. Historian Hugh McCall wrote that a man named Corker died as a result of Dooly's failed campaign in Burke County in June 1779 and that Dooly's killer was also a man named Corker. McCall, *History of Georgia*, 2:296, 306.

56. Robert S. Davis, "The Georgia Militia at the Siege of Savannah," *Atlanta Historical Journal* 25 (Winter 1981): 43–56; *Plan of the Siege of Savannah* (1794), map 601, Georgia Historical Society, Savannah.

57. For the politics of George Wells and his faction, see Edward J. Cashin, "'The Famous Colonel Wells': Factionalism in Revolutionary Georgia," *GHQ* 58 (suppl., 1974): 137–56, and Harvey H. Jackson, "The Rise of the Western Members: Revolutionary Politics and the Georgia Backcountry," in Hoffman et al., eds., *An Uncivil War*, 276–320.

58. Candler, *The Revolutionary Records*, 2:117, 223, 225–26, 359; Davidson, *Early Records of Georgia*, 1:33; Cashin, *The King's Ranger*, 99, 107–8; House Journal, January 31, 1787, p. 241, GAr.

59. Ferguson, "General Andrew Pickens," 93–99.

60. Joseph Johnson, *Traditions and Reminiscences: Chiefly of the American Revolution in the South* (Charleston, S.C.: Walker & James, 1851), 149–50; Lucian Lamar Knight, comp., *Georgia's Roster of the Revolution* (1920; repr., Baltimore: Genealogical Publishing

Company, 1967), 178; Stephen Heard to Richard Howley, March 2, 1781, Keith Read Collection, Hargrett Rare Books and Manuscripts Collection; Revolutionary War pension files of Joshua Burnett, Ga. S 32154, Jesse Gordon, Ga. W 13280, Peter Strozier, Ga. R 10279, and David H. Thurmond, Ga. S 32010 (Microfilm M804, rolls 306, 863, 2195, and 2264, NARA).

61. Inventory of estate of Joseph Duncan, Probate Court packets, Richmond County courthouse. Augusta, Ga.; Dooly to Alexander McGowan, August 8, 1780, Georgia Historical Society, Savannah.

62. Klein, "Frontier Planters and the American Revolution," 63; Shy, *A People Numerous and Armed*, 232; Bicheno, *Rebels & Redcoats*, 179; J. H. Cruger to Charles Cornwallis, September 28, 1780, Cornwallis Papers, 30/11/64, p. 116, National Archives of the United Kingdom, Kew; Heard Robertson and Edward J. Cashin, *Augusta and the American Revolution* (Darien, Ga.: Printed for Richmond County Historical Society by Ashantilly Press, 1975), 48–50; Elijah Clarke to "Gov. Campbell," November 5, 1780, Thomas Sumter Papers, 4 VV 272–73, Draper Collection. Burwell Smith died fighting at the battle of Cedar Spring, South Carolina, on August 24, 1780. Lyman C. Draper, *King's Mountain and Its Heroes* (Cincinnati: P. G. Thomson, 1881), 97.

63. Knight, *Georgia's Roster of the Revolution*, 178; *Gazette of the State of Georgia* (Savannah), February 5, 1784; Clarke to Cornwallis, November 5, 1780, Cornwallis Papers, 30/11/4, p. 20.

64. That loyalist commander J. H. Cruger made no mention of John Dooly in a letter he wrote from Dooly's home suggests that Dooly had died before that date (September 23, 1780) and after Dooly had written to Alexander McGowan on August 8, 1780. J. H. Cruger to Cornwallis, September 23, 1780. Cornwallis Papers, 30/11/64, pp. 104–5; Dooly to McGowan, August 8, 1780, Georgia Historical Society, Savannah. Confusion remains over the details of Dooly's death. An undocumented history has loyalists breaking into the Dooly home late at night and killing him for refusing to join the king's militia. His wife and other children fled, but John Mitchell Dooly, then a small boy, hid under the bed and witnessed the murder. A. C. Whitehead, *Makers of Georgia's Name and Fame* (Boston: Educational Publishing Company, 1913), 101. The first biography of John Dooly has a McCorkle of South Carolina, whom George Dooly later killed, as his murderer. Sherwood, *A Gazetteer*, 198. Revolutionary War veteran Samuel Beckhaem told McCall that the loyalist who ordered the killing was Captain William Corker. Deposition of Samuel Beckhaem, June 1, 1812, Peter Force Collection, vii–E, 3, Manuscripts Division, Library of Congress. John Watkins remembered Dooly as being murdered by one of his own men after Dooly surrendered and disbanded his regiment. A John Smith would claim to have heard of the plot to kill Dooly nine days before it happened and to have tried, unsuccessfully, to warn him. Another John Smith, who lived with the Dooly family, claimed that a loyalist Captain Wilder murdered John Dooly. Revolutionary War pension claims of John Smith, Ga. R31967, John Smith, Ga. R9769, and John Watkins, Ga. R11190, (Microfilm M804, rolls 2219 and 2505, NARA).

65. *South Carolina and American General Gazette* (Charleston), September 27, 1780.

66. Davis, *The Wilkes County Papers*, 30–32; Bowen, *Chronicles of Wilkes County*, 22. For the loyalist politics of the Georgia frontier during this period, see Heard Robertson, "The Second British Occupation of Augusta," *GHQ* 58 (Winter 1974): 422–46.

67. Thomas Brown to Alexander Leslie, July 1, 1782, Thomas Addis Emmett Collection, New York Public Library; Cashin, *The King's Ranger*, 128, 152; David Cockran, *The*

Creek Frontier, 1540–1783 (Norman: University of Oklahoma Press, 1967), 321; John Martin to Tallasee King, July 19, 1782, in *GHQ* 1 (1917): 313. For the campaign to recover Georgia from the British, see Edward J. Cashin, "Nathanael Greene's Campaign for Georgia in 1781," *GHQ* 61 (Spring 1977): 43–58. James Jackson attributed part of the success at the battles of Blackstocks and at Cowpens to the ability of the Wilkes County riflemen to reload while rolling on the ground. This ability actually existed across the frontier. Lilla M. Hawes, comp., "The Papers of James Jackson, 1781–1793," Georgia Historical Society *Collections* 11 (Savannah, 1955), 17–18; Thomas U. P. Charlton, *The Life of Major General James Jackson* (Augusta: Printed by G. F. Randolph & Company, 1809), 21; Baika Harvey to Thomas Baika, December 30, 1775, Orkney Island Archives, Scotland.

68. Davis, *The Wilkes County Papers*, 30; Clarke to Dr. McDonald, December 9, 1794, Georgia, Alabama, and South Carolina Papers, 1V11, Draper Collection. For Turner, see Allan G. Bogue, *Frederick Jackson Turner: Strange Roads Going Down* (Norman: University of Oklahoma Press, 1998).

69. George Dooly vs. Hannah Caudle, Joseph M. Toomey Collection, GAr; Leslie Hall, *Land & Allegiance in Revolutionary Georgia* (Athens: University of Georgia Press, 2001), 153. No records of Robert Dooly or William Dooly (John Dooly's brother, presumed to be in the South Carolina Continentals) having survived the Revolution have been found. Robert Dooly did have a wife. Revolutionary War pension claim of Edmund Forns, SC W 9446, (Microfilm M804, roll 1003, NARA).

70. E. Merton Coulter, "Elijah Clarke's Foreign Intrigues and the 'Trans-Oconee Republic,'" *Mississippi Valley Historical Review*, extra number (November 1921): 260–79. For a description of the Waters plantation, see Davis, *The Wilkes County Papers*, 25, and Peter W. Coldham, comp., *American Loyalist Claims* (Washington, D.C.: National Genealogical Society, 1980), 515.

71. Thomas Lee reportedly lived to the age of 115. Flora B. Dotson to author, December 1, 1976; David Ramsey, *The History of South-Carolina from Its First Settlement in 1670, to the Year 1808*, 2 vols. (Charleston, S.C.: Published by David Longworth for the author, 1809), 2:223; will of Thomas Lee, probate box 108, packet 2952, Probate Court, Abbeville Courthouse, Abbeville, S.C.

72. George Dooley (his spelling) became a large landowner in Lincoln County (named for Benjamin Lincoln in 1780), Kentucky, and died there in 1821. He emancipated his slave wife, Sarah, and their children, including sons John and Clark Dooley, to whom he left most of his property. Will of George Dooley. For Williamson's problems for having surrendered, see Edward J. Cashin, "The Trembling Land: Covert Activities in the Georgia Backcountry during the American Revolution," *Proceedings and Papers of the Georgia Association of Historians* 4 (1983): 34–36.

73. Candler, *The Revolutionary Records*, 2:359–60; Farmer, comp., *Wilkes County, Georgia Deed Books*, 546; legal notice, John Dooly estate, *Augusta (Ga.) Chronicle and Gazette of the State*, July 17, 1790, February 14, 1801. Thomas Waters claimed to have reached Savannah with one thousand Cherokees. Coldham, *American Loyalist Claims*, 515. Some Thomas Waters researchers believe that he even returned to South Carolina after the American Revolution and lived there for many years. For Waters and his family history, see Sharon P. Flanagan, "George Morgan Waters: A Social Biography" (master's thesis, University of Georgia, 1987), and Don L. Shadburn, *Unhallowed Intrusion: A History of Cherokee Families in Forsyth County, Georgia* (Forsyth, Ga.: privately printed, 1993), 11–2.

74. E. Merton Coulter, "A Famous Duel That Was Never Fought," *GHQ* 43 (December 1959): 365; Stephen F. Miller, *The Bench and Bar of Georgia: Memoirs and Sketches,* 2 vols. (Philadelphia: J. B. Lippincott, 1858), 1:333; Mary E. Moragne, *The Neglected Thread: A Journal of the Calhoun Community, 1836–1842,* ed. Delle Mullen Craven (Columbia: University of South Carolina Press, 1951), 156, 171–72, 200. The widow Dianna "Dinah" Mitchell Dooly married Randolph Griffin. Details of her later life are not known except that she, through her new husband, appears to have been repeatedly sued over John Dooly's debts. John Dooly estate papers, Record Group 257–2–10, Wilkes County grants of administrations and guardianships, April 4, 1787, microfilm drawer 44, roll 31, and Superior Court minutes (1788–1794), April term 1788, microfilm drawer 45, roll 29, GAr; Hendrix, *Edgefield County South Carolina Abstracts of Deed Books 1–12,* 7–8.

3

Practice

Fourteen

Moral Allegiance

John Witherspoon and Loyalist Recantation

ROBERT M. CALHOON AND
TIMOTHY M. BARNES

When the Continental Congress returned to Philadelphia on July 7, 1778, following the British evacuation of the city, printer Benjamin Towne solicited several delegates for news and contributions to the *Philadelphia Evening Post*. One of the delegates, John Witherspoon of New Jersey, refused to cooperate unless Towne first publicly apologized for his collaboration with the British during General William Howe's occupation of Philadelphia. Out of either naïveté or servility, Towne asked Witherspoon to compose a suitable apology for him. Later, when Towne saw what Witherspoon had written, he realized what a blunder he had made in entrusting the rehabilitation of his public image to so didactic and judgmental a figure as the Scottish Presbyterian and academic. Towne refused to sign Witherspoon's statement without substantial deletions. Witherspoon thereupon circulated the document in manuscript around Philadelphia and it was published the following October in the Fishkill *New York Packet.*[1] Over the following weeks Witherspoon composed a wholly unsolicited recantation for another notorious loyalist printer, James Rivington. It was even more elaborate and demeaning than Towne's. These two bizarre documents[2] illustrate the nature of cultural and moral conflict in the Revolution; they reveal Witherspoon's elaborate behind-the-scenes leadership; and they provide important new insights into the development of patriot attitudes concerning allegiance, public morality, and the ethical underpinnings of republicanism.

1

Benjamin Towne was an emigrant from Lincolnshire, England, and a marginal figure in the Philadelphia printing community before the Revolution. In 1769, he had been employed by part-owner Joseph Galloway of the *Pennsylvania Chronicle* to serve as a watchdog over the paper's headstrong printer, William Goddard. Towne left this post a year later and worked irregularly as a coppersmith and journeyman printer until 1776, when he began printing the *Evening Post,* a paper which was generally nonpolitical but which occasionally carried pieces written by delegates to Congress. When the British occupied Philadelphia in September 1777, however, Towne's was the only newspaper that continued to appear, and it consistently supported British rule. A week before the British departed, in June 1778, Towne naively signaled his intention to support the American cause.[3]

As a confession of cowardice and civic irresponsibility, Witherspoon's "humble confession, declaration, recantation, and apology of BENJAMIN TOWNE" was a heavy-handed but powerful piece of satire. The pathetic admissions that Towne "never was, nor ever pretended to be a man of character, repute or dignity," and that he had become habituated to "meanness" and "scurrility" provided just the sort of titillation and groveling that Witherspoon needed to guarantee wide circulation and discussion of the confession. He wanted to underscore the way in which virtue could be utterly debased by prolonged subservience to the likes of Joseph Galloway. Incapable of purposeful and consistent civil conduct, Towne had degenerated into equivocation. Opportunistic neutrality and the shifting of loyalty, the apologia insisted, were respectable and understandable kinds of behavior. "[C]hanging sides is not any way surprising in a person answering the above description," Towne blandly contended. Did not Cato of Utica as well as "another senator of inferior note whose name I cannot recollect" commit suicide rather than adapt to the death of the Roman republic? Witherspoon here aimed an elaborate insult at Towne's supposedly skimpy knowledge of the classics; Cato of Utica did commit suicide rather than live under the tyranny of Caesar, but "another senator" could only be a reference to Statilius, an adherent of Cato, who announced his intention of following Cato's example but who was dissuaded by friends acting on Cato's instructions, and who later died in battle defending the republic.[4] Presumably, self-preservation was preferable to self-destruction. To be sure, Witherspoon had Towne concede, if an Adams or a Hancock had defected to the British, the patriots might understandably have punished his treachery severely. But "what occasion is there for the public to pour out all its wrath upon poor Towne? . . . why so much noise about a trifle?" After all, far more important Pennsylvanians—notably John Allen, Tench Coxe, and the Reverend William Smith—had switched from opposition to support of the Crown during the Revolutionary crisis.[5]

Witherspoon's Towne flaunted stylish and superficial knowledge as the only protective garment available to a morally deficient individual with no deep roots in the civic values of his community. Witherspoon had Towne explain how

> the rational moralists of the last age used to tell us that there was an essential difference between virtue and vice. . . . Now, with all due deference to these great men, I think I am as much a philosopher as to know that there are no circumstances of action more important than those of time and place. Therefore if any man pay no regard to the changes that may happen in these circumstances, there will be little virtue and still less *prudence* in his behaviour. . . . [A]sk any plain Quaker in this city, what he would say to a man

who should wear the same coat in summer as in winter in this climate? He would certainly say, "Friend, thy wisdom is not great."

This passage, which expressed Witherspoon's deep suspicion about learning not firmly grounded in personal virtue, revealed the inner logic of the Towne apologia: the buffeting of a loyalist by sensual impressions which he was unable to evaluate with normal discrimination, the perpetually whining tone when confronted with criticism, and the pathetic need to assume any available protective coloration, even that of an apolitical Quaker. So Towne pleaded that he "had no more regard for Gen[eral] Clinton, or even Mrs. Loring, or any other of the *chaste nymphs* that attended the Fête Champêtre, alias "Mischianza" of May 18, 1778.[6] Probably in consideration of these demeaning but revealing sentiments, Witherspoon included the more authentic remark: "I was neither Whig nor Tory, but a printer."

Witherspoon's "*Humble* Representation *and earnest* Supplication of James Rivington," written in late 1778, was another harsh parody of the dilemma faced by loyalist printers. Whereas Towne had inadvertently collaborated with Witherspoon in initiating his apology, there is no evidence that Rivington knew anything about the recantation Witherspoon attributed to him. Building on his experience with Towne, Witherspoon undoubtedly saw Rivington as a still more revealing example of loyalist printer amorality. Rivington was not originally a printer at all, but rather a bookseller in London. At the invitation of Governor William Tryon, Councillor William Smith, and others, he agreed to publish a newspaper of broad appeal which would offer, among other viewpoints, writings supportive of royal authority. Rivington was told that he could expect favors from the royal government if he would execute such a project.[7] Late in 1773 Rivington's *New-York Gazetteer* became the focus of attacks by those who demanded ideological conformity to the resistance movement. By the spring of 1775, increasingly shrill patriot criticism forced Rivington to sign an oath in support of the Continental Congress. The question of the printer's allegiance had become so important to the leading revolutionaries that his oath was acknowledged in Congress and even outside of that body as a recantation. This fact, however, did nothing to prevent a mob from destroying his print shop and forcing him to flee, eventually to London.[8] The attack on his newspaper was meant to chasten Rivington, but in London he was even more willing to put his press at anyone's disposal. Early in 1776, he urged the ministry to reestablish and subsidize his press in New York; the purpose would be to defend the ministry against critics at home and to attack the rebellion they supported in America.[9]

In the fall of 1777 Rivington returned to occupied New York with the title of "King's Printer" and began printing a newspaper that for the next six years would be unmatched in its assault upon the patriots and that would make him the object of their undying condemnation. However, it has never been recognized that Rivington's attack was being directed by William Tryon and William Smith. This oversight accounts for the myth that the *Royal Gazette* was an expression of Rivington's consistent and deep personal allegiance to toryism. As the King's printer, Rivington was the last person to be suspected of serving as a spy for Washington's secret service. Yet prompted by his own political indifference and disappointment at the unfulfilled promise of a royally subsidized press, Rivington in 1779 began to pass military intelligence to Washington's agents in New York.[10]

Oblivious of any of these complexities and nuances, Witherspoon again used florid, obsequious language to condemn loyalist motivation in a highly judgmental fashion and to expose the debilitating effect of Loyalism on a person's character and self-respect. "Your petitioner has no desire at all, either to be roasted in Florida, or frozen to death in Canada, or Nova Scotia," Witherspoon had Rivington explain in a formal memorial; "having been a bankrupt in London, it is not impossible that he might be accommodated with a lodging in Newgate.... In this dreadful dilemma, he hath at last determined to apply to your High Mightinesses, and ... to *lay himself at your feet,* which he assures you is the true modish phrase for respectful submission, according to the present etiquette of the court."

For all his superficial familiarity with the events of the Revolution, Rivington—as caricatured by Witherspoon—understood nothing of the spirit and values of the patriot cause. In order to ingratiate himself with patriot leaders who were "Presbyterians and Religionists," Witherspoon had Rivington take "pains to find out a scripture warrant of example for his present conduct ... in the advice given" to Syrian King Benhadad humbling himself before the rulers of Israel in I Kings 20:31. Though Witherspoon allowed Rivington artificially plausible ground for arguing that he should not be punished by the victorious American regime, those very claims affronted patriot concepts of political morality. Even if it were true that "a Tory heart" possessed "a rancour of spirit and rottenness of heart, unattainable by any other class of men," Rivington could reassure the patriots that he was personally powerless and that, like Towne, he would write and circulate whatever views authorities told him to publish.

Witherspoon's Rivington went on to heap mortification upon himself by piteously explaining how impotent and defanged the adherents of the Crown had become by 1778. The "barbarity" with which loyalist officials abused American prisoners would surely behoove all former Tories to observe the strictest good conduct toward the new American regime. Confessing that the loyalist press had shamefully slandered the patriots—"We never once made you *retreat;* seldom even to *fly* as a routed army; but to *run into the woods; to scamper away through the fields;* and to *take to your heels as usual*"—Witherspoon had Rivington indulge in language of unmanliness and cowardice. Rivington reminded the patriots of the public scourging they had received in British and in American garrison town newspapers: "You must remember the many sweet names given you in print in England and America,—Rebels—rascals—ragamuffins—tatterdemalions—scoundrels—black-guards—cowards and poltroons." Considering "what a miserable affair it must be for a man to be obliged to apply with humility and self-abasement to those whom he hath so treated," Rivington's apology concluded, many loyalist "refugees" and "friends of government" were immobilized by "fear and trembling" and the tory printer Hugh Gaine, "is so much affected, that some say he has lost, or will soon lose, his reason."

Fear of political retribution did not, however, prevent the recanting Rivington from being in "the very pink of courtesy, a genteel, portly, well-looking fellow." Though he was confessedly chastened, Rivington's assumption that his opponents would overlook past faults and indeed draw on his talents in the future revealed, in Witherspoon's portrayal, that Rivington had not truly undergone any inner reformation of attitudes. "I understand and possess the *bienséance,* the manner, the grace, so largely insisted upon by Lord Chesterfield," boasted the printer, betraying his misunderstanding of the nature of republicanism.[11] To maximize the effect of Rivington's inadvertent self-condemnation, Witherspoon made himself the butt of Rivington's smug remarks. "I have been informed," the "Supplication" explained,

> that a certain person, well known to your august body, has clearly demonstrated that virtue and severity of manners are necessar to those who would pull an old government down, which feat is now happily accomplished; but that luxury, dissipation, and a taste for pleasure, are equally necessary to keep up a government already settled ... [N]ow that you have settled governments in all the states, you are looking out for proper persons to soften the rigid virtue of the Americans, or as ... Dr. Johnson would have said, to *somnify* them[12] ... and lay them asleep.... I am proud to say, that there is not a man on this continent more able to serve you in this respect, than myself.

Precisely because he was, in Witherspoon's eyes, a stylish, transient, chameleon-like figure, Rivington could perform as a printer whatever services the shapers of opinion required of him. He could pander to their love of power and authority as readily as he had to British and loyalist interests.

In the "Recantation of Benjamin Towne" and the "Supplication of James Rivington," Witherspoon sought not only to pillory the moral bankruptcy of these two loyalist printers, but more importantly to teach his patriot contemporaries a lesson about their own republicanism. Out of the mouths of these two political trimmers came warnings about how easily human virtue could be perverted, how readily falsehood could circulate in a free society, and how plausibly scoundrels could speak in their own defense.

2

Witherspoon's fascination with ritual humiliation and his agitation in the face of evil were both rooted in painful experience with political conflict. For a quarter century prior to his emigration to the colonies, he had led Scottish evangelical Calvinists in an unsuccessful fight to wrest control from a moderate intellectual elite, determined to accommodate Presbyterianism to the Enlightenment. During these controversies, Witherspoon had twice published devastating satires of his opponents. In the colonies, however, he moderated this abrasive, combative style in order to preside over a consensus within American Presbyterianism.[13] Initially hesitant to participate in the pre-Revolutionary controversy, Witherspoon was appalled by American attachment to John Wilkes, who was, in his view, a mob leader who had opportunistically whipped up anti-Scottish hatred in his attack on the King. By the summer of 1774, however, Witherspoon was privately convinced that colonial protest was neither the result of Wilkesian "pride, resentment, . . . sedition,"[14] nor a desire to encourage Wilkes's vicious assault on the king's family. As a result, Witherspoon began open resistance by joining New Jersey's Somerset County Committee of Correspondence and by becoming a member of a colonywide convention to select delegates to the First Continental Congress. Although he was not selected as a New Jersey delegate, he went to Philadelphia to argue against compensating the East India Company.[15] In the following summer Witherspoon became the undisputed leader of New Jersey's independence movement, and in June 1776 he was elected to Congress.

During his first two years in Congress, Witherspoon's radical credentials seemed confirmed by his opposition to any attempt at reconciliation, by his support of the alliance with France, and by the death of his own son at the battle of Germantown. Yet over the course of his six-year tenure in Congress, Witherspoon's colleagues assigned him to only three major committees out of the hundreds on which he served. His friend Benjamin Rush attributed his peripheral role to his being the only clergyman in Congress.[16] More significant, probably, was the fact that he was Scottish, a member of the minority that his New Jersey associate William Patterson called "the worst vermin under Heaven."[17] Anti-Scottish prejudice caught Witherspoon in such a maze of suspicions that his best efforts to secure a fair hearing for himself and other Scots seemed self-serving and hypocritical. His "Address to the Natives of Scotland Residing in America," published in July 1776, freely admitted that he felt "an attachment of country, . . ." to the land of his birth, but he insisted, only "as far as it is a virtuous or laudable principle." Many Scots, he explained, suffered from suspicion that they were less opposed to British encroachments than were colonists of English and Scots Irish stock, and he conceded that some Scots were "too much inclined" to acquiesce in British policy.[18]

His "Address" was, then, as much an explanation of Scottish political sensibilities as an attempt to change those views. Many Scots, he explained, had been justifiably offended by the American adulation of John Wilkes for appropriating the name *North Briton* and the symbolic number 45 for a scurrilous attack on George III. Sensitivity to Scottish feelings could make the colonial case stronger and more defensible. "If you want to establish a case for liberty," L. Gordon Tait writes, paraphrasing Witherspoon, "do not drag in examples of real or imagined injustice in Britain. . . . Leave Britain and Wilkes out of it." The advantage of this restraint, Witherspoon felt, lay in the fact that it allowed him to base his case for independence on American potentialities rather than on British misdeeds. America had a glorious and God-given destiny that was about to be realized; only "criminal inattention" could blind observers to the "singular interposition of providence . . . in behalf of the American colonies." The rare historical opportunity to create a new political order, coupled with the confidence of the people in their representatives, would motivate American leaders to choose and act wisely. "Too much Scoticism," snorted Ezra Stiles. "He wants to save his countrymen who have behaved most cruelly in the American conflict."[19]

Widespread loyalism and neutrality in New Jersey also prompted Witherspoon to contrast authentic allegiance with Rivington's gross disloyalty. Throughout the Revolution Witherspoon believed that the "great number of Tories in every state" was a more important danger to the Revolution "than the [military] force sent against us."[20] In New Jersey between 1776, and December 1778, when the Supplication was written, unusually strong disloyalty was exhibited in the form of loyalism, neutrality, and allegiance-switching. Among the states, New Jersey ranked fourth in the percentage of active loyalists, and it would have placed higher had it not been for the British army's brutality against loyalists as well as patriots. Despite these indiscriminate atrocities the counties nearest New York and Philadelphia had a proportion of loyalists that probably went as high as one-third or even one-half. By the fall of 1776, Witherspoon and other New Jersey radicals faced a huge problem in maintaining affection for the Revolution. Six New Jersey Provincial Congressmen as well as Witherspoon's friend and colleague in Congress, Richard Stockton, had departed for the British lines. Furthermore, large numbers of those "of inferior rank" had defected.[21] In a fury, Witherspoon referred to such defectors as: "Hypocrite[s] . . . , Fools[s] . . . , Robber[s] . . . , Rogue[s] . . . , Blasphemer[s] . . . , Sycophant[s] . . . , and Liar[s] . . . ,"[22] and would soon use the example of James Rivington to instruct others concerning a firm and proper allegiance.

This harsh condemnation of turncoats masked Witherspoon's apprehension and uncertainty over how to deal with the deteriorating political situation in New Jersey. He knew, for example, that Stockton's defection represented no overt change in loyalty. Both Witherspoon and Stockton had fled Princeton on November 29, 1776, just ahead of advancing British troops. Witherspoon and most other leading whigs had reached safety in Pennsylvania, but Stockton had inexplicably sought refuge in tory-infested Monmouth County, perhaps because Washington had just dispatched troops to keep order there. Stockton and his host John Cowenhoven were dragged from their beds and taken in freezing weather to New York City where Stockton was kept in a cold cell without food for twenty-four hours and then given only scant rations. Anxious for the safety of his family and exhausted by his ordeal, he had taken General William Howe's prescribed oath to cease participation in the rebellion and was released. A painful cancer, which developed from a badly chapped lip in November 1778, and the destruction of his home and property, despite the fact that Howe's oath was obtained from him under duress, precluded Stockton's rejoining the American cause. He died from the cancer in 1780.[23]

Witherspoon was aware of these facts and he even ridiculed the charge that Stockton had pleaded to his captors that he was preparing to surrender to Howe at the time of his arrest.[24] Yet he included in the Rivington recantation a veiled but unmistakable attack on Stockton and on Governor William Livingston: "We have often heard of Hortensius the governor of N—— J—— a gentleman remarkable for severely handling those he calls traitors; and indeed has exalted some of them (*quanquam animus meminisse horret luctuque refugit*[25] [although my mind shudders to remember and has recoiled in grief]) to a high though dependent station." Here Witherspoon alluded to the first election for governor under the 1776 New Jersey constitution. In the election, Stockton and Livingston at first tied in the voting and then Stockton was offered, but declined, the post of Chief Justice.[26] By savagely attacking the pitiable Stockton and by ridiculing Livingston's handling of the tory problem, Witherspoon could vent his rage at what he considered the real issue, the "secret enemies" of the Revolution in New Jersey, including loyalists and allegiance-switchers as well as passive opponents of the patriot cause among the middle and lower classes of society.[27] Even the militia was "tinctured with Toryism" and could not be trusted. So Witherspoon agreed with Governor Livingston to the dispatch by Congress of a small group of Continental troops "to strike a Terror into the disaffected." These numerous equivocating enemies, who Witherspoon believed "more or less abound[ed] in every New Jersey county,"[28] did not disappear however.

So in late 1778, in Rivington's mock recantation, Witherspoon once again took up satire—that form he believed "most agreeable to the public"[29]—to attack the morality of those "chicken-hearted" creatures who failed to rally to the American cause "for no other reason, than that they might avoid fighting" altogether. Congressional military force had failed to deal with these overly prudent people. Now he hoped to humiliate and shame them, beginning with Rivington.

In the "Supplication," Witherspoon sought to vindicate fidelity to the principles of the Revolution. Here again the recantation of a well-known and widely hated loyalist provided an ideal device. Witherspoon had come to America on a mission. As Witherspoon was leaving Scotland, a fellow clergyman had reminded him of his wish to transport the "seat of truth and righteousness . . ." from the Old World, where it had been defeated, to America.[30] After his arrival Witherspoon had been disturbed by the "outrage and sedition" which accompanied colonial resistance. When he realized, however, that resistance in America offered the possibility of moral regeneration, he suddenly became a radical. By 1776, he was looking forward to the turmoil of a revolution as an opportunity for Americans "to shake off the encumbrances of sloth and self-indulgence," and to improve the "temper, . . . morals, national . . . manners and . . . public virtue" of their country. He urged "humility, . . . restraint, and moderation" as imperative for success. "The riotous and wasteful liver," he wrote, "whose craving appetites make him constantly needy, is and must be subject to many masters . . . [b]ut the frugal and moderate person, who guides his affairs with discretion, is able to assist in public councils by a free and unbiased judgment. . . ."[31] Witherspoon saw this moral republicanism in formation in 1776, and, like the Calvinist clergy elsewhere in America, he would make a crucial contribution to the idea. Virtue, he insisted, was the necessary ingredient for a successful republican revolution and an even greater need if a republic was to stand permanently.[32] During the war Witherspoon's mission would take on forms as varied as the rehabilitation of Scottish prisoners,[33] the self-conscious wearing of clerical gowns in Congress,[34] various journeys to Princeton to reopen the College,[35] and intermittent attempts to improve male-female relations. His commitment to the process of moral education for America[36] would remain the same. The "Supplication" was part of this process of moral instruction.[37]

3

The character of Witherspoon's political thought and the degree of continuity and consistency between the Scottish and American phases of his career have been the subject of a long, poorly focused historical disagreement. According to a traditional viewpoint, Witherspoon's leadership of the orthodox wing of the Church of Scotland in the 1750s and 1760s and his opposition to the influence of Francis Hutcheson and other moral philosophers conditioned him to prize order and moderation in American politics.[38] More recent scholarship, however, has emphasized Witherspoon's combativeness and the political orientation of his religious thought. His so-called "moderate" foes in Scotland were closely allied with the aristocracy which, in 1712, had gained control of clerical appointments and continued to prefer genteel preaching leavened with Enlightenment rationalism. In Scotland, therefore, Witherspoon had attacked Enlightenment ideas as part of his larger struggle to reinstate congregational control of ministerial selection.[39] This effort at reform was not necessarily a democratic impulse but was rather part of a struggle between rival elites, the aristocracy and the ruling elders.

Witherspoon's political writings in 1774–1776, Fred J. Hood has observed, were "a blending of American experience, Common Sense philosophy, and Reformed theology" which made conscientious, pious resistance and revolutionary discipline into moral imperatives.[40] So complete was Witherspoon's acceptance in America of Common Sense realism, Mark A. Noll has recently argued, that he "set aside an Augustinian distrust of human nature" in favor of "a value-free science of ethics" in which science and reason would mutually substantiate Christian revelation. In drawing heavily, though with only fragmentary acknowledgment, on Francis Hutcheson, he utilized a writer deeply concerned with reconciling Enlightenment rationalism to Christian belief.[41]

Witherspoon's two loyalist recantations do not resolve the problem of how he reconciled his republicanism and his conservatism, but they both relied on

Common Sense assumptions to argue that falsehood and vice were so corrosive as to imperil society's slender resources of virtue and civic responsibility. So Witherspoon had Towne boast pathetically that sensual stimuli rather than consistent principle made him a chameleon-like political lackey. The "lies" he had printed for the British, he declared, were harmless precisely because they were so gross and absurd. The more craven and pathetic Towne could be shown to be—and the more drastic the loss of his public reputation due to his collaboration—the safer the people would be from the moral contamination spawned by shallow, opportunistic allegiance. Witherspoon's fascination with the details of loyalist immorality and his determination to explain Towne's and Rivington's behavior as a deviation from republican norms underscore Noll's suggestion that Witherspoon deemphasized human depravity as a theological concept and subordinated theology to moral philosophy. Towne and Rivington were not, according to the recantations, partakers of a common human infirmity so much as they were specific sources of moral contamination and products of exotic kinds of ethical vulnerability.

By concluding Towne's apology with the assertion that "I hope the public will consider that I have been a timorous man, or if you will a coward from my youth, so that 1 cannot fight—my belly is so big that I cannot run—and I am so great a lover of eating and drinking that I cannot starve," Witherspoon drove home the argument that the failure to cultivate an intrinsic moral sense left men prey to corruption, folly, and connivance with despotism. Similarly, he had Rivington predict that he would conform to the demands of victorious patriot opinion as readily as he had for the British: "A man that has run the gauntlet of creditors, duns, and bailiffs, for years in England, and has been cudgelled, kicked, and pissed upon in America, is in no danger of losing his reason . . . so long as there is the least prospect of saving his life."

Witherspoon had a good republican's understanding of a republic's fragility. And he was frantic in his efforts to weed out the "detestable selfishness" he saw in some leading revolutionaries. He feared that some of his congressional colleagues were "set upon nothing but making money."[42] Among the body of uninstructed Americans the possibility of a weak republican character could only be greater. The "Supplication of James Rivington" was written, therefore, to define for a popular audience the character necessary to the survival of the republic. Witherspoon believed that satirization of the widely known printer could encourage an appropriate public spirit.[43] Rivington's almost universal reputation as a traitor to the "liberties of this country" and a "vile ministerial hireling"[44] made him an ideal object lesson. Between 1774 and 1776 Committees of Correspondence from the middle colonies and New England had engaged in regular attacks on Rivington, more because of what he symbolized than the danger he posed to resistance.[45] After 1776, the rise of "luxury, effeminancy, and the . . . dissipated life" heightened Witherspoon's conviction that Rivington's example was a public menace.[46] Witherspoon assumed that most of the reading public knew how Rivington, before arriving in America, had gathered a small fortune from an illegal printing scheme and then had quickly gambled it away. Instead of liquidating his property to pay his creditors, he had declared bankruptcy and fled. In America he was a sycophant who again ruined himself while seeking to ingratiate himself with the provincial aristocracy.[47] Witherspoon did not exaggerate Rivington's reputation among contemporary printers and booksellers. They saw in his career a thoroughly self-destructive pattern of behavior. In William Strahan's view, he lacked "manliness and spirit," and in the face of a second financial ruin he had married for money to maintain his pretensions to class. Furthermore, he was shallow, flippant, dissipated, arrogant, and so corrupt he was "indulged beyond what a person of integrity could expect."[48]

To clinch his argument for Rivington's moral baseness and psychological insecurity, Witherspoon drew on a vocabulary of degradation which he knew intimately—that of anti-Scottish stereotypes. "I can assure your High Mightinesses," he had Rivington implore, "that I am as great a coward as King James the VI of Scotland, who never could see a naked sword without trembling, having been, it is said, frightened in his mother's belly, when the fierce barons of that country came in, and killed David Rizzio in her presence." Presenting Rivington as a person who would pander to any public prejudice, Witherspoon also had his victim invoke the opinion of the sixteenth-century Scottish historian George Buchanan, that "*Perfervidum est Scotorum ingenium* [the Scot is by nature zealous]" to the point of unpredictable instability. These qualities, far from endowing Rivington with manliness, only reinforced his tendency to opportunism: "I hope . . . your Honours will consider my sufferings as sufficient to atone for my offenses, and allow me to continue in peace and quiet, and according to the North-British proverb, to *sleep in a whole skin*."[49]

The Towne-Rivington recantations Witherspoon wrote illuminate in unusually graphic detail the transactions which arose from conflicts of allegiance. As Stephen Botein observed in his brief treatment of the controversy, "lack of principle" in Towne and Rivington invited public exposure and humiliation. The older professional standards of printers—service, utility, and adaptability—abruptly became the public face of corruption and sinister motivation.[50] This transformation can be seen not only in Witherspoon's contempt and denunciation but also in elements of the older professional code which possibly survived Witherspoon's recasting of loyalist arguments, as when he allowed Towne to plead, "it is pretended [falsely] that I certainly did in my heart incline to the English, because I printed much bigger lies and in greater number for them. . . ." The coercion which the Revolution inflicted on its internal foes, therefore, was often that of moral castigation. The embarrassing abundance of pain and pathetic, self-serving remonstrance in the recantations served to confirm the triumph of virtue over vice—what the Rivington document called "the dreadful mortification, after our past puffing and vanity[51] of being under the dominion of the Congress."

Through the Towne and Rivington recantations, Witherspoon struggled to locate and vindicate the moral authority of the Revolution at a time when that authority had not yet become fully institutionalized nor hammered into fully recognized behavioral norms. Placing requirements of civic purity and righteous intention at the core of the authority of the Revolution, Witherspoon situated Towne and Rivington beyond the periphery of a morally defined political order. His territorial, exclusionary, and judgmental strictures were the kind of radicalism most congenial to his experience and intellect.

Notes

1. Isaiah Thomas, *The History of Printing in America* (Worcester, 1810), vol. 2, p. 74ff.

2. "The humble confession, declaration, recantation, and apology of BENJAMIN TOWNE, Printer in Philadelphia," *New York Packet* (Fishkill, N.Y.), 1 Oct. 1778, was printed later in *Miscellanies for Sentimentalists* (Philadelphia, 1778), appendix; in *Sermons to Ministers of State* (Philadelphia, 1783), pp. 76ff.; in Thomas, *History of Printing*, 2:453ff.; and in *The Works of the Rev. John Witherspoon* (Edinburgh, 1804–1805), 9:192ff. "The humble Representation and earnest Supplication of James Rivington, Printer and Bookseller in New York," *The United States Magazine: A Repository of History, Politics, and Literature* (Philadelphia), I (Jan. 1779), 34ff., was later reprinted in Witherspoon, *Works*, 9:180–91 and in Thomas, *History of Printing*, 2:495ff. All quotations are from the earliest extant editions in the *New York Packet* and *United States Magazine* respectively. Witherspoon's "Supplication of . . . Rivington" carries the date Dec. 5, 1778, which we accept as authentic. Leroy Hewlett and Ashbel Green both misdated the Supplication to Nov. 1783, misconstruing internal evidence—references to Loyalists and imminent British evacuation which Witherspoon added to lend the document verisimilitude and which referred to the departure of 3,500 British troops bound for Savannah under Lt. Col. Archibald Campbell on Nov. 25, 1778. See Hewlett, "James Rivington, Loyalist Printer, Publisher, and Bookseller of the American Revolution: A Biographical and Bibliographical Study, 1763–1783" (Ph.D. diss., University of Michigan, 1958), 480, and Green, *The Life of the Revd. John Witherspoon, D.D., L.L.D., with a Brief Review of His Writings; and a Summary Estimate of His Character and Talents,* Henry L. Savage, ed. (Princeton, N.J., 1973), 190.

3. Robert Aitken, Waste Book, 229, Historical Society of Pennsylvania, Philadelphia; Dwight L. Teeter, "Benjamin Towne: The Precarious Career of a Persistent Printer," *Pennsylvania Magazine of History and Biography,* 89 (July 1965), 316–30.

4. Bernadotte Perrin, trans., *Plutarch's Lives,* Loeb Classical Library (New York, 1914–1926), 6:243; 8:395–411.

5. "Diary of James Allen, Esq., of Philadelphia, Counsellor-at-Law, 1770–1778," *Pennsylvania Magazine of History and Biography,* 9 (1885), 177.

6. On May 18, 1778 the British Arm in Philadelphia held an extravagant day-long celebration called the "Mischianza" as a farewell to General William Howe; Witherspoon called it a "Fete" to indicate that it was a vulgar unrepublican display.

7. Hewlett, "Rivington," 39ff.; Benjamin Booth to Henry Drinker, 28 Oct., 24 Nov. 1773; 4, 9, 13 July; 8 Aug.; 22 Oct. 1774; Henry Drinker to [?] Pigou & [Benjamin] Booth, 4, 9 Aug. 1774, Henry Drinker Papers, 1772–1786, ibid.; Peter Force, comp., *American Archives,* Ser. 4 (Washington, 1837–1853), 2:726.

8. Ibid., 2:836f., 899.

9. James Rivington to [George Germain], 6 Mar. 1776, Germain Papers, William L. Clements Library, University of Michigan.

10. James Rivington to Richard Cumberland, 23 Nov. 1778, Colonial Office Papers, 5/155: 175f., Public Record Office, London; Catherine S. Crary, "The Tory and the Spy: the Double Life of James Rivington," *William and Mary Quarterly,* 3rd ser., 16 (Jan. 1959), 61–72; Philip Ranlet, "James Rivington, Secret Agent," *Journal of Communication Inquiry,* 8 (Summer 1984), 21–30; Witherspoon assigned Rivington a different covert role by comparing him to Pandarus of Troy, whom the gods employed as an agent provocateur to sabotage a truce in the Trojan wars, *The Iliad,* Richard Lattimore, trans., (Chicago, 1951), book 4, lines 88–99.

11. See, *The Letters Written by the Earl of Chesterfield to his Son, Philip Stanhope . . .* (London, 1774) and James Boswell, *The Life of Samuel Johnson, D.D.* (London, 1872), 2:13.

12. The versions of the "Supplication" in Witherspoon's *Works* and Thomas's *History of Printing* substituted the words "in the lap of self-indulgence" following "asleep." In quoting Dr. Johnson, Witherspoon again subtly ridiculed Rivington's shallow literary knowledge; "somnify" does not appear in Johnson's Dictionary, in the concordance to his poetry, or in his two essays on sleep, *Idler* No. 32 and *Adventurer,* No. 39; the *Oxford English Dictionary* entry on "somnify" does not cite a Johnson usage.

13. George A. Rich, "John Witherspoon: His Scottish Intellectual Background" (D.S.S. diss., Syracuse University, 1964) and note 38 below.

14. Witherspoon, *Works,* 5:202f., 219f.; other Presbyterians could not make the move from Crown supporters to patriots; Jonathan Powell, "Presbyterian Loyalists: A 'Chain of Interest' in Philadelphia," *Journal of Presbyterian History,* 57 (Summer 1979), 135ff.

15. Varnum Collins, *President Witherspoon: A Biography* (Princeton, N.J., 1925), 1:160f.

16. Benjamin F. Stevens, ed., *Facsimilies of Manuscripts in European Archives Relating to America, 1773–1783* (London, 1889–1895), 14:doc. 1399; Elias Boudinot, *Journal, or Historical Recollections of American Events during the Revolutionary War* (Philadelphia, 1894), 6.

17. William Patterson, *Glimpses of Colonial Society and the Life at Princeton College, 1766–1773, by One of the Class of 1763,* Weymer Jay Mills, ed. (Philadelphia, 1903), 48.

18. Witherspoon, *Works,* 5:218ff; Stiles remained sceptical, see Literary Diary of Ezra Stiles, 23 July 1777, Papers of Peter Force, Series 8–E, Box 67, Library of Congress, Washington, D.C.

19. L. Gordon Tait, "John Witherspoon and the Scottish Loyalists," *Journal of Presbyterian History,* 61 (Fall 1983), 305, 308.

20. Stevens, *Facsimiles,* 1:doc. 58.

21. Howe to Germain, 25 Mar. 1777, CO 5/177:64.

22. "Caspipina's Catechism," [n.d.], Papers of John Witherspoon, Library of Congress; Witherspoon to David Witherspoon, 17 Mar. 1777, Paul H. Smith, et al. eds., *Letters of Delegates to Congress, 1774–1789* (Washington, 1976–), 6:454ff.; see also John Cowenhoven to Elias Boudinot, 30 Jan. 1778, Elias Boudinot Coll., Princeton University Library.

23. Alfred Bill Hoyt et al., *A House Called Morven: 1ts Role in American History* (Princeton, N.J., 1954, rev. 1978), 39–51.

24. Witherspoon to David Witherspoon, Mar. 17, 1777, Smith, ed., *Letters of Delegates,* 6:454ff.

25. H. Rushton Fairclough, trans., Virgil, *Aeneid,* Loeb Classical Library (Cambridge, 1916–18), 1:295.

26. Lucius Q.C. Elmer, *The Constitution and Government of the Province and State of New Jersey . . .* (Newark, 1872), 63.

27. "Witherspoon's Speech in Congress, [Sept. 5?], 1776," Smith, ed., *Letters of Delegates,* 5: 112.

28. William Livingston to Witherspoon, May 7, 1777, C. E. Prince et al., eds., *The Papers of William Livingston* (Trenton, 1979), 1:322ff.

29. "The Druid" #1 [John Witherspoon]. *Pennsylvania Magazine, or American Monthly Museum* (May 1776), 206.

30. Thomas Randall to Witherspoon, 4 Mar. 1767, John Witherspoon College, Princeton University Library; for evidence that he considered his mission in America to be spiritual rather than political, see Witherspoon to [?], 10 July [1776?], Papers of John Witherspoon, Library of Congress.

31. Witherspoon, *Works,* 5:209, 214; Collins, *Witherspoon,* 1:140; "Druid #1" [Witherspoon], *Pennsylvania Magazine* (May 1776), 208.

32. Witherspoon, *Works,* 5:266; Stevens, *Facsimiles,* 51:doc. 487.

33. "Acknowledgment of Recept of four Prisoners of War," Aug. 25, 1779 in Board of War to Witherspoon, [n.d.], John Witherspoon College, Princeton University Library.

34. Green, *Witherspoon,* 161.

35. Witherspoon to the Rev. [?] Carmichael, Oct. 2, 1779 and to Jonathan Sargeant, Nov. 22, 1774, John Witherspoon College, Princeton University Library.

36. "X.Y." and "Epaminodas" [Witherspoon], *Pennsylvania Magazine* (April 1775), 150ff.; (May 1775), 197ff.; (June 1775), 262f.; (Sept. 1775), 408ff.; (Dec. 1775), 543ff., 557ff.; (Dec. 1776), 109ff.

37. "The Druid" #1 [Witherspoon], ibid., (May 1776), 205ff.; (June 1776), 253ff.; (July 1776), 301ff.; Witherspoon, *Works,* 9:224–91.

38. Lyman H. Butterfield, *John Witherspoon Comes to America . . .* (Princeton, N.J., 1953), 12f.; Rich, "Witherspoon," chapter 5.

39. Mark A. Noll. "The Irony of the Enlightenment in Nineteenth-Century Religious Thought," *Journal of the Early Republic,* 5 (1985): 154–59; Roger J. Fechner, "The Godly and virtuous Republic of John Witherspoon," Hamilton Cravens, ed., *Ideas in America's Cultures . . .* (Ames, Ia., 1982), 9–21.

40. Fred J. Hood, *Reformed America . . .* (Tuscaloosa, Ala., 1980), 14; James L. McAllister "John Witherspoon: American Advocate of Academic Freedom," Stuart C. Henry, ed., *A Miscellany of American Christianity . . .* (Durham, N.C., 1963), 183–224; and James H. Smylie, "Madison and Witherspoon: Theological Roots of American Political Thought," *Princeton University Library Quarterly,* 22 (1961): 118–32.

41. Noll, "The Irony of the Enlightenment," 5; Norman S. Fiering, *Moral Philosophy at Harvard: A Discipline in transition* (Chapel Hill, N.C., 1981), 198–206; Jack Scott, ed., *An Annotated Edition of Lectures on Moral Philosophy by John Witherspoon* (Newark, 1982), 27–43, 128ff., 165ff., 182ff.

42. Witherspoon to Benjamin Rush, 17 Nov. 1776, Smith ed., *Letters of Delegates,* 5:511.

43. Witherspoon, *Works,* 5:208f., 218; letter for the *Federal Gazette,* [n.d.], Papers of John Witherspoon, Library of Congress.

44. *Rivington's Gazette,* Mar. 2, 1775; *New York Journal,* Feb. 9 and 23, 1775.

45. *Rivington's Gazette,* Mar. 16, 1775; *New York Journal,* Feb. 9 and 23, 1775.

46. Witherspoon, *Works,* 5:269f.

47. Thomas, *History of Printing,* 2:111.

48. William Strahan to David Hall, June 21, 1760 and June 12, 1767, David Hall Papers, American Philosophical Society, Philadelphia, Pa., and "Correspondence between William Strahan and David Hall, 1763–1777 . . . ," *PMHB,* 10 (1886): 327; see also Strahan to Hall, July 11, 1758; Mar. 24, 1759; Jan. 7, Feb. 13, 1760; Hall to Hamilton and Balfour, Dec. 22, 1760; Hall and Benjamin Franklin to Daniel Warner, Dec. 22, 1760, David Hall Papers; Rivington to William Alexander, Jan. 7, 1767, William Alexander Papers, New York Historical Society, New York City; *New York Journal,* Oct. 6, 1768.

49. George Buchanan (1506–1582) was author of *The History of Scotland* (London, 1690); we have not located the source of this quotation; the "North-British proverb" may be found in James Kelly, ed., *A Complete Collection of Scottish Proverbs . . .* (London, 1721), 220.

50. Stephen Botein, "Printers and the American Revolution," Bernard Bailyn and John B. Hench, eds., *The Press & the American Revolution* (Worcester, 1980), 46f.

51. The versions of the "Supplication" in Witherspoon's *Works* and Thomas's *History of Printing* substituted "vaunting."

Fifteen

Aedanus Burke and Thomas Burke

*Revolutionary Conservatism in the Carolinas**

ROBERT M. CALHOON

1

The American Revolution was—as Robert R. Palmer argued thirty years ago—part of a larger political transformation occurring throughout the Atlantic world.[1] Not only did major upheavals in America and France and simmering discontent in Ireland, Poland, the Low Countries, Russia, and elsewhere mutually reinforce each other, as Palmer demonstrated; political discourse also spread widely and intermingled in ways that hastened what Jack P. Greene has called "the modernization of political consciousness."[2] The radical ideas that circulated throughout the Atlantic world during the eighteenth century and that undermined traditional notions of hierarchy and stability were curiously either backward or inward looking. The English "country party" opposition to Walpole and "monied-politics" hankered for a simpler agrarian past. The Scottish Common Sense philosophers were more in tune with newer currents of commercial expansion and development, but they focused their attention on the nature of the human mind and psyche in search of the psychological or "moral" roots of civic consciousness. Caroline Robbins carefully distinguished between the English and Scottish as well as republican and dissenting religious sources of libertarian thought in the British Isles from the Restoration to the American Revolution, and historians have filled several shelves with books amplifying these themes.[3]

*At the symposium at the College of Charleston in 1988 honoring Professor George Rogers, the author of this essay read a paper titled "Evangelicals and Conservatives in the Early South: An Interpretation," adapted from the then-forthcoming *Evangelicals and Conservatives in the Early South, 1740–1861* (Columbia: University of South Carolina Press, 1988). While both Burkes appeared briefly in that book, this essay is the first comparative discussion of the two men and was written expressly for *The Meaning of South Carolina History: Essays in Honor of George C. Rogers, Jr.,* ed. David R. Chesnutt and Clyde N. Wilson (Columbia, University of South Carolina Press, 1991).

One of Robbins's chapters, however, "The Case of Ireland," has provoked little scholarly activity. Irish Protestant political writers combined in a unique way qualities of passion and rage with a capacity for disciplined rational analysis of institutions and principles. "The Irish Protestants," she writes, "were not republican"—that is, believers in a virtuous social order devoid of privilege— "but their own situation forced from them expression of ideas potentially revolutionary and useful to rebellious colonists, to critics of mercantilism, and to supporters of full civil and religious liberties for all mankind."[4] From William Molyneux's *The Case of Ireland's Being Bound by Acts of Parliament Stated* (1698) through Edmund Burke's searing assaults on conventional English whiggery in *Thoughts on the Cause of the Present Discontents* (1770), Irish Protestant intellectuals produced a powerful body of moral criticism against English oppression, complacency, mediocrity, and guile. Anglican, but not anti-Catholic, they combined English political traditionalism with an Irish capacity for passionate human solidarity.

The Anglo-Irish politician Arthur Dobbs, who eventually served as governor of North Carolina from 1754 to 1765, not only defended Ireland's claim to generous commercial treatment from London; early in his career he wrote a stunning manuscript history of colonization in the Western world in which he identified two motives for empire: "thirst for dominion" at the outset of expansion and a mature appetite for trade and commerce in established colonial systems. Even the later variety of empire, however, carried within itself the seeds of destruction, greed, and vicious internal conflict. Without a mature metropolitan economy to absorb wealth and free institutions (especially churches) to channel and tame the passions and desires of the colonial populace, even a trading empire risked internal convulsions and decline. The dispossession of Indians from their land and the exploitation of slaves in the British Empire would, left uncorrected, destroy those colonial societies and bring vengeance and even divine wrath down upon planters and merchants. "Shall we, who by the precepts of our Lord and Saviour ought to love our neighbors as our selves," he asked, "pride our selves by our superior knowledge in arts and sciences and despise them as . . . inferior [and] not worth reclaiming?"[5] Dobbs's ability to place a radical indictment of exploitation within the context of centuries of European conquest and expansion—to substitute analysis for polemics—was typical of Irish-Protestant political discourse like Jonathan Swift's brooding lament that "all forms of government, having been instituted by men must be mortal like their authors . . . ; there are few who . . . examine . . . those diseases in a state . . . that hasten its end."[6] Or like Edmund Burke's astringent faith in the possibility, however narrow, of political responsibility: "Minds that have long been crushed under the weight of privilege and pride or of misery and despair are not equally distant from all rational ideas of the dignity of man. . . . Even these classes may be brought back by degrees to be useful members of the state."[7] Only an Irish-Protestant intellectual and political thinker could have analyzed the tensions between Britain and the American colonists in the late 1760s with such uncanny penetration as Burke:

> The Americans have made a discovery, or think they have made one, that we mean to oppress them; we have made a discovery, or think we have made one, that they intend to rise in rebellion; we know not how to advance; they know not how to retreat.[8]

Two patriot leaders, Thomas Burke of North Carolina and Aedanus Burke of South Carolina, both immigrants from Ireland, friends though apparently not kinsmen, brought precisely these intellectual, moral, and psychological resources to the struggle for American independence and the creation of a republican political and social order. Thomas Burke left Ireland in 1759 or 1760 at the age of fifteen and settled in Northampton County, Virginia, where he became a self-educated physician, lawyer, and poet. Aedanus at age 25 or 26 left Ireland in 1769 and also made his way to Virginia, where he met Thomas Burke, who put him in touch with several Irish-born South Carolinians who assisted his resettlement in Charleston sometime in the early 1770s, about the same time that Thomas moved to North Carolina.[9]

2

Three weeks after his first appearance as a delegate to the Continental Congress, Thomas Burke entered a debate on a recommendation authorizing local officials to apprehend suspected army deserters and lodging coercive authority in the hands of local committees of inspection until such time as states enacted enabling legislation. Burke and James Wilson of Pennsylvania saw the deep constitutional implications in this technical matter of Revolutionary administration. Jack N. Rakove depicts the debate as a turning point in Revolutionary history. Supporting the measure, Wilson envisioned a broad supervisory role for Congress over the efforts of the states to conduct the War for Independence; opposing it, "Burke argued, repetitively but convincingly, that it was inherently dangerous to allow Congress to exercise coercive power within the states." "The states alone," Burke thundered, "have the power to act coercively against their citizens" because only to state governments had citizens given their "consent." Unlike any other previous delegate to Congress, Burke audaciously conceived of himself as "an ambassador from a sovereign state" and from that perspective announced the need of the new nation for a theory of congressional-state relations based on popular sovereignty. In Thomas Burke, Rakove finds "personality and politics fused: assertive and unyielding in debate, acutely sensitive to private honor and personal privilege, this youthful and ambitious Irish immigrant felt few compunctions about calling Congress back to . . . the first principles of republican government." Rakove speculates that "a sensible reaction to the history of his native Ireland" alerted Burke to the dangers of centralized "corruption" and the "dangers" inherent in allowing piecemeal expansion of congressional decision making to shape the yet undrafted constitution of the new confederacy. In the debate over the proposed Articles of Confederation, Burke moved an amendment holding that "all sovereign power" resided "in the states separately," and, except for "expressly enumerated" powers of Congress, each state would exercise all the "rights and powers of sovereignty, uncontrolled." The version adopted was more ambiguous: states retained "sovereignty, freedom, and independence and every power, jurisdiction, and right . . . not . . . expressly delegated" to Congress.[10]

Burke's conception of the states as sovereign entities rested on his conventional (though passionately held) whig view that the people alone possessed the virtue and nerve necessary for a revolutionary seizure of power. In November 1777 he drafted Congress's "Address to the Inhabitants of the United States"—a major appeal for public support of the Revolution. Thomas did so by identifying the popular sources of Revolutionary authority. The defense of American liberty arose, he contended, from collective acts of "the people" acting on "natural" instincts and suppositions: remonstrances by colonial assemblies, avoidance before 1774 of extralegal associations of protesters, the eschewing of "tumult and disorder" even as the breach with Britain became unavoidable, and arising from all of these precedents a "spirit of humility, moderation, and loyalty" that characterized the summoning of the first Continental Congress. In return, the people experienced the indignity of witnessing their "most loyal humility" brutalized by a "military tyranny" by the British that left them "no choice but to oppose arms with arms." The swarms of "slaves, savages, and foreign mercenaries" dispatched by the British finally destroyed any hope of reconciliation, which now "became the same thing as slavery, independence the same thing as freedom."

> Your own experience, fellow citizens, will best bear testimony to the truth of the facts here set forth. Your own experience can best prove the falshood of the suggestion that you are deluded by individuals who aim at nothing but power. You know how little influence individuals have over you. You know that every man trusted or employed by you is a creature of your free choice, and by every choice you make and every act you do you manifest that you feel you are sovereign and supreme, and influenced by nothing but a conviction that you ought to be free, a determined resolution to remain so and to transmit freedom unimpaired to your children.[11]

The contention that "individuals" have little influence over "the people," and that the people "know" this intuitively, represented for Burke the essential difference between a New World republic and the traditional political systems of the Old World "where only the shadow of liberty remains." The Irish coloration of Thomas Burke's radicalism came to the surface when he equated British arrogance with the view that "the people . . . are for nothing but to toil [so] that men of high birth and fortune may live in ease and splendor. . . . They [the British] know not the plenty which the fruitful soil of America yields to the hand that gives it cultivation" nor that "penury and oppressive landlords" are "here equally unknown."[12]

Belief in the innate capacity of the people to make moral and political judgments likewise made Burke suspicious of factionalism and infighting, especially the activities of Thomas Paine in destroying the reputation of Silas Deane. Deane was a Connecticut merchant and American diplomatic representative in France, whose greed became the focus of an extremely acrimonious controversy in Congress in 1779, and the subject of one of Burke's many poems:

> Hail, mighty Thomas! In whose works are seen
> A mangled Morris and distorted Deane;
> Whose splendid periods flash for Lees defence,
> Replete with every thing but common sense. . . .
> Shall Common Sense, or Comus greet thine ear,
> A piddling poet, or puft pamphleteer;
> Behold around thee, how thy triumphs lie,
> Of reputations hosts before thee die;
> On envy's altars hecatombs expire,
> And Faction fondly lights her pupil's fire.
> That pupil most devoted to her will,
> Who for the worthless wags his quibbling quill;
> And with a true democracy of spirit
> Bravely attacks the most exalted merit.
> Thou pupil worthy her attentive care,
> By Satan granted to her earnest prayer.[13]

Burke objected to partisan efforts of Deane's enemies to convert Congress from a solemn assembly of deputies of sovereign states into a fluid, acrimonious legislative assembly and their use of "conjectures, surmises, and inuendoes" against him. "When Ministers of such high trust [are] accused of Such Enormities," Burke insisted, "nothing less than a full and clear Investigation . . . ought to Satisfy the public." In his hasty departure from France, Deane had left behind the financial records that might well have proven his innocence, and without the testimony and cross-examination of Benjamin Franklin and Arthur Lee—Deane's erstwhile colleagues and denouncers—Congress could reach no deliberative verdict about his guilt or innocence. Two years later Thomas Burke demanded that Congress censure fellow delegate John Sullivan, of New Hampshire, for Sullivan's alleged incompetence at the Battle of Brandywine. In the dispute that followed, Burke was a quintessential republican; Sullivan, a staunch Lockean, in that Burke burned with pain when mistakes of others jeopardized the safety of the commonwealth while Sullivan sought vindication of "my own reputation" through an appeal to "Justice, & Propriety." Sullivan's demand for due process, in Burke's view, contaminated public discourse by placing personal reputation above humble submission to the cause of liberty.[14]

Burke doubtless believed that his private investigation of Sullivan represented the kind of thorough inquiry that Congress denied Deane and that Sullivan's demands for justice were tainted with self-interest while Deane's were not. His republicanism was instrumental: what served the republic merited charitable construction, what jeopardized it earned his contempt. His beliefs in states' rights, in natural standards of justice, and in the dangers of selfish factionalism all hinged on his sense of integrity in a political world swirling with opportunism and aggression. When Burke became governor of North Carolina in 1781, this self-image and cluster of precepts served him well. He understood the state he was to govern as a complex system of human capacities and social maladies "everywhere unprepared for defense, without arms, without discipline, without arrangements, even the habits of civil order and obedience to laws changed into a licentious contempt of authority and a disorderly indulgence of violent propensities."[15]

This assessment of North Carolina in the wake of General Charles Cornwallis's invasion of the state was accurate and realistic. Not only was there a residue of tory partisans in the state waiting for a chance to avenge themselves but also the occupation of Wilmington by Major James Craig made North Carolina's disrupted administration extremely vulnerable to counterrevolutionary actions. Just how vulnerable would become clear in July and August 1781 when David Fanning's loyalist militia arrived from Georgia and began operating in Duplin County. Fanning was the first loyalist military commander to realize the value of discipline, respect for noncombatants, psychologically potent attacks on patriot jails and seizure of public officials, and tactics that John S. Watterson aptly characterized as "quickness, mobility, deception, and improvisation."[16]

Receiving reports of Fanning's activities (a rash of robberies, murders, and assaults by individual tories, and brutal retaliation by patriot soldiers), Burke recognized the futility of dispatching forces to each besieged locality or of allowing the pattern of vengeance and brutality to continue uncontrolled. He agreed with General Stephen Drayton's view that "civil wars are always attended with something horrid. The bare idea of friend against friend and nearest relatives in armed opposition shocks human nature! But good God! Sir, let us not countenance barbarities that would disgrace the savage! If we cannot totally stop, yet we may check [the] wanton exercise of cruelty."[17] He concurred with Nathanael Greene that the enemy "act in small parties, . . . appear in so many different shapes, and have so many hiding places and secret springs of intelligence that you may wear out an army and still be unable to subdue them."

In 1777 Thomas Burke had written a series of war poems titled "Colin and Chloe," which were a conventional pastoral dialogue between a man and his beloved, a younger woman, probably inspired by Burke's romance in Virginia with Betsy Harmanson, whose intellectuality he worshiped and whose combination of "beauty and spirit" apparently aroused Burke's admiration and desire.[18] In this poetry Colin made the case for the patriotic martial spirit:

> Now tyrant Ambition extends his dire Arm
> And threats our free Land to enslave:

> No Music is heard but the Drum's hoarse Alarm,
>   No Song but the Dirge of the Brave.
>
> No more soft Emotions become the firm Breast:
>   To these, fiercer Passions succeed:
> Indignation for Rapine and Beauty distress'd,
>   And Vengeance for Brothers who bleed.

Chloe, in reply, bespoke Burke's deep misgiving about the depletion during war of his society's slender reserve of civic virtue:

> *Does lordly Ambition wage War in our Land?*
>   *If so, of that Demon beware;*
> *Nor let fiercer Resentment your Counsels command,*
>   *Lest the Fate of old Satan you share.*
>
> But as Friends and Protectors of Virtue and Truth,
>   Prove these to your Measures gave Birth;
> And the World shall confess you, in Age and in Youth,
>   Delegated by Heaven and Earth.[19]

Understanding warfare as an elusive process that frustrated human intellect and tested men's integrity,[20] Thomas assessed the military situation in North Carolina in the summer of 1781. He realized that Cornwallis's march north to Virginia, far from relieving pressure on North Carolina, held the state in ransom to external events by tying down in the Chesapeake the Continental forces necessary to rescue the patriot administration in North Carolina. He devised a policy, therefore, that would husband available resources and hold together the semblance of a structure of government while Fanning's men did their worst. Burke and Greene, in short, understood quite as well as Craig and Fanning the nature of irregular warfare at the very moment and place in the war where the British had perfected its use. And Burke's geopolitical sense of North Carolina as a tilting plane now sloping to the advantage of the British but liable to shift suddenly in the patriots' favor (depending on events in the Chesapeake) endowed his leadership of the state with vision and cunning.[21]

In the short run, however, it made him personally vulnerable. Staying just out of reach of Fanning's forces but close enough to the action to keep his administration visible and credible, Thomas Burke and other state officials were in Hillsborough on September 13, 1781, when Fanning and Hector MacNeil raided the town and took Burke prisoner. Carried to Wilmington and then confined under parole on Sullivan's Island near Charleston, Burke worried about his family and fumed about the failure of the Continental Army to exchange him for a British officer. In this agitated state, he escaped, returned to North Carolina, and took Nathanael Greene's advice, that he return to his "government," to mean that he should resume his duties as governor.

Greene, on the contrary, simply meant that Burke should return home; he regarded Burke's return to office a violation of his parole that undermined military authority over prisoner exchanges—endangering American officers in British hands and violating comity between opposing armies on the subject of prisoner exchange. Shortly after leaving the governorship in April 1782, Burke justified his conduct in a long letter to Greene. Caught as governor between "the particular interests of the state" he served and "the general interest of the confederacy" to which Greene was responsible, Thomas pointed to "the vast prevailence of the former over the latter"; that is, the multitude of individuals dependent on the integrity of state government, as against the relative handful involved with officials of the United States, justified Burke's violation of parole and his reclaiming of the governorship.[22]

At issue was the priority of prisoner exchanges of regular army officers over militia officers. Thomas Burke strongly denied that militia officers should rank lower than regular officers in consideration for exchange: "All such as assume the character of soldiers for the public ought by the public to be regarded and protected as soldiers"; to do otherwise would devastate "the martial spirit," the willingness of citizen soldiers to leave home and safety and face the "danger of death, captivity, or dishonor" only to have the "enemy" to treat militia captives with "contempt and scorn." Burke vindicated the militia, and the essential moral equality of soldiers and civilians, governors and generals, by audaciously warning that aggrieved militiamen might well cluster into dangerous factions and strive for control of the state:

> Militia leaders will always have their eyes on civil honor and emolument for which military men seldom have any relish. . . . It is not for the eternal preservation of liberty that militia are so necessary for a free people. It is because industry is encouraged, obtains and enjoys property as its reward, and, therefore, few are found so indigent as to make the condition of a common regular soldier eligible. In that species of force they must always be deficient and must fall a prey to invaders, were not the want supplied by the well regulated and well provided militia.

Here was an intriguing twist on the post-Revolutionary controversy over the superiority of regular versus militia forces.[23] The militia deserved incorporation into the body politic, Burke argued, because warfare contagion and social upheaval drew ordinary men into the risky pursuit of power and preeminence. His antidote to the instability of republics was, therefore, the republican remedy of social equality. But it was an antidote that might at any time prove inadequate. "In a country where power is in many hands and fluctuating among several hands," he wrote to Aedanus Burke in 1782, "the spirit and operation of the government will always depend upon the state of society, and this . . . upon the manners and *moral* principles of the people. . . . Are the people needy, rapacious, of low and servile recreation? Narrow, prejudiced, and illiberal? Averse to labor and industry? Familiar with crimes and unaccustomed to restraint? If they be, no form of government can give security, and liberty is as much an empty name amongst them as the natives of Indostan."[24] This analysis was not so much the lament of a "disillusioned democrat" as it was a comment on the inherent fragility of republicanism with its intimate connection to the moral health of society. He had harbored these misgivings long before the misfortunes of his governorship.

3

In 1781–1782 Aedanus Burke also encountered Revolutionary violence and responded to it as a problem in political ethics and a challenge to the republican teaching that shared communal virtue provided society with a tissue of defense against tyranny and anarchy. He believed that deeds of courage and risk, which enabled a republic to defend its liberty, had a corrosive underside jeopardizing all that the people had achieved. As a judge in the backcountry in early 1782, Burke observed an ominous change in the "temper of the people," a rising spirit of vengeance "in the breasts of our citizens" as even "the very females talk as familiarly . . . as the men . . . of shedding blood and destroying the tories . . . who live in swamps and make horrid incursions, . . . destroy our people in cold blood and when taken are killed in their turn."[25] This self-perpetuating cycle of violence and retribution angered Burke because it injected bestial qualities of human behavior into the life of the community. "A fat sheep, a fat sheep—prick him! prick him!" muttered legislators a few months later in Aedanus Burke's hearing as they contemplated the confiscation of loyalist estates; another observer heard the words, "slay, slay utterly the Amalekite," uttered in the tone of "voice of a long eared animal."[26]

For Burke, the spirit of retribution was nothing less than "the pretensions of a few [with] pretensions to superior political merit over the whole aggregate of the people."[27] His model for opposition politics was John Milton and the mythic angel in *Paradise Lost,* Ithuriel, who encountered Satan disguised as a toad waiting close to the ear of the sleeping Eve for a chance to tempt her with "vain hopes, vain aimes, Inordinate desires / blown up with high conceits ingendering pride." "Like a latter day Ithuriel," John C. Meleney writes, "[Burke] would aim the spear of his rhetoric at incipient despotism wherever he found it, so that, as anti-republican threats appeared, the people might be warned and grapple with the enemy before it was too late."[28] The invocation of John Milton not only revealed Aedanus Burke's extensive knowledge of seventeenth-century England but also his understanding of the English civil wars as a crisis in Christian civilization that provoked Puritan ideologues to draw deeply on Renaissance civic humanism. "The great Milton, Harrington, and other men of genius," Burke explained,

> employed all the charms of eloquence to cherish and support [liberty]. But their liberties under their favourite republic they did not maintain a moment. Not because the conjecture of affairs was unfavourable, . . . but [because] the members of the new legislature, *forgetting that they were young beginners in*

the art of governing, instead of endeavouring to reconcile all parties to the republic by temperate administration of law and justice, set to work immediately to gratify personal malice and vengeance in much the same fashion as the South Carolina legislature did in 1782 by instituting confiscation or amercement proceedings against more than 300 South Carolina loyalists. "Machiavel himself," Burke continued, "tho' for violent measures on other occasions, . . . strongly recommend[ed] an act of oblivion after a revolution, and he censure[d] the conduct of the Roman republic on the expulsion" of losers in civil upheaval.[29]

"The momentous decision that precipitated the American Revolution," John Higham wrote in "Beyond Consensus: The Historian as Moral Critic" in 1962, "has not yet had close attention as a problem in political ethics. Given the political and social institutions of the day, what real alternatives were present? Who erred most culpably? What balance of folly, insight, and constructive purpose can we discern in each of the major participants?"[30] In the years since Higham laid down that challenge, the discovery of republicanism of the Machiavellian and Harringtonian variety, which Burke admired, has immeasurably enhanced our understanding of the moral assumptions and commitments of the patriots—as had knowledge of the immense inhibitions against innovation in Augustan English thought helped us appreciate how little room for maneuver and compromise existed in Whitehall and Westminster.

As a judge in the backcountry with an acute eye for the vagaries of human nature he observed from the bench, and perhaps also as an Irishman with an appreciation of the ways injustice arose from contending passionate groups rather than from identifiable villains, Aedanus Burke was a particularly astute political ethicist. His reflection on Milton and Harrington highlighted several ethical problems: whether legislative inexperience mitigated evil done at the behest of the people; where the responsibility lay for bringing "genius" and "eloquence" to bear on the formative early stages in the creation of a republic; and the appropriate ways of indoctrinating discipline in a fragile republican polity.

Inexperience and Seizing the Moment

Burke emphatically agreed with Governor John Rutledge's assessment of South Carolina politics at the time of the Jacksonborough Assembly in 1782: "Private men are thrown frequently into passions and extravagances" like cries of vengeance toward loyalists and other British sympathizers; "but the representatives of a state, when they meet on a public duty, are supposed to be without passion."[31] Greed for confiscated estates, an animal-like craving to devour the despised and vulnerable, a shortsighted expediency of paying Revolutionary soldiers with confiscated slaves, and the cunning psychological ploy of pressuring loyalists in British-held Charleston to defect to the American side before rather than after their estates were confiscated combined in Burke's thinking to contaminate policy making in the Jacksonborough legislature. Burke saw this complex of motives and attitudes as an interrelated whole, "a conflagration" that "ravages" the community, including "the incendiaries who helped to light it. . . . Most of them were staunch Republicans and passionately fond of liberty. But from their wanton, extravagent abuse of their power as legislators, . . . the very name of a democracy or government of the people begins to be hateful and offensive."[32]

This contagion of opportunity, aggression, and guile gratified the passions of individuals, but it did nothing for state. "The experience of all nations has shewn that where a community splits itself . . . and has recourse to arms . . . a law to bury in oblivion past transactions is absolutely necessary," Burke wrote using the pen name "Cassius" (whom Caesar had pardoned following Pompey's uprising in Roman republican history). 'My idea of managing internal enemies, or seditious revolters, is . . . either to drive them out of the state altogether, at least the leaders of them, or make them our friends by pardoning."[33]

Genius and Eloquence

A year later Burke denounced the newly formed Society of the Cincinnati as a hothouse form of nobility. The problem was not the character of most officers in the Continental Army; the danger lay in any self-perpetuating, and hence hereditary, group encapsulating itself as a class of socially distinguished and politically influential persons. The aristocracy in the Roman republic, which eventually split that society into self-destructive categories of the clamoring many and the corrupt few, had its origins in "the disorderly, plundering banditti who first built their cabbins on the foundation of Rome" and comprised the "small stream" from which the ruin of the republic flowed. However innocent the intentions of the founders of the Society, the effect of the privileged incorporation of former military officers into a group set apart from the citizenry at large was to divide America into "the patricians or nobles and the rabble," a "departure" from "our open professions of republicanism that must give a thinking mind most melancholy forebodings."[34] Widely reprinted, Burke's attack on the Cincinnati apparently persuaded Thomas Jefferson that however well intentioned its founders, the society could become a bastion of hostility toward "the natural equality of man" and a conduit of foreign influence, military hauteur, "habits of subordination," and ultimately a threat to liberty itself. "Blow yet the trumpet in Zion," was Aedanus Burke's epigraph for his pamphlet. "Its effect," Jefferson noted, "corresponded with its epigraph."[35] At Jefferson's urging, George Washington threatened to dissociate himself from the society unless it forswore any hereditary perpetuation of membership that was "particularly obnoxious to the people"—and rejected financial contributions from foreigners.[36]

Republican Indoctrination

The moral core of Burke's politics was the creative use of jealousy as an antidote to the impurities of ambition and corruption lurking within every political system. As John Meleney observes, this habit of mind limited Burke's effectiveness as a congressman in the 1790s and relegated him to the fringes of power.[37] But it also focused his energies and his intelligence on tasks such as a history of the ratification of the Constitution that prompted him to send detailed questionnaires to Samuel Bryan and Elbridge Gerry concerning ratification in Pennsylvania and Massachusetts. One of his questions bespoke especially well the tension he perceived between disinterested republican leadership and prominence undergirded by the notoriety: "Was there in 1786 or at any time before that period any influential men, or any, and what party, and in what states, whose view, interests or sentiments were unfavorable, or otherwise to the popular govt. or favorable to a regal one? Or if so from what motives? Or was there any party and who were they inclined to avail themselves of the popularity of a certain *personage* [General George Washington?] to bring about any, and what revolution in the government?"[38] The potency of regal figures in the public imagination, the concentration of scheming ambition to effect a secretive revolution in government under the guise of acclaim for a figure like Washington, and the suspicion that sinister and ascertainable motives were at work in this high-toned approach to nation building pervaded Aedanus's thinking about the Constitution.

To counter these tendencies he sought to stir and invigorate the republican consciousness of his contemporaries. In 1792 he wrote to Ezra Stiles, the president of Yale College, urging the raising of public contributions to erect in New Haven a monument to William Goffe, Edward Whalley, and John Dixwell, three of the judges who voted for the execution of King Charles I in 1649 and who fled to New England in fear of their lives following the restoration of Charles II in 1660. The trio lived in hiding or in obscurity in New Haven, and only Dixwell had a fully marked grave.[39] Americans in the 1790s needed to honor and recall these republican heroes from the seventeenth century, Burke exhorted Stiles;

> the wretched prejudices of the old world ought not to extinguish our reverence for the memory of Whaley, Goffe, and Dixwell who lye buried in New England. They stood forth for the cause of Liberty in dark dismal times in the Parliamentary Army. They were eye witnesses of all the miseries, the infinite slaughter on the field and scaffold, the entire ruin and wretchedness of families which it was the fate of that nation to suffer from the tyranny of their King. They did what they deemed their duty . . . [only to spend] 16 or 17 years . . . in concealment and distress, hunted . . . by hues and crys and pursuivants of King Charles the Second!

Burke's reason for recalling this episode in "commonwealth" politics from the Restoration era arose directly from his understanding of the American Revolution as a moral drama that would sear deeply into the consciousness of the people or else become evanescent: "It is scarcely possible that their fate can be a matter of indifference to any man whose head or hand held a share in our late Revolution: for had the Republicans of America failed as those of Britain did, our illustrious Washington himself, Handcock, and Sam Adams with the rest of our gallant patriots would have been hunted down by royal proclamations." But this irony of history did not need to be forgotten. Providence was on the side of the people and was an intangible, but distinguishing, mark of republicanism: "Tho' the world and these affairs may change, tho' generations of men and upwards of an age may pass away, yet after all, rewarding Providence may, out of some circumstances or other produce a resurrection to their fame and reserve it from oblivion."[40] It is difficult to imagine any American patriot but one with a background in Irish patriotism connecting the regicides of 1649 to the survival of liberty in America in the 1790s. Aedanus Burke did not expect or even want to be remembered. He even ordered that his personal papers be burned lest they fall into the hands of enemies who would posthumously destroy his reputation.[41]

4

The 1990 version of this chapter categorized the ideas and beliefs of the Carolina Burkes as "revolutionary conservatism." The two men were dedicated revolutionaries in their defense of American liberty and, at the same time, historic conservatives in their fierce opposition to the partisan excesses of their fellow patriots and in their commitment to preserving the organic integrity of American society. Revolutionary conservatism seemed then an instructive oxymoron. But it was more than that. Viewing the late-eighteenth-century South through that prism eventually indicated that Aedanus and Thomas Burke were, in reality, *moderate historic conservatives*. Historically, moderation has been the simultaneous adherence to principle *and* prudence. The principles may be conservative or liberal or some unorthodox combination of the two, but in moderation political stances are always qualified by caution, self-preservation, open-mindedness, even stubborn ambivalence. The American Burkes were among the most highly principled and least prudential of moderates.

Thucydides, the historian of the Peloponnesian War, made moderation a proposition in political philosophy, and his successor in Greek thought, Aristotle, formalized the concept of virtuous middle ground between contrasting extremes in his *Nichomachean Ethics*. Although the Roman republican statesman Cicero deeply enriched moderation as a source of ethical guidance and social constraint, political moderation largely became subsumed during the Middle Ages under Augustinian ideals of the blessed community or discredited by Thomist warnings against ethical presumption. Then in the fourteenth century, Florentine humanists rediscovered Cicero, and in the sixteenth century, French Huguenots and humanist Catholics joined to embrace a bold new moderate rationale for ending the French Wars of Religion. From those new beginnings, political moderation reemerged as a coherent tradition between the 1570s to the 1680s. Eventually, Lockean political philosophy supplanted moderation as a belief system, leaving moderate beliefs and practices circulating, in a somewhat disheveled state, widely in the Atlantic world. At the pinnacle of this early modern revival of moderation, the eve of the English civil wars in 1641, the Anglican theorist Thomas Fuller defined moderation as "a mixture of charity and discretion" and, emphatically, "not a halting betwixt two opinions. . . . Nor . . . lukewarmness."

A century later the Irish intellectuals whom Caroline Robbins included among "the eighteenth-century commonwealth men" placed special emphasis on Renaissance and Reformation moderation. The American Burkes were educated and socialized in *that* Irish libertarian environment. As observed above, Jack Rakove first noticed Thomas's Irish predisposition to detect systemic corruption in the very bowels of centralized government, and John Meleney's astute biography demonstrates that Aedanus's considerable capacity as a political ethicist was deeply Irish in its diagnosis of political passion as arising from incestuous groups rather than from deluded individuals.

Both of these Irish insights—Thomas Burke on systemic centralized oppression and Aedanus Burke on pernicious radical socialization—were republican rather than Lockean political insights. As such they were pessimistic and urgent rather than contractual and measured. But that frenetic, jagged quality in their political style did not vitiate the moderation espoused by the Burkes. By bringing government back to the states and arguably closer to the people, the Articles of Confederation, they believed, would inoculate Revolutionary society from the misdeeds of Revolutionary ruffians by pitting them against militiamen—neighbors who had risked their lives to make local society coherent, stable, and rewarding to the small property owners who were the backbone of American society.

Moderates like the Burkes illustrated the fact that although moderates were not always successful, attractive, or wise, they could be useful and beneficial even when they appeared ineffective. The Revolutionary War's endgame, from Cornwallis's departure from North Carolina in the summer of 1781 through the final British evacuation of New York in December 1783, was just such a delicate period when moderation in the patriot ranks paid large, unexpected dividends. During the early stages of this interval, Governor Burke of North Carolina maintained the semblance of a patriot regime until Washington's victory at Yorktown removed the threat of loyalist resurgence and British reinvasion of the state; during the later stages of the endgame, Judge Burke of South Carolina took the heat for many patriot officeholders in the Palmetto State by making a powerful case that leniency toward the loyalists was sound public policy.

Thomas Burke's 1782 letter to Aedanus is the only known communication between the two men since they had conferred in Virginia in 1769 or 1770, but the letter sounds like a continuation of a steady flow of messages between them— letters Aedanus ordered his executor to burn and would have urged Thomas to do likewise. Aedanus and Thomas Burke were shadowy conspirators in the most civilized and decent of human adventures.[42]

Notes

1. Robert R. Palmer, *The Age of the Democratic Revolution: A Political History of Europe and America, 1760–1800* (Princeton, N.J.: Princeton University Press, 1959, 1964).

2. Jack P. Greene, "Paine, America, and the 'Modernization' of Political Consciousness," *Political Science Quarterly* 93 (Spring 1978): 73–92.

3. Caroline Robbins, *The Eighteenth-Century Commonwealthman: Studies in the Transmission, Development, and Circumstance of English Liberal Thought from the Restoration of Charles II until the War with the Thirteen Colonies* (Cambridge, Mass.: Harvard University Press, 1961).

4. Ibid., 135.

5. Robert M. Calhoon, *Evangelicals and Conservatives in the Early South, 1740–1861* (Columbia: University of South Carolina Press, 1988), 59–60.

6. Donald T. Torchiana, *W. B. Yeats & Georgian Ireland* (Evanston, Ill.: Northwestern University Press, 1966), 137.

7. Isaac Kramnick, *The Rage of Edmund Burke: Portrait of an Ambivalent Conservative* (New York: Basic Books, 1977), 17.

8. Michael G. Kammen, *A Rope of Sand: The Colonial Agents, British Politics, and the American Revolution* (Ithaca, N.Y.: Cornell University Press, 1968), 167.

9. John Sayle Watterson, *Thomas Burke: Restless Revolutionary* (Washington, D.C.: University Press of America, 1980), and John C. Meleney, *The Public Life of Aedanus Burke: Revolutionary Republican in Post-Revolutionary South Carolina* (Columbia: University of South Carolina Press, 1989), are the major sources for this essay. In addition, Watterson, "The Ordeal of Governor Burke," *North Carolina Historical Review* 48 (July 1971): 95–117 (hereafter *NCHR*), is a superb source of insight into military and political history of the closing stages of the War for Independence in the South.

10. Jack N. Rakove, *The Beginnings of National Politics: An Interpretive History of the Continental Congress* (New York: Alfred A. Knopf, 1979), 164–76. Rakove's subsection, "Thomas Burke and the Problem of Sovereignty," ranks with Watterson, "The Ordeal of Governor Burke," and Elisha P. Douglass, "Thomas Burke: Disillusioned Democrat," *NCHR* 26 (April 1949): 150–86, as major interpretive achievements on Burke and on the politics of the American Revolution.

11. Paul H. Smith et al., eds., *Letters of Delegates to Congress, 1774–1789* (Washington, D.C.: Library of Congress, 1976–), 7:144–52, quote on p. 148.

12. Ibid.

13. Ibid., 13:226. See also Eric Foner, *Tom Paine and Revolutionary America* (New York: Oxford University Press, 1976), 158–61.

14. Smith, ed., *Letters to Delegates*, 13:226–27; 14:112; 16:628–32, 712–14. See also Richard Walser, ed., *The Poems of Governor Thomas Burke of North Carolina* (Raleigh, N.C.: Division of Archives and History, 1949), 66–67.

15. Watterson, "Ordeal," 96.

16. Ibid, 98.

17. Ibid, 99.

18. Watterson, *Thomas Burke*, 4. Supporting this hint of Burke's passionate attachment to an earlier love, see James Iredell to Helen Blair, April 1, 1783, Don Higginbotham, ed., *The Papers of James Iredell* (Raleigh, N.C.: Division of Archives and History, 1976), 2:387.

19. Walser, *Poems*, 41–42.

20. Charles Royster, *A Revolutionary People at War: The Continental Army and American Character, 1775–1783* (Chapel Hill: University of North Carolina Press, 1979), 147.

21. Watterson, "Ordeal," 102.

22. Ibid., 108–11.

23. Burke to Greene, May 5, 1782, Walter Clark, ed., *The State Records of North Carolina* vol. 16 (Winston and Goldsboro: State of North Carolina, 1895–1914), 312–19, 320–27.

24. Draft of a letter from Thomas Burke to [Aedanus Burke], August 4, 1782, Thomas Burke Papers, North Carolina Archives, Raleigh, North Carolina. This letter is the only extant communication between the two Carolina Burkes; written in blank portions of Burke's ledger, it is difficult to locate by date in his papers. It appears on reel 5, frames 259–65 of the microfilm of the Thomas Burke Papers. For identification of Aedanus Burke as its intended recipient, see Watterson, *Thomas Burke,* 267n5. Cf. Douglass, "Thomas Burke: Disillusioned Democrat," 184–85.

25. Robert S. Lambert, *South Carolina Loyalists in the American Revolution* (Columbia: University of South Carolina Press, 1987), 222. See also Jerome J. Nadelhaft, *The Disorders of War: The Revolution in South Carolina* (Orono: University of Maine Press, 1981), 128.

26. Robert M. Weir, "'The Violent Spirit,' the Reestablishment of Order, and the Continuity of Leadership in Post-Revolutionary South Carolina," in *An Uncivil War: The Southern Backcountry during the American Revolution,* ed. Ronald Hoffman, Thad W. Tate, and Peter J. Albert (Charlottesville: University of Virginia Press, 1985), 80–81.

27. Aedanus Burke, An Address to the Freemen of the State of South Carolina . . . by Cassius (Charlestown, S.C., 1783), 9.

28. Meleney, *The Public Life of Aedanus Burke,* 11.

29. Aedanus Burke, *Considerations on the Society or Order of Cincinnati* (Charleston, S.C., 1783), 27–29.

30. John Higham, "Beyond Consensus: The Historian as Moral Critic," *American Historical Review* 67 (April 1962): 623–24.

31. Weir, "'The Violent Spirit,'" 81.

32. Burke, *Considerations,* 27.

33. Weir, "'The Violent Spirit,'" 85. See also George C. Rogers, Jr., "Aedanus Burke, Nathanael Greene, Anthony Wayne, and the British Merchants of Charleston," *South Carolina Historical Magazine* 67 (April 1966): 76–83.

34. Burke, *Considerations,* 22–23.

35. Meleney, *The Public Life of Aedanus Burke,* 89.

36. Minor Myers, Jr., *Liberty without Anarchy: A History of the Society of the Cincinnati* (Charlottesville: University of Virginia Press, 1983), 60–61.

37. Meleney, *The Public Life of Aedanus Burke,* 4, 16, 207.

38. Saul Cornell, "Reflections on 'The Late Remarkable Revolution in Government': Aedanus Burke and Samuel Bryan's Unpublished History of the Ratification of the Federal Constitution," *Pennsylvania Magazine of History and Biography* 112 (January 1988): 119–20.

39. *Oxford Dictionary of National Biography,* 61 vols. (Oxford: Oxford University Press, 2004), 5:1035; 8:71–73; 20:1305–7.

40. Aedanus Burke to Ezra Stiles, Ezra Stiles Papers, Sept. 20, 1792, Yale University Library, New Haven, Conn. Quoted with permission.

41. Meleney, *The Public Life of Aedanus Burke,* 2.

42. Robert M. Calhoon, *Political Moderation in America's First Two Centuries* (New York: Cambridge University Press, 2009), 9–11, 110–18.

The Reintegration of the Loyalists
and the Disaffected

ROBERT M. CALHOON
WITH THE ASSISTANCE OF
TIMOTHY M. BARNES

1. A Decentralized Infrastructure

The reintegration of the loyalists and the disaffected began with one of the earliest and most authentically revolutionary actions by the patriots—the First Continental Congress's recommendation that local committees enforce the non-importation, non-exportation, and non-consumption provisions of the Continental Association and publicly discredit "as the enemies of American liberty" violators of its provisions.[1] The astounding result of this clause in the Continental Association was the creation of a network of more than 7,000 committeemen by the spring of 1775, a virtually indestructible infrastructure of local revolutionary leadership. "The success of the Whigs in tying so substantial a group of local leaders to the enforcement of the Association," David Ammerman rightly emphasizes, "was a psychological victory of the first magnitude."[2]

These bodies quickly concluded that it would be futile to try to catch violators of non-importation red-handed. Perhaps guided by the Manichaean language of Congress about "enemies" and "foes to the rights of British America," committees hit upon the dynamic tactic of collecting the names of potential or actual Crown supporters, summoning them for public interrogation, and thereby acting as protectors of the community as well as agents of resistance.

Exchanges between revolutionary committees and suspected tories were part of what Peter Shaw calls "the ritual language" of the American Revolution, and ritualization of these proceedings was nowhere clearer than in the evolution of the loyalist recantation as documents dramatizing the bonds holding revolutionary communities together as well as tensions threatening to shatter community unity.[3] When six men in Marblehead, Massachusetts, apologized in May 1775 for signing a farewell address to Thomas Hutchinson a year earlier, each admitted that he had unintentionally jeopardized the safety of the town by signing the address, and then each declared that the hostility of the community was a cleansing force which could restore his public reputation and render him once again a fit participant in the affairs of the body politic.[4]

"As My comfort in life does so much depend on the regard and good will of those among whom I live," wrote Enoch Bartlett of Haverhill, Massachusetts, in September 1774, "I hereby give it Under my Hand that I will not buy or Sell Tea or Act in Any public office Contrary to the Minds of the people in General ... and will yet hope that all My errors in Judgment or Conduct meet with their forgiveness and favour which I humbly ask."[5] Similarly, when David Wardrobe, a British schoolmaster in Virginia, apologized to the Westmoreland Committee of Inspection on November 29, 1774, for having written an indiscreet letter to a correspondent in Scotland about Virginia politics, he "implor[ed] the forgiveness of this country for so ungrateful a return made for the advantages I have received from it, and the bread I have earned in it, and hope, from this contrition for my offence, ... to subsist among the people I greatly esteem."[6]

There was a difference in tone between recantations from New England which were apologies to the whole community and those in the Chesapeake, where a newcomer and outsider admitted his dependence on the sufferance and hospitality of the aristocracy. Recantations reflected local patterns of deference and social control and, in the midst of revolutionary turmoil, an elaborate etiquette of superiority and inferiority. The use of ritualized public language as a means of admitting errant loyalists into a republican polity indicated that the healing of political wounds was integral to the Revolution itself. The dramatization of political conflict, which Rhys Isaac has found at the core of the Revolution in Virginia, sprang directly from the manifold group antagonisms instigated and exacerbated by the Revolution.[7]

2. Moral Republicanism

John Witherspoon's ritual recantations for Benjamin Towne and James Rivington, described in a preceding chapter, were not authentic rituals of purgation and reintegration, but they did seek to educate a wide readership which enjoyed satire about the nature of republicanism, the fragile condition of republican virtue, and the ease with which scoundrels might sound plausible and innocent.[8] Witherspoon was deeply suspicious of learning that was not grounded in personal virtue. It was not that he believed that people were capable of goodness—though he moved surprisingly close to this repudiation of Calvinism—but that he especially despised those contaminated by dependence on British favor and habituated to servility. Such loyalists were, in Witherspoon's eyes, capable of insidious, chameleon-like mocking of republican virtues like sacrifice, duty, or the covenanted obligation to promote the common good. Witherspoon took special delight in exposing the intellectual emptiness of pro-British functionaries by having Towne and Rivington mouth parodies of Plutarch, Homer, and Samuel Johnson, which truly educated readers would recognize as shallow and obtuse. The superficiality and rhetorical excess of the Towne and Rivington recantations make them appear a minor episode in his career and a vacuous contribution to the discussion of reintegrating the loyalists and the disaffected. Witherspoon was the earliest patriot to deal extensively with the issue of reintegration. He not only produced an elaborate depiction of what Samuel Adams called a "Christian Sparta," he endowed moral castigation of loyalists, neutralists, and allegiance-switchers with a kind of curative power. Like debased currency, condemnatory rhetoric was an asset the patriots possessed in abundance and could employ beneficially in the short term.

Loyalist reintegration arose as a political problem early in the war because of the existence of British garrison towns where people like Towne and Rivington—and their readers—could imbibe British corruption and arrogance. In Boston until March 1776, New York from September 1776 until November 1783, Newport from December 1776 until October 1779, Philadelphia from September 1777 until June 1778, Savannah from December 1778 until July 1782, Charlestown from May 1780 until December 1782, and Wilmington, North Carolina, from January to November 1781, loyalist exiles found refuge, British military and economic power acquired a concentrated base, and an unstable culture of violence, deprivation amid wealth, and martial law pervaded the conduct of the war. In those towns which returned to American control during the war, those who had collaborated with the British but had not departed had to come to terms with the patriots. Surrounding each of these towns was a no man's land where illicit trade, crime, and patriot-loyalist violence flourished. The British found administration of the garrison towns a vexing problem; indirectly, these towns nourished the Revolution by providing places to dispatch defiant loyalists. Even illicit trade, which drained resources needed by the Continental Army, provided a valuable injection of British spending into the fringes of patriot-held territory. The garrison towns, therefore, created a large body of defectors for patriot justice to process back into American society as well as a visible demonstration of British power, corruption, and vulnerability.[9]

3. Volitional Allegiance

The most important scholarly discovery about the reintegration of the loyalists and the disaffected is James H. Kettner's "idea of volitional allegiance" as a way of thinking about citizenship in Revolutionary America.[10] Simply stated, volitional allegiance was the notion that American citizenship should be a matter of "individual choice." This seemingly straightforward republican principle, however, was the product of a complex legal, political, and ethical situation—complexity central to the nature of the Revolution itself.

In the process of tracing the development of allegiance from *Calvin's Case* in 1608 to the Fifteenth Amendment in 1870, Kettner illuminates the conceptual problems peculiar to the study of allegiance. In Anglo-American tradition, he shows, concepts of allegiance have not taken the form of gradual accretions resulting from prolonged trial and error; rather, concepts of allegiance at any given time consisted of clusters of theory, practice, law, and tradition, which often coalesced suddenly under the pressure of events that thrust individuals and the state into new and ill-defined relationships. Very much like a Kuhnian paradigm, allegiance embodied contrasting and divergent elements complementary enough to meet the demands of specific situations and consequently fraught with potential internal stress—stress that became more pronounced as a particular definition of allegiance was applied to thorny political and legal cases.

Revolution and war disrupted the fragile web of suppositions undergirding obligation in British America. Drawing on traditional ideas, Revolutionary leaders insisted that George III had forfeited the allegiance of his colonial subjects and that their prior consent to British rule—expressed in the colonial charters—reserved ultimate constitutional authority to the whole body of the people as expressed by their representatives. But Anglo-America tradition provided little guidance in dealing with the question of individual allegiance in situations of revolution and civil war. Could state governments impose American allegiance on all their inhabitants? Did the ultimate success of American arms by 1783 entitle the new nation to the allegiance of all the people by right of conquest? Republican principles and practical realities dictated a negative answer to both questions. The sheer impracticality of prosecuting large numbers of loyalists for treason, the emerging conviction that in a civil war everyone should have a reasonable interval to decide which side to join, and the diplomatic need to strike a compromise between the sovereignty of the new nation and Britain's obligations to her loyalist supporters were all among the constituent elements of the concept of volitional allegiance.

Loyalists documented the formulation of volitional allegiance in two important instances. First, Peter Van Schaack privately expressed in the winter of 1775–1776 the view that "every individual has the right to choose the State of which he will become a member" when that person is caught up in the overthrow of an old government and formation of a new one. Van Schaack limited this right of personal choice to allegiance to the narrow interval between revolutionary overthrow and creation "for I admit that once a society *is* formed, the majority of its members undoubtedly conclude meaning to decide for the rest."[11] Chief Justice Thomas McKean of Pennsylvania took exactly the same position in 1781 when he ruled in the treason trial of Samuel Chapman that in Pennsylvania the interval of individual choice extended from May 14, 1776 (the date before Congress annulled the effect of the Penn charter) until February 11, 1777 (when the state enacted a treason statute making allegiance and protection reciprocal). At the time of Chapman's alleged offense of joining the British Legion in late December 1776, McKean ruled, "Pennsylvania was not a nation at war with another nation, but a country in a state of *civil war*."[12]

The presence in Pennsylvania of a variety of large communities of religious pacifists both provoked the radicals to a program of coercion and served as a moderating buffer against revolutionary zeal. Mennonites were willing to sell farm produce to the Continental Army and to pay commutation fees in lieu of military service, but they refused to take the oath prescribed by law in 1777 because they would not abjure allegiance to a King who had done nothing to forfeit his claim to their obedience and because they had no reason to trust the new regime in Philadelphia. Moravian pacifism did not proscribe any bearing of arms, but regarded military service as sinful, if contrary to the conscience of the individual or performed under coercion. Schwenkfelders were the most apolitical and literalistic of the German pietist sects; one of their number, George Kriebel, told a judge that he could not take the oath of allegiance because the outcome of the war was still in doubt and therefore he did not yet know "upon what side God almighty would bestow the victory." The most visible pacifists and the most politically controversial were Quakers—a sect deeply split by the Revolution. Much of the traditional leadership of the Philadelphia Quaker merchant aristocracy refused on religious grounds "to join in any of the prevailing seditions and tumults," as one Quaker leader, Samuel R. Fisher, put it. Under Congressional pressure, Pennsylvania officials arrested more than forty prominent Philadelphia Quakers and sent them to detention in Winchester, Virginia, during the British occupation of Philadelphia. Beyond that harsh gesture, the discipline of the religious pacifists, the variety of the form of their noncompliance with Revolutionary dictates, and the weakness of coercive machinery all blunted punitive policies. Pluralism proved a powerful solvent of Revolutionary persecution.[13] Volition allegiance was the resulting equilibrium in this fluid situation.

A more complex and less studied setting for Revolutionary allegiance took shape in New York. Pressed to affirm allegiance to the Revolution in early 1777, Cadwallader Colden II told the New York Committee for Detecting and Defeating Conspiracies that "he conceived the former oath of allegiance which he had taken to the King of Great Britain to be binding upon him & professed a desire on being permitted to observe a state of neutrality." It took until the following October for the cumbersome machinery of revolutionary justice in New York to come to terms with this concept of allegiance. "No such state of neutrality can be known by the Council [of Safety]," Colden was told. Given time to reconsider his position, the stolid, apolitical son of New York's last royal lieutenant governor persevered in his claim to be "a faithful & true Subject to that State [New York] from which he receiv'd protection" and, while still bound by his allegiance to the king, he promised to be "a true and faithful Subject to the government of the Said State, So Long as it shall remain an independent State, and I reside therein."[14]

Colden's plight was emblematic of the situation of many loyalists and neutralists in New York. "The contest between Whigs and Tories is not what was most important about Revolutionary Queens [County]," Joseph S. Tiedemann concludes in a detailed study of early Revolutionary mobilization across the East River from Manhattan; "the truly significant reality was that a decisive majority remained neutral in the contest between Great Britain and her thirteen colonies." These neutralists were "traditional agricultural people, ... more concerned with the soil, the weather, and the prospects for the next crop than with debating the merits of Britain's imperial administration." Whig and tory activists represented neither class nor generational constituencies; rather, they were a politicized minority already accustomed to elections, polemicism, public gatherings, and other forms of public display as ways of asserting virtue and denouncing vice.[15]

The keys to understanding most New York loyalists are a sensitivity to apolitical language and gesture and an intimate knowledge of the local history. Jonathan Clark brought both qualities to his study of loyalists and patriots in Poughkeepsie, New York. Clark tracked down personal and political data on nearly three-fourths of 329 male inhabitants of the town. He found 101 committed patriots and 61 staunch loyalists; the remaining 69 "pristine fence sitters" included 29 "occasional patriots" and 40 "occasional loyalists." The people in these four categories knew one another and to a large extent were intermarried. Clark's 69 "occasional" loyalists and patriots embodied the impulses and circumstances framing choices of allegiance. One occasional loyalist, Peter Leroy, refused to sign the Association and had two sons fighting for the British, but under the influence of a patriot brother-in-law remained inactive in the struggle. Another, William Emmot, had agreed to take the oath of allegiance to the state and received, as a consequence, permission from Governor George Clinton to visit Long Island— behind enemy lines. That provoked a storm of protest from neighbors sceptical of Emmot's allegiance to the American cause. Known as a "sligh Designing fallow," Emmot took care to give no more offense and after the war emerged as a prosperous justice of the peace. In terms of wealth, both patriots and loyalists spanned the social scale in Poughkeepsie, but on the average patriots had more wealth in 1775 and even more of them were among the very well-to-do. Supporting the Revolution was a gamble, but those who had the most to lose feared British victory more than they did independence. Forty of the 69 "occasional" loyalists and patriots remained within the town and in possession of their property. "The resolution of the loyalist problem," Clark explains, "rested in the hands of men who, having made themselves noticeably large fish in a small pond, were as intent on saving their town as on saving their country. The destruction of their community, as they knew it, was not a price they would pay for victory."[16]

Finally, Michael Kammen's essay on "The American Revolution as a *Crise de Conscience*: The Case of New York," places the reintegration of the loyalists within a spacious intellectual framework, which included an ironic subsection on "The Meaning and Consequences of an Oath"—one of the first mechanisms used in New York to validate citizenship. New Yorkers knew that oaths were often meaningless, that people swore allegiance insincerely to save themselves from injury or legal punishment, and that in an atmosphere of upheaval unprincipled opportunism flourished. Why then were oaths widely employed? In the first place, Kammen argues, because they were means of rehabilitating the disaffected and the disloyal. An oath could serve as a written record of submission to the new state; its imposition was a stern warning to behave well in the future; and the language of oaths summarized past behavior, including lapses of allegiance, and therefore functioned as individualized prescriptions for conduct. An oath was a cheap, quick, uniform procedure that worked more often than it failed. Moreover, oaths gave individuals opportunities to verbalize and objectivize the hazards and pitfalls that entrapped the unprincipled and the naive in a revolutionary setting. As the Albany Committee of Safety discovered in late 1777, some people sided with Britain "thro' Fear, some thro' the persuasions of artful and designing Persons, others thro' the Allurements of Gain and the prospect of seeing their oppressed Country in the Hands of its base Invaders."[17] The clinical quality of such patriot diagnoses and loyalist admissions resembled what Gordon S. Wood has called "the Whig science of politics"—the confident belief early in the Revolution that political behavior could be understood and handled by the careful discernment of virtue and corruption in the body politic. And the recognition of the contingent character of affiliation and even allegiance implicit in these documents was part of a "new emphasis on piecemeal and the concrete in politics" which, according to Wood, soon replaced that body of classical principles.[18] In these terms, loyalist reintegration was part of the interface between whig assumptions and republican practice.

4. Military Triangularity

During the mid-1960s two quantitative estimates put the maximum number of loyalists at approximately 18 percent of the adult male population. Then in 1971 John Shy called attention to "the essential triangularity" of the War for Independence, that is, to the way British and American forces "contended less with each other than for support and control of the civilian population."[19] The triangularity hypothesis enables historians to make sense of a plethora of information about British frustration and American weakness. Despite the best efforts of conservative commanders on both sides, the war spilled off the formal battlefield and into the surrounding society in what the Rev. Samuel E. McCorkle called an "invasive" conflict. The politicizing and brutalizing of noncombatants hurt both sides but did far more damage to the British because it mocked their pretensions as protectors of the King's faithful subjects and guarantors of order in the colonies. The dual task of holding society together while conducting a socially divisive war, moreover, involved Revolutionary leaders in desperate experimentation, much of which ran counter to their basically conservative predilections. A sizeable body of recent scholarship on local conflict during the war bears on the problem of loyalist reintegration.[20]

In one of the best studies of the social dynamics of the war years, Ronald Hoffman discovered on the Eastern Shore of Maryland, especially in Dorchester County, a kind of tory populism among small farmers who defied the whig elite that had overthrown the Proprietary government in 1775.[21] Harold B. Hancock identified the same sort of loyalist defiance of a new state government in neighboring Sussex County, Delaware—for example, a bizarre episode in which a group of tory refugees descended on the home of constable Robert Appleton in Bombay Hook, Delaware, and ordered him to read a Methodist sermon, destroy legal papers pertaining to loyalists, and submit to being whipped by a black man.[22] The racial and religious references to the Appleton incident highlighted two intriguing features of Eastern Shore/Delaware tory insurgency. News of Dunmore's appeal to Virginia slaves to join him in suppressing rebellion in 1775 reached the ears of Eastern Shore blacks and may have prompted fearful Maryland officials into overreaction, which may have alerted yeoman farmers to the tenuous authority of the Revolutionary regime. As the war progressed, loyalist activity became increasingly identified with the influence of Methodist preachers who seemed intent, as they did in Virginia, on building a new kind of spiritual order among poor whites and some slaves and free blacks and were oblivious to the patriots' presumptions to serving a divine purpose.[23]

Everywhere loyalist deviance tested the discrimination and resiliency of patriot administration. Legislators, governors, and higher level judges were conscious of the practical difficulties of drawing and enforcing tight legal norms; ordinary citizens and local officials were aware of the dangers to their safety from failing to do so. Two recent studies examine this process, one in Connecticut and the other in North Carolina. In both states, a legal vacuum existed at a critical moment in the Revolution. In Connecticut it occurred in 1774–1776; David H. Villers argues that local committees played their role to the hilt, but when committee authority proved insufficient, as it often did, they relied on what Villers calls "'Liberty' gangs," which waylaid and terrorized suspects, extracted confessions, destroyed property, and in one sensational case broke into a jail to release patriot rioters convicted of illegally burning personal goods belonging to a New London customs collector. State officials, though uneasy about such vigilante justice, found these methods a useful supplement to the tenuous authority of the state and cumbersome machinery of the courts.[24] Jeffrey J. Crow found the same tension between official and popular justice in North Carolina. Here the vacuum occurred in the summer of 1781, when the government was exhausted by Cornwallis's invasion of the state and suppression of the loyalists fell into the hands of individuals like Andrew Beard, "a person in the Practice of Shooting down peoples whom he is pleased to suppose disaffected to the . . . Government," in the words of Thomas Cabune, who nearly became one of Beard's victims. General Stephen Drayton saw events of this kind as part of a rough process of "convicting, reclaiming, or punishing of Tories" in which "our own imprudencies & irregular proceedings made more enemies than had ever become so from mere inclination."[25]

Both the Cabune and Drayton documents date from July 1781. Events in North Carolina during that summer provide a model for explaining regular and irregular warfare in the Revolution. Major James Craig occupied Wilmington in January 1781 and in July appointed David Fanning commander of loyalist militia, already operating under Fanning's leadership. Craig and Fanning had finally learned how to fight irregular war in America successfully. Fanning devised a new guerrilla strategy based on what John S. Watterson calls "quickness, mobility, deception, and improvision." Fanning's raids concentrated on freeing tory prisoners, capturing the most notorious persecutors of the loyalists, operating widely in eastern North Carolina under cover of darkness, "plundering and destroying our stock of cattle and robbing our houses of everything they can get." Fanning's men were disciplined and violence was carefully targeted against key officials. Throughout Cumberland, Bladen, Anson, and Duplin counties, pockets of dispirited loyalists felt emboldened by Fanning's exploits. General Nathanael Greene and Governor Thomas Burke sensed almost immediately what was happening. The only safe remedy was to hunker down and wait for events outside North Carolina to shift advantage away from the British irregulars. The use of retaliatory terror against known or suspected loyalists only played into Craig's and Fanning's hands, enabling them to represent themselves as agents of justice for the oppressed and targets of barbarity.[26] The Fanning-Burke duel in North Carolina in the summer of 1781 therefore pitted for the first time in the war adversaries who thoroughly understood military triangularity.

In South Carolina, loyalist reintegration arose not only from patriot victory or from a stabilizing equipoise but from violence itself. The fierce civil war that convulsed South Carolina from late summer 1780 until the spring of 1782 played out memory of a previously learned experience with frontier lawlessness in the mid-1760s and harsh repression later in the decade by the South Carolina Regulators. The savagery employed by both whigs and tories in 1781 and 1782 frightened and shocked South Carolina patriot leaders. General William Moultrie did not exaggerate when he found, in early 1782, a shattered society of brutalized, frightened, impoverished people for whom "a dark melancholy gloom appears everywhere and the morals of the people are almost entirely extirpated." Even moderate, self-critical leaders like Aedanus Burke had felt an almost uncontrollable rage against the British and their loyalist lackeys in South Carolina.[27]

All of these examples of military triangularity involved either geographical conditions hampering the establishment of whig hegemony (as in Eastern Shore Maryland), or geopolitical fields of force giving Britain a competitive edge in dealing with the populace (as in areas adjacent to garrison towns in the middle states), or else the interplay of delicate social tensions making disaffection an understandable choice and reintegration a social and political imperative (as in South Carolina). One major variant remains: the state of Vermont, which lay beyond British or American control during the war and was for both sides an eagerly sought and finally elusive prize. Here military triangularity meant that the segment caught between Britain and America had the muscle to fight back. Within Vermont, patriots, loyalists, and, among both groups, Vermont separatists, were bound together by common ties and interests that would make reintegration of the disaffected a natural consequence of the creation of a state independent of both Congress and Crown.

Peter S. Onuf places this story in the context of the jurisdictional territorial disputes of the Revolutionary era. Vermonters had to deal fundamentally with a problem that arose elsewhere in America only as an incidental feature of continental politics—the basis of statehood. The very existence of Vermont and the daily conduct of politics hinged on defining statehood in ways that would maintain cohesion within and cause the necessary degree of "havoc" in the affairs of grasping neighboring states. Vermont punished its loyalists, then quickly forgave all but the most egregious of them, nearly negotiated its way back under British protection, and finally won a kind of reintegration into the American nation for loyalists and separatists alike through admission as the fourteenth state.[28]

5. Cosmopolitans and Localists

The severity or lenity of the treatment of the loyalists at the conclusion of the Revolution has, for much of the twentieth century, been a test of the radicalism or moderation of the Revolution. That is not the only approach which can be taken to the postwar reintegration of the loyalists. Paul H. Smith's article on General Guy Carleton as British commander in New York in 1782–83 selects a different perspective. Carleton believed with good reason that even after Yorktown, British possession of the port of New York was an immense asset. He proposed to the ministry that Britain simply refuse to budge unless the Americans agreed to some symbolic acknowledgment of allegiance to the king. The Rockingham ministry rejected Carleton's suggestion, not because the idea was faulty but because the capacity to pursue British interests in North America had been temporarily unhinged by the fall of the North government.[29]

Out of such divergent contingencies as London's unwillingness to let Carleton test the discipline and cohesiveness of the New York state government in 1782–83 and Britain's continued hold on the city during those two years, the loyalists may have found the time and opportunity to make their way into republican society. Drawing on the sociology of conflict resolution, Joseph S. Tiedemann clusters those contingencies under four broad categories: withdrawal, imposition, compromise, and conversion. Using Queens County, New York, supposedly a tory stronghold, as a test case, he estimates that no more than 6 percent of the adult males in the county went into exile and that the imposition of terms on those who remained was a matter of mutual adjustment rather than arbitrary prescription. New York's harsh anti-tory legislation became in practice a kind of "psychic assurance" for the patriots "that their efforts had not been in vain" and haphazard enforcement an inducement to former loyalists to accept the new order.[30]

The legislative search for such solutions, Jackson Turner Main demonstrates in his massive roll call analysis of the Confederation period, brought into the open and solidified two distinct orientations toward politics in the new republic, outlooks Main calls "localist" and "cosmopolitan." On roll call votes dealing with two major loyalist issues, 75 percent of localists favored confiscation against only 33 percent of the cosmopolitans; 61 percent of localists opposed readmission of returning loyalists as against 16 percent of cosmopolitans.[31]

In her dissertation "The Treaty and the Tories: The Ideological Reaction to the Return of the Loyalists, 1783–1787," Roberta Tansman Jacobs generally concurs with Main's profile of the supporters and opponents of loyalist reconciliation, although she suggests a strong surge of anti-loyalist sentiment and legislation in 1783–84, a sharply focused and influential nationalist response in 1784, and a dismantling of barriers to loyalist reintegration in 1785–86.[32]

David E. Maas's exhaustive study of loyalist reintegration in Massachusetts confirms Jacobs's finding that localist hostility toward returning and remaining loyalists in 1783 was short-lived.[33] Of 1,423 adult male loyalists in Massachusetts (2 percent of the population), Maas has identified 627 who remained in the state and 233 who returned. Approximately a quarter of physicians, whose occupational skills were in short supply, and Anglican ministers, who went into exile, were able to return.[34] As in New York and Philadelphia, merchants possessed abilities needed to reinvigorate the economy, and those with friends among the patriots also found reintegration relatively easy. Maas attributed the tolerance of former loyalists in Massachusetts to what he has called "honest graft"—the systematic plunder of loyalist property by patriot politicians, creditors, and court officials during the War for Independence which substantially depleted the value of the estates returning loyalists might have hoped to reclaim.[35] "Maryland's Samuel Chase . . . was an early advocate of leniency toward Loyalists," Norman K. Risjord notes in a similar instance, "even while he busily bought and sold their property."[36]

The most weighty contingency favoring loyalist reintegration was the belief that strict compliance with Articles IV through VI of the Treaty of Paris was an essential precondition to establishment of a national reputation for justice and civility. The earliest and most complete linkage between the treatment of the loyalists and the formation of a reputable national state appeared in Alexander Hamilton's defense of Joshua Waddington in a trespass action arising from a dispute over the rental of a brewery held by British merchants in New York City during the war. Hamilton's brief to the New York court in 1784 and his *Phocion* letters made justice and moderation toward the loyalists and scrupulous observance of Articles IV to VI a unique opportunity to inculcate the right kind of civic habits. He set forth a theory of federalism that made state law clearly inferior to national law and treaty-making, and he lodged in the judiciary power to set aside state laws that contradicted national law or treaties. Other publicists followed Hamilton's lead. The need to attract capital to restimulate the economy, the useful entrepreneurial skills of many departed loyalist merchants, the danger that persecuted loyalists would provide Britain with a pretext for hostile intervention, and the conviction that a country "formed for commerce" had to open its marketplace to British creditors and loyalist merchants lest "Private Resentment . . . distract the Tranquility of Government, Trade forsake our Shores, and Contempt and

Reproach . . . of consequence take [its] place" all appeared as themes in a well-orchestrated campaign. If Hamilton was the legal theorist of loyalist reintegration, Benjamin Rush was its social interpreter. The Pennsylvania Test Acts of 1777–1779, Rush declared, were tyrannical measures reflecting the insecurity of the constitutionalist regime because they denied nonjurors the right to grant or withhold assent to taxes imposed on them, offended conscientious pacifism, and damaged the prosperity of the community by excluding productive members of society from full citizenship.[37]

If the political reintegration of the loyalists was a nationalist imperative, reconciliation of loyalists, patriots, and neutralists within American churches was a necessary first step in the adjustment of the churches to a republican polity and culture. Each of the European religious traditions transplanted to the colonies in large or concentrated enough numbers to become a nascent denomination had members on both sides of the Revolutionary struggle—and some outside of it as well. One of the catalysts for the formation of Protestant denominations in the 1780s was the need to heal divisions arising from the Revolution within and between sects and confessional traditions.

No church had such a deep stake in legitimizing its place in American culture following the Revolution as the Anglicans. Anglicans in the South and around Philadelphia who had been predominantly patriots, or like the Rev. William Smith very passive loyalists, were willing to accept lay participation in church governance and forego for the time being strict adherence to episcopal ordination. High Church traditionalists in Connecticut, led by Samuel Seabury, many of them staunch opponents of the Revolution, moved vigorously to secure sanction from the new state government as a necessary prerequisite to consecration in England of a bishop. The Church of England shrank from any such intrusion into American civic life, though Seabury thereupon secured consecration as bishop of Connecticut from the Scottish Episcopal Church in 1783. Over the next six years, the two Anglican factions finally coalesced to form the Protestant Episcopal Church. What is not generally recognized in this familiar story is that Episcopalians, like other Protestant churches, opted for denominational polity as a way of resolving internal ecclesiastical problems and also establishing for themselves a stable position in the culture of the new republic.[38]

Quaker history contains another suggestive case of the origins of denominationalism. Torn like the Anglicans between English-based orthodoxy and acculturation in the new republic, the Revolution forced the Society of Friends to admit that it was not the True Church to which all believers would some day repair but rather a distinct kind of Protestant church. This movement toward a conventional definition of their sect was a positive reflection of American religious pluralism and a negative response to the hostility engendered by Quaker pacifism during the War for Independence. Similarly, the taint of toryism among Methodists arose not only from John Wesley's harsh attacks on the Revolution or because the earliest preachers were apolitical Englishmen but also because Methodists disregarded social norms, shunned politicization, and alienated patriot elites. The potency of that impulse in a democratic society and the suitability of circuit-riding organization in an extensive, rural setting made what had been social liabilities before 1783 into cultural assets in the years which followed. A reputation for political intolerance may well have prompted Presbyterians to present a more moderate and congenial face to their fellow citizens as they sought to heal Old and New Side divisions and to identify national prosperity with the operation of divine providence.[39]

Scholarship on the Revolution has produced a fragmented but richly varied portrayal of loyalist reintegration as a social and political process, but historians have been far less successful in recreating the interior experiences that underlay that process. There are isolated exceptions; of the serious biographies of loyalists,[40] two of the best deal with men successfully integrated into the life of the new republic: Tench Coxe of Pennsylvania and William Samuel Johnson of Connecticut. Coxe sided with the British in 1776 and traded actively in Philadelphia during the British occupation. Johnson operated at the highest levels of the whiggish provincial government in pre-Revolutionary Connecticut but temperamentally could not support independence and was jailed briefly in 1779 when his attempts to mediate between a British raiding force and frightened neighbors in Stratford were deemed "treasonous" by patriot officials. Both men had distinguished post-Revolutionary careers—Coxe as merchant, Treasury official under Hamilton, Jeffersonian publicist and journalist, and far-sighted advocate of industrialization; Johnson as influential delegate to the Constitutional Convention who was instrumental in the Great Compromise of July 1787, United States senator, and president of Columbia College.

Their parallel experiences were illuminating. Both were Anglicans, Johnson actively and Coxe inactively, but neither was doctrinaire in religion. Both secured political rehabilitation in 1779, well ahead of the charged and confusing atmosphere of 1783. Both had professional talents that were widely respected and not in overabundant supply in the new nation. Both had powerful friends within Revolutionary society and each handled himself with considerable discipline and sophistication at the crucial moment. "The Propriety, Modest, and Prudence of your Conduct will probably in a little Time wholly remove the Impressions which have been made and fully restore you to your Friends and Country," Joseph Reed wrote to Coxe in early 1779, in a statement alluding to the delicacy of the task of winning forgiveness and understanding from moderate Pennsylvania patriots.[41] When Johnson came before the Connecticut Council of Safety on July 28, 1779, he saw only four familiar faces from his pre-Revolutionary days and nine newcomers to political power with whom he had never dealt. After three years of painful isolation, he took only two weeks to accept the Council's terms that he swear an oath of allegiance.[42] Opportunity, ability, and luck rank high in American success stories.

Conclusion: Causal and Contextual History

A long tradition of loyalist historiography has presented the loyalists as a self-contained category of historical experience: victims of a popular seizure of power, exponents of a coherent philosophy of subordination and obedience, a military force willing to risk life itself in service of the Crown, and exiles who paid in concrete terms part of the human price for success of the Revolution.[43] A study of loyalist reintegration, based on these assumptions, ought to be written. Conceptual insights favoring such an approach can be found in the novels of James Fenimore Cooper, William Gilmore Simms, Harold Frederic, and Kenneth Roberts, through which the loyalists entered the literary consciousness of the United States;[44] in the gilded age historians' appreciation of the loyalists, which Bernard Bailyn has brought to light;[45] and in Canadian nationalism, which has preserved the memory of loyalist political philosophy carried to Nova Scotia and New Brunswick in the 1780s and 1790s.[46]

This chapter, in contrast, regards the loyalists as fragments of historical experience within the larger context of the Revolution. The distinction between loyalism as a subspecialty of scholarship and as a topic inextricably linked to the whole of the Revolution resembles the choice between what Ronald G. Walters calls "causal" and "contextual" history. Causal history identifies the participants in a historical event and studies what they did; contextual history asks what that event and those actions meant to affected individuals and to the people and culture surrounding them. "Contextual history," Walters explains, "is a history of commonality and structure rather than of distinctiveness and movement."[47] The scholarship examined in this chapter illuminates the shared social space inhabited by patriots and loyalists and the common dilemmas they encountered. But neither a causal nor a contextual interpretation of loyalist reintegration can be completely satisfactory, and historians need to devise a way of integrating the two approaches into a single, coherent vision of the subject.

The five interpretive insights employed here as organizing devices indicate both the utility and intrinsic limitation of a contextual treatment of loyalist reintegration. The committee infrastructure in 1774–1775, the work of moral arbiters of republicanism in 1776–1777, the legal and political evolution of volitional allegiance in 1778–1779, the increasing military triangularity of the conflict in 1780–1781, and the cosmopolitan-localist dispute over treatment of the loyalists in 1782–1785 emphasize that the social logic of the Revolution was unplanned and unanticipated and was shaped first by ideas and visions and next by social needs. In that sense, the treatment of the loyalists served to reinforce and protect an initially fragile republican polity constructed from grassroots politics, moralistic revolutionary norms, philosophical and legal dilemmas, violence, and partisanship.

This formulation cannot contain all the complexities and paradoxes of the situation. The best town studies show many local leaders just as anxious as their cosmopolitan counterparts to ease the rehabilitation of the loyalists.[48] Volitional allegiance was so egalitarian and libertarian in its implications that during the early nineteenth century the law of allegiance sharply curtailed free blacks, Indians, and women from the enjoyment of citizenship. Linda K. Kerber has shown that courts in New York and Massachusetts refused to hold wives of male loyalists accountable for their behavior on the ground that republican society had a transcendent interest in upholding the authority of husbands and preserving wives in a state of political innocence and impotence.[49] Runaway slaves and Native American supporters of the Crown—and ultimately all blacks and Indians— faced a post-Revolutionary regime that was much more monolithic in its assertions of racial hegemony than pre-Revolutionary British-Americans had thought of being.[50] The unexpected removal of large numbers of British, French, and Spanish operatives from the lower Mississippi Valley and Great Lakes regions during the Napoleonic wars deprived some former loyalists of a potentially historic role in thwarting manifest destiny.[51] Finally, the return of large numbers of the Canadian descendants of loyalist exiles to the United States during the nineteenth century indicates that reintegration was a century-long rather than a decade-long process.

Notes

1. Merrill Jensen, ed., *American Colonial Documents to 1776* (London, 1955), 815.

2. David Ammerman, *In the Common Cause: American Response to the Coercive Acts of 1774* (Charlottesville, Va., 1974), 109.

3. Peter Shaw, *American Patriots and the Rituals of Revolution* (Cambridge, Mass., 1981), 2.

4. Quoted in Robert M. Calhoon, *The Loyalists in Revolutionary America, 1760–1781* (New York, 1973), 304.

5. Ibid., 305. Congress apparently distinguished between committees of inspection created in consequence of the Continental Association and the existing network of committees of correspondence that had existed in New England since early 1773.

6. *Virginia Gazette* (Pinckney), Feb. 9, 1775, in Robert L. Scribner, ed., *Revolutionary Virginia: The Road to Independence*, vol. 2, *The Committees and the Second Convention, 1773–1775: A Documentary Record* (Charlottesville, Va., 1975), 179–80.

7. Rhys Isaac, "Dramatizing the Ideology of Revolution: Popular Mobilization in Virginia, 1774 to 1776," *William and Mary Quarterly*, 3rd ser., 33 (1976): 357–85.

8. Timothy M. Barnes and Robert M. Calhoon, "Moral Allegiance: John Witherspoon and Loyalist Recantation," see above, chapter 14.

9. For a listing of scholarship on the British garrison towns, see Robert M. Calhoon, *Revolutionary America: An Interpretive Overview* (New York, 1976), 158–59; see also Janice Potter and Robert M. Calhoon, "The Character and Coherence of the Loyalist Press," in Bernard Bailyn and John B. Hench, eds., *The Press and the American Revolution* (Worcester, Mass., 1980), 262–72; Robert Ernst, "Andrew Eliot, Forgotten Loyalist," *New York History*, 57 (1976): 284–320; Milton M. Klein. "An Experiment that Failed: General James Robertson and Civil Government in British New York, 1779–1783," *New York History*, 61 (1980): 228–54; Milton M. Klein and Ronald W. Howard, eds., *The Twilight of*

British Rule in Revolutionary America: The New York Letterbook of General James Robertson, 1780–1783 (Cooperstown, N.Y., 1985); Elaine F. Crane, *A Dependent People: Newport, Rhode Island, in the Revolutionary Era* (New York, 1985); and Barnes and Calhoon, "John Witherspoon and Loyalist Recantation."

10. James H. Kettner, *The Development of American Citizenship, 1608–1870* (Chapel Hill, N.C., 1978), chap. 7.

11. Ibid., 188–89.

12. Ibid., 195–96. See also G. S. Rowe, *Thomas McKean: The Shaping of an American Republicanism* (Boulder, Colo., 1978), 138–40; Henry J. Young, "Treason and Its Punishment in Revolutionary Pennsylvania," *Pennsylvania Magazine of History and Biography*, 90 (1966): 278.

13. Peter Brock, *Pacifism in the United States from the Colonial Era to the First World War* (Princeton, N.J., 1968), chap. 4; Henry J. Young, "The Treatment of the Loyalists in Pennsylvania" (Ph.D. diss., Johns Hopkins University, 1955), 267–71.

14. Eugene R. Fingerhut, *Survivor: Cadwallader Colden II in Revolutionary America* (Port Washington, N.Y., 1983), 58, 84–85. See also my review in *American Historical Review*, 89 (1984): 1388–89. For a similarly complex dilemma of a leading garrison town loyalist leader, see Sheila L. Skemp, "William Franklin's Fight for Equality," paper read at the Southeastern American Society for Eighteenth-Century Studies, Columbia, S.C., February 28, 1985.

15. Joseph S. Tiedemann, "Communities in the Midst of the American Revolution: Queens County, New York," *Journal of Social History*, 18 (1984): 58–87.

16. Jonathan Clark, "The Problem of Allegiance in Revolutionary Poughkeepsie," in David D. Hall, John M. Murrin, and Thad W. Tate, eds., *Saints and Revolutionaries: Essays on Early American History* (New York, 1984), 285–317.

17. Jack P. Greene, Richard L. Bushman, and Michael Kammen, *Society, Freedom, and Conscience*, Richard M. Jellison, ed. (New York, 1976), 135, 139.

18. S. Wood, *The Creation of the American Republic, 1776–1787* (Chapel Hill, N.C., 1969), 606.

19. John Shy, "The American Revolution: The Military Conflict Considered as a Revolutionary War," in Stephen G. Kurtz and James H. Hutson, eds., *Essays on the American Revolution* (Chapel Hill, N.C., 1973), 126. This essay is conveniently available in John Shy, *A People Numerous and Armed: Reflections on the Military Struggle for American Independence* (New York, 1976), a book that contains several essays amplifying his views on the social configuration of the War for Independence; see chaps. I–II, VI–IX

20. Samuel McCorkle, "The Curse and Crime of Plundering: A Sermon," McCorkle Papers, Duke University Library. See in general my review of Jeffrey J. Crow and Larry E. Tise, eds., *The Southern Experience in the American Revolution* and Don Higginbotham, ed., *Reconsiderations of the Revolutionary War: Selected Essays*, in *Journal of Interdisciplinary History*, 10 (1979): 367–70.

21. Ronald Hoffman, *A Spirit of Dissension: Economics, Politics, and the Revolution in Maryland* (Baltimore, 1973), 183–95, 223–41.

22. Harold B. Hancock, *The Loyalists of Revolutionary Delaware* (Newark, Del., 1977), pp. 37, 82, 96 and Keith Mason, "Localism, Evangelicalism, and Loyalism: The Sources of Discontent in the Revolutionary Chesapeake," *Journal of Southern History*, 56 (1990): 23–54.

23. Hoffman, *Spirit of Dissension,* 227–30; Hancock, *Loyalists of Delaware,* 80–86; Mason, "Localism, Evangelicalism, and Loyalism," 20–23, 33–35; see also William Henry Williams, *The Garden of American Methodism: The Delmarva Peninsula, 1769–1820* (Wilmington, Del., 1984).

24. David H. Villers, "'King Mob' and the Rule of Law: Revolutionary Justice and the Supression of Loyalism in Connecticut, 1774–1783," unpublished paper based on Villers, "Loyalism in Connecticut, 1763–1787" (Ph.D. diss., University of Connecticut, 1976.)

25. Jeffrey J. Crow, "Liberty Men and Loyalists: Disorder and Disaffection in the North Carolina Backcountry," in Ronald Hoffman, Peter J. Albert, and Thad W. Tate, eds., *An Uncivil War: The Southern Backcountry during the American Revolution* (Charlottesville, Va., 1985), 129, 138, 140, 143–48, 161–62, 167–74. See also Paul D. Escott and Jeffrey J. Crow, "The Social Order and Violent Disorder: An analysis of North Carolina in the Revolution and the Civil War," *Journal of Southern History,* 52 (1986): 373–402; Jeffrey J. Crow, "Tory Plots and Anglican Loyalty: The Llewelyn Conspiracy of 1777" and "What Price Loyalism? The Case of John Cruden, Commissioner of Sequestered Estates," *North Carolina Historical Review,* 55 (1978): 1–17 and 58 (1981): 215–33; and Clyde R. Ferguson, "Functions of the Partisan-Militia in the South during the American Revolution: An Interpretation," in W. Robert Higgins, ed., *The Revolutionary War in the South: Power; Conflict, and Leadership* (Durham, N.C., 1979), 239–58.

26. John S. Watterson III, "The Ordeal of Governor Burke," *North Carolina Historical Review,* 48 (1971): 95–102; Lindley S. Butler, ed., *The Narrative of Col. David Fanning* (Charleston, S.C., and Davidson, N.C., 1981), 6–10; Robert M. Calhoon, "Civil, Revolutionary, or Partisan: The Loyalists and the Nature of the War for Independence," *Military History of the American Revolution* (Washington, D.C., 1976), 93–108; Harry Eckstein, "On the Etiology of Internal Wars," *History and Theory,* 4 (1964): 133–163.

27. Robert M. Weir, "'The Violent Spirit,' the Reestablishment of Order, and the Continuity of Leadership in Post-Revolutionary South Carolina," in Hoffman et al., eds., *An Uncivil War,* 76, 77, 85. Robert S. Lambert, *The South Carolina Loyalists* (Columbia, S.C., 1987), devotes a detailed chapter to Loyalist rehabilitation. See also the Loyalist recantations in the *Journals of the House of Representatives, 1783–1784,* Theodora J. Thompson and Rosa Lumpkin, eds., (Columbia, S.C., 1977), 39, 46, 127, 178–79; George C. Rogers, "Aedanus Burke, Nathanael Greene, Anthony Wayne and the British Merchants of Charleston," *South Carolina Historical Magazine,* 67 (1966): 76–83; and Jerome J. Nadelhaft, *The Disorders of War: The Revolution in South Carolina* (Orono, Maine, 1981), chap. 4. Rebecca K. Starr, in "Loyalism on Daufuskie Island, South Carolina, 1775–1783," unpublished paper, explains the postwar reintegration of loyalists who sought refuge on one of the sea islands as an extension of wartime "cultural memory, investing peace-keeping in authorized groups" among conflicting loyalist and patriot communities in the islands. Cf. article by Joseph S. Tiedemann, note 30 below.

28. Peter J. Onuf, *The Origins of the Federal Republic: Jurisdictional Controversies in the United States, 1775–1787* (Philadelphia, 1983), chap. 6. For a discussion of earlier scholarship on the Vermont Loyalists, see Calhoon, *The Loyalists,* 330–34 and "The Floridas, the Western Frontier, and Vermont: Thoughts on the Hinterland Loyalists," in Samuel Proctor, ed., *Eighteenth-Century Florida: Life on the Frontier* (Gainesville, Fla., 1976), 1–15. A similar set of circumstances in Georgia produced the same narrow line between patriots and loyalists. See Albert H. Tillson, Jr., "The Localist Roots of Upper Valley Loyalism: An Examination of Popular Political Culture," *Journal of Southern*

History, vol. 54 (1988): 387; George R. Lamplugh, "Up from the Depths: The Career of Thomas Gibbons, 1783–1789," *Atlanta Historical Journal,* 25 (1981): 37–44 and *Politics on the Periphery: Factions and Parties in Georgia, 1776–1806* (Newark, Del., 1986); C. Ashley Ellefson, "Loyalists and Patriots in Georgia during the American Revolution," *The Historian,* 24 (1962): 347– 56; Robert S. Lambert, "The Confiscation of Loyalist Property in Georgia, 1782–1786," *William and Mary Quarterly,* 20 (1963): 80–94; and James A. Henretta, "Southern Social Structure and the American War for Independence," in *The American Revolution: The Home Front, West Georgia College Studies in the Social Sciences,* 15 (1976): 1–14.

29. Paul H. Smith, "Sir Guy Carleton, Peace Negotiations, and the Evacuation of New York," *Canadian Historical Review,* 50 (1969): 245–64. See also Eldon Jones, "The British Withdrawal from the South, 1781–1785," in Higgins, ed., *Revolutionary War in the South,* 259–85.

30. Joseph S. Tiedemann, "Loyalism, Conflict Resolution, and New York Politics in the Critical Period, 1783–1787," *New York History,* 68 (1987): 27–43. Tiedemann's model applies closely to the dealings between patriot officials and native-born Virginia loyalists studied in Adele Hast, *Loyalism in Revolutionary Virginia: The Norfolk Area and the Eastern Shore* (Ann Arbor, 1979), 140–188.

31. Jackson Turner Main, *Political Parties before the Constitution* (Chapel Hill, N.C., 1973), 32, 44–47, 348–53. Sigmund Diamond, in a prepared comment on a paper by Main read at the Southern Historical Association in Memphis, Nov. 10, 1966, suggested the application of the cosmopolitan-localist concept to Confederation-period partisanship.

32. Roberta Tansman Jacobs, "The Treaty and the Tories: The Ideological Reaction to the Return of the Loyalists, 1783–1787" (Ph.D. diss., Cornell University, 1974), chapters III–VI. See the seminal and quite durable articles by Oscar Zeichner. "The Loyalist Problem in New York after the Revolution," *New York History,* 21 (1940): 284–302 and "The Rehabilitation of the Loyalists in Connecticut," *New England Quarterly,* 11(1938): 324–29; and a fascinating case study, John M. Sheftall, "The Sheftalls of Savannah: Colonial Leaders and Founding Fathers of Georgia Judiasm," in Samuel Proctor and Louis Schmier, eds., *Jews in the South* (Macon, Ga., 1984), 73–75.

33. David E. Maas, *Divided Hearts: Massachusetts Loyalists, 1765–1790, A Biographical Directory* (Boston, 1980), xvi–xxvi.

34. David E. Maas, "The Massachusetts Loyalists and the Problem of Amnesty, 1775–1790," paper read at the American Historical Association, December 1975, Atlanta, tables 1 and 5. Another notorious loyalist physician who secured quick readmission from American officials was Dr. John Pyle of North Carolina. See Carole Watterson Troxler, *The Loyalist Experience in North Carolina* (Raleigh, N.C., 1976), 28–29.

35. David E. Maas, "Honest Graft in Revolutionary Massachusetts," *Boston Bar Journal,* 23 (1979): 7–15.

36. Norman K. Risjord, *Chesapeake Politics, 1781–1800* (New York, 1978), 193, and R. Don Higginbotham, "James Iredell and the Revolutionary Politics of North Carolina," in Higgins, ed., *Revolutionary War in the South,* 79–97.

37. Jacobs, "The Treaty and the Tories," 117–121. See also Robert Michael Dructor, "The New York Commercial Community: the Revolutionary Experience" (Ph.D. diss., University of Pittsburgh, 1975), and Philip Ranlet, *The New York Loyalists,* (Knoxville, Tenn., 1986), and Hendrik Hartog, Public Property and Private Power: The Corporation

of the City of New York in American Law, 1730–1870 (Chapel Hill, N.C., 1983), 82–86, 103–105.

38. Bruce E. Steiner, "New England Anglicanism: A Genteel Faith?" *William and Mary Quarterly*, 27 (1970), 133–35 and *Samuel Seabury, 1729–1796: A Study in the High Church Tradition* (Athens, Ohio, 1971) chap. 6. For an excellent analysis of the subject, and a valuable discussion of scholarship on post-Revolutionary Anglicanism, see David L. Holmes, "The Episcopal Church and the American Revolution," *Historical Magazine of the Protestant Episcopal Church*, 47 (1978), 283–88.

39. Sydney V. James, "The Impact of the American Revolution on Quakers' Ideas about Their Sect," *William and Mary Quarterly*, 19 (1962): 360–82; Donald G. Mathews, *Religion in the Old South* (Chicago, 1977), 29–37; Rhys Isaac, *The Transformation of Virginia, 1740–1790* (Chapel Hill, N.C., 1982), 260–64; Jonathan Powell, "Presbyterian Loyalists: A 'Chain of Interest' in Philadelphia," *Journal of Presbyterian History*, 57 (1979): 135–60; and Young, "Treatment of Loyalists in Pennsylvania," 294–304.

40. Bernard Bailyn, *The Ordeal of Thomas Hutchinson* (Cambridge, Mass., 1974); Carol Berkin, *Jonathan Sewall: Odyssey of an American Loyalist* (New York, 1976); Don R. Byrnes, "The Pre-Revolutionary Career of Provost William Smith, 1751–1778" (Ph.D. diss., Tulane University, 1969); John E. Ferling, *The Loyalist Mind: Joseph Calloway and the American Revolution* (University Park, Pa., 1977); Lawrence Henry Gipson, *American Loyalist: Fared Ingersoll* (New Haven, 1971); Leroy Hewlett, "James Rivington, Loyalist Printer, Publisher, and Bookseller of the American Revolution: A Biographical and Bibliographical Study, 1763–1783" (Ph.D. diss., University of Michigan, 1958); Albert Lawrence Lorenz, *Hugh Gaine: A Colonial Printer-Editor's Odyssey to Loyalism* (Carbondale, Ill., 1972); Alice M. Keys, *Cadwallader Colden* (New York, 1906); Eugene R. Fingerhut, *Survivor: Cadwallader Colden II in Revolutionary America*; Lawrence Shaw Mayo, *John Wentworth* (Cambridge, Mass., 1921); Bruce E. Steiner, *Samuel Seabury*; L. S. F. Upton, *The Loyal Whig: William Smith of New York & Quebec* (Toronto, 1969); and Anne Y. Zimmer, *Jonathan Boucher: Loyalist in Exile* (Detroit, 1978). As their titles suggest, not all of these books are biographies in a strict sense of the term, but all employ a biographical framework and define the genre of loyalist biography against which the books by Cooke and McCaughey, below are judged.

41. Jacob E. Cooke, *Tench Coxe and the Early Republic* (Chapel Hill, N.C., 1978), 45.

42. Elizabeth P. McCaughey, *From Loyalist to Founding Father: The Political Odyssey of William Samuel Johnson* (New York, 1980), 189.

43. For a discussion of this tradition, see Robert M. Calhoon, "Loyalist Studies at the Advent of the Loyalist Papers Project," *New England Quarterly*, 46 (1973): 284–85.

44. Donald G. Darnell, "'Visions of Hereditary Rank': The Loyalist in the Fiction of Hawthorne, Cooper, and Frederic," *South Atlantic Bulletin*, 42 (1977): 45–54; Michael Kammen, *A Season of Youth: The American Revolution and the Historical Imagination* (New York, 1978), 24–26, 52, 154–56.

45. Bailyn, *Ordeal of Thomas Hutchinson*, 394–98.

46. Jane Errington and George Rawlyk, "The Loyalist-Federalist Alliance of Upper Canada," *American Review of Canadian Studies*, 14 (1984): 157–76 and Janice Potter, "'Is This the Liberty We Seek?': Loyalist Ideology in Colonial New York and Massachusetts" (Ph.D. diss., Queen's University, 1977), 353–96.

47. Ronald G. Walters, *The Anti-Slavery Appeal: American Abolitionism after 1830* (Baltimore, 1976), 147.

48. Clark, "Problem of Allegiance in Poughkeepsie"; Fingerhut, *Survivor,* chap. 9; John J. Waters. *The Otis Family in Provincial and Revolutionary Massachusetts* (Chapel Hill, N.C., 1968), chap. 9; Calhoon, *Loyalists,* 292–94, 340–49; Francis T. Bowles, "The Loyalty of Barnstable in the Revolution," *Publications* of the Colonial Society of Massachusetts, 25 (1922–24): 265–345; Nathaniel Freeman Papers, 1775–1785, William E. Clements Library, Ann Arbor, Mich.; and Robert J. Wilson, III, *The Benevolent Piety of Ebenezer Gay and the Rise of Rational Religion in New England, 1696–1787* (Philadelphia, 1984), 225–29.

49. Linda K. Kerber, *Women of the Republic: Intellect and Ideology in Revolutionary America* (Chapel Hill, N.C., 1980), 130–36.

50. Peter Marshall, "First Americans and Last Loyalists: An Indian Dilemma in War and Peace," in Esmond Wright, ed., *Red, White, and True Blue: The Loyalists in the Revolution* (New York, 1976), 33–53.

51. J. Leitch Wright, *Anglo-Spanish Rivalry in North America* (Athens, Ga., 1971); *Britain and the American Frontier* (Athens, Ga., 1975); and *William Augustus Bowles: Director General of the Creek Nation* (Athens, Ga., 1967). I am also indebted to Paul Perry, "They Did Not Wish Us Well: European Intrigues in America, 1782–1798," unpublished research paper, University of North Carolina at Greensboro, 1979.

Conclusion

A Special Kind of Civil War

ROBERT M. CALHOON

Much can be said about the American Revolution without taking the loyalists into account. To the extent that neither were the patriots primarily interested in punishing the loyalists nor were the British chiefly concerned with vindicating and protecting their American allies, the loyalists *were* secondary figures in the Revolution. But they were also integral participants. Hauled before committees of safety, vilified in whig ideology, dispossessed, uprooted, and threatened with injury or death if they refused to acquiesce, and enrolled in large numbers in loyalist military regiments, the loyalists witnessed the Revolution firsthand and were the most immediate victims of the upheaval. Multifaceted and constantly shifting, the loyalists' experiences can be readily described. But *explaining* the loyalists' historical significance entails comment on the nature of the Revolution itself.

The Revolution was in some respects a civil war—protracted hostilities between irreconcilably antagonistic segments of society within the same country to exclude one another from political power and social advantage and extirpate one another's beliefs and principles. During the course of the War for Independence, some nineteen thousand colonists served in forty-two loyalist provincial corps.[1] These troops served as occupation forces in support of the regular British army in New Jersey, in 1776; in the environs of Philadelphia, in 1777 and 1778; at the outpost at Augusta, Georgia, between 1779 and 1781; and in backcountry South Carolina, between 1780 and 1782. Loyalist forces bore the burden of battle in the St. Leger and Baum offensives in upstate New York, in 1777, and in Ferguson's disastrous drive into North Carolina, at the end of 1780. When Sumter and Marion resorted to irregular warfare in South Carolina in 1780 and 1781, William Cunningham and other loyalist guerrilla fighters retaliated in kind, just as Butler's Rangers had in the Wyoming and Mohawk valleys during the year following Sullivan's destructive campaign of 1779. David Fanning, in the summer of 1781, perfected a mobile and disciplined loyalist force that temporarily disrupted the Revolutionary government in eastern North Carolina, but only after Cornwallis had failed to pacify the state and had marched north to Yorktown.

In spite of the impressive scope and intensity of this fighting between loyalists and patriots, the loyalists differed significantly from participants in a civil war. Loyalists in arms never enjoyed or really earned the support of a sizable civilian constituency capable of supplying, financing, and supporting military activities with impunity. The loyalists were not fighting to retain control of colonial government or to preserve particular British policies. They were not fervent monarchists or partisans for an eighteenth-century version of British imperialism. They thrust forward no charismatic leaders, carried into battle no fully developed and widely shared vision of what America might become under continued British rule, nourished no common hatred of particular whig leaders. In the beginning what strength of purpose they shared derived, as John Randolph realized while a loyalist exile in London, from the intense parochialism insulating some regions and communities and many individuals from the growing national identity that the pre-Revolutionary controversy had strengthened and accelerated among other Americans.[2] Only late in the war, in the loyalist communities of occupied New York City and London, did their common paranoia at the apparent injustices visited on them by American cruelty and British incompetence create a strong group consciousness. The realization of the bitter irony of their situation was the beginning of an ideology that would sustain many loyalist exiles in years to come. It was, at the same time, a useless impediment to those who returned to or remained in the United States.[3]

A more satisfactory way to set the loyalists in historical perspective is to consider the Revolution as a special kind of civil war—a struggle for national liberation.[4] It consisted of a number of stages that have reoccurred in mid-twentieth-century wars against colonialism: a colonial elite embracing an ideology of liberation, then a struggle for self-determination, and, finally, a debate within the Revolutionary party over the organization of the new state. What distinguishes the American Revolution from its mid-twentieth-century African and Asian counterparts is the relative ease and bloodlessness with which it passed through these stages. Yet, like recent colonial societies, pre-Revolutionary America was in a state of profound disequilibrium; their links to an imperial metropolis had endowed colonial leaders with an intellectual and cultural sophistication, an economic prowess, and an awareness of international power politics that were heady stimulants to their aspirations. Patriot leaders in 1775 and 1776 innocently disregarded the practical difficulties of waging war against the greatest military power on earth—an apparent lapse in judgment that the loyalists found inexplicable and that beguiled British officials into believing that they possessed sufficient military power and economic resources to crush the rebellion.

At every point, the loyalists became enmeshed in the tragedy of an ill-conceived exertion of national power. Britain proceeded to fight a limited war in a wilderness setting, across an ocean, where it lacked the manpower and logistical capability to occupy every disaffected locality or to destroy the enemy's main force. It was a struggle in which the pro-British partisans were, at best, politically, numerically, and militarily inferior to those of the rebel government. Such limitations on British power dispirited and disillusioned even those loyalists willing to sacrifice for the Crown, thus costing Britain the very resource on which the ministry had counted to keep the expense of the war within politically acceptable limits. It became a war so futile and contrary to the best traditions of imperial power that only gross misrepresentation of Britain's actual standing in the conflict could induce a suspicious Parliament to continue to finance the venture. Finally the war so drained Britain that it sorely tempted her international rivals to intervene, and when Britain finally faced the realities of the situation and negotiated a withdrawal, some loyalists believed they had been cruelly betrayed.[5] Considering the Revolution as a war of national liberation explains why Britain lost the struggle and why many loyalists suddenly found themselves out of phase—applying the assumptions of the 1750s to the conditions of the 1770s. Appropriate as a study of the weaknesses of the imperial connection, this approach, however, fails to touch the deepest roots of American behavior.

In the final analysis the Revolution was an effort to discover the legitimate sources of authority within American society. British policies restricting colonial autonomy and impinging on traditional liberties forced the colonists to examine in detail and with furious intensity the nature of the compact between themselves and the Crown as well as the proper role of parliamentary power in their political life. They concluded that the ultimate power to review the legitimacy of governmental policy rested in the whole body of the people and could be exercised only by representatives of the people. British actions that transferred more and more decision making from the colonies to London jeopardized this vital theoretical arrangement; subsequent measures coercing recalcitrant colonists raised the specter that British power was brutish and ravenous. Deeply concerned with the need to preserve social coherence and harmony, whig leaders sought to enlist the entire community in resistance against British authority and in the creation of stable insurrectionary institutions.

This cluster of belief and action—this ideology of constitutionalism and resistance—created fierce antagonisms within colonial society. It turned the rage of the community against royal officials and allies of the Crown, who appeared to have become lackeys of British tyranny, and it created incredibly self-righteous and humorless standards of public virtue. In retaliation, victims of public outrage and dissenters from whig orthodoxy challenged specific whig arguments, questioned the prudence and realism of whig tactics, ridiculed whig assumptions, and castigated individual agitators for their misdeeds. Loyalist beliefs and preferences, however, never coalesced into a common, vital persuasion with its own logic and momentum. The very nature of the controversy inhibited such a development; except under peculiar circumstances in South Carolina in 1780 and 1781 and among religious pacifists in Pennsylvania in 1777 and 1778, there was little explicit discussion of personal allegiance—the conscious act of making oneself the subject of a ruler. The focus was, rather, on the feelings, expectations, intellectual and cultural heritage, and standards of public morality that subtly shaped the varieties of political behavior and that predisposed men to be receptive to certain appeals and to engage in certain kinds of conduct. The opponents of revolution spoke knowledgeably about each of these components of allegiance, and they began the arduous task of justifying continued colonial acquiescence. But events moved too rapidly for them, constantly cutting the ground of their arguments out from under them and frustrating their belated and often clumsy attempts to rally their adherents to action. "Loyalty was the normal condition," Claude H. Van Tyne wrote in the loyalists' defense in 1902; "it was the Whigs . . . who [had to] do the converting, the changing of men's opinions to suit a new order of things which the Revolutionists believed necessary for their own and their country's welfare."[6] All of the historical insight available to Van Tyne had indicated that allegiance to the Crown and acceptance of colonial subordination were the norm for most people on the eve of the Revolution. It is now clear that the entire process of revolution was a consuming, transforming experience that deeply touched the lives of people in every part of the society. Republicanism and revolution became the norm, the common touchstone of American life, by 1775 and 1776. This is not to say that the loyalists were deviants; it is only to say that the search for legitimate political authority in America thrust loyalists and patriots onto diverging courses. "I discern the goddess, but on the other side of the river," William Smith, Jr., wrote of independence in November 1776. "Most men are for plunging into it to embrace her. I am for going over to her in a boat, distrusting my power to swim across the stream."[7] Others feared to cross the river by any means or regarded the water as a forbidden domain.

Notes

1. Paul H. Smith, "The American Loyalists: Notes on Their Organization and Numerical Strength," *William and Mary Quarterly,* 3rd ser., 28 (April 1971): 259–67.

2. Mary Beth Norton, ed. "John Randolph's 'Plan of Accommodations,'" *William and Mary Quarterly,* 3rd ser., 28 (January 1971): 105.

3. Robert M. Calhoon, *Revolutionary America: An Interpretive Overview* (New York: Harcourt Brace Jovanovich, 1976), 108, 120–21.

4. Thomas C. Barrow, "The American Revolution as a Colonial War for Independence," *William and Mary Quarterly,* 3rd ser., 25 (July 1968): 452–64.

5. On these patterns of war, see Paul H. Smith, *Loyalists and Redcoats: A Study in British Revolutionary Policy* (Chapel Hill: University of North Carolina Press, 1964), chap. 10, and David V. J. Bell and Allan E. Goodman, "Vietnam and Revolution," *Yale Review* 61 (Autumn 1971): 26–34.

6. Claude H. Van Tyne, *The Loyalists in the American Revolution* (New York: Macmillan, 1902), 2–3. For a different view of this issue, see Mary Beth Norton, *The British-Americans: The Loyalist Exiles in London, 1774–1789* (Boston: Little Brown, 1972), 7–8.

7. L. F. S. Upton, *The Loyal Whig: William Smith of New York & Quebec* (Toronto: University of Toronto Press, 1969), 119.

Bibliographical Essay

The best introduction to the loyalists remains, after a half century, William H. Nelson, *The American Tory* (1961), which anticipated the interest of the next quarter century of scholarship in both pre-Revolutionary motivation and wartime victimization of the loyalists. Also valuable are Claude H. Van Tyne, *The Loyalists in the American Revolution* (1902), and Moses Coit Tyler, *The Literary History of the American Revolution, 1763–1783* (1897), chapters 13–17 and 27–29, which respectively charted the legal and intellectual history of the loyalists with a vigor and acuteness that is still instructive. Lorenzo Sabine, *Biographical Sketches of Loyalists of the American Revolution* (1864), considerably expanded and expertly updated by Greg Palmer, *Biographical Sketches of Loyalists of the American Revolution* (1984), provides a vivid picture of the sufferings and experiences of more than twelve thousand individuals. Clifford K. Shipton, *Sibley's Harvard Graduates*, volumes 7 to 17 (1951–1975), presents, through biographical sketches, a portrait of a whole generation of New England leadership. Shipton was sympathetic to the loyalists; they constituted about 15 percent of Harvard graduates alive during the 1770s. See also David E. Maas, *Divided Hearts: Massachusetts Loyalists, 1765–1790: A Biographical Directory* (1980). Wallace Brown, *The Good Americans: The Loyalists in the American Revolution* (1969), is knowledgeable and also sympathetic to its subject; North Callahan, *Royal Raiders* (1963), and Callahan, *Flight from the Republic* (1967), are fast-paced episodic accounts; Robert M. Calhoon, *The Loyalists in Revolutionary America, 1760–1781* (1973), relates the loyalists to a wide range of interpretive questions about the ideological, social, political, and military nature of the Revolution; Esmond Wright, ed., *A Tug of Loyalties* (1975), and Wright, ed., *Red, White, and True Blue: The Loyalists in the Revolution* (1976), are wide-ranging collections of original essays; Mary Beth Norton, *The British-Americans: The Loyalist Exiles in England, 1774–1789* (1972), utilizes the exile experience in England as a perspective from which to reinterpret the entire loyalist experience. Catherine S. Crary, ed., *The Price of Loyalty: Tory Writings from the Revolution* (1973), is an excellent anthology of primary sources. When revised and published, Aaron Nathan Coleman, "Loyalists in War, Americans in Peace: The Reintegration of the Loyalists, 1775–1800" (Ph.D. diss., University of Kentucky, 2008), will become the standard one-volume treatment of the loyalists in Revolutionary society. Likewise, Maya Jasanoff, "The Other Side of the Revolution: Loyalists in the British Empire," *William and Mary Quarterly* (2008), previews her forthcoming book on the loyalist diaspora—the loyalists who were banished or foreswore return to American society.

After comprehensive studies of this kind, readers should next turn to biographical writings. Edmund S. and Helen M. Morgan, *The Stamp Act Crisis: Prologue to Revolution* (1953), and W. W. Abbot, *The Royal Governors of Georgia, 1754–1775* (1953), contain some of the finest chapters ever written on individual Crown officials and supporters, several of whom were colonists who became loyalists. William A. Benton, *Whig Loyalism: An Aspect of the Political Ideology of the American Revolutionary Era* (1969), describes the experience of nine pre-Revolutionary whigs who became loyalists after 1775 or 1776, unfortunately omitting John Jacob Zubly, the most whiggish and defiantly loyal of all those who supported resistance but opposed independence. In addition to these biographical chapters, a growing body of full-scale biographies includes Bernard Bailyn, *The Ordeal of Thomas Hutchinson* (1974); Carol Berkin, *Jonathan Sewall: Odyssey of an American Loyalist* (1974); Jacob E. Cooke, *Tench Coxe and the Early Republic* (1978); Brian C. Cutherbertson, *Loyalist Governor: Biography of John Wentworth* (1983); John E. Ferling, *The Loyalist Mind: Joseph Galloway and the American Revolution* (1977); Eugene R. Fingerhut, *Survivor: Cadwallader Colden II in Revolutionary America* (1983); James Thomas Flexner, *States Dyckman: American Loyalist* (1980, 1992); Lawrence Henry Gipson, *American Loyalist: Jared Ingersoll* (1971); Alfred Lawrence Lorenz, *Hugh Gaine: A Colonial Printer-Editor's Odyssey to Loyalism* (1972); Alice Mapelsden Keys, *Cadwallader Colden* (1906); Elizabeth P. McCaughey, *From Loyalist to Founding Father: The Political Odyssey of William Samuel Johnson* (1980); Lawrence Shaw Mayo, *John Wentworth, Governor of New Hampshire, 1767–1775* (1921); Bruce E. Steiner, *Samuel Seabury, 1729–1796* (1971); Earle Thomas, *Sir John Johnson: Loyalist Baronet* (1986); L. S. F. Upton, *The Loyal Whig: William Smith of New York and Quebec* (1969); and Anne Y. Zimmer, *Jonathan Boucher, Loyalist in Exile* (1978). More recent additions to loyalist biography are Sheila L. Skemp, *William Franklin: Son of a Patriot, Servant of a King* (1990); Edward J. Cashin, *Thomas Brown and the American Revolution on the Southern Frontier* (1989); Kinloch Bull, *The Oligarchs in Colonial and Revolutionary Charleston: Lieutenant Governor William Bull II and His Family* (1991); Geraldine M. Meroney, *Inseparable Loyalty: A Biography of William Bull* (1991); and Doris Begor Morton, *Philip Skene of Skenesborough* (1995). James Kirby Martin, *Benedict Arnold, Revolutionary Hero: An American Warrior Reconsidered* (1997), is a magisterial account of the Revolutionary war background of Arnold's loyalist apostasy. Ian Margeson, "Defender of the Atlantic Empire: Reverend William Smith and His Miranian Vision," *Utopian Studies* (2005), is the newest addition to biographical studies of loyalist thought.

After perusing the general introductory volumes and biographical studies, still curious readers should examine various attempts by historians to distinguish loyalists from patriots along broad lines of ideology, social standing, economic interest, and psychology. Of these the most inventive—in the best sense of that word—is Edwin G. Burrows and Michael Wallace, "The American Revolution: The Ideology and Psychology of National Liberation," *Perspectives in American History* (1972), which argues that "the prospect of living without a system of external supports and control filled ... the loyalists ... with anxiety" and determined their choice of allegiance. Kenneth S. Lynn, *A Divided People* (1977), makes the same case, stressing that loyalists in his sample had a pattern of unsatisfactory relationships with their fathers while patriots tended to imbibe the more liberating influence of restrained parental authority. N. E. H. Hull, Peter C. Hoffer, and Steven L. Allen find a pattern of traits—need for order, intolerance of dissonance and ambiguity, submissiveness, esteem for the powerful, aggressive hostility toward dissenters, fondness for harmony, peer group acceptance, and stereotypic thinking about outsiders—among New York loyalists in "Choosing Sides: A Quantitative Study of the Personality Determinants of Loyalist and Revolutionary Political Affiliation in New York," *Journal of American History* (1978).

A different kind of diagnostic study of loyalists as qualitatively different from patriots combines a variety of ideological, social, and cultural considerations. William Pencak,

War, Politics, & Revolution in Provincial Massachusetts (1981), finds that "loyalists tended to be inductive thinkers, materialists and individualists" while patriots "thought deductively and acted idealistically and communally." Just the opposite pattern appears in Thomas S. Martin, *Minds and Hearts: The American Revolution as a Philosophical Crisis* (1984), which depicts the patriots as "individualistic or self-assertive" and the loyalists as "integrative or corporatist." John A. Schutz, "Those Who Became Tories: Town Loyalty and Revolution in New England," *New England Historical and Genealogical Register* (1975), finds the patriots both self-assertive and integrative in the context of most New England towns and loyalists there to have been marginal and random figures.

L. F. S. Upton, "The Dilemma of the Loyalist Pamphleteers," *Studies of Burke and His Time* (1977), and Jeffrey M. Nelson, "Ideology in Search of a Context: Eighteenth Century British Political Thought and the Loyalists of the American Revolution," *Historical Journal* (1977), both connect the loyalists to English conservatism of the late seventeenth century and Augustan political conservatism of the early eighteenth century.

Heading the list of specialized works that attribute loyalism to a coherent conservative English ideology are Janice Potter, *The Liberty We Seek: Loyalist Ideology in Colonial New York and Massachusetts* (1983), and William Pencak, *America's Burke: The Mind of Thomas Hutchinson* (1982), as well as Jonathan M. Atkins, "Novanglus and Massachusettensis: Different Conceptions of a Crisis," *Historical Magazine of Massachusetts* (1985); Robert J. Chaffin, "Whig vs. Tory: The Ideological Response to the Townshend Acts of 1767," *North Dakota Quarterly* (1977); John Ferling, "The American Revolution and American Security: Whig and Loyalist Views," *Historian* (1978); Leopold Launitz-Schurer, "A Loyalist Clergyman's Response to the Imperial Crisis in the American Colonies: A Note on Samuel Seabury's Letters of a Westchester Farmer," *Historical Magazine of the Protestant Episcopal Church* (1975); Thomas S. Martin, "The Long and the Short of It: A Newspaper Exchange on the Massachusetts Charters, 1772," *William and Mary Quarterly* (1986); James E. McGoldrick, "1776: A Christian Loyalist View," *Fides et Historia* (1977); Rodney K. Miller, "The Political Ideology of the Anglican Clergy," *Historical Magazine of the Protestant Episcopal Church* (1976); and James C. Spalding, "Loyalist as Royalist, Patriot as Puritan: The American Revolution as a Repetition of the English Civil Wars," *Church History* (1976). Among the best published primary sources on loyalist ideology are Douglass Adair and John A. Schutz, eds., *Peter Oliver's Origin and Progress of the American Rebellion: A Tory View* (1961); Jonathan Bouchier, ed., *Reminiscences of an American Loyalist, 1738–1789* (1925); Bouchier, "Letters of Jonathan Boucher," *Maryland Historical Magazine* (1912–1913); Bernard Bailyn, ed., "A Dialogue between an American and a European Englishman (1768), by Thomas Hutchinson," *Perspective in American History* (1975); Thomas Hutchinson, *History of Massachusetts Bay* (repr., 1936); Catherine B. Mayo, ed., "Additions to Thomas Hutchinson's *History of Massachusetts Bay,*" *Proceedings of the American Antiquarian Society* (1949); Wallace Brown, ed., "An Englishman Views the American Revolution: The Letters of Henry Hulton, 1769–1776," *Huntington Library Quarterly* (1972–73); and Joseph S. Tiedemann, Eugene R. Fingerhut, and Robert W. Venables, eds., *The Other Loyalists: Ordinary People, Royalism, and the Revolution in the Middle Colonies* (2009).

A somewhat different approach to the cleavages between loyalists and patriots examines fault lines in the social and political structure along which Americans divided during the Revolution. Christopher S. Carson, "The Oliver Family in Peace and War, 1632–1860," *New England Historical and Genealogical Register* (1976), and Peter C. Hoffer and N. E. H. Hull, *Impeachment in America, 1635–1805* (1984), are the best treatments of Peter Oliver and his family and associates who, as a social group, were driven from power in Massachusetts in 1776. John H. Cary, "'The Juditious are Intirely Neglected': The Fate of a Tory," *New England Historical and Genealogical Register* (1980); Robert C. Coughlin, "Jonathan Ashley: Tory Minister," *Historical Journal of Western Massachusetts* (1979); Eduard M. Mark, "The Reverend Samuel Peters and Patriot Mobs in Connecticut," *Connecticut Historical Society Bulletin* (1975); Glen Weaver, "Anglican-Dissenter Tension in Pre-Revolutionary Connecticut," *Historical Magazine of the Protestant Episcopal Church* (1957); and Joel A. Cohen, "Rhode Island Loyalism and the American Revolution," *Rhode Island History* (1968), are other New England studies of loyalist social cleavage. One of the finest primary sources on the actual event of a community fracturing along whig-tory lines is Albert Mathews, ed., "Documents Relating to the Last Meetings of the Massachusetts Royal Council, 1774–1776," *Colonial Society of Massachusetts Publications* (1937), which contains vivid eye-witness accounts of patriot demonstrations in front of the homes of Crown sympathizers in the Bay State. Keith Mason, "A Loyalist's Journey: James Parker's Response to the Revolutionary Crisis," *Virginia Magazine of History and Biography* (1994), explains the fusion between the social circumstances of resident Scottish merchants in Norfolk and their tory ideology.

For the same process in the middle colonies, see Carl Becker, "John Jay and Peter Van Schaack," in *Everyman His Own Historian* (1935); Rick J. Ashton, "The Loyalist Congressmen of New York," *New York Historical Society Quarterly* (1976); Philip Ranlet, *The New York Loyalists* (1986, 2002); Ranlet, "British Recruitment of Americans in New York during the American Revolution," *Military Affairs* (1984); Ranlet, "James Rivington, Secret Agent," *Journal of Communication Inquiry* (1984); Ranlet, "Tory David Sproat of Pennsylvania and the Death of American Prisoners of War," *Pennsylvania History* (1994); Ranlet, "Yorktown, Loyalism, and a British Spy at West Point," *Journal of America's Military Past* (2002); Ranlet, ed., "Richard B. Morris's James Delancey: Portrait in Loyalism," *New York History* (1999); L. S. Lauritz-Schurer, "The Loyalist Response to the American Revolution: Whig Loyalism in Colonial New York," *Australian National University Historical Journal* (1971); and Dorothy Colburn, "No More Passive Obedience and Non-Resistance," *Historical Magazine of the Protestant Episcopal Church* (1977). Two Maryland studies are Anne Alden Allan, "Patriots and Loyalists: The Choice of Political Allegiances by Members of Maryland's Proprietary Elite," *Journal of Southern History* (1972), and John R. Wennersten, "The Travail of a Tory Parson: Reverend Philip Hughes and Maryland Colonial Politics, 1767–1777," *Historical Magazine of the Protestant Episcopal Church* (1975). See also Richard T. Irwin, *American Loyalists in Morris County, . . . New Jersey* (1996). Henry J. Young, "Treason and Its Punishment in Revolutionary Pennsylvania," *Pennsylvania Magazine of History and Biography* (1966), laid the groundwork for subsequent study, notably in "The Pennsylvania Loyalists," the Summer 1995 special issue of *Pennsylvania History.*

For loyalist-patriot division in Virginia, see Patrick Henderson, "Smallpox and Patriotism: The Norfolk Riots, 1768–1769," *Virginia Magazine of History and Biography* (1965); J. H. Soltow, "Scottish Traders in Virginia, 1750–1775," *Economic History Review* (1959); Courtlandt Canby, ed., "Robert Munford's *The Patriots*," *William and Mary Quarterly* (1949); Benjamin Quarles, "Lord Dunmore as Liberator," *William and Mary Quarterly* (1958); George M. Curtis III, "The Goodrich Family and the Revolution in Virginia, 1774–1776," *Virginia Magazine of History and Biography* (1976); and Larry

Bowman, "The Virginia County Committees of Safety, 1774–1776," *Virginia Magazine of History and Biography* (1971). For North Carolina, see Charles G. Sellers, Jr., "Making a Revolution: The North Carolina Whigs, 1765–1775," in J. Carlyle Sitterson, ed., *Studies in Southern History* (1957), and Laura Page Frech, "The Wilmington Committee of Public Safety and the Loyalist Rising of February, 1776," *North Carolina Historical Review* (1964). For South Carolina, see David H. Villers, "The Smythe Horse Affair and the Association," *South Carolina Historical Magazine* (1969); B. D. Bargar, ed., "Charleston Loyalism in 1775: The Secret Reports of Alexander Innes," *South Carolina Historical Magazine* (1963); George C. Rogers, Jr., "The Conscience of a Huguenot," *Transactions of the Huguenot Society of South Carolina* (1962); Edmund and Dorothy Berkeley, *Dr. Alexander Garden of Charles Town* (1969); Gary D. Olson, "Loyalists and the American Revolution: Thomas Brown and the South Carolina Backcountry, 1775–1776," *South Carolina Historical Magazine* (1967–1968); James H. O'Donnell, ed., "A Loyalist View of the Drayton-Tennent-Hart Mission to the Upcountry," *South Carolina Historical Magazine* (1966); Marvin L. Cann, "Prelude to War: The First Battle of Ninety Six, November 19–21, 1775," *South Carolina Historical Magazine* (1975); Rebecca Starr, "'Little Bermuda': Loyalism on Daufuskie Island, South Carolina, 1775–1783," in Robert M. Calhoon, Timothy M. Barnes, and George A. Rawlyk, eds., *Loyalists and Community in North America* (1994); and Robert Stansbury Lambert, *The South Carolina Loyalists in the American Revolution* (1987). Finally on Georgia, see Edward J. Cashin, "Sowing the Wind: Governor Wright and the Georgia Backcountry on the Eve of the Revolution," in Harvey H. Jackson and Phinizy Spaulding, eds., *Forty Years of Diversity: Essays on Colonial Georgia* (1984); Kenneth Coleman, *The American Revolution in Georgia, 1763–1789* (1958); Robert G. Mitchell, ed., "Sir James Wright Looks at the American Revolution," *Georgia Historical Quarterly* (1969); and Randall M. Miller, ed., *"A Warm & Zealous Spirit": John J. Zubly and the American Revolution: A Selection of His Writings* (1982). For a loyalist perspective on the Revolution, stressing the extreme localism existing just beneath the surface of American life and jeopardizing the unity of the patriots, see Mary Beth Norton, ed., "John Randolph's 'Plan of Accommodations,'" *William and Mary Quarterly* (1971).

Loyalist activity during the Revolution was, to be sure, not entirely reactive and defensive. Some viable loyalist communities maintained a precarious, if short-lived, existence outside of the reach of rebel administration. Stephen P. McGrath, "Connecticut's Tory Towns: The Loyalty Struggle in Newtown, Redding, and Ridgefield," *Connecticut Historical Society Bulletin* (1979), and Catherine Crary, "Guerrilla Activities of James Delancey's Cowboys in Westchester County: Conventional Warfare of Self-Interested Freebooting?" in Robert A. East and Jacob Judd, eds., *The Loyalist Americans: A Focus on Greater New York* (1975), depict such communities in region adjoining New York City. See also Jean F. Hankins, "A Different Kind of Loyalist: The Sandemanians of New England during the Revolutionary War," *New England Quarterly* (1987). A similar situation on the Delmarva Peninsula of southern Delaware and Eastern Shore Maryland and Virginia has attracted several historians: Edward C. Papenfuse, "Economic Analysis and Loyalist Strategy during the American Revolution: Robert Alexander's Remarks on the Economy of the Peninsula or Eastern Shore of Maryland," *Maryland Historical Magazine* (1973); Ronald Hoffman, *A Spirit of Dissension: Economics, Politics, and the Revolution in Maryland* (1973); Harold B. Hancock, *The Loyalists of Revolutionary Delaware* (1977); Keith Mason, "Localism, Evangelicalism, and Loyalism: The Sources of Discontent in the Revolutionary

Chesapeake," *Journal of Southern History* (1990); William Henry Williams, *The Garden of American Methodism: The Delmarva Peninsula, 1769–1820* (1984); and Adele Hast, *Loyalism in Revolutionary Virginia: The Norfolk Area and the Eastern Shore* (1982). A loyalist populace coalesced early in New Jersey; see Adrian C. Leiby, *The Revolutionary War in the Hackensack Valley: The Jersey Dutch and the Neutral Ground* (1962), and Paul H. Smith, "New Jersey Loyalists and the British 'Provincial' Corps in the War for Independence," *New Jersey History* (1969). Almost evenly split between loyalist and patriot factions, Barnstable, Massachusetts, began the war tilting to the British side and later shifted to the rebel cause; see John J. Waters, *The Otis Family in Provincial and Revolutionary Massachusetts* (1968), and Francis T. Bowles, "The Loyalty of Barnstable in the Revolution," *Colonial Society of Massachusetts Publications* (1924). Similar stories are told in John M. Bumsted, "Orthodoxy in Massachusetts: The Ecclesiastical History of Freetown, 1683–1776," *New England Quarterly* (1979); Bruce G. Merrit, "Loyalism and Social Conflict in Revolutionary Deerfield," *Journal of American History* (1970); Phillip Papas, *That Ever Loyal Island: Staten Island and the American Revolution* (2007); and in Jonathan Clark, "The Problem of Allegiance in Revolutionary Poughkeepsie," in David D. Hall, John M. Murrin, and Thad W. Tate, eds., *Saints & Revolutionaries: Essays on Early American History* (1984). A particularly cohesive ethnic loyalist community existed among the Dutch of Albany, New York; see Alice P. Kenney, "The Albany Dutch: Loyalists and Patriots," *New York History* (1961). Vermont was a mosaic of loyalist and patriot communities that sometimes struggled for supremacy with each other and more often cooperated in defense of Vermont separatism, a story told in Gwilym R. Roberts, "An Unknown Vermonter: Sylvanus Ewarts, Governor Chittenden's Tory Brother-in-Law," *Vermont History* (1961); Hamilton V. Bail, "Zadock Wright: That 'Devilish' Tory of Hartland," *Vermont History* (1968); Sarah V. Kalinoski, "Sequestration, Confiscation, and the 'Tory' in the Vermont Revolution," *Vermont History* (1977); and M. Christopher New, *Maryland Loyalists in the American Revolution* (1996). Judith L. Van Buskirk, *Generous Enemies: Patriots and Loyalists in Revolutionary New York* (2002), comprehends Revolutionary America—patriot and loyalist alike—as common cultural space (as does Robert Scott Davis in chapters 12 and 13 above).

More often, Revolutionary efforts at community building simply overwhelmed fragments of loyalist communities, but the process was never easy. In New York, Staughton Lynd found sharp class conflict at the core of this struggle in "Who Should Rule at Home? Dutchess County, New York, in the American Revolution" and in "The Tenant rising at Livingston Manor, 1777," both in *Class Conflict, Slavery, and the United States Constitution: Ten Essays* (1967); Michael Kammen found an acute moral crisis in "The American Revolution as a *Crise de Conscience:* The Case of New York," in Richard Jellison, ed., *Society, Freedom, and Conscience* (1976); and Philip Ranlet found only weak, episodic loyalist opposition to the Revolution in *The New York Loyalists* (1986, 2002), a view supported by Joseph S. Tiedemann, "Communities in the Midst of the American Revolution: Queens County, New York," *Journal of Social History* (1984), Tiedemann, *Reluctant Revolutionaries: New York City and the Road to Independence, 1763–1776* (1997, 2008), and Eugene R. Fingerhut and Tiedemann, *The Other New York: The American Revolution beyond New York City, 1763–1787* (2005). For variants on these themes, see William F. Willingham, "The Strange Case of Eleazer Fitch: Connecticut Tory," *Connecticut Historical Society Bulletin* (1975); Richard C. Haskett, "Prosecuting the Revolution," *American Historical Review* (1954); Thomas R. Meehan, "Courts, Cases, and Counselors in Revolutionary and Post-Revolutionary Pennsylvania," *Pennsylvania Magazine of History and Biography* (1967); Henry J. Young, "Treason and Its Punishment in Revolutionary Pennsylvania," *Pennsylvania Magazine of History and Biography* (1966); Anne M. Ousterhout, *A State Divided: Opposition in Pennsylvania to the American Revolution* (1987); James O. Lehman, "The Mennonites of Maryland during the Revolutionary War," *Mennonite Quarterly Review* (1976); Richard A. Overfield, "A Patriot Dilemma: The Treatment of Passive Loyalists and Neutrals in Revolutionary Maryland," *Maryland Historical Magazine* (1973); Peter G. Yackel, "Criminal Justice and Loyalists in Maryland: *Maryland vs. Caspar Frietschie*, 1781," *Maryland Historical Magazine* (1978); Emory G. Evans, "Trouble in the Backcountry: Disaffection in Southwest Virginia during the American Revolution," in Ronald Hoffman, Thad W. Tate, and Peter J. Albert, eds., *An Uncivil War: The Southern Backcountry during the American Revolution* (1985); Jeffrey J. Crow, "Liberty Men and Loyalists: Disorder and Disaffection in the North Carolina Backcountry," in Hoffman, Tate, and Albert, eds., *An Uncivil Civil War* (1985); Jeffrey J. Crow, "Tory Plots and Anglican Loyalty: The Llewelyn Conspiracy of 1777," *North Carolina Historical Review* (1978); Robert M. Weir, "'The Violent Spirit,' the Reestablishment of Order, and the Continuity of Leadership in Post-Revolutionary South Carolina," in Hoffman, Tate, and Albert, eds., *An Uncivil Civil War* (1985); and Edward J. Cashin, "'But Brothers, It Is Our Land We Are Talking About': Winners and Losers in the Georgia Backcountry," in Hoffman, Tate, and Albert, eds., *An Uncivil Civil War* (1985); Paul V. Lutz, "The Damnation of the Disaffected," *Manuscripts* (1979); and Lutz, "The Oath of Absolution," *Manuscripts* (1976). For a study of women that illuminates the entire process of redefining community in Revolutionary America, see Mary Beth Norton, "Eighteenth-Century American Women in Peace and War: The Case of the Loyalists," *William and Mary Quarterly* (1976), as well as individual examples in Wallace Brown, *The King's Friends: The Composition and Motives of the American Loyalist Claimants* (1966). For comparative studies of loyalist community formation and disintegration, see David H. Villers, "'King Mob' and the Rule of Law: Revolutionary Justice and the Suppression of Loyalism in Connecticut, 1774–1783"; Jean F. Hankins, "Connecticut's Sandemanians: Loyalism as a Religious Test"; Albert H. Tillson, Jr., "The Maintenance of Revolutionary Consensus: Treatment of Tories in Southwestern Virginia, 1775–1783"; and Cynthia Dubin Edelberg, "Jonathan Odell and Philip Freneau: Poetry and Politics in the Garrison Town of New York City," all in Calhoon, Barnes, and Rawlyk, eds., *Loyalists and Community* (1994).

For the loyalists' treatment by and contribution to American law, see J. Willard Hurst, *The Law of Treason in the United States* (1971); Bradley Chapin, *The American Law of Treason: Revolutionary and Early National Origins* (1964); Linda K. Kerber, *Women of the Republic: Intellect and Ideology in Revolutionary America* (1980); James H. Kettner, *The Development of American Citizenship, 1608–1870* (1978); and David E. Maas, "The Massachusetts Loyalists and the Problem of Amnesty," and Joseph S. Tiedemann, "Patriots, Loyalists, and Conflict Resolution in New York, 1783–1787," both in Calhoon, Barnes, and Rawlyk, eds., *Loyalists and Community* (1994).

Communities of loyalists in British garrison towns—many of them exiles from patriot-held areas—are a fascinating and insufficiently understood feature of the loyalist experience. For the British occupation of Boston from the imposition of the Coercive Acts in July 1774 through British evacuation in March 1776, see John Richard Alden, *General Gage in America* (1948), and Allen French, *The First Year of the American*

Revolution (1934). There is no adequate study of the British occupation of Newport, Rhode Island, from 1776 to 1779, but see Elaine Forman Crane, *A Dependent People: Newport, Rhode Island in the Revolutionary Era* (1985), and Ralph Adams Brown, "The *Newport Gazette*: Tory Newssheet," *Rhode Island History* (1954–1955). For the major British garrison town, New York, held from 1776 until 1783, there is an abundant literature: Oscar T. Barck, *New York City during the War for Independence, with Special Reference to the Period of British Occupation* (1931); Thomas Jefferson Wertenbaker, *Father Knickerbocker Rebels: New York City during the Revolution* (1948); Robert Ernst, "Andrew Elliot, Forgotten Loyalist of Occupied New York," *New York History* (1976); Milton M. Klein, "An Experiment That Failed: General James Robertson and Civil Government in British New York, 1779–1783," *New York History* (1980); Milton M. Klein and Ronald W. Howard, eds., *The Twilight of British Rule in Revolutionary America: The New York Letter Book, of General James Robertson, 1780–1783* (1983); William B. Willcox, *Portrait of a General* (1964); William A. Polf, *Garrison Town: The British Occupation of New York City, 1776–1783* (1976); and Robert Ernst, "A Tory-Eye View of the Evacuation of New York," *New York History* (1983). For the occupation of Philadelphia in 1777–1778, see John M. Coleman, "Joseph Galloway and the British Occupation of Philadelphia," *Pennsylvania History* (1963); Jacob E. Cooke, "Tench Coxe: Tory Merchant," *Pennsylvania Magazine of History and Biography* (1972); and Ira D. Gruber, *The Howe Brothers and the American Revolution* (1972).

John S. Watterson III, "The Ordeal of Governor Burke," *North Carolina Historical Review* (1971), is useful on the brief British occupation of Wilmington, North Carolina, in 1781. George Smith McGowen, *The British Occupation of Charleston, 1780–82* (1972), and Patrick J. Furlong, "Civilian-Military Conflict and the Restoration of the Royal Province of Georgia, 1778–1782," *Journal of Southern History* (1972), are the standard works of the British garrison towns in Charleston, South Carolina, and Savannah, Georgia, respectively. Otto Lohrenz, "The Discord of Political and Personal Loyalties: The Experiences of the Reverend William Andrews of Revolutionary Virginia," *Southern Studies* (1985), deals with the brief British occupation of Portsmouth, Virginia, in 1781. The foundation for study of the loyalists in the southern backcountry is Robert Stansbury Lambert, *South Carolina Loyalists in the American Revolution* (1987). On wartime South Carolina and Georgia, see Heard Robertson, "The Second British Occupation of Augusta," *Georgia Historical Quarterly* (1974), as well as other articles by him cited in chapters 12 and 13 above; Kathryn Roe Coker, "The Artisan Loyalists of Charleston," in Calhoon, Barnes, and Rawlyk, eds., *Loyalists and Community* (1994); Coker, "The Case of James Nassau Colleton before the Commissioners of Forfeited Estates," *South Carolina Historical Magazine* (1986); Coker, "Absentees as Loyalists in Revolutionary War South Carolina," *South Carolina Historical Magazine* (1986, 1995); and Coker, "The Calamities of War: Loyalism and Women in South Carolina," in Virginia Bernhard, Betty Brandon, and Elizabeth Fox-Genovese, eds., *Southern Women: Histories and Identities* (1992).

Songs and poetry emanating from garrison town presses were important expressions of loyalist anger and allegiance; see Margaret H. Hazen, "Songs of Revolutionary America," *New England Historical and Genealogical Register* (1976); Bruce Granger, "The Hudibrastic Poetry of Jacob Bailey," *Early American Literature* (1982); Thomas B. Vincent, "Keeping the Faith: The Poetic Development of Jacob Bailey, Loyalist," *Early American Literature* (1979); and Cynthia Dubin Edelberg, *Jonathan Odell: Loyalist Poet of the American Revolution* (1987).

The history of the loyalists in the War for Independence rests on the solid foundation laid in Paul H. Smith, *Loyalists and Redcoats: A Study in British Revolutionary Policy* (1964), and in John Shy, "The American Revolution: The Military Conflict Considered as a Revolutionary War," in Stephen G. Kurtz and James H. Hutson, eds., *Essays on the American Revolution* (1973). Shy reprinted that essay—which presented the war as a triangular struggle among the patriots, the British with their loyalist allies, and an apolitical mass of the population subject to coercion and cajolery by the other sides—in *A People Numerous and Armed: Reflections on the Military Struggle for American Independence* (1976). That volume contained important essays—on Thomas Gage, on Charles Lee, and one titled "Armed Loyalism: The Case of the Lower Hudson Valley"—that amplify the triangularity thesis as applied to the loyalists. He developed it further in "British Strategy for Pacifying the Southern Colonies, 1778–1781," in Jeffrey J. Crow and Larry E. Tise, eds., *The Southern Experience in the American Revolution* (1978), and in his "American Society and Its War for Independence," in Don Higginbotham, ed., *Reconsiderations on the Revolutionary War: Selected Essays* (1978).

For more accounts and studies of the loyalists and the War for Independence, see Jim Piecuch, *Three Peoples, One King: Loyalists, Indians, and Slaves in the Revolutionary South, 1775–1783* (2008); John S. Pancake, *1777: The Year of the Hangman* (1977); Paul H. Smith, "The American Loyalists: Notes on Their Organization and Numerical Strength," *William and Mary Quarterly* (1968); Philip Katcher, "The Provincial Corps of the British Army, 1775–1783," *Journal of the Society for Army Historical Research* (1976); Rene Chartrand, "Sergeant Vrooman, Butler's Rangers, c. 1783," *Military Collector and History* (1982); David L. Mann, "Bennington: A Clash between Patriot and Loyalist," *Historical New Hampshire* (1977); Wyman W. Parker, "Recruiting the Prince of Wales Loyalist Regiment from Middletown, Connecticut," *Connecticut Historical Society Bulletin* (1982); David H. Villers, "The British Army and the Connecticut Loyalists during the War of Independence, 1775–1783," *Connecticut Historical Society Bulletin* (1978); Barbara Graymont, *The Iroquois in the American Revolution* (1972); Philip Klingle, "Soldiers of Kings," *Journal of Long Island History* (1976); Philip Katcher, "Loyalist Militia in the War of Independence," *Journal of the Society for Army Historical Research* (1976); Carole W. Troxler, *The Loyalist Experience in North Carolina* (1976); Lindley S. Butler, "David Fanning's Militia: A Roving Partisan Community," in Calhoon, Barnes, and Rawlyk, eds., *Loyalists and Community* (1994); Clyde R. Ferguson, "Functions of the Partisan-Militia in the South during the American Revolution: An Interpretation," in W. Robert Higgins, ed., *The Revolutionary War in the South: Power, Conflict, and Leadership* (1979); Robert D. Bass, "The South Carolina Regiment: A Forgotten Loyalist Regiment," *Proceedings of the South Carolina Historical Association* (1977); Randall L. Miller, "A Backcountry Plan to Retake Georgia and the Carolinas, 1778," *South Carolina Historical Magazine* (1974); Louis D. F. Frasche, "Problems of Command: Cornwallis, Partisans, and Militia, 1780," *Military Review* (1977); Martha C. Searcy, *The Georgia-Florida Contest in the American Revolution, 1776–1778* (1985); Gary D. Olson, "Thomas Brown, Loyalist Partisan, and the Revolutionary War in Georgia, 1777–1782," *Georgia Historical Quarterly* (1970); James H. O'Donnell, *Southern Indians in the American Revolution* (1973); and W. Calvin Smith, "Mermaids Riding Alligators: Divided Command on the Southern Frontier, 1776–1778," *Florida Historical Quarterly* (1976).

The failure of the British to secure control of any of the thirteen rebelling colonies and reward supporters with security, prosperity, and a bright future contrasts vividly with the North American colonies where that scenario became reality, British East and West Florida. See Carole W. Troxler, "Refuge, Resistance, and Reward: The Southern Loyalists' Claim on East Florida," *Journal of Southern History* (1989); J. Leitch Wright, *Florida in the American Revolution* (1975); J. Barton Starr, *Tories, Dons, and Rebels: The American Revolution in British West Florida* (1976); Robin F. A. Fabel, *Bombast and Broadsides: The Lives of George Johnstone* (1987); Fabel, *The Economy of British West Florida, 1763–1783* (1988); Robert R. Rae, "'Graveyard for Britons': West Florida, 1763–1781," *Florida Historical Quarterly* (1969) (and his many other articles conveniently listed in Starr, *Tories, Dons, and Rebels* [1976], p. 260), as well as Robin F. A. Fabel, "Loyalist West Florida: An Ambiguous Community," and Carole W. Troxler, "Allegiance without Community: East Florida as the Symbol of a Loyalist Contract in the South," both in Calhoon, Barnes, and Rawlyk, eds., *Loyalists and Community* (1994).

For an additional bibliography on the loyalists and American society, see the notes to chapter 16, above. The loyalists' contribution to the post-Revolutionary peace settlement is described and explained in Mary Beth Norton, *The British-Americans* (1972); Wallace Brown, *The King's Friends* (1965); Richard B. Morris, *The Peacemakers: The Great Powers and American Independence* (1965); Charles R. Ritcheson, *Aftermath of Revolution: British Policy toward the United States, 1783–1795* (1969); and Ritcheson, "'Loyalist Influence' on British Policy towards the United States after the American Revolution," *Eighteenth Century Studies* (1973).

For loyalists' thrust to the periphery of United States territory during and after the Revolution and their efforts to establish pro-British or pro-Spanish enclaves along the frontier, see J. Leitch Wright, *Britain and the American Frontier, 1783–1815* (1975); Madel Jacobs Morgan, "Sarah Truly, A Mississippi Tory," *Journal of Mississippi History* (1975); Robert W. Sloan, "New Ireland: Men in Pursuit of a Forlorn Hope, 1779–1784," *Maine Historical Society Quarterly* (1979); and Michael John Prokopow, "'To the torrid zones': The Fortunes and Misfortunes of American Loyalists in the Anglo-Caribbean Basin, 1774–1801" (Ph. D. diss., Harvard University, 1996).

Far and away the most important accomplishment of the loyalists was their role in creating new British colonies in the future country of Canada. For this story, see David G. Bell, *Early Loyalist Saint John: The Origin of New Brunswick Politics, 1783–1786* (1983); Phyllis R. Blakeley and John N. Grant, eds., *Eleven Exiles: Accounts of Loyalists of the American Revolution* (1982); Ann Gorman Condon, *The Envy of the American States: The Loyalist Dream for New Brunswick* (1984); E. T. Crowson, "John Saunders: An Exiled Virginia Loyalist and a Founder of New Brunswick," *Virginia Cavalcade* (1977); Jane Errington and George Rawlyk, "The Loyalist-Federalist Alliance of Upper Canada," *American Review of Canadian Studies* (1984); Doris W. Jones-Baker, "The Huguenot Factor in American Loyalism, 1775–1785," *Proceedings of the Huguenot Society of London* (1985); John G. Leefe, "'And They Shall Devour Israel,'" *Nova Scotia Historical Review* (1981); Neil MacKinnon, *This Unfriendly Soil: The Loyalist Experience in Nova Scotia, 1783–1791* (1986); W. S. MacNutt, "The Loyalists: A Sympathetic View," *Acadiensis* (1976); Christopher Moore, *The Loyalists: Revolution, Exile, Settlement* (1984); H. V. Nelles, "Loyalism and Local Power: The District of Niagara, 1792–1837," *Ontario History* (1966); Larry Turner, *Voyage of a Different Kind: The Associated Loyalists of Kingston and Adolphustown* (1984); Mason Wade, "Odyssey of a Loyalist Rector," *Vermont History* (1980); and David Mills, *The Idea of Loyalty in Upper Canada, 1784–1850* (1988); William D. Reid, *The Loyalists in Ontario: The Sons and Daughters of the American Loyalists in Upper Canada*

(1973); Ann Gorman Condon, "The Loyalist Community in New Brunswick," in Calhoon, Barnes, and Rawlyk, eds., *Loyalists and Community* (1994); Jane Errington and George A. Rawlyk, "Creating a British-American Community in Upper Canada," in Calhoon, Barnes, and Rawlyk, eds., *Loyalists and Community* (1994); Neil MacKinnon, "The Nova Scotia Loyalists: A Traumatic Community," in Calhoon, Barnes, and Rawlyk, eds., *Loyalists and Community* (1994); and Janice Potter-MacKinnon, *While the Women Only Wept: Loyalist Refugee Women* (1993). Jessica L. Harland-Jacobs, *Builders of Empire: Freemasons and British Imperialism, 1717–1927* (2007), reconstructs the infusion of American loyalism into Canadian settler ideology. In her intensive local study of two communities settled by New Englanders in the 1760s, Macchias, Massachusetts, and Liverpool, Nova Scotia, Elizabeth Mancke, *The Fault Lines of Empire: Political Differentiation in Massachusetts and Nova Scotia* (2005), has produced the most precise comparison between similarly circumstanced patriots and loyalists.

For the black loyalists who sought a new homeland first in Nova Scotia and finally in Sierra Leone, see Mary Beth Norton, "The Fate of Some Black Loyalists of the American Revolution," *Journal of Negro History* (1973); James W. St. G. Walker, *The Black Loyalists: The Search for a Promised Land in Nova Scotia and Sierra Leone, 1783–1870* (1976); and Ellen Gibson Wilson, *The Loyal Blacks* (1976). Simon Schama, *Rough Crossings: Britain, the Slaves, and the American Revolution* (2006), magisterially narrates the Nova Scotia / Sierra Leone experience. Graham Russell Hodges, *The Black Loyalist Directory: African Americans in Exile after the American Revolution* (1996), is the basic reference work.

The *Oxford English Dictionary* entries for "Whig" and "Tory" trace these terms to "country bumpkin" and "Irish outlaw," respectively, before they became labels for the opponents and supporters of James, Duke of York, during the Exclusion Controversy in England, 1679–83. Sidney Forman, letter to the editor, *William and Mary Quarterly* (October 1987), discusses the meanings of the terms "loyalist" and "tory." Allegedly John Adams estimated that the American populace consisted of equal thirds of loyalists, patriots, and neutralists; for the controversy over this point, see page 368, note 4, of Robert M. Calhoon, reviews of *The Southern Experience in the American Revolution*, by Crow and Tise, eds., and of *Reconsiderations on the Revolutionary War*, by Higginbotham, in the *Journal of Interdisciplinary History* (1979).

For earlier bibliographical essays on the loyalists, see Wallace Brown, "The View at Two Hundred Years: The Loyalists of the American Revolution," *Proceedings of the American Antiquarian Society* (1970); George Athan Billias, "The First Un-Americans: The Loyalists in American Historiography," in G. A. Billias and Alden T. Vaughan, eds., *Perspectives on Early American History: Essays in Honor of Richard B. Morris* (1973); and Bernard Bailyn, "The Losers: Notes on the Historiography of Loyalism," in *The Ordeal of Thomas Hutchinson* (1976).

Index

LaVergne, TN USA
05 May 2010
181503LV00004B/5/P